Land Legislation in
Mandate Palestine

Land Legislation in Mandate Palestine

VOLUME 2:

STANDARD REFERENCE WORKS, PART II

Editor: Martin Bunton

CAMBRIDGE ARCHIVE EDITIONS

an imprint of

CAMBRIDGE
UNIVERSITY PRESS

CAMBRIDGE UNIVERSITY PRESS

Cambridge, New York, Melbourne, Madrid, Cape Town, Singapore, São Paulo

Cambridge University Press
The Edinburgh Building, Cambridge CB2 2RU, UK

Published in the United States of America by Cambridge University Press,
New York

www.cambridge.org
Information on this title: www.archiveeditions.co.uk

© Copyright in this edition including research, selection of documents, arrangement, contents lists and descriptions: Cambridge Archive Editions Ltd 2009

Cambridge Archive Editions is an imprint of Cambridge University Press.

Facsimiles of original documents including Crown copyright material are published under licence from The National Archives, London, England. Images may be used only for purposes of research, private study or education. Applications for any other use should be made to The National Archives Image Library, Kew, Richmond, Surrey TW9 4DU. Infringement of the above condition may result in legal action.

Subject to statutory exception and to the provisions of relevant collective licensing agreements, no reproduction of other parts of the work may take place without written permission of Cambridge University Press.

Every reasonable effort has been made to contact all copyright holders; in the event of any omission please contact the publisher.

First published 2009

Printed and bound by CPI Group (UK) Ltd, Croydon, CR0 4YY

British Library Cataloguing in Publication Data
Land Legislation in Mandate Palestine.
  1. Land tenure–Law and legislation–Palestine–History–
  20th century. 2. Land tenure–Law and legislation–
  Palestine–History–20th century–Sources. 3. Palestine–
  Politics and government–1917-1948.
  I. Bunton, Martin P.
  346.5'6940432-dc22

ISBN-13:   978-1-84097-260-3 (set) (hardback)
           978-1-84097-258-0 (volume 2)

Land Legislation in Mandate Palestine

CONTENTS

VOLUME 2:

STANDARD REFERENCE WORKS, PART II

The Land Law of Palestine, F.M. Goadby and M. Doukhan. 1
(Tel Aviv, Shoshany's Printing Co., 1935)

The Land Law of Palestine, F.M. Goadby
and M. Doukhan

Standard Reference Works, Part II

THE LAND LAW OF PALESTINE

BY

FREDERIC M. GOADBY, D.C.L.,

of Lincoln's Inn, Barrister at Law. Sometime Director of Legal Studies to the Government of Palestine.

AND

MOSES J. DOUKHAN, O.B.E.,

Advocate. Member of Palestine Bar. Assist. Director, Department of Lands, Government of Palestine. Lecturer Government Law School Jerusalem.

Tel-Aviv—Palestine
1935

Copyright
1935.

Shoshany's Printing Co. Ltd.

PREFACE.

In 1927 the Palestine Government commissioned us to prepare a Statement of the Land Law then in force in Palestine for the use of Officers engaged in the work of Land Settlement.

The Statement then prepared has been given a wider circulation than was, perhaps, at first intended and, copies having been made for sale, it has proved useful both to practitioners and students.

Circumstances appear now to call for a republication of the Statement in a more convenient form and this has been made possible with the consent of the Government.

We have taken the opportunity of revising the original Statement very thoroughly and of adding Chapters upon the Protection of Agricultural Tenants, Expropriation, Town Planning, Taxation of Land, etc. These are matters of interest to the student and practitioner though less relevant to the work of the Settlement Officers for whom the original Statement was designed. We have also inserted a Chapter dealing with the Cadastral Survey and setting forth the law under which Land Settlement operations take place.

References to legislation and, as far as possible, to Court decisions, have been brought up to date. Unfortunatély no adequate reports of decided cases are published in Palestine. Use has been made of the reports given in the Palesine Post for wich all persons interested are very grateful, and also of some other sources of information.

The Land Law of Palestine.

A Volume of Reports under the editorship of His Honour the Chief Justice has just been published and it is to be hoped that the practice of official publication once established will be maintained.

Unfortunately the publication of the Volume of Reports took place at too late a date to allow of reference in the text to the cases included in the Volume. The most important of the Land Cases in the Volume of Reports have been summarized for reference in an Appendix to this book.

The original Statement was in the nature of an official report and though much of it has been rewritten from a somewhat different point of view yet it is possible that this book still in the main preserves the character of its origin. We have, however, aimed at making it as comprehensive a treatise on the Land Law of Palestine as is possible in the present circumstances.

FREDERIC M. GOADBY.
MOSES J. DOUKHAN.

Jerusalem.
April, 1935.

TABLE OF CONTENTS.

		Page
PREFACE		III—IV
BIBLIOGRAPHY		VII—VIII
INTRODUCTION		1—16
CHAPTER I.	Miri Land	17—36
CHAPTER II.	Mulk Land	37—43
CHAPTER III.	Mewat Land	44—51
CHAPTER IV.	Metruki Land	52—59
CHAPTER V.	Public Lands, State Domain	60—68
CHAPTER VI.	Waqf and Trusts	69—95
CHAPTER VII.	Succession and Inheritance	96—124
CHAPTER VIII.	Appropriation of Land of another and use thereof.	125—128
CHAPTER IX.	Disposition by sale, Exchange and Gift	129—146
CHAPTER X.	Pre-emption and Preference	147—160
CHAPTER XI.	Rights of Secured and Unsecured Creditors.	161—180
CHAPTER XII.	Leases	181—198
CHAPTER XIII.	Co-ownership and Partition.	199—213
CHAPTER XIV.	Rights in the nature of Servitudes; Ways; Watercourses and Walls	214—231
CHAPTER XV.	Protection of Agricultural Tenants.	232—249
CHAPTER XVI.	Limitation of Actions and Prescription	250—268
CHAPTER XVII.	Cadastral Survey and Land Settlement	269—293
CHAPTER XVIII.	Registration of Land	294—314
CHAPTER XIX.	Expropriation of Land	315—331
CHAPTER XX.	Town Planning.	332—343
CHAPTER XXI.	Incapacity and Absence.	344—353
CHAPTER XXII.	Corporations	354—357
CHAPTER XXIII.	Taxation of Land	358—367

VI The Land Law of Palestine.

	Page
CHAPTER XXIV. Land Registration Fees	368—372
CHAPTER XXV. Courts dealing with Land Suits	373—385

APPENDICES.

APPENDIX I.	Note on the Palestine (Amendment) Order-in-Council 1935	386—387
APPENDIX II.	Bills recently published	388—390
APPENDIX III.	Summary of Cases concerning Land Law in the Law Reports of Palestine 1920-1933	391—396
APPENDIX IV.	Mewat and its Reviver	397—398
APPENDIX V.	The Transfer of Land (Fees) Rules 1935	399—400

TABLES.

Table of Palestine Cases Cited, Arranged in Alphabetical Order of Titles	401—404
Table of Cyprus Cases Cited, Arranged in Alphabetical Order of Titles	405—406
Table of English Cases Cited, Arranged in Alphabetical Order of Titles	407
Table of References to Ottoman Legislation	408—415
Table of References to Palestine Legislation	416—419
Table of Abbreviations	420

CORRIGENDA 421

INDEX . . . . 422—458

BIBLIOGRAPHY.

1. OTTOMAN LAND LAW [1].

BELIN. — Essai sur la propriété foncière en pays mussulmans. (Published in Journal Asiatique 1861—2).

CHAOUI (J). — Le Régime Foncier en Syrie. (Aix en Provence, 1928).

CHIHA (N). — Traité de la Propriété immobilière en Droit Ottoman. (Cairo, 1906).

FISHER (SIR S). — Ottoman Land Law; Translation and Notes. (Oxford, 1919).

NORD (E). — Die Reform des türkischen Liegenschaftsrecht, 1911.

ONGLEY (F). — The Ottoman Land Code; Translation and Notes. (Revised edition by H. E. Miller—London, 1892).

PADEL (W) AND STEEG (L). — De la législation foncière Ottomane. (Paris, 1904).

TUTE (R. C.). — The Ottoman Land Laws with a commentary. (Jerusalem, 1927).

2. OTTOMAN LAW.

ARISTARCHI. — Législation Ottomane; Recueil des lois, etc. de l'Empire Ottoman. (Constantinople, 1873—1881).

BILLIOTI (A) AND SEDAD (A). — Législation Ottomane depuis le Rétablissement de la Constitution. (Paris, 1912).

CARDAHI, SHOUKRY. — La Possession en droit Ottoman. (Paris, 1926).

GRIGSBY (E). — The Mejelle or Ottoman Civil Law, translated into English. (London, 1895).

[1] The leading Turkish Commentaries are those of Aly Haidar Eff. (New Commentary on the Land Code, Constantinople, A.H. 1311); Alif Bey (Commentary on the Land Code, Constantinople, A.H. 1319) and Khalis Eshreff Eff. (Complete Commentary on the Land Code, Constantinople, A.H. 1314).

VIII   The Land Law of Palestine.

TISHENDORF,
ANDREAS VON.   Das Lehnwesen in den Moslemischen Staaten. (Leipzig, 1872).
HOOPER C. A.   The Civil Law of Palestine and Trans-Jordan, Vol. I. containing a translation into English of the Mejelle. (Jerusalem, 1933).
TYSER (SIR C.).   The Mejelle—translated into English. (Nicosia, 1901).
VOUNG (G)   Corps de droit Ottoman. (Oxford, 1906).

3. WAQF.
KADRY PASHA.   Du Waqf. (Cairo, 1896).
OMAR HILMY Eff.   A gift to Posterity on the Laws of Evqaf; translated by Sir C. Tyser and D. Demetriades. (Nicosia, 1922).
TYSER, ONGLEY
AND IZZAT.   The Laws relating to Immovable Property made Waqf. (Nicosia, 1922).

4. MUHAMMEDAN LAW.
HAMILTON (C).   The Hedaya or Commentary on the Mussulman Laws; translated by Chas. Hamilton (Second edition by S. G. Grady, London, 1870).
SAVVAS PASHA.   Etude sur la théorie du Droit Mussulman. (Paris, 1902).
KADRY PASHA.   Code of Muhammedan Personal Law according to the Hanafite School; translated by W. Sterry and N. Abcarius. (London, 1914).
KADRY PASHA.   Statut Réel Mussulman. (Cairo, 1893).
VESEY
FITZGERALD (S).   Muhammedan Law according to its various Schools. (Oxford, 1931).

INTRODUCTION.

The Palestine Order in Council, 1922, Art. 46, provides that the jurisdiction of the Civil Courts shall be exercised in conformity with the Ottoman Law in force in Palestine on November 1st, 1914, (A.H. 1332) and such later Ottoman Laws as had been or might be declared in force by Public Notice and such Orders in Council, Ordinances and Regulations as were in force at the date of the commencement of the Order (1st September, 1922) or might thereafter be applied or enacted.

The law governing interests in immovables in Palestine is, therefore, the Ottoman Law of Land, as it stood on the 1st November, 1914, supplemented and modified by the legislation of the Palestine Government. The Ottoman Land Law has its roots in a distant past. In general character it conforms to the Moslem Religious Law, as modified, however, by custom. Its principal rules are to be found stated in the Land Code of A.H. 1274 (A.D. 1858) though this has been supplemented and modified by much later legislation. The Ottoman Civil Code (The Mejelle) first published in A.H. 1285 (A.D. 1869) also contains much important matter relating to interests in land.

The Land Law of the Turkish Empire applied, in name at least, throughout the whole of the Sultan's wide dominions. In practice its application in the territories more remote from the capital was much modified by local custom. This was certainly the case in Iraq[1] and to a less extent also in Palestine and Trans Jordan. It still applies, subject to this reservation and to local legislation in Syria, Palestine, Trans Jordan and Cyprus and partially also in Iraq. In the Turkish Republic it has been superseded. In Egypt it does not appear to have ever applied.

---

[1] In Iraq an attempt was made about 1870 to model land holding there upon the principles stated in the Ottoman Land Code and to introduce land registration. The attempt failed and appears to have merely increased the existing confusion of land rights in the country. Theoretically, indeed, the Land Code still continued to apply, but in practice its application was very partial. See fully Sir Ernest Dowson, "Inquiry into Land Tenure in Iraq" presented to the Iraq Government, 1931.

2   The Land Law of Palestine.

It is not necessary here to enquire to what extent, if at all, the Moslem conquerors permitted the survival of pre-existing Byzantine Land Law and customs. Traces of Byzantine institutions may be still discoverable in the present Land system, but for practical purposes we make the Arab and Ottoman Law our starting point.

The original Arab conquerors of Egypt and Syria did not in general dispossess the existing inhabitants. The land of the conquered countries seems from an early date to have been divided into two main classes, Ushuri land (Tithe paying) and Kharaji land (Tribute paying). The Ushuri land, neglecting certain minor distinctions, was land which was delivered over to the Moslem conquerors or which was left to the inhabitants who embraced Islam. Owners of Ushuri land paid a tithe of one-tenth of the gross yield. The Kharaji land was land left in the hands of non-Moslem inhabitants. This land was of two kinds. Upon some land the Kharaj was Moukassamah, i. e. proportional to the gross yield but never less than the Ushur. Upon other land the Kharaj was Mouwassaf, i. e. fixed, and due from the land as soon as it was fit for cultivation and whether it were actually under cultivation or not. Land of these two classes was in private ownership. It was the property of the proprietor, his mulk [1]).

The rights of the private owners of Ushuri and of Kharaji lands appear to have been recognised by law in the most ample manner, though, no doubt, the actual extent of protection granted depended upon the conditions of the Government. Art. 2 of the Ottoman Land Code of A.H. 1274 (A.D. 1858) classifies all Ushuri and Kharaji land as mulk, i. e. land in the full ownership of a private proprietor. With these two classes of land we find that the Code also classifies as mulk : —

(a) "sites" for houses within towns and villages, irrespective of area, and pieces of land not exceeding half a dunam situated on the confines of towns and villages appurtenant to dwelling houses.

(b) Land made mulk by special grant of the Sovereign.

It is these two latter classes of Mulk property which are of the greatest importance in Palestine at the present day. But far the greater part of the cultivated land of Palestine falls under a different category, and is not in the full (mulk) ownership of private persons.

---

[1]) See Belin in Jour. Asiatique, 1861, p.p. 414 f.f.

Introduction.

The earliest Moslem law appears to have treated all land in private ownership as mulk land, of one category or another. But much land in conquered countries remained in the hands of the Sovereign as Commander of the Faithful to whom, indeed, a certain proportion of the conquered lands was allotted as of right. Furthermore, we find it stated that land originally Kharaji was not infrequently seized by the Sovereign upon the death of the proprietor and thus passed under his control. Even if heirs presented themselves, a difficulty in collecting the Kharaj (Tribute) might result from the multiplicity of claims and would serve as a pretext for seizure by the State.

These causes resulted in the accumulation of land in the hand of the State, and the extensive Ottoman conquests both of Moslem and Christian lands may be assumed to have led to the same result. In the Ottoman Empire, therefore, a very large part of the lands of the conquered countries belonged to the class of Emirieh (State) Land. Some part of them may possibly have been cultivated directly for the benefit of the Imperial Treasury but cultivation was more usually secured by a system of grants of a temporary nature. The Sovereign could, and still can, grant out State lands as pure mulk, but the practice more usually followed was to give to the grantee a temporary right, reserving the ownership (Raqabe) to the Treasury.

The Sacred Law permitted the Sovereign to make grants of the State lands (Iqtaa) to private individuals. The grantee of an Iqtaa was obliged to cultivate the land granted to him, subject to the liability of being dispossessed if he failed to do so; thus, according to the Hadith: "Every individual who, during three years, shall leave uncultivated a piece of land of which he has possession, shall lose his rights over the same; and if a third party appears, who will cultivate it, this latter shall have a greater right to possess it than the former owner". This grant of State lands by the Sovereign might either confer on the grantee a right of mulk, or simply a restricted and temporary right [1]; which was, according to the

---

[1] It is stated that even in the case of Mulk the condition applied and if the land remained uncultivated the grantee would be dispossessed. This is, however, not the case in Palestine to day.

The principle that ownership is limited by use is a very ancient one. A Constitution of Valentinian Theodosius and Arcadius (Code XI-59-8) provides that cultivation of deserted lands (agri deserti) by a squatter bars the claim of the previous owner who has neglected for two years to take proceedings for recovery. This text has given rise to much controversy but is very probably an

4   The Land Law of Palestine.

Sharia, personal to the grantee, and did not pass to his heirs after his death.

It was in accordance with this system that the settlement of Christian lands conquered by the Ottomans appears to have been made. Concerning the settlement of Hungary, we read in a fetwa by Abou Sounoud, Sheikh El Islam: "Cultivated land should be left in the possession of the inhabitants but, though their houses and gardens remain in their full (mulk) ownership, the cultivated lands are not their mulk property. These should be reckoned as belonging to the class of land called in other parts of the Empire Miri land (i.e. State land). The Raqabe (ownership) of these lands is reserved for the Treasury of the Faithful and the land can only be treated as let out to the Rayahs" [1]).

The grants of conquered lands of this temporary nature were frequently made not direct to the peasants but to soldiers and military leaders as a reward for their services and an obligation to serve military service was often attached thereto. "An extension of the system of Iqtaa was made and a system of military tenure existed in Turkey from a very early date. This military tenure was of two kinds, Ziamet and Timar, and the holders were called Sipahis [2]).

The Timar was the smaller fief: and the holder had in time of war to provide a certain number of armed horsemen proportionate to the amount of the revenue; the Ziamets were larger and were held by a similar tenure; each was transmissible to the elder son on death. The Sipahis were obliged to reside on their estates in order to be in a better position to perform their duties of military services; but apparently the duties of cultivation were performed by a class of persons living on the land in a position of subordination to the Sipahis. The tenure of these cultivators is not clear, but it seems that they were obliged to remain on the land at their superior's pleasure, that they could not alienate or pledge the lands they cultivated, that the superior could compel them to work for him, and that if they did not cultivate the land they were liable to be deprived of it at their lord's pleasure.

---

exceptional law intended to confirm the customary law followed among the Arabs on the eastern borders of the Empire. See Chauvin, La Constitution du Code Théodosien sur les Agri deserti — Mons, (1900).

[1]) Quoted in Padel and Steeg, De la legislation foncière Ott. p. 20.

[2]) See more fully, Scott, Law affecting foreigners in Egypt, p. 117.

The military fiefs of Islam are elaborately discussed by M. Belin in Jour. Asiatique, 1870, pp 187 ff.

Introduction.

These cultivators appear for the most part to have been Christians[1]).

No evidence is available as to whether military fiefs of this description existed in Palestine. But as we find that the situation of the actual cultivators of Emirieh land was not dissimilar in the Moslem parts of the Empire, we are led to assume that the same general causes operated throughout. The intervention of the feudal lords of this kind between the peasantry and the State may probably have affected adversely the rights of the peasant cultivators; but in general the situation of the holders of State land appears to have continued to be regulated on the principles applicable to grants of Iqtaa.

In some parts of the Ottoman Empire the Sultan made use of the system of tax farming to secure revenue with the least trouble.

About 1839 the Ottoman Government abolished the system of Ziamets and Timars, and replaced the feudatories by Tax Farmers (Multazims) and later, by Muhassils (Tax Collectors). It seems certain that in the first half of the last century, the greater part of the cultivable area of the Ottoman Empire was Emirieh land and that all cultivators of such land paid a tithe of the produce. It appears that the Sipahis collected the tithe under some arrangement with the State, in which case their replacement by Tax-Farmers (Multazims) and later by Tax-Collectors (Muhassils) is comprehensible. There is no doubt that the actual grants of the right of possession to cultivators were made by the Sipahis, who presumably received and retained whatever sums were payable by way of premiums, on admission, etc. When, therefore, the Sipahis were replaced by the Multazims, it would be natural that the latter should make the grants. But in view of the obscurity which surrounds the process of change, it is not possible to be certain of anything save the conclusion, which is revealed by Art. 3 of the Ottoman Land Code of 1858: —

"State Land, the legal ownership of which is vested in the Treasury, comprises arable fields, meadows, summer and winter pasturing grounds, woodland and the like, the enjoyment of which is granted by the Government.

Possession of such land was formerly acquired, in case of sale or being left vacant, by permission of or grant by feudatories (sipahis) of "Timars" and "Ziamets" as lords of the soil, and later through the "Multazims" and "Muhassils".

---

[1]) Scott, op. cit. at p. 116.

6   The Land Law of Palestine.

"This system was abolished and possession of this kind of immovable property will henceforth be acquired by leave of and grant by the agent of the Government appointed for the purpose. Those who acquire possession will receive a title-deed bearing the Imperial Cypher.

The sum paid in advance (muajele) for the right of possession which is paid to the proper official for the account of the State, is called the tapu fee."

The State Land of which this article speaks is that type of land usually designated Miri Land in Palestine. The term Miri will be used throughout this book in this sense. In one view the name is a misnomer since State (Miri) land should include all land in which the State has proprietary rights as owners. But custom has narrowed its meaning in this connection to land vested in the State which is granted out to cultivators in accordance with the provisions of the Land Code [1]).

The Government agents through whom grants were at first made were the officials of the Treasury (Malia) and afterwards those of the Land Registry (Tapu). The change, therefore, seems to have been mainly fiscal in purpose and no serious alteration in the established customary rights of the cultivators was presumably intended but, thenceforth, whatever advantages may at one time have been drawn by the holders of Ziamets and Timars from their rights over the cultivating peasantry were enjoyed by the State. Consequently, throughout the Ottoman Empire from 1858 onwards, the cultivating peasantry received grants directly from the State and not through an intermediary and their possessory rights were enjoyed in accordance with the provisions of the Land Code and the accompanying laws [2]).

This is the actual position in Palestine to day. The greater part of the cultivated land is Miri in the sense that the ultimate proprietary interest is in the State; but a cultivating interest is enjoyed by grantees whose right, though assignable and heritable, is yet less than ownership. Land which is in the full (Mulk) ownership of the holder is rare, except within the confines and on the outskirts of towns and villages.

---

[1]) In Iraq the term Miri is applied primarily to such State lands as remain at the free disposition of the Government. Land which is granted out to Tapu holders is termed Tapu land. This Iraqi usage has much to commend it though it does not accord with the terminology of the Code. In this book, however, the terms used by the Code will be adopted throughout.

[2]) See Tute in Jour. Soc. Comp. Leg. for Nov. 1927 at pp 166 ff.

Introduction.

The peculiar position of the State with reference to Miri land is usually explained in legal language by saying that the State retains the Raqabe (or ownership), while the grantee has only a right of possession (tessaruf). Ottoman legislation more recent than the Land Code has amplified the right of the Miri holder (or possessor); and to describe his present position as that of a "possessor" only is misleading. But the term "tessaruf" of which the English equivalent is "possession" has become a technical term to denote the interest of the Miri holder; and in spite of its misleading implications it is still frequently employed. In this compilation we shall speak of the mutessariff (or person entitled to tessaruf of Miri land) as a "holder" and of his right as a "holding".

The State retains certain important rights in connection with Miri land as contrasted with Mulk. The scope of these rights will be considered in detail in the Chapter dealing with Miri land. The dominant fact to be borne in mind is that, while the State has no proprietary rights in Mulk, it continues to claim a vague though well established proprietary right in Miri. The theory of the law does not allow to a Miri holder more than a "limited" interest.

The theory upon which the law governing Miri land is based is that a limited interest (tessaruf) in the land is granted by the State to a grantee for the purposes of cultivation. The grantee is bound to make the land productive and thus enable a tithe to be levied for the benefit of the revenue. Upon the produce tithe is levied but the holder must upon his entry make to the state a payment for the grant itself. This is the Bedl Misl, Tapu Misl or Tapu fee[1]) chargeable as a premium or fee on admittance. The grantee's interest, though heritable and assignable, may nevertheless come to an end, and upon its termination, the beneficial interest once more accrues to the State. The causes and incidents of the cesser of the Miri interest will be considered later.

A considerable part of the land in the Ottoman Empire, and particularly in Syria and Palestine, is not under cultivation. Some part of it is incapable of cultivation. Most, if not all, of such land in Palestine, outside urban areas is owned and possessed by the State. Woodland and pasture grounds may be the subject of Tapu grants (Land Code, Arts. 24, 30) but there remains much land which is not so granted. It is termed Mewat (Dead) land. Provisions are

Mewat.

---

[1]) Tapu is an old Turkish word for soil. A tapu grant or a tapu fee is, therefore, a grant of or fee payable for the soil. The term Bedl Misl will be normally used throughout this book to designate the sum paid to the State in advance by the grantee of Miri.

made by the law for bringing such land when possible under cultivation and making it the subject of Tapu grants.

Metruki. There remains a special class of land which is withdrawn from private use and is, therefore, called Metruki (withdrawn) land. Such land is left for the use of the public, either for general use (e. g. highways), or for the special use of the inhabitants of one or more villages or towns (e. g. common pasture lands, threshing floors, etc.).

Mevqufe. To these four classes the Land Code and many writers add a fifth, namely Waqf land (Mevqufe). Art. 4 of the Land Code classifies Mevqufe (dedicated) land as of two kinds:—

(a) that which having been true mulk originally was dedicated with the formalities prescribed by the Sacred (Moslem) Law;

(b) land which being separated from Miri land has been dedicated by the Sultan or others with the Imperial Sanction.

Though the Land Code speaks of Mevqufe land as "originally mulk" or "separated from State land by dedication" it will generally be found more convenient to regard land which is dedicated not as a special species of land but as Mulk or Miri land of which the mode of enjoyment has been modified by the dedication. The distinction between undedicated and dedicated land is analogous to that which exists in England between land which is the property of a beneficial owner and land which is held in trust for beneficiaries.

The Moslem Religious Law recognises the power of an owner of land to dedicate it for a religious purpose. It then became Waqf, so called, because the effect of the dedication was to arrest or detain the ownership and to leave it unchangeable, while the enjoyment and revenues of the land continued in perpetuity available for the purpose marked out by the dedicator. A dedication of this description could be made only of land in the full ownership (mulk) of the dedicator. Consequently only mulk land can be made Waqf. The "holder" of Miri cannot dedicate it as Wakf unless the land is transformed into Mulk so that the Raqabe was included in the dedication.

However, a dedication of Miri is possible though such dedication is said to be "untrue". Art. 4 of the Land Code tells us that the dedication of Miri consists in the fact that some of the State imposts, such as tithes and other taxes on the Miri land, have been appropriated by the Government for the benefit of some object. Such a dedication constitutes an untrue Waqf. The only effect of the dedication is that part or all of the revenue which the State enjoyed from the land is paid henceforth to the Waqf.

Introduction.

Art. 4, therefore, provided "the ownership of land, which has been so dedicated, belongs to the Treasury and the provisions and enactments hereinafter contained (i.e. the provisions of the Land Code) apply to it. Provided that whereas in the case of pure Miri, (i.e. Miri in respect of which there is no dedication), the fees for transfer and succession and the price for acquiring vacant land are paid into the Treasury, for this kind of Mevqufe land such fees shall be paid to the Waqf concerned". Such Waqfs are termed "Takhsisat". But there may, with Government sanction be a dedication of the tessaruf itself, and this may or may not be accompanied with a dedication of the State revenues from the land. If the "tessaruf" is dedicated, there can thereafter be no transfer thereof or succession thereto. The land will "be cultivated or occupied on behalf of the waqf directly or by letting it". If the taxes on such land have not been dedicated, they will be payable by the Waqf to the State. If the taxes are also dedicated the interest of the State is practically annihilated, though, as it would appear, that the land remains Miri, the interest of the Waqf is limited to such interests as a Miri holder can have. Throughout the Land Code the term Mevqufe is used without any restrictive prefix to mean, land which belongs to the Miri category and some interest in which is dedicated. The same usage is adopted in other Ottoman legislation as to Miri interests. In this compilation Mevqufe (or Mauquf) land must be assumed to be used in the same sense unless the context shews clearly that the terms are being used in their literal signification as referring to dedicated land in general.

Mussaqaf, (pl. Mussaqafat) means a building from which income is derived and which has a roof. Mustaghil, (pl. Mustaghilat) means income bearing property. The two terms are freely used of dedicated property which produces an income, the term Mussaqafat being specialised in application to property built upon, while Mustaghilat has a more general connotation. When, however, the two are contrasted Mustaghilat is contrasted with Mussaqafat, and means income bearing property other than that covered by buildings (e.g. plantations). *Mussaqafat and Mustaghilat.*

Where a Waqf [1]) is the owner of land it must either use the property itself for the purpose for which it is dedicated or raise a revenue for that purpose by direct exploitation or by leasing it at a rent. *Ijara Wahida and Ijaratein.*

---

[1]) The language used often seems to imply that the Waqf is a person, a kind of corporation owning the property. This is not so in Moslem Law. But the language though theoretically misleading is convenient.

The Land Law of Palestine.

The administrator of property dedicated cannot sell it. To raise a revenue it is desirable to grant a lease, but the powers of leasing allowed are very restricted.

If dedicated property is simply leased in the ordinary way, it is said to be let on Ijara Wahida, i.e. single rent. This method of dealing was, however, inadequate. The device which has most frequently been employed to mitigate the lack of flexibility in the law regulating the disposition and administration of waqf property is known as Ijaratein (double rent). This double rent was treated as conformable with the Law of Waqf, because in theory it was a lease from year to year only, but a right of perpetual renewal was given to the "lessee". The grantee of the lease by Ijaratein paid what may be termed a premium to the Waqf (the first "rent") and further undertook to pay an annual rent. Subject to the payment of the rent, he enjoyed what was in fact a perpetual beneficial interest which was assignable and eventually became heritable also. The similarity in the legal position of the holder in Ijaratein to that of the holder of Miri land is obvious. Both have an interest in land which is strictly not their property. In the case of the Ijaratein Waqf the Raqabe belongs to the Waqf, but the holder in Ijaratein has a perpetual beneficial interest subject to the obligation of making periodic payments. So also the holder of Miri enjoys a perpetual beneficial interest in property of which the Raqabe is in the State. If the holder in Ijaratein terminates, the property escheats to the Waqf [1]).

Another device employed by the Administration of Waqf property was the creation of what are known as Muqata'a Waqfs. Muqata'a is the annual rent paid for land to the Waqfs (i.e. to the person charged with the administration thereof) by the person in possession of property of which the ground is dedicated as Waqf and the buildings, trees and vines thereon are Mulk. In effect, the administrator of the Wakf made an agreement with a person intending to build or plant that in return for a fixed rent (Muqata'a) the lessee should be deemed the Mulk owner of the buildings or plantations though they stood on land belonging to the Waqf. The incidents of Takhsisat, Ijaratein and Muqata'a Waqf are more fully considered in the sequel.

---

[1]) The contract or tenure of Ijaratein is also well known in Egypt under the name of Hikr. There is a close similarity between it and the Roman Emphyteusis, so much so that a historical connection has been plausibly suggested. "Le contrat de Hekr est un contrat consensuel portant des fortes présomptions de sa dérivation de l'emphytéose des Romains". (per curiam in Debbane and Wakf El Noubi. Gaz. Trib. Mixtes. XV p. 265).

Introduction. 11

I. Religious Law.
a) Moslem.

The Moslem Law applied in Palestine is the law of the Sunni School and of the Hanafite rite.

The Sunnis derive their law from: —

(I) the Koran;

(II) the Hadith (or Sunnat) i.e. traditions handed down from the Prophet by any person who heard or saw him;

(III) the Ijmaa el Ummat (Concordance among the followers) including all the explanations and decisions of the leading disciples and especially of the first four Caliphs.

Upon these bases the law was worked out by the use of Kyas, i.e. the exercise of private judgment based on analogy.

There are four schools (or rites) of Sunni Law:

(a) the Hanafis;
(b) the Shafies;
(c) the Malikis; and
(d) the Hanabalis.

The Shafi, Maliki and Hanabali rites are followed in parts of Arabia and Northern Africa. The Hanafi rite is followed by Sunni Moslems in India, and was adopted by the Ottomans. It has consequently become the dominant rite in Egypt, Syria and Palestine, though the bulk of the peasantry are still by tradition Shafites. Hanafite sources are, however, used in the Moslem Courts of Palestine and the Grand Mufti of Palestine is Hanafite, though there is also a Shafite Mufti. In this book references to Moslem law may be assumed to be references to the law according to the Hanafite rite[1]).

The Moslem Law applied in Palestine is in part common law applicable to all the inhabitants whatever their religion or nationality. The Common Law is contained in the Mejelle (Ottoman Civil Code). This Code was compiled in A.H. 1285 (1869) by a Commission appointed by the Sultan. It is intended to be a statement of the Moslem law as to the matters with which it deals, according to the doctrines of the Hanafite rite. In interpreting the Mejelle it is, therefore, permissible to refer to other authorities upon Moslem Law of the Hanafite rite. The Hedaya or Guide to Moslem Law (12th century) which is referred to with approval by the compilers of the Mejelle has been not infrequently used for this purpose.

---

[1]) For further information as to the different rites and their characteristic doctrines see Vesey FitzGerald, Muhammedan Law, Chap. II. No reference will be made in this book to Shia law since this is of no practical interest in Palestine.

12 The Land Law of Palestine.

The Mejelle contains a great number of provisions touching the Law of Immovable Property. It has, however, to be borne in mind that when speaking of owners of land and their rights the Mejelle refers only to Mulk ownership. The existence of the special interests of the grantees of State (Miri) land is barely referred to and they are not regulated. What is said in the Mejelle as to the rights of owners must not, therefore, without further enquiry be extended to Miri holders.

Moslem Religious Law has further application in Palestine not as common law, but as law applicable to Moslems only. This is due to the fact that the Moslem Religious Courts have exclusive jurisdiction in matters of personal status concerning Moslems; and for the purpose of such jurisdiction matters of personal status include suits regarding (inter alia) succession, wills and legacies. (Palestine Order in Council, 1922, Arts. 51, 52). Moslem Religious Courts have also exclusive jurisdiction in cases of the constitution or internal administration of a Waqf constituted for the benefit of Moslems before a Moslem Religious Court. (Art. 52). As regards these matters and within these limits the Religious Law finds application.

(b) the Jewish Religious (Rabbinical) Law; and (c) the Canon Law of certain Christian Communities. Jewish and Christian Canon law have a limited and similar field of application, since Rabbinical and Patriarchal Courts are given jurisdiction in matters of personal status of persons who are members of their respective communities, and jurisdiction over any case as to the constitution or internal administration of a Waqf or religious endowment constituted before their Court and according to their law. This jurisdiction, though exclusive as to such waqfs or religious endowments, is concurrent with the Civil Courts in all matters of personal status except marriage, divorce, alimony and wills. Thus the right of inheritance to a deceased Jew or Christian Palestinian may come to be decided by the Civil Courts who will not normally apply the Religious Law of the deceased's community. The exercise of this concurrent jurisdiction and the law applicable in this matter by the Civil Courts are regulated by the Succession Ordinance, 1923.

Finally it is necessary to remark that the Religious Law of the various communities having jurisdiction in matters of succession is applicable only to mulk interests in immovables. A special Ottoman Law applicable in Palestine governs the inheritance of Miri interests. Every Court (Religious or Civil) having jurisdiction in matters of succession must determine rights of inheritance to Miri interests by reference to this Law to the exclusion of its own Religious Law, Moslem, Jewish, or Christian.

Introduction. 13

The law applicable to interests in Miri land is primarily to be found in the Ottoman Land Code of A. H. 1274. The rights of the Miri holder and the rights of the State are dealt with in detail. The Code applies also to Miri land which is dedicated as Waqf, and contains certain provisions with reference to Metruki and Mewat land.

II. Secular Law
(a) The Ottoman Land Code of A.H. 1274 (1858).

The provisions of the Land Code were not as a whole a new creation of the Ottoman legislator. A Code upon the subject had been promulgated several centuries earlier and various laws modifying it had been enacted. The fundamental ideas set forth in the Land Code conform with those of the Moslem Law, but it is probable that the Code represents in the main the accepted customary law applicable to the classes of land contained therein.

The Ottoman Government did not content itself with a formulation of the law governing Miri land. It conceived the more ambitious scheme of a settlement of existing Miri possessors and the establishment for the future of a regular system of registration. To this end a series of laws were enacted, notably the law as to granting of Title Deeds for State Land, briefly termed the Tapu Law of 8 Jamad El Thani, 1275 (1858), followed by the Regulations as to Title Deeds of 7 Sha'ban, 1276. A new administration, that of the Daftar Khani (Imperial Registers) was established charged with the function of securing the registration of all titles to land. The system of registration in the Daftar Khani was at first confined to Miri. A system of registration of mulk titles by the Sharia (Moslem Religious) Courts had long existed, and by a law of 28 Rejeb, 1291, the registration of mulk was transferred to the Daftar Khani. A later law of Rabi El Awal, 1293, dealt with the issue of title deeds for interests in Waqf property by the Daftar Khani, e. g. the interests of the holders in Ijaratein.

(b) Later Ottoman Laws.

Another series of laws aimed at the modernisation of the Ottoman Law of Land and also at the enlargement of the interest of the Miri holder. Of these some, such as the Forest Law of 1285, the Expropriation Law of 1295, and the Mining Law of 1304, have been superseded in Palestine. Other laws of this period are the Law of 17 Moharrem, 1284, which extended the rights of inheritance in Miri, the Law of 7 Sefer, 1284, which gave to foreigners the right to hold immovables in the Ottoman Empire, the Law of 15 Shewal, 1288, as to sale of immovables for payment of debts; the Law of 4 Rejeb, 1292, as to succession to private interests in Mustaghilat and Mussaqafat Waqfs possessed in Ijaratein.

14   The Land Law of Palestine.

After the Turkish revolution of 1909, the proposal was made to reformulate the Land Law with far reaching simplifications. Though this scheme was never carried out, a group of laws was enacted which did effect a very considerable simplification of the law, mainly in the direction of unification of the law governing Miri interests and that governing Mulk. These laws were strictly speaking provisional only, that is to say, they were in the form of Decrees and had no parliamentary authority. Nevertheless, they were put in force, and are, therefore, applicable in Palestine under the provisions of Art. 46 of the Palestine Order in Council [1]).

The most important of these later Ottoman Laws are : —

Law relating to the Inheritance of Immovable Property, of 27 Rabi-el-Awal, 1331	Promulgated 3 Rabi-el-Thani, 1331 [2]).
Law concerning the Right of certain corporate bodies to own immovable Property of 22 Rabi-el-Awal, 1331	Promulgated 27 Rabi-el-Awal 1331.
Law for the Mortgage of immovable property of 1 Rabi-el-Thani, 1331.	Promulgated 6 Rabi-el-Thani 1331
Law regulating the right to dispose of immovable property of 5 Jamadi-el-Awal, 1331	Promulgated 11 Jamadi el-Awal, 1331.
Law of Partition of joint immovable property of 14 Moharrem, 1332	Promulgated 20 Moharrem, 1332

There is also an Imperial Iradeh on the leasing of immovable property of 25 Jamad-el-Awal, 1299, amended by a Provisional Law of 18 Rabi-el-Awal, 1332.

---

[1]) Art. 46 provides that the jurisdiction of the Civil Courts shall be exercised in conformity with the Ottoman laws in force in Palestine on 1st Nov. 1914.

[2]) Under the Law of Promulgation, 1289, a Law was effective 15 days after the promulgation unless in the law itself a specific day is fixed for putting the law into effect. Promulgation is effected by publication of the Law in the Official Gazette in Constantinople. (Young, Corps de dr. Ott. Vol. 1, page 13).
    This Law was repealed by the Imperial Iradeh of 1329. Sec. 4 of this Iradeh provides that all Laws shall come into operation over the whole of the Ottoman Empire from the date specified in the text. In cases where no date is specified, the Law came into force after a period of 60 days beginning from the date of promulgation.

Introduction.

15

Since the British Occupation many Ordinances have been promulgated making changes in or additions to the Land Law.

These Ordinances have not on the whole seriously modified the substantive Land Law as it existed in Turkish times, though some important changes have been made, notably by the Land Transfer Ordinances, the Mahlul Land Ordinance 1920, the Mewat Land Ordinance 1921, the Succession Ordinance 1923 and the recent Land Law Amendment Ordinance 1933. Ordinances have, however, provided new or modified methods for Expropriation, creation of Charitable Trusts, Land Settlement, Protection of Cultivators, etc. Reference will be made in the text to the provisions of the various ordinances in the appropriate context.

(c) Ordinances of the Government of Palestine.

Finally, it may be remarked that under Art. 46 of the Palestine Order in Council, the Civil Courts are empowered to apply the principles of the English Common Law and the doctrines of Equity in force in England, subject to and so far as the Ottoman Law does not extend and apply, and so far as the circumstances of Palestine and its inhabitants permit.

In view, however, of the abundant authority as to the substantive Ottoman Law of Land, recourse to this provision can seldom be necessary in this connection.

In order to ascertain whether a particular law was in force on November 1st, 1914, and whether, consequently, it is in force in Palestine, the following information will be useful. The months in the Moslem year are: —

Note upon the Calendar.

1. Moharrem
2. Sefer
3. Rabi-el-Awal
4. Rabi-el-Thani or Rabi-el-Akhir
5. Jamad-el-Awal
6. Jamad-el-Thani or Jamad-el-Akhir
7. Rejeb
8. Sha'ban
9. Ramadan
10. Shewal
11. Zil Quade
12. Zil Hijje.

The Moslem years are reckoned from the Hegira (A.D. 622) and are designated A.H. to distinguish them from the Christian era. As the Moslem year is lunar it is shorter than the European (Gregorian) year.

16   The Land Law of Palestine.

The dates of Turkish Laws are in this compliation given according to this reckoning. In the Dastour (Collection of Turkish Statutes, etc.) they are also dated according to the Turkish financial year (Malia) which varied slightly from the Moslem epoch.

The months of the Turkish year are:

1. Kanun Sani   (January)
2. Shubat   (February)
3. Mart   (March)
4. Nissan   (April)
5. Mais   (May)
6. Haziran   (June)
7. Tamuz   (July)
8. Agostos   (August)
9. Elul   (September)
10. Tishrin Awàl   (October)
11. Tishrin Sani   (November)
12. Kanun el Awal   (December)

The 1st of November, 1914, according to the Arabic mode of reckoning is 12th Zil Hijje, 1332, and according to the Turkish mode of reckoning is 19th Tishrin Awal, 1330 (Malia).

CHAPTER I—MIRI LAND.

The term Miri Land is here used to mean land over which a heritable right of possession (tessaruf) is granted by the State to a private person, though the Raqabe (ownership) remains in the State.

The Ottoman Commentators speak of the Miri holder (Mutessarif) as holding land from the State under a lease of indefinite duration at a double rent of which one consists in the Tapu payments (Bedl Misl) and fees payable upon transfer and succession, and the other takes the form of tithe or taxes, or analogous periodical payments (Ijara Zemin)[1]. This is the classical view of the nature of a Miri holding. The resemblance of a Tapu grant to a lease is less obvious to-day than in earlier times, but, though the rights of a Miri holder were at one time much more limited than they are at present, yet there remain certain special limitations or incidents attaching to possession of Miri which distinguish it from Mulk ownership. These are consequences of the fact that a holder of Miri interest can only exercise such rights as can be shown to have been accorded to him by the State, while the Mulk owner must be presumed to be entitled to do as he pleased with the land, subject to any express limitations imposed by the State upon owners.

The right of the holder of Miri is subject to the eminent domain of the State. It exists only in virtue of an express grant from the State, though a right to have such a grant may in certain circumstances arise. It is a right to exclusive possession of the surface for the purpose (normally) of cultivation. The holder has no right of property in the subsoil.

No private interest in Miri land can exist save under a grant issuing out of the Tapu Office. Every interest, therefore, has its origin in a Tapu grant. Upon every devolution or transfer of the interest so created application must be made for the issue of a

---

[1] See fully Nédjib Chiha. Traité de la Propriété Immobilière en droit Ottoman. Le Caire, 1906, p. 129. For an account of the origin and nature of Miri see the judgment of the Cyprus Court in Tzinki v King's Advocate, 10 C.L.R. at p. 57 ff.

The Land Law of Palestine.

title deed in favour of the new holder. It is most explicitly provided by the Ottoman legislation that no one can for any reason whatever hold Miri land without having a title deed (Kushan)[1]). The issue of the title deed involved registration of the new holder as the holder of the interest under the Tapu grant.

In fact, owing to numerous causes, a very large number of occupiers of Miri land in Palestine do not possess title deeds; and until they do, and until the extent of their holding is precisely known, great difficulty must continue in determining rights to land. Certain of the defects in actual administration have been dealt with by Palestine legislation, notably by the Correction of Land Registers Ordinance which will be discussed later. But these meet only one class of cases in which the Register of Title Deeds does not correspond with the facts of possession and enjoyment. It is the main object of Land Settlement to bring about an exact correspondence between the Register and the facts.

The issue of title deeds (Kushans) and the registration of transactions was early entrusted to a department known as the Daftar Khani (Administration of Imperial Registers) which is now represented in Palestine by the Land Registry. The course of legislation with reference to registration of various interests and the procedure at present followed upon registration will be discussed in a subsequent chapter. It is sufficient here to note that the Registry is primarily a Registry of transactions between persons (Registry of Deeds), and not a Registry of transactions with reference to defined plots of land (Registry of Title). Although every devolution of land was by law required to be completed by the grant of new kushans at the Daftar Khani, no attempt was made to locate precisely on the ground the area of land to which each transaction referred and index all transactions by reference to a suitable map defining the area. Such a course could not be adopted in the absence of a reliable cadastral survey maintained up to date, and this did not exist. Consequently the Registry was primarily personal and not territorial. It aimed at revealing the series of transactions affecting a parcel of land not always specified by a survey. Under the present Administration an attempt is made to relate a series of transactions to a specified parcel, but until an exact survey has been made and maps exist showing the situation, extent and features of the land, registration of Title as contrasted with registration of Deeds is impracticable.

---

[1]) see Regulations as to Title Deeds, 7 Sha'ban A.H. 1276, Art. 1.

Chapter I—Miri Land.

Title deeds of Miri land are in form personal only, but new kushans will be given gratuitously (without Tapu payments and on payment of Land Registry fees only) to assignees and heirs, and we may, therefore say that the rights of a Miri holder are assignable and heritable. If there is no heir entitled to succeed under the Miri Law of Succession, the land should in principle escheat to the State, since, the limited right having terminated, the beneficial interest becomes once more merged in the Raqabe. The merger may occur for other reasons also. In particular it is an ancient rule of the Moslem Law that "where a person has brought waste land under cultivation with permission of the chief he obtains a property in it, but if land be left uncultivated for three years it may be resumed and assigned to another"[1]. "It is clear", it has been stated in Cyprus, "that the principle of the law is that the possession of Miri is granted for the purpose of cultivation and of cultivation exclusively, in order that the State may derive a tithe from the land"[2]. Consequently Miri land is in principle cultivable land (tarla) and it is an implied term of the grant that it shall be kept under cultivation. But the State may make Tapu grants of land not intended to be cultivated but intended to be used as pasture, meadow, or woodland, (Land Code Arts. 24, 10, 30) in which case no obligation to cultivate falls upon the holder[3]. The use to which the land is to be put is specified in the column of the Kushan in which the category of the land is stated, e.g. Mera (pasture), Ghair (Meadow), Kurou, (Woodland), Akhrash (Forest), Tarla (cultivated land).

The termination of the interests of a holder under a Tapu grant is said to render the land Mahlul (vacant). The State is then free to make a grant to someone else and to exact payment therefor.

But such termination does not necessarily leave the State free to grant the land to any person whom it chooses. Certain persons have preferential rights to obtain a grant by Tapu, i.e. on payment of the Tapu value. So long as these rights exist the land is not pure Mahlul, but is said to be subject to the Right to Tapu (Mustaheki Tapu).

We shall now proceed to state the law which determines the circumstances under which Miri becomes vacant (Mahlul) or subject to rights to Tapu and the results which follow.

---

[1] Hedaya. Book XLV "On the cultivation of waste lands".
[2] Per curiam in Ragheb v Gerasimo. C.L.R. III at p. 138.
[3] Cf. Economou v Queen's Advocate, cited in C.L.R. II at p. 11.

The Land Law of Palestine.

Want of cultivation.

The state has a right to resume the land, if it has remained uncultivated for three years. An act of resumption is necessary and the former holder has a right to Tapu.

Land Code, Art. 68.

"Except for one of the following reasons, duly established namely:—

(I) Resting the soil for one or two years, or even more if owing to its exceptional nature and situation it is requisite;

(II) Obligation to leave land which has been flooded uncultivated for a time after the water has subsided in order that it may become cultivable;

(III) Imprisonment of the possessor as a prisoner of war; land which has not been cultivated, either directly, by the possessor, or indirectly, by being leased or loaned, and remains unproductive for three years consecutively becomes subject to the right to Tapu, whether the possessor be in the locality or absent. If the former possessor wishes to recover the land, it shall be given to him on payment of its Tapu value. If he does not claim it shall be put up to auction and adjudged to the highest bidder"[1].

Land Code, Art. 69.

"Land, by whomsoever it is possessed, which has been flooded for a long time and on which the water afterwards subsides does not for this reason become subject to the right to Tapu, the former possessor keeps it in his possession and under his control as before. If the former possessor is dead, his heirs shall have possession and enjoyment of it, and failing them it shall be given on payment of the Tapu value, to those who have the right to Tapu. But if on the water subsiding, and when the land can be cultivated the possessor, or his heirs do not enter into possession of it, and leave it unproductive for three years without valid excuse it shall then become subject to the right of Tapu".

So also if meadow land held by Tapu is not reaped and remains idle for three years it becomes subject to the right to Tapu. (Art. 85).

Where pasture land is held by Tapu grant the holders pay dues in lieu of tithe to the State. If without excuse (Art. 68) they do not use the land and fail to pay the dues for three years the land becomes subject to the right of Tapu. (Art. 84).

There is no express provision as to the circumstances in which woodland held by Tapu becomes Mahlul. Presumably the woodland becomes subject to the right to Tapu for causes analogous to those specified in Arts. 84 and 85.

---

[1] The Cypriot case Houston v. King's Advocate, (1922) 11 C.L.R. at p. 72 deals very fully with confiscation of land for want of cultivation, but the decision was under a special Cypriot law of 1885 by which Art. 68 of the Land Code had been repealed.

Chapter I—Miri Land.

It does not suffice that the land should have been left uncultivated for three years. It must have been left uncultivated while in the possession of a particular holder.

If land which has been abandoned and left unproductive by the possessor for two consecutive years without valid excuse, is then transferred by him, or owing to his death devolves on his heirs, and is left uncultivated as before for a further one or two years by the transferee or by the heirs without valid excuse it shall not become subject to the right of Tapu. (Land Code, Art. 70).

But if it has been left uncultivated for three years by a particular holder and has not been granted to another before his death, his heirs have a preferential right to a grant on payment of the Tapu value (Art. 71).

Art. 72 of the Land Code makes provision for the rare cases of a partial or total abandonment of a village by its inhabitants who emigrate to another country. Art. 73 deals with the special case of a soldier leaving his land while on active service.

Under the older law the right of succession to Miri was very limited. It is now widely extended. Consequently it is less frequent for land to become Mahlul by reason of failure of heirs. The law as to succession to Miri will be considered in a subsequent chapter. *Failure of successors*

When the right of the Miri holder comes to an end the Tapu value must again be paid by a person desiring to acquire a tessaruf of it. *Right to Tapu.*

In cases when the tessaruf is forfeited for want of cultivation and analogous causes it is the holder himself, who is called upon to pay the Tapu value. Apparently he must promptly exercise his right to Tapu. If he does not do so the land becomes pure Mahlul.

In cases where the tessaruf comes to an end by reason of failure of successors under the law of inheritance, rights to Tapu are given in succession to—:

(a) those who have inherited Mulk trees or buildings on the land;

(b) co-owners;

(c) inhabitants of the village in which the land is situate. (Land Code, Art. 59, as amended by the law of 17 Moharrem, A.H. 1284).

These rights need not be exercised at once. Periods are fixed during which they are exerciseable; namely, for those of class (a),

10 years from the death; for those in class (b), 5 years, and for those in class (c), 1 year. (Arts. 59, 61) [1]).

These rights were formerly of much importance, but failure of successors under the modern law is not frequent. In particular, cases of class (a) are seldom likely to occur since it will not often happen that there exist heirs to the Mulk, but no successors to the Miri. But though in actual practice the case can seldom occur its mention makes explanation necessary.

The law of inheritance governing Mulk interests differs from that governing Miri. Now a Miri holder may own as Mulk the trees and buildings on his land.

Where trees and buildings were lawfully planted or erected on Miri land, they did not accede to the land but became the Mulk property of the planter or builder and the land upon which they are planted or built became subject to the Mulk plantations or erections. An owner of Mulk trees or buildings on Miri of which he was the holder cannot sell the trees without also transferring the land subject to them. (Land Code, Art. 49). And, by Art. 81, upon the death of an owner of Mulk trees or buildings on Miri of which he was the holder heirs to the Mulk are entitled to a grant of the land subject to the trees without payment of Bedl Misl.

A Mulk heir exercising the "right" to Tapu granted by Art. 59 must, of course, pay the Tapu value. Seeing that by Art. 81, he has the right to obtain a grant of the land subject to the trees gratuitously, it seems clear that his right to Tapu under Art. 59 must be exerciseable over other Miri land of which the deceased died possessed. And the accepted view is that this right to Tapu may be exercised over Miri occupied and used by the deceased in connection with the land on which the trees or buildings actually stand though not strictly subject to the trees or buildings in the sense of Art. 81.

---

[1]) It is now provided by the Land Law (Amendment) Ordinance 1933 (Sec. 7) that in every provision of the Ottoman Land Code and any other Ottoman Law concerning immovable property in Palestine fixing the period within which any action may be heard or any right may be exercised, the terms "month" and "year" shall be deemed to refer to a calendar month or year respectively, according to the Gregorian Calendar. Compare as to the meaning of the terms in Ordinances of Palestine Government, Interpretation Ordinance 1929 Sec. 3. C. (12), (33). In Cyprus it has long been definitely held that whatever originally may have been the meaning assigned by the terms of the Ottoman Empire to the term year, the term by universal custom in Cyprus means a year of 365 days. (Yemenji v Andonian 2 C.L.R. at p. 140).

Chapter I—Miri Land.

Owing to changes made by the Law of Disposition, A.H. 1331, Art. 5, discussed hereafter, where trees and buildings are planted or erected on Miri since that date, they accede to the land and partake of its Miri character. No rights under Art. 59 (1) can, therefor, arise in connection with them.

Strangers who are owners of Mulk trees or buildings on Miri land are also entitled in preference to third persons to have a grant of the land upon the death of a holder without successors and upon the payment of Bedl Misl. The right of preference can be exercised subject only to the preferential rights granted by Art 59. (Land Code, Art. 66).

The periods during which the rights to Tapu can be exercised in the case of the death of a Miri holder are in some cases inconveniently long. In an extreme case a person might come forward and claim a right to Tapu at any time within 10 years, and this is perhaps the reason, why the period is fixed in several articles as the period during which undisturbed enjoyment of Miri gives rights by prescription. (Arts. 77, 78, 87).

Rights to Tapu are not inheritable.

A refusal of any one of the persons, having a right to Tapu of the same degree to take the land at the Tapu value, e.g. of several co-possessors, does not forthwith leave his share at the free disposal of the State; the others of the same rank have a right to take the share [1]. (Art. 62.)

If there is a person having a right to Tapu who is prepared to pay the Tapu value, the land cannot be granted to a stranger even though he offers more than the Tapu value. (Art. 86).

Besides the cases already mentioned rights to Tapu may arise, when Mulk trees or buildings on Miri have ceased to exist. The Miri land "merges" in the Mulk plantation or constructions while they exist, but on their disappearance it becomes once more subject to Miri incidents. The person who owned the trees or buildings, has then the right to take the land as Miri on payment of Bedl Misl. (Arts. 82, 83).

Rights to Tapu on disappearance of Mulk trees or buildings.

The wording of these two articles is confused and misleading. A careful examination reveals that several possible cases are really envisaged, though the solutions are not kept separate in the text.

Under Art. 82 we may distinguish the following cases:—

---

[1] The exercise of rights of Tapu by or on behalf of minors, lunatics and absentees is discussed in a subsequent chapter.

The Land Law of Palestine.

1. "A" has erected buildings on Miri land which belongs to another person "B". "A" is the Mulk owner of the buildings and "B" is the Miri owner of the land. A tax (rent), the so-called "Muqata'a Bedl Ushur" is to be paid to the State for the ground on which the buildings stand. In case the buildings have fallen into ruin so that no traces have been left, the land on which the buildings stood becomes subject to the right to Tapu and the owner of the buildings can claim the site upon payment of the Tapu value.

2. An owner of Miri land has erected buildings (which prior to A. H. 1331 are considered Mulk). Such an owner of Mulk buildings on Miri land is liable to the payment of the "Muqata'a Bedl Ushur" for the site occupied by the buildings. If the buildings have fallen into ruin and completely disappeared so that no trace has been left the land (in case the owner of the buildings is not paying the "Muqata'a Bedl Ushur") becomes subject to the Rights to Tapu. If he pays the tax (the fixed rent) he cannot be deprived of the land and the land remains in his possession.

3. An owner of Miri land erected buildings on a part of his Miri land. After his death the buildings (prior to A. H. 1331) devolved by inheritance under the Sharia Law as Mulk and the remainder of the land devolved by inheritance to the heirs mentioned in Art. 82 (as amended by the Law of 17 Moharrem, A. H. 1284, and later by the Law of Inheritance to Miri of A. H. 1331). If the deceased owner paid the "Muqata'a Bedl Ushur" and the heirs to his Miri estate continue to pay the "Muqata'a" they are not deprived of the land and the land remains in their possession. The mulk heirs who would succeed under the Sharia Law to the buildings had the buildings not fallen into ruin have no right to the land.

Art. 83 is similarly constructed. No mention of payment of a Muqata'a Bedl Ushur is requisite, since tithe would be payable on the produce of the trees. (See Land Code, Art. 25).

Disposal of the land where Rights to Tapu are not exerciseable or exercised.   Subject to the exercise of Rights to Tapu, if such exist and have not been lost, the land is vacant (Mahlul) at the disposition of the State. (Arts. 77, 78, 87). The State authorities seek to ascertain what persons have a right to Tapu before proceeding to make a grant to a stranger and provision was made by Art. 16 of the Tapu Law of A. H. 1275 for an enquiry on this point by the local Administrative Council. These Councils no longer exist and local enquiry by the officials of the Lands Department has now to suffice, but if persons in fact have Rights to Tapu which

Chapter I—Miri Land.

remain undiscovered and which are afterwards claimed within the stated periods, the rights must be admitted.

The valuation having been made, the land is offered at that value to the persons having the right to Tapu but no delay in making the valuation is to prejudice such persons (Tapu Law, Arts. 12, 16). If they refuse, their rights are forfeited and the land is at the disposition of the State as Mahlul. The offer should be made to each of the persons in turn in the order in which the rights are given. (Art. 64).

The State has, therefore, an interest in ascertaining when circumstances have caused land to become Mahlul or subject to a right to Tapu.

Some provisions for the notification to the authorities of land which has become Mahlul were made by the Turkish Law (Tapu Law, Art. 20), but further provision has been made by the Mahlul Land Ordinance, 1920, as follows:—

1. Every person who at any time previous to the issue of this Ordinance has taken possession of any land which owing to failure of heirs or non-cultivation became Mahlul is required to inform the Administration within 3 months of the date of this Ordinance.

No action will be taken against any person who has held such lands and who complies with the requirements of this Article. The Administration will in a proper case lease the land to the person who has possessed it.

The right of inheritance will be determined according to the Provisional Law of the 27 Rabi el Awal, 1331, relating to the inheritance of immovable property.

2. Every Mukhtar of a town, village or mazzraa is required to inform the Administration within 3 months of all Mahlul lands of which at any time previous to the issue of this Ordinance illegal possession was taken, stating the names of the persons who have so taken possession.

3. Any person who having taken possession of Mahlul lands fails to inform the Administration will be liable to a fine of L.E. 50 or imprisonment not exceeding 3 months or both these penalties.

Any Mukhtar who having reason to know of such illegal possession fails to inform the Administration in accordance with Art. 2 will be liable to a fine of £E.25 or imprisonment not exceeding one month or both these penalties.

The Land Law of Palestine.

It is to be remarked that this Ordinance only holds out a hope that the land will be leased (not granted by Tapu) to the person who complies with the terms. The policy of the Ottoman Government so far as it appears from the Land Code aimed at leaving Miri in the hands of holders under Tapu grants. Where no right to Tapu was exerciseable or exercised and the land became Mahlul it was the practice that the land should be regranted to a stranger (Land Code, Art. 60).

Indeed the language of the Land Code both in Art. 60 and in other articles (63, 71, 77, 78) appear to make it obligatory that Miri Mahlul should always be offered by auction to the highest bidder, failing the exercise of rights of Tapu. It has, however, been suggested that the imperative form of the language used was mainly intended to make clear that the land was not to be granted out as Mulk but only by Tapu grant as Miri and that it should not be taken as throwing on the state any obligation to grant it out by Tapu if development as part of the Public Domain seemed desirable.

That the policy of the Land Code was directed to separate Miri (Tapu) land from land formerly part of the public domain is probable. Though the texts are not clear the older law seems to have been that a cultivating squatter on Miri who had reported his occupation was entitled to a grant by Tapu on paying the Tapu value, saving, of course, the rights of a previous grantee and of persons having preferential rights to a grant [1]). If this was so, the implication is that Miri land could not be resumed by the State as against a cultivator who was prepared to pay the tithe. The terms of the Mahlul Ordinance (Sec. 1) are difficult, however, to reconcile with this view of the law. Though the Ordinance itself applies only to land occupied prior to its date, yet it certainly implies that the State has discretion as to the manner in which it will deal with Miri Mahlul.

The Land Law (Amendment) Ordinance 1933. The question for all practical purposes has been set at rest by a provision of the recent Land Law (Amendment) Ordinance 1933. Sec. 3 of this Ordinance provides that Miri land which is or may become Mahlul under the provision of the Land Law may, subject to the rights of persons having a right of Tapu be declared by the High Commissioner to be "public" land within the meaning of Art. 12 (1) of the Palestine Order in Council 1922. If such a declaration is made the land clearly remains at the disposition of

---

[1]) See Tute in Jour. Soc. Comp. Leg. Nov. 1927, p.p. 174, 175.

Chapter I—Miri Land.

the State and need not be put up to auction. Indeed, the Ordinance, when enacting provisions (Sec. 4 (2)) for the conduct of the auctions expressly states that these provisions only apply to land not declared "public land".

It is, however, to be noted that the declaration of land as public land is expressly stated to be subject to the rights of Tapu. No doubt if it is known that there exist persons having a right of Tapu the land will not be declared public land until their claims have been disposed of in accordance with the provision of Sec. 4 (1). But there is nothing in the Ordinance to affect the Tapu rights of these to whom the land has not been offered. These, therefore, continue to be exerciseable during the prescribed periods notwithstanding the fact that the lands have been declared public lands.

The Tapu value is fixed by a Commission composed of the District Officer in charge of the sub-district in which the land is situate and two unofficial members nominated by the District Commissioner, but the value so fixed is subject to the review by the Director of Lands whose decision is final.

The value having been fixed the Director of Lands invites persons having a right of Tapu in order of their priority to accept within a period of thirty days from the date of the invitation the grant of the land on payment of the value so fixed. If any such person accepts, the grant will be made to him. Failing acceptance by any person having a right of Tapu the land is to be put up for auction at a reserve to be fixed by the Director of Lands and provision is made for proper publicity of the sale. If the reserve is not reached the land will automatically become "public" land at the expiration of six months from the date of the auction.

Although not expressly provided in the Ordinance, it is a fair inference from its provisions that where the auction is abortive but subsequently and within the six months period some person offers to pay the reserve price a grant could be made to him. Again, since land offered at an abortive auction becomes public land subject to the rights of persons having a right of Tapu, it seems that any such person to whom the land has not in fact been offered may still claim to exercise his Tapu right within the periods fixed by the Land Code.

A grant by Tapu once made is irrevocable. But Art. 87 (Land Code) provides that if within 10 years of the grant of Mahlul it appears that the grantee paid much less than the Tapu value, he may be called upon to pay the balance, and, failing pay-

The Land Law of Palestine.

ment, the land will be granted to another. So also where the grant was made to a person possessing a right to Tapu. This article was mainly intended to avoid grants made corruptly by the Daftar Khani officials, and the provision has perhaps been impliedly repealed by the terms of Sec. 4 (1) of the Land Law (Amendment) Ord. 1933 according to which the decision of the Director of Lands as to the Tapu value is to be final. In any case it is of no practical significance.

The rights and powers of the Miri holder. The law upon this subject was completely transformed by the Ottoman Law of Disposition A. H. 1331. Acquaintance with the older laws is, however, still necessary. The provisions of the Land Code are, therefore, here summarized and the changes made by the Law of A. H. 1331 then explained.

The law prior to A. H. 1331. The normal purpose of a grant by Tapu was to secure cultivation of the land and thereby obtain a tithe. This being so, the rights given to the grantee were limited generally to those requisite to enable the land to be cultivated, all other rights of user remaining attached to the Raqabe [1]).

User of Miri land. According to the theory of the Ottoman Land Law, Miri is normally arable land and is only exceptionally pasture or woodland. The holder must use his land for the purpose of which it was granted. The possibility of forfeiture for non-cultivation has been already sufficiently considered.

The holder of Miri has rights only over the surface. This is clear from the provisions of Art. 107 of the Land Code which provides that minerals found in State Lands belong to the Treasury [2]).

Art. 7 of the Law of Disposition gave to the holder of Miri a right to use the soil, subject to the provisions of special laws, and thereby impliedly repealed Art. 12 of the Land Code. But Art. 7 must be read subject to the Mining Ordinances.

A few articles of the Land Code make reference to user of Miri for cultivation or otherwise. If registered as such, the land could be used for rice fields (Art. 128), as also for pasture, meadow or woodland. Remark also Art. 9 which gives freedom to sow any grain, Art. 11 which gives to the holder the profits of the grass called Kilimba, and Art. 28 which gives him the profits of trees growing naturally [3]).

---

[1]) The English lawyer will be inclined to compare the position of a Copyholder with that of a Miri holder. The analogy is not complete but is suggestive and helpful.

[2]) Mining in Palestine is now fully dealt with in the Mining Ordinances 1925-1933.

[3]) An Iradeh of 16 Sheval, A.H. 1286, abolishes the right of the Treasury

Chapter I—Miri Land.

Exclusive possession is secured by Arts. 13 and 35. Burial in Miri land is prohibited by Art. 33. Meadow land, as also woodland (pernallik) might be broken and cleared and cultivated by the holder (Arts. 10, 19) though the permission of the official (i.e. the local representative of the Daftar Khani) was requisite (Art. 10). In general, indeed, it may be said that Miri holders were forbidden to change the character of the land. They could not, without the leave of the official, turn arable land into a garden or vineyard, (Art. 25) or into woodland (Art. 29), nor build on the land (Art. 31). With permission these things could be done. The law upon this subject has been radically altered by the Law of Disposition, A. H. 1331.

It has already been pointed out that Moslem Law allows plantations and constructions on land and the land itself to be held by separate titles.

So far as regards Miri land this separation generally arose owing to the extension of the rule that things added to the land remained the Mulk of their owners.

Trees growing naturally on Miri land are subject to the land, i.e. the Raqabe of the trees as of the land is vested in the State. (Arts. 28, 106). An Irade of 18 Rabi el Awal, A.H. 1293, gave to the possessor of Miri the right to cut fruit-bearing and non-fruit-bearing trees growing naturally on his land, notwithstanding the provisions of Land Code, Article 28 [1]).

Trees.

If trees growing naturally in Miri were grafted by the holder, they became his Mulk. (Art. 26).

Vines and fruit trees planted by a Miri holder upon his land with leave, as also those planted without leave, if left for three years, were the Mulk of the holder.

No one can plant vines or fruit trees on land in his possession and make it a vineyard or orchard without the leave of the Official. Should he do so the State has the right, for three years, to have what has been planted removed. At the end of that period trees which have reached a fruit-bearing state must be left as they are. Trees and vines planted with the leave of the Official and those planted without leave which have been left for three years, are not considered as subject to the land but belong in full ownership to the possessor of the land. But tithe is taken

---

under Arts. 28 and 30 to take the standing value of trees unlawfully cut by a third party.

[1]) Young, op. cit. VI, p. 53.

of the produce annually. Fixed rent (muqata'a) shall not be charged on the site of such vineyards and orchards on the produce of which tithe is taken. (Land Code, Art. 25).

So also non-fruit-bearing trees planted by a Miri holder upon his land with leave are his Mulk.

Everyone who, with leave of the Official, plants non-fruit-bearing trees on land in his possession and makes it woodland (kurou) has full ownership of them; he alone can cut them down or uproot them. Anyone who cuts them down must pay their standing value. On this kind of woodland a ground-rent (Ijara-i-Zemin) is charged, equivalent to tithe, taking into consideration the value of the site according to its situation. (Land Code, Art. 29).

So long as the Mulk trees and vines remain on the Miri the land is "subject to the Mulk". The land, however, remains Miri, though the owner of the trees has special rights over it (Arts. 81, 44, 49, 59). The obscurity of these articles has already been remarked. Upon one interpretation it would appear that the land upon which the trees or buildings stand is so completely subject to them as to lose its separate character. Thus the Cyprus Courts held that where a Miri holder owned Mulk trees upon his holding, the land subject to the trees ceased to be a separate assignable entity and became "merged" in the Mulk [1]. And this result seems necessarily to follow where the trees are so closely planted that any user of the land would interfere with the enjoyment of the trees. But the Mulk trees may be scattered sparsely over a wide area and cultivation or user of the land by the holder may be possible without danger to the trees. In such cases the land can be used by the Miri holder though the trees are the Mulk of another and his interest would seem to be an assignable entity.

If Mulk trees or vines on Miri die or disappear the land on which they stand once more becomes subject to Tapu. The Mulk in which it was merged having ceased to exist its Miri character again becomes dominant. (Arts. 83, 90). The right to Tapu is primarily exerciseable by the Mulk owner of the trees or vines, but if by inheritance or otherwise he had come into the possession of the land already, no fresh grant by Tapu is necessary.

Buildings. The land Code (Art. 31) forbad the erection of buildings upon Miri land without leave and declared that if erected without

---

[1] Gavrielides v Kyriakou. 4 C.L.R. at p. 84.

Chapter I—Miri Land.

leave, they could be pulled down by direction of the Government. But if leave was obtained buildings might be erected.

With the leave of the Official a possessor of State land can erect, in accordance with the necessity of the case, farm buildings such as mills, mandras, sheds, barns, stables, straw-stores, and pens upon it. A ground rent, equivalent to the tithe, is assessed and appropriated for the site, according to the value of the situation. But for building a new quarter or village by erecting new dwelling-houses on bare land, a special Imperial Decree must be obtained; in such a case the leave of the Official alone is not sufficient. (Land Code. Art. 32).

The prohibition to erect new buildings was based upon the doctrine that the Miri holder was in reality only a lessee and could not add buildings without the consent of the landlord. The rule was frequently broken, and successive efforts were made by the Ottoman Government to secure its observance while overlooking past infractions [1]).

By a Decree of 1900, however, the rule of prohibition appears to have been finally superseded. In the absence of special reasons, as for instance, military requirements, buildings erected on Miri without leave were to be left as they were, a tax being levied upon them in place of the tithe. By a later Circular of the Daftar Khani it was ordered that the amount of the tax was to be written in the title deed [2]).

The Land Code does not expressly state what is the legal status of buildings erected on Miri with leave. It is however to be inferred from various provisions, and particularly from Arts. 44 and 82 that such buildings became the Mulk of the possessor who erected them. Though the building erected with authorisation remains Mulk, the land on which it stands continues to be Miri; and a tax in lieu of tithe was payable therefor. (Land Code, Art. 32).

So also buildings erected without express leave but permitted to remain under the Decree of 1900 must be deemed the Mulk of the builder and are subject to the tax in lieu of tithe.

The Miri site of Mulk buildings is subject to the buildings in the same way as the Miri upon which Mulk trees stand, and the rules already stated governing this subjection in the case of

---

[1]) Chiha, op. cit. p. p. 150 ff. Compare per Tyser C. J. in King's Advocate v Petrides (1904) 6 C.L.R. at p. 96.
[2]) Young, op. cit. VI, p. 54, note 29.

The Land Law of Palestine.

Mulk trees apply also as regards Mulk buildings. If, however, the buildings disappear, the Miri site once more becomes subject to the right of Tapu. (Land Code, Arts. 82, 89).

Wells. The Code contains no express provision as to Wells on Miri. The subject was much considered in the important Cyprus case Ragheb Beg v. Abbot of Kykko [1]). The following extract from the judgement of the Court in that case is instructive.

"What is the nature of the property in a well? A well sunk on mewat land with the Sultan's permission, is the mulk property of the person sinking it, and it appears to us that a well sunk on arazi-mirié would also be mulk. It would appear to have lost its character of arazi-mirié as from the nature of the case it is impossible to cultivate it, the surface has gone, and it has become merely a receptacle to hold water; and if it is no longer arazi-mirié, it appears to us to have of necessity become mulk. But no one can without permission change the category of arazi-mirié into mulk, and hence it would follow that a well cannot be sunk on arazi-mirié without permission of the State. Notwithstanding the silence of the law on the subject, we incline to the opinion that, on general principles, wells cannot be sunk on arazi-mirié without permission. The question was discussed before us, but not exhaustively. It is not necessary for our decision in the present case, and we have perhaps gone out of our way in discussing the considerations that appear to us to be applicable to it" [2]).

The law since A.H. 1331- (1913). Arts. 5 and 6 of the Law of Disposition, 1331, provide as follows:—

Art. 5. Whoever owns by virtue of a formal title-deed, miri or mevqufe land may transfer it absolutely or subject to redemption, and may lease it and lend it and mortgage it as security for a debt, and he alone has the right to all increase and to the full use of it

---

[1]) (1894) 3 C.L.R. at p. 139.
[2]) In the important case of Tzinki v. King's Advocate (1920) 11 C.L.R. at p. 10 on appeal to the Judicial Committee from the Supreme Court of Cyprus it was held by the Judicial Committee that the Miri holder has not the right without the special permission of the Government to sink wells or to connect a chain of wells for the purpose of supplying water to a village as distinguished from the exclusive purposes of cultivation. Whether he can do so for the exclusive purposes of cultivation was left undetermined. The Committee, however, observed that the provisions of Art. 14 of the Land Code were irrelevant to the question. "Their Lordships are of opinion that the expression of this prohibition is not in itself enough to afford sanction for the claim to sink wells for purposes even of mere cultivation apart from Government sanction. If the claim to do this can be sustained, it must rest on the general law."

Chapter I—Miri Land.

and to all the crops which grow naturally upon it; he is also entitled to cultivate the fields, pastures and gardens and cut down the timber or vines upon it, and, if there are buildings upon it, to destroy them or pull them down and convert the land on which they are erected into cultivated land. He may also convert his land into gardens by planting vines or trees or fruit-trees provided that the ownership remains with the State. He may erect and construct on the land houses or shops or any buildings for industrial or agricultural use provided that the buildings do not form a village or mahalla (quarter). He may set apart a piece of the land as a threshing floor. In all cases in which any alteration is made a new formal title-deed in correction and in place of the first shall be obtained. The rules for disposal and transfer in the manner specified above, of vines and trees, plants, and buildings together with the fixtures and additions constructed on miri or waqf land will be the same as for the land itself. A sum will be fixed as an annual tax on land if it is used in a manner which does not permit of the tithe being levied.

Art. 6. The building of a new village or mahalla (quarter) on all land owned by virtue of a formal title-deed is subject to the rules of the Vilayet Law, and the persons who are to inhabit these villages or mahallas as a community must be Ottoman subjects.

This translation is that given in the Iraq compilation. The translation of the penultimate paragraph of Art. 5 is, however, misleading, and the Turkish text would, it would seem, be more correctly represented by the statement that vines and trees planted and buildings erected upon Miri land are to be governed as regards the right of possession and the rights of inheritance by the rules which govern the land itself. This makes clear what appears to have been the intention of the law that the trees and buildings planted or erected by a Miri holder on his own land should accede to the land and become part of the Miri in contrast to the old law under which, when erected with authorisation, they remained Mulk. As is expressly stated by Nord [1] "The Miri holder now receives only the usufruct of the trees and the newly erected buildings", that is a right of possession (tessaruf) in the trees and buildings similar to that which he has in the land.

The provisions of these articles were the outcome of a long struggle on the part of the Government to secure the observance

---

[1] Die Reform des türkischen Liegenschaftsrechts p.110, note 3.

The Land Law of Palestine.

of the law as stated by the Land Code. The struggle ended in a sort of compromise under which the Government recognises the right of a Miri holder to deal with the surface as he pleases, abolishing at the same time the ancient rule which treated accretions effected by a Miri holder upon his holding with authorisation as the Mulk of the holder. The new provisions recognise the right of the Miri possessor:—

(1) to break up Miri pasture, notwithstanding Land Code, Art. 10.

(2) to plant trees and erect buildings, provided that the buildings do not form a village or a quarter, notwithstanding Land Code, Art. 25.

(3) to cut down timber, notwithstanding Land Code, Art. 28.

(4) to set apart a piece of the Land as a threshing floor without thereby incurring forfeiture for non-cultivation.

Under the older law, it would appear, Miri could only be set apart for a threshing floor by special kushan. (Cf. Land Code, Art. 34).

The new article is so wide that it may legitimately be deemed to authorise any user of the surface of the land not incompatible with its development. A right to use the land as a cemetery cannot be included but such use would be contrary to the provisions of Art. 264 of the Ottoman Penal Code and of Sec. 17 ff. of the Public Health Ordinance, No. 2 of 1919, unless authorised by the Government. Presumably a right to sink wells is included, and the older rule to the contrary is abrogated [1]). The erection of buildings is limited to houses, i.e. dwelling houses, and buildings for agricultural and industrial purposes.

It is further to be remarked that the building of a new quarter or village is expressly forbidden. If the land falls within an area declared to be a town planning area under the Town Planning Ordinances, 1921-1929, the construction of streets and the erection of buildings thereon is regulated by their provisions and in particular by Secs. 35 and 37 of the Town Planning Ordinance, 1921. Numerous Orders have been made declaring town planning areas. By a Notice of 16th July, 1924, it is provided that any person or corporation desiring to establish a new village or quarter outside a town planning area must submit a plan to the District Commissioner. This Notice is designed to adapt to

---

[1]) See, however, the Cyprus case of Tsinki v. King's Advocate to which reference is made at p. 32.

Chapter I—Miri Land.

Palestine conditions the provisions of the Vilayet Law referred to in Art. 6 of the Law of Disposition, A.H. 1331, and provides as follows:—

"Whereas the Ottoman Law regulating the right to dispose of immovable property dated the 30th March, 1329 [1]), provides that the building of a new village or quarter is subject to the rules of the Vilayet Law:

And whereas the Vilayet Law provides that the establishment of a new village shall be carried out only after the approval of the Government has been obtained:—

"Notice is hereby given that any person or corporation desiring to establish a new village or quarter outside a town planning area shall first make application to the District Commissioner; and submit plans which shall indicate the site of the village or quarter, the position of the roads which it is proposed to construct, and any system of drainage or water-supply which it is proposed to introduce. No permanent building and no construction of roads shall be begun till the approval of the District Commissioner has been communicated".

Although there is no express provision to that effect it may be safely assumed that where towns are extended or new towns and villages erected in accordance with the provisions of the Town Planning Ordinance or the Notice of July 1924 [2]), the building of the new quarter or village is authorised. The Law of Disposition does not state whether the buildings of a new quarter or village on Miri when duly authorised will themselves be Miri as is the case with buildings not forming a new quarter or village. But any other solution seems improbable. The question is one of importance in view of recent building extension in Palestine. The conclusion appears to be that while the State reserves its right to require the demolition of unauthorised building of a new quarter on Miri (Land Code, Arts. 31, 32) the buildings if erected before 1913 remain Mulk, and if erected since that date become Miri.

As originally conceived the interest of the Miri holder was personal only. Even to-day, inheritance of Miri is governed by special laws and the right of testamentary disposition is denied, nor can Miri land be dedicated to waqf [3]). (Land Code, Art. 121,

Disposition of Miri.

---

[1]) According to the Turkish mode of reckoning (Malia).

[2]) The provisions of the Ordinances and of the Notice apply, of course, to buildings on land of every category and not exclusively to Miri land.

[3]) As stated in the Introduction (at p. 8), an "untrue" dedication was possible with Imperial authorisation.

Law of Disposition, 1331, Art. 8). Miri interests are, however, today assignable by sale or gift. Miri may be leased (Land Code, Arts. 9, 23 [1]).

Since the Law of 1331 the most important remaining differences between Miri and Mulk are therefore as follows —

1. Miri now cannot be left by will and descends according to a special law of succession. 2. Miri cannot be made waqf. 3. Miri is subject to tithes.

The growth of towns and villages in modern Palestine leads to a great increase of non-agricultural Miri, assuming, as is our opinion, that Miri is not changed automatically into Mulk by the extension of urban boundaries. It is very undesirable that land formerly Miri should be made Mulk since this might lead to an increase of waqf in Palestine. The consequences of such an extension might be very unfortunate. Nor is it desirable to extend the application of the religious laws of succession.

On the other hand this refusal to allow Miri holders to dispose of their holding by will is inconvenient and serves little if any purpose in present day circumstances.

---

[1]) These matters will be more fully dealt with in the relevant chapters below.

CHAPTER II—MULK LAND.

Mulk means "property". From the point of view of pure Moslem Law, everything which is owned is Mulk. All movables are Mulk, i.e. no other form of property in movables is recognised, though, of course, real and personal rights less than ownership may exist over movables, (e.g. the rights of a pledgee, of a hirer, and so on). The form in which the Ottoman Land Law is now presented to us makes it necessary to distinguish between Mulk land and other species of land, Miri, Metruki, and Mewat.

Immovable property classified as Mulk is in the absolute ownership of the proprietor [1]). "Each man" says the Mejelle (Art. 1192), "can deal as he likes with his Mulk". The owner of a site, i.e. of a Mulk site, is the owner of things above and below it (Art. 1194). No one can be hindered from the use of his own Mulk, unless from this use excessive injury results to another person, then he can be hindered. (Art. 1197).

This general statement as to the use of Mulk must be read, subject to the provisions of the law, limiting by general rules the use of property. The Mejelle itself refers to the limitations imposed by the law prohibiting user which causes excessive damage to neighbours. And we find limitations upon the use of property

---

[1]) "Immovable property" is stated by the Mejelle (Art. 129) to consist of property such as houses and land which cannot be transferred to another place. Cf. Interpretation Ordinance 1929 Sec. 3 (C) (7) where the term is treated as equivalent to "land" and is to include "everything attached to the earth or permanently fastened to anything which is attributed to the earth". "Land" must (semble) be treated as including water when attached to land; according to Mejelle, however, possession cannot be taken of flowing water, i.e. it cannot be owned while flowing, though people may have rights to take water from the stream (Art. 1251).

European law treats certain rights connected with the land as themselves immovables. Thus servitudes are treated both by French law as immovables (French Civil Code, Art. 526) and English law to day treats them as "incorporeal hereditaments" and part of the realty. No corresponding conception seems to be known in Moslem law, the distinctions between movables and immovables relating solely to material objects. The distinction between Movables and Immovables is of minor importance in Moslem law.

The Land Law of Palestine.

in the Town Planning Ordinances, the Antiquities Ordinance [1]), the Mining Ordinances, and the Forests Ordinance. Mulk may be expropriated and is otherwise subject to compulsory process of sale. But these limitations are general and not peculiar to Mulk.

Although a Mulk owner is, in general, owner not only of his land, but of everything therein and thereon, certain exceptions occur. Grass and plants growing naturally are common property (Mejelle Arts. 1242, 1257) though trees growing naturally belong to the owner of the soil. (Art. 1244). But that which is sown, planted, or built on the Mulk of another does not accede to the soil, e.g. the product of seed which a man sows is his own property (Art. 1246). The position, however, of a person who builds, plants or sows upon the property of another, is dealt with in a subsequent Chapter [2]).

Ways of acquiring Mulk.

Art. 1248 (Mejelle) states that the causes or ways of acquiring ownership (Mulk) are three: (a) Transfer during life; (b) Succession; (c) Occupation. From the examples given in Arts. 1249 ff. it seems clear that Occupation is only applicable to things which have no owner. At any rate, under present conditions in Palestine, it can have no application to land. The other two methods of acquiring ownership are, of course, applicable to all real rights whether they amount to Mulk ownership or to something less than Mulk, e.g. a Miri interest. What is of more immediate importance is to determine the nature of the right transferred or inherited. We need to know how a Mulk interest can arise.

Art. 2 of the Land Code mentions four classes of Mulk:—

(I) Sites (for houses) within towns or villages, and pieces of land of an extent not exceeding half a dunum situated on the confines of towns and villages which can be considered as appurtenant to dwelling houses.

(II) Land separated from State land and made Mulk in a valid way to be possessed in the different ways of absolute ownership according to the Sacred Law.

---

[1]) The very learned judgment of Tyser J. in the Cypriot case of Lambro v. King's Advocate (1905) 6 CLR pp. 115 contains valuable statements relative to the Ottoman law governing property in Antiquities found in Mulk or in Miri.

All rights of the landowner or finder are subject to the legislation existing in Palestine concerning Antiquities. See in particular Antiquities Ordinance 1929.

As to rights of a finder of buried treasure in Moslem law See Hedaya p. 16 (Hamilton's Translation).

[2]) See below Chapter dealing with Appropriation of land of another and use thereof.

Chapter II—Mulk Land.

(III) Tithe-paying land, which was distributed at the time of conquest among the victors, and given to them in full ownership.

(IV) Tribute-paying land which (at the same period) was left and confirmed in the possession of the non-Moslem inhabitants.

Of the four classes of Mulk here referred to, only the first two are of importance in Palestine. Mulk of the two other classes is stated to exist, but is very rare [1]).

Though it is the site for the house which is described as Mulk, the house itself is necessarily Mulk.

Though the Land Code only speaks of "sites" for houses, yet in fact all land situated within the boundaries of towns and villages is treated as Mulk and not only the actual sites of the buildings. "Land situated within towns and villages is Mulk"; says Chiha, "even though the area exceeds half a dunum. It matters not whether the land is cultivated or not. Waste land and gardens within the town are examples". The word "sites" must, therefore, be broadly interpreted for this purpose. As regards land lying outside the confines of the town or village, a strict limitation is enacted by Art. 2. Only land appurtenant to the dwelling house and not exceeding half a dunum in area is Mulk. The legislator aimed at preventing people from escaping the tithe by making large extensions of the curtilage of their houses, and claiming that they thereby became Mulk owners thereof. (Chiha, p. 25).

<small>Land which is Mulk because it lies in a town or on the confines thereof.</small>

Difficulty arises in applying these provisions to modern conditions in Palestine. It is clear, that the mere building of a house on Miri land outside a town can have no effect upon the character of the land. If the erection is authorised and was prior to the Law of Disposition of A.H. 1331, the building is Mulk, but the site remains Miri. If, however, a group of houses is erected either forming a new village or a new quarter of an existing town, the situation is more obscure. Prior to A.H. 1331 the Ottoman Government took the view that only the buildings of a new village or quarter became Mulk and that a tax (Bedl Ushur) was payable in respect of the land, which remained Miri and of which the Raqabe continued to be vested in the State. An exception was only made in respect of villages formed by immigrants and established with Imperial authorisation, though only in favour of the original immigrants.

---

[1]) Mulk of the Kharaji category still exists in the Lebanon (Chaoui, Le Régime Foncier en Syrie, p. 47).

The Land Law of Palestine.

Art. 32 of the Land Code expressly provides that for building a new quarter or village on Miri land by erecting new dwelling houses, a special Imperial Decree is requisite. It has, indeed, been argued that where Imperial authorisation was obtained for such building the site became Mulk and did not remain Miri, a point in favour of this view being that Art. 32 does not expressly provide that any ground rent is due, while such express provision is made in the case of erection of an isolated building [1]). But this opinion is not supported by any official or judicial authority.

The view consistently taken by the Turkish authorities and by the Court of Cassation was that the character of Mulk only attached to sites within towns and villages which existed and within the limits within which they existed at the date of the promulgation of the Land Code (1858) and to the areas limited by Art. 2 on the confines of villages and towns as then existing. There is no official or judicial authority in favour of the view that an extension of a town beyond its then existing limits automatically changed the character of the site. The prevailing opinion appears to be that Miri cannot be changed into Mulk save by the express declaration of the Sovereign, i.e. by a grant of the Raqabe. The burden certainly falls upon any person claiming that land has become Mulk by interpretation of law.

The situation where new quarters or villages are erected on Miri subsequently to the Law of Disposition, 1331, was considered in the last chapter.

Land which is Mulk by transmutation of Miri. Miri land cannot be transmuted into Mulk save by express permission of the Sovereign.

By the recent Palestine (Amendment) Order in Council 1933 a new article to be numbered 16A is added to the Palestine Order in Council 1922 and provides as follows:—

"The High Commissioner may, if he thinks fit, by order under his hand to be published in the Gazette, convert such land in Palestine of the category termed "Miri", as may be described in such order, into land of the category termed "Mulk".

The need for this express provision is not very obvious. It was long ago stated in Cyprus that "since the Convention of 1878 acts required by law to be performed by the Sultan could doubtless be validly performed by H.M. the Queen or those to whom she has delegated the powers i.e. the High Commissioners

---

[1]) Chiha, op. cit. p.p. 26-27, quoting Khalis Eshreff.

Chapter II—Mulk Land.

of the island"[1]) and there seems no reason to suppose that the position was different in Palestine. However, the Order in Council now removes every scintilla of a doubt. It is, however, to be hoped that the power to change the category of this land will not be freely exercised.

No provision is made by the Land Code or elsewhere as to the form in which a transmutation of the lands from Miri to Mulk is to be effected.

It is, however, expressly provided by Land Code, Art. 121, that Miri land cannot be dedicated as Waqf unless the holder has been previously invested with Mulk ownership thereof by Imperial Patent (Mulkname). Cf. Law of Disposition, 1331, Art. 8 [2]).

The commentators tell us that a grant of the Raqabe by the Sovereign should be made only for the public benefit and in consideration of payment to the Treasury of the value of the land or in some cases, of double the value. It is admitted, however, that the consideration may be "moral" only [3]). Where the transfer has been effected for money consideration, it should be treated as a sale, and is void if there be excessive damage within the meaning of Art. 165 of the Mejelle.

Two other forms of Mulk should perhaps be mentioned in this connection. Art. 1272 of the Mejelle appears to suggest that Mewat land cultivated by authorisation of the Sovereign may become the Mulk of the cultivator. The interpretation of this Article is, however, disputed, and, having regard to the provisions of Art. 103 of the Land Code, we may assume that such cultivation makes the land Miri and not Mulk. However, land reclaimed from the sea with Imperial sanction becomes the Mulk of the person reclaiming it. (Land Code, Art. 132 [4]).

Further it is to be remarked that trees, buildings, and constructions may be held by Mulk title separate from that of the land. A case in which this may occur has already been considered in the chapter dealing with Miri land.

Also, where a well is dug on Mewat land by leave of the Sovereign, the well becomes the Mulk of the digger (Mejelle

---

[1]) Per curiam in Constanti v. The Principal Forest Officer. (1895) 3 C.L.R. at p. 155.

[2]) The right of action by the State claiming the Raqabe of Miri land is barred after 36 years. (Law of Disposition, 1331, Art. 15).

[3]) Chiha, op. cit. p. 32.

[4]) As to land reclaimed from the sea or river or a lake see also Land Law (Amendment) Ord. 1933 Sec. 3.

Art. 1280) who further becomes entitled to a circuit (harim) of 40 pics in every direction round the well for its protection. (Art. 1281 ff.). The circuit of wells is the property (Mulk) of the owner. No other person can open a well within the circuit. (Art. 1286).

Similar principles are applied to trees planted on Mewat with the leave of the Sovereign (Art. 1289) as also to springs which have been opened on Mewat with similar permission. In each case a circuit (harim) is allowed of which the owner of the tree or spring has exclusive possession. So also as regards channels, aqueducts and underground canals (kanat) (Mejelle Arts. 1282, 1284, 1285). These provisions of the Mejelle merely reproduce the law as stated in ihe Hedaya, Book, XLV [1]).

Mulk trees and buildings may also exist on Mulk land, but be held by a separate title. Thus, in the case of Muqata'a Waqf, the trees and buildings are the Mulk of the "lessee" but the land remains the property of the Waqf. And, in general, where there are trees or buildings on Mulk land, the trees or buildings or even parts of the buildings may be separately owned and separate kushans issued therefor. (Cf. Mejelle Art. 1192).

Disposition of Mulk.

Since Mulk is the absolute property of the owner, it follows that the State has no proprietary interest therein. Upon failure of heirs of a deceased owner of Mulk, the property, in default of testamentary disposition, falls to the State as bona vacantia and not by way of escheat; i.e. the State takes in virtue of its sovereignty, and not in virtue of any claim as proprietor. Rights to Tapu can, of course, never arise as against Mulk, though Mulk owners may have Rights to Tapu over Miri. (Land Code, Arts. 44, 59). Mulk falling to the State is sometimes spoken of as Mulk Mahlul (cf. Law of Disposition, 1331, Art. 15); and by Art. 15 of the Law as to Mulk Title Deeds, A.H. 1291, the Mulk property of persons who died without leaving heirs and intestate was directed to be sold by auction like Miri Mahlul. But Mulk, though falling to the State does not thereby become Miri (Tapu) land. It remains Mulk in the hands of the State. However, Art. 2 Land Code expressly provides that Tithe-paying and Tribute-paying Mulk shall become Miri where the State takes on account of failure of heirs. Though the scope of this provision is not clear, it is ap-

---

[1]) The law relating to Harim of Wells, Springs and Channels is considered in the judgement in Ragheb v. Abbot of Kykko 3 C. L. R. p. 105. Further reference will be made to the Subject below.

Chapter II—Mulk Land.

parently intended to make applicable the Miri law from the date of the death in case of failure of Mulk heirs.

Of his Mulk property the owner has full power of disposition. He can sell it, lease it, dispose of it by way of gift or dedicate it by way of Waqf. In this respect, there is no difference in principle between Mulk Immovables and Movables.

The Moslem law places little insistence upon the distinction between movables and immovables so familiar in European law. But Mulk immovables were brought within the scope of the Law of Registration by the Law of 28 Rejeb, A.H. 1291, which provides (Art. 7) that new Mulk Title Deeds with the Imperial Cypher at the head shall be issued for all Mulk property in cities, towns, villages and nahiyets and thenceforth possession of Mulk property without a title deed was forbidden.

CHAPTER III.—MEWAT LAND.

Definition of Mewat land. The following definitions or descriptions of the nature of Mewat land have authority:

Dead land (Mewat) is land which is occupied by no one and has not been left for the use of the public. It is such as lies at such a distance from a village or town from which a loud human voice cannot make itself heard at the nearest point where there are inhabited places, that is a mile and a half, or about half an hour's distance from such. (Land Code, Art. 6).

The expression dead land (Mewat) means vacant (khali) land, such as mountains, rocky places, stony fields, pernallik and grazing ground which is not in the possession of anyone by title-deed or assigned ab antiquo to the use of inhabitants of a town or village, and lies at such a distance from towns and villages from which a human voice cannot be heard at the nearest inhabited place. (Land Code, Art. 103).

"Arazi-mewat" are those lands which are not the mulk property of anyone, and are not the grazing ground of a town or village, or for their collecting firewood, that is to say, the locality in which the inhabitants of a town or village have a right to cut firewood, and are far from the distant parts of a village or town, that is to say, the sound of a person who has a loud voice cannot be heard from the houses which are at the extreme limit of the town or village. (Mejelle, Art. 1270).

The description of Mewat land given in these authorities is of a primitive character. The Hedaya informs us that the special conditions as to the land being distant from any village was inserted, according to the opinion of Abu Yousef, because if the ground is contiguous to a village it cannot be said to be entirely useless to the inhabitants. Mohammed, however, held that land contiguous to a village may be Mewat land if the villagers do not in fact make use of it. It has been suggested in Cyprus that uncultivated land lying near a village, (i.e. within a mile and a half) may happen, as the result of the provisions of the Land Code, to belong strictly to none of the recognised categories of

Chapter III—Mewat Land.

land, being excluded from the Miri class because it is not cultivated and from the Mewat class in accordance with Arts. 6 and 103 of the Land Code. It has been there laid down that where land is of an indeterminate class it should be deemed to be regulated by the law relating to that class of land to which it comes nearest. This normally would be Mewat, at least unless the land had been cultivated within living memory and might, therefore, be regarded as Miri Mahlul [1]). This conclusion seems reasonable and accords with that of the Imam Mohammed quoted in the Hedaya. If such land adjacent to villages has, however, been assigned as village Metruki by immemorial or by express assignment it is, of course, withdrawn from the Mewat class. Art. 1271 of the Mejelle refers to land of this category.

Land lying more than the prescribed distance from a town or village and which is not cultivated is not necessarily Mewat. It may be Miri pasture or woodland. It may be neglected Miri or Miri Mahlul. It may be Metruki pasture or woodland. (Arts. 91, 97, 101). It may be Mulk, though this is very unlikely. But when these possibilities have been explored and the land found to belong to none of these categories, there remains only the category of Mewat into which we can place it.

It is clearly both economically and financially desirable that Mewat should be brought under cultivation, if possible, and it is an ancient rule of Moslem Law, stated in the Hedaya that "whosoever cultivates waste (Mewat) lands with the permission of the Chief, obtains a property in them; whereas, if a person cultivate them without such permission, he does not in that case become proprietor, according to Hanifa". The Mejelle provides as follows:—

If a person, with the leave of the Sultan, takes and improves (Art. 1275) a place from arazi-mewat he becomes the mulk owner of it. *Mejelle Art. 1272.*

And if the Sultan or his representative gives permission to someone to improve the land, upon the condition that he is to have the use of the land only, and not to have the ownership, that person, in the way he has received permission, has the right of disposition (tessaruf) over that land, but he does not become mulk owner of the land.

When a person has improved a quantity of a piece of land, and the remainder of it is left, the remainder does not belong to him, who is the mulk owner of the places improved. But if there *Art. 1273.*

---

[1]) See Kyriako v. Principal Forest Officer, (1894) 3 C.L.R. at p. 87.

remains a quantity of khali land in the middle of the land, which he has improved, that land also belongs to him.

Art. 1274. After someone has improved land from arazi-mewat, if others also come and improve the lands which are on his four boundaries, a road for the first person is set apart in the lands of him who improved last, that is to say, there is a road for him from there.

These provisions merely reproduce the statements of the law made in the Hedaya from which they appear to be derived.

The Land Code provides:—

Land Code Art. 103. "Anyone who is in need of such land, can, with the leave of the Official plough it up gratuitously and cultivate it on condition that the legal ownership (Raqabe) shall belong to the Treasury. The provisions of the law relating to other cultivated land shall be applicable to this kind of land also. Provided that if anyone after getting leave to cultivate such land, and having had it granted to him leaves it as it is for three consecutive years without valid excuse, it shall be given to another".

Comparing the terms of Mejelle Art. 1272 and Land Code Art. 103, we infer that in the usual case permission to cultivate Mewat will be subject to the condition that, when cultivated, the land will be Miri and the Raqabe will still be vested in the State. It would appear that according to Art. 103 this condition must always be imposed by the official.

Art. 103 of the Land Code provided in its last paragraph that, if a person cultivated Mewat without authorisation he should pay the Tapu value (Bedl Misl) and might be given a Tapu grant. It was held in the Cyprus case of Kyriako v. Principal Forest Officer that the making of such a grant was discretionary. In Palestine, the Mewat Land Ordinance, 1921, provides that not only has the person who breaks up Mewat without authorisation no legal right to a Tapu grant, but that he is doing a wrongful act and will be treated accordingly.

This Ordinance repeals the last paragraph of Art. 103 of the Land Code and substitutes the following provisions:—

"Any person who without obtaining the consent of the Administration breaks up or cultivates any waste land shall obtain no right to a title-deed for such land and further, will be liable to be prosecuted for trespass".

An exception was, however, made in the case of persons who had broken up Mewat before the Ordinance, the Ordinance providing as follows:—

Chapter III—Mewat Land.

"Any person who has already cultivated such waste land without obtaining authorisation shall notify the Registrar of the Land Registry within two months of the publication of this Ordinance and apply for a title-deed".

This last paragraph can only be interpreted as meaning that no claim to a title-deed on payment of Bedl Misl will be recognised unless the notification was given to the Registrar within the two months, i.e. before the 18th April, 1921. But, in fact, a more lenient view was taken and it became the practice to make Tapu grants on payment of Bedl Misl to persons who showed that they broke up Mewat and revived the land before the Ordinance though without authorisation to do so. Where the land was revived since the Ordinance, no scintilla of claim arises [1]. The provisions of Art. 5 of the Regulations as to Title Deeds, A.H. 1276 must also be read subject to the Ordinance.

The Tapu Law of A.H. 1275 contains provisions relative to grants of Mewat with a view to its being cultivated.

The grant of khali and kirach (stony) land to persons intending to break it up in pursuance of Art. 103 of the Land Code is made gratuitously and without fee. A new title-deed is issued to them on payment of three piastres for the price of paper, and they are exempted from payment of tithes for one year or for two years if the land is stony. Tapu Law Art. 12.

Administrative and fiscal authorities must take care as part of their duty, that dead land is granted only to persons who intend to break it up and cultivate it as above mentioned and that no one should seize such land in some other way. They must take special care that for land on mountains (moubah) and land left and assigned for purposes of public utility, title-deeds are not granted to any one, and they are not occupied by anyone. It is incumbent on them also to cause land to be cultivated which for want of cultivation has become subject to the right of tapu. Art. 13.

For the purpose of the application of these articles of the Mejelle and of the Land Code, it is necessary to determine what amounts to revival. The Mejelle has several articles upon this

---

[1] The technical term of Moslem law for the process whereby Mewat land is made cultivable is Ihya (Revival) which is defined by Art. 1051 of the Mejelle as equivalent to Ja'mir (making land prosperous) and to consist in making the land fit for agriculture.

It is understood to include any operations which make the land productive, e.g. sowing of seed, plantation of trees etc.

The Land Law of Palestine.

subject which are in the main only an abstract of the statements in the Hedaya.

Mejelle, Art. 1275. The sowing of seed and the planting of young trees are the improving (ihya) of a place and so is the ploughing of it twice for sowing, or the irrigation or the making of a water channel, or conduit for the irrigation.

Art. 1276. If a man makes a wall round a place from arazi-mewat, or raises and makes a dam around it which will protect it from the rain water, that place has been improved.

The Hedaya states that according to the opinion of Mohammed digging up the land is not alone sufficient. (Hedaya, p. 611, Col, 1).

It appears clear from the terms of the Mejelle that irrigation of the land is sufficient, as indeed any proceeding whereby the land is rendered productive, e.g. plantation. (Hedaya, passim).

Following the Hedaya the Mejelle also distinguishes between reviver and mere enclosures.

Art. 1277. Putting stones or thorns or the dead branches of trees to enclose the four sides of land, or to clear away the grasses of the land, or to burn the thorns which are in it, or to sink a well, is not called improving the land, it is only enclosing it.

Art. 1278. If a person cut the grasses, or thorns on arazi-mewat, and merely puts them round the land and puts earth on them, and does not complete a dam in a way that will keep out the overflowing water, that land is not improved, but it is enclosed.

A right of preference over the land enclosed is given for three years.

Art. 1279. If a man encloses a place from arazi-mewat he has a better right to that land than others for three years. If he has not improved it in three years, his right does not remain, and it can be given to another to improve.

These provisions are only summaries from the statements of the Hedaya from which it appears that the enclosures must have been authorised with a view of reviver. If this is so, it would seem that the provisions of Art. 1279 do not go beyond those of the Land Code, Art. 103, whereby a period of three years is allowed during which the person authorised must revive the land.

The nature of reviver was considered by the Jaffa Land Court in 1926 in the case of Dajani and others v. Colony of Rishon le Zion and Att. Gen. where a claim was made that certain sand dunes had been "revived" by planting. The learned Judge (Blake-Reed J.) said:

Chapter III—Mewat Land.

"Cultivation, in my opinion, must be effective and I consider that it must further mean "maintained" cultivation. Operations must be carried out which result in a permanent and definite change in the quality of the land. The wilderness must be made to blossom. With the best intentions the would-be cultivator may fail in his purpose. The land may possibly prove to be entirely incapable of cultivation. The cultivator may be compelled to abandon his experiment by the mere nature of the soil. Or he may go the wrong way to work. His cultivation may be unscientific and he may fail on account of his ignorance. Or, having begun his work, he may later abandon it. Or he may not be able to afford to carry it on. In any of these cases it seems to me he is not entitled to claim any credit for an attempt which has failed. And, of course, the question whether cultivation has been in fact achieved must be decided with some sense of proportion. Obviously, a man cannot claim that he has revived a large tract of land by the planting of a single tree, or a tree at each corner".

In this case also the plaintiff claiming the land sought to bring forward evidence to shew that whatever the existing state of the land then was, it had been cultivated land once, seeking thereby to shew that the land had been in process of reclamation but had relapsed again into its original state before it had been definitely reclaimed or at least before it had been recognised as Miri by the Government. This evidence was rejected as irrelevant, and the Court held that Mewat land, even though reclaimed, but which had never been recognised as other than Mewat by any competent authority, could not be regarded as reclaimed for ever. The title of the cultivator in fact never acquired could not be regarded as permanently held in store for him as a reward for alleged cultivation, all traces of which had vanished from the face of the earth [1]).

Land which was formerly the subject of a Tapu grant as Miri, does not, upon ceasing to be cultivated, become Mewat. It remains Miri in the hands of the Government and is vacant (Mahlul). Mewat land cannot be Mahlul in this sense, but the State may (Semble) transform uncultivated Mewat which is pasture or woodland into Miri by granting it by Tapu. There is no recognised procedure whereby Miri which has become Mahlul can be

---

[1]) An unsuccessful attempt was made in this case to induce the Court to apply Art. 78 Land Code which clearly applies to Miri Mahlul land only, and not to Mewat.

changed into Mewat. Mere temporary want of cultivation would have no such effect. But where land has not only ceased to be cultivated, but by long neglect or other causes has reverted to its primitive condition or has, by drifting sand, landslides or the like, become incapable of cultivation without a process of reclamation, it should be classified as Mewat even though it may be probable that it was once cultivated.

The question whether land is Mewat or Miri, which has become Mahlul is of importance principally in the application of the Laws of Prescription, and in particular of Art. 78 of the Land Code. For example, a question arose in Cyprus whether land left by the receding of the water of an ancient lake or river was Mewat or Miri Mahlul. Land Code, Art. 123, directs that if such land is fit for cultivation it shall be put up for auction, i.e. granted as Miri to the highest bidder. This would appear to show that it is to be treated as Miri and not Mewat. Consequently a right to a gratuitous grant by Tapu cannot be acquired by reviver under Art. 103 [1]).

Under the head of Mewat Land the Land Code mentions two special classes of land: 1. Mubah; 2. Otlak.

Mubah. Art. 104.

The term "Mubah" means that which is permitted to all and is, therefore, used to designate that which is for common use. (Cf. Mejelle Arts. 1234 ff.).

In Art. 104 of the Land Code the term is used of hilly land having trees or shrubs upon it which is not Baltalik within Art. 91.

Art. 104 recognises a general right for the public to cut wood for fuel or building where the woodland is not specially allotted for the use of a particular town or village, and, of course, is not private property, and various articles of the Mejelle make reference to the right of the public to take plants, etc. growing on land which belongs to no one. (Mejelle, Arts. 1241, 1243, 1256, 1259).

These provisions, as also those of Land Code, Art. 104, must, however, be read subject to any special legislation relative to forest lands [2]).

---

[1]) The High Commissioner may now declare such land to be public land in accordance with. Sec. 3 of the Land law (Amendment) Ord. 1933.

[2]) Mejelle Arts. 1253, 1258 are, however, to the same effect as Art. 104 of the Land Code.

Chapter III—Mewat Land.

Chiha states that Art. 104 ceased to be applicable in consequence of the issue of the Ottoman Forest Regulations of 1870. These Regulations are no longer applicable in Palestine, it being expressly provided by Sec. 27 (2) of the Forest Ordinance, 1926, that "all other laws or regulations concerning forestry shall be no longer applicable". Art. 104 is not expressly mentioned nor does it appear to be a "law concerning forestry". In any case the provisions of the Forest Ordinance alone are clearly applicable as regards any forest lands which are, by proclamation of the High Commissioner, brought under the control and management of the Government as Forest Reserves (Forest Ordinance, Sec. 3). Many such proclamations have already been made. Within all these Reserves it is forbidden to take any "forest produce" (defined in Sec. 2). It is, however, provided by Sec. 6 that the prohibition to take forest produce shall not prohibit the collection and removal from forest reserves (other than Closed Forest Areas) of dead and dry wood or brushwood to be used solely for firewood for the use of the inhabitants of villages who have been accustomed to supply their wants in this respect from the forests in the vicinity of their village, but such inhabitants shall not remove roots or stumps or fell standing timber or cut branches. The provisions made by the same Section for the exercise of legal rights or customs by inhabitants of villages in Forest Reserves can have no reference to Art. 104 which conferred such rights as it did confer on the public generally.

This article appears intended merely to make clear that grazing land adjacent to a village over which ab antiquo usage or definite allotment for the use of the village as village Metruki cannot be established, is open to all comers for grazing purposes though the State may in the case of strangers collect a fee. Although the terms of the Article are imperative it should not be assumed that the villagers have a right against the State to prevent enclosure of Otlak grazing ground or its grant by Tapu as Miri. The object of the Article is not to secure a right but to establish a distinction between the villagers and strangers as regards exaction of a fee.

Otlak (Grassy). Art. 105.

CHAPTER IV—METRUKI LAND.

Land left for the use of the public (Metruki) is of two kinds: —

(I) That which is left for the general use of the public, like a public highway for example;

(II) That which is assigned for the inhabitants generally of a village or town, or of several villages or towns grouped together, as for example pastures (Meras). (Land Code, Art. 5).

It is perhaps not strictly accurate, to classify Metruki land as land differing in class from Miri, Mulk and Mewat. It remains somewhat uncertain whether so called Metruki land is not really only Miri or Mulk land subject to certain public or communal rights which prevent its use for any other purpose. The correct view appears to be that if for any reason the public or communal rights come to an end, e.g. by stopping up a highway or by enclosure under statutory powers of common grazing ground, the land will fall at once into that class of land to which it originally belonged, or to which by its situation it naturally belongs.

Metruki left for the general use of the public. This class of Metruki is sometimes termed "Mehmie" or protected [1]. The Land Code contains no clear indication as to how land becomes Metruki of this class. Presumably ab antiquo usage will create public rights in accordance with the principle laid down in Art. 6 of the Mejelle. "The ab antiquo is left in its ab antiquo state". Art. 102 Land Code which, in accordance with the principle laid down in Mejelle Art. 1675, denies the possibility of claims by prescription against public rights, appears to treat dedication (assignment) to public use and ab antiquo usage as creative of Metruki land of both classes specified in Art. 5. Where land is expropriated by the Government or a Municipality and opened to the public as a public road it should presumably be thereafter treated as Metruki, having been dedicated for public use. (Cf. Mejelle Art. 1216). Land which is subject to public use as a highway is (semble) the property of the Government. This

---

[1] See Sec. 264 Ott. Penal Code. Young, op. cit. Vol. VII, p. 53.

Chapter IV—Metruki Land.

seems to follow from the provisions of Mejelle Art. 1217, which permits the Treasury to sell the surplus of a road to a private person if the passersby are not thereby injured. And rivers, i.e. public rivers (Mejelle Art. 1235), are grouped with public roads in Mejelle Art. 1675 as lands of common use [1]).

Any member of the public has a right to bring an action to protect a public right in this class of Metruki (Mejelle, Art. 1644). Thus, any obstruction of a public road [2]) could be made the subject of an action by any member of the public as a public nuisance. And a prosecution is also possible under Art. 264 of the Penal Code as is the case in England. If the obstruction, e.g. stopping up of a public road was ordered by the Government without satisfactory authority, the action would be against the responsible officials. Statutory powers to stop up a public road exist under Sec. 18 of the Expropriation of Land Ordinance, 1926.

The expropriation of land for the construction or widening of roads as for other public purposes is dealt with in a later chapter. Attention may, however, here be drawn to the Village Roads and Works Ordinance 1927 which facilitates the construction and maintenance of roads, tracks and paths connecting villages with one another or with a main road. A series of Ordinances known as the Width and Alignment of Roads Ordinance 1926-1927 authorize the High Commissioner to prohibit the erection of permanent works within a certain distance from the centre of a road and make provision for widening others. It is to be remembered that by Sec. 9 of the Village Roads and Works Ordinance 1927 it was provided that the Ottoman Regulations as to Roads of 16 Jamad el Awal A. H. 1286 and the Ottoman Provisional Law 14

---

[1]) Compare further as to use of public roads, Mejelle Arts. 926, 927, 1215, 1218, 1223.

As to public rivers, lakes and seas, see Mejelle Arts. 1321 (cleansing), Arts. 1237, 1264, 1265, 1266.

The beds of public rivers, of lakes and seas, foreshores and the like may be classified as Metruki of this class.

Open spaces in or near towns for use for public purposes also fall within Metruki of this class.

So also do market places and spaces reserved for fairs and public gardens and all other such spaces as are dedicated to public use. (Land Code, Arts. 94, 95.)

Note that special provision is made by Art. 95 for market and fair dues payable to the Treasury and see Chiha, op. cit., pp. 98 ff. for a discussion of certain problems thence arising.

[2]) Obstruction of public roads is dealt with in Mejelle, Arts. 1213, 1214, and Land Code, Art. 93.

The Land Law of Palestine.

Rabi el Akhir A.H. 1332 should cease to have effect in Palestine. The Regulations of A.H. 1286 had already in part been declared unapplicable under Sec. 6 of the Width and Alignment of Roads Ordinance 1926 as also certain articles of the Ottoman Regulations of 18 Moharrem A.H. 1309.

<small>Metruki assigned for the inhabitants of a village or town or of several villages or towns.</small>

This class of Metruki is sometimes termed "Murfaca" or subject to a Servitude. Several examples of Metruki of this class are mentioned in the Land Code.

Threshing floors set apart ab antiquo for the inhabitants of a place in general, shall neither be sold nor cultivated. No one shall be allowed to erect any building thereon. Possession thereof cannot be given by title-deed either to an individual, or to persons jointly. If anyone takes possession of such a place the inhabitants can eject him. Inhabitants of other villages cannot bring their crops and thresh them on such threshing floor. (Land Code, Art. 96).

In a pasturing ground (Mera) assigned [1]) ab antiquo to a village, the inhabitants of such village only can pasture their animals. Inhabitants of another village cannot bring their animals there. A pasturing ground assigned ab antiquo to a group of two, three or more villages in common shall be the common pasture of the animals of such villages, no matter within the boundaries of which of the villages the pasturing ground is situated, and the inhabitants of one of the villages cannot stop the inhabitants of another of the villages from using it. Such pasturing grounds assigned ab antiquo for the use of the inhabitants of one village exclusively, or of several villages collectively, can neither be bought nor sold, nor can sheepfolds, enclosures or any other buildings be erected on them. If anyone erects buildings or plants trees thereon the inhabitants may at any time have them pulled down or uprooted. No one shall be allowed to plough up or cultivate such land like other cultivated land. If anyone cultivates it he shall be ejected, and the land shall be kept as a pasturing ground for all time. (Land Code, Art. 97).

Whatever number of animals an inhabitant of a village has been accustomed to send to a pasturing ground, whether it be that of a single village or common to several, the succeeding offspring of such animals cannot be prevented from grazing there

---

[1]) The assigned grazing grounds refferred to in Arts. 100, 101 must be distinguished from the unassigned land referred to in Art. 105. See further Tute. The Ottoman Land Laws, pp. 95, 96 and as to "assignment" ibid, p. 93.

Chapter IV—Metruki Land.

also. An inhabitant of a village has no right to bring animals from elsewhere there and so prejudice the animals of his fellow inhabitants. A person who comes from elsewhere to a village and takes up his residence there and builds a house can bring animals of his own from elsewhere and pasture them on the pasturing ground of the village, provided that he does not prejudice the animals of the village. Anyone who acquires the dwelling of an inhabitant of a village can pasture without hindrance, the same number of animals on the pasturing ground of the village as did the owner of the dwelling. (Land Code, Art. 100).

These articles deal with pasturing grounds (Mera) attached to a village or a group of villages over which the inhabitants of the village or villages have exclusive rights of common of pasture. According to Chiha not merely ownership but actual occupancy of property in the village is required to give a right to share in the common pasture.

Art. 99 emphasizes the distinction between right of pasture in the common grazing lands of the village and private pasturing grounds attached by ab antiquo usage to a Jiftlik (or Farm). Such grounds are not Metruki at all but are Miri land held by Tapu and kushans must be provided for them.

The extent of the common grazing lands of a village are fixed by ab antiquo usage [1].

So much assigned land as has been left and assigned as such ab antiquo is deemed to be pasturing ground. Delimitations subsequently made are of no validity. (Land Code, Art. 98).

From a note in Young [2], it would seem that only land delimited in the Land Registry as common grazing ground can be claimed as such. Art. 98 appears to bear this out since it expressly states that delimitations subsequently made are of no validity. It is not, however, clear to what delimitation reference is made, and Chiha (p. 105) appears to hold that immemorial usage, though not used for a number of years, must fix the actual extent of the land intended in the grazing grounds. The preferable view, however, seems to be that only grazing grounds registered as such can be deemed to be a grazing ground by immemorial usage. The mere fact that a greater extent of land has for a good many years been used as common grazing ground by the villagers is not in itself sufficient.

---

[1] Oral evidence is not sufficient to support a claim to a right of pasture as agaist a registered title. Badr v. Hanem L.A. 13/33. (Palestine Post 22 June 1934).

[2] Corps de droit Ott., Vol. VI, at p. 72.

The Land Law of Palestine.

In practice it may be convenient to make use of the principles established in an analogous case by Art. 47 of the Land Code where there is a contradiction between the area and the boundaries as stated in the Register. Reference may also be made to Land Code, Art. 126 as to the restoration of ancient boundaries [1]).

Art. 101 deals with summer and winter pasturing ground assigned for the benefit of the inhabitants of particular villages.

Winter pasturing grounds (Kishlak) are lands which on account of the mildness of their climate, their sheltered situation and the abundance of grass and of water are more specially suitable for cattle in winter. Summer pasturing grounds (Yaylak) are lands sheltered from fierce heat and which on account of the abundance of grass and water are particularly suitable for the grazing of cattle during the summer.

Registration at the Daftar Khani is expressly required, as well as ab antiquo assignment. The dues chargeable by the State (Yaylakie and Kishlakie) are to be charged on the villages benefiting by the pasturage. (Land Code, Art. 127).

The fact that evidence is forthcoming to show that the land belonged to a different category at some time within, what may be termed, "the period of legal memory" is not necessarily conclusive against a claim that land is now Metruki provided adequate evidence of dedication is obtainable. This seems to be a necessary inference from the decision of the Cyprus Court in the case of Constanti v. The Principal Forest Officer [2]), in which the origin and nature of Metruki Mera was considered. The case concerned the right of the Cyprus Government to include certain alleged village Mera land within the limits of a State forest. It appeared from the evidence that the villages had for many years paid a wergo in respect of the land as assessed by the Land Registry official, yet there could be no doubt that at no long time since the land had been dealt with as Miri. Ab antiquo usage being thus disproved, it was necessary to consider the possibility of an express or implied dedication of Miri as Metruki. "Whatever the proper designation to be given to the word 'Mera' we do not see", remarked the Court, "why the State cannot grant arazi-mirié as a Mera on any terms it pleases, or why it cannot, under circum-

---

[1]) Boundary disputes were referred to the Civil (Nizam) Courts by Iradeh 20 Ramadan, 1296. In L. A. 15/28 the Court held that Art. 47 Land Code applies only to registration on sale. We doubt the soundness of this.

[2]) (1895) 3 C.L.R. p. 151.

Chapter IV—Metruki Land.

stances such as the present, be taken to have assented to this particular land, whether it should be termed Mera or Yaylak or Kishlak, being assigned to the inhabitants of the village on the terms of their paying 36 piastres per annum". The Court consequently decided that, as the land had been registered as village Mera for many years and an annual tax had been received by the State from the inhabitants in respect of it, there was, in effect, sufficient evidence of dedication by the State and the Forest Officer could not now be heard to assert that the land was not village pasture ground assigned to the inhabitants.

It is our opinion that the Raqabe of communal Metruki lands must be deemed to be vested in the State and not in the villagers enjoying the rights of the pasture, whether under Art. 97 or Art. 101. Any opinion on the question can be only an inference from the language used. As regards Metruki, as also with regard to Waqf, the law regulates user of the land while leaving the question of ownership obscure as being normally irrelevant.

It has also been a moot question whether the inhabitants of a village having exclusive rights of pasture are owners of the grass in the sense that they can claim the value of the grass consumed by any stranger who permits his cattle to pasture thereon. Art. 91, as we shall see, expressly recognises this right as belonging to villagers having exclusive rights to cut wood, and Chiha is of opinion that the same principle must apply to villagers having exclusive rights of pasture [1]). If this is so, the right of pasture must be deemed not a mere right of servitude (such as is the right of common pasture in England) but a right of ownership, not in the soil, but in the products of the soil.

Metruki land cannot be used save for the purpose for which it is allotted. Art. 97 makes it clear that the enclosure of any land is forbidden even with the consent of the commoners. The same rule applies presumably to any thing done which changes the character of the land as pasturing ground. However, by Sec. 99 (4) of the Mining Ordinance, 1925, (added by Mining Amendment Ordinance, 1926) the High Commissioner may grant to the inhabitants of the village without payment of fee, a licence to extract stone, gravel, sand, or clay from the common lands of the village for their own use, but not for sale.

The trees of woods and forests called "Baltalik" assigned ab antiquo for the use and for the fuel of a town or village shall

Baltalik.

---

[1]) Op. cit., p. 104.

The Land Law of Palestine.

be cut by the inhabitants of such town or village only, no one of another town or village can cut wood there. So also with regard to woods and forests assigned ab antiquo for the same purpose to several towns or villages, the inhabitants of such places alone shall cut wood there and not the inhabitants of other places. No due shall be taken in respect of such woods and forests. (Land Code, Art. 91).

Neither individual nor joint possession of part of a wood or forest assigned to the use of the inhabitants of a village can be given to anyone to make it into a private wood or to cut it down and plough up the ground for cultivation. If anyone acquires such possession the inhabitants can at any time stop it. (Land Code, Art. 92).

Baltaliks (Balta, an axe) are literally woods fit for the axe. The villagers enjoy an exclusive right and, as is clear from the Addendum of A.H. 1293, they can maintain an action for wrongful appropriation (Ghasb) against any person who unlawfully cuts wood in the Baltalik. By art. 23 of the Ottoman Forest Regulations of 1870, it was forbidden to private persons to acquire any portion of the soil of a Baltalik. Whether the soil of a Baltalik can be deemed to be vested in the villagers enjoying the right or not, the terms of the Articles certainly lead to the conclusion that the trees themselves are their private property and their right of property, though not expressly stated, seems implicit in the Ottoman Forest Regulations. These Regulations are no longer applicable. (Forest Ordinance, 1926, Sec. 27).

If the evidence were clear that by ab antiquo usage the trees of some forest had been assigned for the exclusive use of the same village, this would serve to show the existence of a Baltalik. But, unless there is clear evidence that the right was exclusive, it would not constitute a Baltalik.

The Forest Ordinance, 1926, makes no specific mention of Baltaliks, though Sec. 6 (2) regulates the taking by villagers of forest produce within a forest reserve in pursuance of a legal right or custom. Presumably woodland which is Baltalik must be deemed to be private property for the purpose of this Ordinance and could, therefore, only be declared Forest Reserve under Sec. 20 thereof, and not under Sec. 3. But if forest land, including a Baltalik, be taken under the protection of the Government under Sec. 20, the management, etc. of the woods is subjected to all the provisions of this Ordinance. In such case, therefore, the villagers would only be able to cut wood subject to the strict conditions laid

Chapter IV—Metruki Land.

down in Sec. 6. A Licence by the Forest Officer is necessary and this may be granted or refused by him at his discretion, or cancelled if the conditions are not fulfilled.

It may here be remarked that save in Art. 91 there is no reference in the Ottoman Law to any legal right or custom of the kind mentioned in Sec. 6 (2) of the Ordinance. Possibly village customs of this kind established by immemorial usage might be recognised in conformity with the general principle enunciated in Art. 6 of the Mejelle. But there is no express provision.

Under Sec. 9 of the Sand Drifts Ordinance, 1922, land reclaimed by villagers under the provisions thereof is to be applied as Metruki for the benefit of the inhabitants of the villages, which carried out the work. Such land can apparently be applied for whatever purposes it is most suitable, either under Land Code, Art. 2, 96 or 97, or as public Metruki under Art. 94. *[New Metruki.]*

It is also open to the Government to grant Mewat land as Metruki to a village for the benefit of the inhabitants as a whole. This has, at least in one instance, been done by way of confirmation of an Ottoman grant.

Moreover, if the view taken by the Cyprus Court in Constanti v. Principal Forest Officer be adopted, the Government may dedicate Miri land as Metruki, though such a dedication could not be made save by express or implied grant of the supreme authorities of the State, the permission of a subordinate official would not (semble) suffice [1]).

Neither private persons nor the state can interfere with or obstruct (save under statutory powers) any public or communal right of the Metruki class. Interference with the enjoyment of rights of common of pasture or of other similar rights gives a right of action, but the exercise of such a right is apparently restricted by the provisions of the Mejelle. *[Remedies.]*

In an action about things, like rivers and pasture lands, the benefit of which is jointly owned between two villages, the inhabitants of which are not a limited number, the presence of some on each side is sufficient. But in case the inhabitants are a limited number, the presence of some is not sufficient, the presence of wekils of the two sides, or of the whole of them is necessary. *[Mejelle, Art. 1645.]*

The inhabitants of a village, when they are more than 100, are not considered a limited number. *[Art. 1646.]*

---

[1]) Miri may now be turned into "Public Land" at the disposition of the Government under the provisions of the Land Law (Amendment) Ordinance 1933. Whether this was possible under the Land Code is doubtful.

CHAPTER V—PUBLIC LANDS, STATE DOMAIN.

Definition of Public Lands.
We owe the term "Public Lands" and its definition to the Palestine Order-in-Council, 1922, Art. 2 [1]).

"Public lands means all lands in Palestine which are subject to the control of the Government of Palestine by virtue of Treaty[2]), convention, agreement or succession, and all lands which are or shall be acquired for the public service or otherwise".

The fundamental characteristic of Public Lands as so defined is that they are subject to the control of the Government. This is borne out by the provisions of Arts. 12 and 13 of the Order-in-Council 1922.

Art. 12.
"(1) All rights in or in relation to any public lands shall vest in and may be exercised by the High Commissioner for the time being in trust for the Government of Palestine.

(2) All mines and minerals of every kind and description whatsoever being in, under, or on any land or water, whether the latter be inland rivers or seas or territorial waters, shall be vested in the High Commissioner, subject to any right subsisting at the date of this Order of any person to work such mines or minerals by virtue of a valid concession".

Art. 13.
"The High Commissioner may make grants or leases of any such public lands or mines or minerals or may permit such lands to be temporarily occupied on such terms or conditions as he may think fit, subject to the provisions of any Ordinance.

Provided that such grant or disposition shall be in conformity either with some Order-in-Council or Law or Ordinance now or

---

[1]) The Interpretation Ordinance, 1929, does not contain any definition of the term "Public Lands". There is, however, a definition of this term in the Mining Ordinance, 1925, which follows the definition contained in the Order-in-Council, 1922.

[2]) The Treaty of Peace (Turkey) Amendment Ordinance, 1926, adds Article 60 of the Treaty of Lausanne to the Schedule of the Treaty of Peace (Turkey) Ordinance, 1925. Article 60 of the Treaty of Lausanne provides that the States in favour of which territory is detached from the Ottoman Empire by the Treaty shall acquire without payment all the property and possessions of the Ottoman Empire situated therein.

Chapter V—Public Lands, State Domain.

hereafter in force in Palestine, or with such instructions as may be addressed to the High Commissioner under His Majesty's Sign Manual and Signet, or through a Secretary of State, for the purpose of executing the provisions of the Mandate".

As used in the Order-in-Council the term public land appears, therefore, to include only such land as the State exploits or is free to exploit in such way as it pleases, uncontrolled by any law or custom determining the methods of exploitation. In this sense it would not include the Raqabe in Miri or Metruki [1]. Mewat land is, however, strictly part of the public lands, for, indeed, the term Mewat really denotes a method by which uncultivated land may come under cultivation rather than a species of land holding or land user.

The Mandatory in Syria has made much more complete provision as to the Public Domains by Decrees (arrêtés) of 10th June, 1925, (Domaine Public de l'Etat) and 5 May, 1926 (Domaine Privé de l'Etat). In these Decrees the various species of public lands and public rights in land and water are classified and their exploitation regulated.

Public Lands may be considered under the following heads:— *Different Categories of Public Lands.*
1. Miri which has become Mahlul.

Under the Ottoman Land Law the State may have a proprietary interest in land over the exploitation of which it does not exercise control. Thus the Raqabe of land subject to a Tapu grant is vested in the State, as is also (semble) that of Metruki land. In a broad sense land subject to a Tapu grant remains State land and the use of the term Miri to designate it, is, from this point of view, accurate though misleading. But it is only when Miri land becomes vacant (Mahlul) that the State obtains control of its exploitation. And, as was remarked above, Mahlul will, in fact, be re-granted by Tapu unless the High Commissioner has declared it to be "Public Land" within the meaning of Art. 12 of the Order-in-Council. (Land Law (Amendment) Ordinance 1933).

In view of the use of the term "Public Land" in this Ordinance, it appears that Miri Mahlul which has not been the subject of a "declaration" under it should not be classified under that head. It retains the character of Miri unless such a declaration is made.

2. Jiftlik (Mudawara) Lands.

---

[1] If this is so, there does not appear to be any clause in the Order-in-Council explicitly vesting the Raqabe in the High Commissioner.

The Land Law of Palestine.

Jiftlik is derived from Turkish words meaning "double". It is thus defined in the Land Code, Art. 131. "Jiftlik, in Law, means a tract of land such as needs one yoke of oxen to work it, which is cultivated and harvested every year. But ordinarily speaking "Jiftlik" means the land of which it is comprised, the buildings there, as well as the animals, grain, implements, yokes of oxen, and other accessories, built and procured for cultivation". The Article goes on to consider the situation which arises if the owner of a Jiftlik dies without heirs and without a right to Tapu to the land. In this passage, it is clear that the Jiftlik is considered as a farm with accessories, in private ownership, the land being Miri. Such Jiftliks exist in Cyprus and there are several references in the Land Code to privately owned Jiftliks of this kind. (See, for example, Land Code, Arts. 99, 130; Cf. Tapu Law, 1858, Arts. 31—33).

In Palestine, there exist farms formerly belonging to the Sultan as his private property and at a later date taken over by the Ottoman Government as part of the State Domain. They are usually termed Mudawara lands (i.e. turned round, hence transferred) because they were transferred from the Sultan to the Treasury after the Turkish Revolution of 1908. The history of these lands is obscure. It is said that many years ago the holders of lands, presumably Miri, on the confines of Palestine, particularly in the Ghor and in the neighbourhood of Rafa, suffered much from the inroad of nomadic Bedouins. They, therefore, arranged to transfer their holdings into the name of the Sultan, so that they might become Crown lands. This was thought would make them more secure as the Bedouins would refrain from interfering with the Sultan's own property, and the event proved this surmise correct. The former holders were retained as tenants and they paid in addition to tithe which would have been due from them as possessors of Miri, a further 1/10 of the produce, the whole payment being popularly known as Khums (the fifth).

The account of the origin of the Mudawara lands is not, however, fully borne out by official statements of the Ottoman authorities. These appear to show that the cultivators, owing to their fear of Arab incursions deserted the villages and left the lands uncultivated. They consequently became Mahlul, but were withdrawn from auction and allotted to the Sultan Abdel Hamid and registered in his name. Whatever may have been the origin of the arrangement, it is at least a fact that it still prevails and is continued by the present administration with modifications.

Chapter V—Public Lands, State Domain.

In the case of certain Mudawara lands situated in the Jordan valley, it has, however, been arranged that the legal tessaruf should be transferred to the actual cultivator under an agreement made the 19th November, 1921. This agreement provides for a settlement of the lands, in accordance with its provisions upon the basis that the present cultivators shall become Miri owners. This settlement is now completed.

The principal conditions of the agreement were as follows:—

1. The cultivators of the Mudawara lands mentioned in the Schedule to the agreement were to be constituted owners of the land as Miri, and Miri kushans are to be issued to them.

2. The kushan was to contain a clause that in case an adverse claim were made to any land granted by the Government, the Government should refund to the transferee the Bedl Tatweeb (transfer price) paid by him for the land, together with interest and damages as may be determined by the Court.

3. No registration fee was to be taken from the transferee, except the payment of P.T.1 for the title deed.

4. No transfer price was to be paid in respect of land on which houses or other buildings have been erected by the transferee.

5. Each head of a family who purchased or acquired by succession, or exercised for ten years or more successively cultivation rights was to be entitled to a transfer of the land to him, and to be registered as Miri holder of the whole of the area on which he has cultivated summer and winter crops during the previous two years.

6. A family which was found to have cultivated less than 150 dunums was entitled to an area of 150 dunums. If the family consisted of more than five individuals, 30 additional dunums were transferred for each additional member.

7. Where the transferees were members of a tribe, the land transferred to all the members of the tribe constitute one tribal area. The title deed for the tribal area was to contain a list of the heads of the families comprising the area.

8. The Chief of the tribe was entrusted by the Government with the just allotment of areas between individuals and with the collection and payment of taxes and tithes to the Government; and of the instalments of the transfer price (Bedl Tatweeb) due from the members of the tribe for the area pertaining to them.

9. Tribes living principally on flocks and herds were given additional areas known as the tribal grazing area. The additional

area was to be leased to the tribe at an annual rent so long as the tribe used it fully for grazing purposes.

10. The transfer price which was to be paid to the Government is P.T.150 per dunum of arable land, and P.T. 125 per dunum of non-arable land, payable with the tithes in fifteen equal annual instalments.

11. If the transfer price were not fully paid by the end of the 15 years the transferee was deemed to have forfeited his right to the title deed, and to have been a tenant of the Government.

12. The land was to be demarcated by a special Commission with the powers of an arbitration tribunal for the purposes of carrying out the agreement and for settlement of any dispute which arose in connection with the allotment of areas. The award of the Commission is subject to reference to the Courts in the same way as the award of any arbitration tribunal.

As from the date of the Agreement [1]) persons entitled under its provisions as transferees were to be deemed owners of Miri land and free to exercise all the rights and privileges of such owners, provided that no disposition except by way of mortgage to the Government or of succession should be made until the whole transfer price had been paid. (Art. 16). The High Court has, however, held [2]) that this clause does not affect the right of creditors who can attach the land and have them sold in satisfaction of their claims. The persons to whom lands are thus sold, being necessarily aware of the restrictions are bound by the conditions of the Agreement.

Although the greater part of cultivated land in Palestine is Miri land held under Tapu grant or is Mudawara land, there remains, particularly in the South (Beersheba District), a considerable stretch of country which is cultivated at intervals by semi-nomadic tribes, but of which the tribesmen have not been given possession by Tapu grants. Tapu grants can only be made to determinate persons. (Land Code, Art. 8).

Tapu grants have in some cases been made to Tribal Sheikhs for the benefit of the tribes and the land included in such grants becomes Miri.

3. Mines and Minerals.

"Mines and Minerals" are distinguished from "Public Lands" in Arts. 12 and 13 of the Order-in-Council, but this is merely for convenience of phraseology.

---

[1]) The Ghor-Beisan Agreement was signed on the 19th of November, 1921. See P. G. No. 388 of 14.9.1933. [2]) High Court No. 18/32 and No. 19/32.

Chapter V—Public Lands, State Domain.

Strictly speaking minerals in the land are part of the land and minerals under Public Lands became vested in the High Commissioner in trust by the effect of Art. 12(1) [1]).

As already explained the Miri holder has rights in the surface only and is not owner of the mines and minerals under the land [2]). These latter are the property of the State and fall within the Public Domain. Properly speaking land subjacent to a Miri surface appears, therefore, to form part of the Public Lands as being "subject to the control of the Government of Palestine". The terms of Art. 12 (1) appear to be wide enough to vest in the High Commissioner in trust all State rights in minerals under Mewat, Metruki, Miri and State Domain proper and the term "land" may reasonably be interpreted as including the suprajacent water. Following this interpretation, Art. 12 (2) merely provides a closer definition of the High Commissioner's powers over the minerals already vested in him in trust by the effect of Art. 12 (1) [3]).

The view has been advanced that Art. 12 of the Palestine Order-in-Council 1922 vests in the High Commissioner not only minerals in or under Public Lands, including Miri, but also minerals under Mulk. Though Art. 1194 of the Mejelle [4]) does not mention minerals specifically yet its broad terms imply that the Mulk owner of the surface owns all minerals beneath the land and its terms are not compatible with any other interpretation. More specific language would have been used in Art. 12(2) had it been the intention of the legislator to confiscate existing rights without compensation, and the terms of Sec. 35 of the Mining Ordinance 1925 show that the rights of the Mulk owner in the minerals are still recognized by the State [5]).

---

[1]) A Mine is by Moslem law regarded as a constituent part of the land in which it lies. This is the Hanafite doctrine. Hedaya, at p. 15. (Hamilton's Translation).

[2]) By the Law of Disposition A. H. 1331, Sec. 7, he is permitted to take sand, etc. His right in this respect must be deemed to be controlled by the provisions of the Mining Ordinances 1925-33.

[3]) The suggestion that each paragraph is an independent vesting clause leads to the odd conclusion that minerals would be vested in the High Commissioner personally and not in trust.

[4]) Mejelle, Art. 1194, states that the owner (i.e. Mulk owner) of any site is the owner of things above it and below it. The special rights of Mulk owners are protected by Sec. 35 of the Mining Ordinance.

Mining rights or Mining oil leases can only be granted over Mulk or Waqf Sahih with consent of the owner or competent authority (Sec. 35(1)). See subsec. (2) as to compensation and Royalties where consent is dispensed with.

[5]) The fifth part of the Royalty deducted under the provisions of Sec. 35

The Land Law of Palestine.

The Mining Ordinance 1925 defines Minerals (Sec. 2 (i) as "all materials of economic value forming part of or derived naturally from the crust of the earth". Minerals in solution, timber, etc. are explicitly reserved and by Sec. 3(2) nothing in the Ordinance is to derogate from the rights of the High Commissioner with regard to minerals in solution or mineral springs. The Ordinance of 1925 has been amended by later Ordinances of 1926 and 1933. It is to be observed that the Ottoman Mining laws as detailed in the Second Schedule to the Ordinance of 1925 including Art. 107 of the Land Code ceased to have effect by the effect of Sec. 97 of that Ordinance. The provisions of Art. 107 of the Land Code followed the Moslem principle, rewarding the finder of minerals on Mewat and Metruki with four-fifths of their value and taking one-fifth of the value of those found in Mulk as a double tithe to the State.

4. Forest Reserves.

Forest land which is not private property may in one sense be said to fall within the class of Mewat, unless, at least, it is covered by trees grown for timber. The forests of the Turkish Empire were divided into four classes:—

1. State forests. 2. Waqf forests. 3. Communal forests (Baltaliks). 4. Private forests.

State forests were regulated by an elaborate Règlement des forêts of 1870, which also contained some provisions as to Baltaliks. The subject is now dealt with in Palestine by the Forests Ordinance 1926-1928 which provide that no other laws or regulations concerning forestry are to be applicable in Palestine.

Forests lands not being private property may by Proclamation of the High Commissioner be brought under the control and management of the Government. (Forests Ordinance, 1926, Sec. 3). Thereafter the provisions of the Ordinance apply to them. These provisions are directed to secure the care of the forests and their exploitation in accordance with sound principles of forestry.

Forest lands which are private property may also be taken under the protection of the Government in accordance with Sec. 20 of the Ordinance, and are then deemed to be Forest Reserves within the meaning of this Ordinance, but such reserves do not, of course, fall within the scope of the State Domains, though subject in all respects to the restrictions as to management, creation of new rights thereon, powers of disposition, etc. provided by the Ordinance as to Forest Reserves generally.

---

is apparently intended to represent the Zakat or Khums levied on mines under the Moslem Law (Hedaya, ibid). Land Code, Art. 107.

Chapter V—Public Lands, State Domain.

5. Land and buildings the property of the State by purchase.

Within the category of Public Domains must also be placed land and holdings the property of the State by purchase or otherwise used and exploited directly by the State. Such property is not Metruki because it is not subject to public or communal rights; nor is it Mewat because it is already developed and not left open to access. This class includes Government Buildings, Harbours, Experimental Farms and the Railway premises. We may also place under it expropriated archaeological sites and the like.

This class includes Miri Mahlul which has been declared to be public land and any land which is Mulk in the hands of the State by purchase or escheat or other form of appropriation. If the State expropriates or buys the tessaruf of a Miri holder, the land appears thereafter to be the Mulk of the State without the necessity of any declaration under the Land Law (Amendment) Ordinance 1933.

6. Mewat land.

All Mewat land appears to fall within the definition of Public Lands. In a Cyprus case [1] it was stated that, according to Ottoman Law, Mewat land was the property of the Sultan as Caliph, and was in Cyprus vested (prior to the annexation of the Island) in the British Government (i.e. the Crown) as representative of the Sultan. This being so, Mewat land appears by virtue of the Treaty of Lausanne to fall within the definition of Public Lands.

A very large part of the area of Palestine is Mewat. Forest Reserves are probably in most cases Mewat. The nature and incidents of Mewat have been already considered.

7. Land and Water of the Metruki class.

Land and Water of the Metruki class which are Mubah are also sometimes classified as forming part of the Public Domain. It is, however, better to place these in a class apart since they are "public" in the sense of being open to common use, and the ownership of them must (semble) be regarded as vested in the State. But Public Domain proper is not by law open to common use, but possessed and controlled by the State as representing the Community.

The State may and does grant concessions and rights to private individuals in respect of land and water which is Mubah, but could not (semble) save under statutory powers restrict public

---

[1] Kyriako v. Principal Forest Officer (1894) 3 C.L.R. at p. 99.

The Land Law of Palestine.

rights of user. There is, however, no Ottoman authority upon this part of the subject. No doubt the tendency of the Palestine Courts would be to apply principles of English law in the determination of any questions which arise as to the respective rights of the State and the public in this connection.

It may be added that the importance of irrigation to the development of the country has led the Cypriot Government to take steps towards the public control of water (Cf. Irrigation and Water laws 1887-1926; Government Waterworks Law 1928). The desirability of similar legislation has been considered in Palestine but no definite steps have yet been taken.

The only provisions made public as to the exploitation of State Domain consist in

(1) An early Public Notice of 23 June 1920 which refers expressly to Mahlul and is apparently to be read in connection with the Mahlul Land Ordinance of October 1920 as showing the view adopted by the authorities as to the treatment of Miri Mahlul.

(2) The Public Lands Ordinance 1926 conferring certain powers of management on The Director, Department of Lands.

CHAPTER VI—WAQF AND TRUSTS.

The institution known as Waqf is peculiar to Moslem Law. In its effects and incidents it bears a resemblance to the Trust of English Equity, but there are striking differences.

Where a Waqf is made of property, we are told[1]: "the proprietary right of the grantor is divested and it remains thenceforth in the implied ownership of the Almighty. The usufruct alone is applied for the benefit of human beings and the subject of the dedication becomes inalienable and non-heritable in perpetuity". Such dedication must be for a pious purpose. Every object which tends to the good of mankind, individually or collectively, is a pious purpose. A dedication to a mosque signifies the support of a place of worship for human beings; to a caravanserai, the maintenance of a place of rest for travellers. Similarly, a provision for one's children and descendants, kindred or neighbours, is a pious object under the Musulman Law.

Accordingly a waqf may be made for a body or individuals one after another, and afterwards for the poor generally, or for a mosque, madrassa (school or college), hospital, etc.

"There is no essential formality or the use of any express phrase requisite for the constitution of a waqf. A waqf can be constituted by the use of any expression which conveys distinctly the intention of the donor to dedicate the property to a pious purpose.

"It may be created either in writing or verbally. When it is in writing the document is called the "Waqfnamah" (Waqfieh).

An intention to dedicate is essential. To make a dedication irrevocable there must be a judicial decision in favour of the dedication or the dedication must be testamentary. The Waqfieh is the 'hodget' of the Sharia Court in which is contained the declaration of the dedicator about the dedication and the judicial declaration of its validity. It is in general correct to say that a

---

[1] Syed Amir Aly. Student's Handbook of Mohammedan Law, from which this and the succeeding extract are taken.

The Land Law of Palestine.

Waqf is constituted by waqfieh or by will, but there is no law which requires that the terms of the dedication must be set out in a waqfieh so that there may be a valid dedication without a waqfieh". Thus if a man built on waqf land and gave the building for the benefit of the waqf, there is no need for a Waqfieh since the dedication is irrevocable [1]). Other cases of dedications which are irrevocable without the decision of a judge occur when property is given for a mosque and worship has taken place, or when a person has dedicated a building site to be used as a cemetery, gives permission to bury the dead there, and a dead person is burried in it, that building site becomes waqf by irrevocable dedication [2]). Art. 33 of the Land Code which prohibits burial on Miri land is presumably intended to prevent a claim being made that the land is Waqf [3]).

Since a "provision for one's family" is an act of duty, a Waqf constituting the settlor's (Waqif's) own family or descendants the primary recipients of the benefaction is valid in law and meritorious. And under the Hanafi law the Waqif may constitute himself the first beneficiary, and, if he does so, he can lawfully reserve the benefit for himself either wholly or partially. Advantage has been taken of this doctrine to create very many family Waqfs.

The statement of the rules relating to the constitution of Waqfs and of the formalities requisite thereto does not, however, fall within the scope of this work. Reference must be made to treatises on Moslem law. It is important to note that no Waqf can be created of land in Palestine otherwise than by will, unless the settlor has first obtained the written consent of the Government (Land Transfer Ordinance 1920, Sec. 2—5). The Civil Courts would, therefore, treat as void any Waqf of land created since this Ordinance without such consent. It seems, however, that the necessary consent will be given on application provided that the settlor shows that he has a Mulk title to the land concerned. There is nothing, therefore, in the Land Transfer Ordinance to check the multiplication of Waqfs in Mulk land.

---

[1]) See Khanim v. Dianello, (1903) 6 C.L.R., at p. 59, where the principle was applied to buildings on Ijaratein Waqf land.

[2]) See Omar Hilmy. The laws of Waqf, from which book most of the propositions in this paragraph and many others in this chapter are derived.

[3]) Lands not expressly dedicated for a cemetery but covered by graves are regarded as Waqf. Where there are only one or two graves the particular spots where the bodies are buried are regarded as sacred. (Syed Amir Aly. op. cit., 160).

Chapter VI—Waqf and Trusts.

The general effect of dedication of land or other property as Waqf is that it is thenceforth immobilized. The dominant results of dedication are well brought out in the following statement quoted from a learned writer.

Inalienability of Waqf property.

"The constitution of Waqf consists in an irrevocable and perpetual gift of the enjoyment of property capable of immobilization and made inalienable as the result of such constitution. The gift must be made for some religious or charitable purpose but there may be prior provision made for benefits to be enjoyed by persons designated by the settlor, either from among the members of his family and descendants or from among strangers, without regard to the general law of inheritance. The beneficiaries obtain their successive rights to enjoyment of the property dedicated directly from the settlor" [1].

Much ink has been spilt over the question as to what happens to the "ownership" of the Waqf property. Some writers take refuge in the meaningless statement that God is the owner. The tendency of French writers is to treat the Waqf as a juridical person and to vest the property in the person thus created. The whole question is, probably, one of words only. There can, at least, be no doubt that the "ownership" of Waqf property is not vested in the Mutwally who in this respect occupies a very different position from that of an English "trustee". The Moslem theory is that the property is immobilized and only the enjoyment is dedicated.

The feature of Waqf law which is of most importance for the purposes of the Land Law is the inalienable character of property dedicated as Waqf. It is this peculiarity which leads to the strange institutions known as Hıkr and Ijaratein which are, in effect, legal devices for escaping from the grave inconveniences which necessarily result from the rule of inalienability. These will be discussed later. Nor is it necessary to say here anything as to the social effects of the rule which in the eyes of many observers are regarded as gravely injurious. All we need note is that the rule is absolute and cannot be avoided even by agreement of all the beneficiaries [2].

An apparent exception to the rule of inalienability permits Waqf property to be exchanged for other property, or even in some cases to be sold, provided that the sale price is invested in the

---

[1] Lale in L'Egypte Contemporaine, I, at p. 604.
[2] Kadry Pasha. Du Waqf, Art. 77.

The Land Law of Palestine.

purchase of other property, which becomes thus dedicated as Waqf. The exception, though of practical importance, does not seem to be theoretically inconsistent with the general inalienable character of Waqf property, since (we are told) that not the property but the enjoyment is dedicated, and the substitution of a new "corpus" thus enables the enjoyment to continue as before [1]).

Statutory powers of expropriation of Waqf property are, however, given in Palestine Ordinances as will be mentioned below.

Jurisdiction in matters of Waqf. Waqf is an institution of Moslem law and both in its relation to religion and to family is of great importance in Moslem society. Following a well established Turkish tradition, jurisdiction over Waqfs has, therefore, been left to the Moslem Courts and, in accordance with the policy generally adopted, a similar jurisdiction over Jewish and Christian religious endowments has been left to the Rabbinical and Patriarchal Courts respectively. These provisions are made by the Palestine Order-in-Council 1922. But though the Order-in-Council recognizes the jurisdiction of both Moslem and non-Moslem Courts in connection with Waqf, the limitations should be carefully noted. Religious jurisdiction exists in general, both as to questions of constitution and as to internal administration [2]), but (a) the Moslem Courts have no jurisdiction unless the Waqf was created for the benefit of Moslems and before a Moslem Court (Art. 52); (b) the Jewish Courts have no jurisdiction unless the Waqf or religious endowment was constituted before the Rabbinical Court according to Jewish law (Art. 53); (c) the Christian Courts have no jurisdiction unless the Waqf or religious endowment was constituted before the Religious Court according to the religious law of the community if such exists (Art. 54).

The jurisdiction of the Civil Courts in respect to Waqfs under Moslem law created for the benefit of non-Moslems before the Moslem Courts prior to the Order-in-Council is modified in certain particulars by the provisions of the Jurisdiction of Civil and Religious Courts Ordinances 1925. The matter is not one

---

[1]) The rules regulating exchange and sale are set forth by Kadry Pasha, op. cit., Arts. 129, ff.

[2]) The Religious Courts have jurisdiction both to determine whether the Waqf has been validly constituted and to settle questions of administration. Remark, however, that in the case of certain Awqaf questions as to constitution are within the jurisdiction of the Civil Courts. As to the distinction between constitution and administration, see the Egyptian cases referred to in Goadby, Private International and Inter-Religious Law in Palestine, page 129 and note.

Chapter VI—Waqf and Trusts.

which requires detailed notice here. It is, however, of great importance to note that where land is claimed as Waqf and the claim is denied, the issue is within the jurisdiction of the Civil Courts. This had already been declared to be the law by a decision of the Court of Appeal, but it is now expressly so enacted by Sec. 5 of the Jurisdiction of Civil and Religious Courts Ordinance 1925, which provides as follows, "Every action or other proceeding concerning the ownership or possession of immovable property shall be decided by a Civil Court notwithstanding any claim by any party or person that the land is Waqf".

In this book, the word Waqf will be used exclusively to designate Waqfs created under Moslem law.

The Mūtwally of the Waqf is charged with the duty of administration. Subject to the terms of the Waqfieh, the appointment of a Mutwally of a Moslem Waqf rests with the Moslem Court. The Mutwally is not the legal owner of the property as is the English trustee. He occupies an office only. It is not necessary to consider here the powers, duties, and liabilities of a Mutwally. According to Moslem theory he appears to be regarded bailee of the property, but not insurer. He cannot sell, but may under certain conditions exchange. He has limited powers of leasing. _{Administration.}

The appointment of the Mutwally, his powers of administration, his remuneration, his liability to account and his dismissal are considered in detail in every adequate book on Moslem law. To such reference must be made by the reader desirous of further information [1]). The law upon these topics is not peculiar to Palestine nor can it be regarded as part of the Ottoman Land Law except so far as Moslem law becomes applicable to land in Palestine on its subjection to an institution of Moslem law.

When a Waqf has been originally created for a purpose benefiting the community as a whole, it is termed a Waqf Amumy (Public Waqf). Such Waqfs include Mosques, Cemeteries, Colleges, Wells, Bridges, Reservoirs, etc. Property may, of course, be didicated to provide for their upkeep, and the maintenance of preachers, teachers, etc., and such property by its use becomes income bearing Mussaqafat or Mustaghilat. The community for whose benefit such a waqf is created is primarily the community of the Faithful, i.e. Musulmen. But the benefit of a waqf is not necessarily limited to Moslems. Classification of waqfs.

---

[1]) Special reference may be made to the work of Omar Hilmy, above mentioned, and to Kadry Pasha's compilation published by the Egyptian Government.

The Land Law of Palestine.

The majority of Awqaf have, however, been created primarily for the benefit of the dedicator or his family. Property, once made waqf, must remain waqf, subject to special rules as to Istibdal (Exchange), and, therefore, the failure of the heirs of the dedicator or cesser otherwise of the purposes, for which the dedication was made, does not bring the waqf to an end. The waqf property must thereafter be administered for the benefit of the community, e.g. the relief of the poor, education, or the like. The waqf then falls into the class of Awqaf Mazbuta, which are thus defined.

Awqaf Mazbuta (i.e. waqfs which are seized) are those, of which both the Towliet (administratorship or trusteeship) and the administration (Idara) or the administration only is held by the Awqaf Administration and of which all the affairs are administered by the Awqaf Administration. So long as the special purposes, for which the dedication was made, continue the Mutwally (Administrator) of the family waqf administers the family waqf. Such a waqf is Ghair Mazbuta, or as it is more often termed Mulhaqa (attached) because the Idara (administration) does not belong to the Awqaf Administration, but is only under its supervision.

There are also Waqfs which are termed Mustesna (Exceptional) since they are not even attached to the Awqaf Administration, but are administered exclusively by their special Mutwallys [1]).

The manner of administration of the Waqf depends in general upon the terms of the dedication as expressed in the Waqfieh.

In Palestine there is no Ministry of Waqf, but by Orders dated 12th March, 1921, and 12th December, 1921, a Moslem body was constituted for the control and management of the Moslem Awqaf and affairs in Palestine, to be known as the Supreme Moslem Council. General and Local Waqf Committees were to be established, subject to the general supervision of the Council. It was provided (Sec. 8 (2) of Order 12th December, 1921) that the Sharia Courts were not to take any action affecting Hikr [2]), Ijaratein and Istibdal (Exchange) except with the unanimous consent of the Council. Art. 15 provides that the Mutwallys shall administer Mulhaqa Waqf in accordance with the existing laws and they shall

---

[1]) See Omar Hilmy, Arts. 33-35.

[2]) Hikr is a term used for a perpetual lease of Waqf property, and also for the rent thereby reserved. A contract of Hikr and one of Ijaratein are possibly distinguishable in law, but are practically identical in their effect. The term Hikr is not much used in Palestine. In Syria it seems to be used of rural Waqf of the Ijaratein class (Chaoui, Le Régime Foncier en Syrie, at p. 67) which in this book are denoted Muqata'a Waqfs. See also supra, p. 10 (note).

Chapter VI—Waqf and Trusts.

be under the orders of the Waqf Administration (i.e. the Supreme Moslem Council) and shall submit their accounts annually to the Local Committees for examination. The functions of the Local Committees were to be those specified in the Ottoman special law of 11th June, A.H. 1320 and they were to replace the Administrative Council referred to in that law (Art. 14).

Mulk and Miri Waqf.
In Moslem law property can only be dedicated as Waqf by the owner. It follows that only land held in Mulk ownership can be made Waqf. The Miri holder cannot declare a Waqf of his Miri holding.

Nevertheles, as we shall see, a species of dedication by way of Waqf has come to exist with respect to Miri land. But the only true Waqf (Waqf Sahiha) is that of land which at the time of dedication was the mulk of the dedicator.

Mulk of all kinds may be dedicated as Waqf. We are not concerned with Waqf of movables not attached to the soil, but such property may be Waqf if permanency is assured [1]. A dedication of buildings and trees separately from the land is, therefore, valid, but not if the dedicator is also Mulk owner of the site. (Omar Hilmy, Art. 85; Cf. Art. 95). But Mulk trees and buildings on Miri can be dedicated, though the Miri site remains undedicated. (Cf. Land Code, Arts. 89, 90). The latter article envisages the possibility of the trees being dedicated to one object; and the Miri site being dedicated to another.

Awqaf Sahiha are governed only by the Sacred Law and are not subject to Ottoman Statute Law. Since they can only be created over Mulk, a check upon the growth of Waqf results from any restriction upon the creation of Mulk interests. Having regard to the wide-spread and unfortunate consequences, both social and economic, which are due to the abuse of the Waqf system, it is easy to understand the anxiety of the Ottoman Government manifested in modern legislation to prevent the increase of Mulk.

Miri Waqf (Ghair Sahiha).
No true dedication of Miri is possible. Miri made Waqf without being granted as mulk remains Miri. Miri made Waqf in that way belongs to the dedicator as before, and can be sold to another. On the death of the dedicator it passes to those who have the right of succession, and if there is no one having the right to succeed, it belongs to the Beit-el-Mal. In short, the

---

[1] Cf. the curious Guedik Waqf. The "guedik" is the tools, apparatus or appliances of a special trade placed on property permanently established. There were (possibly) no guediks in Palestine. For the Provisional Law of 22 Rabi-el-Awal, 1331, as to Guediks in Constantinople, see Nord, op. cit., pp. 74 ff.

dedication of Miri made Waqf without any grant as Mulk and without the leave of the Sultan cannot be given effect to and cannot be valid [1]. And the grant of the Raqabe must be by way of gift.

Although a true dedication by way of Waqf is only possible in the case of Mulk, a very important modification of the law permits a kind of untrue or customary dedication of Miri interests. Such dedication is untrue (Ghair Sahiha) because it is not in accordance with the Sacred Law. An untrue dedication of Miri leaves the Raqabe vested in the State and does not, therefore, change the category of the land. It is merely a dedication of the interests, which the State has in the produce of the land and in the fees arising therefrom. The land does not really become Waqf. It is called "Irsad" in the Sacred Law, but in the legislation it is called Mevqufe, though properly speaking it is not Mevqufe at all. An untrue dedication of Miri is described as creating a Waqf of the Takhsisat category because the Waqf is created by a special appropriation of revenue (takhsis). Clearly no such Waqf can be created except by dedication by the Sovereign himself or by his authorisation. (Land Code, Art. 4).

Waqfs of the Takhsisat category are of three kinds and are thus explained by Omar Hilmy [2].

"Miri, which has been made Waqf of the Takhsisat category by a dedication which is not a true dedication, is of three kinds:

(a) Lands of which only the tithes and taxes (rusumat) have been dedicated and consecrated by the Government, while the right of possession (tessaruf) over them, as well as the ownership (raqabe) belong as before to the Beit-el-Mal.

(b) Lands of which the tithes and taxes belong as before to the Beit-el-Mal and only the right to their possession has been dedicated and assigned to some object by the Government.

(c) Lands of which both, the right of possession as well as the tithes and taxes have been dedicated and assigned to some object by the Government.

The tithes and such taxes as the tax on grant or inheritance and the price of unowned land (Mahlul) belong to the dedication of the first kind.

---

[1] Tyser and Ongley. Laws Relating to Waqf, p. 11, quoting Khalis Eshreff.
[2] Art. 137. Takhsisat waqf in Miri are alone considered here. There may be Takhsisat waqf in Mulk where the Tithe or Kharaj of Ushur or Kharaji lands are dedicated. (Omar Hilmy, op. cit., Art. 139).

Chapter VI—Waqf and Trusts.

Since the rights over the lands of this sort belong to the State they are granted as other Miri land by the State for cultivation.

The lands of the second and third sort are possessed by the Waqf, whether sown, cultivated or rented to others or given on an agreement to be cultivated in partnership.

But the tithes of the second sort are paid to the State while the tithes of the third sort are not paid.

Of these three sorts, only the first is regulated by the rules of the Land Code.

Since the right of the possession of the other two sorts does not belong to the State, the rules of the Land Code are not applied to them".

From this statement it appears that if, as is usually (if not always) the case in Palestine, the tithes and taxes only are dedicated, the change in the law relating to the land is analogous to that which occurs in England when tithe has been "appropriated" by a lay appropriator. In England tithes were originally ecclesiastical. In Palestine tithes are presumably secular, but are sometimes appropriated by dedication as Waqf. This does not affect the land but only the destination of part of its produce.

Not only the tithes but also the taxes (rusumat) are appropriated. In Art. 4 Land Code it is stated more clearly that it is the fees on sale and inheritance and the equivalent value (Bedl Misl) of vacant land which belong to the Waqf. In Turkish times it appears that varrying proportions of transfer fees were paid over to the Waqf Administration. Under the Fee Schedule dated 13th September, 1920, and made under Sec. 15 of the Transfer of Land Ordinance, 1920, one half of the fees levied in respect of the constitution of Waqf or the transfer of Waqf are to be paid to the Waqf and one half of the Treasury [1]).

Takhsisat Waqfs of the first kind, therefore, merely involve certain payments to the Waqf and do not affect the possession of the land by private persons. But if, as rarely happens, the possession (tessaruf) is dedicated, the right to cultivate the land itself and enjoy it belongs to the Waqf.

Messrs. Tyser and Ongley (Laws Relating to Waqf, p. 7) remark:—

"As explained in the text of Art. 4 of the Land Code only the first of these three kinds is discussed in that Code. As regards the second and third kind, transfer, succession, right to Tapu for

---

[1]) This applies, however, to Moslem Waqfs only.

non-cultivation, or its becoming pure Mahlul by the death of the Mutessarif, when there is no one with a right to Tapu or a right of succession and such rights under the enacted Laws are not in force they are not held by Tapu Sanad. They are possessed by Berat of the Sultan or Imperial Firman or by registration in the Land Registry Office, by the Waqf or by the person taking the benefit under the dedication and if the person taking the benefit under the dedication dies, they are occupied by some one who will be appointed in his place".

The difference between the three kinds of Takhsisat Waqfs is further explained by Khalis Eshreff (Commentary on the Land Code):

"Since these three kinds are different the one from the other, and because doubts have at first sight arisen in people's minds, as for instance whether there is any benefit to the Waqf from the second kind, we propose to explain by examples the differences between them and the benefit which the Waqf takes from each. For example when from Miri land 100 dunums in extent and bringing 1000 P.T. benefit to the State, only the benefit derived from the State is specially assigned (takhsis) to some object by the Sultan or by some one else with the Sultan's leave, that land is made Waqf as Mevqufe Ghair Sahiha of the first kind, and while it is cultivated by the Mutessarif (i. e. the holder) the tithe of its produce and, if the Mutessarif sells or dies, the duty payable on sale or succession or its price as Mahlul is given to the Waqf. When the tessaruf is specialy assigned that land is let at a rent by the Waqf itself. The 1000 P. T. tithe on the produce is paid to the State and the rent is paid by the lessee to the Waqf. Or, if it is cultivated by the Waqf itself, the benefit of the Waqf is the surplus produce. When there is specially assigned to a College or School the rights of tessaruf, taxes and tithes, both the tithe and rent, or, if it is cultivated by the Waqf itself, the surplus produce, belong to the Waqf".

This explanation makes clear the division of the revenue. It has, however, to be borne in mind that when there has been no grant as Mulk, the dedication of the tessaruf leaves the Raqabe vested in the State, the Waqf is Ghair Sahiha, and the land remains Miri [1]). From this it appears to follow that the interests of the Waqf are limited to those which are possible in the case of Miri land.

---

[1]) Cf. Tyser and Ongley, op. cit., p. 10, at bottom.

Chapter VI—Waqf and Trusts.

Takhsisat dedication is of two kinds:

(a) A true Takhsis which consists in the special dedication of the income belonging to the Treasury (Beit-el-Mal) to some object supported by the Beit-el-Mal;

(b) An untrue Takhsis which consists in the special dedication of part of the income of the Beit-el-Mal to some object not supported at the expense of the Beit-el-Mal (Treasury).

The income of the first sort being specially dedicated is spent on the object, for which it was dedicated and does not admit of revocation. The second sort can be revoked and maid invalid at the will of the Sultan [1]).

As to the sale of Mahluls of Takhsisat it is provided by a law of 6 Rejeb, 1292, that "sales and declarations and sales by auction according to the law of Mahluls of mevqufe land paying tithe or a fixed ground rent equivalent to tithe, and for vineyards and gardens the vines and trees whereof are waqf shall be carried out and heard by the officials of the Daftar Khani in the Sanjaks and by Clerks of the Tapu Office in Kazas in accordance with the formalities followed ab antiquo with regard to Miri and Mevqufe land". (Fisher's translations).

The terminology of this part of the subject is somewhat confused and terms well-known in one Moslem country are hardly known or used in a somewhat different sense in another. *Mussaqafat and Mustaghilat Waqf.*

Waqf property being inalienable and no mortgage of it being possible its development was often difficult and various mitigations of the rigidity of the law or devices for evading it have come into use.

Of these the most important is that of the long (or perpetual) lease of the land whereby a revenue is secured to the Waqf without corresponding capital expenditure by it. When Waqf property is so used it is sometimes said to form a Must-

---

[1]) Mr. Barron in his pamphlet with reference to Moslem Waqfs in Palestine makes the following observations as to Takhsisat Waqf of the second sort. Speaking of such Waqfs in Palesitne he says:

"The tithes of these Waqfs have been diverted at different times into State revenues, but the State has recognised its obligation by compounding the tithe and paying a fixed annual sum to the local Waqf Administration. The expression "object supported by the Treasury" is taken to mean an object for which it would be the duty of the State to provide. The legality of this resumption is open to question, but there can be no doubt that the Moslem authorities of the Ottoman Government acquiesced in their revocation, and instances are numerous in which Moslem rulers have taken lands out of Waqf. The Government of Palestine is undoubtedly entitled in law to adopt the action of its predecessors".

aghilat Waqf. "Mustaghel", says Omar Hilmy [1]), "is the name given to property dedicated for providing the persons who have the management of philantropic establishments with the income required". Often the Waqf property is let to some one who builds upon it, or buildings of Waqf are let to persons who undertake to repair them. Waqf property so used is sometimes said to form a Mussaqafat Waqf. "Mussaqaf", says Omar Hilmy [2]), "means a building from which income is derived and which has a roof".

Mustaghilat and Mussaqafat Waqfs are common in Cyprus and Palestine — more particularly, of course, in the towns. They were created by the use of leases, either by an ordinary Ijara Wahida or by the use of the device already explained known as Double Lease (Ijaratein).

Strictly speaking it would seem that the lessee under an Ijara Wahida Waqf is no better off than an ordinary lessee at a rack rent in England. But leases on Ijara Wahida are sometimes beneficial and the interest of the lessee is inheritable by his heirs. The lessee has not, however, a renewable interest. The letting of a Waqf at a rent to a beneficiary under the dedication is valid, and in fact in very many cases this is done.

Ijarateinlu Waqf. Various circumstances led to the transformation of many Ijara Wahida Waqfs (i.e. Waqf property let on Ijara Wahida) into Ijaratein. The principal source of our knowledge of the transformation and of the nature of Ijaratein is the Report of a Commission appointed by the Sultan dated A.H. 1284 [3]).

The Report is referred to and the nature of Ijaratein considered in the judgment of the Cyprus Court in Khanim v. Dianello. "The Commission in their Report say that on the ground that it had become necessary to extend the time of possession of the tenant of Waqf properties, it was decided that the system should be that where a person desired to have the occupation and enjoyment of a place which was Waqf property, it should be given into his possession after having paid the Waqf a small sum of money called the Ijara-Muajele, with the condition of his paying each year something to be called the Ijara-Muajele, and that repairs should fall upon him and whatever he should build with the permission of the Mutwally should be a free gift to the Waqf" [4]).

---

[1]) Op. cit., Art. 14.
[2]) Op. cit., Art. 15.
[3]) There is a translation of the Report in Tyser and Ongley, op. cit., pp. 14 ff.
[4]) (1903) 6 C.L.R. p. 52. See particularly pp. 55 ff.

Chapter VI—Waqf and Trusts.

Using the terms to which we are accustomed in dealing with Miri land, we may say that the Raqabe of the Ijarateinlu Waqfs is in the Waqf, i.e. remains dedicated, but the tessaruf belongs to the holder in Ijaratein. He has an assignable and heritable interest in the property comparable to that of the Miri holder, but, while in the case of Miri the Raqabe is in the State, in that of Ijaratein it is in the Waqf.

"The lessee", says M. Chaoui [1]), "obtains a real right over the Waqf property, not unlike that of the Miri tenant in Miri land but wider in its scope than his since many of the restrictions applicable to the enjoyment of the Miri holder do not apply to the tenant by Ijaratein". Contracts of Ijaratein could, according to the old practice, be formed only after authorization had been obtained from the Cadi.

The property was then, it is stated, put up to auction to be let to the highest bidder. The final letting only took place after a Decree of authorization had been issued by the Sultan. Whether this elaborate practice was invariably and meticulously followed in all cases there seems good reason to doubt.

The similarity in practical effect of contract of Ijaratein to holding by Tapu grant is shown by the use of the same terminology as applicable to each. Thus if the interest of the holder by Ijaratein comes to an end the land is said to be Mahlul—but of course, for the benefit not of the State but of the Waqf.

As regards Mahluls of Ijarateinlu it is provided (Art. 10 of Law 25 Ramadan, A.H. 1281) as follows:—

"As there will be no right to Tapu in Mussaqafat and landed property held in Ijaratein those of them which have become entirely Mahlul will be leased to the candidate at auction according to the former system. When a small or large share of a not entirely Mahlul khan, bath, shop, garden, and such like thing of the landed property category becomes Mahlul, it will be sold to the candidate at auction. But houses are exempt from this law; if a share becomes vacant it will not be sold by auction, but leased to a shareholder on the valuation of a competent person". (Translation by Ongley).

See also, Law concerning Mahlul Waqf, 19 Zil Hijje, A.H. 1288, and as to the sales being conducted by the Muhasebejis of Awqaf, Law of Rabi-el-Awal, A.H. 1293, Art. 16.

For practical purposes the holder in Ijaratein is owner of the property subject to a kind of rent charge in favour of the

---
[1]) Op. cit., p. 68.

Waqf. But the property must be classified as being Waqf though the interest of Waqf is reduced to the receipt of the annual fixed payment. The Raqabe which remains vested in the Waqf is, of course, unassignable, and uninheritable. But the Ijaratein interest is, by modern legislation made assignable and inheritable. All such interests are for purposes of transfer and succession governed by the Ottoman Provisional Laws and by the Palestine Ordinances. These will be considered in the relevant chapter below. Reference may be made to the work of Omar Hilmy for further detail as to Ijaratein. A few extracts must here suffice.

"The Mutwally cannot, contrary to the condition of the dedicator, let property as Ijaratein which has been dedicated under the condition that it shall be let at a wahida rent. But in case Mussaqafat property, directed to be let at a wahida rent, falls down, and the property of the dedication has not sufficient income to repair it, and no one can be found to rent it at a wahida rent and repair it, setting off the expenses against the rent, then the Mutwally may, with the approval of the judge and the permission of the Sultan, let the Mussaqafat as Ijaratein. But if the Mutwally of his own motion let it as Ijaratein without the decision of the judge and the leave of the Sultan, such letting has no force or validity". (Art. 275).

"The possessor of Ijaratein Waqf property is the owner of the benefits derived from the property, but is not the owner of its Raqabe. Consequently, if one pulls down a building on a Mussaqafat Ijaratein Waqf property and sell and deliver the materials to another, and consume them, the Mutwally demands and recovers from him, as damages, the worth of the property as it stood". (Art. 263).

"When the possessor of Ijaratein Waqf property lets it to another and puts him in possession, and goes to another country, the jabi Waqf (collector of the rents of the Waqfs) has no right to demand from the lessee the Muajele which is in arrear". (Art. 264).

"It is not allowed to change the ancient state of Mussaqafat Waqf. But when the necessity for a change, and, that it will be beneficial to the Waqf, is shewn, then a change is allowed with the approval of the judge and the permission of the Mutwally". (Art. 267).

Omar Hilmy proceeds to give examples of what kind of change would be deemed a necessary one. He proceeds:

Chapter VI—Waqf and Trusts.

"If the owner of an Ijaratein Waqf site wish to erect a building on it, with the intention that it shall be his own property, the Mutwally can prevent him". (Art. 268).

In such a case, if the possessor without the leave of the Mutwally erects a building on the site, in order that it may be his own property, the following rules are observed:

If the pulling down of that building will not damage the site, it is pulled down.

If the pulling down is hurtful, the value of the building and materials is given to the person who built it, from the Waqfs and by his consent it is bought for the Waqf.

In such a case, the Mutwally of that site, cannot contend that the building is the property of the Waqf by reason only that in the title deed of the land a condition is inserted that whatever the possessor builds on it should be given to the Waqf. In Khanim v. Dianello [1]), the question was raised as to the ownership of buildings on Ijaratein erected with the consent of the Mutwally, and it was held (in spite of certain suggestions to the contrary) that such buildings must always be regarded as "a free gift to the Waqf". In Delegates of Awqaf v. Kenan [2]), where buildings had been erected on Ijaratein and had been separately registered as the Mulk of the holder, the Court held that the registration was wrong and the builder could not acquire a prescriptive title to the buildings as against the Waqf by the mere fact of occupying them for 36 years. It appears to have been admitted that the buildings when erected became Waqf.

A Muqata'alu Waqf is created when Waqf land is leased at a fixed rent on the terms that buildings and trees thereon shall be the Mulk of the lessee. They, therefore, are not Waqf at all. The position, therefore, resembles that which exists when Mulk trees or buildings stand on Miri land, and the law already explained, which governs that state of facts is in principle applicable here also. This is made clear in the following passages of Omar Hilmy:—

Muqata'alu Waqf.

Art. 277. The land of Waqfs let at a Muqata'a rent is subject to the buildings, trees or vines upon it.

Consequently, into whosoever's ownership the buildings, trees or vines may come, the Waqf land as subject to them comes also into his possession.

---

[1]) (1903) 6 C.L.R. 52.
[2]) (1910) 9 C.L.R. 48.

The Land Law of Palestine.

E. G. If someone sell to another a house, of which the site is Muqata'alu Waqf and the buildings pure Mulk, or trees of which the site is Muqata'alu Waqf but the trees Mulk, or vines of which the site is Muqata'alu Waqf but the vines are Mulk, the site also comes into the possession of the buyer.

Consequently, there is no necessity for a special grant of the site with the permission of the Mutwally of the Waqf.

However, if the seller declare clearly at the time of the sale that he keeps possession of the site, the site does not come into the possession of the purchaser.

But if he grants, by leave of the Mutwally, the land to another, he does not include in the sale the Mulk property upon it, buildings, trees, or vines, since he grants only the site, it is not considered that he has sold to the person, to whom he made the grant, the buildings, trees, and vines upon it.

Again, when the owner of Mulk buildings, trees or vines, situated on a Muqata'aly Waqf site dies and either the persons entitled to a share of his property or the heirs in the male and female line inherit the buildings, trees or vines, the land also comes into the possession of the said heirs gratis, without payment, as subject to the buildings, trees and vines". (Cf. Land Code, Art. 81).

Art. 278. "When one is owner of buildings on a Muqata'alu Waqf site and of trees and vines planted on it, and possesses the site at a Muqata'a rent, and dies without children, and his heirs wish to take the buildings, trees and vines by virtue of their right of inheritance and the site as subject to them, without payment, the Mutwally cannot prevent the heirs occupying it, on the ground that, since the site is Waqf, the buildings, trees and vines on it also belong to the dedication".

Art. 279. "When one possesses Muqata'alu Waqf which has no buildings, trees or vines upon it, and grants it to another, in order that the grant may be valid the leave of the Mutwally is required.

Consequently, in such a case, if he grants the site without the leave of the Mutwally, the grant has no force or validity.

When if one possesses the Muqata'alu Waqf site of a property, and another owns the buildings, trees or vines, when the person in possession grants that site, he must obtain the leave of the Mutwally.

In the same way, if there are Mulk buildings, trees or vines on a Muqata'alu site, but their owner grants only the site, not

Chapter VI—Waqf and Trusts.

selling the buildings, trees or vines, in order that the grant may be valid, the leave of the Mutwally is required".

Art. 282. "As long as there are traces of buildings, trees or vines on a Muqata'alu Waqf site, the owner of the buildings, trees or vines keeps possession of the site.

But as long as the person who possesses the site duly pays the rent at the right time, the Mutwally cannot cancel this rent and take the site out of the hands of the possessor, even if no trace of buildings, trees or vines remain".

As to inheritance to interests in Muqata'alu Waqf, see Chapter VII—Succession and Inheritance.

As to partition of Waqfs, see Chapter XIII—Co-ownership and Partition.

The usual Muqata'alu Waqf is as above described. It sometimes happens that the holder of a Muqata'a Waqf dedicates his Mulk trees or buildings in Waqf. The Waqf to which these are dedicated will then be bound to pay the Muqata'a to the Waqf from which the Muqata'a lease is held. Two different Waqfs will thus have interest in the same property. It may further happen that the Waqf holding the trees or buildings makes a second lease of them at a fixed rent (Muqata'a) so that in a sense two Muqata'a Waqfs exist together. It is stated that a second Muqata'a created in this way is termed a Muqata'a Qadima.

As to Registration of Mussaqafat and Mustaghilat Waqf, See chapter dealing with Registration.

The Ottoman Forest Law of A.H. 1286[1]), contains provisions as to Waqf forests and it is said that some woodland in Palestine is claimed as Waqf[2]). The Forest Law (Art. 20) states that forests administered directly by the Waqf Administration are to be subjected to a regular supervision. Sales and exploitation are to be made in accordance with the rules adopted as regards State Forests. Presumably if the existence of Waqf forests in Palestine is substantiated they might be brought under State regulation by an Order made under Sec. 20 of the Forests Ordinance. *Waqf Forests.*

Moslem rulers permitted their Christian and Jewish subjects to dedicate property as Waqf, though certain restrictions were imposed. The object of the Waqf must, it is stated[3]), "be one *Non-Moslem Waqf.*

---

[1]) Yong, op. cit., VI p. 6.
[2]) It is not clear to what category a Waqf forest belongs. Possibly it is Miri woodland of which the tessaruf had been dedicated.
[3]) Kadry Pasha. Du Waqf, Art. 87.

The Land Law of Palestine.

which would be regarded as pleasing to God both by Moslems and by non-Moslems". This rule seems, however, to have been liberally construed and though a Christian for example could not create a Waqf solely for the benefit of the Church yet if it were provided that should the Church become useless the income should be devoted to the "poor", the Waqf would be good [1]).

It is stated that by the tolerance of the Ottoman ruler Waqfs created by Jews or Christians were not left under the supervision of the Waqf Administration but were placed under the supervision of the Head of the Religious Community concerned. They were Mustesna (Exceptional).

The language of Art. 52 of the Order-in-Council shows clearly that such Mustesna Waqfs remain free from the jurisdiction of the Moslem Courts; only Waqfs created for the benefit of Moslems are subjected to such jurisdiction. It is, however, provided by the Jurisdiction of Civil and Religious Courts Ordinance, that the Moslem Courts may be given jurisdiction by consent of parties, where questions as to the constitution or validity of the Waqf are in issue. Whether any new Mustesna Waqf of this kind can be created since the Order-in-Council is doubtful. In spite of the use of the word "Waqf" in the closing paragraphs of Arts. 53 and 54 of the Order-in-Council, the better opinion seems to be that a Waqf governed by Moslem law can now only be created for the benefit of Moslems and that any similar foundation created before the Jewish or Christian Courts must be created in accordance with the law of the Community concerned. If the Jew or Christian endeavours by will to dedicate his Mulk by way of Waqf in accordance with Moslem law the dedication would (semble) be bad as a Waqf but might be good as creating a Charitable Trust by application of the provisions of Sec. 37 of the Charitable Trust Ordinance 1924, if, but only if, the purpose were charitable within the meaning of that Ordinance.

Land attached to Monasteries. Much land has been purchased by or passed into the possession of monastic bodies. A special article of the Land Code deals with the position thus created.

Art. 122 Land Code. "Land attached ab antiquo to a monastery registered as such in the Imperial Archives (Daftar Khani) cannot be held by title-deed; it can neither be sold nor bought. But if land after having been held ab antiquo by title-deeds has afterwards passed by some means into the hands of the monks, or is in fact held without

---

[1]) Kadry Pasha, op. cit., Art. 58.

Chapter VI—Waqf and Trusts.

title-deed, as appurtenant to a monastery, the procedure as to State land shall be applied to it, and possession of it shall be given by title-deed as previously".

The purpose of Art. 122 is not very clear. One infers that monks and monasteries had tried to attach Miri land to the monastery as part of its permanent property. This obviously illegal proceeding led to the enactment of Art. 122 which is intended to declare that only land legally immobilized (as Waqf) can be so attached. Miri of which monks are holders devolves in accordance with the Miri law, unless no doubt a special concession (by Firman) provides to the contrary. Thus it is provided in the Code of Succession in the Orthodox Community, Art. 134, that "as to the inheritance of the Monk the estate (in certain events) belongs wholly to the monastery, except the Miri land and Consecrated lands as to which special laws are in force".

The situation as regards so-called monastic lands in Palestine is somewhat obscure but there can at least be no doubt that Miri land cannot be immobilized without a precise grant of the Raqabe by the State. The situation in Cyprus was to some extent simplified by the Ecclesiastical Properties Law of 1893. Certain Cypriot cases, however, though evidently decided by a somewhat embarassed Court, yet throw light upon the meaning of Art. 122 and emphasize the impossibility of attaching Miri to a monastery in the absence of a State grant.

In Sophronios v. Principal Forest Officer [1]) the monks of a Monastery sought to restrain the defendant from including land, which they alleged to be their pasture land, within the limits of a State Forest. In dismissing the claim, the Court stated: "As we understand this Article it seems that the law will not recognize the annexation of any State land to a monastery, as monastery property, unless its annexation is recorded in the Imperial Archives; and that where the right to possession of State lands has been granted to individuals, and any owner of it has purported to dedicate it to pious uses, the dedication is in the eyes of the law inoperative, and the right to possession remains vested in the person who so purported to dedicate it, and descends to his heirs on his death. Such right could not be handed over by him to any grantee, without the permission of the competent authority (Art. 36), and must either remain vested in him or his heirs or revert to the State.

---

[1]) (1890) I C.L.R p. III.

The Land Law of Palestine.

"The right to possession of State lands is throughout the law treated of as a personal right, and as we have in effect already stated, the law speaks always of the State as the owner of the land, and does not recognize the possibility of the existence of any right on or over it, save a right of possession, which may be assigned by permission of the proper representative of the State and may pass by inheritance, but which becomes revested in the State on failure of heirs.

"We may also mention that State land cannot in the eyes of the law be made the subject of a dedication for the benefit of any Moslem Religious institution, and the means by which such lands are dedicated is, by their first being granted by the Sultan as a Mulk property, on which the grantee dedicates them to the religious institution".

"It would be very remarkable if the words of Art. 122 had been intended to recognize a right as belonging to Christian Religious institutions, which is not recognized in the case of establishments belonging to the Moslem Religion, and having regard to the considerations we have referred to, we feel it impossible to hold that it does".

The decision of the Court, therefore, was that Miri land could not be "attached to a Monastery" within the meaning of Art. 122 unless its annexation was recorded in the Imperial Archives (Daftar Khani). In the absence of such record, personal rights over it could alone exist, and these would be regulated by the ordinary Law of Miri, and would be transmitted to the heirs of the person in whose name the property was registered. This view is restated in the later case of Emphiedji v. Law [1]).

The decision of the Cyprus Court is undoubtedly right since land attached to a Monastery within the meaning of Art. 122 is certainly Waqf [2]) though the Waqf is of the Mustesna variety, that is to say it is Christian Waqf which, by complaisance of the Ottoman government, was not subject to the Moslem authorities.

If land is Miri it cannot be dedicated as Waqf without a grant of the Raqabe. Miri land cannot be claimed as attached to a Monastery within the meaning of Art. 122.

In the present state of things is Palestine persons who wish to give land to Monasteries or other charitable or religious non-Moslem institutions, should create Charitable Trusts thereof under

---

[1]) (1890) I C.L.R. 122.
[2]) Chaoui. op. cit., p. 69. Tute. Ottoman Land Laws, p. 116.

Chapter VI—Waqf and Trusts.

the Charitable Trusts Ordinances about to be considered. It is more than doubtful whether a new Mustesna non-Moslem Waqf can be created and any attempt to make use of alleged communal (Jewish or Christian) law for the creation of religious endowments would in all probability only lead to grave legal problems in the future. The benefactor is, therefore, to be advised to fall back on the Charitable Trusts Ordinances.

If land is now registered in the name of a person who has in fact purchased on behalf of a Monastery or other religious body, but there is no record of annexation, the proper course is (semble) for an application to be made under Sec. 37 of the Charitable Trusts Ordinance, 1925, for a declaration that the property is held in charitable trust.

Special powers as to expropriation of Waqf property will be found in Sec. 21 of the Expropriation of Lands Ordinance, 1926, and Sec. 22 of the Acquisition of Land for Army and Air Force Ordinance, 1925. As to the grant of mining leases or mining rights on Waqf property, see Sec. 35 of the Mining Ordinance, 1925. *[Statutory powers in connection with Waqf property.]*

Waqfs and Religious Endowments under the jurisdiction of Moslem or other Religious Courts may be transformed into Charitable Trusts under the Charitable Trusts Ordinances 1924—25 in accordance with the provisions of the Public Trustee of Charities Ordinance, 1925, Sec. 11.

It is not necessary to do more than to refer briefly to the Charitable Trusts Ordinances, 1924-25, which have made possible the creation in Palestine of Trusts for charitable purposes. *[Charitable Trusts.]*

The institution of such Trusts is designed to enable persons to devote property to charitable uses otherwise than under the Religious Law. All such Trusts are subject to the jurisdiction of the Civil Courts only.

The Charitable Trust Ordinances are based on English law and in part reproduce provisions of English statutes. But the immediate model used was the Ceylon Trust Law from which, however, the Palestine legislation differs in certain important particulars, and more definitely so since the amending Ordinance of 1925.

The principle of the English trust is that the trustee is the owner of the property entrusted to him but that the ownership is, in equity, charged with a trust in favour of the beneficiaries marked out to enjoy the property. In England trusts may be private or charitable. A private trust is one which is declared for the private benefit of the settlor, his family or strangers. But English law will not permit a private trust to be perpetual. Trusts declared for charitable purposes may, however, be perpetual. It has been recently held that a private trust governed by English law and created with reference to property in Palestine will not be recognized as valid by the Palestine Courts [1]). It was open to the Courts to import the English law of trusts into Palestine, under the authority of Art. 46 of the Palestine Order-in-Council, and the use of so flexible a legal instrument might be a convenience. But it seems that the Courts prefer to leave to the legislator the responsibility for its introduction.

The Charitable Trusts Ordinances, however, specifically provide for the creation and recognition of Charitable Trusts on the English model.

Normally the property subject to these Trusts will be movables. It is only exceptionally that immovables will be so devoted, and, in accordance with the principles of the English Mortmain and Charitable Uses Acts, where immovables are so devoted they must usually be forthwith converted unless they are required for the actual use for the purposes of the trust. Using Palestinian terms, we may say that the law seeks to prevent the erection of Mussaqafat and Mustaghilat Waqf under the guise of charitable trust.

Nature of a Charitable Trust. The nature of a charitable trust is stated in Sec. 2(1) of the Ordinance of 1925 as follows —

"(1) Property is held in trust for charitable purposes in any case in which there is an obligation annexed to the ownership thereof and arising out of a confidence reposed in and accepted by the owner or declared and accepted by him that, while the ownership is nominally vested in the owner, such property and the income and proceeds thereof shall be exclusively used and enjoyed for charitable purposes".

Sec. 2(2) defines the purposes which are to be deemed charitable in the following terms —

For the purpose of this Ordinance, the term "charitable purposes" shall include all purposes for the benefit of the public or any section of the public within or without Palestine, or any of the following categories :—

(a) For the relief of poverty.

---

[1]) Eliash v. Director of Lands. High Court No. 77/31. The case only decided that a disposition creating a trust could not be registered at the Land Registry.

Chapter VI—Waqf and Trusts.

(b) For the advancement of education or knowledge.

(c) For the advancement of religion or the maintenance of religious rites or practices.

(d) For any other purpose beneficial or of interest to mankind not falling within the preceding categories.

This section reproduces the definition of "charitable" purposes given by Lord Macnaghten in his judgment in a well-known English case, Commissioners of Income Tax v. Pemsel[1]).

There are a very great number of English cases in which the question at issue has been, whether a particular purpose was or was not charitable. As the Palestine Ordinance reproduces English law in this matter, the practitioner in Palestine will be safe in referring to and citing English cases on the point. It is not possible here to do more than to refer the reader to English authorities[2]).

Charitable trusts may be declared by Will or during life by a signed written instrument. If, however, the trust extended to affect immovables the written instrument must be "notarially executed" (Sec. 3 (a)). *Declaration of Trust.*

The declaration of trust by a non testamentary instrument appears to be a "disposition" within the meaning of Sec. 2 of the Land Transfer Ordinance, 1920. It is analogous to a "dedication of Waqf" which, as above stated, is a "disposition". This is obviously the case where the immovables have been transferred to trustees accompanied by a declaration of trust, but it would seem also to be the case where the creator of the trust declares himself to be trustee. Dispositions are not valid unless the provisions of the Transfer of Land Ordinance, 1920, are complied with.

Immovable trust property is not inalienable but it can only be sold, exchanged or mortgaged by order of the Court or a Judge (Sec. 12 (1)). And as is the case with Waqf property a lease of immovable trust property for a longer period than three years requires the permission of the Court or a Judge (Sec. 12(3)). It is, however, only exceptionally, that immovable property can remain in trust even where a trust has been declared of it. The policy of the law aims at securing that land, of which there is necessarily only a limited supply, should not be permanently withdrawn from the market as it would be likely to be, if vested in trustees upon a charitable

---

[1]) L.R. (1891) A.C. 531 at p. 583; 65 L.T.R. 621.

[2]) The difficulty of reconciling all the English cases is pointed out by Mr. Bentwich in a recent article in the Law Quarterly Review, Vol. XLIX, pp. 520 ff.

trust. It has long been recognized that serious economic and social dangers arise, when the law allows land to be immobilized in the hands of a group or family. In mediaeval Europe vast stretches of land came into the hands of ecclesiastical corporations. The English Parliament as early as the thirteenth century prohibited the alienation of land into "mort main" that is in such a way that they should come to be held not by an individual but by a corporation or body. Permissions (licences) from the King to hold land in mortmain, were, however, often granted. These ancient provisions are now represented in England by the Mortmain and Charitable Uses Act 1881. An exception is made to-day as regards Limited Companies of a commercial nature (Companies Act 1929, Sec. 14) and as regards certain other corporations.

So again the peculiar land system of England lent itself to the creation, of what were called "entails" of land whereby land was tied up in a particular family and could not be alienated for several generations—it then became a kind of family Waqf though the English law never went so far as the Moslem law in permitting perpetual family Waqfs. Modern legislation has for all practical purposes made these family "Waqfs" of land impossible in England. The charitable trust is on much the same footing. Land held by trustees for charitable purposes, is unlikely to be sold even though the trustees may not form a corporation and this falls under the Mortmain Acts. These and other considerations have led the English legislature to lay down special conditions as regards the alienation of land upon charitable trusts (Mortmain and Charitable Uses Act 1888, Sec. 4 ff), and in particular to provide that if land is left by will upon a charitable trust it must be forthwith sold unless an order is obtained permitting its retention in the hands of the charity. (Mortmain and Charitable Uses Act 1891 Secs. 5 ff).

The Charitable Trusts Ordinance 1925 contains provisions obviously suggested by the English law intended to secure the same results. The dedication of Mulk as Waqf of course withdraws the land from the market but as only Mulk can be made true Waqf, the Government has itself to blame if by transforming Miri into Mulk it makes increase Waqf land possible.

The restriction existing in Palestine upon the acquisition of land by corporations will be considered in detail in a subsequent chapter. If, however, land is held whether by a corporation or by an individual or individuals upon charitable trusts within the meaning of the Charitable Trusts Ordinance the special provisions

Chapter VI—Waqf and Trusts.

of that Ordinance apply, and these are fairly stringent. Under Sec. 39 of the Ordinance of 1924 as amended by Sec. 10 of the Charitable Trusts (Amendment) Ordinance 1925, where immovable property is devised, transferred or otherwise comes to be held upon trust for charitable purposes the trustees must within one year from the date at which the property became subject to the trust apply to the Court or a Judge for an order for sale and the order is to be made accordingly. If the trustees fail to apply for such an order, then the Attorney General may at any time, if satisfied that immovable property is held subject to a trust for charitable purposes make application to the Court or judge for an order for sale. And it is further provided that these provisions are to apply to immovable property held by any limited company in respect of which a licence has been granted under Sec. 22 of the Companies Ordinance 1921 (now Sec. 23 of the Companies Ordinance 1929) unless the company is recognised as having purposes of public utility by certificate of the High Commissioner under Sec. 8 of the Companies Ordinance, 1921, now Sec. 15 of the Companies Ordinance.

These provisions appear to indicate reluctance on the part of the Government to permit land to continue to be held in charitable trust. The exceptions are important: Sec. 39 (4) provides that the provisions just stated are not to apply in the following cases:—

(a) Where the immovable property consists of houses or buildings in, or required for, the occupation of the trustee for the purposes of the trust; or

(b) Where the permission of the High Commissioner has been obtained; or

(c) Where Mulk immovable property was at the date when this Ordinance came into force held upon a charitable trust within the meaning of this Ordinance; or

(d) Where the immovable property is acquired by the trustees in substitution for property sold by them, which was not subject to the provisions of this Section.

In general it may, therefore, be said, that land cannot continue to be held whether by corporations or by individuals as trustees of a charitable trust unless the licence of the High Commissioner has been obtained or the land was so held at the date at which the Charitable Trusts Ordinance came into force. And it should be borne in mind that under Sec. 37 power is given to the Court to declare that property in Palestine is held upon charitable trust if the evidence shows that the holder is under an obligation to use it for charitable purposes.

The Charitable Trusts Ordinance makes full provision for the devolution of trust immovables and for its registration. (Sec. 32 ff).

The term "immovable property" is not defined in the Ordinance, but it is clearly intended to include buildings (Cf. Sec. 3(2); 39(4)(a)) and it may, therefore, be safely assumed that trees and buildings, though movables according to Moslem law, are to be treated as immovables. This being so, the provisions in the Ordinance applicable to immovables would apply to trees and buildings separately owned.

The Ordinances do not expressly state that Miri land cannot be dedicated upon a charitable trust though Sec. 43, as amended by Sec. 12 of the Amending Ordinance 1925, provides that nothing in the Ordinance is to be construed to validate a devise of Miri land for charitable purposes. This latter provision seems hardly to have been necessary.

In practice the Land Registry refuses to allow the registration of a trust of Miri, relying upon the general provisions of the Ottoman Law, e.g. Land Code, Art. 121, Law of Disposition, 1331, Art. 8.

A charitable trust, it is argued, is of the nature of a Waqf and it is common law that Miri land cannot be made Waqf without the consent of the Sovereign. A trust of Miri is, therefore, merely void, just as a Waqf of Miri would be. In order that the trust (or Waqf) may be valid the Sovereign must transform the land into Mulk.

There is indeed nothing to show that the Ordinances were in any way intended to enlarge the powers of disposition possessed by a Miri holder [1]). The distinction between Mulk and Miri, which theoretically is so fundamental, is, however, frequently ignored in practice and is seldom referred to in recent legislation. It is, therefore, possible that the legislator did not intend to restrict the creation of trusts to the Mulk of the settlor. But remark, that save in the special cases mentioned in Sec. 39(4) (a) and (d), the permission of the High Commissioner is necessary to the continuance of a charitable trust of any land and the provision

---

[1]) In Eliash v. Director of Lands, No. 77/31, the High Court remarked obiter, that no charitable trust could be created of Miri land, but the point was not argued.

Chapter VI—Waqf and Trusts.

would in most cases enable the Government to prevent Miri being held in charitable trusts. It need hardly be said that if in any case Miri land is dedicated on a charitable trust, the land does not change its category; it continues to be Miri and rights of Tapu arising on the death of the holder and other rights special to Miri are not affected.

See 43 of the Ordinance makes it clear that whatever view we are left to take as to the possibility of conveying Miri in trust "inter vivos" the Ordinance is not to be construed as giving any power to devise Miri in trust. The Section provides as follows.

"Nothing in this Ordinance shall affect property devoted to charitable purposes which is the subject of a Waqf or religious endowment constituted before a Religious Court in accordance with the provisions of the Palestine Order-in-Council, 1922; nor be construed to validate a devise of Miri land for charitable purposes".

CHAPTER VII—SUCCESSION AND INHERITANCE.

The law regulating succession on death to immovables in Palestine is complicated. Mulk and Miri interests follow different canons of inheritance, and though the law governing Miri interests is the same in the case of Miri land in Palestine, the law governing Mulk inheritance varies according to the religious or national status of the deceased person. So again, while no testamentary disposition of Miri is valid, the rules governing the validity of testamentary dispositions of Mulk vary with the religious or national status of the testator. The interest of a lessee in Ijaratein is for this purpose assimilated to Miri.

Jurisdiction under the Palestine Order-in-Council, 1922.

The Palestine Order-in-Council, 1922, gives to the Civil Courts jurisdiction in all matters and over all persons in Palestine (Art. 38). This general rule is, however, subject to an important reservation under Art. 51, which provides, that jurisdiction in matters of personal status shall be exercised by the Court of religious Communities established and exercising jurisdiction at the date of the Order (1st Sept. 1922). For the purpose of this provision matters of personal status mean (inter alia) suits regarding successions, wills and legacies.

The ecclesiastical jurisdiction in successions, wills and legacies is further regulated by Arts. 52-54. Moslem Religious Courts have exclusive jurisdiction in all matters of personal status of Moslems (Art. 52). Rabbinical (Jewish) Courts and Patriarchal (Christian) Courts have also exclusive jurisdiction in matters of confirmation of wills of members of their community other than foreigners but only have jurisdiction in any other matter of personal status (e.g. determination of legal heirship, administration) where all the parties consent to their jurisdiction (Arts 53, 54). In all other cases the general jurisdiction of the Civil Courts is effective.

The limits of the jurisdiction accorded to the communities under the Order-in-Council are traced with reference to pre-existing usage, and in particular by reference to the practice established under the Ottoman Hatt Hamayoun of 1856 [1]). This document

---
[1]) See Young, Op. cit., II, p. 3 ff.

Chapter VII—Succession and Inheritance.

was in intention at least, a charter of liberties for non-Moslem Ottomans, but its provisions lack precision, and have been the subject of much dispute. A distinction is drawn by it between purely religious matters, as to which the exclusive jurisdiction of the communal Courts is clearly recognised, and "other civil matters such as succession", as to which communal jurisdiction was given only in case of consent of the parties. In Egypt an elaborate but varying jurisprudence has given more precision to this distinction, and it seems that in that country, as well as in Iraq and Trans-Jordan, as also in Syria, the limits of non-Moslem religious jurisdiction must still be determined in accordance with the provisions of Hatt Hamayoun.

The Order-in-Council does not prescribe the law, which is to be applied by the Religious Courts, but the implication is, that each will apply its own religious law. Each community in fact possesses a traditional law. This includes in the case of the Moslem, Jewish and Orthodox bodies at least, a complete body of rules governing succession, testate and intestate, but some of the other Christian communities e.g. the Latins, have no traditional laws of succession. These matters, however, are less clearly of a religious character and less objection could be taken to the application to them of Moslem law. In Palestine before the War the Christian and Jewish Courts do not appear to have administered the estates of the deceased members of their communities and the only law of intestate succession actually applied was the Moslem law. The established practice in Palestine in the case of a deceased Christian Ottoman was that a statement of filiaticn should be drawn up by the religious authority of the community, to which the de cujus belonged, and presented to the Moslem Courts which, thereupon, authorised the distribution of the property among the heirs by a certificate of heirship drawn up in accordance with the rules of Moslem law.

This practice could not continue under the Palestine Order-in-Council since the jurisdiction of the Moslem Courts was thereby restricted to Moslems. The choice, therefore, lay between the traditional law of the community and the Civil law administered by the Civil Courts.

This system has, so far as regards Succession, been given more definite form by the Succession Ordinance 1923.

The Succession Ordinance 1923.

As already stated the jurisdiction of the non-Moslem communal authorities in matters of Succession rests on consent, and

The Land Law of Palestine.

it was surmised, that persons interested would generally exercise their alternative right to have recourse to the Civil Courts.

A Civil law of Intestate Succession was set forth in the Succession Ordinance and made applicable in all cases in which the persons interested had recourse to Civil in preference to Religious jurisdiction, subject, however, to certain reservations intended to secure rights to legitim. This Law is modern in character and is identical with that some years since (A.H. 1331) enacted by the Ottoman Government to regulate rights of quasi-succession in Miri.

The Palestine Administration, by adopting the canons of succession established by this Law as a general law of inheritance, aimed at unifying the Law of inheritance for all non-Moslems whenever the parties interested chose to secure its application by recourse to the Civil Courts, a result which would not necessarily follow if the persons interested preferred to invoke the jurisdiction of the Communal Courts. In that latter case rights of preference in the Miri land would still be governed by the "Ottoman" law of A.H. 1331, but rights of succession in other kinds of property, movable and immovable, would be governed by the traditional law of the religious community, if such existed.

The Succession Ordinance 1923 was designed as an amplification of the provisions of the Order-in-Council dealing with inheritance. It has, however, to be borne in mind that the jurisdiction of the Religious Courts established at the date of the Order-in-Council may be varied by the High Commissioner (Order-in-Council 1922, Art. 57) and this power seems necessary to involve, or perhaps to be identical with a power to alter the jurisdiction of the Religious Courts as established by the Order. Thus it by no means follows, as is sometimes stated, that any contradiction, if such there be, between the jurisdiction of the Religious Courts as stated in the Order and as stated in the Succession Ordinance is to be resolved merely by treating the Order-in-Council as the governing document.

Under the Succession Ordinance the allotment of jurisdiction in matters of succession is as follows:—

1. All questions relating to the succession to a deceased Moslem, whether a foreigner [1]) or not, are within the exclusive competence of the Moslem Religious Courts;

---

[1]) It is very necessary to bear in mind that the term "foreigner" both in the Order-in-Council and in the Succession Ordinance does not include all non-Palestinians, but only subjects and citizens of European and American States and of Japan (Order-in-Council, Art. 59). This peculiar definition is a survival of

Chapter VII—Succession and Inheritance.

2. All questions relating to the succession of a deceased foreigner not being a Moslem are within the exclusive competence of the Civil Courts;

3. When the deceased was a member of a Christian or Jewish Religious Community recognised as having had jurisdiction in matters of personal status at the date of the Order-in-Council, it is competent for the persons interested to apply to the Court of the deceased's Community for the determination of all questions relating to the succession, and it is obligatory to apply to such Court for the confirmation of the deceased's will.

But it is also permissible to apply instead to the Civil Courts (save as regards confirmation of a will) and the Civil Courts may upon such application prohibit further proceedings in the Religious Court if such proceedings are pending.

4. Jurisdiction under the Order-in-Council and consequently under the Succession Ordinance can be exercised only by the Courts of Religious Communities established and exercising jurisdiction at the date of the Order. The schedule to the Succession Ordinance gives a list of these Communities having jurisdiction under that Ordinance. They are:—

> The Eastern (Orthodox) Community;
> The Latin (Catholic) Community;
> The Armenian (Gregorian) Community;
> The Syrian (Catholic) Community;
> The Chaldean (Uniate) Community;
> The Jewish Community;
> The Armenian (Catholic) Community;

To these have been added as having established their claims since the Ordinance:

> The Greek Catholic (Melkite) Community (1st Sept. 1923).
> The Maronite Community (1st Sept. 1924).
> The Syrian Orthodox Community (11 Dec. 1929).

The Moslem Religious Courts did not require express sanction. And it may be observed that their jurisdiction is not strictly communal. It is exercised over matters of personal status of all Moslems, and not merely (as in the other cases) over members of the Community.

---

the Capitulatory system. Persons who are not "foreigners" in the narrow sense are for purposes of religious jurisdiction treated as Palestinians. Stateless persons are not "foreigners". (In re Feinstein, 12 Feb. 1933, judgment of the Jerusalem District Court).

The Land Law of Palestine.

Law of Inheritance applied in Civil and Religious Courts Miri and Waqf Land.

As has been already explained, the right of tessaruf of a holder of Miri was originally personal only. The children of the holder had, indeed, a right of preference (Right of Tapu) but this right was exerciseable only on payment of Bedl Misl. A right of gratuitous transfer upon death was, however, eventually accorded, and its scope extended by successive laws, notably by the law of 17th Moharrem A.H. 1284. But the right thus accorded to the persons designated not being a right of inheritance according to the Moslem law, the person entitled to take the holding upon the death could not be correctly described as heir to the deceased. He had merely a statutory right to a grant in his place. This distinction between inheritance is marked by the use of the special term Intiqal to denote the latter. Precisely the same principle is applied to the transmission of the rights of the lessee under Ijaratein.

By successive laws statutory rights to transmission (Intiqal) on the part of various persons are admitted. The Law of 4 Rejeb, A.H. 1292, with reference to succession to Mussaqafat and Mustaghilat Waqf possessed in Ijaratein was specially noteworthy in this connection. The details of the system prevailing before the Law of A.H. 1331 to be hereafter considered, were complicated. Extension of the rights of transmission was not in all cases compulsory. The law was only applied at the option of the holder in Ijaratein and subject to conditions. The full account of the successive changes in the law will be found in Chiha, pp. 408 ff., but the Law of A.H. 1331 has made the old provisions practically obsolete. The extensions of the rights of transmission in Waqf land was, of course, injurious to the Waqf, since it seriously diminished the probability that the Waqf would benefit by an escheat and would take the interest of the deceased as Mahlul. In the Law of 4 Rejeb, A.H. 1292, we find therefore (Art. 4) a special provision for the augmentation of the rent payable to the Waqf by the holder in Ijaratein where the right of inheritance was extended.

The Law of 4 Rejeb, A.H. 1292, did not apply to Mussaqafat and Mustaghilat Waqf properties held under the Muqata'a system on which there were trees and buildings. These trees and buildings were the Mulk of the lessee and were inherited by his heirs in accordance with the Law applicable to Mulk. The land on which such trees and buildings stood was subject to the trees or buildings and followed the trees and buildings, and no extension of the right of inheritance was, therefore, necessary. Consequently

Chapter VII—Succession and Inheritance.

in case of transfer or devolution of such properties the old Muqata'a was to be levied at the proper rate. (Art. 12).

The law as regards inheritance of the tessaruf of Miri and the assimilated forms of property was completed by a Provisional Ottoman Law of 27 Rabi-el-Awal, A.H. 1331 (Law of Inheritance) applicable in Palestine. This is the law by which all rights of inheritance to these properties is at present governed in Palestine. It supersedes the Law of Moharrem, A.H. 1284, and that of Rejeb, A.H. 1292.

The Law of Inheritance of A.H. 1331 is stated to have been modelled upon the German Law [1]). It is particularly remarkable as giving no preference to males over females in contrast to the older religious laws still applicable in Palestine where Mulk and not Miri interests are concerned. The popular objection to female succession leads, however, not infrequently, to pressure exercised upon the female heirs to renounce their claims. Where such renunciation takes place as regards a succession to Miri, the Land Registry requires that the judgment (or order) of the Religious Court presented as a basis for registration (Succ. Ord. 1923, Sec. 23) should specify the share to which the woman is entitled, and should further contain a statement establishing the renunciation by consent. The Registry charges Transfer fees on the value of the share renounced as on a sale.

A few words of explanation are necessary as to the scope of the Law of A.H. 1331. In the first place, it is applicable only in the case, where the death occurred after the promulgation of the Law of 27 Rabi-el-Awal, A.H. 1331 (Art. 11). Secondly, although expressed to apply to Miri and Waqf land (Art. 1) its precise application as regards Waqf land is stated in Art. 8. Three interests in Waqf are mentioned. As regards one of them, Ijaratein, there is no difficulty, and as to Ijaratein interests the law of A.H. 1331 clearly supersedes that of Rejeb, A.H. 1292. It applies, also, to interests under Ijara Wahida Qadima and Muqata'a Qadima. These two forms of interests in Waqf land must not be confused with Ijara Wahida and Muqata'a of the ordinary type explained above. They are, indeed, variants

---
[1]) Nord, Op. cit., p. 83.

The translation of Art. 9 of the Law of Inheritance as given in the Iraq collection is defective. 8¹/₂ per thousand should be 2¹/₂ per thousand. See Nord, op. cit, p. 94.

The term "Muqata'a Bedl Ushur" in this Article is used to designate a Muqata'a (fixed rent) conceived as a payment in lieu of the tithe of the produce (ushur) which is the customary share of the owner as compared with the occupier.

of these, but of a peculiar kind. In view, however, of the fact that they do not (it is believed) occur in Palestine, it is unnecessary to enter into more detailed explanation. The trees and buildings erected by the holder of a Muqata'a Waqf are his Mulk and follow the Mulk Law of Succession. So also the land is subject to the trees and buildings and consequently follows them. (Law 4 Rejeb, A.H. 1292, Art. 12).

An important amendment had been made of the old law of A.H. 1284 by an additional article dated 29 Rabi-el-Thani, A.H. 1289. This addition gave right of inheritance to the surviving spouse, where a spouse died after a revocable divorce, but before the expiration of the legal delay or period of prohibition (Idda) within which the husband may recant the divorce according to the Moslem personal law, as also where the spouse died after the celebration of the marriage but before its consummation. So also where an irrevocable divorce had been pronounced by the husband in a state of mortal sickness the wife was declared entitled to inherit if the husband actually died before the expiration of the Idda. Those provisions are in accordance with the Moslem Law [1]), but they are not reproduced in the Law of Inheritance of 1331. Since, however, the older law is not repealed but only superseded by the new law, the addition of 29 Rabi-el-Thani would seem still to be applicable, it not being inconsistent with any of the provisions of the Law of A.H. 1331.

The Succession Ordinance, 1923, does not alter the law as to inheritance of Miri and Waqf land. Sec. 19 thereof declares as follows:—

"Every Court having jurisdiction in matters of succession shall in all cases determine the right of succession to Miri land in accordance with the provisions of the Ottoman Law set forth in the Second Schedule hereto" (i.e. the Law of Inheritance, A.H. 1331). "And the said provisions shall be applied notwithstanding any disposition made or power of attorney given by the deceased intended to take effect after death whether by way of will or otherwise".

Though this Section makes express reference to Miri interests only it is to be interpreted to apply also to interests in Waqf assimilated to Miri. (Sec. 26 (III)).

Sec. 19 expressly denies to the holder of Miri, as also by implication to the lessee in Ijaratein, etc., any power to dispose

---

[1]) See Syed Amir Aly, Handbook, para 110.

Chapter VII—Succession and Inheritance.

of his interest by will or by the use of any device intended to take effect on death, e.g. a power of attorney giving to the attorney power to transfer the land after the death of the principal to persons designated by him.

This would not affect the validity of a transfer made in mortal sickness, the validity of which is recognised by Art. 120 of the Land Code, provided that the provisions of the Transfer of Land Ordinance, 1920, had been fulfilled. But it may be safely assumed that an admission made in mortal sickness which has the effect of a bequest under Art. 1596 ff. of the Mejelle, could have no effect as regards Miri land. The acknowledgment is clearly to be deemed a will [1]). So also a gift in mortal sickness under Mejelle Arts. 877 ff. would in order to be valid as a transfer have to be completed in accordance with the terms of the Transfer of Land Ordinances.

Primarily the law relating to inheritance to and wills of Mulk is the Sacred (Moslem) Law. The law applies in Palestine in all cases, in which the deceased is a Moslem. The law applicable is the Sunni Law of the Hanafi rite. The Succession Ordinance (Sec. 4(II)) gives power, however, to the High Commissioner, where the deceased Moslem was a foreigner of any other than the Sunni rite (e.g. a Shia) to direct the constitution of a special Moslem Court for the determination of any question relating to the succession or otherwise [2]).

<small>Law regulating testamentary and intestate succession to Mulk. (a) Where the deceased was a Moslem.</small>

The Sunni Law as to inheritance of Mulk is set forth in numerous works of authority in English. It is not proposed even to summarise it here [3]). It aims at a meticulous division of the estate with a general preference for males, though not to the exclusion ef females. It is stated,-with what truth we are not in a position to determine,-that the hostility to the succession of daughters and other females has led to the creation of family Waqfs which by the terms of the Waqfieh gave more pronounced preference to males.

The Moslem Law permits bequests by will of Mulk. The law is laid down by Syed Amir Aly [4]), as follows:

---

[1]) Cf. per Bertram J. in Hypermachos v. Dmitri (1908) 8 C.L.R. at p. 53.

[2]) Owing to the peculiar definition of "foreigner" in the Succession Ordinance, following Art. 59 of the Order in-Council, the power does not appear to extend to some of the persons for whom it was designed, i.e. Persian Shias, nor to Iraqian Shias.

[3]) The reader will find adequate particulars both of the Sunni and the Shia law of inheritance in Vesey FitzGerald, Muhammedan Law, Chapters XIV ff.

[4]) Handbook of Mohammedan Law, pp. 67 ff.

The Land Law of Palestine.

"According to all schools, a bequest to any one of the heirs is not valid, without the consent of the others. Whether the person in whose favour the devise is made is an heir or not must be determined not at the time of the will but at the testator's death. When the disposition is in favour of a non-heir or of a pious or charitable purpose it is valid and operative in respect of one third of the testator's estate without the assent of the heirs and in respect of more than one third with their consent. Under the Hanafi Law, it must be given after the testator's death. When a bequest to a non-heir exceeds one-third of the testator's estate, and some of the heirs consent, whilst others do not, the excess, like a bequest to an heir, will come out of the shares of the consenting heirs".

The will or testamentary instrument of a Moslem need not be in writing. A verbal, if proved, is as valid as a testamentary instrument reduced to writing. A valid will can, however, only be made by a person who has attained his majority and is in full possession of his senses and not acting under compulsion (Jabr) or undue influence (Ikrah).

A will is revocable in nature as being ambulatory. In the chapters of the Mejelle dealing with admissions occur certain articles relevant to the subject of wills. In accordance with the general theory of Evidence in Moslem Law great stress is placed upon a man's admissions (acknowledgments). Admissions of ownership of another may operate as a gift (Art. 1591; Cf. Art. 1592[1]). So also if a man in mortal sickness acknowledged that another was the owner of his property this acknowledgment might operate as a will.

"Therefore, if a person who has no heirs, in mortal sickness, denies ownership by an admission that all his property belongs to someone, it is good, and after his death, his estate (tereke), cannot be interfered with by the officer of the Beit-el-Mal. Likewise, if a person who has no heirs but his wife, in mortal sickness makes denial of ownership by an admission that her property belongs to her husband, it is good, and there can be no interference with the estate (tereke) of either of them by the official of the Beit-el-Mal after death".

The Mejelle is Common Law in Palestine and it is arguable, therefore, that this Article applies not only where the deceased was

---

[1] These admissions appear to be ineffective as transfers since the law of Disposition, A.H. 1331, and the Land Transfer Ordinances.

Chapter VII—Succession and Inheritance.

a Moslem, but in other cases as well. But since the power to confirm wills of persons who are members of any of the specified communities is within the exclusive jurisdiction of their religious Courts it may be argued that it would be for them to determine whether such acknowledgment should be recognised as having testamentary effect. The matter is one upon which it is difficult to give a decisive opinion [1]). It seems, however, clear that gifts of Mulk made in mortal sickness within the limits specified in Art. 877 ff. of the Mejelle are valid as transfers only if the provisions of the Land Transfer Ordinance, 1920, have been fulfilled.

If the deceased was not a Moslem the Law governing the succession to his Mulk varies according to his religion and his nationality. The religion of the deceased is only material if the deceased was not a foreigner within the meaning of Art. 59 of the Order-in-Council, 1922.

(b) Where the deceased was not a Moslem.

If the deceased was a foreigner in this restricted sense jurisdiction over the administration of the estate belongs to the Civil Courts before which any contentious matter must be brought [2]). The law applicable to the inheritance of the Mulk of foreigners is the national law of the deceased but if such law imports the law of the domicile of the deceased or the law of the situation of the immovable the law so imported is to be applied. The validity in form of a Will made by a foreigner and his capacity to make a Will is determined by identical rules.

Since the law of both countries treats the law of the situation (lex situs) of an immovable as the proper law to govern rights of inheritance in the immovable it will probably in most cases happen, that Palestine law will be held to be the proper law governing the inheritance to the Mulk immovables of which a foreigner dies possessed in Palestine. It is submitted that the Succession Ordinance should be interpreted as making the "Ottoman Law" of A.H. 1331 the common law of succession throughout Palestine, applicable in all cases in which Religious or Foreign law is not, by exception, applied [3]).

The same rules apply to the succession to persons who, though not foreigners in the sense of Art. 59 are yet not Pales-

---

[1]) Goadby, Private International and Inter-Religious Law in Palestine, p. 139 and note 25.

[2]) As to consular non-contentious jurisdiction see Off. Gaz. 1st. Dec. 1922.

A Religious Court may have jurisdiction by Consent (Order-in-Council Art. 65) or by Order of the Court (Succession Ordinance, Sec. 5).

[3]) See more fully, Goadby in Law Quarterly Review, (1929) Vol. XLV, pp. 498 ff.

tinian citizens nor members of a specified Religious community. Thus a Chinaman is not a foreigner, but neither is he a Palestinian citizen, and it is highly improbable that he is a member of any of the specified communities. The Civil Courts have jurisdiction in the administration of his estate in Palestine and will apply his national law subject to the provisions already mentioned in connection with the estates of foreigners.

If the deceased was a Palestinian citizen or not being a foreigner was a member of one of the specified religious communities jurisdiction over the administration of his estate belongs to the Civil Courts unless application to the Court of the deceased's community is preferred. If the religious Court is used it will primarily determine rights of succession according to its own law. If, however, application is made to the Civil Courts, these Courts will apply the same law to determine rights of succession to Mulk (and movables) as to Miri and Waqf, i.e. the "Ottoman Law" as contained in the Law of Inheritance, A.H. 1331, scheduled to the Succession Ordinance, 1923 [1]).

In Goldberg and Palestine Land Development Co. [2]) the Jerusalem District Court had to deal with a certificate of heirship, granted by a Rabbinical Court in connection with the estate of a deceased foreigner (a Russian) the Court having also appointed an Administrator of the estate. The District Court expressed itself as not satisfied that even consent could give jurisdiction to a Religious Court in such a case [3]) but as there was no evidence that any consent had been given [4]) the jurisdiction of the Religious Court to give either a certificate of heirship or to appoint an Administrator could not be recognized. The District Court pointed out that Religious Courts had no power to distribute an estate save in accordance with their own law or the "Ottoman" law. As the distribution of the estate of a deceased foreigner necessarily

---

[1]) As above remarked the provisions of the additional Article (29 Rabi-el-Thani) to the Law of 17 Moharrem, A.H. 1284, were not reproduced in the Law of inheritance, A.H. 1331, and its provisions do not, therefore, form part of the "Ottoman Law" for the purpose of the Succession Ordinance, 1923. But the article is mainly of importance where Moslems are concerned and the Mulk of Moslems can never descend according to the Miri Law.

[2]) Civil No. 317/33. Palestine Post 13 March 1934.

[3]) Such jurisdiction exists (semble) only under an Order made in pursuance of Sec. 3 of the Ordinance.

[4]) Consent to the jurisdiction must be in writing. See judg. District Court Jerusalem No. 401/32. Palestine Post 10 April 1933.

Chapter VII—Succession and Inheritance.

followed his national law[1]) this circumstance appeared to make the Religious Court incompetent to deal with the matter.

If the deceased was not a member of any of the specified Religious Communities or was a foreigner, application must be made to the Civil Courts. In the case of a foreigner the Civil Courts will apply the National law of the deceased to govern his succession. In the case of a Palestinian who was not a member of any of the specified Religious Communities they will apply the "Ottoman Law" as above stated. Wills of Mulk (which includes movables) are effective. If the deceased was a member of one of the specified Religious Communities and was not a "foreigner" the validity in form and substance of his will must be determined by the Court of his Community which will presumably apply the Communal Law[2]). In other cases the will must be proved in the Civil Courts which will uphold the validity of the will of a foreigner if it complies with his national Law and will in all cases within its jurisdiction uphold a will made in accordance with the conditions set forth in Secs. 10 and 11 of the Succession Ordinance, such a will being termed a will in Civil Form.

The application of the Ottoman law to Mulk will, however, be subject in all cases to the provisions of the Will of the deceased. And Sec. 9 of the Succession Ordinance provided that when the Civil Courts are administering the estate of a deceased member of one of the specified communities they are to take into account any restriction upon the power of disposition contained in the law of the community concerned and to distribute any reserve thus created among the persons in whose favour it was made under the law of the deceased's community. Thus the object of Sec. 9 is to secure :

(1) That the deceased should not be allowed by the Civil Courts a wider power to dispose of his estate by his testament than he would be allowed under his Religious Law.

---

[1]) Order-in-Council, Art. 65. Of course the argument only applies to Mulk. Miri land necessarily follows the "Ottoman Law" of A.H. 1331.

[2]) The provisions of Sec. 5(1) of the Ordinance appear explicitly to reserve for the Courts of the specified communities jurisdiction to confirm the wills of the members. Sec. 10, however, states that the Civil Courts "shall hold a will to be valid in Civil Form" if it complies with certain conditions therein stated. It has been argued that the provisions must be taken to confer upon every person a right to make a will in Civil Form and that such a will will be held valid by the Civil Courts whatever the religion of the testator. Convenience would undoubtedly be served by this solution but its correctness is dubious.

The Land Law of Palestine.

(2) That the deceased should not be allowed by the effect of his will to deprive his wife or children in particular of any share in his estate (legitim) which they would be entitled to receive under the Religious Law, notwithstanding any disposition by the will.

Subject to securing these objects the Civil Courts are to distribute the estate in accordance with the provisions of the will of the testator or, so far as such will did not or was not allowed to extend, in accordance with the provisions of the "Ottoman Law". The section operates so as to secure that the provisions of the will or of the "Ottoman Law", as the case may be, should govern the distribution of the estate subject to these two corditions, namely, that the testator should not have any wider power of disposition by will than he had under his Religious Law, and that notwithstanding any contrary provisions in the will, the wife and children should be secured in the enjoyment of any legitim which the Religious Law secured to them.

Sec. 9 has of course no application to Miri land since no will made by the deceased can in any event affect the rights of inheritance in Miri.

The provisions of the Succession Ordinance as to the concurrent jurisdiction of Civil and Religious Courts over the estates of non-Moslems who are members of any of the specified Religious Communities are somewhat special. The law applied does in some degree depend upon the Court, to which recourse is made but the full discussion of the provisions would not be in place here. A few remarks only will be made.

As already stated the administration of the estates of deceased persons who were not foreigners formerly fell in practice to the Moslem Courts even in cases in which the deceased was not a Moslem. Under the new system established before but definitely authorized by the Palestine Order-in-Council 1922 the Moslem Courts were treated as having jurisdiction only over Moslems and Jews and Christians were delegated to their own Courts. They began, therefore, to apply to these latter for certificates of heirship and the practice was not only admitted by the Order-in-Council but seems to be encouraged by the Succession Ordinance though the latter (Sec. 7) reserved to any person interested the right to ask for a transfer to the Civil Courts at any time before the estate was fully distributed. Representations were made at the time on the part particularly of members of the Jewish Community, that the old Jewish law of Succession was not acceptable

Chapter VII—Succession and Inheritance.

to the modern Jews, who yet desired to maintain the jurisdiction of Rabbinical Courts. It was, therefore, suggested that the non-Moslem Courts should be allowed, upon application of the parties interested, to distribute not only the Miri land, but also the Mulk of the de cujus, in accordance with the canons of Succession, set forth in the Ottoman Law of A.H. 1331. This suggestion was adopted, and at the same time the jurisdiction of the Communal Courts was extended to include the certification of rights of quasi Succession in Miri. The result in practice is that recourse to the Civil Courts is comparatively infrequent; the certificate of heirship is usually obtained from the Religious authorities who not infrequently distribute the Mulk land and movables, in accordance with the same rules, as necessarily govern that of the quasi Succession to Miri. It is, indeed, stated that some of the communities ignorantly apply the Moslem law, but this alternative is hardly legitimate in the case of a non-Moslem community.

It seems that neither the jurisdiction of the Religious Courts to confirm the Wills of members of the Community nor the concurrent jurisdiction in matters of succession ab intestato is affected by the fact that some of the claimants or persons interested are not members of the community or are foreigners. In all cases of concurrent jurisdiction the consent of the "parties" is requisite, to give jurisdiction to a religious court; but if such consent is given, jurisdiction exists notwithstanding the differences of nationality or religion. The rule thus established in Palestine varies from that which obtained under the Firmans and the Hatt Hamayoun. Thus, in the case of the Orthodox Community, the Ecclesiastical Courts had jurisdiction only where all the beneficiaries or heirs were also Orthodox and Ottoman [1]). The simpler rule adopted by the Palestine Administration involves a considerable extension of Religious jurisdiction [2]).

Arts. 53, 54 of the Order-in-Council specifically require that the "parties to the action" should consent in order to give to a

Consent to the jurisdiction of the non-Moslem Religious Courts.

---

[1]) Compare the provisions of the Vizieral Order of 3 February, 1891, in Young, Op. cit., II, p. 20.

[2]) In a recent case before the Judicial Committee (Abdullah Bey Chedid v. Tenenbaum) it was held that a Certificate of Succession given by an Egyptian (Maronite) Court with reference to an Egyptian Maronite was rejected by the Supreme Court (Palestine) and by the Judicial Committee on the ground that the "religious Courts in Palestine are the only Courts which have jurisdiction under the Succession Ordinance". The certificate had reference to Miri land in Palestine.

The Land Law of Palestine.

non-Moslem Religious Court jurisdiction in any matter of succession [1]). The provisions of Secs. 6 and 7 of the Succession Ordinance permit a Religious Court to undertake the administration and distribution of an estate upon application made without requiring a preliminary consent to be filed on the part of all persons interested nor does the Ordinance make any provision with the object of securing that the Court has before it as parties all persons interested, before it proceeds to distribute the estate. In fact certificates of heirship are given by the Religious Courts on ex parte application. It may happen that when issuing the certificate the interest of some person entitled to a share is overlooked. The certificate cannot be treated as binding any such person in the absence of any consent which would have given the Religious Court jurisdiction to make an order against him in contentious proceedings. Nor does there appear to be anything in the Succession Ordinance inconsistent with this view that no Order of a Jewish or Patriarchal Court relative to the distribution of Miri or Mulk of an intestate should be regarded as binding upon persons who have not consented thereto. Although the Ordinance (Sec. 7(1)) directs that the Civil Courts shall not undertake the redistribution of an estate already distributed under the Order of a Communal Court, this provision does not destroy rights of heirship nor prevent a person entitled to rank as an heir from claiming his right in a proprietary action in the Civil Court, if he has not consented to the jurisdiction of the Religious Court.

It must, however, be admitted that the Order-in-Council and the Succession Ordinance have left some obscurity remaining in the relations between the jurisdiction of Civil and Religious Courts in matters of succession in Palestine. But it does not appear that in practice many difficulties arise, and such cases as are reported throw little light upon the subject.

In the case of Bruchstein v. Barakat [2]) an ex parte order had been made by the President of a District Court under Sec. 7 of the Succession Ordinance prohibiting the Rabbinical Court from dealing further with the succession to the estate of the late Zwi Bruchstein. The order was opposed by the appellant on the ground that the Rabbinical Courts had already granted a certificate of heirship and that no further proceedings were pending. The

---

[1]) See below, p.p. 120 ff., Appendix, for some further remarks as to the Consent to the Jurisdiction.

[2]) C.A. 141/32; Palestine Post, 23 March 1933.

Chapter VII—Succession and Inheritance.

Respondent had, it appears, signed a consent to the jurisdiction of the Rabbinical Court but alleged that this consent had been obtained by the appellant's fraud. The President set aside his order and an appeal against his decision was dismissed without any reasons being given [1]. It is not clear whether the Court was of opinion that a consent obtained even by fraud was sufficient to give jurisdiction to the Rabbinical Court or whether it considered the application to the Civil Courts to be too late [2].

The Succession Ordinance, Secs. 10 ff., contain provisions as to the formalities to be observed in making a will, such as would be held valid in form by the Civil Courts. *Will in Civil Form.*

The "Civil Form" for a will provided by these sections of the Succession Ordinance is based upon the form of an English will as stated in the English Wills Act 1837 [3]. In any dispute which may arise as to the validity in form of a Will in Civil Form reference may sometimes be usefully made to the very considerable body of cases which have been decided under the English Act. The English provisions as to form of wills stands midway between the system of informal (verbal) wills represented by the Moslem law and the system of highly formal registered wills, which is that generally in use in the Christian communities. The English will is secret but formal. It must be in writing, but need not be in the testator's handwriting. In every case, even if it is holograph, it must be signed (or sealed) [4] by the testator or by some other person by his direction. This signature (or sealing) must take place in the presence of two witnesses at least and they must be present at the same time and must attest [5] the will in the testator's presence. All these requirements are specified in the Palestine Ordinance but since the Palestinian provisions are not exact reproductions of those of the English Act though clearly

---

[1] In a recent case the Court of Appeal held that an Order under Sec. 7 of the Succession Ordinance is a judicial order and can, therefore, only be reversed by a higher Court. Morcos v. Morcos C.A. 70/33. Palestine Post, 6 June 1934.

[2] See below, p.p. 120 ff, Appendix, for some further remarks as to the interpretation of the phrase "where all the parties consent".

[3] 7 Will IV J 1 Vict. c 26. See particularly Sec. 9 thereof. Formerly a distinction as to form was made in England between wills of personal (movable) and of real (immovable). This no longer exists.

[4] An English will is signed, not sealed.

[5] The English Act says "attest and subscribe" which clearly involves the writing of the witnesses' names. The Palestine Ordinance says "attest" only, but the word would in the context probably be interpreted to involve a written attestation.

The Land Law of Palestine.

based upon them, it may well happen that a will which would be good in form in Palestine would be bad under the English law and vice versa. The Palestine Ordinance (Sec. 10 (1) (c)) requires that both the witnesses should be 18 years of age and of sound mind at the time of the execution of the will [1]) and further that an attesting witness shall not take any interest under the will [2]). If, therefore, a legacy is given by the will to one of the persons who attested the execution the will is valid but the legacy lapses.

The testator must be 18 years of age at the time of the execution of the will and must not be suffering from mental infirmity or otherwise incompetent to make a will according to the law governing his personal status applicable to him in Palestine [3]). It is not clear whether the expression "suffering from mental infirmity" should be regarded as equivalent to "not of sound mind". It is unfortunate that two such closely allied expressions should have been used in the same section when the context suggests that the same idea is intended to be conveyed by both [4]).

It is to be noted that even though the testator was 18 years of age and suffered from no mental infirmity yet his will is invalid if he was "incapable" according to his personal statute. Thus the will in Civil Form of a foreigner will be invalid if he was "incapable" according to his national law, and so also in the case of any non-Palestinian who was not a member of a specified religious community. It is far from clear as to what scope is to be given to the word "incapable" in this connection. No doubt, it covers cases in which the age of majority under the personal law is later than 18 years, and presumably it would cover "incapacity" arising from "civil death" and the like but not an incapacity which is not personal in character [5]).

---

[1]) Succession Ordinance, Sec. 10(1) (a), requires that a will shall be in writing.

[2]) Ibid. Sec. 11.

[3]) Ibid. Sec. 10(11).

[4]) In colloquial language people might be spoken of as suffering from mental infirmity who would not be regarded as of unsound mind. The English law requires that the testator should have a sound and disposing mind (Sutton v. Sadler (1857) 3 C.B N.S. 87) but partial unsoundness, not affecting the general faculties does not render a person incapable (Banks v. Goodfellow (1870) 22, L.T R. 813). It may be doubted whether the Palestine legislator intended to suggest any distinction between the terms under discussion.

[5]) e.g. if in a Communist State all wills of property are invalid, this would not invalidate the will of a national as to property abroad.

Chapter VII—Succession and Inheritance.

The Palestine Ordinance further requires [1]) that the testator should not have been induced to make the will by fraud or undue influences. Reference is clearly made here to English equitable doctrines and, in the application of the law, English cases would be relevant [2]).

Probate and Administration.

In its provisions as to proof (Probate) of Wills in Civil Form [3]) and as to appointment of administrators of estates of deceased persons [4]) the Palestine legislator was obviously inspired by English precedent.

According to English practice the executor of the will or if there be no executor some other person interested takes steps after a testator's death to have the will "proved". If there is no dispute as to the validity of the will the proceeding is very simple. Affidavits are lodged at the Probate Registry in accordance with the forms required by the Probate Rules and the will is attached to the affidavits and lodged with them. The Registry will thereupon grant "Probate". A certified copy of the will is handed to the applicant, the original will being retained at the Registry. Before Probate is granted all duties payable upon the death have to be paid and in order that this may be done sworn inventories of the property passing upon the death are lodged when application is made for probate.

If the will is disputed its authenticity or validity needs to be settled in a Probate action in which one party "propounds" the will for Probate and the other opposes the grant of Probate.

Sec. 12 of the Succession Ordinance is clearly inspired by English precedent. The will made in Civil form needs to be "proved" and the probate is obtainable upon affidavits which include affidavits as to Mulk, movables and immovables.

Rules relating to grants of Probate and Administration have been made by the Chief Justice under Sec. 24 of the Succession Ordinance [5]). By the British and Colonial Probates Ordinance 1929 provision is made for the "re-sealing" in Palestine of Probates and Letters of Administration granted in the United Kingdom or in a British possession or by a British Court in a foreign country. Rules of Court under this Ordinance regulating applications thereunder were made by the Chief Justice in 1929.

---

[1]) Succession Ordinance, Sec. 10 (III).
[2]) Compare such cases as Tyrrell v. Painton, (1894) 70 L.T.R. The matter will be found fully treated in any English text book on Equity.
[3]) Succession Ordinance, Sec. 12.
[4]) Ibid. Secs. 13 ff.
[5]) Rules of Court 26 October 1923; 17 September 1929.

The Land Law of Palestine.

The English Colonial Probate Act 1892 authorizes the resealing in the United Kingdom of probate and letters of administration granted in a British possession or by a British Court in a foreign country, if an Order-in-Council has been made applying the Act thereto. The Act has been extended to Palestine by Order-in-Council dated 7 May 1929 [1]).

It is to be remarked that only wills in Civil form can be proved under Sec. 12 of the Succession Ordinance and that only probates granted by the Civil Courts appear capable of being resealed under the Colonial Probate Act 1892.

Special powers are contained in the Succession Ordinance authorizing the District Court to appoint administrators of the estates of deceased persons in cases in which the administration and distribution is within the jurisdiction of the Civil Courts (Sec. 13(I)). In English practice administrators of estates of deceased persons are always appointed if the deceased has not by his will nominated an executor, or if the executors so nominated refuse to administer the estate or for some other reason fail to undertake it. Administration is granted by the Court by so called "Letters of Administration" issued to the person appointed who is, in the case of a solvent estate, usually one of the persons entitled to share in the estate. The provisions of the Succession Ordinance as to the powers and duties of administrators etc. are obviously modelled on English law and practice and it is expressly provided that when probate of a will is granted to an executor or other person the person to which it is granted is to be deemed an administrator within the meaning of the Ordinance (Sec. 13 (IV)).

It has been held that religious Courts are not competent to appoint administrators to administer and distribute Miri [2]) since "the administration of an estate of a deceased person is not one of the matters of personal status in which Religious Courts have jurisdiction under Art. 51 of the Order-in-Council" and "whatever power a Religious Court may have to appoint an administrator to administer and distribute the movable and Mulk property of an intestate in accordance with the Law of the Community" (a matter on which the Court did not express any opinion), "there is no such power as regards Miri land for the reason that the admin-

---

[1]) The Courts of Palestine are "British Courts in a foreign country". This term includes "any British Court having jurisdiction in the (King's) dominions in pursuance of an Order-in-Council". (Colonial Probate Act 1892).

[2]) Vijansky v. Khojainoff. Land Appeal No. 55/32. Palestine Post 25 April 1933.

Chapter VII—Succession and Inheritance.

istration of Miri land is not a matter to which the Law of the Community can apply" [1]).

Assuming the decision to be correct so far as regards Miri for the special reasons there given, it is nevertheless necessary to bear in mind that Sec. 6 of the Succession Ordinance expressly empowers a Religious Court to "administer" as well as to "distribute" the estate of a deceased member of the Community in accordance with the law of the Community [2]). It must, therefore, include power to give directions as to payment of debts and direct the distribution of assets. In most cases no doubt the administration of the estate is in the hands of the heirs in accordance with the practices established in systems of law other then the English [3]), but it is not clear why in case of need a Religious Court should be precluded from appointing an administrator if its own law gave it such powers [4]).

"Vineyards and gardens made on State land possessed by title-deed by planting, after taking possession, mulk trees and vines thereon with the leave of the official, as also Mulk buildings newly erected thereon, pass on the death of the owner of the trees, vines or buildings to the ownership of his heirs in the same way as his other Mulk property. A fee in the nature of succession duty (intiqal) shall alone be charged upon the assessed value of the land upon which the trees are and the land shall be granted gratuitously to the heirs in proportion to the shares of the trees, vines and buildings which they respectively inherit, and the records in the registers deposited at the Daftar Khani shall be amended accordingly and a note thereof made in the margin of the title-deeds given to the parties". *Special provisions as to Mulk Trees and Buildings on Miri or Waqt. Land Code, Art. 81.*

---

[1]) It is submitted that in the language of the Ordinance the "administration (Sec. 6) but not the distribution (Sec. 19) of the Miri is to be "according to the law of the community". See also the remarks as to this point in the judgment of the Supreme Court in the Vijansky case, Palestine Post 14 Nov. 1933.

[2]) As already suggested a jurisdiction recognised by the Succession Ordinance may be valid even though not expressly authorised by the Order-in-Council.

[3]) Compare the case of Re Achillopoulos (1928) 139 L.T.R. 62 in which the English Court treated an "heir" to a foreign estate as the person corresponding under the foreign law to the "representative" of the deceased under English law (executor or administrator).

[4]) For a fuller discussion of the history and present situation of religious jurisdiction in Palestine and the Near East see Goadby, Private International and Inter-Religious law in Palestine (Jerusalem, 1926) Chaps. IV and V. See also an article on Religious Communities in Palestine by the same author in Tulane Law Review Vol. VIII, No. 2 (Feb. 1934) in which the sources of the respective religious laws are considered.

The Land Law of Palestine.

As to the procedure see Regulations as to Title-Deeds, A.H. 1276, Art. 3. The principle laid down in Art. 81 is in accordance with the theory already explained that the land on which Mulk trees and buildings stand, though not changing its character, is, while the trees and buildings exist, subject to the plantations and erections thereon. The same principle is applicable in the case of Muqata'a Waqf. In accordance with a practice established by decision of the Courts the Land Registry adopt the following rules:—

(a) If the trees were planted or buildings erected before 11th Jamadi-el-Awal, A.H. 1331, the land should follow the trees or buildings and division among the heirs of both land and trees or buildings will be according to the Moslem Law, (i.e. where the deceased was a Moslem).

(b) If the trees were planted or buildings erected after 11th Jamadi-el-Awal, A.H. 1331, the trees or buildings should follow the land and division among the heirs of both land and trees or buildings will be according to the law of Inheritance of 27 Rabi-el-Awal, A.H. 1331.

<small>Exclusion from succession by reason of nationality or religion.</small> The older law did not permit the land of a Moslem to devolve upon a non-Moslem, nor the land of a non-Moslem to devolve upon a Moslem (Land Code, Art. 109), nor could the land of an Ottoman subject devolve on any heir of his who was a foreign subject (Land Code, Art. 110). The same rules applied to enjoyment of Rights to Tapu. These provisions, though contained in the Land Code, were of general application and applied to all forms of immovable property [1]).

The Succession Ordinance, 1923, provides as follows:

<small>Sec. 22.</small> "(1) No person shall be deemed to be under a legal incapacity to take any share in a succession to property in Palestine or to take under a will, by reason only of his nationality or religious belief.

(2) Where, under the law then applicable in Palestine, any person has been excluded from a share in the succession to a person who has died possessed of property in Palestine, since the 31st day of December, 1918, by reason only of his nationality or religious belief, the person so excluded or his heirs may apply to the District Court, which, upon such application and upon consideration of all the circumstances, may make such order as

---

[1]) A law of 7 Moharrem, A.H. 1293, gave inter-religious rights of transfer between living persons.

Chapter VII—Succession and Inheritance.

they think fit reopening the succession and granting to the applicant such share in the succession as may, under the circumstances, appear equitable, provided that the share so granted shall in no case exceed the share to which such person would have been entitled under the then existing law if he had not been excluded therefrom by reason of his nationality or religious belief, and provided also that no such applicant shall be entitled to receive any sum in respect of rent, interest or profits arising from the share to which he is admitted by the order of Court between the date at which the succession opened and the date of the order".

It should be remarked that Sec. 22 refers only to shares in succession to property. As has been before pointed out the Ottoman Law did not treat the "heir" to Miri as entitled by way of succession strictly so called. This was a right of gratuitous transmission (intiqal) only. The point is referred to in the judgment in a Cyprus Case [1]), where it was doubted whether the religious Law of personal status could in the case of a Christian be applied to determine the status of illegitimate children in a succession to Miri, since such law was applicable only in case of succession strictly so called. It appears clear, however, that the Succession Ordinance does not perpetuate this distinction, and in speaking of rights of succession intends to refer not only to succession to Mulk, but to succession to Miri. Any doubt which might have existed upon this point has, however, now been set at rest by the provisions of Sec. 10 of the Land Law (Amendment) Ordinance 1933 according to which Arts. 109, 110 and 111 of the Land Code are no longer to have effect.

The special provisions of Art. 108 of the Land Code and of the Addendum of 28 Rabi-el-Thani, A.H. 1292, still continue in force. These exclude manslayers or accessories to the homicide from the succession of the victim.

Certification and Registration of the rights of Succession.

Earlier Ottoman Laws made provision for the certification of rights of inheritance. Thus Art. 5 of Tapu Law, requires the Imam and the Mukhtar of the village or quarter to issue a certificate as to rights of inheritance in Miri land for the use of the Land Registry. Art. 13 of the Law as to Mulk Title-Deeds, provides that on the death of the owner of Mulk property the Local Administrative Council shall be obliged to proceed in accordance with the Register of Successions (Daftar Kassam) or if there is not

---

[1]) Della v. Michael (1902) 6 C.L.R. at p. 30.

The Land Law of Palestine.

one in accordance with the Mazbata signed and sealed by the Sharia (Moslem Religious) authorities based on the certificate of the Imam and Mukhtars of the Quarter shoving the number of heirs. By Sec. 13 of the Land Transfer Ordinance 1920, it is provided that when any immovable property passes by operation of a will or by inheritance the legatees or heirs shall be responsible for registration of the property in their names within a year of the death of the registered owner. The registration was to be made on the certificate of a competent Court, stating that the persons acquiring registration are legatees or heirs or upon a certificate signed by the Mukhtar or Imam and two notables.

More precise provisions are made by the Succession Ordinance 1923, which provides as follows:—

Sec. 23.

"(1) Any person claiming to be entitled to any share in immovable property, forming part of a succession may apply to the Director of Lands, to enter his name upon the Register in respect of his interest, and such entry shall be made accordingly upon payment of the prescribed fees and upon production to the Director:—

(a) Where the deceased was a Moslem, of an Ilam Sharia from the competent Religious Court;

(b) In any other case —

(I) of an order of the President of the competent District Court in any case in which there has been registered at the Land Registry a memorandum of an order under subsection (2) of Sec. 7 hereof, or the probate of a will;

(II) of an order of the President of the competent District Court in any case in which the deceased was a foreigner as to whose succession no order to refer had been made in pursuance of Sec. 3 hereof; and in any case in which the deceased was not, at the time of his death, a member of one of the specified religious Communities;

(III) in any other case, of an order of the competent Court of the Community of which the deceased was a member at the date of his death¹).

(2) The Director of Lands may refuse to make any entry upon the Register in pursuance of an Ilam Sharia or other order of a Religious Court in any case in which he has reason to believe

---

¹) Cf. Judicial Committee case (Abdullah Bey Chedid v. Tenenbaum) referred to at p. 109 supra. It was held by the J. C. that the only competent Court of the Community is the religious Court in Palestine. The Certificate of the Egyptian Court was rejected.

Chapter VII—Succession and Inheritance.

that the persons thereby entitled to be entered as heirs are not the only heirs of the deceased, unless such order is stated on the face of it to contain the names of all persons then known to be the heirs of the deceased.

(3) Where an application for entry on the Register is supported by an Ilam Sharia or other order of a Religious Court, and the Director of Lands entertains a doubt whether the Court had jurisdiction to make the order, he may require the parties to refer the matter to the competent authority for determining cases of conflict and shall enter on the Register a note of their application and reference".

This section makes it clear that no entry in the Land Register of the interest of any person claimed in virtue of a succession, testamentary or not, can be made save on production of a certificate or order of heirship issued by a Religious or Civil Court as the case may be. It is of course the duty of the Court concerned to make all proper enquires as to the persons entitled to share in the succession under the law applicable to the case and to issue its order in strict accordance with the law. The certificate should contain an express statement that the persons named in the order are all the persons due however to be heirs of the deceased. If the order does not contain such statement the Director of Land Registries is entitled to refuse to make the requisite entries in the Land Register [1]).

Assuming that the statement is contained in the Order the Director cannot refuse to make the entries unless he entertains a doubt as to the jurisdiction of the Court making the Order. The independence enjoyed by the Religious Courts makes it difficult to control them if they incorrectly apply the Law, or if they deliberately ignore the rights of persons entitled to claim as heirs. Reluctance to recognise female heirship may not improbably sometimes lead to indifference to the claims of women heirs. The Civil Courts have not yet had occasion to decide to what extent an order by a Religious Court under Sec. 22 binds them in a suit instituted by persons for recovery of property from which they have been improperly excluded under a distribution made by a Religious Court.

In the case of orders made by Moslem Courts, however, the Civil Courts are not entitled to question the accuracy of an order

---

[1]) The term "heirs" must presumably be interpreted to include persons entiteld under a will.

The Land Law of Palestine.

relative to the distribution of the estate of a deceased Moslem. Such orders are not founded on consent.

Appendix to Chapter VII.

Consent to the Jurisdiction.

Concurrent jurisdiction in certain matters of personal status, and, in particular, in matters of succession, ab intestato, has long existed in Palestine. Before the British Occupation such jurisdiction was exerciseable by the Moslem Courts and by the Patriarchal or Rabbinical Courts, the Jurisdiction of the two latter depending on consent. Under the Order-in Council the alternative jurisdiction is that of the Civil Courts, but the jurisdiction of the non-Moslem Courts still rests on consent. It appears certain that the intention of the legislator was to continue the jurisdiction on the same basis as that upon which it was established under the Hatt Hamayoun according to which "Special Civil suits such as those relating to succession and others of a like nature between subjects of the same Christian rite or other non-Moslems may on their application be brought before the Court of the Patriarchs or of the Communities". (Art. 12). In the English form of the Order-in-Council the use of the words "action" and "parties" suggest the application of the provisions to contentious proceedings only. And this limitation of the terms is somewhat confirmed in the Arabic text by the use of the word "Ikhsam" as corresponding to parties [1]).

Nevertheless, it is doubtful whether any inference should be drawn from these circumstances. It cannot be doubted that jurisdiction is intended to be given to non-Moslem Courts to make orders in non-contentious proceedings which make up much of the work of any Court of personal status. Such work comprises the authorisation of adoptions, the appointment of guardians and curators, grants of probate and administration, issue of certificates of heirship etc.; all of which may be effected in non-contentious proceedings. The Order of 1st December 1922, defining the limits of non-contentious Consular Jurisdiction in Palestine illustrates this.

There is no doubt that the non-Moslem Courts are competent to hear and decide upon such applications even though they may not be correctly described as "actions".

On the other hand it would be unreasonable to treat appointments made or certificates issued in such proceedings upon the application of persons interested as binding upon persons who were not parties to the proceedings and who did not consent

---

[1]) An action according to the legal meaning of the term is a proceeding by which one party seeks in a Court of Justice to enforce some right against or to restrain the commission of some wrong by another party (Halsbury).

Chapter VII—Succession and Inheritance.

thereto. The assumption is that not merely the actual applicants have consented to the jurisdiction, but that all persons having an interest have consented. We are driven to conclude that the "parties" whose consent is requested include, at least in non-contentious proceedings, not merely those who chance to have brought the matter before the Court, but also those who would properly be parties in any contentious proceedings affecting their interests [1]).

The Succession Ordinance 1923, Sec. 7, recognizes on the part of certain persons interested (Sec. 8) a right to dissent from the administration of an estate by a non-Moslem Court. They are not bound by the fact that an application for administration has been made to such a Court provided that the estate has not been actually distributed. This appears to show clearly that the consent of the actual applicants does not suffice to give jurisdiction as against other interested persons who have not consented.

The Succession Ordinance while recognising a limited statutory right, does not destroy any wider right which might be possessed under the Order-in-Council. If we are right in assuming that an Order made by a non-Moslem Court, acting without the consent of all interested persons, is not effective against those who did not consent, it seems to follow that, even after distribution of the estate, it would still be open to a person claiming interest and who has not consented to the jurisdiction of the Religious Court, to claim his share, if not by asking for a redistribution, yet by bringing a Civil action against those who had obtained possession of the property for restitution. In the absence of any rules as to advertisement and citation binding upon the non-Moslem Courts and securing at least a measure of publicity, it seems unreasonable to refuse redress to such a person.

In connection with some of the questions which arise, reference may usefully be made to Egyptian cases since in Egypt the like duplication of authorities in matters of personal status exists and the principles established by the Hatt Hamayoun are still followed.

1. As to the parties whose consent is necessary. Though for the purpose of exercising non-contentious jurisdiction the consent of the applicant alone is requisite, yet for the purpose of giving a judgment binding, generally either all persons whose interest would be affected must be consenting parties or at least, adequate

---

[1]) The Jewish Community Regulations 1927, Reg. 6, requires the consent of "all persons legally concerned". See Off. Gaz. No. 202 of 1.1.1928.

The Land Law of Palestine.

citations must have been issued and published, and adequate opportunity given for all persons so interested to appear and to consent or to object.

In a succession case these would include all persons entitled to a share in the estate. The provisions of Sec. 8 of the Succession Ordinance 1923 suggest that we must reckon among them (a) persons who would be entitled to a share in the succession under the Religious Law of the Community; (b) persons who would be entitled to a share under the Civil Law i.e. the law of A.H. 1331. And if a person who would have no share under the Religious Law but who would be entitled to a share under the Civil Law consents to the jurisdiction of the Religious Court, the creditor of such renouncing person is to be permitted to ask that the distribution of the estate should be transferred to the Civil Court so that the application of the Civil Law should be secured (Succession Ordinance 1923, Secs. 7 and 8). This latter point was raised in an Egyptian case reported in the Gazette of the Mixed Courts Vo. 11 at page 86 (Ades v. Geargeoura) in which it was decided by the Mixed Court of Appeal that in the absence of an express provision, the creditors of an heir who renounced the succession cannot accept for him. The decision is explained in a note in the third volume of the Gazette at page 15 from which it appears that the debtor had opted together with his co-heirs for the application of the Religious Law to a succession in which he was interested. It appeared that under such law he would not have any share in the succession but that if the Moslem Law were applied he would be entitled to a share. It was held that his creditor could not take his place and by objecting to the jurisdiction of the Religious Court secure the application of the Moslem Law. Sec. 8 of the Succession Ordinance gives creditors in Palestine the right denied to them by the Egyptian Courts.

2. As to the time at which the consent must be given. It may be safely assumed that if at any time during the proceedings a party interested has appeared and has pleaded, his consent to the jurisdiction must be assumed and should be irrevocable, so far as regards these proceedings. If such party has been cited and has appeared only under protest, not consenting, such appearance does not, it is submitted, constitute consent, provided, of course, the appearance is only for the purpose of objecting to the jurisdiction.

Two cases reported in Vol. XXII of the Official Bulletin to the Native Courts of Egypt are relevant though neither deals with the precise point in question. No. 21, Court of Appeal, lays down

Chapter VII—Succession and Inheritance.

that parties may, if they are agreed, bring a matter of personal status before a Patriarchal Court and that if a party has appeared in such Court and submitted to the jurisdiction he cannot set up a plea of want of jurisdiction after the decision has been given. (Compare Succession Ordinance 1923, Sec. 7(1) proviso).

No. 136 (Superior Meglis Hasby) lays down that in matters concerning appointment of guardians for non-Moslem infants, the non-Moslem Courts are competent only where the parties are agreed explicitly or impliedly upon submitting to the jurisdiction. Where a party has applied to a Moslem Court for such appointment disputing the jurisdiction of a non-Moslem Court (in this case Armenian) he cannot afterwards dispute the jurisdiction of the Moslem Court (i.e. by applying to the Moslem Court he irrevocably refused to consent to the Patriarchal jurisdiction in the matter).

3. What is the effect against third parties of an Order made without consent?

It is clear that third parties acting in good faith upon an Order of a non-Moslem Court purporting to be founded on consent should be protected against any defect of jurisdiction afterwards appearing. Two recent Egyptian cases may be cited. The first of these is reported in Volume XVI of the Gazette of the Mixed Courts No. 191. It suggest that a distinction is to be drawn between a certificate of heirship given by a Religious Court in the application of parties interested (Ishad Sharia) and judgment in an action (Ilam Sharia).

The case concerned the succession of a Russian. The Egyptian Government, having in 1923 declared that it no longer recognized the Russian Consul in Egypt, application was made to the Moslem Courts on the ground that they were the Common law Courts of personal statute and Ishad Sharia was obtained to the effect that the applicants were the heirs of the de cujus. Money forming part of the estate was in the hands of the National Bank of Egypt, who, on facts within their cognizance, were satisfied that the Ishad Sharia was incompatible with certain circumstances in connection with the family of the deceased. They declined to hand the money over and the action was the consequence. The Court held that they were fully justified in their action in view of their knowledge. It was pointed out that an Ishad Sharia was obtained merely on a statement of the parties interested who appeared before the Qadi and had a relative value as was clear from the provisions of the decree regulating procedure in Moslem Courts.

124 The Land Law of Palestine.

The Court suggested that the parties might by agreement bring their differences for adjudication before the Court of the Orthodox Community to which they all belonged, and with reference to this suggestion the learned editors asked who are the "interested parties" where "consent" is necessary. The answer to their question would appear to be that the jurisdiction exists so long as it is not contested. In another Egyptian case (Imperial Ottoman Bank v. Youssounan) reported in Volume XVI of the Gazette No. 187 it was decided that a Certificate of heirship given by a non-Moslem Religious Court was binding upon third persons so long at any rate as such persons were not aware of any objection taken to the jurisdiction. Consequently a Bank would be entitled to act upon and would be fully protected in acting upon such a Certificate, and might safely hand over any moneys in their hands to the persons named in the Certificate. Neither the Ishad Sharia nor the Certificate of heirship were judgments properly so called. They appeared to have been obtained by non-contentious proceedings, or, at least, by proceedings which could not have been described as constituting a suit. The Certificate which was the subject of the second case cited could (semble) have been upset had an heir who had not consented to the jurisdiction intervened; but subject to such intervention the Certificate was treated as a sufficient protection for third persons.

CHAPTER VIII—APPROPRIATION OF LAND OF ANOTHER AND USE THEREOF.

Exclusive possession of his land, whether Miri or Mulk is secured to the holder or owner. Cf. Land Code, Arts. 9, 10, 11 and 13; Mejelle Arts. 1192, 1197.

It may, however, happen that land is wrongfully appropriated by a person to whom it does not belong, and that the appropriator cultivates, plants or builds upon it. Or again a person may plant or build upon his own land with plants or materials which are not his property.

The situation thus created gives rise to interesting problems but only a brief reference to the solutions is here proposed. The most interesting cases are those raised by the planting or building on the land of another.

The principles of Moslem law on this matter differ, therefore, very much from those adopted in English law. The latter follows the maxim that what is planted in the soil, acceds to it, though modern statute has much modified its application, more particularly as between landlord and tenant. In Moslem law trees and buildings are in general regarded as movables and do not accede to the soil, when the owner of the soil is not the owner of the trees or buildings. This leads to very different solutions of the problems presented than those which be reached by the English law. *Planting or Building on the land of another.*

We will deal first with the law as to Mulk laid down in the Mejelle.

Though alluvion which accumulates imperceptibly belongs to the owner of the land to which it adheres if a landslide occurs or a piece of land is torn away by a stream and attaches itself to the land of another ownership is not changed [1]). *On Mulk land.*

But Mejelle, Art. 902, tells us that in case of a landslide the property which is of lesser value is subject to that which is of greater value; the owner of the land of greater value is, however, bound to indemnify the owner of the land of lesser value.

---

[1]) Cf. Chaoui, op. cit., p. 142; Cf. Mejelle, Art. 1240.

The Land Law of Palestine.

Wild grasses and the like growing on Mulk are free (mubah), though the owner of the land may exclude others from entering to pluck them [1]). This applies, of course, only to plants which are not cultivated [2]) and whether, in view of Art. 11 of the Land Code, it also applies to Miri is, it seems, disputed [3]).

If an owner of land plants thereon trees belonging to another or uses materials belonging to another in erecting buildings, he is not, semble, required to restore the plants or materials. This case is not expressly dealt with in the authorities but the principle laid down in Art. 27 of the Mejelle is thought to justify this solution [4]). Indemnity and damages would be due to the owner of the plants or materials.

If a person plants or builds on the land of another, he is to restore the land after uprooting the trees or pulling down the buildings [5]). In this case, however, the principle of Art. 27 is also to be applied and the owner of the land may take the plants or buildings upon paying the pulling down [6]) value if the uprooting or pulling down would be injurious to the land. And further, but only if he acted in good faith, the owner of the trees or material of the buildings may claim to have the land vested in him when the value of the trees or buildings is greater than that of the land. Of course, in such a case the price of the land must be paid to the owner.

The wrongful appropriator of land must make good to the owner any decrease in value of the land arising from his act. If he has cultivated the land he must pay for any decrease in value

---

[1]) Mejelle, Art. 1257. Cf. Arts. 1241, 1242. In practice a similar result seems to be reached in England though on different grounds. Cf. Gardner v. Mansbridge (1887) 57 L.T.R. 265.

[2]) Compare, Mejelle, Arts. 1244 and 1257.

[3]) Chaoui, op. cit., p. 143.

[4]) Chaoui, op. cit., p. 144.

[5]) Mejelle, Art. 906.

[6]) As to "pulling down" value and "standing" value see Mejelle, Arts. 882—885.

The principle was applied in a case before the Judicial Committee on appeal from Zanzibar (Secretary of State v. Charlesworth (1901) 84 L.T.R 212). Their Lordships quoted and relied upon a passage from the Hedaya (Hamilton's Translation at p. 539). The compensation is there stated to be "equal to the value the trees or houses would bear when removed from the ground" which is to be understood to mean "the value which the trees or houses bear upon the proprietor being directed to remove them". The expense of the removal is to be deducted (Cf. Mejelle, Art. 885). See further FitzGerald, Muhammedan Law, pp. 190, 193-4.

Chapter VIII—Appropriation of Land of Another.[127]

arising from such cultivation [1]). And if he has increased the value of the land by clearing it he cannot claim the cost of clearing [2]). But all produce arising from seeds sown by any person for himself is such person's property [3]).

In the case of land dedicated to pious purposes or the property of a minor an equivalent rent seems also to be payable for the time of occupation by the appropriator [4]). If one co-owner cultivates the land alone without permission the other co-owner is entitled to "Noksan Arz" on taking his share [5]).

The rules now applicable to Miri are in effect much the same as those applicable to Mulk under the Mejelle. As already mentioned, a doubt has been suggested whether Mejelle Art. 1257 is applicable to Miri but the doubt is probably unsound. Art. 35 of the Land Code contains some provisions as to planting or building by a bona fide occupier on the land of another but they are now practically obsolete [6]). The position is now regulated by provisions of the Law of Disposition A.H. 1331.

On Miri land.

Thus Art. 11 of the Law of Disposition provides that if a person erects buildings or plants trees or vines on Miri or Miri Waqf land without the consent of the holder, the holder may destroy them, but if their removal is injurious to the ground he can appropriate them while indemnifying the other party for their value, but deducting the amount which their removal would have cost [7]). This is in accordance with the principle laid down in Mejelle, Art. 906, as to buildings or trees on Mulk.

However, in accordance with a principle of which other applications have already been considered, the land may accede to the trees in the sense that the person who in good faith has built or planted on the land of another will be entitled to become the owner of the land on paying its value to the true owner, but only in cases where the value of the trees or the buildings is greater than that of the land. So Art. 9 of the Law of Disposition

Appropriation in good faith.

---

[1]) Mejelle, Art. 907. This is the "Noksan Arz" (Mejelle, Art. 886) which represents the difference between the rent of land which is its value before cultivation and the rent which is its value after cultivation. See also Mejelle, Art. 900 and the remarks of Bertram J. in Tzapa v. Tsolaki, 9 C.L.R. at p. 80.

[2]) Mejelle, Art. 908

[3]) Ibid., Art. 1246. But crops e.g. fruit growing naturally belong to the owner of the property (Art. 903). See more fully as to the law relative to the products of soil wrongfully possessed Cardahi in Revue Critique, April 1925 at p.p. 211–213.

[4]) Mejelle, Art. 596. The rent (Ijr Misl) is a rent fixed by disinterested experts. (Mejelle Art. 414).

[5]) Mejelle, Art. 907.

[6]) See Tute, op. cit., Note (1) on Art. 35.

[7]) This translation follows Nord, op. cit., p. 118. The translation given in the collection published by the Iraq Government is almost unintelligible.

The Land Law of Palestine.

provides that if the holder of Miri or Miri Waqf by virtue of a formal title deed has erected buildings or planted trees upon it and another person proves that he is the true holder of the tessaruf, then if the value of the buildings or the plantations is greater than that of the land, the land will be left in the possession of the person who erected the buildings or made the plantations upon payment of its value; but in the contrary case the buildings or trees will be delivered to the claimant and their value will be paid by the claimant to the person who erected the buildings or planted the trees[1]). This provision again accords with the principle laid down as to Mulk by Art. 906 of the Mejelle.

Unlawful appropriation. Under the Land Code[2]), where Miri land had been taken and cultivated unlawfully but the taxes had been paid neither the Official i.e. the Government, nor the rightful holder was entitled to claim from the usurper either damages for depreciation (Noksan Arz) nor equivalent rent (Ijr Misl) for the period during which the usurper held it.

And it was held in Cyprus that Art. 906 of the Mejelle did not apply to Miri[3]). This provision of the Land Code has, however, been superseded by Art. 14 of the Law of Disposition A.H. 1331 whereby the owner is given a right to claim rent for the period of unlawful occupation but not compensation for decrease in value, and the rule is declared applicable to Mussaqafat and Mustaghilat Waqf. Art. 22 of the Land Code further lays down that, though the true owner can have the crops of the usurper removed, he has no right to take them for himself, though if they have not sprouted above the ground, he may take them on paying the value. (Addendum of 1302). But this article is probably superseded by the Law of Disposition[4]).

The Law of Disposition further provides (Art. 13) that the rules of Art. 11 apply if one co-owner erects buildings or plants trees on the whole land without permission of the other co-owners, or if he does the same on land which upon partition falls to the lot of another co-owner. We may compare with this the provisions of Art. 907 of the Mejelle as to cultivation by one co-owner without the permission of the other.

---

[1]) Here again Nord's translation is preferable to that of the Iraq Government. This method by which the value of the buildings or trees (qa'iman qimet) is to be ascertained is explained in Mejelle, Art. 882.

[2]) Land Code, Art. 21.

[3]) Tzapa v. Tsolaki (1910) 9 C.L.R. 73. See per Bertram J. at p. 81.

[4]) Tute, op. cit., Note (I) to Art. 22. For a case in which it was applied see Loizo v. Hanoum (1894) 3 C.L.R. at p. 46.

CHAPTER IX—DISPOSITIONS BY SALE, EXCHANGE AND GIFT.

It has already been pointed out that the distinction between the law of movable (personal) property and that of immovable (real) property is by no means so fundamental in Moslem law as it is in the feudalised law of Western Europe. In England the distinction is now of less importance than in earlier days but it still occupies a very important position in the arrangement of the law. Thus, in dealing with the law of sale the distinction between the law as to sale of goods and that which deals with sale of land is of first importance. Sale of goods is now governed by the Sale of Goods Act 1893 and it is by reference to the provisions of this act rather than to the special rules applicable to sale of land that comparison with the Moslem law of sale as laid down in the Mejelle is most fruitfully made.

The general principles of this law of sale in any country must be those governing Contract generally since sale in its inception is a species of contract. In the case of a sale of goods, particularly when the sale is for cash, the sale takes the form of a contract and a conveyance which are practically simultaneous. But even in the case of a sale of goods and still more frequently in that of a sale of land the contract (agreement) to sell precedes, sometimes by a long interval, the actual conveyance (transfer) of the legal interest in the land.

Thus while under English law the ownership of goods (movables) passes from the vendor to the purchaser forthwith upon the agreement to sell being made [1] the ownership of land is normally only transferred by the execution (signing and sealing) of deeds of conveyance, though an agreement to sell land gives certain "equitable" rights to the person who has agreed to buy which need not, however, be further considered here. The radical distinction between the effect of an agreement to sell goods and that of an agreement to sell land is typical of a system of law such as

---

[1] Sale of Goods Act 1893, Sec. 18.

The Land Law of Palestine.

the English which has its origin in feudal ideas. In systems in which the distinction between movable and immovable property is less fundamental the difference is not so great.

Sale of land. The usual procedure in a sale of land in England is as follows. The parties having reached an agreement as to the terms of the sale, these are embodied in a written agreement which the parties sign and a day is appointed at which the formal conveyance will be executed and handed over. Until this deed of conveyance is signed and sealed the vendor remains owner of the property. After the agreement has been signed the lawyer of the vendor produces to the lawyer of the purchaser evidence that the vendor is the owner of the property which is to be sold or is entitled to sell it. In areas in which no registration of property exists, this evidence takes the form of title deeds showing how the vendor came to be entitled to the property. This process is called Investigation of Title and is very important; indeed most provincial lawyers in England are mainly occupied in producing or investigating the title to land which is being sold or bought by their clients. When the purchaser is satisfied that the vendor is entitled to sell the land, he draws up a deed of conveyance and this when approved by the vendor is signed and sealed by him. On the day appointed or such other day as may be arranged, the purchaser's lawyer attends at the office of the vendor's lawyer, pays the purchase price and receives in exchange the deed of conveyance of the land signed and sealed by the vendor and also all the earlier deeds of title in the possession of the vendor. The purchaser thus becomes owner of the property. A similar procedure with necessary modifications is followed in the case of other dispositions of land e.g. by mortgage etc.

The details of the procedure of course vary if the land is registered in the Land Registry. But compulsory registration of land only applies in certain areas. And in any case the distinction between the agreement to sell and the sale (transfer, conveyance) of the ownership in the land is almost always very clearly marked. No doubt when land registration as contrasted with mere registration of documents of title has been established in Palestine it will become impossible to transfer ownership in land except by entries in the Register. At present, however, the situation is less simple. Its operation depends upon the distinction between Mulk and Miri, upon the provisions of the Land Code, upon provisions of Ottoman Law and upon those of the Land Transfer **The Law** Ordinances. We will first consider the law as to Mulk. The Mejelle **as to Mulk.** in which the principles of this law is to be found, makes no

Chapter IX—Sale, Exchange and Gift.

distinction between sale of goods and sale of land. According to the original Moslem law there reproduced sale is concluded by offer and acceptance (Art. 167) and the effect of the conclusion of a sale is that the purchaser becomes the owner of the thing sold (Art. 369). Offer and acceptance may be by writing as well as by word of mouth (Art. 173) [1]). Consequently if one person verbally offers to sell land and the other party accepts the offer, the acceptor forthwith becomes the owner of the land and can sell it before he has taken delivery (Art. 253).

The Mulk Titles Law of 28 Rejeb, A.H. 1291 made it obligatory for owners of Mulk land to obtain a title deed from the Land Registry (Daftar Khani) and possession of Mulk without such a title deed was prohibited. At first it was supposed that the effect of this law was to make sales of Mulk land inoperative unless made through the Registry but the Court of Cassation of Constantinople subsequently took a different view and held that sales outside the Registry were quite valid though, of course, they could not avail against registered titles [2]). In Palestine, however, it is now provided by the Land Transfer Ordinance 1921, Sec. 3, that no disposition of immovable property shall be valid unless the provisions of the Ordinance have been complied with. The term "immovable property" is not defined in the Land Transfer Ordinance but it is stated (Sec. 1) that the Ordinance is to apply (inter alia) to Mulk land [3]). Disposition includes sale (Sec. 2) and every person wishing to make a disposition of immovable property must obtain the written consent of the Administration (the Government) (Sec. 4) without which it is null and void (Sec. 11). Entry into possession upon a disposition made without such consent is punishable by fine (Sec. 12).

Mulk Titles.

The Ordinance states (Sec. 4) that the consent required is to be obtained by petition to the Land Registry. The petition is to be accompanied by proof of title and to contain an application for registration of a deed to be executed for the purpose of carrying the disposition into effect. The Land Transfer Ordinances in their

---

[1]) The provision must now of course be applied subject to Arts. 80 ff. of the Civil Procedure Code. See also the Notary Public Law.

[2]) See Chaoui, op. cit., pp. 149 ff. The Cypriot Courts, apparently, took another view. Cf. Christofides v. Tofaridi (1885) I C.L.R. 21. Cf. also L.A. 88/25.

[3]) The term "land" is defined in the Land Transfer Ordinance to include houses, buildings and things permanently fixed in the land but the Interpretation Ordinance 1929 defines the term "immovable property" or "land" to include land of any tenure (Sec. 7).

The Land Law of Palestine.

application to Mulk must be read as in part superseding the provision of the Law as to Mulk Title Deeds of A.H. 1291; Art. 11, which regulated the procedure requisite upon alienation of Mulk. They appear also to supersede the provision of Art. 17 of that Law whereby transfer of Mulk immovable property by way of gift or under a will could not be effected without an Ilam of a Sharia Court. It is further to be observed that the Transfer of Land Ordinances apply to all forms of Waqf land. All dealings with Waqf immovables of every description must follow the procedure directed under these Ordinances; as also (semble) even the creation of a Mulk Waqf.

It is, therefore, now clear that a sale of Mulk land cannot operate to transfer ownership unless consent has been obtained through the Land Registry. These provisions of the Land Transfer Ordinance apply, of course, not only to dispositions of Mulk but to dispositions of all kinds of immovable property and not only to dispositions by way of sale but to all other dispositions as stated in the Ordinance. They will be referred to in other connections in this chapter but their application to Mulk land is here noted.

Subject to various reservations and exceptions the general law of sale laid down in the Mejelle may be taken to apply to sale of all property rights which are subject to alienation. It will be, however, most convenient to consider them primarily as applying to sales of Mulk since strictly speaking this is the only kind of interest recognized by the pure Moslem law as possible for private persons in undedicated property.

The law of Sale in the Mejelle. The principles of the law of sale are to be found set forth in a somewhat unsystematic form in Book I of the Mejelle. They follow those of the Moslem law upon the subject and cover a large number of subjects forming a fairly complete body of law. It is not the purpose of this book to expound Moslem law as such even where, as in the case of sale, it constitutes part of the general law of Palestine. It must, therefore, suffice here to refer to some of the most important articles and provisions relative to sale, and in particular sale of immovable property.

Offer and Acceptance. Sale is concluded by offer and acceptance (Arts 101—104; 167) and consist of exchanging property for property (Art. 185). The law of offer and acceptance is treated in Arts. 167—180; Chapter II (Arts. 197—236) treats of the subject matter of the sale. In this connection it is to be remarked that the Moslem law does not recognize the sale of a thing not in existence, e. g. a future crop

Chapter IX—Sale, Exchange and Gift.

(Arts. 205—206)[1]. Immovable property may be sold by boundaries or by the pic or the dunum (Art. 221). An important group of articles (Art. 230 ff.) treats of things included in a sale.

There is included in a sale, though not mentioned, everything which by the custom of the town is comprised in the thing sold. This rule is explained with illustrative examples in Arts. 230 ff. Special reference should be made in this connection to Art. 231 ff. Thus, Art. 231 provides that things which cannot be separated from the thing sold having regard to the object of the purchase are included in the sale without being specifically mentioned. Thus, when a lock is sold the key is included. And things actually attached to the thing sold are included in the sale even though not specifically mentioned. These latter would in England be called fixtures. In the sale of a house is thus included fixed cupboards and the like and, in the sale of a garden, trees go with the land even though not specifically mentioned (Art. 232[2]). So also (Art. 235) things comprised in any general expressions added at the time of the sale are included in the sale. Thus if a house is sold "with all rights" this will include rights of way or of taking water which are attached to the house. It is of course the law as laid down in the Mejelle which is alone strictly law in Palestine but these provisions will be found to accord with the pure Moslem law to which reference may be made for their interpretation. Thus the Hedaya tells us that in a sale of land the trees upon it are included but not the corn unless particularly specified, nor the fruit upon the trees, nor the seed sown in the ground[3]. Again the sale appears necessarily to include rights essentially connected with the subject of the sale e.g. in the purchase of a house, the right of passing through a road which leads to it or in the purchase of a well, the right of drawing water from it. Interesting solutions are also offered as to cases in which an upper storey passes in a sale of a lower storey, or a well or a drain in the sale of a house and so on[4].

---

[1]) By an amendment to Art. 64 of the Code of Civil Procedure of the year A. H. 1332 contracts the subject matter of which comes into existence in the future are recognised.

[2]) As has already been shown, a Miri holder may own as Mulk trees or buildings upon his land, if these were constructed or built prior to the Law of Disposition A.H. 1331. It is provided by Art. 49 of the Land Code that if such a person transfers the trees or buildings he is bound also to transfer the land; the land is accessory to the trees or buildings.

[3]) Hedaya, Book XVI, Chap. I. (Hamilton's Translation, p. 245).

[4]) Hedaya, Book XVI, Chap. IX, pp. 293, 294.

The Land Law of Palestine.

The Mejelle states in general that what is not capable of delivery cannot be sold (Art. 209) but this must not be taken in too broad a sense. An undivided share can be sold (Arts. 214, 215); a right of way, a right of taking water and a right of flow [1]) attached to the land can be sold with the land, but (semble) not in gross [2]).

Delivery. Delivery is not an essential condition of sale (Art. 262), and a purchaser of immovables can pass a good title even before he has received delivery (Art. 253). The Mejelle, however, carefully states how delivery of immovable property can be effected (Arts. 265, 266, 270, 271) and its consequences (Arts. 267—269). The vendor has a right of retention till the price is fully paid (Art. 375) but loses it if he gives delivery (Art. 281) or if he "transfers" to another his right to receive the price (Art. 282) [3]), or if he gives credit after having sold for cash (Art. 284). Destruction and (semble) damage before delivery falls on the vendor but if occuring after delivery it falls on the purchaser (Arts. 293, 294). Interesting solutions are given as to the claims of creditors in a bankruptcy of the vendor or purchaser and occuring before or after delivery (Arts. 295 — 297). These solutions do not seem to be based on any clear principle, the loss being generally left to rest where it has fallen.

Options. Misdescription and the like are treated as giving rise to options, the purchaser having an "option" to cancel or of paying the price, as agreed (Art. 310). This is also the rule as regards long standing defect (Art. 337). Flagrant misrepresentation amounting to deceit also gives rise to a right of rescission (Art. 356). The distinction between misdescription and misrepresentation is obscure.

The effect of the conclusion of a sale is that ownership passes (Art. 369). A void sale has no effect (Art. 370), but if the sale is only voidable it becomes effective on delivery and ownership then passes. If, therefore, the thing bought is destroyed while in the purchaser's possession the loss falls upon him and he loses his right of cancellation. The same is true if the purchaser disposes of or alters the thing sold while in his possession, e.g. if he plants trees on the land (Arts. 371, 372). Sales by a person suffering from mortal sickness are subject to special provisions (Arts. 393—395). Sales may be subject to a right of redemption by the vendor or

---

[1]) Mejelle Art. 216. As to the definition of the terms, see Arts. 142—144.
[2]) Cf. Hedaya, Book XVI, Chap. V, p. 171.
[3]) Note that this article appears to recognize a right to assign a "chose in action".

Chapter IX—Sale, Exchange and Gift.

of return by the purchaser (Art. 396) in which case the thing sold is unalienable and the right of redemption is heritable (Art. 401). Many of these articles raise as many problems as they solve and the whole section does not form a consistent and complete body of law. Nevertheless the provisions as they stand are good law in Palestine and, subject to conflicting legislation, govern the sale of immovable property.

Seeing that Art. 105 of the Mejelle defines Sale as an exchange of property for property the distinction usually made in European law between "Sale" in which goods or land are transferred for a money consideration (price) and "Exchange" in which other goods or land are given in return, does not appear to have any validity in Moslem law. Sale in the European sense and Exchange are merely different kinds of the same species of contract and the like rules apply to each. The same principle is stated in Art. 379 of the Mejelle [1]). *Exchange.*

Sale is essentially founded on a contract and the usual remedy for breach of a contract is an action for damages. If the vendor fails to deliver the property sold or if the property actually delivered in purported fulfilment of the contract is defective in quality or quantity or in some other particular there is a breach of the agreement to sell. So also if the purchaser fails to pay the price or otherwise make the return for which the agreement stipulates.

English law deals fully with the right to damages and the amount of damages to be allowed for breach of contract. The rules as to the quantum of damages for breach of contract of sale of goods are to be found in the Sale of Goods Act 1893 [2]). In the case of breach of contract for sale of land the damages obtainable by a purchaser against the vendor are usually limited to the amount paid by way of deposit with interest together with the reasonable costs to which the purchaser was put in investigating the vendor's title [3]) though in some cases some general damages for loss of the bargain are given, not amounting, however, to loss of profit upon a possible resale [4]). But the purchaser is often very anxious to get the land itself and damages, particularly when thus limited, are a very poor compensation to him. The Courts of Equity, acting in personam, were able to afford the purchaser, as also sometimes the vendor, a more *Damages for breach of contract of Sale.*

---
[1]) The Interpretation Ordinance 1929 (Sec. 24) provides that "sale" and "sell" include exchange, barter and offering or exposing for sale.
[2]) See Sec. 52.
[3]) Bain v. Fothergill (1870) 7 H. L. 158; 31 L.T.R. 387.
[4]) Day v. Singleton (1899) 2 Ch. 320; 81 L.T.R. 306.

The Land Law of Palestine.

Specific Performance. effective remedy by way of Specific Performance, that is, by compelling the party guilty of the breach to do exactly what he had promised to do — to convey the land, or to accept a conveyance of the land and to pay the price.

"Equitable" remedies are always discretionary, that is to say, the Court is entitled to refuse to grant them if, in the circumstances, it is of opinion that the "common law" remedy by way of damages is adequate or more appropriate. Discussion of the defences open to a claim for Specific Performance would not be in place here, the reader may refer to any good text book on Equity [1]).

The subject of damages is singularly ill regulated by Ottoman law. There are some provisions in the Code of Civil Procedure (Arts 106—112) which differ very much from the principles of English law in the matter. In practice the parties often agree a sum to be inserted in the contract which is to be paid if the contract is not fulfilled and, according to Art. 111 of the Civil Procedure Code, when this is done, no other sum is to be awarded as damages. In practice the Courts in Palestine not infrequently adopt English principles in assessing damages where the parties have not agreed a sum. This they are fully entitled, or even bound to do. Art. 46 of the Palestine Order-in-Council 1922 directs them to apply the substance of the Common Law of England and the doctrines of English Equity so far as local circumstances make necessary where the Ottoman Law is silent.

This provision of the Order-in-Council has not, however, induced the Courts in Palestine to adopt equitable doctrines to the extent of granting the remedy of Specific Performance [2]). They could no doubt do so, but presumably consider it undesirable.

Gift. The law of gift (Hibe) is discussed in Book VII of the Mejelle. A gift becomes a concluded contract by offer and acceptance (Art. 837), but is completed by delivery (Art. 839). The donee becomes owner by receipt and until receipt the gift is revocable (Arts. 861, 862). Revocation is possible even after receipt, but if the donee does not consent application must be made to the judge (Art. 864). Some kinds of gifts may not be revoked e. g. gifts to relatives (Art. 806) or matrimonial gifts (Art. 867). Nor may a gift be revoked if something has been given in return (Art. 868). This latter pro-

---

[1]) Such as Strahan, "Digest of Equity", or Snell "Principles of Equity".
[2]) Compare Litvinsky v. Lippman. Case 88/25. The Court of Appeal held that there was no law whereby Specific Performance of an agreement for sale of land could be enforced in Palestine. If the vendor failed to register at the agreed date, the purchaser could not compel him to do so. The remedy was in damages.

Chapter IX—Sale, Exchange and Gift.

vision seems to indicate a confusion between gift and sale. In sale property is given in return for property (Art. 105) but, apparently, if only a promise is given in return the transaction should be deemed a gift (Art. 855). Nevertheless, the unsystematic character of the law seems evident. If a person gives land on a condition that he shall receive maintenance for life the transaction is a gift and failure to perform the condition renders the gift revocable. Such a transaction would seem to be more logically treated as a sale for a life rent of undeterminate amount [1]).

The right to revoke is purely personal. It is barred by alienation of the thing given (Art. 870) or by death of either party (Art. 872). There is special provision as to gifts made in mortal sickness (Arts. 877 ff) in connection with which similar rules apply to those laid down in the case of sales in mortal sickness (Arts. 393 ff) and the consent of the heirs is requisite (Art. 879) if such exist (Art. 177) [2]).

These general remarks and their indications as to the rules of the pure Moslem law of Sale and Gift must here suffice. For further details reference may be made to works on Moslem Law of which there are many excellent ones in English, French and German. Our particular concern is with the official Ottoman law of land and its Palestinian modifications.

The land outside the towns in Palestine is usually either Mewat, Metruki or Miri. As regards the first two of these classes no question of disposition arises. It is only gradually that the interest of a Miri holder has become alienable. Originally, in law, if not in practice, the Miri holder was regarded as having only a personal interest in the land which was neither alienable nor heritable. It is very probable that, like the English copyholder [3]), the holder of Miri enjoyed by custom greater rights than the general law allowed and that the very limited nature of his interest was due to the oppressive and arbitrary power of the feudal lords in earlier days. However this may be, we are only concerned with the law as stated in the texts. The Ottoman Land Code conferred

Transfer of Miri (Feragh).

---

[1]) As to Gifts in Moslem law, and particularly as to the indeterminate character of the return, see Vesey FitzGerald, Muhammedan Law. Chap. XXV.

[2]) As to mortal sickness, see Vesey FitzGerald, op. cit., Chap. XXI and the Egyptian cases Gaz. Trib. Mixt. XXI Nos. 152, 153. See further Goadby in Jour. Comp. Leg. XIV, Pt. IV, pp. 231-2.

[3]) At Common Law the holder by Copy of Court Roll (copyholder) was at first regarded as a mere tenant by will of the lord of the Manor in which the land lay and was not protected by the Royal Courts.

The Land Law of Palestine.

upon Miri holders a legal right of disposition inter vivos but dispositions could only be made with the leave of the Land Registry (Daftar Khani) given in pursuance of a special formality known as the Takhrir; this was a declaration made before the official by both parties to the transaction (Land Code Art. 36)[1]. Of course, any disposition of a Miri interest by the holder is necessarily limited to the tessaruf of the land; it could not affect the Raqabe, and the right transferred was only the limited right of the holder. In effect the transfer for a determinate return was a sale, but the Ottoman lawyers declined to regard such a transfer as a sale properly so called, because a sale is a transfer of property (Mulk) and the transfer of Miri was only a transfer of a right of enjoyment. Transfers of Miri were, therefore, designated Feragh (transfer) as contrasted with sale (Bey) and Gift (Hibe) which latter terms were consecrated to Mulk. The interest of the Miri possessor was regarded as in the nature of that of a lessee only and this fact gave rise to certain legal consequences in regard to transfers to which it does not now appear necessary to advert[2]).

The peculiarities attaching to the form of transfer of Miri, as also of Mussaqafat and Mustaghilat Waqf, are now, however, swept away and, in form at least, a complete assimilation has taken place between transfers of lands of all categories. But none of the provisions of the Land Code have been expressly repealed; they, therefore, remain in force so far as they can be reconciled with the new law.

The Law of Disposition A.H. 1331. The provisional Law of Disposition, A.H. 1331, required (Art. 1) that every kind of disposition of Miri and Mevqufe (Miri Waqf) land should be made in the Tapu Registry and a formal title deed delivered for every disposition. This provision is made applicable to Mulk land and to Mustaghilat and Mussaqafat land of Waqf Mazbuta and Waqf Mulhaqa and Waqf Mustesna. Art. 2 provides that in all dealings with regard to Mussaqafat and Mustaghilat Waqf if the Mutwally is not present the Mudir or Mamur or Clerk of the Tapu Registry shall act for him. This latter provision supersedes the formal consent of the Mutwally to dispositions of Waqf. Art. 5 recognizes the right of every holder of Miri or Mevqufe to transfer, mortgage, or lease his land without requiring the consent of the "Official", and thus in effect supersedes Art. 36 of the Land Code, and all other provisions making requisite the consent of the "Official" to transfers and mortgages.

---
[1]) See also Land Code Arts. 27—40.
[2]) See more fully Chaoui, op. cit., pp. 152 ff.

Chapter IX—Sale, Exchange and Gift.

And since under the Law of A.H. 1331 vines and trees, plants and buildings on Miri and Miri Waqf land follow the land by mere association and remain Miri, the provisions of Art. 49 of the Land Code are of no effect at least, where the plantations and constructions were made since the Law and are consequently themselves Miri.

This was the situation at the time of the British Occupation. When dealings in land were once more permitted upon the lapse of the period of prohibition, new provisions were enacted by the Transfer of Land Ordinance, 1920. All dispositions of land must now comply with the provisions of this Ordinance as amended by Ordinances of 1921 and 1929. For this purpose "dispositions" means a sale, mortgage, gift, dedication of Waqf of every description, and any other disposition of immovable property except a devise by will or a lease for a term not exceeding 3 years; and "land" includes houses, buildings, and things permanently fixed on the land (Sec. 2). The Ordinances apply to all immovable property subject to the Land Code as well as to Mulk land, all forms of Waqf land, and every other form of immovable property (Sec. I). Though immovable property is not defined it clearly includes "land" and this word is in Sec. 2 stated to include "houses, buildings and other things permanently fixed in the land". It is safe, therefore, to conclude that constructions, trees and plantations which are owned separately from the land on which they are built or in which they are growing are nevertheless to be deemed "immovable property" for the purposes of the Land Transfer Ordinances [1]). *The Transfer of Land Ordinance 1920.*

The principle effect of the Ordinance is to invalidate every disposition of immovable property not made with the consent of the Director of the Land Registries and in accordance with its provisions, but normally such consent is to be accorded if the transferor appears to have a title though no guarantee of title is implied by the consent (Secs. 4 and 9 of the Land Transfer Ordinance) [2]).

In view of these provisions it appears, that transfers of Miri interests are now in Palestine assimilated to those of Mulk, subject,

---

[1]) By Sec. 7 of the Interpretation Ordinance 1929, "immovable property" or "land" is defined to include everything attached to the earth or permanently fastened to anything which is attached to the earth.

[2]) Under Sec. 4 of the Land Transfer Ordinance 1920, as amended by the Transfer of Land Amendment Ordinance No. 2, 1921, the petition for consent is to be presented to the Director of the Land Registries through the Land Registry Office of the District in which the land is situate.

The Land Law of Palestine.

of course, to the continued application of special provisions, which do not conflict with the unrestricted right of transfer now accorded. Transfers of Miri which took place before dates specified in the Proclamations of 18th November, 1918, are valid, but prior to A.H. 1331 the leave of the Official was necessary. If the transfer was made since the law of Disposition, A.H. 1331, this consent was not, however, requisite.

The effect of a contract to sell Miri has been much discussed. It was contended that under the pure Ottoman law a promise to transfer was merely void and of no effect, since it could not operate as a Feragh and no other facility for alienation of Miri was given by the law. This view has, it seems, been more recently definitely disapproved by the Syrian Courts which recognize the binding character of the agreement though, of course, the only remedy for breach is an action for damages [1]). The position in Palestine is governed by the provisions of the Land Transfer Ordinances but there seems no reason why an agreement to sell should not be deemed good as a contract, though specific performance will not be decreed. Thus in a case before the Court of Appeal [2]) it was held that a claim for damages was maintainable upon breach of a contract for the sale of land containing a promise to effect registration. That the contract could not operate as a disposition of the ownership of the land was admitted, but it was held that the provisions of Sec. 11 of the Ordinance of 1920 could not be interpreted as annulling the obligations arising out of an agreement to sell. It was further held that the measure of damages was the difference between the agreed price and the estimated market price at the time when the contract was repudiated [3]).

It is, however, important to note that if the agreement is designed not merely to give rise to a promise to convey but to operate as a transfer of the land it will be wholly invalid since in that case it constitutes a "disposition" of land within the meaning of the Land Transfer Ordinances and consequently requires the consent of the Government in order to be valid [4]).

---

[1]) Chaoui, op. cit., pp. 157, 158 quoting decision of Cour de Cassation, Damascus, 7 April 1926.

[2]) Zeide v. Alealy, Off. Gaz. 1st Febr. 1927.

[3]) In Cyprus such an agreement could be enforced specifically under the Sale of Lands Law, 1885, subject to conditions therein laid down.

[4]) Compare Abu-Ja'afar v. Mustapha No. 130/32, reported in Palestine Post March 1933 following Abu Ja'afar v. Mustapha Bitar, (C. A. 95/31). Compare Harris v. Duchner C. A. 82/33 reported in Palestine Post 4 April 1934.

Chapter IX—Sale, Exchange and Gift. 141

Money paid in respect of such a void disposition is, however, recoverable as is expressly provided by the section itself (Sec. 11).

In a case before the Court of Appeal in 1933 [1]) the appellant had agreed with the Respondent to plant the land with trees, and in consideration for this the appellant was to "be owner of half the land planted at the end of eight years". The Court was of opinion that this constituted a disposition of property within the Land Transfer Ordinances and consequently void since the written consent of the Government had not been obtained.

A transfer of Miri upon which there are growing Mulk trees the property of the vendor will be deemed to include the trees, even though not specifically mentioned unless the ownership of the trees is registered separately from the land [2]). It is not, however, precisely stated whether the trees may not be expressly excluded from the sale. It seems that they may be so. Trees growing naturally on the land follow the land in every case. Such trees are not Mulk even though their growth commenced before the Law of Disposition. Neither Art. 48 of the Land Code nor the Land Law (Amendment) Ordinance mention Mulk buildings on Miri, though in other Articles relating to the subject both trees and buildings are mentioned (Cf. Land Code, Arts. 44, 49). The ommission is probably due to oversight only and it may be assumed that as in the case of trees a disposition of Miri will include Mulk buildings thereon unless, at least, they are expressly excluded, or registered separately from the land. It is expressly stated (Art. 49) that the Miri land will be accessory to Mulk buildings so that the transfer of the buildings involves a transfer of the land. Where, as is always the case as regards buildings erected since the law of A. H. 1331, land and buildings are like Miri, there can be no doubt that the general principles of law laid down in Arts. 231 ff. of the Mejelle will be applicable.

<small>Trees and Buildings.</small>

In general it will be correct to say that the general principles of the law may be applied to dispositions of Miri and Miri Waqf as well as to Mulk, save where these conflict with any special provision of the Land Code or other legislative act. In this connection attention must be drawn to certain special provisions of this nature. Now that for purposes of actual enjoyment so little difference exists between Mulk and Miri, differences in the law

---

[1]) Muhd. Takrouri v. Abdul Rahim Murib (C. A. 90/33), Palestine Post 17 Oct. 1933.
[2]) Land Law (Amendment) Ordinance, 1933, modifying Land Code, Art. 48.

relating to each are less justifiable or convenient. However, note should be made of any case in which such differences still appear to be maintained.

It was provided by Art. 43 of the Land Code, that if by error of the Official a third person had been permitted to dispose of land or of a share therein without the consent of the holder, the latter could recover his holding through the official. Such a provision was, perhaps, necessary lest it should be supposed that the leave of the official given under Art. 36 would suffice to give a good title. Under the present system in Palestine it is clear that the consent of the Director of Lands to a transfer is not an affirmation of title. Sec. 9 of the Transfer of Land Ordinance, 1920, is explicit upon the point. Though a gift is irrevocable a sale can be revoked till the price is paid even though the actual transfer has been carried through (Art. 38, Land Code).

Certain specific provisions of the Land Code as to alienation by infants, lunatics and their guardians will be referred to in a later chapter when the subject of Incapacity is taken up.

Gratuitous transfers of Miri. Arts. 38 and 39, Land Code, contain special provisions as to gratuitous transfers of Miri. Such a transfer once completed with the authorization of the Official appears to be irrevocable. These appear to include the application of the provisions of the Mejelle permitting revocation in certain eventualities — but it is doubtful whether such an interpretation should be adopted. However, the intention to make exceptional provision is supported by the analogy

Alienation in Mortal Sickness. of Art. 120 which provides, that the alienation of Miri and Mevqufe effected in mortal sickness are valid and prevail over the claims of the heirs or of persons, who have a right to Tapu. Comparison may be made with the provisions of Mejelle, Arts. 393, 877 ff., 1596 which, however, are by no means identical in effect. To be effective under Art. 120 the transfer must be complete in form. If otherwise effective it would (semble) not only be available against heirs and persons having a right to Tapu, but would prevent the land becoming pure Mahlul.

Conditional Transfer. Art. 114 as amended by 18 Saefer, A.H. 1306, permits transfers of Miri on a condition such as that suggested in Mejelle Art. 855, namely that the transferee should provide for the transferor during his life. The liability to make provision runs with the land and if the heirs of the transferee fail to carry it out the land reverts to the transferor. The transfer of land subject to such a condition makes the land inalienable during the life of the transferor, but the condition must be recorded in the title deed.

Chapter IX—Sale, Exchange and Gift. 143

The special provisions of Arts. 113 and 119 of the Land Code as to Duress and Fraud call for note. In general no doubt such principles as are expressed or implied in the Mejelle govern agreements for sale, etc. of Miri as well as of Mulk as regards mistake, fraud, etc. According to Art. 113 of the Land Code a tansfer of Miri or Mevqufe land brought about through duress, exercised by one who is in a position to give effect to his threats, is void. If a person who through such duress has become possessed of land transfers it to another, or if at his death it has devolved by inheritance on his heirs as hereinbefore designated, or if on his death without leaving heirs it becomes Mahlul, the transferor, the victim of the duress, or his heirs after his death can bring an action based on the duress. But if he dies without leaving heirs the land shall not be treated as Mahlul, and it remains in the hands of the actual possessor [1]).

<small>Duress Fraud.</small>

Remark that under Art. 113 the State to which Miri would have escheated for failure of heirs of a transferee cannot exercise the right of recission on the ground of duress as against the transferor. Presumably the holders of a Right of Tapu over the land can exercise this right though this is not expressly stated.

Art. 119 states that "Actions for deceit (tagrir) or excessive deception (gabr-i-fahish) between a transferor and a transferee in connection with State and Mevqufe land in general shall be maintainable. After the death of the transferor, the heirs having right of succession shall not have the right, to institute an action and the land cannot be treated as Mahlul".

The provisions of Art. 24 of the Tapu Law, A.H. 1275, with reference to the hearing of actions for deceit under Art. 119 are now superseded by Art. 38 of the Palestine Order-in-Council, 1922, whereby general jurisdiction is given to the Civil Courts.

Transfers of Miri may be set aside by the operation of rights of preference (Rudjhan) under Land Code, Arts. 43, 44, 45. These provisions will be considered in a subsequent chapter.

Art. 47 Land Code lays down the rules applicable in the case of a sale of land by dunums as also in the case of a sale by boundaries. Cf. Mejelle Arts. 224-226 [2]).

To what extent some of these provisions are now to be applied to Miri, may perhaps be doubted. But there seems no good reason for regarding them as in any way affected by the Land

---

[1]) Chiha, op. cit., p. 250.
[2]) Compare L. A. 15/28 referring to Art. 47 Land Code. See p. 56, surd.

The Land Law of Palestine.

Transfer Ordinances, which in effect merely change the form of the disposition.

Unregistered Transfers. It is clear that no person can become owner of registrable Mulk or holder of Miri by an unregistered transfer. The rule is clearly stated by the Cyprus Court in Stavrino v. Queen's Advocate [1]).

"To complete a sale of land the law requires registration. If it were possible for a vendor to confer a benefit on a purchaser which the law says can only be conferred by registration, then the law becomes a dead letter. As to Arazi Miri we have never had any doubt and on looking into the law as regards Mulk, we find in a law of Rejeb, A.H. 1291 (The Law as to Mulk Title Deeds) that it is forbidden for a person to hold Mulk without kushans and Art. 2 lays down special formalities to be followed for the sale of Mulk property. The law, therefore, appears to be as clear about the sale of Mulk as about Miri."

In Palestine where the Law of Disposition, A.H. 1331, is applicable, the law already clear, is abundantly confirmed by Art. 1 thereof [2]).

Again and again, specific mention of the formal title deed as the only proof of ownership occurs. The provisions of the Transfer of Land Ordinance, 1920, are even more explicit. Not only is every "disposition" of "immovable" property null and void, unless the consent of the administration has been obtained (Sec. 11) but penalties are pronounced against a transferor, who lets into possesion a transferee under such an invalid disposition, as also against the transferee who enters (Sec. 12).

The position of an unregistered transferee under the older law has been frequently considered in Cyprus where, of course, the Ottoman Laws prior to 1878 are alone applicable. The decisions form a body of law of great interest, but it is only necessary here

---

[1]) (1888) I C.L.R. 46. As above mentioned the Courts of Constantinople treated sales of Mulk outside the Registry as valid inter partes.

[2]) In spite of the Ottoman Law as to registration a considerable part of the land of Palestine remained unregistered and was habitually dealt with by unregistered deeds. It was held that under such circumstances it would be inequitable to refuse to recognize the validity of a sale of land by unregistered deed, merely for lack of registration; and a number of judgments has been given upholding the validity of the unregistered sale and declaring that as against the vendor, the purchaser is entitled to registration. That principle, however, can only be applied to a case in which the sale took place before the Occupation as the Proclamation of the 18th of November, 1918, rendered all dispositions of immovable property made after the Occupation invalid. (This was held by the Court in Litvinsky v. Lippman & others in L. A. 88/25).

Chapter IX—Sale, Exchange and Gift.

to refer to the main principles which have been adopted. It is fully admitted that an unregistered transfer conveys no legal interest in the property to the quasi-transferee. As a contract, the sale is valid and an action for damages can be brought if the transferor fails to complete, e. g. by attending the Land Registry for the purpose of perfecting the transfer, but only where registration of the sale was contemplated [1].

What usually happens, however, is that there is no contract of sale properly so called, but merely a payment of money against receipt, upon which the quasi-transferee enters into possession. No registration is attempted or intended. The Cyprus Courts in dealing with these cases have laid down that where a purchaser pays the purchase money without demanding registration in his name, so that it is clear that no registration was intended, he acquires only the right to be protected against the vendor, until the latter repays the purchase money. He has no right either to demand registration or the return of the purchase money [2].

If the property remaining registered in the name of the vendor, is sold for payment of his debts, the purchaser under the unregistered transfer has no redress since in a sale of immovable property unaccompanied by registration there is no implied covenant for quiet enjoyment on the part of the vendor [3].

Nor will the Court give damages for breach of an agreement to sell where the facts show that neither party intended to register, though the vendor will not be allowed to recover possession and at the same time retain the purchase money [4].

An order for possession would only be made on the terms that the vendor refunded to the purchaser the amount of the purchase money, in accordance with the English principle that he who demands an equitable remedy, must do equity [5].

A covenant purporting to bind the heirs of the transferor in an unregistered transfer by imposing a penalty is void as against public policy [6].

Where, in Palestine, a transferee has been let into possession under an unauthorised transfer since the Transfer of Land Ordi-

---

[1] Chacalli v. Kallourena (1895) 3 C. L. R. at p. 246.
[2] Topal Ahmet v. Agha (1886) I C. L. R. at p. 31.
[3] Zenobio v. Osman (1893) 2 C. L. R. at p. 168. Cf. Stavrino v. Queen's Advocate, ubi supra.
[4] Gavrilidi v. Georghi (1895) 3 C. L. R. at p. 140.
[5] Pascali v. Toghli (1907) 7 C. L. R. at p. 76.
[6] Petri v. Petri (1893) 2 C. L. R. at p. 187.

nance, 1920, the transferee is entitled to recover his purchase money from the transferor (Sec. 11). A transferor seeking possession against an unregistered transferee would usually have to assert his own wrong doing as a ground of the action, and it is doubtful, whether the Court would grant an order for possession except upon the terms that the transferor repaid the purchase money. The situation appears to be identical with that raised by a void disposition under Sec. 11. And it may be noted that, in a case already noted [1]) the Court of Appeal held that the term "money paid" used in Sec. 11 must be deemed to include "money spent on the land of another" if the spending of such money formed the consideration for the void disposition.

---

[1]) Muhd. Takrouri v. Abdul Rahim Murib. C. A. 90/33, Palestine Post, 17 Oct. 1933.

CHAPTER X—PRE-EMPTION AND PREFERENCE.

"Pre-emption", says Kadry Pasha, "is the right of having transferred to oneself, even by compulsion, the whole or part of an immovable which has been sold upon payment of the price and expences"[1]).

Pre-emption. Shufa.

This right is called "Shufa". The terms are thus defined by the Mejelle.

Art. 950. "Shufa" is the acquisition of possession of mulk property sold, for the amount which the property cost the purchaser.

Art. 951. "Shefi" is a person who has a right of Shufa.

Art. 952. Meshfu'bih is the Mulk property of the person who has the right of Shufa by which there is the right of Shufa.

This right of pre-emption is fully regulated by the Mejelle, Arts. 1008 ff. It applies only to Mulk. Nevertheless, a more limited right analogous to the right of pre-emption is granted in the case of Miri by Arts. 41-44 of the Land Code. This will be explained later. Our present concern is with pre-emption proper. The articles of the Mejelle follow the law as laid down in the Hedaya, Vol. III, Book XXXVIII.

The right of pre-emption cannot be exercised upon lands belonging to the State but granted out for exploitation, i.e. over Miri land. But if there is a sale of the land by the State the right of pre-emption becomes exerciseable, i.e. if the Raqabe be sold[2]).

Pre-emption cannot be exercised either by or in favour of Waqf property[3]) nor upon a partition of property[4]). A voidable sale does not give rise to a right of pre-emption until the right to avoid has been lost, and if a sale is conditional only, the right is not exerciseable so long as the condition remains operative[5]).

There are, says Art. 1008, three grounds for Pre-emption:

---

[1]) Statut Réel Mussulman, Art. 95.
[2]) Mejelle, Art. 1017; Kadry Pasha, op. cit., Arts. 111, 112.
[3]) Mejelle, Art. 1017; Kadry Pasna, op. cit., Art. 113.
[4]) Mejelle, Art. 1027; Kadry Pasha, op. cit., Art. 114.
[5]) Mejelle, Art. 1026; Kadry Pasha, op. cit., Arts. 106, 115, 116. Cf. Nicolaides v. Ierodiaconos (1892) 2 C.L.R. at p. 93 and see further, infra.

1) Where a person is the joint owner of the property sold.

2) Where a person is part owner of a servitude in the thing sold. As where a person shares in a private right of taking water (Shurb Khas) or in a private road (Tariq Khas)

3) Where a person is adjoining neighbour to the thing sold.

Kadry Pasha treates the first two of these cases under one head as both examples of co-ownership but they are usually distinguished [1]. In any case co-ownership only exists when the shares of each co-owner are not distinct; the property must be held in true co-ownership [2]. It is immaterial of how small an undivided share the pre-emptor is owner [3]. And if a person is joint owner of the wall of a house, he is deemed to be joint owner of the house [4] but if the beams of his house rest upon his neighbours wall he is not deemed a joint owner [5].

The most frequent ground for the exercise of the right of pre-emption is that of contiguous neighbourhood. To give rise to the right the properties must actually touch [6].

Owners sometimes seek to avoid the application of the law of Shufa by leaving a strip of land unsold between the parcel sold and the neighbouring property. Subsequently this strip is transferred by gift to the purchaser. The Courts, however, are inclined, to treat such a device as ineffective when its fictitious nature is clear.

Since, in principle, ownership of movables does not give rise to any right of pre-emption [7] the separate ownership of constructions and plantations does not give rise to such a right, though when land is sold together with the trees and buildings the trees and buildings are also subject to the right. If, however, the trees and buildings are sold separately no right of pre-emption can be claimed [8].

In the case of Shukairi v. el-Moghrabi an attempt was made, to induce the Court to apply the rules of Shufa to Miri, subject to Mulk trees and buildings, on the ground that being subject to the Mulk, it should be treated as Mulk. This proposition was

---

[1] Kadry Pasha, op. cit., Art. 97.
[2] Ibid., Art. 98.
[3] Ibid.,
[4] Mejelle, Art. 1012. Kadry Pasha, Art. 98.
[5] Mejelle, Art. 1012. The owner of the beams may, nevertheless, claim pre-emption as adjoining owner (Nicholaides v. Ierodiaconos, (1892) 2 C.L.R. at p. 93).
[6] Kadry Pasha, op. cit., Art. 100.
[7] Mejelle, Art. 1017.
[8] Mejelle, Arts. 1019, 1020. Kadry Pasha, op. cit., Art. 109. Cf. L. A. 94/25 in Re Shukairi v. Nour.

Chapter X—Pre-emption and Preference.

obviously unsound and was rejected by the Court of Appeal [1]). Mejelle, Art. 1011, recognises, however, one exception to the rule that Pre-emption has no application in respect of buildings since a right of pre-emption is allowed as between the owners of the upper and lower stories of a house.

And the right of pre-emption is, in this case, exerciseable even if the stories are not adjacent. Neighbourhood is in the case of parts of the same building "established by the law" [2]). And as has been mentioned the owner of a beam which rests upon the house of another is regarded as the owner of contiguous property.

The cases of co-ownership, which must often give rise to questions are those connected with the ownership of a servitude, as to which the Mejelle contains several specific provisions. The nature of Servitudes will be considered in a later chapter.

The right of pre-emption excerciseable among joint owners of a servitude is exerciseable only between the joint owners of the servitude and over the property in right of which the servitude is enjoyed. Thus if a private right of taking water is enjoyed by the owners of a number of gardens and one of the gardens is sold, the owners of the other gardens have each a right of pre-emption over the garden thus sold, whether the gardens adjoin or not [3]). The object appears to be, to prevent the intrusion of a new claimant to the right into the group of persons enjoying that right.

"When several gardens share in a right of Shurb Khas and one of them is sold, all the owners of the other gardens become entitled to buy the garden sold at the price for which it was sold, whether they are adjoining neighbours or not" [4]).

"Likewise, when a house is sold, whose door opens on a blind alley, the whole of the owners of the other houses having their doors on that blind alley have together the right to purchase the house sold, for the price at which it was sold, whether they are adjoining neighbours or whether they are not" [5]).

The authorities distinguish between the right of a co-owner in the servitude and the right of a co-owner in the land (or water) subject to the servitude.

---

[1]) Off. Gaz. 16th July, 1926. Cf. Kadry Pasha, Art. 110.
[2]) Kadry Pasha, op. cit., Art. 100.
[3]) Mejelle, Art. 1009.
[4]) Mejelle, Art. 1008. Cf. Art. 1239. As to the case, in which an owner possessing a right of Shurb Khas sells the dominant property without the right, see Mejelle, Art. 1015.
[5]) Cf. Kadry Pasha, op. cit., Art. 99.

"A partner in the road (i. e. in the right of way over the road) or the rivulet, cannot be entitled to Shufa during the existence of one who is partner in the property of the land; for his is the superior right"[1]). Though the point is not expressly dealt with in the authorities available, the inference from their language seems to be that the owner of the servient property is not to be regarded as one of the co-owners of the servitude. Consequently there is no right of pre-emption under this head over the servient property itself, nor is the owner of the servient property entitled to a right of pre-emption over any of the dominant properties.

No right of pre-emption exists in respect of common use of a public right. Thus the Mejelle states (Art. 1008):—

"But when a house is sold, which is one of those houses which take water from a river which is for the public benefit, or whose door opens on a public road, there is no right of pre-emption for the owners of the other houses, which take water from that river, or the doors of which are on that public road".

"By a private road", we are told, "is understood a road shut at one end; and by a private rivulet we understand a stream of water in which boats cannot pass and repass", or, according to Abou Yusuf, "a stream which affords water to two or three pieces of ground only"[2]).

Order in which Pre-emption is exerciseable. Mejelle, Art. 1013, lays down the principle that as between all persons of the same rank, the right of all is equal and no regard is paid to the extent of their several properties. But a certain preference is given where there are several "joint" Servitudes. (Mejelle, Art. 1016).

Art. 1009 states the order in which pre-emption can be exercised as between persons claiming on different grounds. The co-owner has the first option. Failing him, the Khalit (joint owner of the Servitude) has the next right and the adjacent owner comes last. Art. 1014 states that "Where two classes of persons

---

[1]) Hedaya, Vol. III, Book XXXVIII, Chap. I at p. 548. (References to Hamilton's Translation 2nd Edition).

As to the order in which rights of pre-emption are exerciseable, see further, infra.

[2]) Hedaya, p. 549. It is the opinion of Abou Yusuf which appears to have prevailed in the Mejelle. Art. 1239 clearly states that no right of pre-emption applies save in the case of private streams which do not flow into vacant land but are exhausted by the joint owners. Indeed, the language of the Mejelle seems to warrant the conclusion that the joint servitudes, to which alone right of pre-emption attaches are really cases of joint ownership of artificial channels or private roads. See further Chapter XIV.

Chapter X—Pre-emption and Preference. 151

having joint shares in a servitude come together the less general right takes precedence over the more general". The examples given illustrate this somewhat cryptic rule.

If there are two persons each having a right of pre-emption and one is absent the person present can exercise his right and will have the property allotted to him. Nevertheless, the absent person may upon his return also exercise his right and half the property will then be allotted to him if he is of the same rank, or the whole if he is of a superior rank to that occupied by the pre-emptor who has already pre-empted [1]).

A claim to exercise a right of pre-emption must, however, be made promptly where no legal excuse such as absence is available. If a possible claimant of a higher rank has failed to make prompt claim or has expressly or tacitly renounced, the claim made by those of the lower rank becomes effective. But renunciation after the property pre-empted has been allotted by the Court does not make effective the claim of any other possible pre-emptor [2]).

A right of pre-emption arises only upon a sale of the property, over which it is to be exercised. (Mejelle, Art. 1021). But a gift with a condition for a gift in return is for this purpose a sale (Art. 1022). For gifts of this kind see Mejelle, Art. 855. A right of pre-emption does not arise by inheritance (Art. 1023) nor when immovables are given by way of dowry (Art. 1025) [3]). The pre-emptor must not have assented to the sale expressly or impliedly (Art. 1024) [4]). *Circumstances giving rise to Pre-emption.*

According to Art. 1026 the vendor must have divested himself of the ownership in the thing sold before the right of pre-emption becomes exerciseable. The provision has been the subject of several Cypriot decisions. It has been held that, until registration, the purchaser could not be regarded as the owner of the property and that consequently proceedings taken before registration were of no avail to establish the purchaser's right of pre-emption [5]). In Palestine and under the Land Transfer Ordinance a disposition of immovables is null and void until the consent of the Government

---

[1]) Kadry Pasha, op. cit., Art. 124.
[2]) Mejelle, Art. 1043; Kadry Pasha, op. cit., Art. 137.
[3]) Even though the forms of a sale have been gone through, evidence may be given that the transaction was not a sale. Demetreades v. Liverdou (1912) 10 C. L. R. at p. 49.
[4]) Compare Musleh v. Yehia L. A. 44/32. Palestine Post 3 May 1933.
[5]) Christofides v. Totaridi (1885) I C. L. R. at p. 21. Compare Constantinides v. Theodosi, 4 C. L. R. at p.59.

has been obtained and proceedings for pre-emption should not, therefore, be taken until such consent has been obtained. Proceedings taken earlier would be inoperative, unless (as is possible) the Courts took the view that the consent when given, are operative retrospectively to validate the disposition as from the date at which it was actually made.

Art. 1026 deals also with the case of a sale subject to an option [1]. A vendor's option is a bar to pre-emption so long as it exists, but the legal options for defect or inspection are no bar [2]. A right of pre-emption is indivisible and not assignable [3]. As we shall see, the pre-emptor does not become owner of the property pre-empted merely by making a claim, the property must have been surrendered to him by the Court. If, therefore, before property has passed he sells the land to which the right is attached, the right disappears [4]. So also, if he died, his right of pre-emption would not pass to the heirs [5].

Exercise of the right of Pre-emption.

The exercise of a right of pre-emption requires -

a) An immediate assertion of the right [6].

b) Assuming that the person entitled to pre-empt has forthwith asserted his right, he must next proceed to make a formal declaration before witnesses.

c) Finally after declaring his right and making a formal declaration before witnesses, the pre-emptor must claim his right by action in the Court. According to the Mejelle one month only is allowed for the commencement of the action, running from the date at which the witnesses were called, but the period may be lengthened if there were lawful hindrances to action [7].

From the language of the Mejelle, and also of the Hedaya upon which the articles of the Mejelle are obviously based, it is

---

[1] See also Constantinides v. Theodosi 4 C. L. R. at p. 59 and Nicholaides v. Ierodiaconos (1892) 2 C. L. R. at p. 93.

[2] Mejelle, Art. 1037.

[3] Mejelle, Art. 1042; Kadry Pasha, op. cit., Art. 135. But if a house be sold by a sole owner to several persons in separate parts, a pre-emptor can pre-empt as to one part only. Ibid.

[4] Mejelle, Art. 1039.

[5] Mejelle, Art. 1038. (Hooper's Translation). The translation of Dr. Grigsby is defective.

[6] In the case of Halevi v. Halperin (Land Case 47/33) the District Court of Jaffa held that a delay in claiming Pre-emption for three weeks was a fatal delay. Palestine Post 13 Nov. 1933.

[7] Mejelle, Arts. 1029-34. For a form of judgment in Pre-emption see Nicholaides v. Ierodiaconos, 2 C. L. R. at p. 97.

Chapter X—Pre-emption and Preference.

clear that these forms of claims are not different and independent forms, but are all essential to the validity of the claim. The right of Shufa, say the Moslem Jurists, is a feeble right and the disfavour with it is shown by the stringent conditions for its exercise. So also under Art. 1035 it appears that if the right is not claimed by the guardian of a minor entitled, it is lost[1]).

As already noted a claim made before ownership has passed to the purchaser is of no avail. According to a decision of the Cypriot Courts[2]) the pre-emptor does not lose his right by not making a first claim so soon as he hears report of the sale unless (a) he in fact believes the report; or (b) receives it from a person entitled to credence. This decision was given after careful consideration of the Moslem authorities and purports to follow them. The Hedaya fully bears out the view adopted in the case. Indeed, according to Abou Hanifa the first claim need not be made unless the news of the sale has been communicated by two men or by one man and two women or by one upright man. If, however, the buyer communicate it, the condition of uprightness is not to be insisted upon[3]).

The Cypriot Courts allow a reasonable delay for the second claim[4]). Fourteen days is not a reasonable delay[5]). If the first claim has been made before witnesses the necessity for a second claim is obviated[6]).

Under Mejelle, Art. 1030, the second claim must be made in the vicinity of the property pre-empted or by the side of the purchaser or vendor, whichever is still in possession[7]). If the pre-emptor is in a distant place he may make the claim through an agent or he may send a letter if he cannot find an agent[8]). In Joannes v. Stavrinou[9]) a claim made four years after date by a pre-emptor, who had been absent in Morocco at the time of the sale was held bad. The Cypriot Court indicated that the law relating to pre-emption must be construed strictly and that persons volun-

---

[1]) If, however, the minor had no guardian a claim can be made on his reaching majority (Kadry Pasha, op. cit., Art. 121).
[2]) Jassonides v. Kyprioti (1907) 7 C. L. R. at p. 80.
[3]) Hedaya, at p. 551.
[4]) Nicolaides v. Ierodiaconos (1892) 2 C. L. R. 93.
[5]) Houry v. Sabba (footnote to p. 84 of 7 C. L. R.)
[6]) Kadry Pasha, op. cit., Art. 119.
[7]) Yosif v. Nami (1905) 7 C. L. R. 28.
[8]) Mejelle, Art. 1030. It is clear that a claim made by letter does not comply with the strict requirements as to the second claim.
[9]) (1922) 11. C. L. R. at p. 56.

tarily absent from Cyprus should leave a representative to look after their interests.

The second claim must be made in such a way that the witnesses must know that the first claim has been made and that they are witnesses to the second claim [1]). The form proper to a second claim is given in Art. 1030 of the Mejelle which may be compared with that given in the Hedaya.

The period during which the action is to be brought, is prolonged in case of absence in a foreign country [2]). It will be brought against the vendor and purchaser jointly unless the property to be pre-empted has already been delivered to the purchaser in which case it is exercised against him alone [3]).

If the claims are not duly made the right of pre-emption is extinguished. It is not, however, extinguished by the purchaser's death [4]), but it is extinguished by action on the part of the would-be pre-emptor which indicates renunciation; such as purchase by him of the property sought to be pre-empted or hiring thereof, or even an offer to buy or to hire [5]). The right is, however, not lost if the pre-emptor's renunciation was based on mistake as to the price for which the land had been sold or the indentity of the purchaser [6]).

Ownership in the property pre-empted only passes to the pre-emptor upon voluntary delivery by the purchaser or upon the order of the judge [7]). The pre-emptor is, therefore, regarded as a new purchaser and has the options of defect and inspection [8]). Indeed, for many purposes the pre-emptor is regarded as having acquired the property direct from the original vendor. Thus acts done by the "purchaser" with reference to the property pre-empted are void as against the pre-emptor, e.g. if the purchaser had constituted the property as a Waqf [9].

---

[1]) Romani v. Skoullou (1922) II C. L. R. pp. 17, 69. Cf. Joannes v. Stavrinou, ibid. p. 56.

[2]) Mejelle, Art. 1034.

[3]) Kadry Pasha, op. cit., Art. 122. Cf. Art. 123.

[4]) Ibid, Art. 139. As to the pre-emptor's death, see Mejelle, Art. 1038.

[5]) Kadry Pasha, op. cit., Arts. 142, 143. The Palestine Courts have held on the authority of Art. 1024 of the Mejelle that a person who, instead of claiming the land by right of pre-emption and complying with the formalities required by the Mejelle, offered to buy the land, lost his right of pre-emption. (Salimeh Bint Abed el Musleh v. Abdallah Yehyia. L. A. 44/32 Pal. Post, 3 May 1933).

[6]) Kadry Pasha, op. cit., Arts. 144, 145.

[7]) Mejelle, Art. 1035; Kadry Pasha, op. cit., Art. 125. Cf. Hedaya, p. 550.

[8]) Mejelle, Art. 1037; Kadry Pasha, op. cit., Art. 126.

[9]) Kadry Pasha, op. cit., Art. 129.

Chapter X—Pre-emption and Preference.

The pre-emptor must pay to the purchaser the amount which the purchaser himself gave [1]) and is not entitled to take advantage of any term allowed for payment by the original vendor [2]). Payment may be made to the vendor, if the price has not yet been received by him [3]). If the purchaser has destroyed buildings or grubbed up trees upon the property their value will be deducted from the amount payable by the pre-emptor and charged against the purchaser alone who must pay the amount to the vendor but will keep the material of the buildings or the timber [4]). Art. 1044 of the Mejelle tells us that if the purchaser has planted trees or has constructed buildings upon the property to which the right of pre-emption attaches the holder of the right has an option to relinquish the right or to pay the value of the buildings or trees [5]). If buildings or trees have perished without fault on the part of the purchaser, no such deduction is made [6]).

Art. 46 of the land Code expressly states that the right of Shufa is not applicable in the case of Miri or Mevqufe land. (Cf. Mejelle, Art. 1017). It is, however, significant that the example given in Art. 46 is that of the exercise of pre-emption by reason of contiguous neighbourhood. And indeed, we find that in the case of co-ownership of Miri or joint interest in a servitude a right of preference analogous to that of Shufa is given to Miri holders by Arts. 41, 42 of the land Code. And it is remarkable that though, as we have seen, Shufa is not favoured yet this right of preference as regards Miri is treated more generously, at least to the extent of being made much more easily exerciseable than the right of Shufa and more burdensome to the purchaser against whom it is exercised. The right of preference is exerciseable only in three cases (1) as between co-owners; (2) as between inhabitants of the same

<small>Right of Preference (Rudjhan; Haq - el - Awlawia).</small>

---

[1]) Mejelle, Art. 950. As to the effect of increases of price, see Mejelle Arts. 258-261. A device sometimes used for evading Pre-emption is to augment fictitiously the price mentioned in the deed of sale but the Courts will permit evidence to be given as to the true price paid.
[2]) Kadry Pasha, op. cit., Art. 127.
[3]) Ibid.
[4]) Kadry Pasha, Art. 131.
[5]) We learn from the Hedaya that the rule to be followed in this case was disputed. The Mejelle here adopts the view of Abou Yusuf. Zahir Rawayet (followed by Kadry Pasha, op. cit., Art. 130) allowed the pre-emptor to insist on removal by the purchaser, since the latter had in law built or planted on the land of another. (Hedaya, p. 556).
[6]) Kadry Pasha, op. cit., Art. 132.

village; (3) by the owner of trees and buildings as against a purchaser of the Miri land on which they stand.

Preference as between co-owners.

In the case of Miri as of Mulk a right exists on the part of a co-owner to secure the transfer to himself of the share of another co-owner of which the latter is seeking to dispose.

Land Code, Art. 41, provides as follows:—

Land Code, Art. 41.

"The owner of an undivided share in State land cannot transfer his share, by way of gift or in consideration of payment, without the leave of the persons jointly interested. If he does so the latter have the right, within five years, to claim from the transferee the restitution of his share, on paying him its value at the time of the claim. The right of claiming back the land lapses at the expiration of the said term, even if there exist the excuses recognised by law, namely, minority, unsoundness of mind, or absence on a jorney.

But if any person jointly interested at the time of the transfer has given his consent to it, or has refused to take the share in question although offered to him, he cannot afterwards maintain any claim.

Addition. 19 Sha'ban 1291. In the event of the person jointly interested dying within the said period of five years, his heirs, having the right of succession, shall have the right to claim possession of the property from the transferee or his heirs in the event of death, and in the event of the death of both the person jointly interested and of the transferee the heirs of the former shall have the right to claim possession from the heirs of the latter".

Although the terms of Art. 41 appear to limit the right of preference to co-owners of the tessaruf, it appears to be generally admitted that, as in the case of Shufa, the right can be exercised by joint owners of a servitude (Khalit) and this view is confirmed by decisions of the Turkish Court of Cassation [1]).

A comparison of the conditions for the exercise of the right of preference under this article with those for the exercise of the right of pre-emption will show that the right of preference is in principle very different to that of Shufa. A co-owner of Miri can never transfer his share without the consent of the other co-owners. Even if the transfer takes place upon death, the other co-owners have a right to Tapu. (Art. 59). If the transfer is during life, whether it be gratuitous or for consideration, the other co-owners can claim preference and, within five years, secure

---

[1]) Compare Tute, The Ottoman Land Laws, Note 3 on Art. 41.

Chapter X—Pre-emption and Preference.

restitution from the transferee on paying the value of the share at the time of the claim. This right of preference is, therefore, not really a right of pre-emption. It is a right to refuse to accept a new person as co-owner. The person exercising the right does not buy the property from the purchaser at the price he gave for it as in the case of Pre-emption; but indemnifies him for the loss which he suffers by having to surrender his property at the time at which he surrenders it. The right of preference much more closely resembles the Right to Tapu. Like the Right to Tapu it can be brought to an end by offer and refusal and it is provided by Art. 11 of the Regulations as to Title Deeds (Sha'ban, A. H. 1276) that if a person wishes to transfer to a third person a share of land possessed in common, it must be first offered to the co-possessor and if he declines to take it, a declaration in writing must be taken from him.

Unlike the Right to Tapu, however, the right of Preference is heritable and passes with the land to the heirs (Addendum to Art. 41) but it must be exercised by them within the original period of five years running from the date of the transfer [1]. As in the case of the Right to Tapu the period for exercise of the right runs notwithstanding incapacity or (semble) ignorance.

If amongst three or more co-possessors there is one who wishes to transfer his share, he may not give preference to anyone of those jointly interested. If the latter wish to acquire the share they can take it in common. If one co-possessor disposes of the whole of his share to one of the other co-possessors, the others can take their proportionate shares in it. The provisions of the preceding Article are also applicable in this case. *(Land Code, Art. 42.)*

This provision may be compared with Mejelle, Art. 1013.

"If the possessor by title-deed of land lying within the boundaries of a village has transferred it to an inhabitant of another village, the inhabitants of the former place who are in need of (zarouret) land have, for one year, the right to have the land adjudged to them at the price at which it has been sold". *(Preference as between inhabitants of the same village. Land Code, Art. 45.)*

Though no right of Preference (Rudjhan) is given by reason of contiguous neighbourhood this special right is similar. The translation of the article is apparently misleading. According to the Turkish text the person taking the land pays the equivalent value (Bedl Misl) and not the price at which the land was sold. The right may be compared to the Right to Tapu given under

---

[1] Chiha, op. cit., p. 308.

The Land Law of Palestine.

Art. 59 (III). The rules laid down in this latter article for application where several inhabitants desire to exercise the right to tapu, are, it is suggested, applicable by analogy in cases under Art. 45.[1]) As in the case of Art. 59, so here, difficulty may arise in determining whether an inhabitant has need of the land. Certainly if he has no land he has need of some. If he has some, the appreciation of his need must be left to the Court. The addendum to Art. 41 can have no application to a right of preference under Art. 45.

Preference as between the owner of the trees and the holder of the land. Land Code, Art. 44.

"The possessor of any land on which there are mulk trees or buildings,- land of which the cultivation and possession are subordinate to the trees and buildings,- cannot part with the land by way of gift or for a price, to anyone other than the owner of the trees or buildings, if he claims to have it transferred to him on payment of its tapu value. (Tapu Misl).

Should such transfer, however, take place, the owner of the trees or buildings shall, for ten years, have the right to claim the land, and to take it on paying the value at the time when he made the claim (Bedl Misl). The excuses of minority, unsoundness of mind, and absence on a journey are not applicable to this case".

As already explained the Moslem Law does not treat trees and buildings as accessory to the land on which they stand. It may happen, therefore, that the owner of trees and buildings is not the holder of the land.

If from any cause there has arisen a separation of ownership, the law has made it an object to facilitate a union. Art. 49 seeks to prevent the separation arising by requiring the vendor of Mulk trees and buildings on Miri of which he is the holder to transfer the land with the trees, etc. Art. 81 gives to the heirs of the owner of Mulk trees and buildings standing upon Miri of which he was holder a right to a gratuitous transfer of the Miri subject to the trees, etc. Art. 66 gives a right to Tapu to the owner of Mulk trees and buildings over the Miri on whicn they stand, exerciseable within 10 years of the death of the Miri holder and in default of superior rights. Art. 44 gives a right of preference to the owner of Mulk trees and buildings in case the Miri holder

---

[1]) The right of prior purchase conferred by Articles 41 & 45 of the Ottoman Land Code of the year A. H. 1274 on a villager to buy land, which has been transferred to an inhabitant of another village, cannot be invoked in a case in which the land was sold by Public Auction in execution proceedings. (Spectroff v. Agricultural, Loan and Land Co-operative Society. L. A. 64/32.)

Chapter X—Pre-emption and Preference.

of the land on which they stand seeks to transfer the land. This right in principle is a right of Tapu exerciseable during the lifetime of the holder of the land. If exercised at once, the Tapu value is paid. If exercised subsequently the value at the time, when the claim is made is paid [1]).

Whether the right is lost by consent given to the transfer or by a written refusal to exercise it, is not stated, but on the analogy of Mejelle, Art. 1024, Land Code, Art. 41, and the above quoted article of the Regulation of 1276, we may assume such loss to take place.

Since the Law of Disposition of A. H. 1331, the creation of new Mulk trees or buildings on Miri land appears to be if not impossible, at least very rare.

The burdensome character of the right of Preference over Miri has been much lightened by the Land Law (Amendment) Ordinance, 1933. Sec. 6 of this Ordinance provides that no right to claim a transfer of land under Articles 41 and 42 of the Ottoman Land Code shall be exerciseable on the part of any person more than one year after the right first occurred and that if a period was running at the commencement of the Ordinance (23 August, 1933) it should expire at the expiration of one year from the commencement of the Ordinance at the latest. The same Section provides that where transfer of the land is ordered under Art. 41, 44 and 45 of the Land Code the Court may order the transfer to be effected within a period not exceeding three months and that if by the default of the person in whose favour the order is made the transfer is not completed within the specified period the right to receive the transfer arising under the judgement or otherwise shall cease and determine.

_{The Land Law (Amendment) Ordinance 1933.}

Special rights of pre-emption are granted by Sec. 20 of the Expropriation of Lands Ordinance, 1926, and Sec. 20 of the Acquisi-

_{Pre-emption under special Ordinances.}

---

[1]) The Land Code clearly aims at securing that the land subject to the trees and buildings shall follow them. As above stated the trees or buildings may be so situated that the Miri holder of the land can make no use of the land at all if the trees and buildings are the Mulk of another. Presumably Art. 44 refers to cases in which the situation of the trees or buildings does not prevent the interest of the Miri holder being purely nominal.

The Court of Appeal in Shukairi v. Nour. L. A. 94/25 held that an owner even of a share in trees has (under Art. 44) the first claim to the land on which they stand.

tion of Land for Army and Air Force Ordinance, 1925. This right is limited to the former owner of expropriated land if still alive and gives to him a prior right to repurchase the land if no longer required for the purpose for which it was expropriated. Under the Law of Corporations, A. H. 1331 (Art. 2) if a corporation desires to sell its land the inhabitants of the village and owners of land in the village have the right to purchase in priority to any other purchaser on payment of the assessed value.

Pre-emption as regards Waqf property.
In respect of Ijaratein Waqf property there is no right of pre-emption. Consequently one joint owner of Ijaratein Waqf property can grant his share to another person without the permission of the other joint owner. (Omar Hilmy, Art. 241—Cf. Mejelle, Art. 1017).

CHAPTER XI—RIGHTS OF SECURED AND UNSECURED CREDITORS.

In this Chapter it is proposed to set forth the provisions of the Law:

a) as to mortgages or other forms of real security;

b) as to the liability of immovable property to be seized in execution and sold for unsecured debts.

As will appear hereafter there is now only one way in which immovable property of any land can be given by way of security for money. It is, therefore, only necessary briefly to note the forms of real security possible or usual in former times. As the Law differed somewhat as regards Mulk and Miri, it is necessary to make this distinction, and we may commence by a consideration of the forms of real security provided by or founded upon the Mejelle. The only form of real security directly contemplated by the Mejelle is the Pledge. Mortgages and other forms of real security before British Occupation of Palestine.

The Pledge is probably the most ancient form of Real Security. It is fully regulated in the Mejelle (Arts. 701 ff.) where the same rules are, in principle, made applicable to both movable and immovable property. As already mentioned, the distinction between these two species of property is of minor importance in Moslem law. Pledge(Rehn).

Pledges of immovables are, however, now rarely made and the law is, therefore, in this connection of little practical interest. It may be thus summarized [1] —

1) Pledge is a "real" contract; it requires the consent of the parties and the delivery of the object pledged (or the pledge) to the pledgee (Mejelle, Art. 706).

2) The pledge must be something which may be validly sold, and must be the Mulk of the pledgor. Miri cannot, therefore, be pledged (Mejelle, Art. 709, Land Code, Art. 116 [2]).

---

[1] Cf. Chaoui, op. cit., pp. 109-111.

[2] A borrowed article may, however, be pledged by the borrower with the consent of the owner (Mejelle, Art. 726. Cf. Arts. 732, 736). As to Pledge of pledged articles see Mejelle, Arts. 743 ff.

3) The pledgee has the right to retain the pledge in his possession (Mejelle, Art. 729). His right is not extinguished by death of the pledgor, nor by his own death (Art. 733). But the pledgee may lend the pledged article to the pledgor and retain his right of preference (Art. 749) [1]).

It is odd to find that the right of the pledgee, to retain the pledge, may survive the contract of Pledge (Mejelle, Art. 718), though the Hedaya states that a contract of pledge is not rendered void, until the pledgee restore the pledge to the pledgor [2]).

4) The pledgee is responsible for expenses incurred in connection with the preservation of the pledge (Mejelle, Art. 732). But the pledgor must pay the expences of maintenance and improvement, e. g. repairs, watering, grafting, cleansing of conduit pipes (Mejelle, Art. 724). The illustrations given have some doubt as to the scope of this distinction which, however, is elucidated in the Hedaya where it is stated that what is requisite for the support of the pledge and the continuance of its existence falls on the pledgor but what is necessary for its preservation or safety on the pledgee [3]). The pledgor is liable if he destroys or damages the pledge (Art. 741) but not if the pledge is destroyed by another (Art. 742). The pledgee has in that case an action against the third person and retains what he receives as a pledge in place of the pledge which has been destroyed [4]). A depreciation in the value of the pledge occasions a proportionate deduction in the claim of the pledgee [5]).

The pledgee may not make use of the pledge without the permission of the pledgor (Art. 750).

5) Neither the pledgor nor the pledgee may sell the pledge without the consent of the other (Mejelle, Art. 756). But the Court may order a sale and if necessary conduct it (Art. 757) as also where the pledge is likely to deteriorate (Art. 759). A power of sale may, however, be given in effect by a power of attorney given by the pledgor which is irrevocable and is not annulled by death of the pledgor (Art. 760).

---

[1]) This provision is a dangerous one and in the absence of a system of registration at the least, might easily give rise to serious injustice. But the Mejelle is here following the strict Moslem law. Cf. Hedaya, Vol. IV, Book XLVIII. Chapter IV (Hamilton's Translation, at p. 650).

[2]) Hedaya, at p. 633.

[3]) Ibid., at p. 634.

[4]) Mejelle, Art. 742. Hedaya, at p. 650.

[5]) Hedaya, ibid. Cf. at p. 653, as to the depreciation of a pledge from a fall in the price.

Chapter XI—Secured and Unsecured Creditors. [163]

The Ottoman Law as to title deeds for Mulk (28 Rejeb, A. H. 1291) contains provisions (Art. 16) as to pledges of Mulk land, and Art. 19 of the same Law provides further that actions based on a pledge or mortgage asserting that a transaction was subject to a condition of which no mention is made in the bond shall not be heard. Thus, after a vendor has sold Mulk property absolutely and a bond (Sanad) of sale has been duly handed to the purchaser, if he brings an action asserting that he pledged or mortgaged it such an action is not heard.

As at Rome and elsewhere, the Pledge proved in many respects an inconvenient form of security practical only as regards immovables. We find consequently that people cast about for other and more convenient forms. In Rome this led gradually to the creation of the modern form of real security known as the hypothec which does not involve any handing over of the possession of the land to the creditor but gives him good security by his power of sale and provides other conveniences. The modern English mortgage though its history is different, may in practice be regarded also as a hypothec.

The inconvenience was even the greater in the case of Miri, *Bei bil Wafa.* since the Miri holder could not pledge his interest. So soon, however, as his power to sell the tessaruf was admitted it became possible for him also to make use of the Bei bil Wafa or sale subject to a right of redemption [1]. The validity of such sales is recognized by the Mejelle (Art. 118). But this mode of giving security was handicapped by the rule that neither the vendor (mortgagor) nor the purchaser (mortgagee) could sell the property transferred subject to a right of redemption (Arts. 118, 379) and in this respect a sale of this land resembled a pledge. To obviate the impossibility thus created of realization of his security by the mortgagee it became the practice to add to the Bei bil Wafa a clause whereby the mortgagor appointed an attorney to whom he gave power to sell in case of non payment of the debt at the date fixed for redemption. A power to sell given in such circumstances was a Wakalat "ma Haq el Ghair" (with the right of another depending) and was irrevocable [2].

---

[1] Mortgages in English law approximate to this conception, Equity having long treated a transfer by way of security as subject to a perpetual "equity of redemption". The maxim of equity was that "once a mortgage, always a mortgage".

[2] Chaoui, op. cit., 113-114. Cf. Mejelle, Arts. 760 and 1527 as to irrevocable powers of attorney in connection with Pledges.

The Land Law of Palestine.

Wakalat Haq el Ghair

The irrevocability of a Wakalat "ma Haq el Ghair" resulted from the provisions of Arts. 1522, 1527 of the Mejelle, which state that a Wakalat is not revocable by the principal of the right of another depending. Nor, in such a case does the death of the principal discharge the attorney (Wakil)[1].

The phrase "if the right of another is depending" is explained by an example given in Art. 1521 as follows:

"When a debtor has pledged his property and at the time of making the contract of pledge or afterwards he has appointed someone wakil to sell the pledge when the time for payment of the debt is come, the pledgor cannot dismiss the wakil without the consent of the pledgee".

A wakalat cannot, however, be inherited. The heirs of the wakil do not stand in his place (Art. 1528).

Even so, however, the arrangement was not entirely satisfactory. Though it gave a good security to the mortgagee it deprived the mortgagor of enjoyment of the property. A further refinement was necessary. The mortgagor received back the property by way of hire from the mortgagee and the interest payable on the loan might, therefore, figure as rent payable under a lease. Art. 119 of the Mejelle contemplates a sale subject to an agreement that the vendor shall retain the use of the thing sold (Bei bil Istighlal).

Bei bil Istighlal.

An arrangement of this nature conjoined with a Bei bil Wafa and containing a power of attorney authorizing sale, combined to constitute a security both ample and convenient.

Miri land was mortgaged by use of the same device and the Land Code fully recognizes its validity. Art. 116 provides:

"State and Mevqufe land cannot be pledged; provided always that if a debtor, against his debt and through the Official, transfers land in his possession to his creditor, on condition that the latter will return it to him whenever he discharges the debt, or if he makes a transfer with right of redemption called Feragh bil Wafa, that is to say, that whenever he discharges the debt he shall have the right to claim re-transfer of the land, the debtor cannot without previously discharging the debt, whether there be a time fixed or not, force a re-transfer of the land; he can only have it back after complete discharge".

The procedure in the case of a Feragh bil Wafa was further elaborated by Arts. 25 ff. of the Tapu Law of A.H. 1275 and extended to Mussaqafat and Mustaghilat Waqfs by a law of 23 Ramadan,

---

[1]) Compare Atalla v. Nima and Khalil (High Court case 93/32).

Chapter XI—Secured and Unsecured Creditors. [165]

A.H. 1286, which further amended the law. The owner of Ijaratein Waqf could not, however, mortgage by Feragh bil Wafa without the leave of the Mutwally of the Waqf [1]).

In the case of a mortgage (Feragh bil Wafa) of Miri the parties were bound to conform to the procedure laid down by the Tapu Law of A. H. 1275. A private mortgage was null and void (Tapu Law, Art. 30). The procedure is stated in Arts. 26, 27 and involved a declaration before the local Administrative Council (Art. 26). After 1869 this procedure was also required in the case of Mussaqafat and Mustaghilat Waqfs. (Law 23 Ramadan, A. H. 1286).

These laws have never been repealed, but by the operation of the later Ottoman and Palestinian enactments to be hereafter considered the greater part of their provisions is, in fact, made inoperative and their application is confined to mortgages made before 18th November, 1918.

With the Feragh bil Wafa was combined as in the case of Mulk, a Wakalat Dawaryia. As to this Art. 117 of the Land Code provides:

"If a debtor after transferring land in his possession to his creditor against a debt, whether on the above mentioned condition or in the form of transfer with right of redemption (Feragh bil Wafa) finds himself unable to discharge the debt at the time agreed upon, and if he gives the creditor a power of attorney (Wakalat Dawaryia) that is to say if he entirely puts the latter in his position, without power of revocation, and gives him power to sell the land or cause it to be sold, to repay himself the amount of the debt out of the purchase money, and pay to him any balance; under these conditions, the creditor so impowered, in case of non-payment at the time agreed, can sell the land during the life-time of the debtor, through the Official [2]) and pay himself the amount due to him; or if the debtor has invested a third person with such powers, the latter can, at the expiration of the agreed period, and in virtue of his power of attorney, sell the land and pay the creditor the debt due by the debtor, his principal".

Wakalat Dawaryia.

It has been argued that the words "during the lifetime of the debtor" must be interpreted as limiting the Wakalat to the period

---

[1]) Omar Hilmy, op. cit., Art. 244.

[2]) The reference to sale "through the Official" is to remind that an unregistered sale is invalid. In Land Appeal No. 135/23 in re Mohamed Yahia v. Shaban Aidi the Court held that so long as the Wakalat Dawaryia remained unexecuted by registration the owner of the land (the debtor) was free to transfer the land to a purchaser by registered transfer, leaving to the creditor only a right to claim damages from the transferor (the debtor).

of the debtor's life, but the words can be otherwise explained and the better view appears to be that the power to sell is not revoked by the debtor's death, though it is not inherited by the heirs of the wakil (Mejelle, Art. 1529)[1]).

Enforcement of the security. In the case of a "Bei bil Wafa" or "Bei bil Istighlal" the mortgagee was owner of the property as a consequence of the bei, though subject to a right of redemption. While in possession the pledgee could not take any benefit from the thing pledged without the pledgor's consent (Mejelle Art. 750). But the mortgagee in possession under a "Bei bil Wafa" would take benefit as if he were a full purchaser (Art. 118). And if the pledgor (or mortgagor) were let into possession under a lease from the pledgee (or mortgagee) rent would be payable.

Sale could, however, be obtained through the Court (Mejelle, Art. 756) or under the Wakalat Dawaryia in which latter case it would be effected through the Land Registry (Orders of Ministry of Tapu, 18 Zil Hijje, 1306; 14 Rabi el Awal, 1308).

It is important to enquire how far the security was enforceable against the heirs of a deceased debtor. No doubt arises in this connection in the case of Mulk. But in the case of Miri and Mussaqafat or Mustaghilat Waqf the inrerest of the holder was, in the older Law, of a personal nature, and different considerations applied. Under the Land Code in its original form very limited rights of Intiqal in Miri were allowed, and by Art. 118 the rights of a creditor secured by a quasi pledge or Feragh bil Wafa were limited to a right of attachment of the land if the debtor left persons capable of succeeding to his property under the rules of Intiqal set forfh in the Code. If there were no persons entitled to a right of Intiqal, the land became Mahlul (subject to rights of Tapu) and was free from the incumbrance of the creditor's security.

The situation was altered by a series of enactments which, though not expressly repealing Article 118, rendered its provisions practically inoperative. In particular a Law of 23 Ramadan, 1286 (Arts. 2, 3) gave to a creditor who held a mortgage over Miri or Waqf land the right to have enough of the land sold after the debtor's death to satisfy the mortgage debt even though the debtor left no heirs with right of succsession and no persons were entitled to a right of Tapu. These provisions are now in turn superseded by the more general provisions of Art. 16 of the Law of Disposition, A.H. 1331, whereby Miri, Mevqufe, Mussaqafat and Musta-

---

[1]) Chiha, op. cit., pp. 336 ff.

Chapter XI—Secured and Unsecured Creditors.

ghilat Waqf owned by a debtor are declared to be security for the debts during his life and after his death even if it become Mahlul. This section refers primarily to unsecured debts but applies a fortiori to those which are secured [1]).

In A.H. 1331 a Provisional Law of Mortgage was enacted by the Turkish Government whereby a new form of mortgage applicable to all kinds of land was introduced. The law was applicable from the date of its promulgation. It is under this Law, as amended and supplemented by Palestine Ordinances, that mortgages of immovables are now effected in Palestine. From the date of promulgation of this Law till 18th November, 1918, it was possible to create real securities either in the forms already considered, or under the Provisional Law. Mortgages created during that period and under the Provisional Law are governed by that law in the form in which it was originally enacted. *Provisional Law of Mortgage, 1331.*

Dispositions of immovables in Palestine were prohibited by the Militaty Proclamations of 18th November, 1918. Mortgages and other dispositions made after that date are void —

a) if made with reference to land in the Sanjak of Jerusalem on or after 1st December, 1917;

b) if made with reference to land in the Sanjaks of Nablus and Acre on or after 1st October, 1918.

During the prohibited period many attempts were made to create a species of security by unregistered Bei bil Wafa or Feragh bil Wafa. Such transactions could, however, have no effect having regard to the terms of the Proclamations.

Wakalats with Haq el Ghair were much used during the prohibited period. They could not be made use of, of course, until the Registry was again open but transfers under such wakalats have since that time been frequently acted upon. Wakalats of this kind are, indeed, still in use though the simplicity of the mortgage under the law of A.H. 1331 makes their use much less frequent than formerly.

The Transfer of Land Ordinance, 1920, whereby provision was made for the resumption of dealing in land enacts (Sec. 10) that no mortgage shall be accepted for registration unless it complies with the terms of the Provisional Law for the Mortgage of Immovable Property of 1 Rabi - el - Thani, A.H. 1331, and the amendments *Mortgages since the British Occupation.*

---

[1]) Fisher gives Art. 118 in a form amended by the later Laws. But strictly speaking it has never been amended but merely superseded by later enactments. The original form is given in Ongley.

The Land Law of Palestine.

of the said Law¹). Certain amendments of this Provisional Law were made by the Mortgage Law Amendment Ordinance, 1920. Mortgages and transfer of mortgages are further stated to be "dispositions" within the meaning of Section 2 of the Ordinance and the provisions thereof with reference to the consent of the Administration to dispositions (Secs. 4, 8, 9, 10) apply to them. Thus under Sec. 11 a disposition by way of mortgage is void unless the consent of the Government has been obtained though money paid thereunder may be recovered by action. And under Sect. 12 taking or permitting possession of immovable property²) under a disposition to which the consent of the Government has not been obtained is punishable. The written consent of the Government implies registration. Consequently no document purporting to be (or which intended to have the effect of) a mortgage will have any operation by way of security for money unless it is presented to the land Registry, and no such mortgage will be accepted for registration in the Registry unless it complies with the Provisonal Law. Moreover, Section 3 of the Mortgage Law Amendment Ordinance, 1920, provides that any person wishing to make immovable property security for a debt must do so in accordance with the provisions of the Transfer of Land Ordinance, 1920, and execute a deed in the form and manner prescribed by rules made thereunder.

In view of these provisions it seems that immovable property cannot now be charged with a debt by way of real security save in accordance with the provisions of the Provisional Law of 1331 as amended by Palestine Ordinances.

The method of giving security by way of mortgage established by the Provisional Law is similar in nature to that known as Hypothec in French Law. The mortgagee does not become the owner or the possessor of the property mortgaged. It is, therefore, unlike the old form of mortgage in English Law whereby the legal estate in the property passed to the mortgagee subject to a right (or equity) of resumption remaining with the mortgagor. The English form resembles more closely the sale with right of repurchase (Bei bil Wafa) of Moslem Law. The Ottoman and French Hypothec and

---

¹) Interest by way of Mortgage registered in an unofficial Land Book may obtain official registration under the provisions of the Correction of Land Registers Ordinances, 1926.

²) As explained earlier "immovable property" though not defined in the Transfer of Land Ordinance, includes all kinds of land (Mulk, Miri 'or Waqf), Mulk buildings and Mulk trees.

Chapter XI—Secured and Unsecured Creditors.[169]

the English Mortgage are, however, not unlike in their practical effects though the legal theory underlying them is different.

Though a creditor may take a mortgage by way of security the loan or other form of debt for which the security is given is not generally merged in the security but remains distinct. Thus after a mortgage has been given, the rights of the mortgagee are generally of a double nature.

In the first place the mortgagor is his debtor for the money lent. This personal obligation to repay created by the loan falls upon the mortgagor and his heirs and remains binding whether the mortgagor sells the land mortgaged or not. In addition, however, to the mortgagee's personal right against the mortgagor and his heirs, the mortgagee holds a real right exerciseable over the land into whose-soever hands it may come which enables him to make good his debt out of it. Whether the claim against the borrower (mortgagor) will pass to the lender's (mortgagee's) heirs on the death of the mortgagee and whether the mortgagor's heirs will be liable for the debts of their ancestor, depends upon the rules as to transfer of personal rights and liabilities. The Palestine legislation clearly contemplates that death does not extinguish either the right or the liability. Clearly in any case the interest of the mortgagee under the mortgage survives to his heirs nor does the death of the mortgagor affect the mortgagee's security, which is as much available against the land of the heirs of the mortgagor as it was when in the hands of the mortgagor himself.

The precise nature of the interest of the mortgagee in the mortgaged land may be disputed. In the case of a Bei bil Wafa the mortgagee is, of course, owner of the property mortgaged though subject to a right of redemption. In the cases of a mortgage under the Provisional Law of 1331 the mortgagee does not (semble) become owner but he has a real right less than ownership in the mortgaged property.

Mortgages of Leaseholds. The nature of a leasehold interest in Palestine is a matter of some doubt and will be further discussed in a subsequent chapter [1]). In this place it is enough to say that the validity of a mortgage of such an interest had been questioned, as it was difficult to treat a leasehold interest as "immovable property" within the meaning of Sec. 1 of the Provisional Law of A. H. 1331. Sec. 2 of the Transfer of Land Ordinance 1920, does, indeed, impliedly treat such interests as immovables for the purpose of the

---

[1]) See Chapter XII dealing with Leases.

The Land Law of Palestine.

Ordinance but sec. 10 of the same Ordinance requires every mortgage to comply with the provisions of the Provisional Law of A.H. 1331.

However, leasehold interests of certain categories were declared capable of being mortgaged to Credit Banks under the provisions of Sec. 3 of the Credit Banks Ordinance 1922. The question as to whether leasehold interests generally can be given in mortgage has now been set at rest by Sec. 9 of the Land Law (Amendment) Ordinance 1933 which provides that the lessee of land who has registered a lease in the Land Registry may, save where the lease contains a condition to the contrary, mortgage his interest in accordance with the law of mortgage for the time being in force and such mortgage may be registered in the Land Registry by the mortgagee either in addition to or instead of the mortgagor.

The provisions of this Section as to mortgage of leasehold interests are not so explicit as those of Sec. 3 of the Credit Banks Ordinance 1922. Thus, under the latter Section, para (II), it is expressly provided that the consent of the lessor shall not be necessary to any exercise by the mortgagee of his power of sale provided that he was notified in due course of the execution of the mortgage. Save in cases of mortgage of leasehold to Credit Banks it is not clear whether the mortgagee is free to sell the leasehold interest without the lessor's consent, if assignment is thus restricted in the lease. Presumably, however, legislative authority to mortgage leaseholds should be taken to carry with it all proper powers to enable the mortgage to be effective and useful.

Text of the Law of Mortgage A.H. 1331.

We shall now proceed to set out the text of the Provisional Law of A.H. 1331 in the form in which it is now applicable in Palestine, i.e. as modified by Ordinance.

Sec. 1.

"Immovable property whether held as separate property or in common, and whether Mulk, Miri, Waqf or Mustaghilat and Mussaqafat waqf land may be given as security for a debt by means of a mortgage.

If the value of the land is greater than the debt, the land may be mortgaged for other debts in the second, third degree or any other degree; and in this case the mortgages of prior degree will have preference over the mortgages of later degree".

This provision assimilates the Mulk and Miri Law of Mortgage. The leave of the Government is no longer necessary to a mortgage of Miri save so far as such leave is necessary to all dispositions of land under the Transfer of Land Ordinance.

Chapter XI—Secured and Unsecured Creditors. [171]

It is noteworthy that the Section expressly recognises the possibility of second, and subsequent mortgages ranking according (semble) to their date of registration. The older law did not permit the creation of second mortgages [1]).

Mortgagees sometimes seek to avoid the provisions of the law by inserting in the mortgage a condition that the mortgagor shall not create any further mortgage upon the property save with the mortgagee's consent. It may be assumed that the existence of such a condition in a prior mortgage would not affect the validity of any subsequent mortgage created in breach of it, whatever personal right of action it might give to the first mortgagee against the mortgagor in respect of the breach.

Sec. 2. The original section so numbered in the Provisional Law of A.H. 1331 and the amendment thereof by the Ordinance of 1920 have been repealed by the Mortgage Law Amendment Ordinance 1929 which has substituted the following provisions —

"Immovable property may be mortgaged to a waqf, or to a bank or company authorized to carry on business in Palestine. Any such bank or company holding a mortgage shall have the like right of buying in the property mortgaged and be subject to the like restrictions, as are applicable to a Credit Bank under Sec. 2 (2), (3) and (4) of the Credit Banks Ordinance, 1922".

The term Waqf may perhaps be interpreted as covering a charitable trust under the Charitable Trust Ordinance 1924-5. But in any case the provisions of Sec. 8 of the Charitable Trust Ordinance 1924 make clear that the trustees of such a trust are entitled to lend trust money on mortgage of immovables.

By a further provision of the Mortgage Law Amendment Ordinance 1929, Sec. 3, it is declared that notwithstanding anything in the Ottoman Provisional Law of Mortgage immovable property may be mortgaged as security for contingent or future debts. Thus a mortgage can be given for future advances a practice very commonly followed.

Sec. 3. The original Section has been altered by the Mortgage Law Amendment Ordinance, 1920. The provisions of this section are as follows:

"In the first place a certificate approved by the Municipality, containing a statement whether the immovable property, which is to be mortgaged has been leased or not, and if so for what period it has been leased, will be produced. Whether such certificate shall be produced or not, the mortgagee shall be deemed to have received

---
[1]) Mejelle, Art. 744. Chiha, op. cit., pp. 341-2.

notice of any existing lease duly registered with the Municipality or with the Land Registry; and if the powers of sale contained in Sec. 9 hereof shall become exerciseable, the property shall be sold subject to and with the benefit of any such lease".

Sec. 4. The Original Section has been amended by the Mortgage Law Amendment Ordinance, 1920, to read as follows:

"Any person who wishes to make immovable property security for a debt must do so in accordance with the provisions of the Transfer of Land Ordinance 1920, and must execute a deed in the form and manner prescribed thereunder. Deeds so executed will be accepted as evidence of the matters therein contained in all Courts and by the Administrative authorities without further proof".

This Section in its amended form will, of course, only apply to mortgages made since the amending ordinance.

Sec. 5. "Buildings, trees and vines already erected or planted, or which may be erected or planted on immovable property mortgaged will be considered as forming part of the property and subject to the mortgage".

Sec. 6. The mortgagors have the right to use and enjoy immovable property mortgaged and in the same way they bear any loss or injury to the same".

Sec. 7. "The mortgagee may transfer his claim to a third person and assign his rights over the immovable property through the Tapu Registry with the consent of the mortgagor, but if the document is payable to "order" the consent of the mortgagor is not necessary [1]).

The mortgagor may sell the immovable property mortgaged with the mortgagee's consent to a third person who undertakes to repay the debt. The rights of the mortgagee over the same remain".

The terms of Sec. 7 appear to show that the mortgagee can only transfer the claim against the mortgagor together with and not separately from his interest as mortgagee in the property mortgaged.

It is clearly contemplated that the personal claim and the mortgage should not be separated. The mortgagor is only permitted to sell the mortgaged property with the consent of the mortgagee and the purchaser is bound to undertake to pay the debt.

---

[1]) In Kardahi v. Sahyoun and the Chief Execution Officer (High Court No. 16/31) the Court held that in the case of a mortgage to "order" the creditor (mortgagee) for the time being, whether he be the original mortgagee or his heirs, may assign his rights under the mortgage in virtue of Sec. 7 and that in consequence of such assignment the assignee acquires the same status as the assignor (the original mortgagee).

Chapter XI—Secured and Unsecured Creditors. [173]

It is clearly intended, though not explicitly stated, that the mortgagee would thus accept the third person as his debtor in place of the original debtor who would be freed from liability (Hawale).

It is clear that the personal claim of the mortgagee on the loan is part of his Mulk and on his death descends as Mulk or passes under his Will. If the land mortgaged is also Mulk the mortgagee's interest will be Mulk and will be governed by the Mulk rules as to succession. But if the land mortgaged is Miri the mortgagee's interest appears to be Miri also. The Succession Ordinance 1923, Sec. 26, defines Miri land as including any registered interest in Miri [1]). Consequently a mortgagee's interest in Miri will descend as Miri and cannot be left by will [2]).

The interest of the mortgagor in the land mortgaged remains, of course, Miri or Mulk according to the intrinsic nature of the land. But in the hands whether of Mulk or Miri heirs it remains charged with the repayment of the mortgage money.

This Section has been altered by the Mortgage Law Amendment Ordinance, 1920. It reads as follows: Sec. 8.

"Save where the mortgage deed contains an express clause to the contrary, mortgagors may pay their debts secured by formal documents together with any additions which may have accrued before the date on which they fell due. In that case the principal sum, together with the amount of damages, if provided for in the document, will be paid to the account of the mortgagee at a Bank authorised by the Government under the name of the Tapu Registry, and after the receipt has been produced to the tapu Registry the Tapu will inform the mortgagee of the action taken, and will cancel the mortgage".

The only change in this Section made by the Amending Ordinance was the insertion of the opening words "Save where the mortgage deed contains an express clause to the contrary".

It is not unusual to insert in the mortgage a provision that the mortgage shall be for a fixed period so that the mortgagor is not entitled to repay until its expiration. Even more usual is a provision that though the debt shall be repayable at any time by

---

[1]) In Agronovitch v. Agronovitch the District Court of Jaffa (Copland J.) held that a Mortgage of Miri was Miri (123/30).

[2]) This inconvenient conclusion is intended to be avoided by the proposed Succession (Amendment) Ordinance 1934 (Gaz. 18 Jan. 1934) under which interests in Miri registered by way of security for money are for the purposes of the Succession Ordinance to be assimilated to Mulk.

the mortgagor repayment shall only be made after notice, and a period of three months notice is often stipulated ¹).

It is to be remarked that where mortgagors pay the debt before the day of payment arrives "damages, if provided for in the document" are payable to the mortgagee. The interpretation of the term "damages" has been the subject of controversy, it being sometimes contended, that the mortgagor is bound to pay interest up to the date, at which the payment was to fall due even though he paid the debt before that date ²).

Sec. 9. "If the period for the payment of the debt has passed and the debt is not paid, or if the debt becomes due under a condition terminating the mortgage, then on the demand of the mortgagee or his heirs, or of any other mortgagee, in a later degree, provided the first mortgagee has made no demand, the immovable property mortgaged may be sold by the Tapu Registry Office in which the mortgage is registered according to the following articles. Even if the mortgagor has died or if he has no heirs or becomes bankrupt it is not necessary to obtain a judgment or decision to have recourse to the inheritance (i.e. the representative of the debtor) or to the trustee in bankruptcy".

Sec. 10. "When, in accordance with the preceding Article, the mortgagee makes a demand to the Registry Office for payment, the Registry Office will notify the mortgagor in accordance with the Rules of Civil Procedure that he must pay the debt within a week. If the mortgagee is dead this notification will be made to his heirs or to their guardians either personally or at their residence or to his trustee in bankruptcy if he is bankrupt.

---

¹) In a case before the Supreme Court sitting as a High Court of Justice, the Court (Baker and Khayat JJ.) held that the mortgage deed containing a condition that the mortgagor was entitled to discharge the mortgage by paying the principal and interest due to the date of repayment provided he served on the mortgagee three months notice in writing of his intention to do so, the mortgagor could not demand the discharge of the mortgage by payment of three months interest in lieu of notice. No such provision appeared in the mortgage and the Court held that it could not be read into the mortgage. (H.C. 37/32 in re Habib Elias Salem v. The Director of Lands and Sa'ad el Din Taha).

It would, therefore, appear that when a three months notice is stipulated the mortgagor, in addition to notice, is bound to pay interest up to the date on which the three months expire and that interest cannot be paid in lieu of notice unless expressly provided for in the deed.

²) This is, however, subject to the rule contained in Art. 4 of the Ottoman Law of Interest of 22 March 1302 (Bagdad Translation, p. 2), which is to the effect that the total interest on a debt shall not exceed the principal amount of the debt, irrespective of the period of the debt.

Chapter XI—Secured and Unsecured Creditors. [175]

If, after this period, the debt is unpaid, the immovable property mortgaged will be sold by public auction during the next 45 days. After this period has expired another period of 15 days is allowed for the offer of further bids in advance of 3 per cent. at least. It is then sold finally and directly to the highest bidder.

If necessary the Execution Officer on the order of the Registry Office will cause the immovable property mortgaged to be vacated and will deliver it to the purchaser.

The proceedings of the auction, sale, or delivery will not be suspended by opposition made before the Court by the mortgagor. Nor will they be suspended by claims as to the existence of leases which were not mentioned in the document referred to in Art. 3.

But an order of the Court that the mortgagee, if a private individual, shall give personal security, or, if a Company authorised to lend money, shall give an undertaking in writing, shall be executed at once".

Sections 9 and 10 contemplate sale only through the Tapu Office and the Execution Office.

Section 11 has been amended by the Mortgage Law Amendment Ordinance, 1920. It reads as follows: Sec. 11.

"(a) The purchase money will be paid into such Court as the Registrar directs; provided that the Court may order that the purchase money be paid into an authorised Bank to a special credit.

(b) The mortgagees shall produce an account setting out their claims, which shall be verified by the Court; and the purchase money, after payment of costs and expenses, shall be distributed according to the rights of the parties on an order of the Court made in Chambers.

(c) Sums due to mortgagees who do not claim payment will be placed to their credit in an authorised bank.

(d) If the price is not sufficient to pay the whole debt, the mortgagee may claim the balance from the mortgagor".

These provisions are substituted for those of the original Sec. 11 which can now have no application.

Other provisions with regard to sale of mortgaged property are as follows:

"Where immovable property is sold under the Provisional Ottoman Mortgage Law the registration thereof in the name of the purchaser shall transfer to him all the estate and title of the mortgagor in the property mortgaged and, as against the mortgagor, the purchaser's title shall be indefeasible" [1]). Mortgage Law Amendment Ordinance, 1920. Sec. 6.

---

[1]) The effect of Sec. 6 is to protect a purchaser under the Law of A.H.

The Land Law of Palestine.

Transfer of Land Ordinance No. 2 of 1921.

"(1) Notwithstanding anything in Art. 22 of the Proclamation of 24th June, 1918, [1]) and the Transfer of Land Ordinance, 1920, the Courts may order the sale of immovable property in execution of a judgment or in satisfaction of a mortgage.

(2) Application for sale should be made to the President of the District Court who may order postponement of the sale if he is satisfied:

a) that the debtor has reasonable prospects of payment if given time; or

b) that having regard to all the circumstances of the case, including the needs of the creditor, it vould involve undue hardship to sell the property of the debtor".

Though the Mortgage Law of A. H. 1331 read in connection with the Land Transfer Ordinance, 1920, and with Sec. 4 of the Mortgage Law Amendment Ordinance, 1920, appears to establish a mortgage under that Law as the only form of Real Security now allowable in Palestine, yet in other respects the rules set forth in the Mejelle, the Land Code, the Tapu Law of 1275, and the Law of 23 Ramadan, 1286, remain unaffected [2]).

The general rules as to the procedure to be followed when morgaged immovables are sold under execution will be found in the Ottoman Law of Execution, 15 Jamad el Thani, 1332 (11th May, 1914). See, in particular, Arts. 67, 98.

The Credit Banks Ordinances 1920-22.

It remains to note certain special provisions as to mortages contained in the Credit Banks Ordinances and other Ordinances.

The Credit Banks Ordinances, 1920-1922, give special facilities for the advance of money on mortgage of immovable property by Companies incorporated as or authorised to act as Credit Banks. These facilities consist —

(a) of special provisions for the sale of land mortgaged to a Credit Bank by Order of an Execution Officer without an Order of Court;

(b) provisions enabling a Credit Bank to obtain possession of the mortgaged property in certain conditions and eventually to obtain a foreclosure Order.

1331 against claims to have the sale declared void on the ground of irregularity of procedure. Khaledi v. Imperial Ottoman Bank. O.G. 16 Sept. 1926.

[1]) The provisions of this Proclamation forbade the Courts to order the sale of immovable property.

[2]) Art. 28 of the Tapu Law and Arts. 2, 3 of the Law of 23 Ramadan, A. H. 1286, appear to treat the general estate of a deceased mortgagor as primarily liable for his mortgage debts, the mortgaged property being liable only in case of insufficiency of assets.

Chapter XI—Secured and Unsecured Creditors. [177]

These include the power to appoint a Receiver of the rents and profits of the mortgaged property (Credit Banks (Facilities) Ordinance 1920, Sec. 2). The Credit Bank is entitled in certain circumstances to buy in the mortgaged property at the sale and may eventually obtain a foreclosure order (Credit Bank Ordinance 1922, Sec. 2)[1]).

(c) As already mentioned the Credit Banks Ordinance 1922 made special provision for the mortgage of leaseholds to Credit Banks (Sec. 3).

(d) Sec. 4 of the same Ordinance makes detailed provisions as to the conditions of loans by Credit Banks, more particularly in connection with loans on the security of Agricultural property in which a condition is always to be implied for the relief of borrowers in a bad season [2]).

The Companies Ordinance 1929 by which earlier Ordinances as to Companies were repealed, contains provisions as to mortgages and debentures of Companies which require here only brief reference. The subject properly belongs to mercantile law. Part VI of the Ordinance (Arts. 120 ff.) is devoted to Debentures Mortgages and Charges and the provisions therein regulate (inter alia) the borrowing powers of Companies (Sec. 121)[3]), debentures and debenture trust deeds (Secs. 121-123, 124, 127 (5), 128, 138) floating charges [4]) (Sec. 123), registration of mortgages of a Company (Sec. 125 ff) and enforcement of security by receivers (Secs. 134 ff). *Debentures of Companies.*

The floating charge by which under Sec. 121 moneys payable under debentures may be secured does not confer any right of preference or priority to the detriment of any registered mortgage or purchasers for value of immovable property of the Company notwithstanding that its existence was known to the mortgagee

---

[1]) As to extension to "Banks or Companies" of the provisions of Sec. 2 (2), (3) and (4) of the Credit Banks Ordinance 1922 see Mortgage Law Amendment Ordinance 1929.

[2]) For the relief of borrowers provision is made (Sec. 4 (1)) that every loan on immovable security advanced by a Credit Bank shall be repayable by instalments; and that a Credit Bank shall accept payment of the whole loan or of any part thereof (not less than one-fourth of the original loan) before the date stipulated for payment, subject to the payment of a commission to the Bank which shall in no case exceed six months interest on the sum so paid in advance. If the mortgagor has given to the Bank three months notice of his intention to repay, the commission payable shall not exceed three months interest on the sum so repaid (Sec. 4 (11)). There is no such statutory relief to mortgagors who borrow from mortgagees who are not Credit Banks.

[3]) For the purpose of Part VI, "Company" includes a Co-operative Society (Sec. 120).

[4]) See "debenture" and "floating charge" defined in Sec. 2 of the Ordinance.

The Land Law of Palestine.

or purchaser at the time of the creation of the mortgage or of the sale (Sec. 123 (3)), but debenture holders or their trustees may apply to the Court for an order restraining the Director of Lands from permitting further registrations of mortgages or sales in respect of the registered lands of the Company (Sec. 123 (4)).

Attachment of Land for Government Debts. It was the practice of the Ottoman Treasury to attach land of tax farmers, and their guarantors for failure to pay sums due to the Treasury.

In the year 1328 (7th Jamad-el-Awal) an order was issued by the Turkish Government to the effect that owners of properties attached by the Government can redeem their holdings on payment of the amounts due.

On the lines of this enactment emanating from the Ottoman Government a Public Notice has been issued by the Government in 1921 allowing the redemption by former owners of lands attached since 1327, and registered in the name of the Ottoman Treasury [1]).

The former owners or their heirs or representatives were to be allowed to pay to the Government within one year from the date of the Notice, the sums owing to the Treasury together with 6% interests per annum for every year that the land has been attached.

The Notice provides that where land in possession of the Government had been leased to the former owner the sum payable should be that with which the land was charged, and no interest should be added. If the land attached had been sold by the Treasury the right of redemption did not apply.

Properties foreclosed by Imperial Ottoman Agricultural Bank. In August 1921 the Government of Palestine by Public Notice ordered the restoration to the former owners of properties foreclosed by the Imperial Ottoman Agricultural Bank which at the date of the Notice were still registered in the name of the Bank. The former owners were allowed to pay to the Bank the amounts of principal and interest due at the date of foreclosure together with interest on that amount from that date at the rate prescribed in the original Deed of Mortgage.

Applications for the return of such properties were to be made to the Public Custodian within 90 days from Sept. 15th, 1921 [2]).

Furthermore, as an act of grace it has been ordered by Public Notice of 1st September, 1921, that no interest shall be charged on outstanding debts due to the Imperial Ottoman Agricultural Bank until the 1st Sept. 1921.

---

[1]) Off. Gaz. 15 Jan. 1921.
[2]) Off. Gaz. No. 51.

Chapter XI—Secured and Unsecured Creditors. [179]

As from the 1st September, 1921, interest of the rate of 6% per annum has been charged in every case of debts that were still unpaid after the 1st Sept. 1921.

By Proclamation of March 1921 the winding up of the operations of the Imperial Ottoman Agricultural Bank in Palestine was ordered and a liquidator appointed. All the property of the Imperial Ottoman Agricultural Bank was vested in the Liquidator who was given power to collect all the outstanding debts, realise the securities of the Bank, grant discharges of any mortgage or other charges registered in favour of the Imperial Ottoman Agricultural Bank and defend proceeding in the Courts.

Agricultural Loans. A considerable sum was advanced by the Anglo-Egyptian Bank in accordance with a special agreement between the Government and the Bank and lent by the Government in small amounts to the agriculturists in the form of agricultural loans to enable them to purchase stock and seeds and to restore their cultivation [1]).

The loans to cultivators bear interest at the rate of 6½ % per annum. Loans were granted in two forms: — (a) Loans for small amounts not exceeding £E. 60. (b) Loans of £E. 60 and over.

In case of (a) when there was no immovable property registered in the name of the debtor in the Tapu the crops of the debtor were by agreement put under attachment.

With regard to loans of (b), which were granted only to persons who have immovable property registered in their names in the Tapu, the immovable property of the debtor was attached under an agreement in the form of a Deed or Mortgage registered in the Land Registry. When the loan is repaid the mortgage is discharged and the property released.

Rights of unsecured creditors to obtain execution against the debtor's immovable property. It has never been doubted that all the Mulk of a debtor is available for payment of his debts and can be seized and sold on behalf of the creditor through the process of execution (Mejelle, Art. 998). This Article instructs the judge when ordering execution to sell first the things of which the alienation causes the least damage to the debtor, and on this principle the immovables are to be sold last.

Under the older Law, however, Miri and Waqf land were not strictly chargeable with the holders unsecured debts (Land Code, Art. 115) but the law was altered by an enactment of 15 Shewal, A.H. 1288, whereby it was provided (Sec. 1) that Mussaqafat and

---

[1]) As to loans for the purchase of seed made by the Government see Seed Loans Ordinance 1929.

Mustaghilat waqfs held in Ijaratein [1]) as well as Miri land could be sold without the consent of the debtor for payment of a judgment debt in the same way as Mulk.

It still remained doubtful whether these latter classes of interests were assets in the hands of the heirs for the payment of the debts of a deceased debtor. But all doubts were set at rest by the provision of Art. 16 of the Law of Disposition, A. H. 1331.

"Miri and Mevqufe land and Mussaqafat and Mustaghilat waqf owned by a person are security for his debts during his life and after his death, even if it becomes mahlul land. But if the debtor is a cultivator that part of the land which is required for his support will not be sold unless it is already the object of a contract of conditional sale or mortgage, or unless the debt represents the price of the land. This rule applies also to the house which is necessary for accomodation of the debtor, or of his family after his death".

It is noteworthy that this Article gives the right to obtain execution even against the State or the Waqf claiming the land as Mahlul. The purchaser under the forced sale would, therefore, presumably have a right to a Kushan of Miri even against persons claiming rights of Tapu, or in the case of Waqf, would be entitled to be deemed lessee in Ijaratein.

The procedure to be followed for attachment and sale is set forth in the Execution Law of A. H. 1332. The unsecured creditor who has obtained a judgment in his favour, can get an order from the President of the Execution Office (i. e. the President of the District Court) for the attachment of the immovable property of the judgment debtor (Sec. 89). The dwelling house of the debtor if suitable to his position is exempt; so also land sufficient for the maintenance of the debtor's family (Sec. 90). The rules regulating the attachment and consequent sale are set forth in those and the ensuing Sections of the Execution Law above referred to.

The Civil Procedure (Execution of Judgments) Bill published for information in the Off. Gaz. for 6 April 1933 [2]) contemplates the repeal of the Ottoman Law of Execution and the substitution of new provisions as to execution. Part IV of the Bill is devoted to execution against immovable property.

---

[1]) Muqata'a waqf interests are Mulk and fall, therefore, under Mulk Law.
[2]) See P. G. No. 437 of 3. 5. 1934 in which the Bill is re-published.

CHAPTER XII—LEASES.

The Mejelle contains a large number of Articles dealing with the Law of Hire (Arts. 404 ff.). The contract of hire is divided into two distinct species, the hire of things and animals and the hire of work (Art. 421). Of these we are only concerned with the hire of things, and of one class of things only, namely immovables. In the Mejelle the rules relating to contracts of hire of the different kinds are not separated. The following provisions relative to such contracts in general or to contracts for the hire of immovables, in particular, are noteworthy.   *Contract of Hire in the Mejelle.*

Contract of hire is formed by offer and acceptance (Art. 422), the contracting parties must be of full age and of sound mind (Arts. 444, 458). Anything which in sale may serve as price serves also as hire (Art. 463). Price (i. e. rent, Ijara) may be paid in advance if so stipulated (Arts. 468, 473). If payment be agreed by month or by year, the price is to be paid at the end of the time (Art. 476). If the use of the thing hired is impossible, the contract of hire is of no effect and consequently payment cannot be required (Art. 478). Hire must be for a defined period (Art. 484). The period begins from the time of the agreement in the absence of contrary stipulation (Arts. 485, 486). Hire for a month and so on from month to month is permissible, in which case the contract may be broken by either party during the first 24 hours of each month (Art. 494). If defects in the thing hired arise, which prevent the enjoyment of the benefit the hirer may dissolve the contract (Art. 516 ff.). The contract of hire of a field should define what the hirer should sow in it or that he shall have the right to sow what he wishes (Art. 524). If the period of hiring expires before the carrying of the crops the hirer can keep the field in his possession until the carrying by paying for the extra time a rent according to valuation (Art. 526). The lessee of a house may sublet (Arts. 528, 586). He must not use the house in such a way as to injure it (Art. 528). Repairs necessary to give proper enjoyment of the thing hired fall upon the lessor and if he fail to keep in repair the lessee may give up the house (Art. 529);

but repairs which are merely for the benefit of the lessee, i. e. not necessary in order to keep the house in good condition, fall upon the lessee in the absence of agreement (Art. 830). If the lessee of a house build on it or plant trees on property which is hired the lessor has an option at the expiration of the tenancy either to claim the destruction of the building or the uprooting of the trees or to keep them on paying their value (Art. 531). The lessee must clear the property from rubbish accumulated during the tenancy (Art. 532). The lessor can ask from the Court a disolution of the contract if the lessee is so acting as to destroy the property.

A co-owner of an undivided thing may let out his part to his co-owner, but not to a third person, unless they take turns in the benefit of the thing (Art. 429) [1]).

Law governing the Hire of Miri. Arts. 9 and 23 of the Land Code imply the existence of a right by the Miri holder to let his holding on lease, and this power is confirmed in the broadest terms by Art. 5 of the Law of Disposition, A.H. 1331. We may safely assume that the rules governing contracts for the hire of land contained in the Mejelle apply as well to hire of Miri as of Mulk. No distinction is suggested and the provisions purport to regulate contracts for hire in general.

Apparently a lease may be granted for any time however long [2]) and the terms for payment of rent are entirely a matter for bargaining between the parties. The term may also be made to commence at a future date [3]).

The law of Hire as thus stated differs much in certain respects from that of England. The English Common Law adopts the principle that if a person has accepted an obligation he is bound in law to perform it or to pay damages, even though the performance may have become much more onerous owing to the new circumstances or indeed, impossible [4]). If a person takes a lease of a house and during the term the house is destroyed without any fault on the part of the lessee, the lessee is nevertheless bound to continue to pay the agreed rent though he has lost the benefit of the house [5]). And if he has agreed to keep the house in repair

---

[1]) Cf. Arts. 1178, 1186. Two co-owners may let the thing in common to another (Art. 431).
[2]) Mejelle, Art. 484, Iradeh as to Leasing, A. H. 1299, Art. 7.
[3]) Mejelle, Art. 408.
[4]) On the other hand if the obligation is one imposed by law, impossibility is a defence.
[5]) Cf. Paradine v. Jane (1648) Aleyn, 26.

Chapter XII—Leases.

he must do so even though the house is destroyed by fire or otherwise and will require rebuilding[1]). The Mejelle appears to proceed from a different point of view. A lease of property is subject to an option for defect such that if, during the currency of the lease, the property become so defective that the primary purpose of the lease cannot be accomplished, the tenant has an option to cancel (Mejelle, Arts. 513-514). The examples given in Art. 514 clearly show how widely this principle is applied. The matter is further explained in Art. 518 from which it is clear that if the lessee cannot get the intended benefit from the hiring he is not required to pay the rent [2]).

It follows that, as stated in Art. 529 of the Mejelle, the lessor is bound to keep the property in proper repair. If he does not do so the lessee may quit. And if the lessee does necessary repairs which are for the permanent benefit of the property the lessor may be called upon to make good the expense even though he had not consented (Art. 530) [3]).

These principles and applications are fully confirmed by other authorities. "If a person hire a house", says the Hedaya, "and then discover a defect in it such as renders it uninhabitable, he is at liberty to dissolve the contract; because the contract was executed with a view to advantage; and as that continually, from time to time, is the object of the hirer, it follows that the deffect discovered in the house had existence previously to his obtaining possession of the thing actually contracted for, although it had occurred subsequent to taking possession of the house". So also Kadry Pasha lays down that "The repair of a house which is let is at the cost of the lessor. He cannot, however, be compelled to do the repairs, but if he fails to do them the lessee may annul the contract". And again "If a house which has been let becomes ruinous so as to be quite unfit for the purpose for which it was let the tenant can annul the contract and is under no obligation to pay further rent [4]).

The Mejelle contains no chapter dealing with contracts in general and its solutions, though often very reasonable and just do not always conform to any general theory [5]). It is not, therefore, easy

---

[1]) Cf. Pym v. Blackburn (1796) 3 Vesey 34.

[2]) Compare Mejelle, Art. 478. No rent is payable if the benefit to be obtained from the thing hired is entirely lost.

[3]) Hedaya III, Book. XXXI, Chap. IX (Hamilton's Translation at p. 509). As to the provisions of the Imperial Iradeh of A. H. 1299 so far as they affect a essee's liability for repairs see further below.

[4]) Statut Réel; Arts. 645, 646. Cl. Art. 655.

[5]) As we have elsewhere stated, the Mejelle recognizes the principle of

to say what the precise effect of a contract by the tenant to keep in repair would be. But it should be borne in mind that Art. 64 of the Code of Civil Procedure lays down that all agreements not forbidden by special laws and regulations and which are not contrary to morality and public order [1]), are valid as regards the contracting parties, and, further, that under Art. 108 of the same Code damages are not awarded for breach of contract due to causes outside the control of the party guilty of the breach.

Nature of interest created by a lease.   An important question arises as to the precise nature of the interest created by a lease. Primarily a lease is merely an agreement between a lessor and a lessee whereby the lessor undertakes for a certain payment that the lessee shall have occupation of the property leased for a specified term. It is natural that persons familiar with the actual working of the leasehold system in England should assume that the lessee has an heritable and assignable interest; and that his interest is available against both the lessor and his heirs and assignees, who are bound to recognise the lease though entitled to the benefit of the rent reserved and the covenants contained in the lease.

We are not, however, entitled to assume that this is the law in Palestine [2]).

There seems ample authority for stating that according to the Moslem Law, upon which the Mejelle is based, a lease is a contract creating obligations only between the immediate parties thereto. Thus Kadry Pasha lays down:

"The lease terminates at the death of the lessor or of the lessee when these persons have contracted in their own name. If they have contracted as agents for others their death has no effect [3]).

---

compensation for improvements (Art. 531). See Chapter dealing with the Protection of Agricultural Tenants, infra.

[1]) Compare Art. 3 of the Iradeh as to Leasing of A. H. 1299.

[2]) The nature of the rights enjoyed by Government tenants of jiftlik lands was considered by the Jaffa Land Court sitting as a Court of Appeal in the case of the Government of Palestine v. the Village Settlement Committee of Sajad and Qazaza Villages (case 18/32). The Settlement Officer Ramle Settlement Area decided that the land occupied by the tenants was Government Miri land subject to "hereditary and assignable rights of occupancy and tenancy".

On appeal the Court (Copland and Shehadeh JJ.) held that such "hereditary and assignable rights of occupancy and tenancy" did not exist, and that they were a form of tenure unknown to the Law of Palestine, being contrary to the provisions of Art. 23 of the Land Code.

[3]) Op. cit., Arts. 664. Compare the Hedaya at p. 510, "If one of the contracting parties die... the contract is dissolved, because if the contract were still to remain in force it would follow that the rent thus becomes the right of a person who was not a party to the contract since it would shift from the deceased

Chapter XII—Leases.

But though the Moslem law is as stated yet one may assume that the Courts of Palestine will make every effort to avoid its strict application which in modern conditions would prove very inconvenient. In practice it is usual in Palestine for rent to be paid in advance and where there is a letting for a period of years the rent for the whole period is often paid in advance when the lessee goes into occupation.

In practice leases usually contain a clause whereby the parties to the contract purport to bind their heirs and assignees. The operation of the clause as against or in favour of heirs has not been judicially interpreted as far as we know. Art. 17 of the Imperial Iradeh on Leasing of A. H. 1299 as amended in A. H. 1332 states that if the contract stamps specified thereon have been duly affixed to the lease then "upon the death of the lessor or of the lessee the contract shall continue to be binding (without payment of additional fees)". These words appear to imply that a contract of lease is normally to be treated as binding on the heirs of both parties, and this conclusion is certainly one which is in accordance with modern expectations [1]).

Heirs and Assignees.

Even in Moslem theory it would not be correct to say, that the lessee gets nothing under the lease save a right in personam against the lessor. No consistent juridical theory on the subject was worked out by the Moslem jurists, but from certain points of view they recognize that the lessee has an interest in the land which is created by the lease. Reffering to the question discussed below as to the effect on the lessee's interest of a sale of the land by the lessor, Sir Anton Bertram J. in his interesting judgement in Tzapa v. Tsolaki [2]) remarked "The Sharia law differs from the Roman law, which regards a lease simply as a contract between the parties; and not as giving a right in rem". It is perhaps a little bold to use Western judicial terms to describe the legal conceptions of the Moslem law. Yet we are bound to recognize that the Moslem law of lease is not fully explicable on the basis of a purely personal relation between lessor and lessee.

Lease a right in Personam.

---

to the heir, which is unlawful". The same principle is subsequently applied to the case in which the lessee has died. See also Baz (Commentary on Art. 443 of the Mejelle) in the same sense. A contract of lease is not annulled by subsequent madness of the lessor or lessee (Art. 458). If the lessee becomes owner of the property leased, the lease comes to an end (Art. 442).

[1]) The interest of lessees in Ijaratein were made heritable by special enactment. It would be strange indeed, if the interest of an ordinary lessee had become heritable by the effect of the cryptic words at the close of Art. 17 above cited.

[2]) (1910) 9 C. L. R. at p. 78.

Kadry Pasha lays down that where a lessee has paid rent in advance and the lessor died before the lease has terminated the lessee is entitled to continue in occupation till the rent for the period which remains unexpired has been returned to him. For this sum he has a right of preference over the sale price of the immovable if the lessor has died insolvent and the immovable has to be sold [1]. Similar rules clearly congruent with Moslem law are to be found in a Decree as to Contracts of Hire dated 6th Sha'ban A. H. 1284 printed in Aristarchi's Collection of Ottoman legislation. Reference to it is not irrelevant as illustrating the attitude of the Ottoman Government. Thus Art. 7 provides that every contract of lease as to immovables is made void by the death of either party. If rent had been paid in advance and the lessor died, the part of the rent corresponding to the unexpired period must be restored by the lessor's heirs to the lessee. If the lessee died in the same circumstances the rent for the unexpired portion of the term must be restored by the lessor to the heirs of the lessee. Sub-leases were not to be allowed without the consent of the lessor (Art. 11). Destruction of the immovable by fire or other chance brought the lease to an end (Art. 12). Sale of the reversion by the lessor would not affect the binding character of the lease (Art. 14) [2], but it is left undetermined what is the relation between the lessee and the grantee of the reversion.

The difficulty which we find in the determining the juridical nature of the lessee's interest, casts doubt upon the question as to whether the lessee can validly assign his lease. An assignment could, of course, be arranged with the consent of the lessor who accepts the assignee as his tenant in place of the assignor, but there is no authority to show that assignment inter vivos without the co-operation of the lessor is possible. Nevertheless the possibility of a transfer of the lessee's interest seems to be taken for granted in some recent enactments though it is not always clear that the transfer may be made without the lessor's co-operation. Thus Article 17 of the Iradeh of A.H. 1299 as amended by the Law of A. H. 1332 provides that: —

"If a lessee desires to transfer his right for a portion of the term of the lease a note shall be made at the foot of the lease".

This provision impliedly recognizes assignments of leases though their operation is not worked out.

---

[1]) Statut Réel, Art. 665.
[2]) Cf. Mejelle, Art. 590.

Chapter XII—Leases.

Sec. 78 (5) and (6) of the Civil Procedure (Execution of Judgments) Bill published in the Off. Gaz. for 6 April 1933 [1]) assume that there exist cases in which lessees may assign their interest without the consent of the lessor, and the Stamp Ordinance of 1927 specifies the stamps to be placed upon a "transfer of lease" (Item 21 of the Schedule).

It seems, therefore, that leases may be assigned [2]). And in certain cases an interest created by a lease may be mortgaged. Sec. 3 of the Credit Banks Ordinance 1922 made provision for such mortgages in specified cases and this provision has now been generalized by Sec. 9 of the Land Law (Amendment) Ordinance 1933. In the case of sale of the leasehold interest mortgaged under the Credit Banks Ordinance express provision is made for dispensing with the consent of the lessor; whether the mortgagee of a leasehold interest could sell without the lessor's co-operation in any other case may be doubted.

Similar doubts arise as to the effect upon the lease of a sale of the property by the lessor. Art. 590 of the Mejelle deals with a sale by the lessor of the property let. Such a sale is good as between vendor and purchaser though its operation is postponed. It is not effective as against the lessee unless he accepts it. And if the purchaser demands delivery before the lease expires the judge may annul the contract of sale. And Kadry Pasha definitely states that "the sale of an immovable which has been leased cannot be executed unless the lessee agrees. If he refuses his consent, the sale remains in suspense till the term expires" [3]).

Sale of property leased.

Nevertheless the Amendment made by the Mortgage Law Amendment Ordinance 1920 to Art. 3 of the Provisional Law as to Mortgages of A.H. 1331 provides that if a mortgagee exercises his power of sale the purchaser is bound by any lease of the property which has been duly registered with the Municipality or with the Land Registry [4]) and is entitled to its benefit. If this is the position in the case of a sale of a reversion of mortgaged property by a mortgagee it is difficult to see why the same rule should not apply in the case of sale by the owner of the property whether encumbered or unencumbered. It is, indeed, generally

---

[1]) See also P. G. No. 437 of 3 May 1934.
[2]) Cf. Art. 64 of the Code of Civil Proc. as amended. All matters, interests and rights are regarded as being capable of both acquisition and enjoyment.
[3]) Op. cit., Art. 663.
[4]) As to registration at the Municipality and at the Land Registry, see further below.

understood that the provision in question must be taken to apply to protect registered leases against all purchasers of the reversion; such purchasers are deemed to have received notice of the lease and are bound by it.

They are also entitled to receive rents and sue upon the agreement since the section expressly gives them the "benefit" of the lease.

If the provision may be thus generalized and interpreted we arrive at the modern conception of the situation as between lessees, their assignees, and lessors and their grantees. In the absence of direct authority much must be left obscure. What covenants in the lease "run" with the lease or with the reversion? To what extent are remedies reserved by the lease available in the hands of grantees of the reversion or against assignees of the lease?

In English law an important body of cases supplemented by statutory provisions has elaborated rules governing the rights and liabilities of assignees of leases and of grantees of reversions and in particular the right of each to sue and liability to be sued on the covenants in the lease. Assuming as we do that leasehold interests are transferable in the modern law of Palestine questions of the sort are bound to arise and would be solved probably by reference to English authority [1]).

To sum up. It seems that a lessee who has registered his lease is protected against a purchaser of the reversion. But whether a lessee can alienate his leasehold interest without the co-operation of the lessor is doubtful. That he can mortgage it is clear, but the extent to which the mortgagee can exercise his power of sale without the co-operation of the lessor is left doubtful, save as stated in the Credit Banks Ordinance. Nor is there any definite statement enabling us to say that leases are either binding against the heirs of the lessor or that a leasehold interest can be inherited or bequeathed by will. It appears to follow a fortiori that an interest under a lease granted by a Miri holder cannot avail against persons claiming a right to Tapu on his death without successors, still less against the State claiming to take the land as pure Mahlul.

But it appears that the lessee can create sub-leases out of his interest [2]), though such a creation would not, of course, free him

---

[1]) The subject is one of considerable complexity. For a brief survey see Radcliffe, Real Property Law, Chapter XXII.

[2]) The Mejelle (Art. 586) appears to limit this to Sub-leases made by the Sub-lessor "before taking delivery" and in Antoniou v. Joannon (1923) 11 C.L.R. at p. 88 this was interpreted to imply that a Sub-lease made "after delivery"

Chapter XII—Leases.

from his personal liability for rent, etc. towards the head lessor, nor would the head lessor have any direct action against the sub-lessee.

In England it is usual for leases to contain provisions giving the lessor power to re-enter if rent is not paid or covenants are not performed. Relief against such clauses is provided by statute [1] in certain cases. In view of the provision of Art. 64 of the Code of Civil Procedure, such clauses might well be treated as binding in Palestine [2]. In a case recently reported in the Palestine Post [3] application was made to the Court of Appeal for cancellation of a lease on the triple ground of misrepresentation, non payment of rent and breach of covenant. The judgment lays down no general principle and refers to no authorities but gives rise to the inference that the Court reserves a right to cancel a lease if misrepresentation inducing it is proved and would also be prepared to cancel the contract, i. e. (semble) to determine the lease, if it considered that there had been a breach of a substantial condition. Non payment of Government taxes by the lessee was held not to be a substantial condition in the case of a lease for a long time (49 years).

Power of lessor to re-enter.

Until recently leases in Municipal areas were registered at the Municipal Offices and leases generally for periods exceeding three years were registered at the Land Registry. The latter form of registration alone now exsists.

Registration of leases.

Registration at the Land Registry is effected in compliance with the Transfer of Land Ordinance, 1920, which defines a "disposition of immovable property" in terms to include all leases thereof for terms exceeding three years as also all leases containing an option by virtue of which the term may exceed three years. Consequently any such lease is void, unless the provisions of that Ordinance have been fulfilled, and these involve registration at the Land Registry. A lessor who lets a lessee into possession under such a lease or lessee who goes into possession thereunder without complying with the Ordinance is subject to heavy penalties (Sec. 12).

In the case of Mamur Awqaf v. Syndic of Barsky [4] the Jerusalem District Court had no difficulty in holding that a lease

---

was invalid. But this is a very doubtful decision. See Kadry Pasha, op. cit., Art. 643. And compare Mejelle, Art. 587.

[1] Law of Property Act. 1925, Sec. 146.
[2] It is not unusual to insert in the leases granted by Government of State Domain a clause giving Government (the lessor) power to re-enter if rent is not paid or covenants are not performed.
[3] Keren Kayemeth Ltd. v. Beigal L. A. 15/33; Palestine Post 19 April 1934.
[4] C. A. 325/32; 326/32; Palestine Post 11 Aug. 1933.

for a term exceeding three years which has not been registered as required by the Land Transfer Ordinance 1920 is bad as a whole and cannot be treated as a good lease for three years. The Court further appears to have held that the lessee was entitled to recover from the lessor any rent which he has paid (Transfer of Land Ordinance, 1920, Sec. 11) less the amount of a fair rent as agreed by experts. But the judgement as reported is not free from obscurity.

In the interesting case of Cornu v. Ali Ahmed [1]) which has been referred to in another connection the Court of Appeal held (Baker and Frumkin JJ.; Khayat J. dissenting) that a lease for three years would be a disposition within the meaning of the Transfer of Land Ordinance if it contained a clause under which extension was possible even though the extension were not the result of an option but followed upon the occurence of some event (Act of God) outside the volition of the parties.

The position of a person who has gone into possession and effected improvements under a void lease was discussed in the Cyprus case of Koukoulli v. Hamid [2]) but in that case the act of going into possession was not in itself an illegal act as it would be under the Transfer of Land Ordinance in Palestine in the case of a lease for a term exceeding three years.

A form of "deed of lease" is provided at the Land Registry and registrable leases are generally made by use of this form. The form is signed or sealed by the parties as certified by the Registrar and a certificate of registration is endorsed on this form. The use of the official form is not, of course, compulsory.

Iradeh of A. H. 1299 and Law of Leases of A. H. 1332.

Registration at the Municipality was effected in accordance with the Iradeh as to Leasing of 28 Jamad-el-Awal A.H. 1299 which regulated the form of contracts of lease of immovable property. This law was amended by a Provisional Law of 18 Rabi-el-Awal, A.H. 1332, and is in force in Palestine in the amended form subject to the provisions of the Municipal Corporations Ordinance 1934, mentioned below.

The object of the enactments was partly fiscal. It secured the payment of certain duties by making requisite the apposition of "Contract Stamps" on the document of lease. This made it necessary to require the parties to make their contracts in writing and the Iradeh contains detailed provisions with this object as follows:-

---

[1]) C. A. 105/32; Palestine Post 8 May 1933.
[2]) (1907) 7 C. L. R. at p. 85.

Chapter XII—Leases.

In order to lease houses, shops, lands, farms or other immovable property, whether at Constantinople or in the provinces, a deed of agreement must be executed by the lessor and lessee. Art. 1.

There shall be set forth in the deed the names of the lessor and the lessee, their occupations, their places of residence, their nationalities, the class and situation of the property, the purpose to which it is applied, the period of the lease and the amount of the rent. If the rent be payable in future instalments, the amount of such instalments shall be stated; if it be payable in advance, it shall be recorded as so payable. Art. 2.

If the property be held by owners in joint possession, the share of each shall be stated separately in the deed of contract. Art. 8.

The deed of contract shall be drawn up in duplicate and each copy shall be signed by both parties and by their sureties, if any. Art. 9.

The lessor and lessee may alter any of the conditions of the lease by entry at the foot of the deed. Art. 18.

The provisions of the Iradeh requiring all leases of immovable property to be in writing are general, but the obligation to affix Contract Stamps was confined to leases of property within a Municipal area[1]. Contract Stamps.

The purpose of these provisions was, as stated above, partly to facilitate the imposition of a tax. To sanction them it was further provided by Art. 22 that "a lessor who fails to execute a written deed of lease should be liable to pay a cash penalty equal to three per cent of the rent of the property for one year", and according to Art. 24 the hearing of any case which required the production of a deed of lease was suspended until the penalties provided have been paid. The Law required that contract stamps of the Municipal Office within the jurisdiction of which the property is situate should be affixed to the deed of lease. It did not state that the lease must be registered but the opening paragraph of Art. 3 of the Law of Mortgage, A. H. 1331, appears to assume that some record was kept in the Municipal Offices of all leases stamped there, and Sec. 1 of the Law of Mortgage Amendment Ordinance, 1920, amending that Article speaks definitely of registration of leases with the Municipality.

In consequence of these provisions it appears that every agreement for tenancy of immovable property for however short a

---

[1] A Public Notice of August 1920 made the Iradeh applicable in the Municipal area of Jerusalem. In fact it was applied to all Municipal areas.

The Land Law of Palestine.

time must, in order to be enforceable, be in writing and comply with the requirements of this law.

The Municipal Corporations Ordinance 1934. Recently, however, the Municipal Corporations Ordinance, 1934, has annulled the sanction for the enforcement of the provision of the Iradeh. By that Ordinance (Art. 133 (1)) it is provided that Arts. 6, 10, 11, 12, 13, 14, 15, 16, 22-29 of the Iradeh shall cease to have effect as also Arts. 17, 18, 20, so far as they relate to Contract Stamps.

As a matter of fact it is many years since Contract Stamps have been placed on leases in accordance with the provision of the Iradeh of A. H. 1299. Originally they were affixed at the Municipal Offices and were a source of revenue for the Municipalities. When about 1923 the stock of such stamps was exhausted the Government refrained from reprinting though the Municipalities were administratively permitted to collect the equivalent amounts as a sort of registration fee. Notification of payment of which was then endorsed on the lease. Leases for terms exceeding three years, registration of which at the Land Registry is required under the Transfer of Land Ordinance 1920, were not usually registered also at the Municipality under the Iradeh. It is to be observed that the protection afforded to leases by Sec. 3 of the Provisional Mortgage Law of A. H. 1331 as amended by the Law of Mortgage Amendment Ordinance 1920 extends to all leases duly registered with the Municipality or with the Land Registry.

Since the promulgation of the Municipal Corporation Ordinance 1934 the fiscal foundation upon which registration at the Municipality rested has been destroyed and such registration has ceased. This being so leases which are registered at the Land Registry can alone obtain the statutory protection given by the provision of the Law of Mortgage Amendment Ordinance just cited. There is no statutory obligation to register leases for three years or less at the Land Registry but as a precautionary measure it may, in view of the provision, be wise to do so.

The Iradeh of A. H. 1299 and Law of A. H. 1332 has not, however, entirely lost its interest as a consequence of the abolition of Contract Stamps or the equivalent Municipal registration fee [1]). The provisions which require all leases to be embodied in a document

---

[1]) Note that the collection of the Stamp duties imposed under the Stamp Ordinance 1927 would not be possible unless the lease were in writing. No action is maintainable if the lease is not properly stamped. See Stamp Ordinance 1927 Secs. 16, 17, 40-43; Schedule, Item 21.

Chapter XII—Leases.

still remain in force and a lease or agreement for a lease which is not so embodied appears to be unenforceable [1]).

Other articles of the Iradeh also remain in force which contain important rules relative to the legal relations of lessor and lessee. Art. 3 provides that "the parties may introduce into the agreement any condition which is not repugnant to law or public morality"; a provision which makes it obligatory for the Courts to treat as valid restrictive covenants of a kind which have become very common in England, and which in some cases are undoubtedly injurious to the public interest though hardly of public morality.

Art. 4 states that "there may be prepared a list of the appurtenances of the property with a statement of the condition of the property at the time of the lease, and in such case such list and statement shall be mentioned in the deed of contract. Upon the expiry of the lease, the lessee is bound to deliver to the lessor the things shown in the said list to have been received by him, and shall deliver the property leased in the same condition as is recorded in the said statement. Provided that the lessee shall not be held responsible for deterioration due to natural causes".

If, therefore, the parties have taken the precaution of compiling the inventory here mentioned the liability for keeping the items in good repair falls definitely upon the tenant. The scope of the proviso is not clear, but the "natural causes" referred to are probably to be treated as including earthquake, fire, water and the like, corresponding in general to what English lawyers would term "Act of God". No exception for fair wear and tear is allowed. As already stated the tenant may annul a lease if the property becomes unusable for the purpose intended. The provisions of Art. 4 of the Iradeh do not seem to affect this rule.

The remaining provisions of the Iradeh so far as they have escaped the Municipal Corporations Ordinance 1934, are of less interest. Art. 5 authorizes the clerk of "the Court" to draw up leases on behalf of minors, etc. and Ijara Wahida of Waqf. Art. 7 forbids the leasing of Waqf on Ijara Wahida for a longer period than three years, but expressly provides that Ijaratein leases may be of any length as also leases of all other immovable property.

Ijara Wahida and Ijaratein Leases.

---

[1]) The earlier Ottoman law of 10 Rabi-el-Awal A. H. 1291 was considered and interpreted in the Cypriot cases of Tritoftides v. Nikola (1900) 5 C.L.R. at p. 31 and Koukoulli v. Hamid (1907) 7 C.L.R. at p. 85. The latter case shows that a lease not in writing is invalid and cannot be sued upon. The Cypriot Court on equitable principles gave compensation to the lessee for improvements made by him upon the land.

Art. 19 somewhat cryptically provides that if the Government acquire for a public purpose property held under a lease the lessee shall vacate the property "within the time fixed". It is not clear whether the "acquisition" of the property referred to is acquisition as owner or mere occupation, nor whether the "time fixed" is a time to be fixed by the Government. The Expropriation Ordinance 1926 provides for compensation to persons having an interest in land taken compulsorily and it is not probable that the Government would act otherwise than in accordance with the provisions of that Ordinance.

<small>Divers enactments relating to leases and leasing. Rent restriction and the like.</small>

Mention may here be made of the steps taken in Palestine to deal with the problem of house shortage which has in England led to such remarkable innovations. By the Landlords and Tenants (By-Laws) Ordinance 1933 Municipalities and Local Councils were empowered with the consent of the High Commissioner to make by-laws providing with respect to premises within their respective areas that subsisting agreements of tenancy should continue in force. By the same or subsequent by-laws the same authorities are empowered to provide "for the regulation of the relationship between landlords and tenants and tenants and sub-tenants for a period not exceeding the end of Zil Hijje A. H. 1352", either generally or in respect of landlords and tenants whose agreements have been extended by reason of any by-law.

Further and more elaborate provision with the same object is made by the Landlords and Tenants (Ejection and Rent Restriction) Ordinance 1934. The Ordinance is to remain in force until 31 March 1935. In view of its temporary character it is not necessary here to consider its provisions in detail. Secs. 4 and 5 restrict the powers of the Courts and execution officers in connection with the eviction of tenants of dwelling houses. Secs. 6—9 fix or provide for the fixing of maximum rents of dwelling houses from and after the end of Zil Hijje A. H. 1352. Secs. 11-13 restrict increases of rent and Secs. 14 ff. provide for the setting up of Rents Commissioners and Rents Tribunals. The application of the Ordinance is dependent upon an Order by the High Commissioner in Council and by Order dated 17 April 1934 [1] the Ordinance was applied in whole to the Municipal area of Tel Aviv.

The Protection of Cultivators Ordinances the object of which is similar in character to that of the Landlords and Tenants Ordinances, are fully dealt with in a later chapter [2].

---

[1] Suppl. 2 to P. G. Extra No. 434 of 17 April 1934.
[2] See Chapter XV dealing with the Protection of Agricultural Tenants, infra.

Chapter XII—Leases.

In conclusion a reference may be useful to certain other provisions of Palestinian Ordinances touching upon power of leasing and the like. In this connection we may note— {Powers of leasing etc.}

(1) As to notice to mortgagee of leases of property mortgaged—See Law of Mortgage A.H. 1331, Sec. 3, as amended by Mortgage Law Amendment Ordinance, 1920.

(2) As to mortgage of leasehold interest—Credit Banks Ordinance, 1922, Sec. 3. Land Law (Amendment) Ordinance, 1933, Sec. 9.

(3) As to powers of leasing:—
   (a) Mortgage Credit Banks in possession—Credit Banks Ordinance, 1922, Sec. 2 (II).
   (b) Trustees of Charitable Trusts—Charitable Trusts Ordinance, 1924, Sec. 12.
   (c) Administrator of estate of deceased person—Succession Ordinance, 1923, Sec. 15 (II) (c).
   (d) In case of property of a minor—Succession Ordinance Sec. 20 (A).
   (e) Possessed by Mutwally of Waqf property, Iradeh on Leasing A.H. 1299, Sec. 7.

(4) As to leasing of Public Lands, see Public Lands Ordinance, 1926.

(5) For mining leases and surface leases in connection with mining operations, see Mining Ordinance, 1925, Sec. 30 ff.

(6) As to the taking of land on lease compulsory—Acquisition of Land for the Army and Air Force Ordinance 1925, Sec. 17. Expropriation Ordinance 1926, Secs. 4, 5, 12, 19. Antiquities Ordinance 1929, Sec. 9 (2) (a).

In the Title of the Mejelle dealing with Partnership mention is made of contracts concerning the taking of land with a view to cultivation either as arable land or for trees. Of these the more important in former times was the contract for cultivation of land by sowing (Muzaraa). Such contracts were formerly not uncommon as owing to the prohibition of interest in Moslem law they were one of the few ways in which capital could be invested without incurring the guilt of usury. They constituted a form of the partnership known as Mudarebe in which one partner supplied the capital and the other the skill. "Muzaraa", said Sir Anton Bertram J.[1] "is an extension of the principle of Mudarebe; for in Muzaraa the capital of the partnership may be land, one party supplying {Contracts of Cultivators (Muzaraa and Musakat).}

---

[1] In Tzapa v. Tsolaki (1910) 9 G.L.R. at p. 77.

The Land Law of Palestine.

the land, and the other the labour, and the various means of cultivation being furnished by the one or the other according to their agreement. But though the agreement is spoken of as a form of partnership, it is in substance not so much a form of partnership as a form of lease [1]. It is an essential condition that the land be given up absolutely to the cultivator (Mejelle, Art. 1436). The contract is naturally one that admits of many combinations, and six possible forms of it are enumerated in the Hedaya and the modern Turkish commentators. Two of these are universally recognized as invalid, and the reason is that they infringe this principle—that the land must be given up to the cultivator. This being to great extent, the real nature of the contract, its legal incidents will be found worked out by the early authorities upon this analogy of the law of lease".

In the Cypriot case just referred to the Court was called upon to consider the incidents of Muzaraa and in particular, whether it was lawful for the proprietor of the land to sell it during the term of the contract. The principle followed was that of the Moslem law that if the contract is one in which the proprietor supplies the seed he may in any year rescind the contract before the seed is sown. Since in this case the land was sold before the seed was supplied the contract was lawfully rescinded and the entry of the cultivator in sowing the land constituted a trespass against the purchaser [2].

Contracts of this kind are not common in Palestine to-day. But recent cases appear to show that they are sometimes resorted to in order to avoid the law as to sale of future crops. In Civil Appeal 105/32 a contract alleged to be in the nature of Musakat was before the Court of Appeal and the nature of this contract was discussed [3]. Contracts of Musakat are, in principle, similar to those of Muzaraa, one partner supplies the trees and the other tends them on the terms that the fruit produced is to be shared between them [4]. In the case in question the contract was termed one of Musakat and provided that in consideration of 990 shares

---

[1] Compare the ancient form of cultivation known in France as "Métayage". Planiol, Droit Civil, vol. II, p. 597 (Paris, 1923). Note that by Sec. 6(1) of the Partnership Ordinance 1930 "partnerships by way of Muzaraa and Musakat... are not to be deemed partnerships for the purpose of carrying on a trade, profession or industry".

[2] As to contracts of Muzaraa see Mejelle Arts. 1431—1440 and very fully in Hedaya, Book XL (Hamilton's Translation), pp. 579 ff.

[3] Cornu v. Ali Ahmed, C.A. 105/32, Palestine Post 8 May 1933.

[4] Mejelle, Arts. 1441—1448; Hedaya, Book XLI, pp. 584 ff.

Chapter XII—Leases.

out of a thousand in the crops of the Respondent's orange grove which the Respondent undertook to give to Apellant for three years, the Apellant undertook to cultivate the trees of the orange grove for the like period.

Another clause of the contract created a lease of the orange grove that could in certain circumstances be prolonged beyond three years. The majority of the Court (Baker and Frumkin JJ., Khayat J., dissenting) held that in the circumstances the agreement constituted a disposition within the meaning of the Transfer of Land Ordinance, 1920, and was void as not having been made with the consent of the Government. For our present purpose the case is of special interest in its relation to Musakat and in that connection the following quotation form the judgement of Frumkin J. is of special value. The learned Judge remarked:—

"Musakat is a partnership based on the same principles as that of Muzaraa partnership. The Muzaraa is dealt with in the Mejelle sections 1441—1448, while sections 1431—1440 deal with Musakat.

Both institutions were created for the benefit of landlords who cannot or do not wish to cultivate their land or their trees respepectively themselves, and anxious to avoid dealing with hired labour, enter into partnership with a cultivator to do for them the cultivation of the land or trees, as the case may be, in consideration of a proportional share in the proceeds of the land or trees so cultivated.

It is in both cases nothing else than a contract between an owner of a farm or grove on the one side and a workman or cultivator on the other side, the latter to work on the land not as a hired workman for a fixed daily or monthly pay but as a partner in the proceeds at an agreed proportion. There is apparently nothing to prevent the parties to a "Musakat" partnership from imposing upon the cultivating partner to invest money of his own on materials or other matters, required for the cultivation. Yet, his principle function would remain to be that of work and cultivation.

Sale or pledge of things not in existence at the time of the contract being prohibited under the Mejelle, growers in this country as in other parts of the Ottoman Empire to which Palestine then belonged, used very frequently to give their contract for the sale or pledge of their crops the form of Musakat. The vendor or pledgor assumes the role of the owner of the trees in the Musakat partnership, and the "workman" is in fact the purchaser of the crops or the money lender, as the case may be. A most striking example of a fictitious Musakat we find in this case. I don't know whether the Respondents, the owners of the groves, could themselves look after their groves but the lady Apellant, herself a town resident, is certainly the last person in the world to assume the function of the workman to do the cultivation of the trees; and the remuneration she gets for her work; nothing less than 99 per cent! The one per cent formerly left to the owner in fact also remains with the "workman" for payment of taxes.

Whatever might have been the intention of the parties to hide under this fiction of Musakat, it is clearly not a contract of Musakat".

The learned Judge later pointed out that since under Art. 64 of the Ottoman Code of Civil Procedure as amended on 21 December 1919 [1]) future goods may be the subject matter of a contract, a contract for the sale of future goods is now valid. But he proceeded as follows: —

"I would like to take this opportunity to make the following remark which is of a somewhat wider aspect.

It has already been stated that it was the practice in olden times to shelter under the Musakat (a form of partnership whereby one gave the trees and the other party tended them) when parties sought to obtain funds advanced on their future crops by way of sale or mortgage.

In absence of clear legislation to meet the point the practice still continues. The present case is not the only example to show that this practice is not to be encouraged as being to the disadvantage not only of the parties to such fictitious contracts, but may often become prejudicial to the interests of non-contracting members of the public.

With the immense development of the Citrus industry which becomes more and more one of the principal resources of the wealth of this country it will be of great assistance not only to orange growers and credit institutions but to the public at large if legislation is passed to meet the demands of the trade providing, on the one hand, for more adequate and up-to-date ways and conditions under which future crops may be sold or mortgaged and, on the other hand, for measures of control to safeguard public interest".

---

[1]) Art. 64. "All matters, interests and rights are regarded as being capable of both acquisition and enjoyment. Agreements relating to things to be produced n the future are also valid".

CHAPTER XIII—CO-OWNERSHIP AND PARTITION.

The ownership of property by two or more persons jointly is fully recognised by the Ottoman Law. Its frequent occurrence in Palestine is due to many causes, which resulted in the prevalence in Palestine of a system of customary joint ownership known as Mesha'a.

The joint ownership of Ottoman Law is analagous to that known to English lawyers as Tenancy in Common [1]). The joint owners are each owners of a separate undivided share of the property, that is to say, each is entitled to a share in every part of the property. Each joint owner, therefore, holds his share on a separate title, and the share may be separately alienated and separately inherited. This type of joint ownership must be carefully distinguished from the true "joint tenancy" of English Law. {Tenancy in Common.}

Joint tenants, as distinguished from tenants in common, do not (in English Law) own separate undivided shares but all together own the whole property. As they do not hold separate shares the death of any one joint tenant will cause the interests of the deceased to accrue by operation of law to the survivors. This form of joint ownership is unknown in Ottoman Law, but it has been introduced into Palestine by the Charitable Trusts Ordinance, for the purpose for which it is actually still in use in England, namely for the regulation of the interests of trustees in property held in trust [2]). {Joint Tenants.}

It is only in this connection that such a joint tenancy exists in Palestine. Property held in joint ownership of this kind cannot be partitioned among the joint tenants. It is merely a legal device

---

[1]) The word "tenant" is used here in its feudal sense and applies to freehold tenants, i. e. owners of the freehold.

[2]) See Charitable Trusts Ordinance 1924, Sec. 25, as amended by Charitable Trusts Ordinance 1925. In the case of the form of joint ownership known as Shirket el Ibaha it would be improper to speak of ownership of separate undivided shares. But, as remarked below, the attempt made by the Moslem law to treat the so-called Shirket el Ibaha as a form of joint ownership is unfortunate and is due to the absence in Moslem law of adequate theoretical legal conceptions.

The Land Law of Palestine.

for securing continuity of ownership and further consideration of it is not necessary. This Chapter, therefore, deals only with joint ownership of the type known to Ottoman Law, in which separate undivided shares belong to the joint owners.

Joint ownership.
Joint ownership is the subject of many articles of the Mejelle. The subject is closely connected with business partnerships and the Mejelle in this connection draws a distinction (Art. 1045) between joint ownership "derived from purchase or acceptance of a gift or from any other thing causing ownership" (Shirket el Mulk), and joint ownership arising from contract, that is, partnership which is constituted by offer and acceptance (Shirket el Akd).

In general terms we may say that where joint owners are partners they agree to exploit the thing owned in common as a capital for their common benefit, and such an agreement implies reciprocal mandates (Mejelle Art. 1333). Shirket El Mulk does not of itself imply reciprocal mandates.

The Mejelle (Art. 1045) speaks also of another kind of joint ownership, Shirket el Ibaha "brought about by the joint acquisition of ownership by the public of things which are free (mubah) and themselves belong absolutely to no particular person". As a consequence of this conception we find that the law with reference to common rights in land and water is comprised in the chapter on "Joint Ownership". It is, however, clear that the joint ownership which is a form of private property and the so-called joint ownership of things subject to the common rights of all, are judicially very different. No serious advantage is gained by an attempt to assimilate the two forms of joint or common enjoyment. They have nothing in common save the fact that in each case we find several people using the same thing as of right and this fact was perhaps enough to mislead the Moslem jurists into assuming a theoretical connection.

In this Chapter we shall deal only with joint ownership of property owned in absolute ownership. Moreover, partnership is excluded from our scope. The law of partnership in Palestine is now governed by the Partnership Ordinance 1930 which, in the main, reproduces English legal principles, by reference to which the Ordinance is to be interpreted (Sec. 75). The application of the Mejelle is excluded (Sec. 69). It will only be necessary to make a few observations as to the law of partnership property under the Ordinance [1]).

---

[1]) The Mejelle still applies to non-commercial or professional partnerships

Chapter XIII—Co-ownership and Partition.

Sec. 3 (1) of the Partnership Ordinance explicitly states that joint or undivided ownership etc. shall not of itself create a partnership as to anything so held or owned whether the owners do or do not share any profits made by the use thereof. Sec. 29 (2) provides that the legal interest in any land which belongs to the partnership shall devolve according to the laws of Succession applicable to the category of land and the general rules applicable thereto but in trust as far as necessary for the person beneficially interested.

<small>Partnership Ordinance 1930.</small>

Both of these provisions are reproduced from the English Partnership Act 1890[1]) and must be interpreted by reference to English law. Partnership in England was within the jurisdiction of the Courts of Equity and it is, therefore, natural to find the scheme of the trust employed freely in partnership law. A partnership firm does not form a legal person in English law and the firm itself could not own property. The ownership of the partnership property is, therefore, treated as vested in the partners jointly, or in one of them though charged with a trust in favour of partnership interests.

It is, however, expressly provided by Sec. 61 (1) of the Palestine Partnership Ordinance that any partnerships registered under the Ordinance shall be legal persons. Partnership property may, therefore, be vested legally in the firm as distinguished from the partners, jointly or separately, and the conception of co-ownership appears consequently to have no place in partnership law.

Resuming now our consideration of the common law of co-ownership in Palestine we remark that the Mejelle is directly concerned only with the joint ownership of Mulk, that being the typical form of absolute ownership. According to Ottoman legal theory Miri holders cannot be regarded as joint owners but only as joint possessors. It may, however, be safely assumed that in the absence of any specific provision as to Miri, the principles of the Mulk law as laid down in the Mejelle would be deemed applicable also to Miri interests. More and more a Miri interest is tending to be treated as merely a form of land ownership and the Raqabe is slipping into the background so as to be regarded as little more restrictive than is the theoretical eminent domain of the King over freehold land in England.

---

which have not been registered under the Ordinance of 1930 (See Partnership Ordinance 1930, Sec. 69 (3)).

[1]) See Partnership Act 1890, Sec. 2 (1) and Sec. 20 (2). Sec. 29 (3) of the Partnership Ord. which follows Sec. 20 (3) of the English Act is also noteworthy.

The Land Law of Palestine.

Joint ownership in the Mejelle.

The general principles of joint ownership of property are set forth in Arts. 1069, 1071 and 1075 of the Mejelle. Art. 1071 tells us that each of the joint owners may deal with the property alone but must not deal with it in such a way as to cause injury to the co-owner. Thus each may sell or mortgage his undivided share unless at least such sale would be injurious to the other co-owner [1]. Neither can, however, compel a sale by to other [2]. Art. 1075 states that co-owners of property held in absolute ownership (Mulk) are strangers to one another as regards their shares. Neither is agent of the other. Consequently neither joint owner may deal with the share of the other without the latter's permission. But in the case of dwelling in a house which is jointly owned and as regards matters pertaining thereto, such as coming in and going out, each of the joint owners is considered to be an absolute owner of such property [3] [4]. The Moslem law in this matter appears to proceed upon the principle that each co-owner is free to make use of his own share as he pleases, but his right as co-owner cannot give him any claims over the shares of the others; if, therefore, while exercising his own rights he has possession of the physical totality, he must be considered merely as a depositary of the undivided shares of the other co-owners and liable as such [4]. "One of two joint owners of a house lives in such a house for a certain period without obtaining the permission of the other. He is considered to be living in his own Mulk property and he cannot be called upon by the other owner to pay rent for his share. If the house is burnt down by accident, he is likewise under no obligation to make good any loss" [5] [7]. But if one of the co-owners lets the property on hire as a physical whole and receives rent he must pay the other owner his share of the rent [6]. And if the value of the property is decreased by the act of the co-owner, he must make good the loss to the other [7].

---

[1] Mejelle, Arts. 215, 1088. The condition that the sale must not be injurious is in accordance with general principles and is specifically stated in Kadry Pasha, Statut Réel, Arts. 751, 752 with an example. As to Pre-emption between Mulk co-owners see Art. 1009 and Chapter X, supra.

[2] Mejelle, Art. 1072.

[3] Mejelle, Art. 1075, Hooper's Translation. Tyser translates "But as regards the things on which habitation depends, like the entrance and exit with respect to a house held in common, they are considered to be, in their entirety, the special property of every one of the owners".

[4] Mejelle, Art. 1087; Kadry Pasha, op. cit., Art. 783, Chaoui, op. cit, p. 90.

[5] Mejelle, Arts. 777, 1075, 1083, Cf. Kadry Pasha, op. cit., Art. 755.

[6] Mejelle, Art. 1077. Cf. Art. 1084.

[7] Compare the example given in Mejelle, Art. 1075 and Art. 1076.

Chapter XIII—Co-ownership and Partition.

Art. 1069 provides that the joint owners of Mulk may by agreement deal with their property in any way they wish in the same way as a single owner of such property. They may also agree to an arrangement by which the benefit of the property is partitioned between them without affecting the co-ownership. Such a partition of benefit is, of course, revocable by either party though third persons who have acquired rights under a partition of this land by consent are to be protected [1]. In the absence of such an arrangement each co-owner appears to enjoy a usufruct over the whole property jointly owned. "The usufruct accruing to two joint owners of a country house is undivided, that is to say, it embraces every part of such house" [2].

A partition of the usufruct may in certain cases be enforced by one co-owner through the Court and in that connection is considered further below.

It follows from the principle of deposit, that co-owners cannot prescribe against one another. This thesis was adopted by the Court of Appeal in the case of co-heirs in Nadim Abdel Rahman Serlan [3] and confirmed in the later case of Musa Shaban v. Abbas el Farawi [4]. It may be generalized [5]. But a modification of the

---

[1] Mejelle, Art. 1188.

[2] Mejelle, Art. 1179. The language of the Mejelle occasionally gives ground for doubting whether the Moslem jurists always kept clearly in mind the undivided character of the shares of respective co-owners (e. g. Art. 1085), but, in general, the solutions proposed are in strict accordance with this conception.

[3] Off. Gaz. 16 July 1927.

[4] L. A. 36/30. The decision laid down the general rule, that in actions for title to land, where the plaintiff claims by inheritance from an ancestor of the defendant, possession by one heir is possession by all the heirs, and not adverse possession. The land of a family is frequently cultivated by one or more members of the family to the exclusion of the other members, who, however, receive a share of the produce. In such a case the possession by the cultivating members is not adverse to those who do not cultivate and they cannot set up a plea of prescription. Compare Sheikh Yusuf v. Khàlil Ghnubeish, L. A. 6/33, Palestine Post 17 Jan. 1934.

[5] Chaoui, op. cit., p. 91. It was, however, stated in a Palestine case that "The rule that possession by one heir is possession by all the heirs should be qualified so that it would not apply to possession by co-owners whose title does not arise from inheritance derived from a common ancestor. A co-owner who is not a co-heir can set up adverse possession as a defence to a claim by another co-owner". (Mahmud Ahmad Salameh v. Saleh Ibn Ibrahim Ismail, L.A. No. 121/26).

In the Cypriot case Pieri v. Philippou (1903) 6 C.L.R. 67 the fact that the defendants who claimed to prescribe were co-owners does not seem to have been considered by the Court.

law has been made by the recent Land Law (Amendment) Ordinance 1933 by Sec. 3 of which it is provided that occupation by one or more co-heirs to the exclusion of others may be a ground for prescription if the occupying co-heir is able affirmatively to prove that his occupation was adverse to the others. In such a case actions between co-heirs for the recovery of the land included in the inheritance are barred if the land is being claimed from a co-heir who has been in adverse possession for the period required for prescription.

As already stated the provisions of the Mejelle apply specifically only to co-ownership of Mulk and can be applied to Miri only by analogy and so far as such analogy extends. On some points the law has made special provision in the case of Miri. We have already noticed the rules governing the right of preference as between co-owners of Miri. Attention may also be drawn to the provisions of Arts. 12 and 13 of the Law of Disposition A.H. 1331 concerning Miri and Mevqufe. Art. 12 runs as follows:—

<small>Law of Disposition A.H. 1331. Arts. 12 and 13.</small>

"If one of the co-owners of Miri or Mevqufe land held in common, which consist of forests or pernalik and the like, ploughs them and turns them into land for cultivation without the permission of the other co-owners, the latter will take their shares of the ploughed land without sharing in the expense and they will also receive their share of the trees cut down or of the value of the trees as they stood; but if the ploughing was authorised by them, they will share in the expense in accordance with their respective share".

So also Art. 13 provides that if the co-owner without the permission of the other co-owner erects buildings or plants trees on the land and the part so built on or planted falls on partition into the lot of another co-owner, the latter may destroy them or may appropriate them and pay their value, in accordance with the general rule laid down in Art. 11. These articles supersede the earlier provisions of Art. 35 of the Land Code [1]).

As is remarked by Chaoui they assimilate the co-owner who has built or planted without consent to a third person who has built or planted in bad faith on the land of another [2]).

It is not, however, clear that these provisions are intended to apply where a co-owner honestly believes himself to be sole owner.

---

[1]) See Chapter VIII, supra. Grafts cannot be destroyed but compensation must be paid to the co-owner in whose lot the grafted trees fall. (Art. 13).

[2]) Chaoui, op. cit., p. 92.

Chapter XIII—Co-ownership and Partition.

Chaoui appears to treat the provisions of the Law of Disposition in this connection as applicable also to Mulk. It is, however, clear from their terms that they apply only to Miri and Mevqufe as also did Art. 35 of the Land Code. The principle upon which the Mejelle deals with such matters appears to be that a co-owner who deals with the land in such a way as to decrease its value is liable to the other co-owners for the amount of the decrease. This is exemplified by Arts. 907 and 1076 of the Mejelle and it is also the principle applied generally in regulating the relations of a proprietor of land with the wrongful appropriator [1]). In Art. 1173 the Mejelle refers to the case, in which one of the joint owners builds upon the jointly owned property without the permission of the co-owner. If upon a partition the building falls to the lot of the other co-owner, the latter can require that it be pulled down. It should be noted that under the Mejelle as under the Provisional Law of Partition of A.H. 1332 the actual distribution of the shares on a compulsory partition is to be made by lot [2]). Presumably the same rule would be applied in the case where one co-owner planted without permission of the other. The general principle suggested by Art. 1080 is that a co-owner must not change the character of the joint property without consent of the others and if by so doing he had diminished the value of the property he would certainly be liable to them.

The repair of property in co-ownership is fully dealt with in Arts. 1308 ff. of the Mejelle. The general principle is that expenses of repairs are to be borne by the joint owners in proportion to their shares (Art. 1308). Where all parties have consented to the work being done by one joint owner the latter has a right of recourse against the others for their shares (Art. 1309). The Court may consent in the place of an absent joint owner (Art. 1310).

If consent has not been obtained the co-owner who executes the repairs is deemed to have done so at his own expense and has no right of recourse against the others for their shares (Art. 1311). This appears to be in accordance with the principle that co-owners are not agents for one another. But if repair is necessary and one of the co-owners refuses to take part in its execution an order may be obtained from the Court for the expenditure of a reasonable sum, if the property is incapable of partition [3]). If, however, it is capable

---

[1]) Mejelle, Art. 1151, 1158.
[2]) Mejelle, Art. 1151, 1158.
[3]) Mejelle, Art. 1313; Kadry Pasha, op. cit., Art. 768. Various further refinements are mentioned by the latter author.

of partition the Court cannot force repair upon an unwilling co-owner but may order partition (Art. 1312). The Mejelle further states that [1]) if the property is incapable of partition, a co-owner who executes necessary repairs to property incapable of partition is entitled to receive a share of his expenditure "calculated according to the value of the building at the time the repairs were carried out". (Art. 1313).

The Mejelle contains many provisions as to the rights of an absent co-owner and the user of the jointly owned property in his absence [2]). A co-owner is absent for the purposes of these articles, if he is not present even though his whereabouts are known.

In general the co-owner who is present may make use of the property "to the extent of his share thereof", the consent of the absent owner being implied (Art. 1078); but such implications only exist if the user causes no harm to the jointly owned property (Art. 1079). A series of articles which follow give examples of the applications of these principles. Application to the Court is possible in order that authority may be obtained where property is likely to depreciate if left unoccupied (Art. 1082) or uncultivated (Art. 1085). The interests of the absent co-owner are meticulously protected by the law [3]).

Mesha'a Land. In many parts of Palestine the lands cultivated by the villagers are held by them under a system of customary joint ownership known as Mesha'a. The Mesha'a system is often described as a system of communal ownership, and the lands held in Mesha'a said to be owned by a corporate body, usually a village, and to be temporarily partitioned among the individual members of the corporation—redistributions taking place periodically [4]). In criticism of this view it must be pointed out:- (1) that the jural institution known as the corporation is unknown to the older Ottoman laws; (2) that the Land Code, Art. 8, expressly forbids Miri land of a village being held as a whole by the inhabitants of a village or by a few of them as representing the others. Each inhabitant must have a separate Tapu Grant; (3) that since A.H. 1331 no action of Nam Musta'ar can be heard so that no person can have a legal

---

[1]) The corresponding article in Kadry Pasha (Art. 768) makes no such concession.

[2]) Arts. 1078 ff., infra. See for this distinction the Chapter dealing with Absence.

[3]) See Kadry Pasha, op. cit., Arts. 757, 758, 760—762; 766.

[4]) This is distinctly stated in the Report of the 1923 Commission as to the Partition of Mesha'a Lands.

Chapter XIII—Co-ownership and Partition.

claim to land as against a registered owner merely on the ground that the registered owner is his nominee, (4) that the Ottoman Law contains no provision whatsoever recognizing in any way any form of joint ownership or joint interest other than those specified in Art. 1045 of the Mejelle.

It apperrs, therefore, impossible to justify the view that so-called Mesha'a land differs in character from land held in joint ownership. It does not, of course, follow that the interests of persons holding in Mesha'a are to be treated strictly according to the rules relating to joint ownership. But the determination of their interests on any other basis is not a matter upon which the enacted law of the country has any bearing. The Government may make other provision, or the Courts may take the view that Art. 6 of the Mejelle (What is from time immemorial will be left in its ancient state) or Art. 36 (Custom is of force) justifies the recognition of rights as to which statute law is silent.

Indeed, in a case, concerning the land of the village of Aslin [1]), the Court of Appeal varying the order of the Land Court held that, on proof of a custom of yearly redistribution of the "village lands" among the villagers, an entry was to be made in the Land Registers in respect of the plots of the appellants registered owners that the land was common land subject to the custom of the village. The grounds for this decision are not given. But it cannot be too plainly stated that the Land Code recognizes no common village land except the Metruki lands referred to in Art. 97 ff. and such land cannot be registered in the names of private owners. The introduction of the idea of cultivated communal land suggested by the decision is contrary to the Land Code and subversive, indeed, of the principles upon which it is based.

A custom which contradicts enacted law has (in England) no validity, and it is difficult to understand how customary claims which nullify the system of Tapu grants and the most explicit statements of the statute law that land cannot be owned save by formal Title Deed can be deemed of any validity in Palestine [2]).

This work is not designed as a statement of any except enacted law. The discussion of Mesha'a save on the basis of the enacted law is, therefore, irrelevant. For purposes of information only it will be convenient to insert certain portions from the Report of the 1923 Commission as to the principal forms of Customary Mesha'a and their prevalence and distribution in Palestine.

---

[1]) Reported Off. Gaz. 16 Sept. 1926, p. 486.
[2]) Mejelle, Art. 7; Cf. Art. 1224.

The Land Law of Palestine.

Extract from Report of Mesha'a Commission.

There are fundamentally two forms of title to a share in the Mesha'a Land of a village :—

Sahm or Hussa:

The commoner form of title apparently arose as follows. At some date beyond the memory of living man, the Mesha'a Land of a village was divided into a number of shares (ashum), one or more of which was assigned to each male member of the village. Very possibly these shares were let out by Sheikhs or Headmen in return for a portion of the produce. On the death of the original assignees, his heirs inherited his Sahm, each being entitled to a fraction of the Sahm determined by the number of heirs. In each succeeding generation the process was repeated. Sometimes by purchase or other means two or more shares might be amalgamated. Hence at the present time a man may be entitled, for example, to 1/17 of 3/23 of 2/9 of a Sahm. It is said that the full denominator of such a fraction sometimes contains ten figures.

Theoretically females are entitled to share in the inheritance, but in practice they are usually induced to waive their rights. The reason for this practice is that, if femals were given their due shares, these shares would often pass by marriage to strangers.

Hamuleh.

There is a common variation of this system. In each village there are usually several "Hama-il", a term which may perhaps be rendered as "Clans". Often each Hamuleh has a fixed area of land allotted to it which is divided among the members of the Hamuleh in the manner described below. Thus in all but name, the Mesha'a system ceases to apply to the village as a whole and comes to apply only to the different Hama-il of the village.

Males alive at Date of Partition (Zukur).

The rarer form of title is based on the present alone. Every male—from the new-born babe to the old man on the brink of the grave—alive in the village on the day of partition is entitled to a share of the Mesha'a land. It is obvious that, under this communistic arrangement, the amount of each share is constantly changing, and that sales or permanent partition are alike impossible.

Variations.

Several peculiarities of local practice were brought to the notice of the Committee.

(1) of persons entitled to a share, only those are allowed to claim their rights who are in a position to cultivate their shares, i.e. who have sufficient oxen, etc.

(2) Other peculiarities are hardly worthy of mention.

Method of Partition.

Division of land

The Mesha'a land of most villages exhibits different qualities. Some is plain land, some is hill land; some is near the village, some is distant; some is reserved for winter crops, some for summer crops; and so on. It is, therefore, usual to divide the

Chapter XIII—Co-ownership and Partition.

whole of the Mesha'a land into a number of Mawaki (sites) in each of which the Hamuleh, family or individual is allotted the due number of shares.

When the Sahm system is followed, repartition is effected by agreement or by lot. There seems to be no evidence of repartition by rotation. In partition no account is taken of the sub-divisions of a Sahm. The Sahm as a whole is assigned an area and the co-owners divide that area among themselves. Usually their shares are situated always in the same position relative to one another. *Partition of shares.*

When the other system (Zukur) is followed, it is usual to put up to a sort of auction the different plots into which it has been found convenient to divide the village land. The entitled males group themselves as they like into parties each under a leader, and the largest party declaring its claims to be satisfied by any given plot is awarded that plot. Each party then sub-divides its plot by agreement or by lot.

The intervals between partitions usually range from one to five years, but occasionally extend to nine years. *Intervals between Partition.*

In some villages the last partition was made a number of years ago and by common consent is regarded as permanent. *"Ifraz Urfi".*

Usually existing holders are responsible for the shares of absentees or minors, but the latter might have difficulty in securing their rights later on.

In some of the villages referred to in the previous Section the permanence of the partition has been reinforced by prescriptive rights acquired through uninterrupted possession for a period of ten years. *"Ifraz Urfi" with Prescriptive Rights.*

The Mejelle deals very fully with the subject of Partition of jointly owned property in Arts. 1114 ff. *Partition (Qesmat).*

Primarily these articles refer to partition of Mulk, but in principle and subject to certain reservations they were applicable also to the partition of Miri also. As regards this latter there were certain special provisions in the Land Code, namely Arts. 15, 16, 17, 18, 35.

The provisional law of 14 Moharrem A.H. 1332 unified and simplified the law of partition of Mulk, Miri and Mevqufe land and for the first time gave to every co-owner a right to obtain a partition, following the French principle "Nul ne peut être contraint à demeurer dans l'indivision" [1]).

---

[1]) French Civil Code, Art. 815.

210   The Land Law of Palestine.

Prior to the Law partition by order of Court of Mulk could have been obtained upon application of some of the co-owners alone provided that the property owned was capable of partition [1]; otherwise no partition could be obtained.

If the object was incapable of partition, it was, however, possible to obtain a "partition of benefit" (Muhayeh) in the case of Mulk; this form of partition was, however, forbidden as regards Miri by Art. 15 of the Land Code. The provisional law of A.H. 1332 states (Sec. 1) that property which is capable of partition, that is, property of which the value is not decreased by partition, may be partitioned, and property which is incapable of partition, may be sold by auction [2].

The purpose of the Provisional Law is primarily the regulation of the process of Partition. It does not affect the provisions of the Mejelle, which remain in force so far as they are not inconsistent with those of the Provisional Law; indeed the Provisional Law itself assumes the existence of the Mejelle [3].

The Law of Partition.   A brief statement of the provisions of the Law of A.H. 1332 will here suffice, together with some reference to certain articles of the Mejelle, which appear particularly noteworthy.

The obvious intention of the legislator was to facilitate and secure partition. Joint ownership of land is generally uneconomical and checks development [4]. Thus the Law definitely provides that the right to apply for partition shall not be restricted by any previously existing contract (Sec. 1) though the co-owners may agree to delay partition for not more than five years (Sec. 2). The procedure to be followed in partition by consent is set forth in Secs. 4 and 5 which are also applicable, mutatis mutandis, where a physical partition is ordered under Sec. 6. Under the Magistrates Courts' Jurisdiction (Amendment) Ordinance 1930 Magistrates' Courts exercise jurisdiction in actions for the partition of immovable property and for Muhayeh though no civil action or counterclaim which

---

[1] Mejelle, Art. 1130.
[2] Compare Chaoui, op cit., pp. 94, 95.
[3] Of course the Mejelle still applies in its entirety when the property jointly owned is not immovable.
[4] Cultivation of land in common was normal in Europe in the Middle Ages. The enclosure and partition of the common fields has certainly assisted production. But the process of enclosure and partition has usually proved dangerous and injurious to the peasantry. Much care is needed if it is desired that the process of partition shall not have the effect of separating the peasants from the land.

Chapter XIII—Co-ownership and Partition.

involves a decision as to the ownership of immovable property may be heard by a Magistrate (Sec. 1 (1) (b) and Sec. 1 (2)).

The actual partition is to be made by dividing up the land into distinct shares of equal value so far as may be and then drawing lots for the shares [1]. Adjustment of value may be made by cash payments (Sec. 5). In the case of roofed property (Mussaqafat) the provisions of Art. 1150 of the Mejelle are to be followed. These, however, do not differ in essence from those of the Provisional Law. Recourse will, however, not infrequently be made in the case of buildings and structures to the provisions of Sec. 8 ff., which regulate the sale by auction of property claimed to be incapable of partition [2]. Experts are appointed to determine the market value of the shares of any co-owner, who so claims, which is then to be offered at that price to the other co-owners. If none of them will take the share at the price fixed, the property as a whole is sold through the Execution Office (Sec. 9). Further provisions relate to the steps to be taken if no bidder for the totality be forthcoming, in which case the co-owner whose share is in question may sell to a third person (Sec. 10) and the other co-owners forfeit their right of pre-emption.

The provisions made by the law of A.H. 1332 have rendered many of the articles of the Mejelle obsolete in practice, as far as immovable property is concerned. Whether partition is advantageous to some only of the co-owners or not is now less material [3] as also the question whether the property is capable or not of partition [4]. In every case partition may be secured or one co-owner may in effect compel the other co-owners to buy him out to avoid a sale by auction of the property as a whole.

The Mejelle contains a series of interesting provisions relating to the effect of partition [5]. Each former co-owner becomes of course

---

[1] The Provisional law (Secs. 4 and 6) allots functions to the "Village Council" in connection with Partition. There are now no village councils and in practice the Magistrate asks each party, i. e. petitioner and respondents to appoint a person and he himself appoints a third to act as Committee of inspection. This follows Art. 63 of the Code of Civil Procedure, the purported repeal of which by Rule of Court in 1926 is generally treated as having been ultra vires.

[2] In practice the functions of the local Administrative Council under Sec. 8 are performed by the Magistrate.

[3] Compare Mejelle, Arts. 1140, 1141.

[4] Mejelle, Arts. 1130, 1131.

[5] The Hedaya also contains in Book XXXIX a mass of learning upon the subject of Partition and in particular prescribes with great particularity the mode in

The Land Law of Palestine.

sole proprietor of his allotted share (Art. 1182). Trees and buildings follow the land without being mentioned (Art. 1163) but crops and fruits remain jointly owned unless expressly mentioned (Art. 1164). Rights of way and of water may be arranged in the partition (Art. 1166) but in the absence of stipulation belong to the person who obtains the share, to which they are attached (Art. 1165). Upon partition of a house a wall separating the two shares may be left as a party wall (Art. 1146). Art. 1170 deals with the case in which upon the division of a building the beams of one part project and rest upon a wall, which belongs to another part.

It is to be borne in mind that on a partition under the Law of A.H. 1332 the official making the partition is directed to take care that the shares are distinct so far as possible in respect of rights of way and of water (Sec. 5). This provision follows Art. 1151 of the Mejelle.

Cancellation of Partition. The law of A.H. 1332 expressly provides (Sec. 11) that after the completion of a transfer of property under Sec. 9 no suit by a co-owner for the cancellation of the sale is to be heard.

It is not, however, stated whether a partition under the Law remains liable to cancellation under the provisions of the Mejelle.

Under the Mejelle partitions may be annulled by consent or for excessive damage.

Mejelle, Art. 1159. "After the partition the co-owners can annul the partition by their own consent; and the things divided can be owned in common between them as before".

Art. 1160. "If it is shown that there is excessive damage in a partition, it is set aside, and a division is made again which is just" [1]).

Art. 1161. "If after the partition of the disposable estate of a deceased person, it appears that there is a debt owing by the deceased, the partition is set aside.

Unless the heirs pay the debt, or the creditors release them from it, or there is property of the deceased other than that which was divided and the debt is paid with it. In those cases the partition is not annulled".

And according to Arts. 1153 and 1154 the options of inspection and options for defect are attached to partitions as in the case of sale. The conditions for the exercise of these are not likely to be very frequent in the case of immovable property.

---

which houses and land are to be partitioned. There seems, however, to be little there of practical value in modern conditions.

[1]) Hooper translates "if flagrant misrepresentation is apparent during the partition" etc. See also Art. 1127.

Chapter XIII—Co-ownership and Partition.

Partition, as also a setting aside of a Partition already made are dispositions of property within the meaning of the Transfer of Land Ordinance and are, therefore, effective only if the provisions of these Ordinances have been fulfilled.

Reference has already been made to this institution which was more particularly of use in the case of jointly owned property incapable of partition. It is regulated by Arts. 1174 ff. of the Mejelle. The partition of benefit may provide, that each of the joint owners shall be entitled to use the whole property for a successive fixed period or that each of them shall be entitled to use a specified part of the property [1]. *Partition of Benefit (Muhayeh).*

The Mejelle proceeds to give examples of each of these methods.

Partition of Benefit could be ordered by the Court in the case of objects incapable of partition (Art. 1188); and once made could only be annulled by agreement of all the co-owners (Art. 1189), unless one of the co-owners wishes to sell his share or obtain a partition of the property (Art. 1190). The partition of Benefit is not avoided by the death of one or all of the co-owners. (Art. 1191) [2].

Partition of Benefit cannot be allowed in the case of Miri (Land Code, Art. 15). The co-owners may, of course, agree for their own convenience to cultivate separate parts of the land, or to cultivate the whole in turn and so on, but such an agreement could not affect the rights of the State. An Imperial Iradeh of 1st Sha'ban, A.H. 1296, permits judicial Partition of Benefit of Ijaratein property subject, however, to the consent of the Mutwally of the Waqf [3].

The provisions with reference to Partition in the Land Settlement Ordinance are of great importance. Full reference is also made to them in the Chapter dealing with Land Settlement, and it is not necessary here to repeat what is there said. It suffices to note that the Provisional Law of A.H. 1332 does not apply to partitions carried on under the Ordinances [4], and to remind the reader that the original provisions in the Land Settlement Ordinance 1928 have been much altered by the Amending Ordinances of 1930 and 1932. No partition in a settlement area of any parcel owned by two or more co-owners or of village Mesha'a is to be effected save as provided by the provisions of the Land Settlement Ordinances [5]. *Partition in Land Settlement Areas.*

---

[1] Arts. 419, 1176.
[2] As to Muhayeh, see also Hedaya pp. 578 ff. Much of the law contained in which is reproduced in the Mejelle.
[3] Chiha, op. cit., p. 204.
[4] Land Settlement Ord. 1928, Sec. 52 (3).
[5] Land Settlement Ord. 1930, Sec. 13.

CHAPTER XIV—RIGHTS IN THE NATURE OF SERVITUDES; WAYS, WATERCOURSES AND WALLS.

The Mulk owner is on general principle exclusively entitled to the possession and enjoyment of his property. The Mejelle lays down the principle in the broadest language. "Any person may deal with his property owned in absolute ownership as he wishes" (Art. 1192). Moreover, he is owner of what is above the land and of what is below it (Art. 1194)[1], but must not infringe upon his neighbours, like possession of the column of air above the land (Art. 1195). This is further exemplified by Art. 1196 which gives the right to have the overhanging branches of a tree on adjoining property cut or tied back.

Nevertheless there are limits to the user of land. Such user must not cause "excessive damage" to the enjoyment of property of others (Art. 1197). And, an owner may find his exclusive possession limited by definite rights possessed by others entitling them to use his land in some limited way. Even the public may have similar rights over private property.

In this chapter it is proposed firstly to consider the rights arising from neighbourhood which limit user of land and thereafter to consider the defined private rights of user of the land of another known to Continental law as Servitudes and to English law as Easements and Profits. Some remarks upon public rights will be added.

Rights arising from Neighbourhood. English law recognizes certain "natural" rights of owners available against the owners of neighbouring property. Natural rights of this kind are not acquired by grant or prescription, but are incidental to the ownership of land. Such are the rights to support by adjacent or subjacent land, rights to uninterrupted flow of natural streams. The Mejelle recognizes even wider natural rights arising from neighbourhood. An owner must not do anything on his land in such a way as to cause excessive damage to his neighbours.

---

[1] This is also a maxim of English law. For speculations as to the origin see a note in Law Quarterly Review for Jan. 1931 at pp. 14 ff.

Chapter XIV—Servitudes, Watercourses, Walls. [215]

What amounts to excessive damage is not dogmatically stated but the examples given show the general character of the conception. Thus, loud hammering or the emission of smoke may constitute excessive damage [1]) as also may a flow of sewage [2]). And if a person allows water to flow along his neighbour's walls or places rubbish near them, so as to cause them to become rotten, this is excessive damage. Moreover, an owner must not build on his land so as to cut off air from a threshing floor, or light from a window. Nor may he open windows which overlook the women's quarters of his neighbours. It is also an excessive injury to do on one's own property anything which will weaken a building on neighbouring property (Art. 1199). The Mejelle appears to treat rights to support of buildings and rights to light as incidental to enjoyment of property. Such rights could in England only be acquired by grant or prescription i.e. long user, though it has indeed been stated that if a building is divided into floors or "flats" the owner of each upper floor is entitled to vertical support from the lower part of the building [3]). But a right of support of a building by adjacent land is not a natural right but must be acquired though there exists a natural right to support of land by adjacent or subjacent land [4]).

Particular attention is given by the Mejelle to the right to light and the right to prevent overlooking of the Harim. As regards the former the test to be applied is a vague one; there is excessive damage "if a person erects a building and cuts off the light from the window of a room belonging to his neighbour, the room being darkened to such an extent that it is impossible to read therein anything written" [5]).

The right to privacy, or in particular to the privacy of the Harim. Harim is even more carefully regulated, as is natural in a body of Moslem law. The Harim includes not only womens quarters proper, but also the places which are frequented by women such

---

[1]) Mejelle, Art. 1200.

[2]) Ibid., Cf. Arts. 1212, 1213.

[3]) Compare Mejelle, Art. 1192, which lays down that the owner of an upper storey of a house has a right of support against the owner of the lower storey, as also a right to have the upper storey covered. Separate ownership of divided parts of a building is now rare in England though common in Palestine. But see per Lord Selborne in Angus v. Dalton (1881) 44 L.T.R.

[4]) The whole subject was fully considered in England in the famous case of Angus v. Dalton.

[5]) As to English law see Colls v. Home and Colonial Stores (1904) 90 L.T.R. 687. The cramped character of the buildings in the City of Jerusalem suggests that the law has not been very strictly observed.

as the kitchen and the head of the well and courtyard (Art. 1262). Even if the women can be seen through chinks in a fence, these must be closed. But the garden is not part of the women's quarters (Art. 1204) and as "no weight is attached to mere supposition"[1]) the fact that a person may reach a point of outlook by a ladder is not a ground for alleging excessive damage (Art. 1203). From Art. 1224 we infer that a right to cause excessive damage cannot be acquired by immemorial user; it appears to follow that mere neglect to take action however long continued, does not destroy the right to complain, though no doubt it might be relevant in deciding whether the damage was, indeed, excessive.

Excessive Damage.

It is further stated that if a person chooses to build in such a way that he suffers excessive damage from operations on the part of his neighbour which were already in existence, he must endure the damage, or, as the Mejelle quaintly puts it, he must himself remove the injury and cannot call upon his neighbour to do anything. Thus, if a man chooses to build near a forge, he cannot prevent the forge working, but must take such steps as he can himself to guard against injury from the hammering. So also if a person builds a new house the women's quarters of which are overlooked by an older house he cannot complain[2]). So also if a person alters his house and thereby enables his women's quarters to be overlooked, he cannot complain (Art. 1209)[3]). No doubt the same principles apply in the case of rights to light and the like.

Servitudes.

The servitude of modern law is a "real" right enjoyed in the property of another, which, however, does not involve the possession of or power of disposition over the servient property but consists in a right to use that property in a defined and limited manner. Such a servitude corresponds to the praedial servitude of Roman law.

The servitude in this sense is always enjoyed with respect to some other property which is spoken of as dominant. Thus A enjoys a right of way over Blackacre as owner of (say) Whiteacre. Of course the owner of Blackacre may give permission to A personally to cross his land or may bind himself by contract to allow A to cross. But the right thus given to A would not be a servitude but a right in personam only; it would not be a "real"

---

[1]) Mejelle, Art. 74.
[2]) Mejelle, Art. 1208.
[3]) The provisions as to privacy have been applied in Cyprus. See Erikzade v. Arghiro (1890) 1. C.L.R. 84 and Ali v. Papa Yanni (1892) 2 C.L.R. 79. See also FitzGerald, Muhammedan Law, pp. 194—5.

Chapter XIV—Servitudes, Watercourses, Walls. [217]

right unless it was granted to A as owner of Whiteacre and belonged to all future owners of Whiteacre as such.

French and English law both contain many important rules as to servitudes and we may be inclined sometimes to make use of them in applying the Mejelle since the law laid down in the latter is incomplete. It is, however, dangerous to do this unless great discretion is used. Rights which resemble closely the servitudes of European law [1] are mentioned in the Mejelle and in some cases these rights are perhaps identical with those of European law, but the similarity is often deceptive.

As the English law is that to which reference is most properly made in Palestine it will be well to explain briefly how these rights are dealt with by it and then to explain the provisions of the Mejelle upon the subject.

English law recognizes two classes of rights of this order, Easements and Profits à prendre. The easement is a right possessed by the owner of one immovable [2] (called the dominant immovable) to make use in some limited way of another immovable (called the "servient" immovable) but such use is not personal to the holder but is only enjoyed in respect of the dominant immovable which he owns. In the case of the easement the right of user is said to be without profit, i.e. it does not involve taking anything from the servient immovable. A right similar to an easement which does involve taking something from the servient immovable is termed a "Profit à prendre". Thus a right of way or a right to light is an easement but rights to take fish or graze cattle or to cut timber are "Profits" [3]. It is a peculiar rule of English law that a "Profit" unlike an "Easement" may be enjoyed "in gross" that is not as attached to and in respect of any "dominant" immovable, but as a "real" right belonging to a man and his heirs irrespective of their ownership of an immovable to which it appertains. The English law as regards Profits is, however, old and in some respects obscure and is mainly concerned with peculiar rights which were enjoyed under the old system of agriculture in existence in the Middle Ages [4].

Easements and Profits à Prendre.

---

[1] Une servitude est une charge imposée sur un héritage pour l'usage et l'utilité d'un héritage appartenant à un autre propriétaire (French Civil Code, Art. 637).

[2] The English lawyer would speak not of an "immovable" but of a "tenement"—but it is desirable to avoid English technical terms.

[3] A right to take water is treated as an Easement not a Profit.

[4] These are the rights of "common of pasture" and the like which have some importance even in modern England.

The Land Law of Palestine.

Natural Rights.

English law also recognizes the important class of so called "natural" rights attached to property merely by reason of its neighbourhood. Classified among these are the right of support by adjacent land enjoyed by every landowner as such and the natural right of a "riparian" owner to take water from a stream for purposes beneficial to the riparian estate. Such rights are generally spoken of as easements, but this term is sometimes limited to rights which are not natural but are acquired by grant or by prescription such as rights of way, rights to light through particular windows and rights to support of buildings.

These general remarks as to Easements and Profits in English law will perhaps help the reader to understand what follows as to the similar rights mentioned in the Mejelle. But it would be in the highest degree unwise to treat the rights recognized in the Mejelle or Land Code as more than analogous to the Easements and Profits of English law.

Rights of Way. Rights to the passage of Water.

Rights to discharge Water.

The rights of way considered in this section are private rights. We are not here concerned with public rights of passage such as highways. Land dedicated as highways is classified as Metruki. It is not clear whether a public right of way over ground privately owned such as is common in England, can exist under the Ottoman law but there does not appear to be anything in the Mejelle which prevents such a right being maintained. Art. 6 of the Mejelle which provides that things which have existed from time immemorial should be left as they were, may be applied to a claim on behalf of the public to enjoy a right of way over land as well as to a private claim [1]).

However, our immediate concern is with private rights of the nature of Servitudes. The Mejelle treats together of three of this class, the right of way, the right of aqueduct and the right of flow i.e. right to discharge water.

The right of way may be a right to passage along a defined path [2]) but this is not stated to be essential. Nor is it anywhere stated whether a right of way can be or is normally limited to foot pedestrians or animals or may cover vehicles. Presumably such questions would be answered by reference to the actual user.

The private right of way must be distinguished from the private road to which rights of pre-emption attach (Art. 1008).

---

[1]) The example of the dirty water flowing on to the public highway given in Art. 1224 shows that the principles of Art. 1224 apply also to public rights.
[2]) Art. 1227. Cf. Art. 1220.

Chapter XIV—Servitudes, Watercourses, Walls. [219]

Such private roads are apparently cases of joint ownership in the soil of a roadway. A person may also own or be joint owner of a roadway which crosses land belonging to another or others, and this state of things is distinguishable and distinguished from the abstract right of way [1]. It must, however, be admitted that the distinction between the "incorporeal" right of passage and the like which constitutes a true easement and the ownership of a road way or water channel enclosed in the land of another is not always clear in the authorities. Rights of aqueduct i.e. rights to lead water through another's land appear generally to be identified with the ownership of the channel itself in which the water is conducted [2].

The juridical theory of Servitudes is imperfectly worked out in the Mejelle and apparently in Moslem law generally but the more acceptable inference from the texts appears to be that private rights of way and rights to the flow of water are conceived as attached, like easements, to a dominant property and are enjoyed over the servient property in respect of this dominant property only. Kadry Pasha states that the servitudes of irrigation and passage of water can be acquired by inheritance but cannot be the object of a gift or a lease and cannot be sold save with the land to which they are attached [3]. The Hedaya also distinctly states that a sale of a right of water is not possible unless the right is attached to some land in respect of which it is enjoyed [4]. But this "attachment" seems to be due rather to practical necessity than to any theoretical conception. It may be doubted whether the Moslem jurists had formed any consistent juridical theory on the subject. The general tenor of Moslem legal thought in this connection suggests that such rights as these now under consideration would be treated as part of some land and identified with it. The abstract idea of an incorporeal right of which possession could not be given by any physical act is foreign to earlier legal systems as the English Common Law shows.

In any case, however, the right of way enjoyed ab antiquo must be carefully distinguished from the mere licence to pass over land. Such a licence is revocable at will (Art. 1226) though, no doubt, if given in pursuance of a contract the revocation would, as a breach of contract, give rise to an action for damages.

---

[1] Mejelle, Arts. 1145, 1168.
[2] Mejelle, Arts. 1228, 1290.
[3] Op. cit., Art. 47. Cf. Mejelle, Art. 216.
[4] See p. 618 (Hamilton's Translation).

The Land Law of Palestine.

A right to conduct sewage through the property of another is of the same character as the right of aqueduct. If the sewer bursts the consequential pollution may cause excessive damage [1].

Another right mentioned in this place in the Mejelle is the right to permit water to discharge itself upon the land of another. This is the right known to European law as Stillicide. It is recognized by Art. 1229 and is created normally by immemorial user [2].

Immemorial User. It is by immemorial user that rights of this character are normally established [3]. Such user must not of course be confused with prescription. It is a form of acquisition of a right or title, while, as we shall see, prescription as understood by the Mejelle is merely a ground for refusing to hear actions upon rights.

It is not easy to explain how immemorial user operates as a title to a right. English law faced with a similar problem evolved the ingenious theory that immemorial user raised a presumption that at some time in the past there had been a definite grant of the right claimed which grant had been lost. The Mejelle does not explicitly refer to any presumption arising from immemorial user, nor does it even state that the rights of the kind now under discussion can be created by grant. Grant is a recognized mode of acquiring ownership [4] and immemorial user is not stated to be such. But it would probably be rash to assume that we are to treat immemorial user in Palestine as giving rise to a presumption of a lost grant. No such theory justified clearly by the texts can be advanced. All that can be said is that if immemorial user be established, the right will be assumed to have risen at some time in the past, supposing always that it is capable of a legal origin [5].

Whether a right of this kind can be newly created by grant or agreement on the part of the owners of the dominant and servient properties is not clear from the authorities though the modern commentators appear to treat such acquisition as permissible [6].

No doubt the conception of a grant of an incorporeal right of which physical possession was impossible or difficult, would be strange to the older law.

---

[1] Mejelle, Art. 1232. Cf. Art. 1200.
[2] Mejelle, Art. 1231, 1224.
[3] Mejelle, Art. 1224, Art. 6.
[4] Mejelle, Art. 1248.
[5] Cf. Aly Haidar quoted in Chiha, op. cit., at p. 179.
[6] Chiha, op. cit., pp. 177, 178 quoting Khalis Eshrefl as stating that new grants of servitude may be made by Miri holders if authorized. Cf. Chaoui, Régime foncier en Syrie p. 82.

Chapter XIV—Servitudes, Watercourses, Walls. 221

Kadry Pasha and the Hedaya agree that a right to passage of water can be the object of inheritance or bequest but Kadry Pasha denies that such a right can be given, therein following no doubt high Moslem authority [1]. Probably the Courts would now be inclined to recognize a new creation of an easement by direct grant or agreement. Such a transaction is a "disposition" of immovable property within the meaning of the Transfer of Land Ordinance and requires the approval of the Government as stated therein. Servitudes must presumably be treated as immovables for the purpose of these Ordinances and an agreement whereby such a right is brought into existence appears therefore to be a "disposition" of a form of "immovable" property [2].

Whether a definite grant of a right of this kind is possible or not, it is at least clear that rights of way and rights to the flow of water can be created by reservation. "If at the time the partition is carried out, it is stipulated that there shall be a right of way or a right of flow over another share the stipulation is valid" [3]. Such rights can also be reserved upon a sale of part of a piece of land [4].

Upon a sale or partition rights of way etc. enjoyed with the land sold may pass with the land, [5] and the sale or partition of the servient property does not, of course, affect the existence of the right [6].

A more difficult question arises when part of a property is sold or property is partitioned, and claims are made to enjoyment by the new owner of one part to ways, etc., actually used over the other part during the period of single or joint ownership. Is the purchaser entitled to use ways or water channels over the unsold portion if they were actually used in connection with the land sold during the time of single ownership? Or again, can a vendor claim a right to use such ways or water channels over the sold portion if during the time of single ownership he actually made use of them in connection with the land unsold? Upon these important questions

---

[1] Kadry Pasha, op. cit., Art. 47; Hedaya, Vol. IV, Book. XLV, Sec. III at p. 616 (Hamilton's Translation).

[2] The Registration Laws ignore Servitudes. In practice it is not uncommon for entries to be made in the Land Registers, establishing the existence of a servitude, and certified copies of the entry are supplied to interested persons.

[3] Mejelle, Art. 1166, Cf. Art. 1167.

[4] Cf. Hedaya, at p. 616; Mejelle, Art. 1145.

[5] Mejelle, Art. 235. If the right is one necessary to the enjoyment of the land sold it will apparently pass without any mention. (Art. 232).

[6] Mejelle, Arts. 1232, 1168, 1169.

the Mejelle is not explicit. It seems, however, that reservation is necessary, though such reservation may be in general terms. (Art. 1107).

Servitudes can be lost by an act which indicates abandonment, of which Art. 1227 gives us an example. Prescription runs against the owner of a Right of Way, etc. [1]).

It may be assumed that the law laid down in the Mejelle as to natural rights and rights of way, etc. is applicable as well to Miri as to Mulk.

Profits. English law, as above explained, couples with easements a class of rights in the land of others known as Profits à Prendre. Rights to take water are not "Profits" but rights to take wood, grass, fish, game, etc. may be Profits.

Neither the Mejelle nor the Land Code contain any provisions which explicitly recognize rights of this nature. Actually in Palestine customary rights of grazing, of cutting wood and of cutting reeds appear to be admitted and reference to them is specifically made in Sec. 18 of the Protection of Cultivators Ordinance 1933, but the nature and origin of these rights is not clear. So again in Sec. 4 of the Land Disputes (Possession) Ordinance 1932 we find reference to alleged rights of user of land or water, of grazing, cutting wood or reeds, watering animals, irrigation, fishing or other like purposes (whether such rights be claimed as a servitude or otherwise). Some of these rights might, of course, be claimed as rights in Metruki, or as public or private rights in water, but it seems that, besides these, which are regulated by the texts, customary rights in the nature of Profits are recognized by the Law, justified probably on the ground of long user [2]).

The rights of grazing and of cutting wood, etc. which exist over village Metruki might be plausibly represented as rights in the nature of Profits resembling the rights of Common of pasture and of turbary known to English law. The older authorities would, however, probably have treated them as rights of communal ownership in the soil [3]). It is only in modern theory that the

---

[1]) Mejelle, Art. 1662. As to Prescription see Chapter below.

[2]) Cf. Mejelle, Art. 6 and as to custom see Mejelle, Arts. 36, 37, 41, 45. The provisions of Art. 125 of the Land Code may be cited as an illustration. The article appears to recognize a right on the part of villagers, established by ab antiquo usage, to graze cattle in fields after the crops have been harvested.

[3]) Cf. Mejelle, Art. 1645. Moslem law was never much concerned to locate the "bare ownership". Its rules deal primarily with user and destination of property. The search for the legal owner, of so much importance in English

Chapter XIV—Servitudes, Watercourses, Walls. [223]

ownership of the soil of Metruki is treated as vested in the State. In any case the rights of the villagers must be thought of rather as a regulated form of public right than as private rights in State lands, as is clear from the provisions of Mejelle Art. 1675.

There is nothing in the text which militates against the recognition by the Courts of private rights in the nature of Profits but no specific example can be afforded [1]). The "sporting" and "fishing" rights known to English law are scarcely represented in Palestine. Game and fish are "mubah" in the sense that wherever caught, they belong to the captor [2]). Exclusive rights of fishery were granted by the Turkish authorities under the Turkish Fishery Law and similar grants have been attempted in the Palestine Administration. On the assumption which seems correct, that the soil and products of unappropriated land and water are to be treated as vested in the State, such grants appear to create rights analogous to "Profits".

In general water is "mubah" that is that any person may take water wherever he finds it [3]). This applies to flowing water, but water may be appropriated if collected and reduced into possession [4]). Seas and great lakes are Mubah. So also are wells which have served immemorially for the needs of all and natural subterranean waters [5]). Public rivers are also Mubah. A public river is one which does not flow in a channel which is the private property (Mulk) of a body of individuals but the water of a public river may by long established usage be appropriated for the use of riparian owners whereby rights are created which cannot be disturbed. This apparently is only possible in the case of small streams [6]).

Rights to take water from Public Rivers, and to dig for Water; Wells.

Every man we are told is free to make use of the air and the light and of seas and of great lakes subject always to the

---

legal theory, was not pursued by Moslem jurists. Cf. in this connection the difference between the Waqf and the Trust.

[1]) In the recent case of Badr v. Hanem L. A. 13/33 (Palestine Post 22 June 1934) the Court of Appeal held that a claim to a right of pasture put forward on behalf of villagers could not be established by oral evidence against a registered title, and, further, that the fact that villagers had been accustomed to graze flocks over certain lands did not give rise to a right of pasture over the land. The claim of the villagers seems to have been that the land in question was assigned village Metruki.

[2]) Mejelle, Arts. 1293, 1295—7, 1300—01.
[3]) Mejelle, Art. 1234.
[4]) Art. 1251, Arts. 1249, 1250.
[5]) Arts. 1235—1237.
[6]) Arts. 1238, 1239.

The Land Law of Palestine.

condition that he does not thereby disturb the rights of others[1]). Nowadays the State in some cases has restricted this freedom by imposing regulations or by creating exclusive rights. But in the pure Moslem law stated in the Mejelle, all persons were free to make such use as they could of the unappropriated natural products of the earth.

The right to use water which was Mubah for irrigation or as a mill race is stated in Art. 1265, but the taker must have respect to the rights of other members of the public, neither accumulating water to such an extent that it overflows, nor withdrawing water so as to make a stream no longer navigable.

As already mentioned the Mejelle, Art. 1239, speaks of a class of public rivers the water of which is jointly owned but to which no right of pre-emption attaches. This class seems to include natural streams the water of which has been appropriated by the riparian owners but which does not flow in an artificial channel made by the joint proprietors. The language of the translated texts is somewhat obscure but the distinction intended appears to be one between water in a channel which is jointly owned and water in a natural stream over which persons have established rights of irrigation by ab antiquo usage. In the case of the channel, the water is appropriated and is owned by the owners of the channel[2]). In the case of the natural stream the riparian owners who have established rights ab antiquo have an exclusive right to take water in the sense that they can prevent others interfering with the flow thereof, but they cannot be said to own the flowing water until it has been led off into an artificial channel. In determining the rights to take water from such natural streams only ab antiquo usage is to be considered; rights to take water from a stream which is public cannot be acquired by prescription[3]). By this appears to be meant that user during a specified period (fifteen years) will not establish such a right. Immemorial user only is adequate. The distinction resembles one well known in the English law of Easements[4]).

Once it is established that the river[5]) is public, i.e. is not the Mulk property of individuals, it is clear that any person may

---

[1]) Mejelle, Arts. 1264, 1265.

[2]) Art. 1251 is not inconsistent with this if the water does not flow beyond the land of the proprietors of the channel.

[3]) Panayi v. Kathomouta (1924) 12 C.L.R. at p. 1; Mejelle, Art. 1675.

[4]) Compare the acquisition of easements by immemorial user and under the Prescription Act. 1832.

[5]) The term "river" is misleading. The word used in the Turkish and

Chapter XIV—Servitudes, Watercourses, Walls. [225]

use the water for irrigation, provided he does not thereby damage others [1]). If there exists among those who use the water any immemorial custom as to turns or the like this custom must alone be taken into consideration (Land Code, Art. 124). But if no such immemorial custom exists then new ways of using the water are not excluded, provided that damage is not done to others. What amounts to damage to others is a matter for the Court. A reasonable use of the water for purposes of irrigation is not inconsistent with the rights of other persons [2]). On the other hand no immemorial custom of user can justify a user which does cause unreasonable (excessive) damage, since Art. 1675 of the Mejelle expressly states, that actions regarding public rivers are never prescribed [3]).

Special attention should be paid to Art. 124 of the Land Code above cited which will probably prove the most important article for the determination of water rights in Palestine.

It seems clear from the texts and from these cases that claims to exclusive enjoyment for irrigation may be maintained by "bodies" or "communities" of people i.e. of the inhabitants of villages or to definite groups of villagers, and that their claims may be treated as a species of property rights when they are claiming the water in an artificial channel or even the water in a natural channel if the natural stream has been appropriated.

Private rights over water are, however, subject to a somewhat

---

Arabic texts (Nahr) signifies "running water" whether in the form of a river or stream, or even (Cf. Mejelle, Art. 1284) artificial channels. (per Curiam in Papa Panayi v. Jasenidou (1904) 6 C.L.R., at p. 88). Any stream may, therefore, be a "river" within the meaning of these Articles.

[1]) The Ottoman Law does not appear to limit the right of user even for purposes of irrigation, to riparian owners. In England riparian owners have a natural right to take water for the domestic purposes and for the use in connection with their riparian land. Unreasonable use of the water may be restrained. See McCartney v. Londonderry and Lough Swilly Railways (1904) A.C. 301. Kadry Pasha says "The right to use the water of public rivers is proportioned to the extent of land to be irrigated. (Statut Réel, Art. 43).

[2]) Ragheb v. Gerasimo (1894) 3 C.L.R. at p. 122. Compare Panayi v. Jasenidou (1904) 6 C.L.R. at p. 85. Speaking of the "river" which was in issue in that case the Court remarked: "The river is not in a channel which is the mulk property of any person; therefore, the water is mubah" .....In the absence of usage, agreement or express law, the Defendant has the right given to him under Art. 1265 to irrigate his fields from this water, ...(the plaintiff) has certainly not proved a usage ab antiquo as defined by Art. 166 of the Mejelle, nor has he acquired the ownership of the water in the manner prescribed by Art. 1251 of the Mejelle.

[3]) Haji Michael v. Georgiades (1905) 7 C.L.R. I.

ill defined general right of the public to drink and to take water for ablution [1]). In a broad sense the water remains mubah; men must not be allowed to die of thirst or to be unable to purify themselves merely to profit a proprietor. Humanity and Religion are to be preferred to Property.

In an earlier chapter [2]) reference has been made to the rights which arise from the digging of a well or the making of a water channel on Mewat land. The matter is dealt with in Arts. 1250 ff. of the Mejelle.

The general conclusion from these articles is that if a person with leave from the Sovereign digs a well, opens a spring or makes a water channel on Mewat land it becomes his Mulk, and he is also entitled to enclose a prescribed circuit or harim for the use and protection of the well, spring, or water channel.

In general subterranean waters are mubah [3]) so that it remains open to anybody to sink a well and appropriate such subterranean waters as he can find. Once collected the occupation gives a good title but the collection must be such as amounts to a storing of the water since water which is in flow cannot be treated as appropriated [4]).

Apart from the special provisions (Arts. 1281, 1287) as regards the circuit (Harim) of wells on Mewat land there is no rule of law whereby an action is given to the owner of a well against a person who reduces the volume of water in his well by sinking another in the neighbourhood.

"If someone sinks a well outside the harim of a well, and the water of the first well goes to this well, it is not necessary to do anything. Like as when someone opens a shop near another's shop, and there is a falling off in the trade of the first shop, the second shop cannot be closed". (Art. 1288).

---

[1]) Mejelle, Arts. 1267; 1268. Hedaya (Hamilton's Translation), p. 614.
[2]) Chapter I, p. 32 and Chapter II, pp. 37, 41, 42, supra.
[3]) Mejelle, Art. 1235.
[4]) Mejelle, Art. 1251. See also Anastassi v. Georghi (1892) 2 C.L.R. 64. In the Cyprus case of Houloussi v. Fiori, 2 C.L.R. 60, the part owner of a watercourse was restrained by injunction from making underground workings on his own land whereby he diverted water which had previously fed the jointly owned watercourse. No authorities were referred to, but the decision may (perhaps) be justified by reference to Art. 124 of the Land Code and Art. 1269 of the Mejelle, since the workings constituted an interference with an immemorial user of water. Refer further to the note on p. 120 of the Digest of Cyprus Cases. In England the distinction drawn is between tapping underground water not flowing in a defined stream and tapping underground streams.

Chapter XIV— Servitudes, Watercourses, Walls. [227]

There is no Harim to a well which has been dug by someone on his own Mulk property. His neighbour can dig another well near it on his own mulk. And the first person cannot prevent the digging of that well, saying "It takes the water of my well" (Art. 1291).

It has been held in Cyprus that the mere fact that the digging of a well has caused damage to a pre-existing neighbouring well does not avail to give a right of action to the person aggrieved [1].

Chapters III and IV of Book X of the Mejelle, treating of Joint Ownership contain a number of articles dealing with rights of ownership in general, obligations of neighbours, rights of way and of water, public rights, game, reviver of Mewat land, party walls, etc. The grouping together of these provisions arises partly from an assimilation of co-ownership as a form of private property with common rights in land which is not privately owned. This assimilation is not happy. Joint ownership of Roads, Watercourses and Walls.

Here we shall refer briefly to such of these provisions as touch upon private roads and streams and party walls.

It seems clear that the so-called private roads and private streams are conceived as land and water jointly owned. The co-owners do not merely possess rights of passage over or rights to take water from them; they are the owners of the soil and water, just as are the co-owners of a party wall. This being so the inclusion of this subject in the present chapter is justified.

Of course a private stream, or a private road may be owned by one person alone and cases of this sort are referred to in the Mejelle; in this chapter, however, we are not concerned with such cases which indeed come within the general principles of the law of ownership.

A private road, says Art. 956, is a road from which there is no exit (Tarik Khas). And Art. 1220 tells us that such a private road is like the jointly owned property held in absolute ownership (Mulk) of persons having a right of way. Private Roads and Streams.

"Consequently none of the owners may make a fresh construction therein without the permission of the other, whether such construction is prejudicial or not".

---

[1] Ragheb v Gerassimo, (1804) 3 C.L.R. at p. 105. In Cyprus the Wells Law, 1896, has since created a statutory harim in the sense of an exclusive drainage area on all categories of land as against the surrounding owners of all property other than Mulk. See Zade v. Tsinki 9 C.L.R. at p. 71. As to Wells in Miri see Tsinki v. King's Advocate in the Judicial Committee, (1920) 11 C.L.R. at p. 10.

The joint owners are not entitled to sell it or divide it by mutual consent, nor to shut the entrance to it, since, though not normally open to public use, it can be so used if the public road is overcrowded. Only the joint owners can open doors on the private way (1219). As to the repair of private roads, see Art. 1328.

A private road may be partitioned [1]) and would fall within the scope of the Provisional Law of A.H. 1332.

A private stream is one "the waters of which are divided between the land belonging to a limited number of persons and which upon arriving at the limits of such land, disappear and do not flow in vacant land [2]). Such a stream is jointly owned by the persons entitled to the water and the right of pre-emption mentioned in Art. 1008 applies [3]).

The co-owners of a private stream cannot, without the leave of the other owners, vary the turns of taking the water established between them by immemorial usage or utilise a turn for irrigating other lands not immemorially served by the stream (Art. 1269). A series of later Articles (Arts. 1322 ff.) deal with the obligations of cleansing of private streams. The same principles apply to sewers owned jointly (Art. 1327). Partition of jointly owned sewers is regulated by Art. 1144.

It is not always clear whether the articles of the Mejelle refer to waterchannels for irrigation or to sewers for the outflow of surplus water.

Where a stream or water channel is the exclusive property of a single person or of a group of persons no right to take water for irrigation exists on the part of others. However, Art. 1267 of the Mejelle allows a right to drink and even to water animals.

"The right of watering animals and crops from streams which are mulk property, that is to say, from water which enters into a channel which is mulk property, belongs to the owner of it. Others have a right of drinking in them. Therefore, from a river

---

[1]) Mejelle, Arts. 1143—1144. Compare Hedaya, at p. 572. (Hamilton's Translation).

[2]) Art. 1239. Compare Art. 955.

[3]) Compare the explicit statement in Art. 1239. Some of the Arts. (e.g. those relating to partition, Cf. Arts. 1144, 1151) appear primarily to refer to artificial channels constructed for the outflow of water, e g. sewers. A person may own as his mulk a channel running across the land of another. Art. 1290 which though comprised in the group of articles dealing with wells, etc. upon Mewat appears to refer to Mulk channels upon the land of another.

Chapter XIV—Servitudes, Watercourses, Walls.

which is the special property of a number of persons, or from a man's water channel, or his water pipe, or his well, without permission, another cannot irrigate his land. But he can drink the water, by reason of his having a right of drinking. And if there is no fear of the destruction of the river, or water channel, or pipe by reason of the number of the animals, he can bring his animals there and water them.

And, moreover, he can get water with a jug, or barrel, and take it to his house or gardens".

The streams now under discussion and which fall within the category mentioned in the second paragraph of Art. 1239 of the Mejelle appear to be those which flow along artificial channels constructed by persons solely for their own use [1]). Such artificial channels may be made to conduct water from a natural stream and the owners of the channel will then have an exclusive right to the water so conducted [2]).

In the Cyprus case of Stassi v. Vehim [3]) a channel made for conducting the water from a public stream to the lands of the parties was treated as a private stream within the meaning of the articles of the Mejelle. In that case it appeared that the water of a public river was conducted into an artificial channel and thence to the lands of a village. A dispute arose as to the division of the water as between the Christian and Moslem inhabitants. Many years previously an Ilam Sharia had recognized or established a decision but since that date the Christians had much increased their holdings in the village lands by purchase from the Moslems. They now claimed, in consequence, to be entitled to a greater share of the water, maintaining that the right to take water ran with the land.

The Court of Appeal held, however, that the position in fact was that there had been a partition of the enjoyment (Muhayeh) of the common property which, in the circumstances, there was no reason to set aside or alter. The decision refers to the provisions of Art. 1269 of the Mejelle of which the following translation occurs in the judgment.

"A person who has a share in a watercourse held in partnership cannot open from it a river, that is to say, a channel or ditch without the consent of the other partners (i.e. joint owners). He cannot change his ab antiquo turn of taking water. He cannot

---

[1]) per Curiam in Panayi v. Kathomouta (1924) 12 C.L.R. at p. 3.
[2]) See Hanim v. Irikzade (1923) II C.L.R. 91.
[3]) (1890) I C.L.R. 91.

utilise his turn for irrigating other land he may possess, not having a right to be irrigated from that river, and if the other joint owners consent to such a use both they and their heirs can revoke their consent".

In another case, Louka v. Nicola[1]), the dispute turned upon the rights of several villages to take water for irrigation by channels from a rivulet. The water was taken by a series of dams which were remade every summer. It appeared that in dry years water did not come down to irrigate both the upper and lower lands and the plaintiffs claimed that in such a year the defendants had taken more than their fair share of the water and had left little or none for the lower lands of the plaintiffs.

No immemorial custom on either side was proved. It does not seem to have been suggested that the rivulet was public and the case was argued on the assumption that it was a private stream. The Court relied upon a passage in the Hedaya (Book XLV, Sec. 3) to the effect that where a rivulet was jointly owned by several persons the distribution must be made according to the extent of land which they severally possessed; and held that, there being no other rule established either by ancient custom or by agreement, the persons entitled to the water were entitled to share in it according to the extent of their lands. Neither in this case nor in Stassi v. Vehim was any immemorial custom proved such as would have made Art. 124 of the Land Code applicable. In the absence of such custom the Court was driven to decide the proper distribution of the water upon principles governing the use of jointly owned property. In Stassi v. Vehim the Court adopted what it deemed to have been a partition of enjoyment by hours previously made, and not to be disturbed unless sufficient reason appeared. In Louka v. Nicola they took the view that in the absence of any other ground for decision, the available water should be divided according to the extent of the cultivable lands of the joint owners. Had an immemorial custom been proved this would have governed the distribution in accordance with Art. 124. The same principle as to the governing force of immemorial custom is stated in Mejelle, Art. 1269.

In Stassi v. Vehim the Court opined that rights such as those with which it was dealing were capable of registration though registration was not compulsory [2]).

---

[1]) 5 C.L.R. at p. 82.
[2]) Per Curiam in Stassi v. Vehim I C.L.R. at p. 103. The Court speaks only of the water. "The water so divided may become mulk but it does not follow

Chapter XIV—Servitudes, Watercourses, Walls. [231]

The dictum applies, of course, to the Turkish law. In Palestine every disposition of immovable property is brought within the Transfer of Land Ordinance 1920—1. Water on land is (semble) part of an immovable and a disposition thereof would, therefore, come within the Ordinance. A fortiori is this the case when the channel itself is jointly owned.

It seems that ownership of a water channel or water must be Mulk ownership. A tapu grant of a stream or of water in a stream is unknown, though an artificial channel upon Miri would, if erected since 1331, be part of the land and partake of its Miri character.

Art. 1239 of the Mejelle mentions another category of streams to which the rights of pre-emption applies, but to the water of which joint owners may be absolutely entitled. This class of stream appears to include natural streams, distinguished from the artificial channels already mentioned. The consideration of the rights of the joint owners of this class of streams will be undertaken in another chapter [1]).

Co-owners of a party wall must not erect structures on it without the consent of the other co-owners, but may rest joists upon the wall though not more joists than are placed there by the others [2]). The position of joists once placed cannot be changed [3]). Party Walls.

If a party wall needs repair and one of the owners declines to co-operate he can be compelled to do so, even though he be guardian of a minor or Mutwally of a Waqf. (Mejelle, Arts. 1318, 1319) [4]).

---

that it need be registered. It is not every kind of mulk property that requires registration".

[1]) In the Cyprus cases it is not always easy to determine whether the Court regarded itself as dealing with a stream included in the first or in the second category of Art. 1239. Streams of the first category are public rivers the water of which has been appropriated by riparain owners. Streams of the second category are private "rivers" which flow (semble) in an artificial channel made and presumably owned by proprietors (per Curiam in Panayi v. Kathomouta 12 C.L.R. p. 3).

[2]) Mejelle, Art. 1210 Tyser's translation is clear in this sense. Hooper's translation is difficult to follow.

[3]) Art. 1211. The article is somewhat indefinite.

[4]) Compare Art. 1316.

CHAPTER XV—PROTECTION OF AGRICULTURAL TENANTS.

Provision for the protection of agricultural tenants was not directly made by the Ottoman law. Under the older rural economy the cultivator was as he still in most cases is, a holder by Tapu grant from the State and his rights and duties were regulated not by the law of Hire but the special Miri Code.

In more recent years, however, land is to an increasing extent cultivated by tenants holding under landlords, usually in accordance with common understandings under which tenants paid a varying share of the produce known as Khums [1].

The general law of hire applicable to immovable property is elsewhere considered, as also certain peculiar forms of hiring of land recognized by the Moslem law. In this chapter, however, special attention will be drawn to the steps taken in Palestine to secure the protection of the tenant cultivator as against his landlord independently of the agreed terms of the contract of hire.

It is as well at once to note that the Moslem law as represented by the Mejelle appears to provide juster rules as between landlord and tenant of cultivable land than those contained in the somewhat landlord ridden Common law of England. Thus it has required special legislation in England [2] to give an agricultural tenant any right to agricultural fixtures which he had affixed in the land during the tenancy, but the Mejelle (Art. 531) recognizes the tenants' right to compensation. And Art. 526 of the Mejelle gives to a tenant a right to crops which had not matured at the time at which the hiring expired. Such a right to "way-going" crops was sometimes secured by special custom or special agreement but was not granted by the Common Law [3]. English legislation

---

[1] The so called "Khums" is not necessarily a fifth; sometimes it amounts to as much as a third.

[2] Elwes v. Maw (1802) 3 East. 35. For the legislation see in particular Landlord and Tenant Act. 1851, and the consolidating Statute, Agricultural Holdings Act, 1923.

[3] Wigglesworth v. Dallison (1779) I Douglas 201.

Chapter XV—Protection of Agricultural Tenants.[233]

has in this and in many other respects sought to give greater protection to the tenant than the Common law afforded [1]).

Agricultural tenants have in Palestine appeared the most to stand in need of special protection against eviction from their holdings and particularly so when a change of landlord has taken place by the sale of the reversion.

The special necessity for protection in Palestine is due to special causes. In part it is a need for protecting the tenant against his own folly and recklessness. In the very early days of the Mandatory regime steps were taken to protect the sitting tenant of land upon a sale thereof.

It was provided by the Transfer of Land Ordinance 1920 that "in all cases of disposition of land the Governor shall withhold his consent to the transaction unless he is satisfied that in the case of agricultural land the tenant in occupation will retain sufficient land in the district or elsewhere for the maintenance of himself and his family". (Sec. 6. O. G. No. 28). The Transfer of Land Ordinance 1920.

The Transfer of Land Ordinance 1920 was modified in the year 1921 by an amending Ordinance to the effect that any person wishing to make a disposition of immovable property must first obtain the consent of the Government to the transaction; such consent is to be given by the Director of Lands who shall be satisfied only that the transferor has a title. In the case of agricultural land which was leased the Director of Lands before giving his consent is to be satisfied that any tenant in occupation will retain sufficient land in the District or elsewhere for the maintenance of himself and his family. (Sec. 2. O. G. No. 60). The Amendment of 1921.

No further consideration of these provisions is now necessary since the repeal of the section by the Protection of Cultivators Ordinance 1929 (Sec. 10). This Ordinance has indeed been since also repealed by the Protection of Cultivators Ordinance 1933 but any question as to the effect of the repeal of a repealing Ordinance is set at rest by the provision of Sec. 5 (2) of the Interpretation Ordinance 1929.

The inadequacy of the protection afforded to sitting tenants in the special circumstances of Palestine has led to further legislation. In Palestine the peasant needs, as already remarked, to be protected against his own lack of foresight.

Experience shows that where existing tenants of land were left on the land by the purchaser of the estate, they did not normally stay on the land, but disposed of their rights to the purchaser

---

¹) In particular recently by the Landlord and Tenant Act, 1927.

or contracted out of their rights of receiving land in consideration of money compensation. The tenants, therefore, become liable to eviction even without notice. Legislation was, therefore, introduced [1]) on the lines in force in England and elsewhere giving protection to agricultural tenants from sudden eviction by requiring a due period of notice, save in cases where the tenant fails to pay the rent or misuses the land; and securing to the tenant compensation for improvements which he carried out during his tenancy and which are not exhausted, and, further-providing that a tenant of long standing who is required by the landlord to leave his holding is entitled to a further compensation. Provision was also made for the constitution of a Board to decide disputes as to whether or not compensation for disturbance or compensation for improvement was payable and as to the amount of any such compensation. In the case of tenants who had cultivated their holdings for a period of five years and more the landlord who terminated the tenancy was required to pay as additional compensation a sum equal to the average annual rent paid by the tenant during the five years preceeding the termination of the tenancy.

The Protection of Cultivators Ordinance 1929. This Ordinance, while repealing Sec. 2 of the Transfer of Land Ordinance 1921, did not contain provisions to the same effect or other adequate provisions tending to check the tendency among the tenants to contract out of their rights for money compensation, thus exposing themselves to eviction. The Ordinance was, therefore, in the year 1931 amended by the Protection of Cultivators (Amendment) Ordinance, the main provisions of which were designed to provide for the better protection of the tenants and occupants of Agricultural land by directing that no Court or Judge is to issue an order for eviction unless satisfied that the tenancy had been validly determined under the Ordinance and further that the High Commissioner is satisfied that equivalent provision has been secured towards the livelihood of the tenant. Similar protection has been given to persons who have exercised continuously for a period of five years a practice of grazing or watering animals or the cutting of wood or reeds or other beneficial occupation of similar character on the land whether by right, custom, usage or sufferance.

Certain of the amendments made by the Ordinance of 1931 were limited in duration [2]) and were to remain in force until 28 May 1932 only. Further amending Ordinances were enacted in

---

[1]) The Protection of Cultivators Ordinance 1929.
[2]) See Sec. 7 of the Ordinance.

Chapter XV—Protection of Agricultural Tenants.[235]

1932[1]) and the duration of all the amendments was extended till 28 May 1933 and subsequently till 31 Aug. 1933[2]).

The Ordinance of 1929 together with all the amending and extending Ordinances of 1931, 1932 and 1933 were repealed by a comprehensive consolidating and amending Ordinance, the Protection of Cultivators Ordinance 1933, which has, however, been itself amended by the Protection of Cultivators (Amendment) Ordinance 1934. The provisions of the consolidating Ordinance as amended will now be explained and in part set out. The two Ordinances are together known as the Protection of Cultivators Ordinances 1933-4. References to them and extracts from them will be given as from the Ordinance of 1934 in the amended form.

The object of the Ordinances is the protection of Cultivators that is to say of cultivating tenants. They apply only to tenants of Miri or Miri Waqf land and only to tenants or persons deemed to be such who are actually cultivating their holding. The terms "cultivator" and "cultivating", are not defined; it covers arable cultivation and possibly orchards and the like [3]), but not dairy farms, or stock raising. Protection is afforded in several ways. (I) The landlord's rights to determine the tenancy and evict the tenant is regulated and restricted. (II) Security is given against disturbance following upon sale or mortgage of the reversion. (III) The tenant who is evicted is in certain circumstances to be given compensation for disturbance. (IV) A tenant is given a right to be compensated for improvements. (V) The right of the landlord to increase rent is restricted.

The Protection of Cultivators Ordinances 1933-4.

The provisions of the Ordinance are in part suggested by

---

[1]) Protection of Cultivators (Amendment) Ordinance (No. 1) of 1932; Protection of Cultivators (Amendment) Ordinance (No. 2) of 1932.

[2]) Protection of Cultivators (Extention) Ordinance 1933.

[3]) The term "cultivate" means properly "to bestow labour and attention upon the land in order to the raising of crops: to till. Probably the word is strictly used in the Ordinance the general purpose of which is to protect fellahin following the customary forms of tillage as a means of livelihood. In Cyprus it has been declared and decided (Houston v. King's Advocate (1922) 11 C.L.R. at p. 72) that planting trees and shrubs is cultivation. But the circumstances of this interpretation were special. In Palestine in a recent case before the High Court the Court held that a person who cultivates land through another's agency is not a "cultivator" within the meaning of Art. 90 of the Execution Law. See Hussein Abu Radwan v. Chief Execution Officer, Jaffa, H.C. 68/34. Palestine Post 21 October 1934.

It is doubtful whether such a person (cultivator) would be considered a "statutory tenant" within the meaning of Sec. 2 of the Protection of Cultivators Ordinances 1933—4.

The Land Law of Palestine.

and to a considerable extent use the phraseology of English Acts. In particular those relating to compensation are based on the English Agricultural Holdings Acts [1] and, though their purpose is not in all respects the same, reference appears also to have been made to the English Increase of Rents Acts [2]. How far the Ordinances must be regarded as superseding the provisions of the Mejelle or affecting their application will be further considered below. It should, however, be noted that as the Ordinances only apply to cultivating tenants of Miri and Miri Waqf there remain outside them all tenants of Mulk or Mulk Waqf and all tenants of Miri or Miri Waqf who do not come within the definition of "statutory tenant" as stated in the Ordinance. To all such the provision of the Mejelle alone apply [3].

The Ordinance of 1933 starts with the usual definition of terms (Sec. 2). Some of these definitions are of fundamental importance since the limits of the application of the Ordinance depend upon them. Of such is the crucial definition of "statutory tenant".

A person, family or tribe, occupying and cultivating a holding otherwise than as owner thereof [4] is "statutory tenant" thereof. The term is enlarged to include a wife or relative who has cultivated with the knowledge of the landlord and also agricultural labourers hired by the landlord, who receive as remuneration a portion of the produce of the holding but only if such labourer cultivates the holding. It also includes the heirs of a statutory tenant.

A "holding" is defined to mean a plot of Miri land (or Miri Waqf land) occupied and cultivated by a tenant and includes land held in undivided ownership.

As a whole the Ordinances apply only to statutory tenants as thus defined, though certain of their provisions apply more widely [5]. It is further to be noticed that nothing in the Ordinance applies to persons who "at the commencement thereof" were occupying and cultivating holdings of which the Government of Palestine was

---

[1] Agricultural Holdings Act 1923.

[2] Increase of Rent and Mortgage Interest Restrictions Acts 1920, 1923.

[3] Such protection as may have been afforded by the provisions of Sec. 2 of the Transfer of Land (Amendment) No. 2 Ordinance of 1921 has also been withdrawn.

[4] In a recent Case before the Land Court of Jaffa sitting as a Court of Appeal (L.A. 13/34. Chibly Ayoub v. Dib Abou Nawas) the Court held that a person claiming ownership cannot come within the definition of "Statutory tenant". Palestine Post 2 Sept. 1934.

[5] Compare Sec. 17. The interesting and exceptional provisions of Sec. 18 have also, of course, no reference to statutory tenants.

Chapter XV—Protection of Agricultural Tenants. [237]

the landlord. (Art. 21). As only Miri or Miri Waqf land is included in the term "holding" tenants of public domain strictly so called would not in any case be affected. But so far, as Miri Mahlul remains Miri in the hands of the State [1], this provision excludes the application of the Ordinances at least as regards persons who were occupying and cultivating at the commencement of the Ordinance, i.e. the day of which it came into force [2]).

The termination of a tenancy of a "Statutory Tenant" is possible only in the way set out in Sec. 3 of the Ordinance which provides:—

Regulation and Restriction of the Landlord's Rights to Evict.

> 3.- (1) Notwithstanding any provision of any contract to the contrary where any statutory tenant has occupied and cultivated a holding for a period of not less than one year, the landlord thereof shall not be entitled to terminate the tenancy unless he shall have given to the tenant in writing notice to quit not less than one year from the first day of October following the date of the notice: Provided that nothing herein shall extend to the case, where any agreement between the landlord and the statutory tenant provides for any longer notice than the notice provided for herein.
>
> (2) Every notice to quit given under this Section shall be void and of no effect unless a copy thereof is served by the landlord on the District Commissioner of the district in which the land is situated within thirty days after the notice has been served on the statutory tenant, and unless the notice contains a declaration by the landlord that its object is to terminate the tenancy in order that the land may be transferred with vacant possession, if such be the object of the notice.

Where, however, a tenant has grossly and wilfully neglected his holding, three months notice suffices, though the tenant has the right to appeal to a Board upon the question of fact as to such neglect. (Sec. 4 (1)).

These foregoing sections, as indeed the Ordinances as a whole, appear to assume throughout, that the tenant cultivator of Miri land in Palestine normally holds land either at will or for short periods, such as a year, only.

---

[1] See supra, p. 25 ff. and the Land Law (Amendment) Ordinance 1933 Secs. 3, 4.
[2] Interpretation Ordinance 1929, Sec. 3 (General Definitions (3)).

The provisions of Sec. 3 may be compared with those of Sec. 25 of the English Agricultural Holdings Act 1923, reproducing earlier legislation. In England in the absence of a formal lease for a period of years, the usual form of agricultural tenancy is that from year to year. The assumption appears to have been made that this was also the case in Palestine. However that may be, occupation by a cultivating tenant of Miri cannot now be normally determined save by a year's notice [1]).

Subject to the provision of the proviso to subsection (1), Sec. 3 is applicable notwithstanding any provision of any contract to the contrary, but it applies only to prevent the landlord terminating the tenancy and does not (semble) apply where the tenancy is terminated without action by the landlord, e.g. by mere effluxion of time. Thus if the landlord and tenant agree together that the tenancy shall last for a fixed period only, the tenancy terminates upon the expiration of the period and it cannot be said that the landlord terminated it. If this is the proper construction of the Ordinance, it appears to open the way to an easy way of avoiding some of its provisions. It is, however, to be remarked that under Sec. 6 orders for eviction cannot be made against statutory tenants unless notice to quit under Sec. 3 has been served. This makes it obligatory in all cases that a year's notice to quit should be given to all statutory tenants whether they hold under a lease for a fixed period or not.

The provisions of Sec. 6 are indeed of striking severity. The assistance of the law in securing his rights is refused to landlords of statutory tenants unless very stringent conditions have been fulfilled. No court, judge or execution officer is to make an order for eviction of a statutory tenant save in accordance with the following provisions:-

(a) Where the tenant has paid when due or has paid within a reasonable time in accordance with the decision of a Board all rent due in respect of the holding, no such judgment shall be given or order made,

1. unless a notice to quit has been given by the landlord in accordance with the provisions of section 3 of this Ordinance, and
2. unless it is made to appear to the court or judge or execution officer that the tenant

---

[1]) The "year" is of course a solar year. See Interpretation Ordinance 1929 for definition of "month" and of "year".

Chapter XV—Protection of Agricultural Tenants.[239]

(a) has been provided with a subsistence area approved by the High Commissioner, or

(b) the High Commissioner is satisfied that the tenant has other land sufficient to enable him to maintain his customary means of livelihood in an occupation with which he is familiar, and

3. unless the questions whether the statutory tenant is entitled to compensation for disturbance and for improvements made by such tenant to the holding have been referred to a Board, and if such questions have been so referred unless those questions have been decided by the Board and any amount of compensation in respect thereof assessed by the Board, shall have been deposited with a Notary Public, and

4. if the statutory tenant has cultivated the holding under the landlord for a period of not less than five years consecutively preceeding the date when the notice to quit expired, unless in addition to any compensation fixed under the preceeding paragraph a sum equivalent to one year's average rent of the holding has been assessed by a Board and deposited with a Notary Public, and

5. if any compensation is payable under the provisions of section 17 of this Ordinance, unless such compensation has been assessed by the Board and deposited with a Notary Public.

If the tenant has not paid all rent due in respect of the holding within a reasonable time he has no claim to provision of a "subsistence area" nor to compensation for disturbance and has a claim only to compensation for improvements (Sec. 6 (1) b). The section further makes provision for payment out to the statutory tenant of sums deposited with the Notary Public under proper safeguards (Subsec. (2)).

The most remarkable provision of Sec. 6 is that which requires that the statutory tenant who has paid his rent shall be furnished with a subsistence area unless in the opinion of the High Commissioner he in fact has such. Detailed provisions as to the area are contained in Sec. 9. The burden of providing a subsistence area falls upon the evicting landlord, though he need not provide such area necessarily upon his own land. The area and situation of subsistence areas are determined by a Board subject to the approval of the High Commissioner (Subsec. (1)). The position of the tenant of a subsistence area is somewhat peculiar and varies from that of an ordinary tenant, though tenants of subsistence areas appear clearly to fall within the definition of statutory tenants in Sec. 2 [1])

---

[1]) Though not expressly so provided it appears to be assumed that sub-

and, therefore, to be entitled to all the rights of the statutory tenant so far as the contrary is not provided. The security enjoyed by a tenant of a subsistence area is, however, greater even than that of an ordinary statutory tenant, since he cannot be evicted save with the approval of the High Commissioner (Sec. 9 (4)). Indeed he is spoken of as having a "tenancy right" which, however, cannot be sold or mortgaged, save that with the approval of the High Commissioner given on the recommendation of a Board, it may in certain limited circumstances be surrendered to the landlord (Sec. 9 (7)). The heirs of the tenant succeed to the same rights and liabilities (Sec. 9 (5)). Presumably the "heirs" so entitled are the "heirs" according to the Ottoman Law of A.H. 1331 and not the "Mulk" heirs, at any rate if as must be normally, if not universally, the case the subsistence area is provided on Miri land. The question as to the proper interpretation of the word "heirs" is, however, arguable. According to the older use of the term the word "heirs" could only include persons succeeding to Mulk. There was no true successor to Miri. But the wide extension made by the Ottoman law of A.H. 1331 has (semble) broken down this older distinction.

Apparently the tenancy right of the tenant of a subsistence area cannot be devised by will and should not strictly be regarded as a form of property. The position of such a tenant is analogous in certain respects to that of the Miri holder and if subsistence areas become numerous one is inclined to foresee the growth of a new form of land holding.

<small>Security against Disturbance following upon Sale or Mortgage of the Reversion.</small>

Sec. 7 provides as follows :-

The rights under this Ordinance of,

(a) any statutory tenant who has occupied and cultivated a holding for not less that one year, or

(b) any person lawfully occupying any subsistence area, shall not be affected by any sale or transfer of such holding or area or of any immovable property of which such holding or area forms part including any sale effected under the Ottoman Provisional Law for the Mortgage of Immovable Property dated the 25th February 1326 [1]), or the Mortgage Law Amendment Ordinances 1920—

---

sistence areas will be provided in Miri or Miri Waqf land, but a subsistence area situate on Mulk is not forbidden. In such a case, of course, the tenant of the area would not be a statutory tenant.

[1]) "1326" is clearly an error. The Turkish date (Malia) was 25 February 1328 corresponding to (Moslem) 1st Rabi-el-Thani A.H. 1331. (See supra, p.p. 14 and 16.

Chapter XV—Protection of Agricultural Tenants. 241

1929 or under any law relating to Execution for the time being in force.

As remarked above tenants of subsistence areas appear to fall within the class of statutory tenants, since they occupy and cultivate a holding otherwise than as the owner thereof. They are, however, protected by this section whether or not they have occupied and cultivated for a complete year.

What is the nature of the protection afforded by this section is far from clear. Art. 590 of the Mejelle states that "if a person giving the thing on hire sells the thing hired without the permission of the person taking the thing on hire the sale is not executory as regards the latter"[1]. There is no reason for supposing that this rule is not as well applicable to hirings of Miri, as it undoubtedly is to hirings of Mulk. A tenant cannot, therefore, be damnified by a sale of a reversion, and the provisions of Sec. 7 seem otiose. In any event a purchaser would be bound as "landlord" by the provisions of this Ordinance restricting and regulating his right to evict.

The provisions of Sec. 14 are designed to give security to a statutory tenant against cesser of a head lease out of which his tenancy is derived. They apply only in cases in which the ground landlord has recovered judgment for possession against the superior lessee[2]. In such a case the occupation of the statutory sub-tenant is not to be affected except that he in future will hold immediately of the ground landlord and be thenceforth treated retrospectively as having been his tenant.

A statutory tenant who vacates the holding or is evicted is entitled to compensation for disturbance (Sec. 10). The compensation is to be assessed by a Board and is to consist of a sum representing such loss or expense directly attributable to the quitting of the land as the tenant may unavoidably incur in connection with the sale or removal of his movable property. No compensation is, however, to be payable in respect of the sale of any such movable property unless the statutory tenant has, before the sale, given the landlord a reasonable opportunity of making a valuation thereof.

Compensation for Disturbance.

As already noted, an order for eviction against a statutory tenant cannot be made unless the Court, judge or execution officer is satisfied that the question whether the tenant is entitled to compensation for disturbance has been referred to a Board, decided

---

[1] Cf. Kadry Pasha, op. cit., Art. 663.
[2] Compare Rent and Mortgage Increase Restriction Act, 1923, Sec. 4 (5).

by a Board, and the compensation paid to a Notary Public (Sec. 6 (1) (a) (3)).

If, however, all rent due has not been paid within a reasonable time an order for eviction may be made, though compensation for disturbance has neither been assessed nor paid (Sec. 6 (1) (b)). Indeed, the terms of Sec. 10 (1) (b) show that if a tenant is evicted under an eviction order he will get no compensation for disturbance unless the order was made under Sec. 6 (1) (a). If, however, a statutory tenant vacates in consequence of a notice to quit, and an eviction order is not required, he is entitled in all cases to compensation for disturbance and the fact that rent is in arrear is immaterial to his claim. The only express exceptions to the general rule that compensation is due to every statutory tenant who vacates in pursuance of a notice, are stated in Sec. 10 (2) which provides that compensation for disturbance is not to be payable :-

(a) Where the landlord has made the tenant an offer in writing to withdraw the notice to quit and the tenant has unreasonably refused or failed to accept the offer, or

(b) If the claim for compensation is not made within three months from the date at which the statutory tenant quits the land.

If a tenant was in occupation under a lease for a fixed period and vacates at the end of it he is clearly not entitled to compensation for disturbance. Though he is a statutory tenant, within the meaning of Sec. 2, he did not "vacate his holding in consequeuce of a notice to quit [1])".

A tenant who has grossly neglected his holding and who has, therefore, become liable to eviction on three months' notice under Sec. 4 (1) does not (semble) thereby lose his right to compensation for disturbance. Indeed, these tenants are given by Sec. 4 (2) a special right to compensation for the way going crop which is to be assessed by a Board. This right is not extended to tenants who receive a year's notice, since in their case the crop will have surely been reaped before the notice expired. Similar provisions are made by Sec. 9 (6) as regards tenants of subsistence areas and these provisions must be read in connection with those of Sec. 9 (5) whereby such tenants who have grossly and wilfully neglected

---

[1]) It is not clear whether an order for eviction against such a tenant can be obtained without notice to quit. Since the landlord does not need to give such a notice in order to "terminate" the tenancy Sec. 3 (1) seems inapplicable, yet the provisions of Sec. 6 are very wide. There are other obscurities in the Ordinance as to the rights, etc. of such a tenant.

Chapter XV—Protection of Agricultural Tenants.[243]

their area are liable to eviction on the recommendation of a Board [1]). It should be borne in mind that Art. 526 of the Mejelle gives a tenant vacating land on which are immature crops a right on payment of an estimated rent for the land, to enter to reap the crops when ripe. This rule is not excluded by any provision of the Ordinances now under discussion and (semble) any tenant can take the benefit of it without prejudice to any claim he may have under the Ordinances.

As already remarked, Art. 531 of the Mejelle gives to every tenant of land a right to claim compensation in respect of buildings and trees erected or planted by him during the tenancy if the landlord does not desire their removal. The compensation to be paid is to be the equivalent of the "value" whatever that may be [2]).

Compensation for Improvements.

The Protection of Cultivators Ordinances, however, while not (semble) in any way impeding the application of the Mejelle so far as it extends, provide much more fully for compensation to the statutory tenant for improvements effected by him in his holding. And the obligation to pay compensation under this head falls upon every landlord of a statutory tenant when the tenancy of the latter terminates "whether by notice to quit or otherwise" (Sec. 11 (1)).

The provisions of the Ordinances as regards compensation for improvements follow in principle and to a considerable extent indeed reproduce the wording of Secs. 1 ff. of the English Agricultural Holdings Act 1923 which reproduce earlier English legislation.

For the purpose of compensation improvements are divided into two classes, the details of which are set forth in Pt. 1 and Pt. 11 respectively of the First Schedule to the Ordinance of 1933. Part 1 contains a list of improvements to which the consent of the landlord is required. This list is an adaptation to Palestinian conditions of Part 1 of the First Schedule to the Agricultural Holdings Act 1923 and the items therein mentioned are mainly such improvements as are expensive, substantial or change the character of the holding. Part 11 contains improvements in respect of which notice to the landlord is required. The list corresponds in the main to the contents of Parts 11 and 111 of the First Schedule to the English Act.

---

[1]) An eviction order must (semble) be obtained if the tenant refuses to quit. And the making of such an order would be subject to the provisions of Sec. 6 since the tenant of a subsistence area appears to be a statutory tenant.

[2]) Kadry Pasha, who lays down the law to much the same effect, adds that the value will be "calculée comme s'ils devaient être démolis et arrachés". (Statut Réel, Art. 677).

The conditions under which compensation for improvements mentioned in each part of this Schedule is obtainable are set forth in Sec. 11. The basis of the compensation is to be the sum which "represents the value of the improvements to an incoming tenant", (Sec. 11 (1))[1]), and benefits given or allowed by the landlord to the tenant are to be taken into account (Sec. 11 (1) proviso)[2]).

The Ordinance proceeds as follows:-

Sec. 11 (2). "Compensation under this section shall not be payable in respect of any improvement comprised in Part 1 of the First Schedule to this Ordinance unless the landlord has previously to the execution of the improvement consented in writing to the making thereof, and any such consent may be given by the landlord unconditionally, or upon such terms, as to compensation or otherwise, as may be agreed upon between the landlord and the statutory tenant, and, if any such agreement is made, the question whether the statutory tenant is entitled to compensation under this section shall be deemed to have been referred to and decided by a Board and any Compensation payable under the agreement shall be deemed to be compensation payable under this section and to have been assessed by the Board".

This subsection corresponds to Sec. 2 of the English Act of 1923.

Presumably if a tenant has without the consent of the landlord planted trees or erected buildings for which compensation under this Section cannot, therefore, be obtained, both parties still have the rights granted by the Mejelle. No doubt it is arguable that the words "compensation ... shall not be payable in respect of any improvements, etc." may be interpreted as excluding such compensation unless the landlord has given written consent to the improvement. But the compensation excluded is only compensation under the Section and the better opinion seems to be that a claim for the value under Art. 531 of the Mejelle would be good, notwithstanding lack of consent by the landlord.

As regards improvements to which the consent of the landlord is not required the Ordinance provides as follows:-

Sec. 11 (3). "Compensation shall not be payable in respect of any improvement comprised in Part 11 of the First Schedule to this Ordinance unless the statutory tenant has given to the landlord not less than two months' notice in writing of his intention to

---

[1]) Agricultural Holdings Act, 1923, Sec. 1 (1).
[2]) Ibid., Sec. 1 (2) (a).

Chapter XV—Protection of Agricultural Tenants.

execute the improvement, and of the manner in which he proposes to do the work:

Provided that: (a) if the improvement consists of application to the land of farmyard manure, it shall be sufficient for the statutory tenant to give notice to the landlord once in each year; and (b) if the improvement consists of repairs to buildings which are necessary for the habitation of the statutory tenant or the proper cultivation or working of the holding, the statutory tenant shall not execute the repairs, unless the landlord fails to execute them within a reasonable time after such notice. Where notice is given under this sub-section, the landlord and statutory tenant may agree on the terms of compensation or otherwise on which the improvement is to be executed; and, if any such agreement is made, the question whether the statutory tenant is entitled to compensation under this section shall be deemed to have been referred to and decided by a Board and any compensation payable under the agreement shall be deemed to be compensation payable under this section and to have been assessed by the Board".

These provisions may be compared with those of Sec. 3 of the English Act of 1923. The second proviso (b) corresponds to a proviso to item (29) in the first Schedule to the English Act.

The remainder of the Section is concerned with procedure; compensation is to be assessed by a Board and claims must be made within the period limited (Sec. 11 (4)).

It is to be remarked that the landlord of a statutory tenant cannot get an order of eviction until the compensation for improvements, like the compensation for disturbance, has been not only referred to and decided by a Board but has actually been paid into the hands of the Notary Public (Sec. 6 (1) (a) (3)). But rent at the accustomed rate is payable from the date at which the notice to quit expired and that of eviction (Sec. 6 (3)).

The provisions of Sec. 17 are applicable not only to statutory tenants but to all tenants who have received notice to quit. They intend to secure compensation to the tenant under notice to quit if he prepares land for cultivation in the ensuing year. As in other cases, compensation is to be assessed by a Board; as in the case of other forms of compensation the assessed compensation must have been deposited with a Notary Public before an order for eviction is made against a statutory tenant (Sec. 6 (1) (a) (6); 6 (1) (b) (III)). *Compensation for Preparation.*

Sec. 13 forbids a landlord to "increase the rent of a holding" without the sanction of a District Officer. The section applies of course only to Miri and Miri Waqf occupied by a cultivating *Restriction of Rent.*

tenant (Sec. 2). The section is probably to be read as forbidding rent to be raised as against a sitting tenant, though at first sight it might appear to forbid the rent of the "holding" being increased even against a new applicant.

In any case the section undoubtedly throws upon District Officers a duty which is trying and difficult. In effect they become the final authority for fixing rents of cultivated land throughout Palestine. Apparently there is no appeal from the decision of a District Officer though on general principle, his decision could be questioned on suspicion of bad faith.

Rent is defined (Sec. 2) as "any payment in money or kind including any share of the produce of a holding". This is a very wide definition. It brings within the Ordinance all forms of tenancy under which the "landlord" shares in the produce whether or not he supplies stock, seeds or the like. Indeed, it seems possible to bring within the definition some forms of co-operative management in which separate holdings are allotted for cultivation by individual co-operators.

Duty of Director of Lands.

In order to secure compliance with the provisions of the Ordinance and to prevent landlords escaping their obligations by transferring the land upon which statutory tenants are settled, Sec. 16 throws a novel duty upon the Director of the Department of Lands. It will be remembered that orders for eviction cannot normally be obtained against statutory tenants unless the compensation due has been assessed and also deposited with a Notary Public. If this has been done the Director of Lands is not called upon to interfere in a transfer of the reversion [1]) (Sec. 16 (3)). But otherwise he is not to record the transfer in the Land Registers "unless he is satisfied that security has been given by the landlord for carrying out any obligations to the statutory tenant under this Ordinance, or unless the purchaser agrees that he will take over the obligations of the former landlord, and that any compensation that has been or shall be found due to the statutory tenant shall be charged on the land" (Sec. 16 (1)). And Sec. 16 (2) charges upon the land all compensation found by a Board to be due. The nature of the charge is not further defined. Presumably it would be treated as a kind of hypotec and sale could be ordered by the Court in case of need. The analogy in English to equitable

---

[1]) The section speaks of "transfer of Miri land". Presumably an assignment of a head lease of "Miri" land out of which the tenancy of the statutory tenant was derived, would be also covered by the term.

Chapter XV—Protection of Agricultural Tenants. [247]

charges would probably be followed in connection with the remedies.

An important reservation is made as to the application of the Ordinances by Sec. 15. This Section gives to a District Commissioner power to "authorize" the "resumption" by a landlord of a holding or any part thereof if he is satisfied

    (a) that such resumption is required for some reasonable and sufficient purpose having relation to the good of the holding or of the adjoining land, including development by drainage or irrigation or by closer settlement or colonization or disposal for building purposes, and

    (b) (I) that the statutory tenant will retain sufficient land of such nature as to enable him to maintain his customary means of livelihood in occupations with which he is familiar, such land being as far as possible in the vicinity of the home from which the transfer may cause his displacement, or

        (II) that the purpose for which the resumption of the holding is sought comprises the provision for the statutory tenant of developed land sufficient for the maintenance of himself and his family, together with adequate subsistence for them, pending the development of such land.

Resumption of Holding.

It seems probable that this section does not entitle the District Commissioner to over-ride the terms of an agreement between a landlord and tenant; all it enables him to do, is to over-ride the application of the Ordinance. If the District Commissioner assents to the landlord's application, the statutory tenant is liable to eviction from the land without notice (save such notice as would be due apart from the Ordinance) and without compensation either for disturbance or improvements. Presumably the District Commissioner would be entitled to make conditions in favour of a tenant in addition to those specified in the section. It is not clear whether the order of the District Commissioner is equivalent to a judicial order for eviction; more probably an order for eviction from the Court is necessary though the landlord would be entitled to such an order on producing the "authority" for resumption granted by the District Commissioner and would not need to satisfy the Court according to the terms of Sec. 16.

How far this Section is workable in practice may be doubted. A recent writer remarks :-

The Land Law of Palestine.

"Section 15 allows the District Commissioner to return to the landlord his leased property, if the land is necessary for the development of the place by closer settlement or colonisation on condition "that the purpose for which the resumption of the holding is sought comprises the provision for the statutory tenant of developed land sufficient for the maintenance of himself and his family together with adequate subsistence for them, pending the development of such land.

The provisions of this paragraph are not sufficiently clear and as far as they can be understood, appear not to be feasible. Is the cultivator to receive developed land as a gift, as compensation, or on lease? And are the means of subsistence until the development of the land is accomplished to be accorded as a gift, or as a place of work? Is it, for instance, meant that the tenant is to receive a planted orchard in place of the unplanted land he has worked hitherto and that it will be necessary to maintain him and his family for 6-8 years until the orchard bears fruits? Or to find him work during this time?" [1]).

Protection of Grazing Customs, etc. The provisions of Sec. 18 are also noteworthy. They forbid the making of eviction orders against "any person who has exercised by himself or his agent habitually at the appropriate seasons for not less than five consecutive years within a period of not more than seven years prior to the date, when application is made for any such order, a practice of grazing or watering animals or the cutting of wood or reeds or other beneficial occupation of similar character on the land whether by right, custom, usage or sufferance, unless the landlord satisfies the court or judge or execution officer that the High Commissioner is satisfied that provision of equal value has been secured towards the livelihood of such person".

Clearly it is the peculiar and somewhat undefined nature of rights to land in Palestine which alone makes such a provision necessary. The persons protected are not tenants but are in actual enjoyment of what English lawyers would be inclined to term a prescriptive right of common of pasture "in gross". Their claim to graze animals, etc. is not, it should be remarked, recognized as a legal right. Even where it is a claim of right it may be over-ridden if the High Commissioner is satisfied that provision such as is required has been made for the livelihood of the claimant. The question as to whether the claim is one of right or of sufferance becomes immaterial, the whole emphasis being laid upon the need of the

---

[1]) Palestine Post 15 Aug. 1933.

Chapter XV—Protection of Agricultural Tenants.[249]

particular individual. In this respect the provision may be said to be the most striking of all the provisions of this somewhat remarkable Ordinance.

Reference has been frequently made to the settlement of questions in issue under the Ordinance by a Board. The constitution of these Boards is laid down in Sec. 8. In general they are to consist of three persons, one being nominated by each of the two interested parties, landlord and tenant, and the District Officer acting ex officio as the third. There is an appeal to the District Commissioner (Sec. 8 (2)). Rules as to procedure and fees may be made by the High Commissioner (Sec. 20 (a) (b)). The Boards and the Commissions.

A striking innovation is contained in Sec. 19 which authorizes the High Commissioner to appoint special Commissions which alone are to have jurisdiction to decide upon any questions arising under the Ordinances, some of them being difficult questions of mixed law and fact.

The disputes in question are as follows:-

(a) as to whether any person is a statutory tenant of a holding, or

(b) as to the length of time that any statutory tenant has occupied and cultivated a holding, or

(c) as to whether any person is the landlord of a holding, or

(d) as to whether any person has exercised continuously any practice of grazing or watering animals or cutting wood or reeds or other beneficial occupation of a similar character by right, custom, usage or sufferance.

Sec. 19 has been modified in certain particulars by the Ordinance of 1934. This later Ordinance fortunately gave an appeal on points of law by case stated to the Land Court this arrangement having been substituted for that in the Ordinance of 1933 according to which the High Commissioner in Council was the final judge both of law and fact.

Sec. 19 (3) as modified by the Ordinance of 1934 requires all Courts to treat decisions given in accordance with the provisions of the Section as binding parties and privies. These questions cannot be litigated but are res judicata.

The High Commissioner is authorized by Sec. 20 (c) to issue regulations as to the practice and procedure to be followed in all enquiries before the Commissions [1].

---

[1] Regulations under this Section appeared in Supplement No. 2 to O.G. No. 419 of 5 Feb. 1934. In the case reported in the Palestine Post 2 Sept. 1934

CHAPTER XVI—LIMITATION OF ACTIONS AND PRESCRIPTION.

All bodies of law attribute some legal effect to long continued neglect to enforce or to long continued enjoyment of a right. Sometimes failure to sue during a certain period is a bar to action thereafter. The right may continue to exist though not enforceable. Or it may be, that the lapse of the period will be deemed to extinguish not only the remedy, but the right itself. Again, actual user of property if continued uninterruptedly for a certain length of time may be deemed to create a legal right to the property, that is to say, long continued user may be deemed to be a title to a right.

The terms used to denote the different effects, which lapse of time may have upon a right, are not always clearly differentiated in meaning. The word Prescription [1]) is often used of them all. In the Mejelle we find a group of Articles (Arts. 1660 ff.) which fix the periods during which actions for debt and actions for the recovery of property must be brought, the circumstances which will prevent or interrupt the running of the periods, etc. The effect of the lapse of the prescribed period appears always to be the same; the remedy is barred, but not the right. Length of time does not destroy a right. The lapse of the period merely renders the right unenforceable by action unless its continued existence is ack-

---

(L.A. 131/34), the Court held that in cases under the Protection of Cultivators Ordinance, the person called before the Commission is entitled to receive a notice setting out the nature of claim and the particular land in which cultivation rights are claimed; that the notice should be served personally on the person to whom it is addressed; that the Commission must state in their decision in what particular area of land setting out the boundaries the claimant has a right of cultivation, and that a tenant claimant must be the "tenant" of a particular parcel of land and not a "tenant" of an indefinite area. (See Chibly H. Ayoub and others v. Dib Abu Nawas. Jaffa Land Court sitting as a Court of Appeal).

¹) The "prescriptio" was a clause in the formula (or statement of issues) in the Roman procedure by which the issue of long continued delay was raised. As it was written first, i.e. at the beginning of the formula, the defence which it stated came to be known as "prescription".

Chapter XVI—Limitation of Actions, Prescription.[251]

nowledged. According to the terminology of English Law we should describe this as a limitation of action rather than a true prescription [1]. The Moslem law treats lapse of time not as causing the extinction of a right, much less as a title to a right enjoyed during the period, but merely as limiting the evidence adducible to substantiate the rights claimed by the plaintiff. Thus in the case of an action of debt the plaintiff will not succeed after the period has elapsed unless the defendant acknowledges his indebtedness before the judge. Again in action for recovery of property if the defendant admits that he was a lessee or if that fact can be proved against him (as a matter of common knowledge) the plaintiff will succeed. With this may be compared the similar provision of Land Code, Art. 20, set forth below. Under this article the plaintiff who has been out of possession for the prescribed period succeeds if the defendant admits that he "arbitrarily" took possession of the land. The lapse of the period, therefore, does not destroy the right of the original owner but it makes it impossible for him to prove his prior right save through the mouth of the defendant possessor [2] or by evidence which shows that the defendant possessor was in possession as his tenant or the like.

Arts. 1660 ff. contain no provision as to the effect of long continued adverse possession upon the legal position of the possessor, but are concerned solely with the effect of such possession upon the remedy of the person out of possession. "Prescription" says Chiha "protects a state of things which has long existed; but the law does not thereby legalise a state of things however long existing, which had an unlawful origin. The Sovereign merely forbids the Courts to entertain claims which have long been neglected [3]. This view of the effect of the Articles is, we are told, accepted by all Ottoman writers [4].

---

[1] The term "Prescription" as a technical English legal term is confined to the acquisition of easements and similar rights by long continued enjoyment. Cf. Prescription Act, 1833. But the term is used not infrequently in a broader sense to mean the destruction of a remedy or of a right as well as the acquisition of rights by long possession.

[2] See Chiha, op. cit., pp. 612-4 as to what constitutes acknowledgment sufficient to prevent a prescriptive claim arising.

[3] Ibid., p. 596.

[4] The view that acquisitive prescription is unknown in Moslem law is strongly contested by Dr. M. Boulis in an article in Gaz. Trib. Lib. Syriens 1932 at pp. 991 ff He contends that the Moslem law on the subject is merely a survival from the Roman law of Byzantine times and that usucapion so far from being unknown is inherent. The doctrine stated in the text is, however, that commonly held. Cf. Cardahi, Revue Critique 1926, pp. 207 ff.

The Land Law of Palestine.

Thus, in common with European law, the Moslem law treats the right of the proprietor as still existent notwithstanding the denial to him of an action for its enforcement. But the manner in which the Moslem law views the matter is nevertheless somewhat different. Its rules as regards limitations of actions are, we are told, primarily intended not so much to put an end to litigation as to prevent fraud [1]). The assumption is that the defendant in a revendication action is really the owner and his reliance upon the lapse of the period of limitation is a method by which he can conveniently rebut a false claim. It follows, therefore, that if he in any way acknowledges that the claimant was once owner he must thereafter rely for his defence upon a title which he has acquired from him. Thus, if he says in defence that he bought the land from the claimant more than fifteen years earlier, his defence based upon the lapse of fifteen years fails and he is called upon to prove his purchase. For though the lapse of fifteen years would be in itself a good defence, and he is not bound also to prove his title, yet it is only a good defence when he is asserting it as an owner. Actions are not prescribed merely because they have not been exercised during the period stated in the law; the right claimed must have also been denied by the defendant during the whole of the period fixed by the law. If the defendant in a revendication is to succeed he must do so as owner though he asks for the rejection of the plaintiff's claim on the ground of prescription and does not put forward his better title [2]).

It is easily comprehensible from what has been said, why long continued possession is not mentioned in Art. 1248 of the Mejelle as a method of acquiring ownership [3]). The occupation of some thing previously without an owner does, however, figure among the methods mentioned. The possession of a thing as owner will, therefore, in the absence of any superior and available claim be a good title to ownership. This conclusion is in effect equivalent to the principle that possession raises a presumption of ownership. If no other person is able to put forward a better claim, the possessor, claiming to be owner, must be deemed owner. "Posses-

---

[1]) See per Wajih Khoury in Gaz. Trib. Lib. Syriens VII at p. 109; see further Cardahi, in Revue Critique 1926, pp. 210 ff.

[2]) Cf. Wajih Khoury, loc. cit. So also in the case of a personal action, the defendat must plead, in effect, that he does not owe the debt and that in any case the claim is too late.

[3]) As stated in the chapter dealing with Servitudes ab antiquo enjoyment is clearly a ground upon which the right to a Servitude may be based.

Chapter XVI—Limitation of Actions, Prescription.[253]

"...sion" as the old English adage says "is nine points of the law". The tenth point which it lacks is that which may be relied upon by the true owner.

In the light of what has been said as to the pure Moslem theory of prescription we may now proceed to consider the provisions of the Mejelle which embody it. Arts. 1660—1661 fix the periods fixed for the limitation of actions relating to immovables as follows:-

Prescription in the Mejelle.

(a) Actions concerning ownership of mulk immovable property and inheritance, as also of dedicated property and inheritance and of dedicated (Waqf) immovable property of the category of Muqata'a or Ijaratein cannot be heard after fifteen years.

(b) Actions by a Mutwally or by the beneficiaries of a Waqf property are heard up to thirty-six years [1]).

Owing to the fact that Arts. 1660 ff. of the Mejelle are concerned solely with the effect of delay upon the right of action, various questions as to the effect of such delay upon the position of the person in possession, are left undetermined. Such questions will not arise when the right of action barred is a personal one only, e.g. action for debt, and it is with rights of action of this kind that the Mejelle is mainly concerned. It may, however, be safely stated that a right of action for recovery of immovable property is only barred by the lapse of the periods specified when the possession of the defendant has been adverse to the claimant, i.e. when the defendant has possessed as owner in such a way as

---

[1]) The "year" referred to in the Mejelle is a lunar year (Cf. Omar Hilmy, op. cit., Art. 448). But in Yemeniji v. Andoniou (1893) 2 C.L.R. p. 140, it was stated that at all events in Cyprus by universal custom the term is construed as meaning a Gregorian or Julian year of 365 days. In Egypt the compilation of Kadry Pasha (Statut Réel) gives 33 years for the action for recovery of land based on a right of inheritance on the constitution of a Waqf (Art. 152).

In Palestine the term "year" in the Mejelle would reasonably be deemed as meaning a lunar year there being certainly no "universal custom" to the contrary. The Interpretation Ordinance 1929 applies only to Ordinances and the like; consequently Sec. 3 C (12) (33) have no application to the Mejelle and Land Code. But it is now provided by Sec. 7 of the Land Law (Amendment) Ordinance 1933 that "in every provision of the Ottoman Land Code and any other Ottoman Law concerning immovable property in Palestine fixing the period within which any action may be heard or any right may be exercised, the terms "month" and "year" shall be deemed to refer to a calendar month or year respectively according to the Gregorian Calendar". The term "Ottoman Law" in the enactment is intended, presumably, to include the Mejelle. It is to be observed that the enactment refers only to provisions concerning immovable property.

to dispossess the claimant. Thus in a Cyprus case[1]) a room had been given by a father to his daughter but the gift had not been perfected by registration. The father continued to be registered as owner. On his death the daughter sought registration and could, of course, only rely on a prescriptive right. On the facts it was clear that she had not during the period of 15 years had possession of the room adversely to her father; on the contrary the father had occupied the room. "The plea of prescription" said the Court (Tyser C.J. and Bertram J.) "implies that, the father being dispossessed, neglected during 15 years to bring an action to recover possession. But how could he have brought an action to recover possession of the room while he was actually living in it[2]). Possession for the period of prescription under a grant or sale not perfected by registration may no doubt operate to supply the defect of want of registration; but such possession in order to be effective must be maintained adversely to the person entitled to dispute it, and be of such a nature as to exclude the donor or vendor continuously and substantially from the enjoyment of his property".

Obviously possession under a lease or similar arrangements cannot be adverse to the lessor. "A person who takes land from the possessor (i.e. the Miri holder) under a lease or loan, acquires no permanent right over the land by reason of the length of the time, for which he cultivates and possesses it, so long as he acknowledges himself a lessee or borrower. Consequently no account is taken of lapse of time, and the possessor will always have the right, to take back his property from the lessee or borrower"[3]).

"A person who holds a thing as hirer or borrower of it cannot while admitting that circumstance defend an action for recovery by the lessor or lender by relying upon the lapse of the period of prescription. If he desires it in the presence of the claimant the latter will lose his right if he abandons his action"[4]).

Special provisions are now made by Sec. 2 of the Land Law (Amendment) Ordinance of 1933 as regards possession by one or

---

[1]) Mourmouri v. Haj Yanni (1907) 7 C.L.R. p. 95.

[2]) This remark must not, of course, be taken to mean that the corporal possession of the defendant is never consistent with the adverse legal possession of the plaintiff; e.g. the defendant might have possession in fact under an agreement of lease from the plaintiff in which case the plaintiff would be deemed to have in law adverse possession.

[3]) Land Code, Art. 23. Cf. Mejelle, Art. 1673. See Chapter XII—Leases, at p. 184 (footnote) as regards the inadmissibility of a claim of occupancy by a tenant.

[4]) Kadry Pasha, Statut Réel, Art. 155.

Chapter XVI—Limitation of Actions, Prescription.[255]

more of several co-heirs. This subject is referred to in Chapter XIII dealing with co-ownership, where the relevant authorities as regards possession between co-owners are considered [1]).

The period of limitation begins to run as from the date at which the plaintiff had the right to bring an action in respect to the subject matter of his claim [2]). Limitation in respect of a person who is bankrupt only begins to run as from the date of the cessation of the bankruptcy [3]). Moreover the effective period must have been allowed to elapse without any excuse. Examples of lawful excuse are given in Art. 1663 as also in Art. 20 of the Land Code set out below.

"The effluxion of time which has occured by reason of some lawful excuse, such as cases where the plaintiff is a minor or a lunatic, or an imbecile, and that whether he has a guardian or not, or where the plaintiff has gone to some other country, or where the plaintiff has been in fear of the power of his opponent is disregarded. Consequently limitation begins to run from the time of the cessation or removal of the excuse".

Ignorance of his rights on the part of the true owner is not an excuse, "at all events where it was not caused by fraud or false statement on the other side" [4]).

Though the Articles appear to deal primarily with the date of commencement of the period, the words suggest that not only does the period not commence to run till the fact justifying delay is removed, but a period which has commenced to run is interrupted so long as the fact justifying delay exists [5]).

---

[1]) Cf. L. A. 121/26; L.A 36/30, 6/33;

[2]) Mejelle, Art. 1667. See the judgment in Saadat Hanum. Mutwally of Ali Pasha Waqf v. The Government of Palestine, L. A. 70/32, Palestine Post 12 November 1932.

[3]) Art. 1668. But this article seems to refer only to debts due from insolvent persons. Compare Tyser's translation. Bankruptcy in the European sense is not a Moslem institution.

[4]) Per Hutchinson C.J. in Muzaffer Bey v. Collet (1904) 6 C.L R. at p. 109. Cf. Omar Hilmy, Laws of Evqaf, Art, 444. As to minority and absence see more fully Chapter XXI infra.

[5]) In Monk v. Nicola (1924) XI C.L.R. 118 the Court indeed stated that "so far as Miri is concerned Art. 20 (Land Code) points to the view, that the disabilities and circumstances, that prevent the period running must be in existence at the time the period begins to run". This dictum was not expressly applied to Mulk, governed by the articles of the Mejelle. The provisions of Art. 1663 apply, however, as well to limitation under Art. 1660 as to that under Art. 1662. Note that Chiha (op. cit. p. 609) says that the established doctrinal view is that the provisions of Art. 1663 as also of Art. 20 of the Land Code are not exhaustive.

The Land Law of Palestine.

The period is also interrupted by presentation of a claim "before a judge" but not if the claim is not made "in the presence of the judge". By these phrases institution of action in Court appear in modern phraseology to be intended [1]).

And it is interrupted by a written acknowledgment of the claimant's right for this would prevent the possession being adverse [2]).

It is not, however, interrupted by the death of the person against whom it is running, nor, if the period has already run, does a right of action revive for the heirs; periods of neglect to bring action are aggregated in the case of all persons "in privity" with one another, such as ancestor and heir, vendor and purchaser, donor and donee [3]).

The Mejelle speaks only of the barring of the action. It appears, that, if the defendant cannot show a possession by himself adverse to the plaintiff during the whole of the prescribed period, his defence is bad. Consequently though the plaintiff has in fact been out of possession for the prescribed period he will nevertheless succeed if the defendant possessor has not himself possessed adversely to the plaintiff for the prescribed period.

Suppose that two different persons, A and B, have consecutively been in possession of the land and the aggregated period of their respective occupations are equal to the whole period requisite to bar the action of the true owner. In this case the action will no doubt be barred if the consecutive occupiers were in privity with each other. But if they were independent squatters, the action of the true owner would not be barred, assuming that B, the person in possession at the date of the action, had not been in possession for the requisite period. This follows from the terms of Art. 1667 of the Mejelle since the right to bring the action against B could not have arisen, until B went into possession and, therefore, time did not commence to run in his favour till that date [4]). But if there was privity between the two consecutive possessors, their periods

---

Any circumstances making action impossible constitute a valid excuse. Cf. Kadry Pasha. Statut Réel, Art. 157; Mejelle, Art. 1666; Mejelle, Art. 1674.

[1]) Mejelle, Art. 1666. Compare Judge Hooper's translation. As to what amounts to a claim made in the presence of a Judge see Joannou v. Michai (1912) 10 C.L.R. 51.

[2]) Mejelle, Art. 1674.

[3]) Mejelle, Arts. 1669, 1670. Action may be barred against one or more of several co-heirs and not against others. Art. 1672.

[4]) The same result is reached in English law under the Statute 3 and 4 Will IV c. 27. See Agency Company v. Short (1888) 13 App. Ca. 793; 59 L.T.V. 677; Samuel Johnson & Sons Ltd. v. Brock (1907) 97 L.T. 294.

Chapter XVI—Limitation of Actions, Prescription.[257]

of occupation may be aggregated. This is not explicitly stated in the Mejelle, but it is certainly the law according to Moslem authorities and might be inferred from general principle and analogy[1]).

Omar Hilmy, referring to Mejelle Art. 1670, states that if someone die after he has possessed waqf property by Ijaratein for a certain period and his heirs, having the right of inheritance, take and possess that property in Ijaratein, relying simply on their rights of succession and the aggregate of these two periods completes the time of prescription, the action of the plaintiff is dismissed if he has kept silence during those times without legal excuse [2]).

It is provided by Art. 79 of the Treaty of Lausanne that all periods of prescription or limitation of action whether they began to run before or after the outbreak of war shall be treated in the territory of the High Contracting Parties so far as regards relations between enemies as having been suspended from the 29th Oct. 1914 until the expiration of three months after the coming into force of the Treaty. This article was brought into force in Palestine by the Treaty of Peace (Turkey) Ordinance, 1925, as from 6th August, 1924.

It was, however, laid down in a Palestine case that "Closure of the competent Court (during the war) is not one of the legal excuses recognized by the Ottoman Law regarding Prescription (Limitation of Actions). When the Courts were re-established after the Occupation it was found necessary to make express provision for this matter by Art. 16 of the Proclamation No. 42 of the 24 of June 1918" [3]).

Art. 1662 of the Mejelle provides that actions relating to Miri including actions relating to private roads or rights to a flow of water or to take water on Miri cannot be heard after the expiration of ten years. *Prescription in Relation to Miri Land.*

Art. 20 of the Land Code makes a similar provision and as this article is often referred to it may be well to set it out in full. It provides that "in the absence of a valid excuse according to the Sacred Law, duly proved, such as minority, unsoundness of mind, duress, or absence on a journey (Muddet Safar) actions concerning Tapu lands the occupation of which has continued without dispute for a period of ten years shall not be maintainable. The

---
[1]) Compare Kadry Pasha, Statut Réel, Art. 153. Mejelle, Art. 1667, and see also judgment in L. A. 70/32 referred to above.
[2]) Laws of Evqaf, Art. 440.
[3]) Mahmud Ahmed Salameh & others v. Saleh Ibrahim Ismail & others, L. A. 121/26.

period of ten years begins to run from the time when the excuses above mentioned have ceased to exist. Provided that if the defendant admits and confesses that he has arbitrarily (fouzouli) taken possession of and cultivated the land no account is taken of the lapse of time and possession of the land is given back to its proper owner" [1]).

Art. 15 of the Law of Disposition A.H. 1331 thus provides:
"The Mamur Tapu represents the State in all actions by or against the State in regard to the raqabe or the diposal of Miri, Mevqufe and Mulk Mahlul lands.

The period of prescription in cases referring to the raqabe of these lands is 36 years".

In the case of Mahmud Diab v. Mohammed Selim [2]) the appellants claimed registration as owners of Miri. More than ten years had elapsed since the right of action arose. The Respondents could show no title save by possession and the appellants claimed that this being so they could not set up a good defence under Art. 20. The Court of Appeal dismissed the appeal, holding that the failure to claim for 10 years constituted a good defence in the absence of an admission by the Respondents. In view of cases cited later it seems clear that the Respondent could not have succeeded in obtaining registration as against a registered owner; whether, if the land was Mahlul he could obtain a Kushan depends upon the interpretation of Art. 78.

Art. 20 of the Land Code follows in principle the provisions of Art. 1662 of the Mejelle. It is the remedy only which is barred and not the right. "Now Art. 1660 of the Mejelle and Art. 20 of the Land Code" it was remarked in a Cyprus case "differ in their wordings but in effect they appear to be the same. It is necessary in either case, that there should be an absence of possession by the person who has the right to the property, and an actual possession by another to create the bar to the action imposed by these articles. The cases in the one article are and have been treated as cases governing the construction of the other article" [3]). As under the Mejelle, so under the Land Code the admission of the defendant that he had no right prevents his taking advantage of the lapse of the prescriptive period. So also if the plaintiff can show that the defendant held under a lease or loan form him prescription will not

---

[1]) As to the translation of this Article see per Curiam in Mehmet v. Kosmo (1884) 1 C.L.R. at p. 14.
[2]) Off. Gaz. 16 Sept. 1926.
[3]) Per Tyser C. J. in Ahmed v. Hassan (1906) 7 C.L.R. at p. 44.

Chapter XVI—Limitation of Actions, Prescription.[259]

un [1]). Art. 20 treats adverse occupation as sufficient to bar the plaintiff's right whether there has been cultivation or not. Non cultivation would however bring into existence the right of the State to the forfeiture under Art. 68.

We turn next to the provisions of Art. 78 which is worded as follows:

"Everyone who has possessed and cultivated State or Mevqufe land for ten years without dispute (bila niza) acquires a right by prescription and whether he has a valid title deed or not the land cannot be regarded as vacant, and he shall be given a new title deed gratuitously. Nevertheless if such person admits and confesses, that he took possession of the land without any right when it was vacant, the land shall be offered to him on payment of the tapu value, without taking into account the lapse of time; if he does not accept it shall be put up to auction and adjudged to the highest bidder".

Art. 78 is designed to give a person who has possessed and cultivated Miri Mahlul land a right to receive from the State a Tapu grant.

Certain very striking variations from the common doctrine of prescription are to be remarked. As between two private persons claiming Miri no real right is conferred by long possession. But as between the State claiming land as Mahlul and a private person who has cultivated the land without a Tapu grant, long possession coupled with cultivation is expressly stated to confer a right to obtain a Kushan. All the claimant need do, therefore, is to satisfy the Land Registry that he has complied with the provisions of this Article and, his title being recognised, he will forthwith be registered and receive a Kushan.

The right to claim a Kushan without payment of Bedl Misl under Art. 78 is by the terms thereof limited to possessors who do not admit that they took the land without right; and by Art. 8 of the Regulations as to Tapu Sanads it appears further to be limited to those who possess by virtue of a claim under a sale or succession or transfer. Art. 8 of these Regulations is so worded as to imply that Kushans are only to be issued to persons claiming a prescriptive right under Art. 78 in cases in which their possesion has been acquired by one of the means in which property can be acquired, namely inheritance, purchase and the like. Though the validity of these instructions as law has been contested, there can

---

[1]) Land Code, Art. 23. See Chapter XII— Leases, at p. 184 (footnote).

be no doubt that it was fully admitted by the Turkish Council of State [1]) and further that the decision of the Turkish Courts accepted the Regulations as constituting a legal modification of Art. 78.

The Ottoman Court of Cassation 9th September, 1328, (Malia) laid down that in conformity with this Art. 8, a claimant to a right of occupancy under Art. 78, must establish his claim under one of the three heads specified and that otherwise his claim will be dismissed. If this decision is correct the right against the State under Art. 78 does not extend to squatters and is enjoyed only by persons whose claim has a legal origin but whose title thereunder is defective by reason of lack of registration. The mere occupant of Mahlul land is not protected and can be ejected unless possession has continued for 36 years and the right of the State to claim the Raqabe is barred (Law of Disposition A.H., 1331, Art. 15 [2]).

The practice followed by the Department of Lands in Palestine is that where a person is shown to have occupied Mahlul for ten years and has cultivated it and paid taxes, but is unable to show how his occupation originated, he is entered in the register as Miri holder and is granted a Kushan on payment of Bedl Misl. The Court of Appeal in the case of Abu Mustafa v. The Government of Palestine [3]) held that Bedl Misl is not payable unless the occupant admits that he occupied without right. This decision does not appear to be reconcilable with the decision of the Ottoman Court of Cassation. The question as to whether the claimant had obtained possession with or without right was not argued. The report as given in the Official Gazette is defective and the decision as reported cannot be regarded as having fixed the significance of Art. 78 and Art. 8 of the Regulations.

---

[1]) Decision No. 3006 of 30 Dec. 1332 (Malia) (Cf. Mahmud Diab v. Mohammed Selim. Off. Gaz. 16 Sept. 1926) quoted also by Wajih Khoury, Gaz. Trib. Lib. Syriens 1932 p. 113. Art. 8 is clearly intended to make temporary arrangements with a view to securing the registration of interests in accordance with the new law. But its terms indicate the scope of Art. 78 as understood by the Ottoman authorities contemporary with the promulgation of the Land Code.

[2]) The import of Art. 78 was considered by the Cyprus Courts in Kyriakou v. Principal Forest Officer (1894) 3 C.L.R. at p. 87 but the attention of the Court was not apparently drawn to the provisions of Art. 8 of the Regulations of A.H. 1276. The subject is discussed by M. Wajih Khoury in Gaz. Trib. Lib. Syriens 1932, pp. 113, 114 who remarks that the Ottoman decisions have invariably followed the Regulations.

See also Padel & Steeg, op. cit., p. 168; Chiha, op. cit., p. 597, where the two views as to the scope of the article are stated.

[3]) Off. Gaz. 16th September 1926.

Chapter XVI—Limitation of Actions, Prescription.[261]

Subject to this important doubt as to the operation of Art. 78 long continued possession of Miri Mahlul gives the possessor a right to a Kushan. By the provisions of Art. 1 of the Regulations as to Tapu Sanads he is not entitled to the rights of the owner (holder by title-deed) until the Kushan has been issued and his title registered. Until he makes such application he cannot be considered as owner. In Loizou v. Philippou [1]) the defendant had been in occupation of the land for 10 years and had then sold it to E. The Plaintiff, a judgment creditor of the defendant, obtained registration of the land in the defendant's name with a view to sale. The Appeal Court set aside this registration on the ground that though at the end of the 10 years possession the defendant had a right to a Kushan, he had not then asked for it but had abandoned his right and given up possession to E. He could not thereafter ask to be registered.

It is perhaps relevant to mention in this connection the provisions of the Mahlul Land Ordinance, 1920.

Persons who under Art. 78 had a right to receive a Kushan are not (semble) affected by its provisions. But if a squatter had been in possession of Mahlul for any length of time prior to the Ordinance, and gave notice of his occupancy under Section 2 thereof he might, in a proper case, obtain a lease (not a Kushan). If, however, his possession had lasted 36 years he would be able to defend himself against claims by the Government in spite of the Ordinance. Persons, who take possession of Mahlul since the Ordinance are penalised, if they fail to give information as to their occupancy. But presumably possession under the conditions stated in Art. 78 (Land Code) and Art. 8 of the Regulations still gives a right to a Kushan notwithstanding the Ordinance.

The Mahlul Land Ordinance, as also Art. 78 Land Code, is applicable only in the case of Miri Mahlul. In the comparatively rare case in which Mulk becomes Mahlul in the sense that it falls to the State as bona vacantia by failure of mulk heirs Art. 78 has no application. The only provisions applicable are those of Art. 15 of the Law of Disposition, A.H. 1331.

As between private owners or holders of Waqf the ordinary periods of prescription are applicable for Mulk and Miri interests respectively (Mejelle Art. 1660; Land Code, Art. 78).

---

[1]) (1904) 6 C L.R. at p. 104. The decision related to Art. 20 of the Land Code, but the principle appears to apply as well to Art. 78.

The Land Law of Palestine.

Prescription as regards Waqf Property.

As against the waqf the period of prescription is 36 years (Mejelle Art. 1661, 1662)[1]. The admission of a Mutwally against the Waqf is not valid. "In actions about philanthropic establishments appointed for the common benefit" says Omar Hilmy, "there is no prescription". For authority for this statement he refers to Mejelle Art. 1675, but it seems doubtful whether the Art. can bear this broad interpretation[2].

It is only actions relating to the "fundamental constitution" of a Waqf, as Judge Hooper translates it, to which the prescription of thirty six years applies. Actions not relating to the "fundamental constitution" such as actions relating to Ijaratein or to revenue of a waqf are subject to the ordinary period of fifteen years as stated in Art. 1660 of the Mejelle. The distinction is illustrated by the Cypriot case of Muzaffer Bey v. Collet[3]. "Where a man claims the possession of property which both he and the other party admits to be waqf, his action is heard up to fifteen years; but where he claims waqf as trustee (Mutwally) or as beneficiary, from a person who denies that it is waqf, his action is heard up to thirty six years"[4].

There is no authority as to whether land could be deemed waqf by prescription. The law is clear that waqf implies dedication and where dedication cannot be proved property cannot be waqf. Certainly mere enjoyment as Waqf during a fixed period does not make property waqf. Presumably where property has been immemorially treated as Waqf a legal origin may be presumed. (Cf. Mejelle, Art. 6).

---

[1] Cf. Mejelle Arts. 1661 and 1667. The true meaning of the expression "from generation to generation" in Mejelle Art. 1667 is explained in Saadat Hanum, Mutwally of Ali Pasha Waqf v. The Government of Palestine (L.A. 70/32, Palestine Post 12 Nov. 1933). The Court held, inter alia, that there was no contradiction between the provisions of Arts. 1661 and Art. 1667 of the Mejelle. Art. 1661 fixes the period of limitation in respect of all Waqfs at 36 years. Art. 1667 does not deal with the length of the period of limitation, but with the date from which such period begins to run in the case of Waqf of a particular nature.

[2] Omar Hilmy, op. cit., Art. 449.

We are inclined by tradition to treat Art. 1675 as an application of the rule "Nullum tempus occurrit regi". The Moslem theory, however, treats the State as a community of believers and the insistence is always placed on the interest of the community rather than of the State in the modern European sense. Thus "public interest" in Art. 1675 be deemed to include interests of the members of the public in a charitable or religious waqf or trust.

[3] (1904) 6 C L.R. at p. 108.

[4] per Hutchinson C.J. at p. 109.

Chapter XVI—Limitation of Actions, Prescription.[263]

Unauthorised possession and cultivation of Mewat for any length of time gives no right. Art. 78 has no application and the latter part of Art. 103 has been repealed by the Mewat Land Ordinance [1]). *Prescription as regards Mewat.*

Speaking of Art. 103 the Cypriot Court has remarked that the true construction of the article appears to be that the law designedly made the provisions which apply to Miri apply also to Mewat cultivated by permission and designedly omitted to make these provisions applicable to Mewat cultivated without permission; in other words Mewat cultivated without permission cannot be regarded as Miri; if cultivated with permission it is so regarded [2]).

Art. 1675 Mejelle and Art. 102 Land Code are explicit as to the impossibility of prescribing against public rights. *Prescription as regards Metruki.*

Both as regards Mulk and Miri land explicit provisions of the Ottoman Law appear to deny title to any person other than the registered owner as regards all save a few interests [3]). *Prescription and Registration.*

Can a prescriptive title avail, therefore, against that of the registered owner? Upon this question there have been numerous Cypriot decisions, the effect of which is summed up in the judgment in Ahmed v. Hassan, as follows:

" (1) Art. 20 of the Land Code and Art. 1660 of the Mejelle which fix a limit of time within which the owner of real (i.e. immovable) property of the kinds mentioned therein must sue for its recovery, confer upon a person who has been in possession for that time a statutory title to the land, and a right to be registered for it.

(2) By virtue of Art. 1 of the Regulations as to Tapu Sanads and the Law of Rejeb A.H. 1291, the statutory title so acquired until perfected by registration does not confer any right which can be enforced in a Court of Law except the right to claim a declaration

---

[1]) In the case of Kaltoum Ghanameh v. the Director of Lands, L.A. 35/27, the Court held that Art. 78 of the Land Code did not apply to Mewat Land.

[2]) Per Curiam in Kyriakou v. Principal Forest Officer (1894) 3 C.L.R. at p. 69. The Court stated however that on the facts it was not satisfied that the land was not Miri in which case Art. 78 applied. Though there was no evidence that it had ever been cultivated before, the fact in itself was not, said the Court, a bar to its being Miri land, provided it was capable of cultivation. Cf. Art. 123 Land Code.

[3]) Servitudes appear to be ignored by the Ottoman Registration Laws. See p. 221.

For the relevant enactments See Art. 1 of Regulation as to Tapu Sanads, 1276; Art. 1 of Law as to Mulk Title-Deeds 26 Rejeb, 1291; Art. 1 of Law of Disposition, A.H. 1331.

of right to registration as against another and to have any existing registration set aside and an injunction to take effect upon registration" [1]).

In this case the early Cypriot decisions were reviewed and their effect considered. It was explicitly stated as having been firmly established since 1895, that length of possession was no defence to an action by the registered owner unless there was a cross action, to set aside the registration. This was clearly laid down in Pieri v. Philippou [2]) in which the Court stated that it considered itself bound by the registration, until set aside but gave a stay of execution to enable the defendant to bring a cross action.

It appears, however, that such a cross action to vacate an existing registration may succeed upon proof of adverse possession by the claimant for the required period.

According to this view of the law, it is clear that the fact, that a person is registered as owner or holder of a right in immovable property does not prevent time running against him. If he has been out of possession for the prescribed period he cannot recover from a defendant who has been in possession during that period. On the other hand the defendant in possession is without title until he has succeeded in having his name substituted in the Register for that of the former registered owner.

Practice in Palestine before the Occupation (like in Cyprus) appears to justify the view that the successful defendant could by application to the Courts in an action against the unsuccessful plaintiff obtain a declaration authorizing the registration of the land in his name.

So long as the prior registration persists transactions may take place in the Registry with reference to the registered interest, such transactions will not prevent the running of the period, if in fact the interest is possessed by another, and his possession is not interfered with.

But if the circumstances of the case show that the possessor neglected to have his own name substituted in the Register for that of the registered owner, he may be estopped from denying the effectiveness of transactions (Mortgages, Sales) by the registered owner as against mortgagees or purchasers in good faith. As a general rule, where there are no exceptional circumstances, it was

---

[1]) per Tyser C.J. in Ahmed v. Hassan (1906) 7 C.L.R. at p. 45.
[2]) (1903) 6 C.L.R. at p. 67. The form of the declaration as to the right of registration used in Cyprus is given in Bishop of Kyrenia v. Paraskeva, 4 C.L.R. at p. 54. Cf. Joannou v. Georghou 4 C.L.R. at p. 62.

Chapter XVI—Limitation of Actions, Prescription.[265]

remarked in one Cypriot case "a purchaser who buys land from a registered proprietor can rely on the title so acquired, and the title cannot be defeated by a claim based upon some title which ought to be and which is not registered, and of which he had no notice"[1]. Statute in Cyprus has modified and strengthened the law but consideration of these provisions is not here relevant[2]).

The view taken by the Palestine Courts appears to fortify still more the position of the registered owner. From the decisions it seems that long continued possession is of no avail in itself against a registered title.

The difficulty of securing by long continued possession a right to registration as against a registered owner has been very amply demonstrated by several decisions of the courts.

Thus in Frank v. Government of Palestine[3]) it was laid down that the effect of Art. 20 of the Ottoman Land Code is to defeat a plaintiff, whose claim has not been asserted by action for ten years in favour of a defendant who has been in occupation during that period. Art. 20 does not give an acquisitive title to the occupier so as to entitle him, as plaintiff, to obtain judgment for registration as owner in the place of a registered defendant.

Again in Abdullah el Hafiz v. Abd el Kasim Salman[4]) it was stated, that having regard to the terms of Art. 20 of the Land Code, a ten years occupier cannot obtain a title (as plaintiff) against a registered owner. Art. 20 prevents the registered owner from enforcing his right by action after ten years adverse possession. But, while it bars his remedy, it does not destroy his right; and so long, as the registered owner has a right to the land, even though he cannot enforce it by action it would be inconsistent to hold, that the occupier had also acquired a right which was capable of registration.

In another case, that of Abu Hijla v. Hamed el Yusuf[5]) claim to a share in land based on purchase and possession for a period of over 10 years was dismissed, the plaintiff having failed to prove the purchase. In this case the claim was made against a registered

---

[1]) Per Curiam in Haji Michael v. Stilli Nikoli (1909) 8 C.L.R. at p. 115, Cf. Sava v. Paraskeva (1898) 4 C.L.R. at p. 71.

[2]) Immovable Property Limitation Law 1885; Ecclesiastical Properties Law 1893.

[3]) L. A. 19/23.

[4]) L.A. 135/26. As to prescription in Settlement areas see Chapter XVII— on Land Settlement and the Registration of Land Ordinance 1929.

[5]) L.A. 113/26.

owner; the plaintiff failed to prove his allegation that his possession was based on purchase from the registered owner's ancestor.

From these cases it may be inferred that, in the absence of fraud, a registered owner has nothing to fear from a claimant who relies only on long continued possession. Such possession is not a good root of title such as will avail to secure registration as against a registered owner. Except in the case of Miri Maḥlul it will not, save under the special legislation applicable in Settlement areas, give the possessor a title of any sort. Yet the registered owner may be barred from his action in revendication, so that he will be unable to recover the land from a person in possession even though that person can make no title to be registered. A separation of registered right and actual enjoyment seems, therefore, to be possible and the resulting situation is obscure and unsatisfactory.

The view that possession of itself will not avail against a registered title is supported by other Ottoman authority. Indeed, the principle that possession available for prescription must commence with a title of some sort appears to be implicit in the law of the Tapu, under which nobody can validly possess immovable property without a title deed [1]).

From the language of the Palestine Courts it is to be inferred that the written evidence produced must prove some title on the claimant as a basis for the possession upon which he relies. The judgments of the Palestine Courts do not unfortunately give the grounds upon which the decisions proceed in any detail though this defect may indeed be merely the consequence of the scrappiness of the published reports. It may, however, be relevant in this connection to refer to the remarks of M. Wajih Khoury in his examination of the Ottoman Laws of Prescription. M. Khoury quotes authority to show that a person relying upon prescription as a title to land must be able to produce a document of title of some kind as the origin of his possession. Citing an Iradeh of 21 October 1318 (Malia) in support he proceeds "In all the countries in which the law of 1290 (Malia) [2]) applies and as regards lands surveyed when the Tabu was established, a title deed is necessary. Of course the Court is not called upon to ask in cases of prescription whether this title deed is derived from a true owner or from a person having capacity to transfer, but only if it is formally valid.

---

[1]) Regulations as to Title Deeds of A.H. 1276, Art. 1; Law of 28 Rejeb A.H. 1291, Art. 2.

[2]) i.e. the law of 25 Rejeb A.H. 1291.

Chapter XVI—Limitation of Actions, Prescription.[267]

The title-deed is not required to prove ownership but merely to show that the possessor was in a position to obtain the benefits of prescription, that is, if his possession was based upon a mode of acquisition of ownership". And again "The Ottoman legislator in instituting possessory actions by the Magistrate's Law of 1329 (Malia) has clearly shown his intention not to allow any value to the mere fact of possession as regards land subject to the Tabu. According to Arts. 24, 25 and 26 of that Law the plaintiff in a possessory action must prove both that he is possessor in fact and that he holds a title deed"[1].

The nature of a registered title is considered more fully in the Chapter dealing with Registration to which the reader is referred. It suffices here to refer again to the decision of the Court of Appeal in Afifeh Elias v. Naim Jurius Abiad and Ahmed Abu Nyma v. Anglo Palestine Bank[2] from which it appears that a registered title will not be set aside except by some evidence in writing sufficient to support an adverse title, or to corroborate evidence in support of such adverse title.

In conclusion it may be remarked that the Law prescribes various periods within which rights of various kinds in connection with immovable property other than claims of ownership, must be excercised. Most of them have been mentioned elsewhere in the course of this compilation. The following will serve as examples. *Periods during which various rights must be exercised.*

The right of the State to demand removal of trees, etc. planted on State land is prescribed after 3 years (Art. 25 Land Code). The right of preference exerciseable by a co-owner of Miri land lapses after the expiry of five years. The right of preference exerciseable by the Mulk owner of trees and buildings on Miri land lapses after the expiry of 10 years (Arts. 41, 44)[3]. The right of preference of a villager lapses after the expiry of one year (Art. 45).

The right of absentee heirs to claim that the land should not become subject to the right of the Tapu lapses after the expiration of three years (Arts. 74 and 75).

The right to Tapu enjoyed by persons who have inherited Mulk trees or buildings on Miri land escheated to the State is prescribed after the expiry of 10 years. The same right by co-possessors or those who have a joint interest is prescribed

---

[1] Gaz. Trib. Lib. Syriens 1932 at p. 114.
[2] L.A. 137/23; L.A. 67/32.
[3] See, however, now Land Law (Amendment) Ordinance 1933. Sec. 6. The right to claim a transfer of land lapses after the expiry of one year.

The Land Law of Palestine.

after 5 years. The right of inhabitants of the same locality expires after one year. (Arts. 59 and 66 Land Code).

The right of the State to claim a fair price for Miri land given to a person who was the highest bidder in a public action and the right to claim a fair tapu value in a case when there is excessive damage to the State, lapses after the expiry of ten years from the date when the land was adjudged (Art. 87).

A permission to cultivate Mewat land must be acted upon within three years (Land Code, Art. 103).

The right of pre-emption (Shufa) concerning Mulk land must be exercised within one month from the time when the claimant has called his witnesses declaring that he is claiming pre-emption (Mejelle, Arts. 1034, 1035).

CHAPTER XVII—CADASTRAL SURVEY AND LAND SETTLEMENT.

There was no Cadastral Survey in Palestine prior to the Occupation. The Ottoman Law of the year A.H. 1331 (1913) concerning Cadastral Survey has not been made applicable here, and by Sec. 68 of the Land Settlement Ordinance 1928, has been declared to have no effect in Palestine [1]).

Cadastral Survey.

In the year 1920 a Survey Ordinance was passed by the Government of Palestine which provided facilities for the Demarcation of Boundaries and for the making of Surveys with a view to a Cadastral Survey. This Ordinance was replaced in the year 1929 by the Survey Ordinance, No. 48, which regulates in a comprehensive manner the survey of lands in Palestine, providing particularly for a Public Survey of Palestine under the directions of the High Commissioner [2]).

A Cadastral Survey rigorously maintained to date whereby the parcels of land affected are accurately defined on a plan is considered to be the foundation of an effective system of Land Registration. Although survey is commenced in advance of Land Settlement, the operations are closely connected with the Land Settlement operations.

The country is topographically surveyed on a suitable scale and plans are in the first place prepared showing all the main visible features such as hedges, fences, wadis, roads, etc. When the stage of Land Settlement is reached the land of a village (or any other Settlement Area) is divided into Blocks of convenient size called Registration Blocks. Provisional Block plans are prepared followed by the demarcation on the ground and by plotting on the Block plan of the mosaic of parcels within the Registration Block

---

[1]) In Sec. 68 of the Land Settlement Ordinance 1928 the Ottoman Cadastral Law is erroneously referred to as the Law of the year (A.H.) 1329. The correct year of this law is (A.H.) 1331 which corresponds to the year 1913. See New Dastour, Vol. 5, P. 79, Law No. 61

[2]) The powers of a Government Surveyor in relation to the Public Survey are set out in Secs. 2, 8 and 10 of the Survey Ordinance, 1929.

The Land Law of Palestine.

according to the boundaries claimed by individuals. At a later stage the areas of the parcels are computed and the registration Block plans which are required by the Land Settlement Ordinance to accompany the Schedule of Rights are to be finally prepared by the Survey Department.

An intermediate stage of survey work connected with the settlement of title to land consists in the correction of boundaries of parcels on the provisional plans in accordance with the decisions of the Settlement Officers [1]).

The Registration Block plans which accompany the Schedules of Rights [2]) show the situation, shape and size of every individual parcel of land within the area described in the Registration Block plan. This method of Survey and record of immovable property incorporated in the plan has made it possible to dispense with a description of boundaries in the Register of Titles. The plan is regarded as the one and only authoritative definition of the area to which the registered title refers. The plan thus constitutes the complement of the written Register. No verbal description of the boundaries by reference to the neighbours (or neighbouring properties) or to visible features on the ground is employed at all. The plans are accurately scaled and survey reference points are fixed on the ground. Upon the information contained in such scientifically drawn plans any boundary can easily be refixed, and the boundary marks replaced. The fixing of the boundaries, marks and features on the ground can be accurately done, so that it is no longer possible for any one to tresspass secretly on the land of another. Finally, no mutation is permitted without an accompanying mutation plan either prepared or approved by the Survey Department after checking on the ground. The corresponding map sheets are kept up to date in the custody of the Survey Department [3]).

As a consequence of this system of Cadastral Survey, no overlapping of area beyond the area indicated on the plan is possible and no correction of areas under the provisions of Art. 47 of the Ottoman Land Code by the inclusion of large areas of land for which application was so frequently made under the Ottoman system of registration of land, can be necessary or possible.

Settlement of Rights.

In 1928 as a beginning in the carrying out of a systematic settlement of rights in land, a Land Settlement Ordinance was

---

[1]) Land Settlement Ordinance 1928, Sec. 12.
[2]) Ibid. Sec. 30 modified and reproduced by the Land Settlement Ordinance 1932.
[3]) Land Settlement Ordinance 1928, Sec. 45.

Chapter XVII—Cadastral Survey & Land Settlement.[271]

enacted [1]). It was based on the Sudan Land Law, which has been in operation for a number of years. The ordinance was designed to meet the requirements of Palestine with regard to the Ottoman system of registration of title to land based on the Ottoman Land Code.

Under the Ottoman System, which may be described as a system of registration of Deeds combined with the registration of a Title, the Title Deed usually refers to a parcel of land (or to a unit of immovable property) the boundaries of which are stated without any reference to a survey, no parcel has usually been located on the ground prior to the registration of the Title Deed and no plan of it was made. This resulted in confusion of title to immovable property. An entry in the Register of Deeds could rarely be identified with the parcel on the ground. In the absence of defined and properly surveyed boundaries Title Deeds were necessarily divorced from the unit of the land to which they purported to refer. Encroachments and boundary disputes took place frequently [2]). In addition, a great number of transactions were effected outside the Land Registry offices and the Title Deeds were not recorded. Successions were as a rule not recorded. The Register of Deeds was, therefore, most defective and, particularly in rural areas, did not show the true ownership of the land.

The Ottoman system has been with certain modifications maintained under the Land Transfer Ordinances 1920-1921. The system if it may be so called is indeed a combination of a Register of Deeds and a Register of Title, but in practice it has not worked effectively and may be described rather than as an aspiration.

The Land Settlement Ordinance 1928 provides for the Settlement and Registration of title to land on a system of recording of immovable properties on a territorial basis in accordance with the best known and only effective practice.

---

[1]) Sectional references in this chapter may be assumed to be references to Sections of this Ordinance (Land Settlement Ordinance 1928) unless the contrary is stated. This Principal Ordinance has been much modified by amending Ordinances of 1930, 1932 and 1933. In particular Sections 16, 30, 34, 35, 49, 50, 51, 53, 56, 61, 63, 64 (2), have been repealed and modified provisions substituted.

The group of Ordinances are cited as the Land Settlement Ordinances 1928-1933.

[2]) The prevalence of boundary disputes cannot of course be to any serious degree atributed to the system of registration. In England conveyance by plan or by description has been the usual and all but universal system for centuries but boundary suits are infrequent.

The Land Law of Palestine.

Block and Parcel.

The stable unit for survey and registration is the Block, which is defined in Sec. 2 of the Ordinance as a subdivision of the land which contains one or more parcels. The Parcel or variable unit of property is defined as a unit of land within the Block, which is owned by a person or body of persons.

Definition of Land.

Land is defined to include any rights arising out of land, buildings and things permanently fixed to land, an undivided share in land and any interest in land, which requires or is capable of registration under the Land Settlement Ordinance.

Settlement Area.

The whole of Palestine has not been made simultaneously subject to the provisions of the Land Settlement Ordinance. The application and operation of the Ordinance in the country is limited to defined areas, called the Settlement Areas, declared from time to time by a Settlement Order of the High Commissioner, published in the Gazette. It is only within such a declared area, that the Settlement of rights to land and Registration in accordance with the provisions of the Ordinance is carried out [1]. An area having been declared a Settlement Area, a Settlement Officer is forthwith appointed by the High Commissioner for the purpose of carrying out land settlement operations in the area. The Settlement Officer proceeds to publish a Preliminary Notice of intended survey, settlement and registration of rights in a village within the Settlement Area [2].

Definition of Village.

A village is defined to include a tribal area or any part of a tribal area and any village lands within or abutting on a Municipal area [3] and such area of land within a Settlement Area, as may be prescribed by a Settlement Officer by Notice [4].

Preliminary Notice.

A Preliminary Notice is required to be published not less than 30 days before the demarcation of the parcels and the presentation of the claims is to begin. The effect of the publication of the Preliminary Notice is that after the publication of the Notice and until the publication of the Schedule of Rights, no action concerning rights to land in the area under notification can be entered in any

---

[1] See Secs. 3 and 4. Areas of sites and houses of small value may, however, be excluded from the operations of the Ordinance, though included within a Settlement Area (Secs. 27 and 30 as amended by the Land Settlement Amendment Ordinance, 1930).

On the other hand provision is made in Sec. 69 of the Ordinance for the application of its provisions to the Ghor Lands (Beisan) which are subject to a special agreement published in the Gazette of the 15th January, 1922, (reprinted in O. G. No. 388 of 14. 9. 33). See supra, pp. 62 ff.

[2] Sec. 5.

[3] Land Settlement (Amendment) Ordinance, 1930.

[4] Land Settlement (Amendment) Ordinance, 1933.

Chapter XVII—Cadastral Survey & Land Settlement.[273]

Land Court or Civil Court, nor can any application under the Correction of Land Registers Ordinance 1926 be entertained. It would seriously hamper and delay the Settlement operations, if disputes about the land were in course of consideration by the Courts at the time a Settlement Officer was dealing with the right to the land in the same village, or if applications under the Correction of Land Registers Ordinance 1926, were before the Director of Lands. Any action entered before the Preliminaty Notice is published is, if possible, to be heard and decided, before the Settlement is begun, or, by leave of the Court, any such action may be withdrawn. Actions pending at the date of notification of Settlement may be completed. The same applies to applications for the correction of the registration: they are either to be withdrawn or, if possible, to be decided before Settlement is begun [1]).

In addition to the Preliminary Notice of intended Settlement, and not less than ten days before the beginning of the Settlement in a village notified under Sec. 5, a further notice, a Settlement Notice, is to be published by the Settlement Officer [2]). The effect of the Settlement Notice is that no parcellation of land purporting to be either a Subdivision of land held in individual shares or a permanent division of land held in common and periodically distributed (Mesha'a) is to have effect thereafter [3]). Any parcellation which was effected prior to the publication of the Settlement Notice may be approved and accepted by the Settlement Officer.

Settlement Notice.

Under Sec. 8 of the principal Ordinance, the Settlement Officer is also authorised to issue Progress Notices recording the progress of the Settlement and stating the order in which the work will be continued. Under Sec. 34, as amended by the Ordinance of 1930, the Settlement Officer is authorised to issue, under Sec. 8 of the Land Settlement Ordinance, notices directing that no fresh entries are to be made in the pre-existing Registers after the publication of the Schedule of Claims. In consequence of this amendment the closing of the pre-existing Land Registers which according to the Ordinance of 1928 was effected at the time of publication of the Settlement Notice is postponed to a later date (or dates) prescribed in the progress notice.

After publication of the Settlement Notice claimants to land are to submit a Memorandum of Claim in the prescribed form and

Memorandum of Claim.

---

[1]) Sec. 6 of the Ordinance of 1928, as amended by the Land Settlement (Amendment) Ordinance, 1930.
[2]) Sec. 7.
[3]) Sec. 23.

produce all the instruments of title affecting the lands. Claimants may appear in person or through an authorised agent [1]). Waqf interests are represented by the Mutwallis of the Waqf or by a representative of the Supreme Moslem Council in the case of Moslem Waqfs. Non-Moslem Waqfs are represented by the guardian of the Waqf or by a person appointed by the authority of the Community [2]). Corporations are to present their claims through an agent appointed for the presentation of claims in Land Settlement [3]). The claims of Government are presented by an officer appointed by the Attorney General [4]).

Village Settlement Committee. In any matter of common interest the villages are represented by the Village Settlement Committee which is constituted by the authority of the District Commissioner and is chosen from amongst persons nominated by the inhabitants and the reputed owners. The Village Settlement Committee is empowered in its own name to bring and defend actions. It is its duty to protect the interests of the absentees, minors and persons under incapacity. It is constituted by the Settlement Officer in connection with Partitions. These provisions of Secs. 13—15 and Sec. 52 of the Ordinance are designed to secure the co-operation of the village authorities in the work of Land Settlement.

Schedule of Claims. All claims are to be entered upon the Schedule of Claims which is posted at the office or camp of the Settlement Officer and at the office of the Sub-District in which the village is situate [5]). Not less than 15 days after the date of the posting of the Schedule of

---

[1]) Sec. 16 of the Ordinance as amended in 1930.
[2]) Sec. 17.
[3]) Sec. 18.
[4]) Secs. 19 and 28. The latter Section defines the rights of Government as follows.

(1) The rights of the Government to land of the category of Miri or Mulk which are required by law to be registered shall be investigated and settled. The rights of the Government to land of any other category shall be investigated and settled only if any claimant puts forward a claim which is in conflict with such right.

(2) Land used for general public purposes that falls within the category of Metruki shall be registered in the name of the Government; any land in the category of Metruki which is used for the purposes of a village shall be settled and registered in the name of the village.

(3) All rights to land in any settlement area which are not established by any claimant and registered in accordance with the settlement shall be registered in the name of the Government. (Sec. 28 as amended by Sec. 8 of the Ordinance of 1930).

[5]) Secs. 21, 24 and 26.

Chapter XVII—Cadastral Survey & Land Settlement.[275]

Claims the Settlement Officer is to commence the investigation and settlement of claims [1]).

The investigation of Claims is required to be done publicly [2]). If there are conflicting claims the Settlement Officer decides the dispute or may, with the consent of the parties, refer them to arbitration. It is within the Settlement Officer's power to designate one party to the dispute as plaintiff and the other as defendant. If he is satisfied that any person who has not presented a claim is entitled to any right to land he may proceed as if such person has made a claim [3]).

After the investigation of the claims to rights in a Block the Settlement Officer draws up a Schedule of Rights which he is to read out to the Village Settlement Committee and the claimants. The Schedule of Rights is to be posted for 15 days. A signed copy of the Schedule of Rights is to be transmitted to the Registrar of Lands together with a signed plan of the parcels comprised in the Schedule of Rights. Upon the determination by the Settlement Officer of the disputed claims, the Settlement Officer informs the Registrar of Lands of his decision and the Registrar records the particulars of the right in accordance with the Settlement Officer's decision [4]).

The powers of a Settlement Officer are of a twofold nature: (a) Administrative Powers; and (b) Judicial Powers. The Administrative Powers of a Settlement Officer are widely defined in Secs. 9, 12, 22 and 61. He has power to order the attendance of claimants to land, to order the marking out of boundaries and to cause the boundaries to be marked out at the expense of any person included in the Schedule of Rights; to order the production of documents and to extend the time prescribed in the Ordinance for the performance of any act to be done under the Ordinance. He has power to settle the boundaries of a Village or a Block; to order the laying out of a fresh boundary in place of the original boundary and adjust the rights of the owners of adjoining lands affected by the laying out of a new boundary by exchange of land of equal value or by the payment of compensation in respect of the alteration of a boundary, alignment of property or right of way; demarcate any existing road or path and indicate any existing right of way

---

[1]) Sec. 25.
[2]) Sec. 27 as amended by the Ordinance of 1930.
[3]) Sec. 27 (4).
[4]) See Sec. 30 as amended by the Ordinance of 1932; Secs. 31 and 32 as amended by the Ordinance of 1930.

The Land Law of Palestine.

or any new right of way to a public road in favour of any owner whose parcel is surrounded by other parcels [1]). The Settlement Officer has power to authorise correction of clerical errors in the Registers of Lands [2]). In his administrative functions the Settlement Officer is subject to the supervision and directions of the Commissioner of Lands [3]).

(b) Judicial Powers.
The Judicial Powers of a Settlement Officer are thus defined in Sec. 10 of the Ordinance.

"(1) The Settlement Officer shall have power to hear and decide any dispute with regard to the ownership or possession of land in a settlement area and may make such order as to costs in any such matter as he thinks fit".

"(3) A Settlement Officer shall apply the Land Law in force at the date of the hearing of the action, provided that he shall have regard to equitable as well as legal rights to land, and shall not be bound by any rule of the Ottoman Law or by any enactment issued by the British Military Administration, prohibiting the Courts from hearing actions based on unregistered documents or by the rules of evidence contained in the Code of Civil Procedure or the Civil Code".

He has thus dual Judicial Powers. He is a Civil Magistrate and a Summary Land Court. He is enabled to deal with disputes as to possession of land and also as to title.

The procedure to be followed in any judicial proceedings by a Settlement Officer is set out in Rules of Court by the Chief Justice under Sec. 10 (2) of the Principal Ordinance [4]).

In matters of personal Status of Moslems the Settlement Officer is assisted by a Religious Judge (a Qadi of the Sharia Court). The Religious Courts of the other communities may likewise appoint a Religious Judge to assist the Settlement Officer in matters of personal status which is within their jurisdiction. In Waqf claims the Settlement Officer is assisted by a Religious Judge who sits as an assessor for the purpose of advising him upon the law of Waqf involved [5]).

---

[1]) Sec. 22 as amended by the Ordinance of 1930.
[2]) Sec. 61 as amended by the Ordinance of 1930.
[3]) The Commissioner of Lands is the Officer appointed by the High Commissioner to exercise general direction and control over Settlement and Registration (Sec. 2).
[4]) See Rules made by the Chief Justice dated 1st August, 1928 (O.G. No. 216), 1st August, 1929 (O.G. No. 240); 16th September, 1930 (O.G. No. 267) 16th December, 1930 (O.G. No. 273); 16th March, 1932 (O.G. No. 303).
[5]) Sec. 11.

Chapter XVII—Cadastral Survey & Land Settlement.[277]

The functions of the Religious Judge are, therefore, of a limited character.

The Settlement Officer has power to refer a question to Court in the circumstances set out in Sec. 29 as follows:

(1) The Settlement Officer may refer to the Land Court or to the competent Religious Court any question which may arise with regard to —

(a) the true construction or validity or effect of any instrument;

(b) the category of any land;

(c) the extent or nature of any right;

(d) the constitution or internal administration of a Waqf affecting any land.

(2) The Court shall allow any party interested to appear before it, and may summon any other party and may order the production of any instrument.

(3) The Court may either give judgment on the question referred or may direct any proceedings to be instituted, or may issue any direction or instruction to the Settlement Officer relating to the matter.

From a Judicial decision of a Settlement Officer an appeal lies to the Land Court of the District in which the land, which is the subject matter of the action is situate. Sec. 56 of the Principal Ordinance as modified by the Ordinances of 1930 and 1932 thus provides— *Appeal from a decision of a Settlement Officer.*

> "(1) No appeal shall lie from the decision of a Settlement Officer as to any right to land save with the leave of such Officer or of the President of a Land Court. An application for leave to appeal shall be made by a petition in writing within thirty days of the notification of the decision of the Settlement Officer in a disputed claim, and shall be submitted to the Settlement Officer. Application for leave to appeal may be made also by a claimant, who is aggrieved by the decision of the Settlement Officer in an undisputed claim, within fifteen days from the date of the posting of the Schedule of Rights or the Partition Schedule containing the decision which is the subject of appeal. If the Settlement Officer refuses the application, the applicant may within fifteen days of such refusal refer to the President of the Land Court stating the grounds for the appeal".
>
> "(2) Where leave to appeal is granted, it shall be heard by the Land Court, and the Settlement Officer shall forward

to the President of the Court all the documents relating to the case".

No time for appeal from a Settlement Officer, after leave has been granted, is mentioned in the Ordinances or the Rules thereunder. In Shehadeh el Aly v. Same the Court of Appeal held that strictly speaking this was not an omission, which could be supplied by analogy, since the Land Court became seized of the appeal upon the documents being forwarded by the Settlement Officer to the President of the Land Court in accordance with Sec. 56 (2) of the Land Settlement Ordinance 1928. The analogy from Sec. 5 (2) of the Magistrates' Courts Jurisdiction Ordinance 1924 is not to be applied [1]).

In Goldberg v. Rabinovich [2]) the Court of Appeal was asked (a) to declare the exercise of judicial power by a Settlement Officer to be repugnant to and inconsistent with the Palestine Order-in-Council 1922 and, therefore, of no effect or in the alternative (b) to reverse the decision of the Land Court upholding the Settlement Officer on a question of fact. The argument in favour of the first contention was based on the terms of Arts. 38 and 42 of the Order-in-Council, which gives jurisdiction to Civil Courts and Land Courts and to no other.

By an interlocutory judgment [3]) the Court held that the provisions of Secs. 56 and 59 of the Land Settlement Ordinance 1928, as amended by the Ordinance of 1930 read in conjunction with Sec. 42, gave such facilities to the litigant to apply to the Land Court, as would comply with the terms of Art. 42 of the Order-in-Council. As regards the second submission the Court was of opinion that having regard to the fact that the Land Settlement Officer is not bound by rules of evidence, there was in the case before him evidence on which he could lawfully find the facts necessary to support his judgment.

Appeals are decided in chambers unless the Land Court directs otherwise [4]).

The powers of the Land Court are defined as follows.

Sec. 57.
(1) The Land Court may either:—
    (a) decide the appeal on the evidence taken by the Settlement Officer; or
    (b) rehear the evidence or hear fresh evidence and give judgment on the appeal; or

---

[1]) L. A. 21/33.
[2]) L. A. 5/33.
[3]) Palestine Post, 18 Febr. 1934.
[4]) See Sec. 56 (3) added by the Ordinance of 1932.

Chapter XVII—Cadastral Survey & Land Settlement.[279]

(c) remit the case to the Settlement Officer for retrial.

(2) An appeal shall lie from the judgment of the Land Court to the Court of Appeal on a point of law. Notice of the appeal shall be lodged with the Court of Appeal within 30 days of the judgment if given in presence, or within 30 days of the notification of the judgment if it was given in absence [1]).

(3) Where no appeal is brought from the judgment of the Land Court within the time prescribed, an authenticated copy of the judgment of the Land Court shall be communicated to the Registrar of the District in which the land is situate and to the Settlement Officer. The Registrar shall on payment of any fees due enter in the Register of the village any order affecting the land contained in the judgment.

After the expiration of the period prescribed in Section 56 no appeal shall lie from any decision recorded in the Schedule of Rights or the Partition Schedule unless in the opinion of the Settlement Officer or of the President of a Land Court to whom application is made:— {.sec Sec. 58.}

(a) any new fact is established which was unknown and could not have been within the knowledge of the interested party at an earlier date; or

(b) owing to sickness, minority, absence from Palestine or other similar incapacity, the claimant to a right has suffered prejudice which he was not able to bring to the attention of the Court previously.

The fees payable in Land Settlement operations are prescribed by Secs. 62, 63 and 64 of the Principal Ordinance as amended by the Ordinance of 1930, and by an Order dated 17 March 1932 made by the High Commissioner under these Sections [2]). {Fees. Penalties and Offences.}

Offences committed in connection with Land Settlement work are defined and the penalties for such offences, particularly penalties for false evidence or fraud, prescribed by Secs. 66 and 67.

There are two pecular difficulties in securing a proper title to land in Palestine (1) a large part of the village land in Palestine is held in undivided ownership, and (2) land is held in shares of bafflingly large fractions which frequently run to several figures. In the {Partition}

---

[1]) The Court of Appeal in a recent case (Faris Hamdan v. Osman Bushnaq and others. L. A. 61/33. Palestine Post 22 Jan. 1935) held that the judgment of the Land Court signed in Chambers should have been read out in open Court, and until that was done, the period within which the appeal must be lodged did not begin, and that there had been no notification of the judgment.

[2]) See O. G. No. 304 of 1 April 1932.

The Land Law of Palestine.

majority of cases these fractions have no real value. The provisions of the Land Settlement Ordinance, 1928, have been so designed as to make it possible in place of the fractions to have the rights in a unit of land recorded in a definite figure of integral metres and to avoid very small fragments of land of no substantial value being made the subject of registration. The owner of such fragments may be required to transfer his share to a neighbouring owner, or in the case of undivided land to the owner (or owners) of the more considerable shares.

Sec. 33 of the Ordinance of 1928 confers power on the High Commissioner to prescribe by order (a) the limitation to a minimum or to different minima of the area of any parcel or the breadth of a parcel; (b) adjustement of boundaries of parcels by exchange, and (c) the method in which fragments of land are to be added to the land of an adjoining owner and compensation fixed.

In general the Settlement Officer has been given power after the rights of the co-owners have been determined to proceed with the partition of any land held in undivided ownership as directed from time to time by the High Commissioner if such partition is deemed to be in the public interest. He is in no way bound by the provisions of the Ottoman Law of Partition of A.H. 1332 [1]).

Partition Schedule. The Settlement Officer has power [2]) on the application of any person registered as the owner of a share in undivided land, to divide the share from the remainder of the undivided land; he has also power on the application of the owners of not less than two thirds of the shares of the village land held in common (Mesha'a) and recorded as such in the Schedule of Rights to divide the Mesha'a among the owners of the shares so recorded. In this case a Partition Schedule is to be prepared by him which is to be posted for a period of 15 days. Upon the expiration of the period of 15 days the Partition Schedule is to be forwarded to the Registrar of Lands for entry of the parcels in the Register. If there is no agreement between the owners as to the method of partition, the Settlement Officer may carry out the Partition in consultation with the Village

---

[1]) The reference to the Provisional Law of Partition of the year A.H. 1329 in Sec. 52 (3) of the Land Settlement Ordinance, 1928, is given according to the Turkish mode of reckoning. The year of enactment according to the Moslem reckoning was A.H. 1332 corresponding to 1913. See New Dastur Vol. 6, No. 41, p. 100.

[2]) Secs. 33, 49, 50, 51, 52, 54 and 55 as amended by the Ordinances of 1930 and of 1932. See also Sec. 5 of the Regulations (O.G. No. 212 of 1st June, 1928).

Chapter XVII—Cadastral Survey & Land Settlement.[281]

Settlement Committee. Save in a case where the High Commissioner directs that partition should be carried out in the public interest the system of partition under the Land Settlement Ordinances is a voluntary partition and not a compulsory one.

Provision was made by the amending Ordinance of 1930 for the rectification of the Schedule of Partition (and/or Schedule of Rights and/or Register) or for compensation to an owner who establishes title to a share after posting of the Schedule of Partition (or Schedule of Rights) in the following manner:—

Where any undivided parcel is periodically redistributed among co-owners, no transfer of any share shall be registered after the posting of the Schedule of Rights unless the undivided parcel has been partitioned. *Sec. 40.*

(1) Where, after posting of the Schedule of Rights or the Schedule of Partition a person establishes his right by action to a share in a parcel of undivided land, the Land Court may order the rectification of the new register, or that compensation shall be paid to such person by the other co-owners in such manner as the Court may direct. Provided that in the case of village Mesha'a, if the right so established affects the total number of shares in the Mesha'a, the Land Court shall not order the rectification of the Schedule of Rights or the Schedule of Partition or of the new register, but shall order compensation to be paid. *Sec. 53 (*)*

(2) Where the Settlement Officer has accepted the parcellation of village Mesha'a in accordance with the proviso to Section 23 hereof, and prior to the posting of the Schedule of Rights or of the Schedule of Partition a person establishes his right to a share in the village Mesha'a, or where after the partition of village Mesha'a has been carried out, but prior to the posting of the Schedule of Partition, a person establishes his right to a share in the Mesha'a the Settlement Officer may award him compensation which shall be paid in such manner as he thinks fit.

(3) Compensation in all cases shall be charged upon the land of the owners of the shares until it is fully paid.

When the period of posting of the Schedule of Rights has expired, the Settlement Officer forwards the Schedule with its accompanying registration block plan to the Land Registrar of the District in which the settled area is situate. The parcels in the *Registration.*

(*) As amended by Land Settlement (Amendment) Ordinance 1930.

The Land Law of Palestine.

registration Block are then entered in the Land Register [1] a separate folio of which is devoted to each parcel [2]. The reference to the property in the Land Register follows the description of the Schedule of Rights. Mortgages, leases and other encumbrances, discharges, etc. are recorded on the back of the folio.

The new Register of title compiled as a consequence of Land Settlement operations conforms to the best modern practice. A parcel of land is taken as a unit of registration. The ownership in this unit of land and all the interests to which it is subject, the charges, cautions, and easements affecting it are all recorded in the registration [3]. Every subsequent dealing with the land is recorded in the Register of Title. To the holder of a Title a certificate or an extract from the Register is issued [4].

When the identity of the parcels disappears, for example, by Subdivision, new folios are opened for the new parcel and the folios referring to the old parcel are closed.

Dual System of Registration. The New Register is defined in Sec. 2 of the Principal Ordinance, 1928, to mean a Register of Title to land established under the Ordinance. This Register is to be distinguished from the Existing Register defined in Sec. 2 of the Ordinance to mean a Register of Title to land existing prior to the Settlement operations. This is the Register purporting to have been one of Title-Deeds compiled in virtue of the provisions of the Ottoman Land Laws and the Land Transfer Ordinances.

A dual system of registration exists in other countries, including England, where registration of deeds is compulsory in Middlesex and Yorkshire and registration of title permissible everywhere but compulsory only in the County of London. In Counties in which neither form of registration is compulsory title is proved by presentation of private unregistered conveyances. This, indeed, has been the practice for centuries past and seems acceptable generally since few persons value advantage of the optional arrangements for land registration, outside the compulsory area.

It is intended that in Palestine the two systems of Registration under the Ottoman Law and registration in the new Settlement

---

[1] Secs. 30 and 35 of the Principal Ordinance as amended by the Ordinance of 1932.

[2] Sec. 8 of the Regulations (O.G. No. 212 of 1st June, 1928).

[3] Sec. 48.

[4] Sec. 37 of the Principal Ordinance and Sec. 9 of the Regulations (O.G. No. 212 of 1st June, 1928).

Chapter XVII—Cadastral Survey & Land Settlement.[283]

Registers shall operate side by side, though in different areas, until eventually the areas included in the New Register absorb the whole of the country. No amalgamation of the two systems is possible owing to difference in the background of each. In Settlement areas the system of registration is based on the frame work of a scientific survey which does not exist in non-Settlement areas.

In order to secure that the New Register shall represent title as it was at the prime date at which it came into force with respect to a village provision is made by Secs. 36 and 38 of the Principal Ordinance, restricting transfers during registration. Sec. 36 provides:

> "(1) No voluntary transfer of rights to land in a notified village shall be made during the interval between the closing of the existing Registers and the posting of the Schedule of Rights, unless the Settlement Officer authorises such transfer to be effected immediately on grounds of urgency.
>
> (2) Any involuntary transfer of rights which occurs by death or other cause during the said period shall be notified to the Settlement Officer by the person claiming such right.
>
> (3) As soon as all the Schedules of Rights in respect of a village have been recorded in the Register of the village, the Schedule shall be in the custody of the Director of Lands".

Sec. 38 provides:—

"Any disposition which occurs after the Schedule of Rights has been posted shall not be valid until it is duly registered in the Register of the village".

The character of a Registered Title. A title once registered after Settlement obtains with certain reservations an indefeasible character. Under Sec. 42 of the Principal Ordinance registration of land in the New Register shall invalidate any right which conflicts with such registration. And the dominating character of the New Register is further shown by the restrictive provisions of Sec. 59 as amended by the Ordinance of 1930. This Section limits the extent to which rectification of the New Register may be ordered by the Land Court as follows:

"After the completion of the settlement, rectification of the Register may be ordered by the Land Court, subject to the law as to limitation of actions, either by annulling the registration or in such other manner as the Court thinks fit, where the Court is satisfied that the registration of any person in respect of any right to land has been obtained by fraud; or that a right recorded in the existing Register has been omitted or incorrectly set out in the Register, provided that, where a person has since the settlement acquired land in good faith and for value from a registered owner, the Court shall not order a rectification of the Register".

Thus a bona fide purchaser will obtain a title free from any claims existing prior to the settlement. The unfortunate person, whose rights have been fraudulently omitted from inclusion in the new Register, is not indeed wholly without remedy but his remedy is very ineffective. Sec. 60 provides that—

"When any registration or any entry in the Register has been made or procured by or in pursuance of fraud and the entry cannot be rectified under this Ordinance, any person sustaining loss thereby shall be entitled to claim compensation against the person responsible for the fraud; provided that nothing herein shall involve either the Government or any officer of the Government in any liability for or in respect of any act or matter in good faith done or omitted to be done in the exercise or supposed exercise of the powers given by this Ordinance or by any Regulation made thereunder".

If without fraud a right recorded in the existing Registers has been omitted or incorrectly set out, and rectification of it is impossible in accordance with the terms of the amended Sec. 59, the victim of the omission or inacuracy appears to be without redress.

Clerical errors.

Clerical errors may be corrected by authority of a Settlement Officer in accordance with Sec. 61 (1) of the Principal Ordinance as amended by the Ordinance of 1930 and the same Section gives powers to insert omissions or correct errors at any time before the completion of the registration of the land in the village and to set right after registration discrepancies as to areas and boundaries between the survey plan and the boundaries or areas as appearing on the land or the area of any parcel as furnished by fresh survey.

Subject to what has been said, the title granted after Settlement appears to be an absolute title [1] without guarantee. When the New Register conflicts with the Existing Register, the former prevails subject to the provision of Sec. 59.

It is clear, that the owner of a conflicting interest has no remedy against the Government in any circumstances. Sec. 41 of the Principal Ordinance provides as follows.

---

[1] As regards the grant of Prescriptive title to land and Possessory title see the Section dealing with the Registration of Land Ordinance 1929, pp. 288 ff., infra.

Chapter XVII—Cadastral Survey & Land Settlement.[285]

"No claim to compensation shall lie, and no action shall be maintainable against the Government—

    (a) on account of any failure during the settlement to locate a parcel to which the record in any existing Registers or any existing title deed or judgment of the Court relates; or

    (b) on account of any failure to establish any right to land which purports to be based on any record in an existing Register or an existing title deed; or

    (c) on account of any error in the establishment of any boundaries, in the partition of any land or in the statement of any area".

In view of the provisions of Sec. 42 of the Principal Ordinance it becomes necessary to determine what rights can be said to conflict with the registration. Only rights which ought to be registered can be said so to conflict; rights which either cannot or need not be registered, would continue to exist notwithstanding registration of the land. Conflicting Rights.

The Ordinances do not state explicitly what rights require registration. Sec. 3 (2) of the Principal Ordinance tells us that within the settlement area rights to "land" shall be settled and registered, and "land" is defined by Sec. 2 as including "any rights arising out of land, buildings and things permanently fixed to land, an undivided share in land, and any interest in land, which requires or is capable of registration under this Ordinance". The phrase "rights arising out of land" is unusual and it is not clear, what species of right is referred to, nor if a distinction is intended between a right arising "out of land" and an "interest in land". Rent charges and the like are sometimes said to issue "out of land" and it is possible, that the intention was to comprise within the definition Ijaratein rents and impropriated tithes.

The term "land", it will be observed, covers also interests in land, which require or are capable of registration.

Thus it appears that the Settlement Officer is to settle and cause to be registered every interest in land, which requires or is capable of registration. The distinction which is drawn between interests which require and those which are merely capable of registration suggests that certain interests fall within the latter category and though in principle they are to be settled and registered by the Officer, their registration is not requisite for their continued validity. The question is of particular importance in connection with easements including water rights, assuming that land is to be interpreted as inclu-

The Land Law of Palestine.

ding suprajacent water. It is clear from the Regulations, issued under the Ordinance, that rights of way at least and leasehold interests for a period of more than three years are deemed capable of registration under the Ordinances [1]). Presumably other rights in the nature of servitudes are also registrable.

The language of the Ordinances suggests that their purpose is to secure registration of the land with a view, primarily to make certain both for the present and future the ownership and power of disposition thereof and that registration of such interests as servitudes is not regarded as important. The Ordinances contain no explicit reference to them. Nor can their existence be said to "conflict" with the title of a registered owner. The conclusion is that though capable of registration they are not invalidated if not registered [2]). Whether existing leases for more than three years, which are also "capable" of registration are invalidated if not registered by the effect of Sec. 42 is more doubtful. The existence of a long lease may more easily be said to "conflict" with the interest of the registered owner. It is not, however, stated in the Ordinances that interests not mentioned in the Schedule of Rights are necessarily invalidated and the question as to whether a leasehold interest omitted from the Schedule can be said to "conflict" and to be consequently invalidated by the effect of Sec. 42 remains open.

Leases of more than three years are, however, dispositions within the Transfer of Land Ordinance 1920-1929 and if created since Sept. 1920 are invalid unless registered. Such interests appear, therefore, to come within the provisions of Sec. 59 of the Principal Ordinance as amended by the Ordinance of 1930, in the sense, that their omission might give rise to a claim for rectification. It appears to follow, that as against a purchase of the land in good faith and for value, a lease of the land would be invalid if mention of it was omitted from the New Register.

---

[1]) Cf. Regulations 11 Sept. 1933 (O. G. 21 Sept. 1933). Servitudes including rights to water were specifically mentioned as subjects for inclusion in the Schedule of Rights by Sec. 30 of the Ordinance of 1928 as originally enacted. The form of the Schedule of Rights is, however, now left to be prescribed by Regulation (Land Settlement (Amendment) Ordinance 1932, Sec. 4).

Water rights and similar interests are capable of, but not required to be registered under the Ottoman Law. Per Curiam in Stassi v. Vehim I C. L. R., at p. 103.

[2]) The provisions of Sec. 22 (c) as amended by the Ordinance of 1930 do not affect the question except so far as they suggest that demarcation of paths is optional for the Settlement Officer.

Chapter XVII—Cadastral Survey & Land Settlement.[287]

Servitudes enjoyed ab antiquo would not necessarily appear in the old Register and to these Sec. 59 has no application.

In the absence of any provisions to the contrary we may assume, that the Land Settlement Ordinances do not affect the continued application of the Transfer of Land Ordinance 1920-1929 within settled areas. No explicit provision declaratory of such non application is contained in the Ordinance but it will seldom if ever be needful to rely upon the provisions of the original Ordinance in view of the even more drastic provisions of Secs. 43 and 44 of the Principal Ordinance which adopt and enlarge the main provisions of the Transfer of Land Ordinance as follows.

Sec. 43. No disposition of land registered in the New Register, other than a lease for a period of not more than three years, and no transmission of land on death shall be valid until it has been registered in the Register.

Sec. 44. (1) No action shall be maintainable on the ground of any unregistered disposition against the owner of any registered right, provided that any person who has paid money in respect of any such invalid disposition shall be entitled to bring an action for the recovery of the sum.

(2) If any person is a party to a disposition, other than a lease for a period not exceeding 3 years, which has not been registered, and either enters into possession or permits the other party to enter into possession of the land, any Civil Court or Land Court in which an action, concerning the land is pending may impose a fine upon him not exceeding one-fourth part of the value of the land.

Remark that the definition of "disposition" given in Sec. 2 of the Principal Ordinance, is much wider than that which applies under the Transfer of Land Ordinance and includes a will of land. Every transmission of land on death indeed, even in an intestacy, is by Sec. 43 invalidated until entry on the Register. It is not clear in whom the property is deemed to be vested pending registration; clear it cannot be treated as still the property of the deceased and one concludes that the State must be entitled to it as bona vacantia. No doubt, however, the transmission is retrospectively validated by registration.

Provision is made by Secs. 47 and 48 of the Principal Ordinance for entry in the Register of judgments of Land Courts or Civil Courts concerning land registered under this Ordinance and for entries of cautions with regard to the disposition of a parcel

The Land Law of Palestine.

or prohibitions against the disposition of any parcel pending the decision of a pending suit.

Possessory and Prescriptive Titles. Registration of Land Ord. 1929.

It seems that in the actual working of the scheme of Land Settlement difficulties arose with reference to the title to lands within the area which made it necessary to empower Settlement Officers to record claims to ownership which were of doubtful or only of potential value. As an administrative expedient for completing the settlement without delay, the Registration of Land Ordinance 1929 was enacted with a view to facilitate such settlement. As explained in another chapter, the Moslem law, according to the best authorities, knows nothing of acquisitive prescription and acquisition of right to land by long continued possession exists only under Art. 78 of the Land Code and as against the State. This being so long continued possession whether as against a registered title or of land as to which there was no registered owner, could not give ownership. It became, therefore, desirable to authorize the Settlement Officer to register the possessor as owner subject or not as the case may be, to reservations in favour of other potential claimants.

The Ordinance envisages four distinct cases—

(a) possession adverse to a registered title has been held for the period sufficient to bar an action for recovery.

(b) possession adverse to a registered title has been held for a period less than that sufficient to bar an action for recovery but the registered owner cannot be traced or makes no claim.

(c) adverse possession has been held for a period sufficient to bar an action for recovery and no person is registered as owner.

(d) the possessor claims under an unregistered title derived from a prior possessor and no person is registered as owner.

It will be observed that these situations fall into two groups. To the first group belong the situations (a) and (b), in each of which case some person other than the actual possessor is already on the register as owner. The first of these situations arises when the possessor has already a prima facie right to plead long possession as bar of all actions for recovery. In this case the Ordinance merely authorizes the Settlement Officer to enter the possessor as owner in the Schedule of Rights; but he is entitled to decline to do so or to impose conditions if the registered owner opposes the possessor's claim. This is provided by Sec. 2 which enacts as follows

"Where a Settlement Officer is satisfied that land is registered in the name of any person and that another person has been

Chapter XVII—Cadastral Survey & Land Settlement.[289]

in possession thereof for such period and under such conditions, as will prevent any action for recovery of the land being heard, he shall enter the name of the person in possession in the Schedule of Rights as owner of the land in respect of the interest therein, which was held by the person registered as owner: Provided that, where the person, in whose name the land is registered opposes the application and the Settlement Officer is satisfied that the person making the application originally obtained possession from the registered owner as tenant or mortgagee, or otherwise than as owner, he shall not be bound to enter the name of the applicant in the Schedule of rights as owner of the land, or he may enter it subject to such conditions as he thinks fit".

The Section, therefore, gives to the long continued possession an acquisitive character. So soon as the possessor is registered as owner in the New Register all rights conflicting with his registered ownership are invalidated by the effect of Sec. 42 of the Land Settlement Ordinance 1928 [1]).

The situation postulated by the proviso is one likely to be of common occurence. It is only when (I) the registered owner opposes the "application" and (II) the applicant is shown to have obtained possession from the registered owner otherwise than as owner, that the Settlement Officer is entitled to refuse to record the possessor as owner.

The peculiarity of the decision under Sec. 2 is, that it may be a decision to record a possessor as owner i.e. in effect to give acquisitive character to long continued possession. It is not very clear how the Settlement Officer's powers under Sec. 2 are related to his very wide power of judicial decision under Land Settlement Ordinance 1928, Sec. 10. The Registration of Land Ordinance 1929 is "to be read together with the provisions of the Land Settlement Ordinance 1928", and appeals may, therefore, be assumed to lie from decisions of the Officer under Sec. 2 as from his decisions under Sec. 10 of the Principal Ordinance of 1928 [2]).

It should be remarked that, to secure registration under Sec. 2 it is not necessary for the "applicant" to show that he has himself possessed for the period required. The Settlement Officer is required to enter the possessor's name as owner in any case in which "another" person than the registered owner has been in possession

---

[1]) Sec. 6 of the Registration of Land Ordinance 1929 saves, however, the rights of persons, who have a lawful excuse. See further below as to this.

[2]) Sec. 56 of the Principal Ordinance as modified by the Ordinances of 1930 and 1932.

for the required period but such other person need not be, though normally he is likely to be, identical with the person in actual possession at the time of the Settlement. The inference from the language of the Section is that if there has been possession adverse to the registered title for the required period, the possessor at the time of the Settlement is entitled to be recorded as owner.

The second situation dealt with by the Ordinance of 1929 arises when another person than the registered owner is in possession but the possession has not continued long enough to present a legal bar to an action for recovery by the registered owner. The probability that possession will continue for the required period is, however, great owing to the fact that the registered owner has disappeared or made no claim. Sec. 3 of the Ordinance provides as follows:—

Where a Settlement Officer is satisfied that land is registered in the name of any person; and—

(a) that another person is in possession thereof in such circumstances that, if his possession continues for the period prescribed by law, any action for recovery thereof by the registered owner will not be heard thereafter;

(b) that the registered owner cannot be traced or makes no claim to the land; he may enter the name of the person in possession in the Schedule of Rights as having a possessory title, and shall state the date on which possession began.

The device of a possessory title is well known to the lawyer. Under English Land Registration Acts applicants for registration may apply for registration either with an "absolute" or with a "possessory" title, the latter being subject to "any estate, right or interest adverse to or in derogation of the title of the first proprietor" [1]. The effect of registration with a possessory title under the Ordinance of 1929 is very completely stated in Section 4 as follows:—

(a) The person previously registered as owner or his heirs shall thereafter be entitled to recover the land by action: Provided that such action is begun within the period prescribed by law.

(b) If action is brought within due time and judgment is given in favour of the registered owner or his heirs and is registered, the registration of any person with a possessory title shall be vacated, and the interest of any person claiming under him shall be deemed to be avoided from the date of registration of the judgment.

---

[1] Land Registration Act 1925, Sec. 6.

Chapter XVII—Cadastral Survey & Land Settlement.[291]

(c) The person registered with a possessory title and his successors shall be deemed to be owners of the land and entitled to the revenue thereof until the date of registration of judgment for recovery of the land by the registered owner.

(d) If no action for recovery of the land is brought by the registered owner or his heirs within the period prescribed by law the Director of Lands, on being satisfied that the person registered with the possessory title, or his successors, are in possession, shall vacate the registration of the registered owner and enter the person registered with the possessory title as the owner of the land. And all rights and interests therein of the person previously registered as owner shall cease and determine.

(e) No disposition or transfer, otherwise than on the death of the registered owner or the person registered with a possessory title, shall operate to create any right to the land, and no entry thereof shall be made in the Land Registers.

Remark that the person registered with a possessory title is in effect given a limited interest in the land. He is deemed to be owner until the date at which a judgment for recovery is registered against him. His limited interest is heritable though neither vendible nor capable of being given as security. The principles stated in an earlier chapter governing the relations between persons who appropriate the land of another and the lawful owners will not govern the relations between the person registered with a possessory title and the registered owner. Until the moment at which the limited interest ceases the person registered with a possessory title is to be deemed owner; he is entitled to the rents and profits. If he has planted or built upon the land in his possession he is not to be treated as a wrongful appropriator, since he was owner at the time at which these acts were done [1]. Owing to the presence of the restrictions upon power of disposition mentioned in Subsec. (e) it is clearly to the interest of the limited owner to secure registration as full owner so soon as may be, and at the first opportunity advantage will, therefore, be taken of the provisions of Subsec. (d) [2]. Claimants in

---

[1]) So far as we are aware the Moslem law does not contain rules which govern the new situation of "limited owner". The Courts might not unreasonably apply the rules relating to compensation for improvements as between landlord and tenant.

[2]) The Director of Lands has only to satisfy himself that the person registered with a possessory title is still in possession. Presumably he must also be satisfied that no action has been brought and that the period prescribed has expired. That the possession was adverse has already been decided by the Settlement Officer.

Land Settlement areas accept registration with possessory title only with great reluctance.

The two other situations dealt with in the Ordinance of 1929 are both cases in which no registered title adverse to the possessor exists. Sec. 5 provides as follows:—

"If a Settlement Officer is satisfied—

(a) that land has been in the possession of any person for such period and under such conditions as will prevent any action for recovery thereof being heard, and that no person is registered at the time of the settlement as owner; or

(b) that a person is in possession of land under an unregistered transfer to himself or his predecessor in title made by a person who was in possession at the date of the disposition but was not registered as owner, and that no other person has a registered interest in the land; he shall enter in the Schedule of Rights the name of the person in possession as owner of the land".

A proviso excludes Mahlul and Mewat land from the operation of this Section and states that nothing therein is to derogate from the provisions of Art. 78 of the Land Code. The operation of Art. 78 is considered in the chapter dealing with Limitation of Actions and Prescription; it suffices here to say that the proviso makes it clear (a) that an interest in Mewat cannot be obtained by long continued possession [1]; (b) that the operation of the Section now under discussion is limited to the possible over-riding claims of private persons against the possessor of Miri. If the land is Mahlul possession for less than the ten years prescribed by the texts will not give the possessor any right to a Tapu grant notwithstanding Section 2; but possession under the conditions specified in Art. 78 of the Land Code will continue to give a right to a Tapu grant without regard to any provisions of Sec. 5.

It is to be observed in conclusion that (Sec. 6) nothing in the Ordinance is to be deemed to affect the right of any person who has a lawful excuse, according to Art. 1663 of the Civil Code, to claim any right to land which has been registered in the name of another person on account of possession for the period prescribed by law.

This Section is apparently designed to save the right of a person out of possession and against whom time has not been running by reason of some available excuse within the meaning of Art. 1663 of the Mejelle. The Settlement Officer may be supposed,

---

[1] Cf. Mewat Land Ordinance 1921, supra, pp. 46 ff.

Chapter XVII— Cadastral Survey & Land Settlement.[293]

either in ignorance or otherwise, to have passed over such persons' right in recording as owner the person in possession. It is indeed stated that before recording the possessor as owner the Settlement Officer must be satisfied that he has possessed (or is in course of possession of) the land under such conditions (Sec. 2) or in such circumstances (Sec. 3) as would bar the action for recovery and this statement appears to imply that the Officer would take into account any excuse which the registered owner would be able to make available. But whatever action is taken by the Settlement Officer, and with whatever knowledge he acts, his record of the possessor as owner and the consequent registration will have no operation as against a person who is able to show that, assuming that the Ordinance had not existed, he would under the ordinary law have been entitled by reason of an excuse to make available his claim as against the possessor.

CHAPTER XVIII—REGISTRATION OF LAND.

The Ottoman System of Registration.
The Ottoman Land Code contains at the end (Art. 132) a rule of a general nature to the effect that all Imperial decrees, old or recent, issued with regard to State and Mevqufe land, which are inconsistent therewith are repealed, and that ancient Laws and Ordinances concerning State and Mevqufe land shall not be observed in the Imperial Divan Office, the Daftar Khani (Imperial Land Registers) or elsewhere.

Shortly after issuing the Land Code the Turkish Government published the Tapu Law, A.H. 1275, and Regulations as to Title Deeds (Tapu Sanads), A. H. 1276. By these enactments a new system of registration of title was established.

At the date (1858) at which the new Land Code came into operation, many persons occupied Miri Land without being able to produce any formal Title Deed, while others possessed Title Deeds issued by Sipahis, Multazims, etc. The Tapu Law, Art. 11, made provision for the issue of Title Deeds to occupiers without title deeds after enquiry and of new title deeds to holders of old ones.

According to Art. 1 of the Law the granting of Miri land was entrusted to officials of the Treasury.

Registration of Miri Titles.
These duties were subsequently transferred to the Daftar Khani. This Administration was primarily a Registry of Deeds, but its functions were later extended and it was charged with the duties of representing the State in suits relating to Miri, of ascertaining the circumstances, in which Miri was left uncultivated, and of supervising the legal formalities where Miri was transferred by Succession or became Mahlul.

The Head Offices of the Daftar Khani were in Constantinople; but in each province (Vilayet) and in each Sanjak were branch offices of which Tapu Mudiri (in the Vilayet) or Tapu Mamouri (in the Sanjak) were in charge. The Sanjaks were subdivided into Kazas and in each of them was a subordinate officer of the Daftar Khani [1]).

---

[1]) In Turkish times the Nablus Sub-District from Lebban northwards lay within the Vilayet of Beyrouth. Jerusalem Sub-District and Southern Palestine

Chapter XVIII—Registration of Land.

When Kushans were issued the counterfoils of the certificates were preserved in the capital of every Kaza. A summary book for each Kaza was kept at the capital of every Sanjak. These books as well as the counterfoils were as a rule deposited in safe places and consulted when required. The title deeds issued were based on the entries in the Tapu books. In cases of doubt arising with regard to the Kushans, instructions were given by the Daftar Khani at Constantinople (Art. 16 Tapu Law). The Kushans issued by the Tapu Offices bore the Imperial Cypher (Tugra) at the top, stated the title of the occupier, the Kaza and village where the land was situated, the boundaries and the number of dunums [1]) and were sealed with the seal of the Treasury Office (Art. 14).

By the Regulations as to Tapu Sanads (Art. 1) it was provided, that no one in future for any reason whatever should possess State land (Miri) without a title deed. Provision was made for the issue of new title deeds in the place of the old ones, and for the issue of title deeds to occupiers who proved a right by prescription but had no title deeds, to persons who held old title deeds issued by Sipahis, Multazims, etc. and to persons who claimed to have lost the title deeds issued prior to the year A.H. 1263 by Sipahis, Multazims or Muhassils (Arts. 8, 9, 10).

From time to time a Youklama (Land Census) was held. Entries in the Tapu books were made on information received through the Youklama and kushans issued to persons who were in a position to establish a title to their holdings.

It was first the practice of the local Tapu Officers acting under the provisions of the Tapu Law and Regulations to issue temporary kushans. Permanent certificates of title were issued from

---

formed an independent Sanjak attached directly to the Ministry of the Interior. What is now Transjordan fell within the Vilayet of Damascus.

¹) According to the Land Code (Art. 131) a dunum is 40 ordinary paces in length and breadth, i.e. 1600 square picks.

By an Ottoman Law of 1869 (See Young, op. cit., Vol. IV, p. 365) the metric system was introduced in the Ottoman Empire but its compulsory application was from time to time postponed. Surface measures of land were different in various parts of Palestine. By Sec. 3 of the Weights and Measures Ordinance 1928—1933 the standard dunum is fixed at 1000 square metres. The equivalence of 1000 square metres is 1/10 part of a Hectar. The use of the Standard dunum has not been made compulsory, but having been adopted in all Government and Municipal transactions and records the standard dunum came into general use. Surveys completed after the coming into force of the Weights and Measures Ordinance 1928—33 are in Standard (metric) dunums, but reservation was made for existing titles and contracts relating to land which have been effected prior to the Ordinance (Sec. 10).

the Daftar Khani in Constantinople. This system was subsequently abolished.

The Kushans now producible in Palestine in support of a claim to Miri have been issued by the Daftar Khani Authorities and it is unnecessary to say anything concerning kushans of earlier date.

As already explained above, the Daftar Khani was charged with the function of securing the registration of all title to land. Transfers of Miri were first effected before commissions which were called "Commissions of Feragh", and the procedure is carefully detailed in the Tapu Law and in the Regulations as to Tapu Sanads [1]).

Transfers of Miri land by inheritance were regulated by Art. 5 of the Tapu Law.

The leave of the Official was required to every kind of disposition of Miri [2]).

Registration of Mulk Titles. The system of registration in the Daftar Khani was at first confined to Miri. A System of registration of Mulk titles by the Sharia Courts had long existed. By the Law of 28 of Rejeb, A.H. 1291 (1874) (Law as to Mulk Titles), the registration of Mulk was transferred to the Daftar Khani. "This law" states the preamble, "regulates the issue of title deeds of pure Mulk properties situate in cities, towns, villages and nahiehs of the Empire, that is to say houses of which the ground and the buildings and trees thereon are Mulk, shops, vineyards and gardens and other immovable property, and buildings, vines and trees situate on Muqata'alu, Mevqufe, and Miri land subject to Bedl el Ushr (tithe)". This enumeration does not exhaust Mulk interests in immovables [3]). Servitudes are not mentioned and were not (semble) bound to be registered. But so far as regards all the species of Mulk interests in immovables enumerated possession thereof without a kushan was thenceforth forbidden (Art. 1). The title deeds were to be of two kinds—(1) for pure, (i.e. undedicated) Mulk; (2) for Muqata'a land with Mulk trees and buildings thereon (Art. 2). A special office at the Daftar Khani was set apart as the headquarters of records of transactions relating to Mulk (Art. 4); and an inspection (Youklama) of Mulk properties was directed at which the old "hodgets" issued for Mulk by the Religious Authorities were to be

---

[1]) See particularly Arts. 3, 4, 15, 21 of the Tapu Law and Arts. 3 and 14 of the Regulations.

[2]) Land Code, Arts. 36, 37 and 40.

[3]) per Curiam in Stassi v. Vehim (1890) 1 C.L.R., at p. 103.

Chapter XVIII—Registration of Land.

produced for examination and new title deeds issued in accordance with the law.

In former times transfers, mortgages, etc. of interests in waqf property were effected through the Waqf Authorities [1]). Subsequently, however, the records of Mevqufe [2]) land, of Mussaqafat and Mustaghilat were handed over to the Daftar Khani [3]) and the registration of transfers, mortgages, etc. of such property conducted in that office.

<small>Registration of Waqf transactions.</small>

Thus all land records and registration came to be centred at the Daftar Khani.

The principle of compulsory registration of Miri and Mulk land introduced by the earlier Laws was confirmed by the Law of Disposition, A.H. 1331. Art. 1 of this Law provides that every kind of disposition of Miri, Mulk and Waqf land must be made only in the Tapu Office.

The Daftar Khani (Land Registers) kept by the Tapu Office were, therefore, intended to be a complete record of all land transactions in the Empire. From time to time and for specific purposes other "Dafatir" were compiled, the names of which occur in dealing with land transactions.

In the past it happened not infrequently that villages were abandoned, the inhabitants having left the country or moved to other places where public security was better [4]).

<small>Daftar Shamsieh.</small>

The Ottoman authorities created special Commissions to investigate and take the census of such villages and the results of the investigations were usually submitted to the Mejlis Idara (Administrative Commission) for approval, and were afterwards embodied in a Daftar Shamsieh, so called because it was a record of vacant lands lying idle and "exposed to the sun" (Shamsieh) which are, therefore, to be recorded as State Domain.

There is no law regulating the keeping of a "Daftar Shamsieh" since it was not treated as a statutory register. Lands recorded in a "Daftar Shamsieh" are normally deemed to be State Lands. Usually the records state the different categories of land found in the abandoned villages, i.e. cultivable land, waste land and forest, the boundaries and the value of the land. In many cases the State disposed of such land by public auction. Big estates were thus disposed of by the Turkish Government in the Lewas of Acre,

---

<small>
1) Law of Jamadi-el-Thani A.H. 1287.
2) i.e. Miri land subject to a Takhsisat Waqf.
3) Laws of 9 Rabi-el-Awal A.H. 1293; Rejeb, A.H. 1299.
4) Cf. Land Code, Arts. 72, 130.
</small>

The Land Law of Palestine.

Haifa, Nazareth, Tiberias, etc. the estates (jiftliks) having been acquired by notables. The auction lists referring to estates so disposed of contain reference to the categories of land, the boundaries and areas as recorded in the "Daftar Shamsieh" prior to the putting up of the estates for sale by public auction.

In many instances the "Daftar Shamsieh" contains reference to persons who have acquired rights by occupancy or otherwise in different parts of the cultivated or cultivable land recorded. The records cannot, however, be treated as constituting a complete legal title.

Daftar Mahlulat. Distinction must be drawn between "Daftar Shamsieh" and "Daftar Mahlulat", and again between "Daftar Shamsieh" and "Daftar Daimi".

The "Daftar Mahlulat" is a book which was regularly kept by the Tapu and in which entries were made of all the lands reverted to the State under Arts. 60 and 68 of the Land Code.

If the persons having a right to take the land by Tapu did not do so, the land became considered Mahlul. An entry in the "Daftar Mahlulat" is prima facie evidence that the land is Mahlul.

Daftar Daimi. The "Daftar Daimi" is the book of the Title Deeds in which all the transactions of the Tapu were finally recorded and on the strength of those entries kushans were issued. An entry in the "Daftar Daimi" is considered to be of the nature of a complete title to the estate recorded in this book.

Unregistered transactions. Although under the Ottoman Regime registration of immovable property was in law compulsory, yet in fact it was seldom enforced. Consequently much land remained unregistered and was held in virtue of private and primitively drawn contracts.

In view of the number of transactions made outside the Tapu, the Turkish registers do not show the true ownership of the property. Frequently the heirs of the vendors dispute the sales, made by their deceased ancestors. Added to this are the complications, arising from unregistered successions and illegal transactions so that, in effect, the majority of the transactions are contested. As a result of the complex nature of the Turkish Land Laws, the difficulties arising from numerous unofficial sales, the survival of local customs governing successions and particularly the habit of not dividing the lands between heirs, so that properties come to be recorded as held in impracticably minute fractions, the complications of the title are extremely difficult to straighten out.

The establishment of a definite system of Registration implied a Cadastral survey and preliminary Settlement of existing titles. A

Chapter XVIII—Registration of Land.

Law to this effect known as the Cadastral Law, A.H. 1331 (1913), was passed, but the reform itself has not been carried out.

On the occupation of Palestine by the British Forces it was found that the Turkish Authorities had removed many of the registers and records. Most of the missing registers were subsequently recovered. During the War many of the inhabitants had heavily encumbered their property in order to provide money to purchase exemption from Military Service and to provide necessaries of life at a period when Turkish currency was depreciated and living abnormally dear. Owing to the financial chaos it was impossible for these people to redeem their mortgages and foreclosure would have meant an utter ruin.

In view of this fact and of the absence of the registers it was decided to close the Registries for a time, and Proclamations were accordingly issued in November 1918 (No. 75 and 76) prohibiting any transactions in immovable property and declaring all transactions effected since the Occupation void. The Proclamations were operative in the Ottoman Sanjak of Jerusalem from 1st December 1917, and in the Ottoman Sanjaks of Nablus and Acre from 1st October 1918. In 1920 the Registries were reopened under the sanction of the Land Transfer Ordinance 1920, which, however, required that transactions should only be valid if made with the consent of the Government. *The Proclamations of 1918 and the Land Transfer Ordinance 1920.*

Certain restrictions, directed mainly against speculation and the aggregation of large estates, were, moreover, imposed.

A Department of Land Registries was thereupon formed which succeeded, as from the 1st day of July 1920, (the day upon which Civil Administration was substituted for Military Administration) to all the functions of the Daftar Khani of the former Ottoman Government in Palestine [1]). *The Department of Land Registries.*

The preparation of all documents affecting immovable property and the investigation of title are undertaken by the Land Registry and registration fees are charged on the capital value of land involved. With a view to preventing future disputes and to enable registration to be reasonably accurate the survey of the properties which are the subject of transactions is undertaken by a Government Surveyor or by a licensed Surveyor. This also ensures that the current areas are recorded in the Wergo Office as a basis on which to assess the Land Tax. The fees vary according to the nature

---

[1]) Public Notice, Off. Gaz., No. 96.

of the transactions—from $1/2\%$ on partition to 5% on the registration of land not hitherto registered [1]).

The Transfer of Land Amendment Ordinance No. 2 of 1921, repealed most of the restrictions imposed upon the disposition of immovable property by the Ordinance of 1920, but re-enacted a provision which provided that in the case of agricultural land which was leased the Director of Land Registries should be satisfied that a tenant in occupation would retain sufficient land in the district or elsewhere for the maintenance of himself and his family (Sec. 2) [2]).

The Department of Lands. In August 1920, the High Commissioner appointed a Land Commission to report, inter alia, upon what steps should be taken to obtain an accurate record of State lands and to advise the best disposition of them in the interests of the country generally and of closer settlement and increased production in particular. This Commission recommended the creation of a Department whose function should be to ascertain, delimit, register and control all State lands. This recommendation was acted upon and the Department of Lands was organised. The Department of Lands was amalgamated with the Department of Land Registries (Public Notice, 15th August, 1922).

Rules of the Land Registry. By Sec. 16 of the Land Transfer Ordinance 1920, the Legal Secretary was empowered, with the sanction of the High Commissioner, to make rules as to the organization, procedure, and business of the Land Registry, the functions and duties of the Registrars, the mode in which the Register is to be kept, the forms to be used, the execution of deeds, fees to be payable, etc. No rules as to organization and procedure have yet been issued under this Section [3]). These powers are now exerciseable by the High Commissioner.

The procedure of registration of dispositions and the business of the Land Registry Offices is, however, regulated by interim Regulations, issued by the Director of Land Registries to his subordinate officers in the Districts. Under these Regulations the formalities of all dispositions between living persons are identical. In every case the parties (grantor and grantee) submit a petition in the form prescribed accompanied by the documents of title to

---

[1]) See Chapter on Land Registration Fees, infra.

[2]) This Section is repealed by the Protection of Cultivators Ordinance 1929. As to the provisions now made for protection of agricultural tenants see fully the Chapter dealing with this subject (XV), supra.

[3]) As to fees see Chapter on Land Registraion Fees, infra.

Chapter XVIII—Registration of Land.

the property and a certificate by the Mukhtar stating that the grantor is the owner of the property specifying its situation, boundaries, and description. The grantor also submits a declaration to the same effect.

The land is, when necessary, surveyed by a Surveyor of the Government Survey Department or a licensed Surveyor.

In each Local Registry a Petition Book is kept in English for the whole District and all petitions presented to the Registry Office of the District are entered under consecutive numbers according to the date on which they are received. Petitions for the approval of sales, mortgages, leases, and partitions, are presented on the prescribed Registry form. Petitions for other dispositions in land and for transfers and discharges of mortgages may be presented on ordinary paper in a form approved by the local Registrar. On receipt of a petition it is checked, together with the documents attached to it.

The Mukhtar's certificate is examined and the seals verified. The petition is then entered in the petition book and the number added. The file is entered in the Despatch Book and is passed to the District Revenue Office for information as to taxes and value.

In cases where the applicant is unable to produce a vergo certificate on account of (1) failure to identify the property in the Wergo Register; (2) loss of the Wergo Register; or (3) the property being unassessed,—the Revenue Officer is informed and asked to assess the property and to inform the Land Registry Office of the amount of the assessment.

Where a sale of property takes place and the Land Registry accepts the price mentioned in the deed of sale as the true value, the Wergo Office is informed before the Land Registry fees are actually determined. If the price is contested by the Wergo Office the matter is settled between the Registrar and the Finance Officer. In case of disagreement the matter is submitted to the District Commissioner for final decision. Where the Land Registry Office does not accept the pirce mentioned in the deed as the market value the value is assessed as also in case of registration of property previously unregistered. The market value is assessed by the Finance Officer or his representative together with the Registrar. They fix the true market value. In case of disagreement the matter is submitted to the District Commissioner for final decision.

Valuation of Land.

In cases of correction of area of properties already registered or of application for registration of Inshaat (erections or trees) the

The Land Law of Palestine.

Wergo.

result of survey and enquiry on the ground is referred to the Wergo Office before completion of registration.

The Wergo Office certifies in each case whether the Wergo tax has been collected up to date, and also (a) the value of the property according to the new correct area and the valuation assessed in accordance with the provisions of the Urban Property Tax Ordinances 1928—1932, which value is inserted in the Register on registration of correction; and (b) the value of "Inshaat" on which "Inshaat" fees should be collected. In cases of registration of succession, partition or bequest, registration fees are collected on the existing wergo value of the properties, no fresh assessment in such cases being made.

When one or more of the undivided shares of Mesha'a land [1]) is transferred by sale, or otherwise, a revaluation of the portion transferred is made but not of the remaining portions not transferred.

A map of the property to be entered in the Register is made and a note made to the effect that the boundaries on it are correct, the note being signed or sealed by the Mukhtar, the Transferor, the Transferee and the neighbours in the presence of the surveyor who also signs it. Two copies of the plan are prepared, one to be attached to the copy of the deed retained in the Registry Office and the other to be handed to the Transferee together with the copy of the deed delivered to him on completion of the registration.

In cases of doubt as to procedure and also in specified cases the local Registrar is required to consult the Director of Lands.

Deeds.

Printed forms of Deeds are used where such are provided, any variation being referred to the Director for approval.

The execution of a deed is carried out in the following manner:—

(a) The deed or document which it is desired to register is drawn up by the parties or the Registrar in the form prescribed in duplicate or multiplicate as required;

(b) The Registrar or official verifying the execution, satisfies himself that the persons appearing before him are the persons they purport to be;

(c) The execution is verified by the Registrar and the note of verification at the back of the deed is filled in and signed by him.

The deed is not handed over till the registration fees are paid. The number and particulars are then entered in the Deeds Book.

---

[1]) As to Mesha'a land see Chapter XIII upon Co-ownership and Partition, supra.

Chapter XVIII—Registration of Land.

In case of a mortgage, the prior Deeds and Certificate of Registration in possession of the mortgagor are retained in the Registry Office.   *Mortgages.*

On discharge of the mortgage the following procedure is carried out:—

(a) The copy of the mortgage is produced by the mortgagee and retained in the Registry Office and both copies of the Mortgage Deed (the office copy and the one produced by the mortgagee) are endorsed with a note thus "Mortgage discharged by Deed No....".

(b) The original Deed and the Certificate of Registration taken from the mortgagor are returned to him.

The following procedure is followed in the case of a mortgage whose term has expired, where the mortgagor desires to repay the loan and obtain a formal discharge, but the mortgagee fails to appear in the Land Registry.

In such cases the Mortgagor presents to the Registrar a statement of the sums due by him under the mortgage, and if the Registrar is satisfied that his statement is correct, he is then directed to pay it to the Treasury as a deposit at the disposal of the Director of Lands. Upon the production of the Treasury receipt to the Registrar the discharge is registered and the mortgage cancelled.

A petition relative to a Succession must be accompanied by (1) a certificate of a Competent Court, stating that the person, or persons acquiring registration are entitled as legatees or heirs; (2) a certificate signed by the Mukhtar or Imam and two Notables. *Succession.*

A Succession is registered:—

(a) In the name of the heirs collectively when all the heirs are named in the registration, or

(b) In the name of each heir for his undivided share, or

(c) In the name of each heir for such proportion of the estate as may have fallen to his share or division.

Further particulars as to the conditions under which registration of Disposition by transfer or mortgage, rights of succession, leases, etc. shall be effective are given in the Chapters dealing therewith.

According to the law of certain religious communities immovables may be subjected to dowry rights, and may be thereby rendered inalienable by the husband. The Ottoman authorities permitted the registration of such rights on the certificate of the religious court [1]). Under the present Administration the same *Dowry.*

---

[1]) Padel and Steeg, op. cit., pp. 130—131 where the Ottoman Circulars are quoted.

procedure would (semble) be followed. Dowry is not expressly mentioned as a matter of personal status in Art. 51 of the Palestine Order-in-Council, but is probably to be treated as included within the term "suits regarding marriage". In the case of foreigners it may be thought more doubtful whether registration of dowry making the immovables inalienable should be allowed; there is nothing in the Order-in-Council which justifies a distinction in this respect between natives and foreigners. The certificate leading to registration should be given by the Civil Courts or possibly by the Consul under the Order of November 1922, relative to Consular powers. Constitution of immovables in dower is a "disposition" within the meaning of the Transfer of Land Ordinance 1920.

<small>Application for Kushans in respect of land for which no Kushan has ever been issued.</small>

Applications presented to the Land Registry for the grant of Kushans in respect of land for which no kushan has ever been issued is made in writing and must be accompanied by a certificate signed by the Mukhtars and at least two notables testifying the following :

(a) the nature, extent, position and boundaries of the property;

(b) the name of the person entitled to registration;

(c) the manner in which such person acquired possession of the property and the period he has been in possession.

The application is then referred for enquiry to officers in charge of the supervision of unregistered land and State Domain.

<small>Inshaat.</small>

When a person applies for the amendment of a registration by the addition thereto of a building erected or trees planted subsequently the applicant is required to produce his Kushan, or an extract from the Tapu books of the existing registration, together with the Wergo receipt and a Mukhtar's certificate. The "Inshaat" is then entered upon the Register.

<small>Correction of Land Registers Ordinances.</small>

Since a very large number of transfers or purported transfers of land had taken place without registration at the Daftar Khani it follows that the entries in the Land Registry records do not correspond with the facts of occupation and enjoyment of the land. It was the object of the Correction of Land Registers Ordinances to bring the records into conformity with the facts of occupation. The first of these Ordinances was enacted in 1920 and permitted (Sec. 1) any person claiming any interest in registered land otherwise than as being the rsgistered owner or mortgagee to apply to the Court for an order that an entry be made in the Register relating to such land to the effect that the applicant claims an interest therein. The evidence upon which such order could be made was specified in

Chapter XVIII—Registration of Land.

Sec. 2 and included a private document, as also payment of wergo in respect of the lands for a period of three years immediately preceding the date of application. This Ordinance was of temporary application only. The period for which it was to be applied was extended and the Ordinance itself amended by Ordinances of 1921 and 1922, but all these have now lapsed. No application for correction of the Registers on grounds mentioned in these Ordinances was receivable after the 20 July 1924.

A further Correction of Land Registers Ordinance, 1926, has, however, been enacted and is still in force. It was discovered that various communities of persons had been in the habit of keeping unofficial Land Registers among themselves, in which were recorded all transactions concerning their land. No registration in the Official Registers was intended or attempted. This proceeding was, of course, an abuse and a cause of serious loss to the Government. At the same time, the circumstances made it difficult to apply the law strictly and decline to recognise the validity of any of these transactions so recorded. The Ordinance of 1926 fixed a period of three months during which all Unofficial Land Books were to be handed over to the Director of Land Registries and it was provided that no Unofficial Land Book which had not been handed over within such period should be pleaded or given as evidence in any Court as affecting any land, and that no entry in any unofficial land book whatsoever subsequent to the date of publication of the Ordinance (1926) should be pleaded or given in evidence. Provision was made for the entry in the Official Register upon application of all interests recorded in the Unofficial Land Books as follows:— *[margin: Unofficial Land Books. Correction of Land Registers Ordinance 1926.]*

Sec. 4. (1) "Where an unofficial land book has been delivered to the Director, any person who has an interest recorded in such book may apply to the Director for the registration of the interests in the official registers; and, notwithstanding anything in the Ordinances of the Chief Administrator dated the 18th November, 1918, concerning the disposition of immovable property, or in the Transfer of Land Ordinance, 1920, and any amendment thereof, any sale, mortgage, lease, partition, or other transaction in land which, prior to the date of this Ordinance has been recorded in an unofficial land book shall not be deemed to be null and void for the reason only that it was not recorded in the official registers [1]).

---

[1]) The value of an entry in an Unofficial Land Book is discussed in L.A. 55/22. Palestine Post 14 November 1933.

The Land Law of Palestine.

(2) The application shall be supported by such evidence relating to the interest claimed as the Director may require".

Sec. 5. "No application under this Ordinance shall be entertained in respect of any interest in land which could have been registered in the official registers in pursuance of the final judgment of a competent Court".

Sec. 8 (as altered by Amending Ordinance of 1926).

"If no adverse claim is made within four months of the publication of the application, or such extended time as the Director may prescribe, the Director may order that the interest claimed shall be registered in the official registers in the name of the applicant, on payment of the fee which is payable on the original registration of such interest".

Sec. 9 makes provision for the hearing of objections.

Sec. 12 provides as follows:—

"If at any time a land settlement is instituted in Palestine, the officer conducting the settlement in an area in which transactions have been recorded in the unofficial land book shall give notice to any person who has an interest recorded in the unofficial land book as well as to the owner registered in the official registers that he proposes to determine the title to the land and is prepared to receive any claim; provided that no such notice shall be given where an objection to registration under this Ordinance has been referred to a Land Court".

Registration in the name of a Nominee. The older Ottoman law, in accordance with a policy by no means confined to Turkey, prohibited foreigners from owing immovable property in the Empire [1]). It was also impossible for corporations, native or foreign, to become owners of land since the juristic person was unknown to Ottoman Law. To evade the difficulties arising from this state of the law it was not unusual that a transfer to a foreigner or to a corporation should be made in the name of a nominee (nam musta'ar, i.e. registration in the name of a nominee).

By a law of Sefer, A.H. 1284, foreigners were invested with the same title as Ottoman subjects to enjoy the right to possess immovable property anywhere within the Empire (except the Hedjaz) and (Sec. 4) the right to dispose by gift or by will of such immovable property, the disposition of which in this way is allowed by law.

---

[1]) Equality of treatment as regards transfer of land inter vivos between Moslem and non-Moslem subjects was granted by a Law of 7 Moharrem, A.H. 1293.

Chapter XVIII—Registration of Land.

The application of this law was, however, confined to the subjects of those powers which accepted the conditions of the law. It appears that under the Mandate the Mandatory Power is under an international obligation not to discriminate between subjects of States which are members of the League of Nations, nor as against American citizens.

By a Provisional Law of 22 Rabi-el-Awal, A.H. 1331, certain corporations were also recognized as lawful owners of immovable property. The precise extent to which and conditions under which corporations may hold land in Palestine will be stated in a later Chapter.

In consequence of these two enactments it became possible to discountenance the practice of nam musta'ar which had previously been tolerated. By Art. 4 of the Law of Disposition, A.H. 1331, it was provided that "no action of Nam Musta'ar was to be heard in respect of Mulk and immovable property owned by virtue of a title deed". The effect of the provision was that thenceforth, no action would be heard in the Courts, in which it was alleged that a person though registered as owner was in fact a nominee [1]. The Law, however, allowed a period of two years for corrections of the registers by the issue of a new Title Deed in the name of the true owner. Compare the Provisional Article of the Law as to Corporations. Since the occurence of War made it impossible in many cases for application for correction to be made, provision for such correction was inserted in the Correction of Land Registers Ordinance 1920, Sec. 3.

Having regard to the provisions of the Law as to Mulk Title Deeds, A.H. 1291, and the prohibition of actions of Nam Musta'ar by the Law of Disposition, the provisions of Arts. 1591-4 ff. of the Mejelle, which determine the effect of admission of ownership appear to have been deprived of effect as regards Mulk immovables.

The law applicable in Palestine is the Ottoman law in force in Palestine on 1st November 1914 as amended or affected by legislation of the Palestine Administration and Orders in Council. *The Value and Validity of a Registered Title.*

Under the Ottoman Administration as now under the present Government the Sanad Tapu, generally known as Kushan is the recognized instrument of title to land. A Kushan bearing the Imperial "Tugra" was considered conclusive as being a document free from fraud and forgery and one upon which a judgment can be based without further evidence.

---

[1] Land Transfer Ordinance 1920, Sec. 5

The Land Law of Palestine.

Art. 90 of the Ottoman Law of Civil Procedure recognizes the entries in the Tapu books as evidence which is sufficient to prove a claim [1]).

The Law of Disposition of A.H. 1331 confirmed the principle as follows (Art. 3):—

"Formal title-deeds are valid and executory. The Civil and Sharia Courts shall give judgment on these deeds and their registration without further proof. A formal title-deed shall not be annulled except by a judgment of a Court based an lawful reasons provided that errors, which contradict unambiguous entries and official documents, may be corrected by the Registry Office on an order given by the Administrative Council after informing the parties interested".

The provisions of the Law of A.H. 1331 have much strengthened the titles of the Kushan holders. The "Hodgets" which used to be issued by the Religious Courts are not considered to be good title to immovable property. The sole legal title is the Kushan based on the entry in the Land Registers.

The form of Kushan now in use does not purport to be a Title Deed, but a Certificate of Registration. It is, however, submitted that, reproducing as it does the entry in the books of the Land Registry, it is entitled to the protection afforded by Mejelle Art. 1737, and Art. 3 of the Law of Disposition, A.H. 1331.

The Turkish form of kushan was styled Sanad Khakany (literally, a Title Deed of the State Book). In form the new Certificate follows the older kushan except that it contains references to Art. 3 of the Law of Disposition, A.H. 1331, and Art. 9 of the Land Transfer Ordinance 1920; and a definite statement that the issue of the Certificate is not to imply a guarantee of title by the Administration. The practice of the Courts has always been to maintain the validity of a Certificate of Registration (Kushan) unless there is evidence of fraud.

The legal value of an entry in the Land Registers and of the corresponding Kushan has been examined in a number of cases before the Palestine Courts, which appear to justify the view that such entry gives more than a merely prima facie title and is conclusive evidence of ownership in the absence of fraud [2]). It is, however, necessary to bear in mind the somewhat cryptic provisions

---

[1]) Cf. Mejelle, Art. 1737.

[2]) In Bishara Assileh v. Fuad Saad (C. A. No. 77/33) the Court of Appeal held that an admission in proceedings in the Land Registry is an irrebutable admission and, therefore, cannot be rebutted by whom it is made.

Chapter XVIII—Registration of Land.

of the Land Courts Ordinance of 1921 Sec. 7 (1) which authorize the Land Courts, to have regard to equitable as well as legal rights to land. The precise meaning of "equitable" rights in this connection has not, it appears, been yet explicitly formulated. The reference does not seem to be to that English conception of "equity", as worked out by the Courts of Chancery but to something of a wider import though British judges are likely to be influenced by the English ideas.

Under Sec. 2 of the Land Courts Ordinance the Land Courts have power to determine disputes as to the ownership of the land or of any rights in or over the land and give a judgment, and it has been held that applications to set aside ownership in a Land Register are causes or matters in which the Land Courts have jurisdiction [1]).

It has further to be borne in mind that under the Land Transfer Ordinance 1920 no disposition of immovable property is valid unless the consent of the Director of Land Registries has been obtained; in effect, as has been already pointed out, this means, that an unregistered assurance does not operate to transfer rights.

We now proceed to mention a few typical Palestine cases, which illustrate the attitude adopted by the Civil Courts towards the rights of the registered owner. We are of course dealing here exclusively with cases under the Ottoman registration laws and the Land Transfer Ordinances. The position of the registered owner in Settlement areas is not in issue. The subject of Land Settlement and its effect upon rights registered under the Settlement is discussed in Chapter XVII.

The following cases are noteworthy:—

1. So far as Mulk property is concerned, possession unsupported by evidence of title is insufficient to enable a Plaintiff to succeed against a Defendant who is registered as owner [2]).

2. The general rule is that evidence of witnesses unsupported by evidence in writing cannot be heard against a Kushan. In other words a formal transaction evidenced by registration in the Land Registry cannot in the absence of documentary evidence be

---

[1]) High Court No. 74/32. Palestine Order-in-Council 1922 Art. 43. Land Courts Ordinance 1921, Sec. 2. But see as to the powers of the Chief Justice, Land Courts Ordinance 1921, Sec. 8 (2) and Notice in Off. Gaz. 1st September 1922. The Land Court is not bound by rules of evidence contained in the Codes of Civil Procedure or in the Civil Code (Mejelle). Sec. 7 (2).

[2]) Abdullah el Hafez v. Abdel Kader Salman L. A. 135/26. Cf. Mejelle, Art. 1248.

disproved by verbal evidence, the rule being that a registered title will not be set aside except by some evidence in writing sufficient to support an adverse title or corroborate evidence in support of such adverse title [1]).

3. Evidence of witnesses unsupported by evidence in writing cannot be heard against a Kushan. But when supported by written evidence or an admission that the Land Registry entries did not correctly record the true facts as to title, evidence of witnesses are admissible against a registered title [2]).

4. Effect has been given by the Courts to a form of a customary tenure of land registered in the name of some persons as holding the land in undivided ownership (Mesha'a) as trustees for the adult males of a village and a plaintiff is entitled to a declaration that an entry is to be recorded in the Land Registers that a certain land forms part of the common lands of the village cultivable according to the custom of the village by the adult male inhabitants of the village. This entry in the Books of the Land Registry should not, however, be in a form which would give the plaintiff a fixed share in the common lands in perpetuity. This share will always depend on the number of adult males in the village at the date of action.

As an exception to the rule, that in the absence of documentary evidence a Kushan cannot be disproved by verbal evidence witnesses can be heard under Section 7 (2) of the Land Courts Ordinance, 1921, to prove against the holder of a Kushan that the land registered in his name, is common land of a village subject to a village customary tenure and his registration is as a trustee for the villagers [3]).

5. The provisions of Section 7 (1) of the Land Courts Ordinance, 1921, to the effect that the Courts shall have regard to equitable as well as to legal rights in land and shall not be bound by any rule of the Ottoman Law prohibiting the Courts from hearing actions based on unregistered documents, has been applied by the Courts to unregistered transactions which took place before the Occupation, in which it appeared from the circumstances, such

---

[1]) Afifeh Bint Elias Abu Rahmeh and others. v. Naim Jurius Abiad and others, L.A. 137/23; Compare Farah Hadad v. Haj Abdul Wahis Sammer, L.A. 109/24.

[2]) Abdel Halik Haj Shaban Tafish and others. v. Ismail Ahmad Ghalayani. L.A. 93/26.

[3]) Zeita village Land Case L.A. 59/24; Aslin village Land Case L.A. 57/25; Beit Lid village Land case L.A. 121/26.

Chapter XVIII—Registration of Land.

as delivery of possession and payment of purchase money, that the parties intended the transaction to take effect as a sale without registration.

It was held that under such circumstances it would be inequitable to refuse to recognize the validity of a sale of land by unregistered deed, merely for lack of registration; and a number of judgments has been given upholding the validity of the unregistered sale and declaring that as against the vendor, the purchaser is entitled to registration. That principle, however, can only be applied to a case, in which the sale took place before the Occupation as the Proclamation of the 18th of November, 1918, rendered all dispositions of immovable property made after the Occupation invalid [1]).

6. A registered owner who sold the land by an unregistered deed, and having received the purchase price, had given an irrevocable Wakala for the transfer of the land in the name of the purchaser, is not prevented, so long as the Wakala remained unexecuted, from conferring a valid title by a registered transfer to another purchaser. Hence the effect of the registered transfer (in the Courts finding) was to destroy any right that the purchaser by unregistered deed might otherwise have had to registration, leaving him only with a right to claim damages from the vendor. (Cf. Mohammed Tewfik Yahya v. Sha'aban Mustafa Aidi. L.A. No. 135/23).

From these cases may it be concluded how firmly the Palestine Courts are opposed to attempts to shake the validity of a registered title. In the later case of Ahmed Abu Nyma v. Anglo Palestine Bank [2]) the Court of Appeal held that the Land Court could not hear oral evidence or receive evidence of wergo payments in support of a claim to land brought by the plaintiff who based his claim upon possession of the land for thirty years but sought on that ground to upset a registered title. The Court followed the earlier decision [3]) above mentioned in which the law had been stated as follows. "The evidence of witnesses, the possession of the Respondents, the admission of the parties interested, however convincing, are not sufficient to over-ride the general rule, that has been established in this Court that a registered title will not be set aside except by some evidence in writing sufficient to support an adverse title or to corroborate evidence in support of

---

[1]) Sara Litvinsky v. Lippman and others. L.A. 88/25. See also p. 144, supra.

[2]) L.A. 67/32; Palestine Post 1st February 1934.

[3]) Afifeh Elias v. Naim Jurius Abiad, L.A. 137/23.

such adverse title. The general rule thus expressed has been followed in this Court subject to a few recognized exceptions as, for example, when the claim is to lands of a village cultivable in common according to the custom of the village".

"Evidence in writing sufficient to support an adverse title" would include entries in the Youklama records and "Hodgets" of the Moslem Religious Courts where these are relevant [1]).

The effect of the views thus accepted by the Courts of Palestine upon the legal consequences of long continued possession are considered in the Chapter upon Limitation of Actions and Prescription.

7. Where a transfer of title has been found to be based on sale or exchange or on similar transactions when consideration was involved, the Courts have held that an innocent transferee, who obtains a title from a registered owner is entitled to hold it but the vendor may be sued for compensation by the owner of an overriding interest.

The Court of Appeal has in a number of cases ruled that the Title-Deed (Kushan) of a bona fide purchaser for valuable consideration, who acquired land without the knowledge of any adverse claim, cannot be upset.

8. The defendant who bought the land in the Land Registry on the strength of a certificate of Succession, issued by the Religious Court, which certificate was afterwards annulled by the Religious Court, was a bona fide purchaser for value without notice and must retain the land. The plaintiff is at liberty to claim from the vendor compensation for the loss he has sustained [2]).

9. A purchaser in the Land Registry who bought from a registered owner in good faith without notice of any right vested in another person (who was not a registered owner) is to retain the land [3]).

10. Improper registration of land is void. The registration of a sale by a guardian of a minor's share without the consent of the Court is void, and the minor is entitled to be re-registered in respect of his share [4]).

In Friedman's case the Respondent was entitled by inheritance from her grandfather to a share in a piece of land, but was not registered, the whole land being registered in the names of his

---

[1]) See Fisher. Ottoman Land Code, pp. 63 ff. The Land Courts have admitted contracts made prior to the Proclamation of 1918. See also Litvinsky v. Lippman L.A. 88/25.

[2]) Abdallah Husein Haj Ali and others v. Aaronson and others. L.A. 27/28.

[3]) Shlomo Friedman v. Badie bint Abdul Karim. L.A. 96/27.

[4]) Nader v. Taher Qaraman. L A. 39/32. Palestine Post 23rd April 1933.

Chapter XVIII—Registration of Land.

older heirs. The Appellant had acquired by registered transfer from a vendor who had bought from the registered heirs by registered transfer. In these circumstances the Court of Appeal had been of opinion that the purchaser had done all that he could be expected to do and the fault lay with the Respondent who had omitted to obtain registration. As between two innocent parties the purchaser had done all that was required by law and since he had the legal title vested in him he clearly had the better claim. But in Nader's case these considerations did not apply and to deprive the Appellant of the land merely as the result of a mistake on the part of the Land Registry Officials to which he had not contributed would be inequitable.

It appears from the judgment that in the opinion of the Court the registration gave to the purchaser a legal title which could only be upset by equitable considerations. As already suggested the terms "legal" and "equitable" used in this connection must not be interpreted strictly by reference to the corresponding English terms. Though no doubt the Court is influenced by the English use; strict adherence to English doctrines as to the relations between legal and equitable rights is not intended. If, however, a purchaser, who had taken reasonable steps to see that a good title was being transferred, would have learned of the defect, his registered title will be liable to be overridden by a claimant who had not been guilty of laches and of whose rights the purchaser would have become cognizant by making proper enquiries. Mr. Justice Khaldi took a stricter view. In his dissenting judgment in Nader's case he lays down that the Land Registrar when issuing a title deed is presumed to have been satisfied that the requirements of the law have been complied with. "The title deed of a person is prima facie evidence of a perfect title and there seems to be no authority whereby ...an obligation is imposed on intending purchasers to examine the document filed at the Land Registry at the time of the transfer to the Vendors".

The following cases may also be remarked:—

11. In the curious case of Baivqari v. Omar el Mughrabi [1]) application was made by the Respondent for a declaration of title to the upper storey of a house of which the appellant was registered as owner. The appellant appears to have contended that there could be no registration of a second storey apart from the first storey. The Court of Appeal in allowing the appeal did not, how-

---

[1]) L.A. 8/33 Palestine Post 28th December 1933.

ever, go so far. They laid down, however, that "Where a fresh storey is added to a registered house, the presumption is that it is built by and is the property of the owner of the registered house". It may be assumed that, the house in this case was Mulk, but even if it were a Miri house, the conclusion arrived at by the Court of Appeal appears certain. Some documentary proof that the upper storey has been transferred to the respondent was clearly demanded. The mere fact, if true, that the building had been undertaken in his name could not give title.

12. In the case of Fahideh bint Nimmer el Murshed v. Muhammed Abd el Razak Daoud & Elia Abraham Matalon [1]) the Court of Appeal held that where a person has allowed land to remain registered in another's name, then he has no recourse against a creditor of that other person who has attached the said land in satisfaction of a debt due to him from that other person [2]).

---

[1]) L.A. 42/33. Palestine Post 14th January 1935.
[2]) See Zenobio v. Osman (1893) 2 C.L.R. referred to at p. 145, supra.

CHAPTER XIX—EXPROPRIATION OF LAND.

Owners of land may be required to surrender for purposes of public utility some or all of the rights they possess in or over their land. The Ottoman Law, like the Law of every European State, made provision for the compulsory acquisition of land for public purposes on payment of compensation to the owner. The principle of expropriation by payment of compensation was generally adopted in the Ottoman Empire [1]). In the year 1879 this principle was embodied in the law entitled "Regulations for Expropriation for Public Purposes" of the 21 Jamad-el-Awal, A.H. 1296 (Dastour, Vol. IV) and also in the law of 17th Nissan 1330 (1914) [2]). The provisions of these laws were, however, inadequate. In addition to the laws of the years 1296 and 1330 which dealt with expropriations by the State there was another law dealing with expropriations by the Municipalities dated 7th Rabi-el-Awal, A.H. 1332 (21 Kanun Sani 1329 (1914) [3]).

This law has been made applicable in Palestine by Public Notice No. 117 of 20th May, 1919, subject to the amendments that (a) the Civil Officer of the Villayet as the person whose consent is required to the scheme of expropriation was replaced by the Chief Administrator of the O.E.T.A.; (b) the power to nominate arbitrators which was vested prior to the occupation in the Mejlis Idara (General Council) of the Villayet in accordance with Art. 4 of the law of A.H. 1332 was vested in the Military Governor of the District; and (c) the right of recourse to the Court of Cassation given to the landowner under Art. 8 of the said law of the year A.H. 1332, was replaced by a right to appeal to the Court of Appeal in Palestine.

Public Notice No. 117 of 1919.

The several laws provided for assessment of compensation by different tribunals and, generally, in an unsatisfactory manner. The machinery set up by the Turks was complicated and made

---
[1]) See Chiha, op. cit., page 379.
[2]) See Translation of Turkish Laws prepared by the Ministry of Justice. Baghdad, 1921, p. 65.
[3]) Ibid., p. 62.

The Land Law of Palestine.

it possible for objectors to obstruct for a considerable period possession by the promoters of a scheme of the land required for carrying it out. The powers for acquiring land for public purposes were wide enough; the procedure, however, was extremely cumbersome and unworkable. One of the principal defects of the Ottoman legislation was the absence in the Law of a definition of "an undertaking of a public nature" and of a "promoter". There was, however, in the law reference to a variety of undertakings, like the construction of hospitals, schools, railways, etc. which made the public purposes wide enough [1]).

Compulsory Acquisition of Historical Sites. In the year 1920 machinery was set up by the Palestine Government for the compulsory acquisition of historical sites (Sec. 20 of the Antiquity Ordinance, 1920), and in the year 1921 provision was made for the compulsory acquisition of land required for the purposes of a Town Planning Scheme. Secs. 18, 19 and 20 of fhe Town Planning Ordinance, 1921, provided for the procedure and rate of expropriation. This Ordinance was amended in the year 1922 and further amended in the year 1929. Secs. 19 and 20 of the Town Planning (Amendment) Ordinance 1921—1929 deal with matters relating to the expropriation of land required for Town Planning Schemes.

In 1924 the Government of Palestine promulgated an Ordinance to provide for the Expropriation of land for Public Purposes. This Ordinance (the Expropriation of Land Ordinance, 1924) amended the Public Notice of May 1919. It was provided that the Public Notice of 1919 should not be deemed to restrict the purposes for which land may be expropriated outside Municipal areas, and that the procedure of Expropriation for all purposes should be that prescribed by the Ottoman Law of the 7th Rabi-el-Awal 1332 (1914) as amended by the Public Notice of 1919, subject to the provisions of the Acquisition of Land for the Army Ordinance, 1920, and the Town Planning Ordinance, 1921.

In 1925 the Mining Ordinance was published dealing with the compulsory acquisition of land required for mining purposes.

Acquisition of Land for the Army. In 1920 came the Acquisition of Land for the Army Ordinance. This Ordinance was replaced in 1925 by a more comprehensive Ordinance dealing with expropriation for the purposes both of the Army and Air Force, modelled on English Statutes as to Compulsory Acquisition of Land for Public Purposes.

---

[1]) See Chiha, p. 375.

Chapter XIX—Expropriation of Land.

The main provisions of the Acquisition of Land for the Army and Air Force Ordinance 1925 are:

(1) The land to be acquired must be required for the purposes of the Army or the Air Force.

(2) The land may be acquired by absolute purchase or by the acquisition of possession or use for a definite period.

(3) If the Officer Commanding shall fail to come to terms with the owner of the land, Notices to Treat approved by the High Commissioner may be served.

(4) If there is no agreement as to the amount of compensation the Officer Commanding may enter into immediate possession of the land.

(5) In default of agreement as to compensation an Arbitration Board is to assess the compensation in accordance with certain rules set out in the Ordinance.

(6) The compensation may be paid into Court.

(7) A compulsory lease cannot exceed the term of 21 years.

(8) If the land is not required for the purposes of the Army and Air Force, it may be sold; in this case the former owner has a right of pre-emption on paying the sum agreed upon or awarded as compensation together with the value of any improvement made upon the land since the occupation of it by the Army or Air Force.

The Expropriation of Land Ordinance 1926. A more comprehensive Ordinance based on the Acqusition of Land for the Army and Air Force Ordinance, 1925, but dealing with expropriation in general was, however, published in 1926. This was the Expropriation of Land Ordinance No. 28, 1926, which repealed the Ottoman Legislation dealing with expropriation of land, the Public Notice of 1919 and the Expropriation Ordinance 1924 and Sec. 20 of the Antiquity Ordinance 1920. Provision was made later by Sec. 13 (c) of the Antiquity Ordinance 1929 for the acquisition of historical sites (or a lease thereof) in accordance with the provisions of the Expropriation Ordinance in force from time to time. Sec. 25 of the 1926 Ordinance provides for the saving of the following laws concerning expropriation: (1) the Town Planning Ordinance 1921 (now 1921-1929); (2) The Mining Ordinance 1925 (now 1925—33); (3) The Acquisition of land for the Army and Air Force Ordinance 1925.

The 1926 Ordinance if compared with the Ottoman Laws of Expropriation does not enlarge the purposes for which the compulsory acquisition of land may be made. But there are in the Ordinance two fundamental principles which should be pointed out:

The Land Law of Palestine.

(1) The Ordinance enables the promoters of an undertaking of a public nature which has been so certified by the High Commissioner to obtain the land without delay; and

(2) Compensation in default of an agreement is to be determined by the Land Court of the District in which the property is situate.

In principle the Expropriation Ordinance 1926 follows the procedure for expropriation established in England under the Lands' Clauses Consolidation Act 1845, though modified and simplified and subject to alterations often derived from later English enactments. We shall now proceed to give a summary account of the Ordinance.

Definition of Land. In Sec. 2 we find a broad definition of "land" which is made to include land of any category or tenure and any building, tree or other thing fixed in the land and any portion of the sea, or shore or a river and any easement in or over land and water. This definition is wider and more detailed than the definition of "land" contained in the Transfer of Land Ordinance 1920—1921 and in the Interpretation Ordinance 1929, particularly as regards the inclusion in the definition of the sea, shore, river and easement in or over land or water; it follows the wider definition contained in the Acquisition of Land for the Army and Air Force Ordinance 1925.

It would appear that buildings cannot be expropriated save with the land on which they stand. Though the definition of the term "land" is wide enough and includes "land of any tenure", it would appear that this definition would not cover the lease of land, otherwise there would have been no necessity for the special power which is provided for in Sec. 19 to obtain compulsory lease of land for a term of years instead of compulsory purchase, a power which is not always found in similar laws of other countries but which in England has been found of great utility. The lease cannot, however, exceed in any case 21 years.

The inclusion of this power of compulsory lease is a benefit rather than a greater burden on the land owner and is also a benefit to the State. When land is occupied by a promoter of a scheme of a public nature and there is no intention that the land shall be diverted permanently from its previous use though for some years public interest requires the land to be taken for some public purpose, it is more satisfactory to give only temporary use of the land at a fair rent. Provision is made in Sec. 10 (5) for the rent to be assessed by the Land Court.

Chapter XIX—Expropriation of Land.

"The Promoters" are defined to include the Government, a Municipality or a Local Council or any other Local Authority, or any person, whether a Company or a private person executing an undertaking of a public nature (Sec. 2). *Definition of Promoter and of Undertaking.*

"Undertaking" is defined to mean any undertaking of a public nature which shall have been certified by the High Commissioner as such (Sec. 2).

The intention would appear to have been to make the scope of the 1926 Ordinance cover all expropriations whether directly for the Government or for the purposes of any public authority including concessionnaires, subject only to the provisions relating to expropriation under the, enactments with regard to which saving has been provided by Sec. 25. It was, however, doubtful whether the wording of the Ordinance, particularly the definitions of "Undertaking" and "Promoters" (though the later expression was defined in wide terms by Sec. 2), when read together with the provisions of Sec. 3 of the Ordinance, should not be limited to undertakings involving works of a "public nature" in the sense of Government (or other public authorities) activities only. It was arguable that other undertakings which are not of a public nature in that sense, such as undertakings by concessionnaires, were not covered by the definitions contained in Sec. 2. This doubt has been removed by Sec. 2 of the Expropriation of Land (Amendment) Ordinance 1932 which is so worded as to cover any kind of a development scheme including works for which concessions have been granted. *The Expropriation of Land (Amendment) Ordinance 1932.*

The amended Sec. 2 reads:

"Undertaking" means any undertaking certified by the High Commissioner to be of a Public nature and any undertaking under a concession granted by the High Commissioner according to the terms of which land as herein defined may be expropriated for the purposes of the concession".

The amended Sec. 3 reads:—

"Subject to the provisions of this Ordinance it shall be lawful for the promoters of any undertaking to treat and agree with the owner of any land required by them for the undertaking and with all persons having an interest in such land either for the absolute purchase thereof or for the possession or use thereof for a definite period, or for the acquisition of any easement required for the purpose of the undertaking".

Certain observations on the legislation dealing with the expropriation of land in England and particularly with regard to the question *Expropriation of Land in England.*

whether it is possible to expropriate land for the benefit of a private person or of a private company are relevant. In general, it would appear that the principle of eminent domain, that is the right of the sovereign body to take land which is required for public purposes, has been more fully explored as a constitutional doctrine in the United State than in England. But, as a matter of practice, the principle has been familiar in England at any rate since the latter part of the eighteenth century. It is best exemplified in the Lands' Clauses Consolidation Act, 1845, which is a "clauses" Act collating the provisions of a large number of private and local Acts, which resulted from the new movement in public health, railway transport and so forth, in the eighteen-thirties and eighteen-forties. At that date Parliament, while prepared to confer powers of compulsory purchase both on the forerunners of the present-day local authorities (Commissioners of Sewers, etc.) and on commercial public utility undertakings (railways, waterworks, etc.), jealously reserved to itself the power to decide what actual land should be liable to expropriation, and as a consequence the precise description of the land in question was scheduled in the Bill. Since 1845, driven by practical considerations of time and expense, Parliament has considerably relaxed that principle. Under the public health legislation of the middle of the century, culminating in the Public Health Act, 1875, land can be acquired by a local authority for public health purposes by means of a provisional order made by the Minister, on the application of the authority, and confirmed by Parliament. Here Parliamentary control is retained, but the procedure by way of provisional order is simpler and cheaper then that by way of private Bill.

About the beginning of the present century a further and important step was taken by permitting the compulsory acquisition of land by means of orders made by the acquiring local authority, and confirmed by the Minister, but not submitted to Parliament at all. This "departmental order" procedure has now become almost common form in the case of local authorities, though for some important purposes, notably public health and road making, the provisional order procedure is still operative.

As regards public utility undertakers, the provisional order procedure was adopted in the case of gas and water undertakings by an Act of 1878, and in the case of electricity by an Act of 1899. Railway companies still have to go to Parliament for a Bill if they wish to obtain fresh compulsory powers of acquiring land.

Chapter XIX—Expropriation of Land.

As regards the possibility of land being compulsory acquired by some Government Department on behalf of a private undertaking, there are two cases which present some analogy (1) it appears that the Secretary of State for War has power to buy land compulsorily for the purposes of a territorial association, and (2) under the English housing legislation a County Council can buy land compulsorily by means of an order, made by the Council and confirmed by the Minister, for the purposes of a public utility society, whose objects include the erection of working-class houses. These societies are, however, bodies which limit the rate of interest for dividend payable on their capital, and are in substance charitable concerns. It would appear that a power of compulsory acquisition on behalf of some body which is not itself an organ of Government, whether central or local, has never been granted, except in the case of bodies whose objects are public or charitable and not primarily profit making.

The criterion of profit making or not profit making does not, of course, apply to the commercial public utility undertakings, but the principle underlying that case is plainly the fact that the particular undertaking, whether it be a railway, a waterworks, or dock, can only be established if the promoters secure the particular land which they require. It might well be convenient for any commercial concern to have power to extend its operations by compulsorily buying land adjoining to its works. No application to Parliament appears ever to have been made for the purposes and if such an application were made and granted, an entirely new principle would, so far as England is concerned, be established.

Certain provisions of the Agricultural Land (Utilisation) Act, 1931, are relevant. The general effect of Part II of that Act is to empower the Minister to provide small holdings and allotments for unemployed persons, and he has been given powers of compulsory acquisition of land in this connection. Under Section 7, the Minister can provide demonstration small holdings, and any land acquired for this purpose may be occupied and managed by such local authorities, societies or persons as the Minister may appoint as his agents. Section 13 (5) of the Act empowers the Minister to delegate his powers in connection with providing allotments (except the power of acquiring or disposing of land) to any local Council or to any Society having as its object or one of its objects the provision for the profitable working of allotments. Thus the Minister could purchase land compulsorily (1) for a Society to run as a demonstration small holding; or (2) for an Allotments Society

The Land Law of Palestine.

to provide allotments with. These powers have never, in fact, been exercised.

Acquisition by Agreement.

It would appear from the wording of Sec. 5 of the Expropriation Ordinance 1926 that expropriation should be proceeded by a genuine effort to acquire by agreement. It is only when the promoters of an undertaking have failed to come to terms with the owner that the land required for the undertaking becomes subject to the expropriation proceedings. After the High Commissioner has certified that the undertaking is of a public nature a Notice to Treat is served upon the owner in the manner prescribed in Sec. 5 (4) of the Ordinance. Every Notice to Treat must be drawn up in the form set out in the Regulations made under Sec. 24 of the Expropriation Ordinance published in O.G. No. 172 of 1926 and must be approved by the High Commissioner. It would appear, however, that the High Commissioner may delegate his power in connection with the approval and signature of the Notices to Treat. This is in accordance with the provisions of Sec. 19 (1) of the Interpretation Ordinance, 1929, which empowers the High Commissioner to depute any person by name, or the person holding an office to exercise any powers or perform any duties prescribed in any Ordinance.

Notice to Treat.

A Notice to Treat must relate to land which is within the project certified by the High Commissioner as an undertaking of a public nature. The usual practice, in accordance with the Regulations, is that a certificate by the High Commissioner to the effect that the undertaking is of a public nature should be issued only after production of a plan shewing the land comprised within the undertaking.

It is not necessary for the ownership of the land which is expropriated to be ascertained before the expropriation proceedings are carried out. By Sec. 5 (4) of the Ordinance a Notice to Treat shall be served on all the persons interested in the land and by Sec. 15 when the compensation has been assessed, if the persons entitled to the compensation cannot be found, or if the persons claiming to be entitled failed to make out a title, the promoters may pay the compensation into Court and they are by such payment entirely discharged from all liability in respect of the compensation awarded. This provision enables promoters to avoid delay in the procedure of expropriation. The Notice to Treat, therefore, may be served on such persons as after ordinary enquiry are found to be interested in the land as owners, mortgagees or otherwise, and if there is doubt whether these persons represent all the parties

Chapter XIX—Expropriation of Land.

interested in the land, the promoter is to pay into Court the sum assessed as compensation.

If all the parties interested in the land are not known, it will be impossible to come to an agreement as to the price to be paid as compensation for the land, and the question, therefore, of compensation will have to be referred to the Land Court in accordance with Sec. 7 of the Ordinance [1]).

The amount of compensation to be paid by the promoter may be determined by agreement between the promoter and the parties having an interest in the land (Sec. 6).

Under Sec. 7 (a) of the Ordinance the promoter can enter into immediate possession of the land if on the expiration of 15 days from the service of the Notice to Treat the promoter and the owner have not agreed as to the compensation payable. If the owner does not voluntarily vacate the land, an order of possession must be obtained from the President of the Land Court (Sec. 2 in part dealing with the definition of "The Court") and Sec. 7 (a). *Entry into Possession.*

In default of agreement, the amount of compensation payable by the promoter is to be determined by the Land Court in whose jurisdiction the land is situate (Sec. 8). Under the Acquisition of Land for the Army and Air Force Ordinance, 1925, an Arbitration Board was constituted in whom the right to assess compensation was vested. It is possible that for army purposes it is expedient to entrust such a function to an Arbitration Board; for ordinary public purposes, however, the principle adopted by the Expropriation Ordinance, 1926, is more correct as it is always preferable to vest the powers dealing with the right of property in the regular judicial authority. In assessing compensation the Court is to act in accordance with the Rules set out in Secs. 10, 12, 13. *Assessment of Compensation by Land Court.*

10. In assessing compensation, the Court shall act in accordance with the following rules:

(1) No allowance shall be made on account of the acquisition being compulsory.

(2) The value of the land shall, subject as hereinafter provided, be taken to be the amount which the land if sold in the open market by a willing seller might be expected to realise.

Provided that the Court in assessing such compensation shall assess the same according to the value of the land on the said basis

---

[1]) Where there are several owners of the land a separate action against each is not necessary. Bayside Land Corporation v. Segal L.A. No. 71/32. Palestine Post 9 March 1934.

at the time when the same was or under the provisions of this Ordinance could have been entered upon by the promoters without regard to any improvements or works made thereon subsequent to such date by the promoters or the owners or any other person, and

Provided further that the Court in assessing such compensation shall be entitled to consider all returns and assessments for capital or rental value for taxation made by or acquiesced in by the claimant.

(3) The special suitability or adaptability of the land for any purpose shall not be taken into account if it is a purpose to which it could be applied only in pursuance of powers derived from legislation or for which there is no market apart from the special needs of a particular purchaser or the requirements of the promoters.

Provided that any bona fide offer for the purchase of the land, made before the passing of this Ordinance which may be brought to the notice of the Court shall be taken into consideration.

(4) Where the land is and but for the compulsory acquisition would continue to be devoted to a purpose of such a nature that there is no general demand or market for land for that purpose, the compensation may, if the Court is satisfied that reinstatement in some other place is bona fide intended, be assessed on the basis of the reasonable cost of such equivalent reinstatement.

(5) In assessing the rent to be paid for the lease of land, the Court shall assess the same on the basis that the said rent shall be a reasonable return to the owner on the capital value of the land assessed in accordance with the provisions of the preceding sub-sections hereof.

(6) The Court shall assess the compensation to be paid by way of damage for the imposition of any easement or other restraint on the exercise of any rights incidental to ownership on the basis of the amount by which the value of the land assessed in accordance with the preceding sub-sections hereof shall have been diminished by reason of the imposition of such easement or restraint.

(7) The Court shall also have regard to

(a) the damage (if any) caused by the severance of the land acquired from other land belonging to the person entitled to compensation by reason of the undertaking; and

(b) the enhancement or depreciation in value of other land belonging to the person entitled to compensation by reason of the undertaking.

(8) Such enhancement or depreciation in value shall be set off against or added to the amount of the value of the land and

Chapter XIX — Expropriation of Land.

the damage thereto assessed by the Court under the provisions of this Ordinance[1]).

12. (1) If part only of any lands comprised in any lease or otherwise subject to any rent or any annual or other payment or incumbrance be acquired under this Ordinance, such rent, payment or incumbrance may be apportioned by agreement between the promoters and the persons entitled thereto or to the land subject thereto, or in case no such agreement be made the same shall be apportioned by the Court.

(2) After such apportionment the apportioned part only of such rent, payment or incumbrance shall be payable out of the residue of the said lands, and all conditions, agreements, powers, and remedies in respect of such rent, payment or incumbrance shall remain in force in respect of the residue of the said lands.

13. (1) Where any damage has been sustained by reason of any undertaking executed in or upon lands acquired under this Ordinance and such damage has not been agreed upon or otherwise determined prospectively, compensation shall be paid when the works have been done and shall be determined by the Court in the manner prescribed under this Ordinance or as near thereto as circumstances admit.

(2) In determining the amount of compensation payable regard shall be had to any increase in the value of the land by reason of any improved drainage and other advantage derived from the undertaking.

Appeal by any party against the decision of the Land Court regarding compensation lies as of a right to the Court of Appeal within 15 days of the notification of the judgment if the award exceeds £P.200 (Sec. 11).

Special provision is made as regards costs. Sec. 15 permits payment into Court by the promoters if the persons entitled thereto cannot be found or fail to make out a title. In a recent case before the Court of Appeal[2]) it was held that where a claimant's title has not been challenged until after judgment awarding compensation it is then too late to invoke the assistance of Sec. 15 which presupposes that a title to land has always been in issue.

---

[1]) The provisions of Subsections (1) to (4) reproduce with slight changes those of Sec. 2 (1) (2) (3) (5) of the English Acquisition of land (Assessment of Compensation) Act 1919. Subsec. (7) (a) is derived from Sec. 63 of the Lands' Clauses Consolidation Act 1845.

[2]) Att. Gen. v. Salah, L.A. 29/33. Palestine Post 20 July 1934.

The Land Law of Palestine.

Withdrawal of Notice to Treat.

A Promoter is allowed under Sec. 16 of the Ordinance to withdraw the Notice to Treat served upon the owner. This power is, however, limited by the following conditions:

(a) The promoter must serve upon the owner a further notice - a Notice of Withdrawal;

(b) He remains liable for damages sustained by any interested person in consequence of the service of the Notice to Treat;

(c) The Notice of Withdrawal, like the Notice to Treat, must be approved by the High Commissioner;

(d) The notice must be given within three months after the service of the Notice to Treat or within six weeks after the delivery by the claimant of the claim for compensation or for rent whichever date shall be later.

The amount of the damage is to be determined by the Land Court in like manner as other compensation.

The 1926 Ordinance does not contain any provision for the cancellation of a certificate given by the High Commissoner certifying that an undertaking is of a public nature. It may be inferred, however, from the provisions of Sec. 16 that such a cancellation is possible. Otherwise no withdrawal of the Notice to Treat could be effected. If the promoters serve a Notice of Withdrawal it means that they have abandoned the undertaking. Unless the certificate is cancelled, the value of the land included in the certificate is adversely affected and it is, therefore, for the promoters to ensure that the certificate is cancelled before or simultaneously with the Notice of Withdrawal being submitted for the High Commissioner's approval.

The land taken by the expropriation becomes vested in the promoters on payment of compensation. A certificate of the Court that the compensation awarded has been duly paid shall be sufficient authority to the Director of Lands, to cause the necessary entries to be made in the Land Registers (Sec. 17).

Sec. 18 of the Ordinance, gives the promoters power with authority from the High Commissioner to divert roads, to alter the level of any road, sewer, drain or pipe; to alter the course or level of any river, stream or water course, subject to their liability for the payment of compensation for any damage done by them to the interested parties.

Promoters have power to sell the land which is no longer required for the purpose of the undertaking. In such a case the former owner if he is still alive has a right of pre-emption on paying back the sum awarded or agreed upon as compensation

Chapter XIX—Expropriation of Land.

with the value of improvements made upon the land by the promoters. The right of pre-emption is to be exercised within one month of notice by the promoters to the previous owner of the intended sale (Sec. 20). The right of pre-emption under Sec. 20 of the Ordinance, appears to be a personal right of the former owner which does not pass to his legal heirs. With the death of the former owner of the land the right of pre-emption lapses.

Gratuitous expropriation as an exception to the principle of expropriation by payment of compensation is allowed for widening of an existing road (Sec. 22). This Section does not speak of "promoters". The power is given only to: (a) the Government and (b) to a Municipality. It would appear, therefore, that the power is not given to a Local Council, neither is it given to any other local authority (except a Municipality) or to a private person or Company. Local Councils, however, (through the Local Commissions of Town Planning) would appear to be vested with a similar power (of expropriation without compensation) under the provisions of the Town Planning Ordinances, since Sec. 22 of the Ordinance of 1921 in the form in which it is re-enacted by the Town Planning (Amendment) Ordinance 1929 allows expropriation of land included in a town planning scheme for the purpose of constructing, diverting or widening of roads. _{Gratuitous Expropriation for Widening of Roads.}

The right of Government or Municipality to expropriate land without payment of compensation under the Expropriation Ordinance 1926 exists only where the land is taken for the purpose of widening of an existing road. If a new road is contemplated, gratuitous expropriation is not possible. From the expression used in the first part of Sec. 22 "...Where any land is taken under this Ordinance..." it would appear that if the Government or the Municipality desire to apply the provisions of Sec. 22 the High Commissioner's certificate is required.

Gratuitous expropriation under the Expropriation Ordinance can be required only if the amount by which the road is widened on each side of the centre line of the road is equal unless the alignment of the road is altered. If this condition is not complied with compensation is payable to the owner of the land. Compensation is only payable if the area taken exceeds one quarter of the whole area of the plot. Where the land taken is less than one quarter of the total area of the plot compensation is payable only in a case of hardship. It is doubtful whether when the area is taken exceeds one quarter of the area of the plot compensation is payable only for the area in excess or for the whole of the plot. The most probable inference appears to be that compensation must in that case be paid for the whole area expropriated. In the Town Planning (Amendment) Ordinance 1929 explicit provision to the contrary is made, but this has little bearing upon the interpretation of the section now under discussion.

Sec. 22 of the Expropriation Ordinance refers to "any land" taken for the widening of "any existing road". The principle of gratuitous expropriation under the 1926 Ordinance is, therefore, not limited to land taken within urban areas and roads outside towns are also subject to this rule. Again, nothing is stated in Sec. 22 of the 1926 Ordinance as to the situation if the land taken is not taken equally on either side. It must be assumed that in such a case compensation is payable. The principle of gratuitous expropriation is an exception to the rule of expropriation by compensation and, therefore, must be interpreted in a limited sense. If all the land taken for widening of an existing road is taken from one owner and the alignment of the road is not changed in such a case the owner has a right to compensation even though the land taken does not exceed 1/4 of his plot.

In certain respects the provisions of the 1926 Ordinance differ substantially from those of Sec. 22 of the Town Planning Ordinance 1921 as now re-enacted by the Town Planning (Amendment) Ordinance 1929. Under the latter Section it is competent for the responsible authority to expropriate without compensation any land which is included in a town planning scheme which is required for the purpose of constructing, diverting or widening any road or street included in the scheme. Gratuitous expropriation is, therefore, not limited to the widening of an existing road as under the Expropriation Ordinance 1926, and this section expressly provides that where more than one quarter of the area of the plot is taken compensation is to be paid only for the land taken in excess of such quarter.

Width and Alignment of Road Ordinance 1926—7.
Reference in this connection should further be made to the Width and Alignment of Roads Ordinance 1926 amended by Ordinance No. 23 of 1927 [1]). The High Commissioner is thereby authorised:

(a) to prohibit the carrying out of permanent works as there defined within ten metres from the centre of any road;

---

[1]) O.G. No. 194 of 1st September 1927. There was an amendment Ordinance No. 8 of 1927 but this Ordinance was disallowed. See O.G. No. 188 of 1st June 1927.

Chapter XIX—Expropriation of Land.

(b) to make orders for the widening of roads and to expropriate lands accordingly. The expropriation is to take place in accordance with the provisions of the law of Expropriation (for roads) in force from to time. The provisions of Sec. 22 of the Expropriation Ordinance 1926 are, therefore, applicable.

It should also be mentioned that under Sec. 19 of the Town Planning Ordinance 1921 in the form in which it was re-enacted by the Town Planning Ordinance of 1929 no certificate is required from the High Commissioner as to the public nature of the town planning scheme before expropriation.

The reason would appear to be that an approved town planning scheme is by itself considered an undertaking of a public nature giving power to the responsible authority to proceed with the expropriation of land required for carrying out of the scheme in accordance with the Law of Expropriation in force.

Sec. 23 of the 1926 Ordinance maintains the right given by the Ottoman Law of Expropriation by Municipalities to recover an improvement charge from the owners of surrounding property where the value of the property has been increased by the widening (or construction) of a road by Government or Municipality. The Ottoman Law provided a betterment tax of $1/4$ of the increased value. The charge is a contribution towards the cost of the work. In practice the betterment tax is levied by the Municipality in relation to the cost of the improvement. And it appears that a betterment charge can be imposed on a person whose property is increased in value even though no land has been taken from him for the purpose of making a new road or widening of an existing road. *[marginal note: Betterment Charge.]*

This section makes it clear that there can be no gratuitous expropriation from a person on whom betterment is imposed. It is provided in Sec. 23 (1) (proviso) that when a betterment charge is imposed under this Section upon the owner whose property has been increased in value by the widening of a road, compensation should be paid for any land taken for the purpose of the widening and the amount of compensation may be set off against the contribution due under this Section.

The principle of setting off the value of the land taken gratuitously against the contribution due by the owner for betterment is adopted also in Sec. 22 of the Town Planning Ordinance 1921 in the form in which it was re-enacted in 1929 in the case of land taken under a Town Planning Scheme.

The Land Law of Palestine.

The provisions of Sec. 23 of the Expropriation of Land Ordinance 1926 with regard to the betterment charge where land has been taken for making or widening of roads may be summarized —

(a) The making of a new road or widening of an existing road must be within a Municipal or Town Planning area;

(b) The land must increase in value;

(c) The right to recover a betterment tax is vested only in the Government or in a Municipality. Other promoters are not entitled to recover a betterment tax;

(d) The claim for a betterment charge must be made within one year of the execution of the work;

(e) The betterment tax which is a contributon towards the cost of the work cannot exceed $1/4$ of the amount of increase in the value of the land;

(f) When a betterment tax is imposed, compensation is payable for any land taken for the purpose of widening of a road, notwithstanding the provisions of Sec. 22 as to gratuitous expropriation for widening of roads;

(g) The amount of compensation payable may be set off against the betterment tax;

(h) Any question whether any land has increased in value and as to the amount of such increase will be determined in default of an agreement by a single arbitrator appointed by the Chief Justice;

(i) The betterment tax is payable in not less than four equal annual instalments and is recoverable as a civil debt by the promoter from the owner of the land.

Expropriation from Persons under disability (Companies, Guardians and Waqfs). Persons under disability, and particularly any Company or trustee, guardian or curator may under Sec. 4 of the Expropriation of Land Ordinance, 1926, and notwithstanding anything to the contrary in any Law, Memorandum or Articles of Association, or other document, sell, lease, or otherwise dispose of land or any interest in land to the Promoters. Sec. 4 has been designed to overcome the difficulties in connection with disabilities in the Law or in the Statutes of any Company as to the sale, lease or exchange of land. This Section should be read together with Sec. 2 (the part dealing with the definition of "land") and Sec. 21 of the Ordinance which provide for the application of the expropriation proceedings to Waqf lands of any category or tenure as well as to land which is subject to a religious, charitable or the like trusts. The Mutwally

Chapter XIX—Expropriation of Land.

of a waqf, the trustee of a trust, in general, the person or authority responsible for the administration of the trust or Waqf are, like other owners of land, enabled to treat with the promoters.

The provisions of Sec. 21 of the 1926 Ordinance are similar to the provisions of Sec. 22 of the Acquisition of Land for the Army and Air Force Ordinance, 1925. In general, it was possible to expropriate a Waqf even under the Ottoman Law. When the parties were not willing to proceed under expropriation proceedings the transaction usually took the form of an "exchange" in accordance with the provisions of the Sharia Law by applying the so called "Tarikat el Istibdal". Such a transaction, however, required the permission of the Qadi and the Supreme Moslem Council (Sec. 8 (2) of the Regulations for the Supreme Moslem Sharia Council of 1921).

CHAPTER XX — TOWN PLANNING.

Town Planning before the Occupation.
Until 1921 there was no Town Planning Law in Palestine. Town Planning good, bad or indifferent did, however, take place before the Occupation.

The Ottoman Law of 1891 [1]) concerning the construction and alignment of streets provided for the taking of land in Municipal Areas for the laying out of new streets or the widening of existing streets without payment to the owners of the land wherever the land has not been already built upon [2]). The expropriation provisions of the Law of 1891 implied the taking of land without payment except where more than one-quarter of the land of the owner is taken for the purpose of the street (Art. 8).

Under the Ottoman Law of 1877 [3]) the Municipalities possessed certain powers with regard to the construction of buildings and the widening and the arrangement of streets [4]).

In April 1918 a Military Proclamation was issued forbidding building in the neighbourhood of Jerusalem without permit.

In a country such as Palestine with a rapidly increasing population, the need of town planning is very great in order to avoid wasteful and unsatisfactory development of new quarters, to provide for laying out of open spaces and gardens and for the gradual reconstruction of such parts of existing towns as are congested and insanitary. The principle of systematic planning of towns as an essential part of the development of a country and an important factor in promoting the health and prosperity of the inhabitants is now recognized in all countries of America and Europe. In England a special Town Planning Department has been attached to the Ministry of Health in London.

---

[1]) Young, op. cit., Vol. VI, pp. 137 ff. (Règlement 18 Moharrem 1309).
[2]) Ibid., Arts. 8, 12 and 18.
[3]) Young, op. cit., Vol. I, pp. 69 ff. (Loi 27 Ramadan 1294 and amendments of A.H. 1304 (1886), of A.H. 1308 (1890) and of A.H. 1330 (1912)). See also the Bagdad Collection.
[4]) Ibid., Arts. 3, 39, 46, 47, 62 and 53. See also Young, op. cit., Vol. IV, pp. 246-252, for the Regulations concerning Roads of A.H. 1286 (1869), of A.H. 1304 (1887) and of A.H. 1312 (1895).

Chapter XX—Town Planning.

In Palestine the principle has been established that the Government should control the growth and laying out of the towns and should see that they develop in a healthy and orderly manner.

A Town Planning Ordinance was, indeed, among the earliest Ordinances enacted by the High Commissioner upon the establishment of Civil Government in Palestine in 1920. This was the Town Planning Ordinance 1921 [1]) based upon the English Housing and Town Planning Act 1909 [2]). It is stated in the Preamble, to be enacted in order "to secure the orderly planning of towns and to control the erection of buildings and the laying out of streets within certain areas with a view to securing the proper development of such areas in the interests of public health, the amenity of the neighbourhood and the general welfare of the community". The Principal Ordinance has been twice amended, namely by Ordinances of 1922 [3]) and 1929 [4]). Rules, Instructions and Bye-Laws were issued in 1923, 1925, 1927, 1929, 1930, 1932 and 1934.

The Town Planning Ordinance 1921—9.

The general scheme of these enactments and their main provisions will now be discussed.

Under Sec. 1. of the Principal Ordinance a Central Building and Town Planning Commission is set up. The function of this Commission is to watch the broader aspects of Town Planning and to bring influence to bear on the Local Commissions in respect of the larger issues which the Local Commissions, harrassed by the problems and requirements of the moment, are most liable to overlook. The Central Commission is also charged with the duty of control of plans of town development and general supervision over the execution of the town planning schemes of Local Commissions.

Central and Local Commissions.

Upon the application of the Central Commission any area may be declared by the High Commissioner to be a Town Planning Area, and provision is made by the Principal Ordinance (Secs. 4—6, amended in 1922) for the establishment of a Local Commission in every such area, the arrangements varying according

Town Planning Area.

---

[1]) Dated 14th January 1921. See Off. Gaz. 1st February 1921.

[2]) The Act of 1909 and various subsequent enactments were repealed so far as they related to Town Planning by the Consolidating Act of 1925 which has in turn been repealed by the Town and Country Planning Act 1932 which is now the operative enactment in England and Scotland.

[3]) Town Planning (Amendment) Ordinance No. 16 of 1922.

[4]) Town Planning (Amendment) Ordinance No. 36 of 1929.

as the area does or does not include the site of a town having a Municipality. if it does include such a town the Local Commission is established by the Municipal Council and when established it is a body independent of the Council but the Council is always adequately represented upon it (Sec. 4 (1) amended in 1922).

In an area not possessing a Municipality the powers and duties of the Local Town Planning Commission are to be exercised and performed by the Central Commission and the powers and duties of a Municipality are to be exercised by the Central Commission unless delegated by it to the Local Commission (Sec. 6).

<small>Powers in a Town Planning Area.</small>
Even in the absence of a Town Planning scheme for the area the Local Commission possesses certain powers and duties under Sec. 35 of the Principal Ordinance [1]. No street may be laid out or constructed nor any building erected, pulled down, reconstructed or structurally repaired within a town planning area unless a permit to that effect has been first obtained from the Local Commission. The Ordinance of 1922 gives to a Local Commission permission to delegate to a sub-committee of itself the power to grant permits and by Sec. 7 of the Principal Ordinance the Central Commission is empowered to make rules and bye-laws and to prescribe fees for grant of permits. This section further indicated that the object of the regulations as to permits is to secure "adequate width and construction of streets, the stability, ventilation and sanitation of all new buildings, and the stability of any structural repair or alteration of any existing building". Rules as to plans, application and grant of permits and the fees payable have been issued by the Central Commission [2] and a body of Model Bye-laws [3] has been published to be brought into force in whole or in part in any town planning area when adopted by the Local Commission. Sec. 37 gives a right of appeal to the Central Commission to any person aggrieved by the refusal of the Local Commission to grant a permit to construct streets or build or repair buildings. Those who carry out work for which a permit is required without having obtained a permit or in contravention of the bye-laws are liable to a pecuniary penalty and "shall be required to demolish the work or pay the cost of demolition" (Sec. 38). As to jurisdiction see Sec. 4

---

[1] The Section appears strangely out of place in its present position in the Ordinance.

[2] O.G. No. 95 of 15th July 1923; No. 152 of 1st December 1925; No. 191 of 16th July 1927.

[3] O.G. No. 150 of 1st November 1925; O.G. No. 261 of 16th June 1930; and P.G. 429 of 22nd March 1934.

of the Ordinance of 1922. In addition to their control over buildings and streets by issue of permits Local Commissions are further required by Sec. 8 of the Principal Ordinance to furnish the Central Commission with certain particulars as to the needs of the town and indications of the probable development of the neighbourhood. They may, with the consent of the Central Commission, require the Municipality to expropriate land, etc. for roads, housing, public gardens, etc., and the Municipality "shall expropriate such lands accordingly".

If a Local Commission has been constituted for a Municipal Area, the powers and duties possessed by Municipal Councils under the Ottoman law of 27 Ramadan A.H. 1294 as to construction of buildings and streets became thenceforth exercisable by the Commission (Sec. 5). This Ottoman law and the amendments thereof are now declared by Sec. 133 of the Municipal Corporation Ordinance 1934 to have ceased to have effect in Palestine. The powers of Municipal Councils under the latter Ordinance include control of streets and buildings (Secs. 96—98). But the powers conferred by Secs. 96—98 are declared to be exercisable subject to the provisions of any other Ordinances or Law. It would, thus, appear that the Local Commissions under the Town Planning Ordinances are not affected by the provisions of the Municipal Corporation Ordinance 1934. Under Sec. 99 (6) of that Ordinance, however, the Municipal Council may make Bye-laws which shall be in force in any town-planning area which includes the Municipal area.

Sec. 4 (4) of the Principal Ordinance provides that the Local Commission is a Committee of the Municipality and its expenditure if approved by the Central Commission is deemed to be Municipal expenditure. A Municipality may, therefore, be burdened with expenditure required by the Central Commission (Cf. Sec. 8).

The constitution of the Local Commission in Municipal areas appears, however, to provide adequate safeguards against serious divergence of policy on the part of the Municipal Council and the Local Commission.

The Local Commission is established by the Municipal Council. The President of the Council is ex officio a member and may be Chairman (Sec. 4 (1) as amended by the Ordinance of 1922), two other members are nominated by the Council and the Municipal Engineer for the time being is also an ex officio member. Only two members can be nominated by the Central Commission. It is unlikely, therefore, that requirements of expenditure would be made to which the Municipality would be disinclined to consent.

Some questions may be raised as to the precise extent as to which the control of buildings and streets is placed under the jurisdiction of the Local Commissions to the exclusion of the Municipal Council. The words used in Sec. 5 of the Principal Ordinance which transfer the powers "so far as they relate to the construction of buildings and the widening and arrangement of streets" refer to the first two clauses ((a) and (b)) of Art. 3 of the Ottoman Law of A.H. 1294 which state that the duties of a Municipal Council include the supervision, etc. of the construction of buildings and the widening and arrangement of streets.

Those clauses are in the Ottoman Law followed by a statement of other matters connected with the streets, namely:—

(a) The construction of pavements and sewers;

(b) The construction and repair of public and private water supplies, etc.; but Sec. 5 does not transfer these from the Municipality to the Local Town Planning Commission. They remain under the control of the Municipality.

This is confirmed by other provisions in the Town Planning Ordinance. Thus Sec. 35 does not require the permit of the Commission for any alteration of a street or operation which may interfere with the street.

It is true that among the matters which a Town Planning scheme may include are drainage, lighting and water supply, and where a scheme is being carried out the Local Town Planning Commission, as distinct from the Municipality, has complete authority. Where, however, there is no scheme the Municipality keep control over such matters as the breaking up of streets for the purpose of carrying out work connected say with a Concession.

Preparation of Town Planning Schemes. The primary object of the Town Planning Ordinance is to secure the proper planning of areas and more especially of areas not yet fully developed. The arrangements now in force with regard to the preparation of Town Planning Schemes are those contained in the new Secs. 9—12 which by the effect of the Ordinance of 1929 have replaced the earlier Secs. 9—12 of the Principal Ordinance. A distinction has under these Sections to be drawn between an "outline" town planning scheme and a "detailed" scheme. Every Local Commission must within a time prescribed by the Central Commission submit to it an outline scheme. Such a scheme must make provision for all or any of the following matters as prescribed by the Central Commission:—

Chapter XX—Town Planning.

(a) construction, diversion, or alteration of streets, main roads, and communications and general building lines;

(b) drainage, including sewerage;

(c) water supply;

(d) the limitation of zones within which special trades and industries may be carried on or which are reserved exclusively for residential or other purposes;

(e) the imposition of conditions and restrictions in regard to the open space to be maintained about buildings and the particular height and character of buildings to be allowed in a specified area [1]).

It is, however, open to the Local Commission to prepare a detailed scheme or to adopt a detailed scheme prepared by the landowners. And Local Commissions may be required by the Central Commission acting on the application of the District Commissioner to prepare detailed schemes with reference to land within the town planning area. Detailed schemes are to deal not only with the matters already mentioned but may deal with any of the following also, namely:—

(a) the plotting out of land as building areas and sites;

(b) the allotment of land for roads, open spaces, gardens, schools, markets and public purposes of all kinds;

(c) dedication of roads to the public;

(d) arrangements for the disposal of refuse;

(e) lighting;

(f) the determination of the situation of buildings designed for specific use, and the demarcation of areas subject to restrictive conditions;

(g) the preservation of objects of archaeological interest or beauty, and the buildings or places used for religious purposes or cemeteries, or regarded with religious veneration;

(h) the abolition and reconstruction of overcrowded and congested areas;

(i) the control of the design of buildings;

---

[1]) In a prosecution before the Chief Magistrate of Jerusalem (Palestine Post 27th February 1933) the learned Magistrate took the view that a restriction on building operations over an entire area, to wit, the Mount of Olives, could not be imposed by an "outline" scheme under Sec. 9, but only by a scheme under Sec. 11. In the particular case a building had been erected without a permit contrary to the provisions of Sec. 38. The Court admitted that it was incumbent upon it to make an order for demolition though, in what were regarded by the Court as the special circumstances, the making of the order was postponed.

The Land Law of Palestine.

(j) the preservation of trees;

(k) the reconstitution of plots by the alteration of their boundaries or by combining, with the consent of the owners, two or more original plots held in separate ownership to be held in ownership in common;

(l) the allocation of plots to any owner dispossessed of land in furtherance of the scheme;

(m) the special powers to be vested in the Local Commission or responsible authority for the purpose of carrying out the general objects of the scheme;

(n) any special conditions for the exercise of such powers as regards notice or otherwise;

(o) the cost of the scheme and any provisions with regard to the recovery of betterment tax on land of which the value will be increased by the execution of the scheme (Sec. 10 (2)).

The scheme in all cases is to be accompanied by a plan of the area.

An interesting and valuable provision, Sec. 11 (2), authorizes the Central Commission notwithstanding the fact that land is already developed to require a town planning scheme to be made with respect to an area if it appears to the Commission that on account of the special archaeological interest in the natural beauty of a locality such a scheme is necessary with a view to preserving the character of the locality. The purpose of the scheme under this provision is apparently limited to the regulation of the space about buildings, the erection of new buildings, and the height and character of buildings [1].

Sec. 36 of the Principal Ordinance makes provisions to which we shall again refer as regards building within the area after a scheme has been approved, but by the new Sec. 12 such building is also regulated before approval of the scheme.

So soon as the Local Commission has published a notice that a scheme is in preparation the Central Commission may prescribe conditions for the grant of building permits and so soon as the scheme has been actually "deposited" no building permit can be granted by a Local Commission save in accordance with the scheme unless the approval of the Central Commission has been first obtained. Indeed, the Central Commission may, after deposit, prohibit the grant of any permit.

---

[1] Housing and Town Planning Act 1925 Sec. 1 (2).

Chapter XX—Town Planning.

The provisions relative to the approval of Schemes are contained in Secs. 13—17 of the Principal Ordinance. Copies of the scheme must be deposited at the office of the Local Commission and notice of deposit posted in the Municipal Offices or at some other public office within the area and published in the Gazette. Religious bodies whose property is affected by the scheme and any Commission established for the protection of holy sites in Palestine are to be notified of the deposit of the scheme in the case of any land which comprises or is in the neighbourhood of land belonging to a religious body or a holy site (Sec. 13). Persons interested in land affected by the scheme may lodge objections to the scheme as prescribed by rules and these are forwarded to be considered and answered by the Central Commission. Modification of the scheme may be made consequent upon such objections (Secs. 14, 15). The scheme is put into force by authority of the High Commissioner given upon application by the Central Commission made not earlier than two months from the publication of notice of deposit. It comes into force fifteen days after publication of the notice of approval (Secs. 16, 17).

Approval of Schemes.

So soon as a scheme is in force the Local Commission acquires very drastic powers as regards buildings and work in the area comprised in the scheme. Permits are not thenceforth to be granted unless the work contemplated fulfils the requirements of the scheme (Sec. 36 (1)) and the Commission may, and indeed if so required by the Central Commission, shall—

(a) remove, pull down, or alter any building or other work in the area comprised in the scheme or in the carrying out of which any provision of the scheme has not been complied with [1]);

(b) execute any work which it is the duty of any person to execute under the scheme in any case in which it appears that the delay in the execution of the work would prejudice the efficient operation of the scheme [2]).

Expenses incurred under the section may be recovered by the Local Commission in accordance with rules made by the Central Commission.

---

[1]) See Housing and Town Planning Act 1909 Sec. 57 (1) (a). But in that Act the powers are strictly limited to buildings and work which contravenes the scheme. Presumably a similar condition should be read into the Palestinian provisions.

[2]) Housing and Town Planning Act 1909 Sec. 57 (1) (b).

The Land Law of Palestine.

Expropriation.

Lands and buildings mentioned in the scheme as destined for expropriation may be expropriated at any time after the scheme has come into force [1]).

The expropriation is carried out in accordance with the Law in force from time to time concerning expropriation of land for public purposes, but no certificate of the High Commissioner is required that the Town Planning Scheme is an undertaking of public nature (Sec. 19).

Sec. 22 as enacted by the Amendment Ordinance of 1929 contains the following provisions as to the expropriation of land for roads :—

"It shall be competent for the responsible authority [2]) to expropriate without compensation any land which is included in a town planning scheme, and is required for the purpose of constructing, diverting or widening any road or street included in the scheme, provided that not more than one-quarter part of the area of the plot of any owner is so expropriated. If more than one-quarter of such area is taken, compensation shall be paid to the owner for the land taken in excess of such one-quarter part. Where a contribution for betterment is imposed under Sec. 27, the value of the land taken gratuitously shall be set off against the contribution due".

With the approval of the Central Commission owners of land taken for a scheme instead of being paid for the land expropriated may be given land in exchange (Sec. 21 (1)). In case of refusal by the owners to accept land offered in exchange, the question as to whether the owners should not be compelled to accept the land so offered instead of the money payment, is to be referred to a single arbitrator appointed by the Local Commission with the approval of the Central Commission (Secs. 21 (3) and 39).

Sec. 23 makes special provisions as to cases in which completion of expropriation is postponed (Sub-sec. 1) and authorizes the resale or reletting with the consent of the Central Commission

---

[1]) According to Sec. 13 of the Principal Ordinance the Municipality is to expropriate on the requisition of the Central Commission. The new Sec. 19 (Ordinance of 1929) says that "the responsible authority may proceed to the expropriation"

[2]) The term "responsible authority" is apparently borrowed from the English Act of 1925, though the term "authority" occurs in Sec. 24 (1) of the Principal Ordinance. It seems doubtful whether the Municipality or the Central Commission is to be treated as the "responsible authority" in Municipal areas. The expropriation is carried out by the Municipality (Sec. 18) but only at the instance of the Central Commission. Outside such areas the Central Commission is clearly the responsible authority (Sec. 6 (2)).

Chapter XX—Town Planning.

of any land expropriated (Sub-sec. 2). It is enacted rather oddly by way of proviso to this sub-section that dwelling houses expropriated for purposes of demolition are not to be evacuated until suitable accommodation for all residents therein is available within the Municipal area. It is also provided that the vendor of property purchased by private treaty or expropriated under a scheme is entitled to the first offer of sale thereof at a price not greater than the sum for which the same was purchased or expropriated. He is, however, to pay any addition of value resulting from the scheme. In case of dispute the price is fixed by arbitration (Sec. 23 (2) (b)).

According to Sec. 24 (1) the cost of a town-planning scheme includes: *Financial Provisions.*

(a) sums payable by the Local Commission under the Ordinance;

(b) sums spent or estimated to be spent by the Local Commission; and

(c) legal and technical expenses of the authority incurred in the making and in the execution of the scheme;

The provisions of the second sub-section of this section are less easily intelligible.

Sec. 24 (2) provides that if in any case the total of the value of the plots included in the final scheme exceeds the total of the values of the original plots, then the amount of such excess shall be deducted in arriving at the costs of the scheme as defined in sub-section (1) hereof.

These costs it is intended should be raised exclusively by a "betterment" tax, levied by the Local Commission on all owners of property (whether included in the scheme or not) which has increased in value by the preparation, making or execution of the Scheme. The recovery of the Betterment tax is regulated by Sec. 26 which gives to the Local Commission a right to recover one half of the increase in value from every person whose property has increased in value, and the right to do so does not appear to be conditional upon the existence of costs to be met by the money so recovered. Claims for the recovery of the betterment must be presented by the Local Commission within a year from the date at which the scheme is in force and questions as to the amount (if any) of the increase and the manner of payment are to be determined (by arbitration) "under the provisions of this Ordinance" (Sec. 26 (a) (b))[1]). It may appear to some a hazardous step to *Betterment Tax.*

---

[1]) The words "by arbitration" do not appear in the original issue of the Ordinance but were apparently omitted by error. They have been inserted by Mr. Bentwich in his compilation.

hand over the determination of all these questions to a single arbitrator appointed by a Local Commission (Sec. 39) but it is to be remarked that under the section of the English Act of 1909 which served as a model, such questions are left to the determination of a single arbitrator appointed by the Local Government Board [1]. Under the Amending Ordinance of 1922 sums recoverable in respect of increase of value are made payable by four annual instalments and are to be recoverable in the same manner as rates due to the Municipality. It is further provided that if the increase in value of the property is the consequence of expropriation of a portion of such property, the share of the increase to which the Municipality is entitled may be deducted from the expropriation price. The payment of any such sum shall liberate the person against whom it is assessed from any liability for increment value under Art. 12 of the Law of Expropriation dated 3rd February 1329 [2]).

Compensation for Injury. Any person whose property is injuriously affected by the scheme otherwise than by the expropriation thereof may, within three months from the date at which the scheme comes into force, by notice in writing served at the office of the Local Commission claim compensation in respect of such injury (Sec. 27). The amount of the compensation will, in default of agreement, be fixed by a single arbitrator appointed by the Local Commission. The section does not, however, state whether if the liability to pay compensation is disputed the same procedure is obligatory for the settlement of the dispute [3]).

The Principal Ordinance by the provisions of Secs. 28—30 materially reduces the scope of claims for injurious affectation.

By Sec. 28 it is provided that "No compensation shall be due in respect of any building erected, street laid out, or other thing done upon land comprised in this scheme after the date of the publication of the notice of deposit of the scheme" [4]).

Under Sec. 29 property is not deemed to be injuriously affected as a consequence of the scheme on account of any provisions

---

[1]) Housing and Town Planning Act 1909 Sec. 58 (4).

[2]) The Ottoman Law of Expropriation has now ceased to have effect in Palestine (Expropriation Ordinance 1926 Sec. 26 (1)). It may be assumed that the principle of liberation stated in the article must now be assumed to apply to betterment charges under the Expropriation Ordinance 1926.

[3]) In Sec. 58 (4) of the English Act of 1909 the question as to whether property is injuriously affected is to be determined by the single arbitrator.

[4]) Housing and Town Planning Act 1909 Sec. 58 (2).

Chapter XX—Town Planning.

inserted therein which prescribe the space about buildings to be erected or prescribe the height or character of the buildings if the provision is certified by the High Commissioner to be reasonable [1]) and under Sec. 30 (1) no compensation is payable in respect of any prohibition contained in the scheme against building on any land affected by the scheme whether such land is included in the scheme or not.

The severity, from the point of view of the landowner, of the provisions of Sec. 30 (1) is in part mitigated by the ensuing provisions of Sec. 30 (2). To obtain compensation, however, the landowner must prove one of the following propositions:

(a) That he has begun building operations on the said land prior to the date of the publication of the scheme, or

(b) That he has before such date actually made preparations, entered into contracts or negotiations or incurred expense in connection with any project for building on such lands; or

(c) That he bought the land with the express intention of building thereon at some date not more than 10 years prior to the publication of the said scheme, and has been prevented from so building on the said land by circumstances beyond his control.

In no case is the amount of compensation to amount to a larger sum than the actual pecuniary loss proved to have been incurred or suffered by the person claiming compensation. The single arbitrator appointed by the Local Commission, with the approval of the Central Commission is to decide all questions at issue under (this section) [2]).

It seems that amounts payable as compensation should be treated as cost of the scheme within Sec. 24 (1) (a). Clearly, therefore, no scheme is feasible which does not increase the value of properties to an amount adequate to provide for all approved claims for compensation.

Later sections of the Principal Ordinance make provision for modifications, suspension or annulment of a scheme, presumably after it has come into force (Sec. 31), for delegation of powers on the part of the Central Commission (Sec. 32) and for the making of Rules by the Central Commission (Sec. 33), etc.

---

[1]) Sec. 59 (2) of the English Act of 1909.
[2]) In the Ordinance as published in the contemporary quarterly volume the provision concludes with the words "last preceding article". The word "section" is substituted by Mr. Bentwich.

CHAPTER XXI—INCAPACITY AND ABSENCE.

Incapacity.

The subject of Incapacity is dealt with in the Mejelle under the head of Interdiction (Hajr), which is defined by Art. 941 as follows:—

"Hajr" is to restrain a particular person from disposing of property at his will.

That person after the restraint is called "Mahjur".

"Izn" (Emancipation, Authorisation) is defined by Art. 942:—

"Izn" is to put an end to a restraint (Hajr) and the removing a prohibition of a right. The person to whom "Izn" is given is called Me'zun.

Minority and Lunacy.

The minor, the lunatic and the idiot are interdicted naturally [1]. The prodigal can be placed under interdiction by order of the Court [2]. Debtors may also be interdicted by the Court [3]. Another variation in capacity known to Moslem law is that caused by Slavery. The status of slavery no longer exists; and reference to it may, therefore, be ignored [4]. It is only necessary here to take note of the provisions of the law relating to minority and lunacy.

The Mejelle fixes the period of minority and the powers and duties of guardians in general. The principles followed are those of Moslem Law. In accordance with this law no definite age of majority is fixed. A distinction is drawn between persons who have attained puberty (baligh) and those who have not done so (saghir). Puberty is a

---

[1] Mejelle, Art. 957.
[2] Ibid., Art. 958.
[3] Ibid., Arts. 998—1002. The Court of Appeal held that civil bankruptcy amounts to interdiction and is, in accordance with the provisions of the Palestine Order-in-Council, a matter of personal status falling within the jurisdiction of the Sharia Court, yet Art. 52 limits the jurisdiction of this tribunal to matters of personal status between Moslems only. In a case between a non-Moslem and Moslem the jurisdiction in matters of interdiction is with the Civil Courts in accordance with Art. 47. In re Mustafa Sakija v. Jacobson, C.A. 98/27. Palestine Post 12th December 1934. Cf. also C.A. 58/32 and Hankin v. Qasem Mustafa, C.A. 161/33. Palestine Post 3rd December 1934.
[4] Land Code, Art. 112.

Chapter XXI—Incapacity and Absence.

matter of fact [1]). Puberty begins in the case of males at the completion of the twelfth year and in the case of females at the completion of the ninth year. From that time until actual puberty the child is said to be "approaching puberty" (Merahik, Merahika) [2]). If the signs of puberty are not exhibited by the fifteenth year, the person is nevertheless deemed to have arrived at puberty [3]).

The minor who is approaching puberty may be emancipated by the guardians but such emancipation is revocable by the guardians, unless effected by the judge [4]). On attaining puberty the child does not at once cease to be under guardianship. The guardian exercises a discretion and should try him first. If he is not of sound mind he continues under interdiction [5]). But if the guardian has handed his property over to him, this emancipation is no longer revocable save by the judge.

But the giving of permission by a brother, or fraternal uncle, or other near relative, is not legal, if he has not been appointed guardian [6]).

Art. 974 determines the order in which persons become the guardians of a minor, as follows:

"In this chapter, an infant's guardian is first, his father, secondly, if his father is dead, the guardian chosen and appointed in the lifetime of his father; thirdly, if the guardian chosen is also dead, the guardian appointed by him in his lifetime; fourthly, his true ancestor, that is to say, the father of the infant's father, or the father of the infant's father's father; fifthly the guardian who has been chosen and appointed in the lifetime of his ancestor; sixthly, the guardian who has been appointed by the guardian; seventhly, the judge, or the guardian appointed, that is to say, the guardian appointed by the judge" [7]).

No maximum is fixed by the law, beyond which it is impossible for guardianship to extend [8]). A law relating to the property

Guardians.

Puberty.

---

[1]) Mejelle, Art. 985; Cf. Kadry Pasha, Muhammedan Personal Law (translation by Sterry and Abcarius), Sec. 495; Hedaya, p. 529.

[2]) Mejelle, Art. 986.

[3]) Ibid., Art. 987.

[4]) Ibid., Arts. 968, 973, 977.

[5]) Ibid., Arts. 981, 982, 984.

[6]) Ibid., Art. 974.

[7]) Comapre Kadry Pasha, op. cit., Sec. 442, which is expressed in clearer language than Art. 974.

[8]) Kadry Pasha, op. cit., Sec. 496 states that guardianship ceases at puberty; but this applies only to the "person" as is clear from the latter part of the Section.

of orphans fixes the 20th year as the extreme date at which maturity must be presumed. But this is not a provision applicable generally [1]).

There is a difference between the Shafi and Hanafi law as to the conditions in which guardianship continues after puberty in cases in which the minor has not an intelligence sufficiently developed to be entrusted with the management of property. Kadry Pasha is explicit that guardianship does not cease in respect of property by the minor attaining majority and aptitude for good administration [2]). This is the Hanafite law [3]), but does not appear consistent with the provision of Art. 989 of the Mejelle. That Article clearly implies that, in the absence of a judicial interdiction, a person who has admittedly arrived at physical puberty can make valid contracts. We are given to understand that the Moslem Courts in Palestine apply the strict Hanafite law and regard a judicial decree as necessary in all cases for the determination of guardianship.

As regards other communities than the Moslem, the Mejelle must (semble) be applied. The Mejelle is Common Law in Palestine and there is nothing in the Palestine Order-in-Council to suggest, that its provisions are not binding on religious courts to the exclusion of the communal law of the court. The Order-in-Council gives jurisdiction in certain cases to the courts of the various communities and may be taken to imply that these courts will apply their own law. As regards most of the matters as to which jurisdiction is given, however, no provisions are contained either in the Mejelle or in any other Ottoman Law. Where, however, as in the case of Minority and Guardianship explicit provisions are to be found in the Mejelle it seems probable, at least, that these are intended to apply to all persons [4]).

Age of Majority.

If this is so the provisions of the Mejelle as to age of majority and such provisions as are given there with reference to the persons to act as guardians and their rights and powers should be followed not only by the Civil Courts [5]) but also by the non-Moslem

---

[1]) Padel and Steeg. De la Législation foncière, p. 60.

[2]) Op. cit., Sec. 496.

[3]) See Vesey FitzGerald, op. cit., pp. 164 ff. and Anastassi v. Hussein (1924) 12 C.L.R. at p. 16.

[4]) Mejelle, Art. 971 provides that determination of guardianship may be effected by the guardian expressly or impliedly. In case of disagreement between the minor and the guardian emancipation of the minor is a matter for the Judge to decide. Mejelle, Art. 975.

[5]) Palestine Order-in-Council 1922, Art. 46. "Capacity" is not mentioned

Chapter XXI—Incapacity and Absence.

Religious Courts, and the same is true as regards the provisions of the Land Code. The alternative view is that the Religious Courts are free to fix the age of majority, etc. in accordance with their own ecclesiastical law.

Special provisions exist, however, as to age of majority in connection with certain transactions. Thus in Art. 2 of the Commercial Code which yet remains unrepealed there is a provision treating 21 as the full age of majority for commercial transactions.

In the very special case for which provision is made by Sec. 2 of the Land Law (Amendment) Ordinance 1933, namely the occupation of land by one or more co-heirs to the exclusion of the other co-heirs it is provided that (Sub-sec. 2) if the claimant shall have been a minor or under any other disability at the beginning of the period of adverse occupation the period is to run from the date at which he ceases to be a minor or under such disability. And Sub-sec. 3 states that "for the purpose of this section (a) the age of minority shall be taken to be eighteen years (b) persons under disability shall be deemed to include persons of unsound mind and persons interdicted by a competent Court.

Sec. 20 of the Succession Ordinance 1923 also treats 18 as the normal age of majority for persons other than Moslems. It provides as follows:—

"Where it appears that any person under the age of 18 years is or may become a person interested in the estate of a deceased person other than a Moslem, the President of a District Court may, upon the application of the person having the custody of the minor, or of any other person interested in his welfare, make such order as he deems fit for the protection of the interest of the minor, and in particular, orders may be made under the Article:—

(a) authorising the sale or lease of the share or part thereof of any minor heir or beneficiary;

(b) directing the application and investment or re-investment of any such share or income of the sale of any such share;

(c) directing payments to be made out of capital or income for the maintenance or otherwise for the benefit of the minor;

(d) appointing any person to represent such minor in any proceedings;

(e) transferring to the Civil Courts the administration and distribution of any estate in which a minor is interested, in any

---

by Art. 51 as a matter of personal status. See more fully, Goadby, International and Interreligious Private Law in Palestine, pp. 177, 183—4.

case in which there is jurisdiction to make such order in accordance with the provisions of Article 7 hereof.

The powers under paras (a), (b), and (c) of this Article may, subject to the Law of the Community, be exercised by the Court of a Community with reference to the property of any minor the administration of which is within the jurisdiction of such Court".

Persons of Unsound Mind. As regards persons of unsound mind, the Mejelle distinguishes between maniacs (majnun), persons suffering from periodical mania (majnun ghair moutbek), and imbeciles (maa'tuh) [1].

It provides that the latter are to be assimilated to minors approaching puberty [2]. The Majnun is to be considered as a minor with no clear judgment, i.e. as a minor not approaching puberty. But if he has lucid intervals he is capable during such periods as ordinary folk [3]. It is not expressly stated who are the guardians of persons of unsound mind. The provisions of Art. 974 already quoted must (semble) be applied. Lunatics and idiots are naturally interdicted, so that, as in the case of minors, their incapacity results from facts and not from a general decree, certification, or the like. Persons may, however, be certified as insane for the purpose of reception into asylums in pursuance of a Decree of 19 Sefer A.H. 1293 and it is therein stated (Sec. 17) that the management of all the property of a lunatic in his house or town belongs to the Government so long as he is detained in the hospital [4].

Provisions of the Land Code referring to persons under puberty. The Land Code contains numerous articles referring to the special position of minors and of lunatics and the powers of their guardians [5]. The term "minor" as used in the Land Code is not defined, but presumably must be taken to refer to all persons under puberty.

It remains doubtful whether the term "minor" should be deemed to include persons who have attained puberty but are not yet deemed to be of sufficiently sound mind to be released from guardianship. The following Articles of the Land Code are specially important:

---

[1] Arts. 944, 945.
[2] Art. 979.
[3] Art. 980.
[4] The power of a Religious Court to appoint a Curator of a lunatic is doubtful under the terms of the Palestine Order-in-Council 1922. Art. 51 does not mention "curatorship" as distinct from "guardianship" and speaks only of "inhibition" of persons legally incompetent as falling within "matters of personal status". Probably, however, such Courts are competent to appoint curators.
[5] Land Code, Arts. 20—21; 50—53; 60—63, etc.

Chapter XXI—Incapacity and Absence.

Partition of land of minors and lunatics must be carried out through their guardians. — Art. 18.

Persons who have not attained puberty, lunatics, and imbeciles, cannot transfer their land. If any such person does so and dies before the age of puberty or recovery the land passes to his heirs and, failing them, it becomes subject to the right of Tapu. — Art. 50.

Persons of either sex who are minors, lunatics, or imbecils cannot buy land. Nevertheless if it is shown that it is for their profit or advantage their natural or appointed guardians can, in their capacity as such, buy land in their name. — Art. 51.

Forfeiture of rights of Tapu by refusal cannot be alleged against minors or persons of unsound mind or their guardians. — Art. 60.

The periods during which rights of Tapu can be exercised run notwithstanding minority or unsoundness of mind on the part of the person entitled. — Art. 61.

But the right of Tapu can be exercised by such persons during the periods allowed, notwithstanding grant of the land to another. — Art. 63.

The right of Tapu can be exercised by guardians on behalf of minors, lunatics or imbeciles. — Art. 65.

Land belonging to minors, etc. does not become subject to the right to Tapu by reason of non-cultivation. The article prescribes the procedure to be followed where Miri held by such persons, is left uncultivated. — Art. 76.

Art. 52 forbids the sale of a minor's land by the parents or guardians save with the permission of the Sharia Court [1]). The Court is bound to satisfy itself that the sale is in the interest of the minor and that a proper price was paid [2]). This applies also to the land of lunatics and imbeciles. Special provision is made by Art. 53 as to trees and buildings [3]). Minority and unsoundness of — Art. 52. Art. 53.

---

[1]) See also Tapu Law A.H. 1275, Secs. 31—33. Cf. Nader v. Qaraman. L.A. 39/32. Palestine Post 23 April 1933. In practice, however, the Daftar Khani allowed the sale of a minor's land by parents guardians even without the permission of the Sharia Court, provided the Qadi certified that the parents were of good behaviour.

[2]) The requisite consent would (semble) now be given by the Civil or Religious Court competent under Arts. 51—54 of the Palestine Order-in-Council 1922, or where there is none such, by the Civil Court. In the case of foreigners the Consul would be competent (Off. Gaz. 1st December 1922). The same would apply also to Exchange, Gift, Lease and Mortgage. With regard to Partition the provisions of Art. 18 of the Land Code and those of Secs. 3 and 6 of the Law of Partition A.H. 1332 would apply. The Qadi's approval would not be required.

[3]) For the "Musaveghat" conditions mentioned in Art. 53 see Note thereon in Fisher's edition of the "Ottoman Land Code".

The Land Law of Palestine.

Art. 20.

mind suspend the running of the period of prescription under Art. 20; the rules of Moslem Law are to be applied.

These articles by implication or necessary intendment apply to Miri only. It appears that in pure Moslem law a guardian may sell the immovable property of his ward without the sanction of the Court, at least, in certain circumstances [1]. This is not explicitly stated in the Mejelle which contains only provisions as to effective or ineffective contracts made by the minor [2]. In the absence of express statement a guardian of a non-Moslem at least, would be well advised to obtain the authority of the competent court to any sale by him of immovables of his ward.

Though no explicit reference is made in the texts to any power of leasing by the minor or his guardian, it may be assumed that contracts of lease made with the guardian's permission are good, when made within the terms of Art. 967 of the Mejelle. Art. 441 of the Mejelle states that if a guardian lets the immovables of a minor for a rent which is less than the "estimated" rent [3] the contract of hire is voidable and the rent must be increased to the "estimated" rent.

This provision implies clearly that guardians have a power of leasing the immovables of their wards.

Reference may also be made to the provisions of Sec. 5 of the Iradeh on the Leasing of Immovables of A.H. 1299 and A.H. 1332 which deals with the drawing up of leases of the immovables of persons under incapacity and to Sec. 3 of the Partition Law of A.H. 1332 as to partitions of their lands.

Prodigals.

Spendthrifts may be interdicted by the Court [4]. Such interdiction falls, it would seem, within the jurisdiction of Religious Courts in Palestine [5]. The interdicted prodigal [6] is under the guardianship of the Court itself which may validate a disposition

---

[1] See Vesey FitzGerald, Muhammedan Law, pp. 107 ff. Kadry Pasha, Muhammedan Law, Sec. 450. See also Secs. 452—455. As to laesio enormis in sales by guardians, see Mejelle, Arts. 165, 365. Vesey FitzGerald, op. cit., p. 110. For sale and purchase of Ijaratein Waqf by guardians of minors, see Omar Hilmy, Laws of Evqaf, 214 ff. As to repair of property held in common by minors, see Mejelle, Art. 1319.

[2] Compare Arts. 966, 967, 978, 989.

[3] Hooper's translation. Grigsby says "for an amount less than the estimated value". See also Vesey FitzGerald, loc. cit.

[4] Mejelle, Art. 990.

[5] Palestine Order-in-Council 1922, Art. 51. Cf Aggelidi v Tudjarbash (1892) 2 C.L.R. at p. 69.

[6] Mejelle, Arts. 990, 993.

Chapter XXI—Incapacity and Absence.

of property made by the prodigal. The prodigal is assimilated to a minor "arriving at puberty" [1]).

By an absent person (mefqud) is meant, in Moslem Law, a person who is not present, whose abode is unknown, and of whom it is uncertain whether he is alive or dead [2]). Such a person is said to be absent under conditions of absolute disappearance (Ghaib el Munqata). A person may, however, be absent and yet known to be alive (ghaib) [3]). Another form of absence known to the Land Law is absence on a journey (Muddet Safar). According to Moslem Law a person who is absent (mefqud) cannot be presumed to be dead until ninety years have expired since the date of his birth [4]).

Absence. Absent Person (Mefqud).

The Moslem law treats the mefqud as a living person until the expiration of this period. His property is held in suspense, including his rights of inheritance, but if there be no evidence of his being alive when the period has elapsed his share in an inheritance which has opened is to be distributed among those who were heirs to the original proprietor at the period of the demise of such proprietor, as in the case of embryos in the womb [5]).

If, however, the land held by or inherited by the mefqud was Miri different considerations apply. Obviously the fact that the holder was absent is no defence to a claim by the State for forfeiture on the ground of non-cultivation. And if the heir of a deceased holder is absent (mefqud) the land becomes forthwith subject to the Right to Tapu, though upon reappearance within three years of the death the heirs may claim the land without payment [6]).

If heirs are present the land devolves upon them and in this case also the mefqud has only three years in which to claim his share. If there are no heirs to the Miri land save persons who are mefqud than if they have been mefqud for three years the land

---

[1]) Mejelle, Art. 990. The subject of interdiction of a prodigal is dealt with in detail in Hedaya, pp 526 ff.

[2]) Hedaya, Book XIII (Hamilton's Translation), at p. 213.

[3]) The Religious Courts have jurisdiction to appoint persons to administer the estates of absent persons (Ghaibeen). In the case of Rabbinical and Patriarchal Courts this jurisdiction is concurrent only (Palestine Order-in-Council, 1922; Arts. 51 ff.)

[4]) Hedaya, at p. 216. Per curiam in Francoudi v. Heirs of Michailides (1895) 3 C.L.R. at p. 229.

[5]) Hedaya, loc. cit. The Qadi may sell immovables likely to waste. Kadry Pasha, op. cit., Sec. 874.

[6]) Land Code, Art. 75. The State (semble) would have to refund the Bedl Misl.

becomes subject to the rights of Tapu or is Mahlul; but if the heirs reappear within three years of the death of the ancestor they can claim the land without payment¹). Of course if the land has been left uncultivated for three years the State may exercise the right of forfeit and no claim is then possible.

Though these Articles (56—57) of the Land Code apply in terms only in cases of succession (intiqal) under the older law, the principles involved are no doubt applicable in cases of succession under the existing Law of Inheritance of A.H. 1331.

Where the heir is not mefqud but only "away" (ghaib) and has not caused the land to be cultivated it is forfeited for non-cultivation after three years ²).

Claim to the exercise of rights to Tapu run notwithstanding absence but are exerciseable during the prescribed periods notwithstanding grants to others ³). All these special provisions as regards Miri are intended to secure the cultivation of the land. The law does not appear to provide expressly for the case of absent heirs to Mussaqafat or Mustaghilat Waqf. Presumably the principles applicable would be those laid down in the Land Code rather than those applicable in the case of Mulk.

Muddet Safar (a long way off). The term "Muddet Safar" occurs in connection with prescription and limitation of actions. Thus under Art. 1663 of the Mejelle the time during which a plaintiff was "a long way off" does not count in estimating the period within which he is required to bring his action. Art. 1664 states that by the term "Muddet Safar" is meant a distance of three days journey or eighteen hours at a moderate rate of travelling. But if in fact the parties have from time to time met, though living at this distance from each other, the period runs (Art. 1665). The same term occurs several times in the land Land Code, e.g. Arts. 20, 61, 63. Its meaning was considered by the Cyprus Courts in the case of Mehmet v. Kosmo ⁴),

---

¹) Land Code, Arts. 56, 57, 75.
²) Land Code, Art. 74. As to soldiers See Arts. 58, 73.
³) Land Code, Arts. 61, 63.
⁴) (1884) I C.L.R. at p. 12. In Muzaffer v. Collet (1904) 6 C.L.R. at p. 108 the Court held that "absence is only an excuse when it is absence of the claimant". In Monk v. Nicola (1924), 11 C.L.R. at p. 118 it was laid down that "where a man has a right of action vested in him he cannot by voluntarily quitting the country suspend the running of the period of prescription". In this latter case the Court was of opinion that the disabilities and circumstances that prevent a period running must be in existence at the time when the period begins to run and that, with the possible exception of compulsory military service, no suspension occurred if the period had once commenced to run.

Chapter XXI—Incapacity and Absence.

where the plaintiff sought to take advantage of his absence from Cyprus for 13 years and residence in Constantinople to maintain against which the defendant contended that the period of limitation had run under the Land Code. The Court held that residence in a foreign country was not absence on a journey.

The Palestine Courts do not, however, adopt this view. In Estrangin v. Tayan [1] it was held by the Supreme Court that where the defendant was living in a foreign country such absence was a cause for suspension of the running of the period, even though the person against whom the plea was put forward had a duly authorised agent in Palestine. Actual presence in Palestine of the plaintiff during the whole period was required if the period was to run against him. *The view of the Palestine Courts.*

A change in the law as interpreted by the Courts of Palestine has, however, been made by the Land Law (Amendment) Ordinance 1933. By Sec. 8 thereof which appears to apply to all forms of land, Mulk as well as Miri, it is provided that "notwithstanding any provision of the Ottoman Law, absence from Palestine of a person claiming to be entitled to bring an action or exercise any right as to land, during the whole or any part of the period limited by law for the commencement of the action or the prescription of the right, shall not prevent the commencement or interrupt the running of the period, and if a person absent from Palestine has appointed an agent in Palestine, the absence of such an agent from Palestine during the whole or any part of the period shall not prevent the commencement or running of the period. Provided that, where a person has been absent prior to the commencement of this Ordinance, the effect of such absence shall be interpreted in accordance with the law in force at the time of his absence". The Ordinance "commenced" on 23rd August 1933 [2]. It appears from the wording of the proviso that the absence which is to be interpreted in accordance with the previous law is absence prior to this date only; a period of absence commencing before that date and continuing cannot be treated as governed as a whole by the previous law. *The Land Law Amendment Ordinance 1933.*

---

[1] Off. Gaz. 16th September 1926. This case has been followed in Fahima Hanem v. Assad Shukairi, L.A. 49/32 (Palestine Post 9 May 1933) in which Mehmet v. Kosmo was quoted.

[2] This is the date on which the Ordinance was signed. It was published in Off. Gaz. 24th August 1933. See Order-in-Council 1922, Art. 24 and Interpretation Ordinance 1929, Sec. 3 (C) (3).

CHAPTER XXII—CORPORATIONS.

Corporations in Moslem Law.

The Moslem law has not developed a theory of juridical personality. The institution of Waqf gave the permanency required in the case of eleemosynary assignments of property and family settlements [1]) and the comparative immobility of capital in earlier days made less necessary the large joint stock company which figures so largely in modern industry. Moslem law has, no doubt, long found difficulty in fitting Christian ecclesiastical bodies into its frameworks and the language used seems to show that the difficulty is really insurmountable.

As has been already pointed out in an earlier Chapter [2]) the Moslem law recognized Waqfs Mustesna for the benefit of Christians and Art. 122 of the Land Code speaks of land attached to a monastery. But the idea of a group of persons forming together one group person and the clear separation of the personality of each member from that of the group are not found in Moslem Law [3]).

The Ottoman Law of A. H. 1331.

At the close of the Ottoman rule, however, implied legislative recognition was accorded to the idea of a Corporation by a Law of A. H. 1331 which was primarily designed to enable Corporations to own land [4]).

The Law of A. H. 1331 declared (Arts. 1, 3) that certain bodies might own immovable property in accordance with their

---

[1]) The Waqf is indeed often spoken of by modern writers as a juridical person. But there is no justification for this in Moslem theory. See Goadby in Jour. Comp. Leg. 3rd Series, XVI, Pt. I, pp. 41 ff.

[2]) Chapter VI—Waqf and Trusts, supra.

[3]) The slow process by which the idea was developed in England more particularly in connection with ecclesiastical communities is described in Pollock & Maitland, History of English Law I, pp. 469 ff. In current usage in Palestine monastic communities are often spoken of as bodies with a representative Head who in fact acts for the whole group. But this language has no legal sanction.

[4]) Corporations of a commercial character had, however, been recognized impliedly at least, by the adoption in 1850 of the French Commercial Law, in the form of an Ottoman Commercial Code. And in fact long before the Law of A.H. 1331 the idea of the Corporation had entered into Ottoman Law more particularly in connection with foreign interests.

Chapter XXII—Corporations.

Charters, Contracts and Regulations sanctioned by the Government and subject in certain cases to special conditions. The bodies in question are as follows:—

Departments of State, Municipalities, Ottoman (Concessionary) Societies, Ottoman Commercial, Industrial and Development Companies, Ottoman Agricultural Companies, Ottoman Charitable Institutions and Ottoman (Religious) Communities.

The law appears to apply only to Ottoman Corporations and in its application to Palestine applies only to Palestinian Corporations. By Sec. 8 of the Land Transfer Ordinance, 1920, the Ottoman Law of Corporations was declared to be in force in Palestine and it was provided that the Director of Lands might authorize banking companies to take mortgages of land and commercial companies in Palestine to acquire such land as was necessary for their undertaking [1]. Companies.

By Sec. 15 (1) of the Companies Ordinance 1929, re-enacting in a modified form the provisions of Sec. 8 of the Companies Ordinance 1921, it is provided that the Registrar of Companies is not to register any Company which has as its objects or one of its objects the acquisition and development of land generally in Palestine unless such Company produces a certificate under the hand of the High Commissioner empowering it to hold lands generally. The High Commissioner is given power by Sub-sec. (2) to revoke any such certificate if he is satisfied that the Company is not cultivating or developing the land and after such revocation the Company may be wound up by the Court [2]. It is further to be remarked that by the effect of Sec. 6 combined with provisions of Schedule 2 to the Ordinance every company registered under the Ordinance has power to purchase, take on lease or in exchange, hire or otherwise acquire or hold for any estate or interest any lands, buildings, etc. and any immovable property of any kind necessary or convenient for the purposes of or in connection with the Companies' business or any branch or department thereof and to explore, manage, cultivate, develop, exchange, let in rent etc., mortgage, sell, dispose of etc. or otherwise deal with all or any part of its property.

Under Sec. 38 of the Charitable Trusts Ordinance, 1924, foreign corporations may be trustees of charitable trusts under the Foreign Corporations as Trustees.

---

[1] Cf. Art. 2 of Mortgage Law of A.H. 1331 modified by Mortgage Law Amendment Ordinance, 1929, Sec. 2. Cf. also Sec. 2 (11) (a) and 2 (1v) of the Credit Banks Ordinance 1920—1922.

[2] By Sec. 269 of the Ordinance similar provisions are made applicable to foreign companies and the provisions of Sec. 15 (2) are extended to them.

Ordinance, provided that they register with the Registrar of Companies. Stringent restrictions upon the power of trustees to continue to hold land are imposed by Sec. 39 as modified by Sec. 10 of the Charitable Trusts Ordinance 1925 and these restrictions are, by Sec. 39 (3) made applicable to immovable property held by a limited company in respect of which a licence had been granted under Sec. 22 of the Companies' Ordinance 1921, (now represented by Sec. 23 of the Companies' Ordinance 1929) unless a certificate had been obtained from the High Commissioner under Sec. 8 of the Ordinance of 1921 (now represented by Sec. 15 of the Ordinance of 1929).

Charitable Institutions and Communities. By Art. 3 of the Law of 22 Rabi-el-Awal A.H. 1331 Ottoman Charitable Institutions and Communties were authorized to hold land in towns and villages and were allowed to continue to hold immovable property in respect of which their title was registered at the time at which the Law came into force [1]). There seems to be no express provision giving power to hold lands to foreign charitable institutions, other than the provisions of the Charitable Trusts Ordinance above cited. Under the Correction of Land Registers Ordinances, 1921—22, numerous applications were made by Charitable and Religious Institutions for registration in their name of land previously registered in the name of a nominee on their behalf. The "national" character of such institutions in Palestine is often somewhat indeterminate. But, in practice, the Land Registry required the institution to register as a Society under the Ottoman Law of Societies, A.H. 1327, or under the Companies or Cooperative Societies Ordinances, and thereby to acquire, it was presumed, Ottoman (i.e. Palestinian) nationality. These Correction of Land Registers Ordinances have now expired and applications of this nature are now governed by the more limited provisions of the Correction of Land Registers Ordinance, 1926, by Sec. 2 of which it is to be observed, "person" is stated to include "a corporate body".

But though there is no quotable text granting to foreign corporations the right to hold land little doubt need be entertained that such right is admitted. Any other solution would be contrary

---

[1]) Cf. Palestine Jewish Colonisation Association Ordinance 1924. The Religious Communities Organisation Ordinance 1926—1934. The Regulations for the Organisation of the Jewish Community 1928 and the Municipal Corporation Ordinance 1934. All these corporations were authorized to hold land and property of every description.

Chapter XXII—Corporations.

to the general tenor of Palestinian Policy [1]). But the right must be allowed subject to the conditions imposed in the case of native charitable institutions, namely, those laid down in Art. 3 of the Law of Corporations, A.H. 1331, and Sec. 39 of the Charitable Trusts Ordinance, 1924.

A "provisional" article of the Law of 22 Rabi-el-Awal imposed upon all corporate bodies an annual tax in respect of all immovable property in their possession, Mulk and Miri owned by Government departments being, however, exempt. This tax has, however, been abolished as from 1st April 1933 by the Tax on Immovable Property of Corporate Bodies (Abolition) Ordinance 1933.

It may be also remarked that a provisional addition to Art. 3 of the same law provided facilities for registration in their own name of charitable institutions and communities which had been registered under a borrowed name. This arrangement has already been considered in the Chapter dealing with Registration [2]).

---

[1]) Cf. Palestine Order-in-Council 1922, Arts. 2, 58, 59 and Interpretation Ordinance 1929, Sec. 3 (c) (14).
[2]) Supra, pp. 304—307.

CHAPTER XXIII—TAXATION OF LAND.

It is not easy to separate the payments which the Ottoman Government received from landholders in its proprietary capacity from those which it received by way of taxation. The distinction is very clear in modern law, but is often obscured in older law. Thus, feudal incidents under earlier English law were a source of revenue to the Crown and, when finally abolished (in the reign of Charles II), new taxation had to be imposed in substitution.

Tapu Fees.   The proprietary interest of the State in Miri land secures to it payments (Tapu Fees) by the grantees on admission. The term Tapu Misl or Bedl Misl (equivalent value) are employed to designate this "fee". This is the Muajele (payment in advance) made for the grant of the tessaruf (Land Code, Art. 3).

The Tapu Misl is payable whenever the State makes a new grant by Tapu of the land; and only then. It may be paid by a person exercising a Right to Tapu or by a person to whom a grant of Mewat is made where he is not entitled to a gratuitous grant, or by a person who obtains a Tapu grant as the highest bidder at an auction of Mahlul. A waqf selling Ijaratein which has become Mahlul obtains, of course, a payment which is analogous in nature, but this must not be confused with Tapu Misl.

Tapu Value.   The principle followed upon making a grant by Tapu was that the grantee should pay to the State the value of the soil (Tapu). This is called the Tapu value. Where Mewat land was revived withot authorisation the person responsible might (under Art. 103 Land Code) obtain a grant on payment of the Tapu value. Art. 5 of the Regulations as to Tapu Sanads, A.H. 1276, tells us 'that such persons would obtain a grant on payment of the Tapu value "at the time of seizure and cultivation". This would be equivalent to the waste value of the land. If, however, they delayed giving information for six months as required by the law (Art. 4) they would have to pay the "present" Tapu value, i.e. the value of the land as improved. The term Tapu value means simply the value of the Land. What will have to be taken into account in estimating Tapu value depends on the circumstances in which the grant is made.

Chapter XXIII—Taxation of Land.

"When payment of the Tapu value is made by a person having a Right to Tapu, the Tapu value which shall be taken for land that is going to be conferred on the possessor of the Right to Tapu does not mean the amount fetched at auction or the amount stated by a person from outside, but its actual value in accordance with the information of disinterested possessors of knowledge having regard to the likes¹) of the land." (Regulations as to Tapu Sanads, Art. 6—Ongley's Translation. Cf. Land Code, Art. 59).

So again Art. 16 of the Tapu Law states that the value for which the land is to be offered to persons having a right to Tapu under Land Code, Art. 59, is to be assessed locally by ascertaining from the inhabitants of the town or village in which the land is situate who are disinterested possessors of knowledge (impartial experts). It is the practice to include in this valuation only the "waste" value of the land, i.e. the value of the land without taking into account its condition as land ready for cultivation. If there are buildings or trees or vines which follow the land the practice is not to include their value in the Tapu value payable by a person having a right to Tapu. The site value alone is taken into account.

Where, however, the land is pure Mahlul and is put up for auction the land will be sold with all its improvements, including houses and trees where these follow the land. But the payment made by the highest bidder may still be termed a Tapu Misl, it being a payment made for a Tapu grant. And it may still be called Bedl Misl because it is an equivalent value. The term Bedl Misl occurs, however, in the Land Code in its more literal sense as meaning any equivalent sum paid. Thus in Art. 117, which deals with sale of mortgaged property by the mortgagee, we are told that it will be sold for its equivalent value (Bedl Misl). So also in Arts. 41, 44, 45, it is used to mean the sum paid by a person exercising a right of preference under these articles.

Bedl Misl.

Of course Land Registry fees are not to be included in the term Tapu Misl. But in the case of a Takhsisat Waqf where tithes and taxes are dedicated the fees on sale and inheritance belong to the Waqf in favour of which the dedication is made (Art. 4)²).

---

¹) Fisher says "according to the ratio of other similar land".

²) In Tapu Law, 1275, Arts 20, 21 Bedl Muajel and Muajel are used in the same sense as Bedl Misl. In Land Code, Art. 4, Bedl Mahlulat is used to mean the Bedl Misl paid on the sale of Mahlul.

The Land Law of Palestine.

For the determination of the Tapu value reference must now also be made to the provisions of Sec. 4 of the Land Law (Amendment) Ordinance 1933. The Tapu value is to be fixed by a Commission consisting of the District Officer in charge of the sub-district in which the land is situate and two unofficial members nominated by the District Commissioner. The value so fixed is to be subject to review by the Director of lands whose decision "will be final". It is not easy to understand the force of these last words. Appeal to the Courts is, of course, out of the question and presumably it cannot be the intention to exclude the general power of supervision which it is as much the duty as the right of the High Commissioner to exercise over subordinate officials.

In assessing the Tapu value the new Commission will undoubtedly follow the established practice and take into account only the site value.

It should be observed and has already been noted that when Mahlul land is put up for auction the reserve price is to be fixed by the Director of Lands, and it may be safely assumed that in doing so this official would take into account all improvements, etc., so as to secure that if the land is to be granted, the State shall make as much profit as possible.

Tithe.   Islamic law treated all lands in private hands as subject either to payment of Tithe or Tribute. The tithe represents the shares of the sovereign, or of the community as a whole, in the produce of the soil. It is not, of course, peculiarly an Islamic institution, but occurs in widely separated countries.

The tribute (Kharaj) was a payment by the non-Moslem population in return for protection and toleration.

Tribute no longer interests us since its payment is not exacted. But tithe is, in principle, still payable by all private owners.

The authority for the imposition and collection of the tithe is contained in the Ottoman Regulations, 24th May, A.H. 1287 (1871)[1], supplemented by Regulations of the 4th January, A.H. 1295 (1880)[2], amended by the Regulations of 9th June, A.H. 1321 (1905)[3], by the Regulations of 24th Shewal, A.H. 1306 (1889)[4] and by a Law of 1906[5].

---

[1] Dastour, Vol. III, pp. 243 ff.
[2] Dastour, Vol. IV, pp. 755.
[3] Dastour, (Supplementary) pp. 391 ff.
[4] Young, op. cit., Vol. V, pp. 112, 302, ff.
[5] Young, Vol. VII, p. 354—8.

Chapter XXIII—Taxation of Land.

Under these enactments all agricultural lands in Palestine were chargeable with tithes but land appurtenant to houses situate in towns and villages and land enclosed by walls or hedges and less than an ancient dunum (919 pics) in extent was exempt. As such land normally belongs to the Mulk class, the idea has gradually become prevalent that Mulk property is not subject to tithe. Historically there is no foundation for this view. As is very clearly stated in Padel and Steeg[1], "Tithe attaches to all cultivable land, pasture lands and woodlands in the possession of private persons whether they be Mulk owners or holders of Miri or Waqf land. Only State forests, Mahlul land not regranted, Metruki land, or land belonging to the Sovereign are exempt. In fact, indeed, the Ottoman Government not infrequently did exempt portions of Mulk from tithe, and this practice coupled with the general exemption of land appurtenant to buildings in a town from tithe, has created a state of facts from which the common doctrinal error has been inferred[2]. The error is made the more plausible by the circumstance that nearly all land which is cultivated and, therefore, titheable in kind is Miri. Yet though in practice Mulk is not deemed subject to tithe, this is not because as Mulk it is not titheable".

The tithe, as its name indicates, is supposed to be equal to one-tenth of the produce. It was increased by an Iradeh of A.H. 1302 (1886) to $11\frac{1}{2}\%$ and by a second Iradeh of A.H. 1313 (1897) to $12\frac{1}{2}\%$. The Palestine Government issued in 1925 a Tithe Reduction Ordinance which reduced the tithe to the original percentage.

Where the soil is in private hands and is not actually cultivated the tithe was replaced by imposts in lieu thereof (Bedl Ushur or Ijara Zemin). Thus, land which is granted by Tapu for use as a threshing-floor, or a salt pan, pays a "rent" equivalent to the tithe. (Land Code, Art. 34). So also where pasturing grounds (Kishlak and Yaylak) are granted by Kushan the possessors pay dues called Kishlakie or Yaylakie in proportion to their yield (Land Code, Art. 24), and a ground rent equivalent to the tithe is assessed and appropriated for the site of buildings erected on Miri land (Art. 32) and for woodland possessed by Kushan (Art. 30).

A decisive step in mitigation of the evils of the tithe was taken by the Commutation of Tithes Ordinance, No. 49 of 1927, (Off. Gaz. No. 201 16th December 1927) and by the Regulations

Commuted Tithe.

---

[1] Op. cit., p. 324.
[2] Op. cit., p. 325, note.

made under this Ordinance (Off. Gaz. No. 205 of 16th February 1928). The 1927 Ordinance was amended by the Commutation of Ttihes (Amendment) Ordinance 1928. These enactments have removed the worst abuses of the Collection. Prior to the application of the Commutation of Tithe Ordinances 1927—28 the value of the crops were estimated on the threshing floors or in the field [1] and 10% of the value of the crop at the harvest month prices was payable as tithe. The estimation of the crops entailed loss on the owner because during the assessment operations, which covered several months each year, the crops were liable to be stolen, eaten by animals, or carried away by storm and as the owner was unable to dispose of them until the assessment was completed, he lost opportunities of selling them when favourable prices were obtainable.

The Commuted Tithe has now replaced the Tithe throughout Palestine, except in the case of a small number of Bedu tribal areas in the Beersheba Sub-District, where the tithe at the rate of 10 per centum of the produce of the land is still collected in money.

The Commuted Tithe is based on the average aggregate amount of tithe assessed as payable during the four years preceeding the application of the Commuted Tithe and is apportioned among reputed owners of titheable land in proportion to the potential productivity of their holdings as ascertained by Village Assessment Committees.

Since the application of the Commuted Tithe the owner has been free to thresh his crops and to dispose of them as and when he pleased.

There is a redistribution annually of the amount of the Commuted Tithe payable by the village:— If there has been a change of ownership, the name of the new owner is substituted for that of the previous owner; If by reason of sale or succession, etc. a parcel of land previously owned by one person is in the joint ownership of a number of persons, the aggregate amount of the Commuted Tithe on the parcel is apportioned among the several owners in the proportion of their shares; If there has been a change of ownership of a parcel and the parcel has been divided into a number of parcels, the tithe payable on the original parcel is distributed among the owners of the new parcels; If at the time of the original application of the Commuted Tithe the lands of a village were held in undivided shares (Mesha'a), which has since been partitioned the Commuted Tithe which had been distributed

---

[1] Cf. Concealment of Crops Ordinance, 1923.

Chapter XXIII—Taxation of Land.

on the basis of the shares, is redistributed among the owners of the parcels resulting from the partition.

Exemption from tithe is granted in respect of fuel wood, vegetables which cannot be preserved, vines grafted on American stock for ten years after planting [1]), hay from village pasture lands, cotton [2]) tobacco [3]) and the produce of land utilized for agricultural instruction or research [4]).

The described system of distribution of the Commuted Tithe among the landlords of the Villages has, however, certain defects. Direct dealing between Government and the individual taxpayers is preferable to the method of distribution of the tax through and by village units. The existing procedure, however, must remain in force until the Settlement of Rights in the villages has been completed and direct dealings between Government and Taxpayer made possible. Among the most important reforms of Land Taxation in Palestine which has been approved and initiated, is the survey and valuation of the village lands by blocks for fiscal purposes. This will make it feasible to replace the existing tithe by a Land Tax.

It will be remembered that in very many cases a quasi Waqf of Miri has been created by the dedication of Tithes as Waqf. Such an impropriation should not tie the hands of the Government in regulating the rate of tithe or even be assumed to imply a promise to continue its exaction. However, when private interests in public revenue are once allowed to exist, experience shows how difficult and odious their reduction or disturbance may become. The present position in Palestine is that the Government has made an agreement with the Supreme Moslem Council as representing Waqf interests, under which the Government collects the tithe and pays a lump sum to the Council on behalf of the Waqfs. It is regarded as improbable that commutation or even abolition of tithe will be allowed to affect the Waqf interests.

Takhsisat Waqf.

The Wergo is a land tax and originated in a tax imposed by the Sipahis [5]). Upon the abolition of Ziamets this was replaced by a land tax (Wergo, or gift established for the benefit of the

The Wergo (House and Land Tax).

---

[1]) Iradeh A.H. 1315. (P.N. of 26th April 1920).

[2]) Cotton Exemption from Tithe Ordinance 1925; continued till 1929 by Ordinance No. 11 of 1927.

[3]) Tobacco Ordinance 1925 Sec. 3 (1).

[4]) Exemption from Tithe Ordinance 1929.

[5]) See Padel and Steeg, op. cit., at p. 329 as to the hearth taxes etc. imposed by the Sipahis and which were superseded by the Wergo.

The Land Law of Palestine.

State). This tax is still levied on land of every class, Mulk or Miri, and whether the land is Waqf or not. It is governed by a Law of 5 Zil Quade, A. H. 1303. The amount of the tax could be varied by Imperial Iradeh. In practice in Palestine and in accordance with Ottoman Iradehs the amount varies with the character of the land.

The Wergo is collected in Palestine under an Order of the Military Administration of 15 November, 1918, validated by the Palestine Order-in-Council, 1922, Art. 73, and by a Public Notice published in O.G. No. 83 of the 15th January 1923.

The Wergo from immovable property in Palestine is assessed on the capital value and is levied at the following rates:

(1) Property not built upon:—   Per mil.
  (a) Lands, fields, vineyards, gardens subject to tithe, or to the equivalent of tithe (Bedl-Ushur) or changed into land of the muqata'a category . 4
  (b) Land destined for building purposes . . . 4
  (c) Lands not paying tithe, nor paying the equivalent of tithe nor changed into muquta'a land . 10

(2) Property built upon:—
  (a) Farm buildings 4
  (b) Farm buildings hired and occupied by tenants not exceeding 200,000 mils capital value . . 5
  (c) Farm buildings hired or occupied by tenants exceeding 200,000 mils capital value . . . 8
  (d) Farm buildings within the area of a town or village 5
  (e) Waqf buildings (mussaqafat waqfiye) . . . 4
  (f) Houses inhabited by the proprietors, the value of which is below 200,000 mils 5
  (g) Houses inhabited by the proprietors, the value of which is over 200,000 mils 8
  (h) Buildings leased or rented by their owners . 10

Additions to this tax aggregating in all 41% on buildings and 56% on lands were made from time to time under Ottoman Decrees [1]). These additions are still collected, except in the case of buildings and lands re-assessed since 1919. Immovable property registered in the name of corporate bodies was formerly subject to an additional tax varying from $1/_2$ to 1 per mille of its assessed value[2]).

---

[1]) Ottoman Law of 16th Feb. 1328(1913) and O.G. No. 84 1st Feb. 1923.
[2]) Abolished by Tax on Immovable Property of Corporate Bodies (Abolition) Ordinance 1933 (O.G. 383 of 24 Aug. 1933).

Chapter XXIII—Taxation of Land.

Exemption from the payment of Wergo is granted in respect of the buildings of recognized Charitable and Religious Institutions and buildings and playgrounds owned and maintained by recognized Educational Institutions, provided the buildings are used solely for charitable, religious, or education purposes and are not revenue producing (Public Notice, 18th Sept. 1922; O. G. No. 75 of 1st November, 1922).

In accordance with the Mussaqafat Law (Roofed Property Law) of 14th June, A.H. 1326, a roofed property tax was levied in lieu of the Wergo in the Township of Haifa, Acre and Shefa Amr. This tax is assessed at $3\frac{1}{2}\%$ of the gross income of buildings with the exception of farm buildings, which are exempted.

Certain doubts as to its proper imposition have been set at rest by the Mussaqafat Tax Validation Ordinance, 1932.

It is intended that the Wergo and Mussaqafat and Bedl Ushur Taxes shall be replaced within all the urban areas by a new tax to be known as Urban Property Tax, the rate of which will be fixed according to the net annual value of the house property and land. Provision for this replacement is made by the Urban Property Tax Ordinance 1928, amended by Urban Property Tax (Amendment) Ordinance, 1929, and the Urban Property Tax (Amendment) Ordinance 1932. *Urban PropertyTax*

The new tax is payable by the reputed owner of the property at such annual rates as may be prescribed for the various categories of property. The Ordinances also provide for a revision every year and a general re-assessment every fifth year. The rates of tax prescribed in all urban areas [1] on house property is not to exceed 15% (For the years 1932-3-4 the tax was $12\frac{1}{2}\%$) (O.G. No. 361 11th May 1933). House property constituted and used for the purpose of industrial undertakings is charged at 10%.

Exemption is granted in the followings cases:—

(a) Properties which formerly enjoyed exemption in respect of House and Land Tax;

(b) House property occupied by the registered owner of which the net annual value is less than the sum specified by order and in no case exceeding £P.20;

(c) Newly constructed house property (the first 3 years).

The High Commissioner may remit wholly or in part the tax on playing fields, open spaces accessible to the public, and

---

[1] All the towns in the country are now subject to the Urban Property Tax replacing the Ottoman House and Land Tax (Wergo).

property on which building is prohibited or restricted under town planning orders.

The Collection of the Tax is regulated by the Collection of Taxes Ordinance 1929—34 and the Regulations made thereunder

It is proposed to introduce the Rural Property Tax from the 1st April 1935. A Rural Property Tax Ordinance has been enacted on the 16th January 1935 (P.G. Extra, No. 486) making provision for the replacement of the Wergo and the Tithe from rural lands by a Land Tax to be paid by the owners of the land and industrial buildings which are not subject to the Urban Property Tax.

The Rural Property Tax is levied at a rate per dunum according to the category of the land, the greater tax being levied on the more highly developed land. No distinction is made between long term lessees and owner occupiers, the owner of the land in all cases being responsible for the tax. The Ordinance provides that the High Commissioner may by Order declare the areas of lands and industrial buildings within such areas, not being urban areas within the meaning of the Urban Property Tax Ordinance, 1928, to be subject to the tax (Sec. 3).

In such areas the Rural Property Tax will replace the tithe, the Ottoman House and Land Tax (Wergo, Mussaqafat, Ijara Zemin and Bedl Ushur) and the Muqata'a tax (Sec. 2). The Commutation of Tithes Ordinance, 1927, and the Decree of 21st September 1920 (Off. Gaz. 15th November 1920) relating to the exemption from tithes of vineyards planted with American stock shall cease to have effect in any area to which the rural property tax shall be made applicable (Sec. 42).

The tax is levied on lands at the rates set out in the Schedule to the Ordinance in respect of the category within which the lands fall, and on industrial buildings at such rate, not exceeding fifteen percentum of the net annual value of such industrial buildings, as shall be prescribed by the High Commissioner (Sec. 4).

Sec. 7 of the Ordinance provides for the appointment of official valuers, and Secs. 8, 9 and 10 prescribe the duties and powers of such valuers with regard to the preparation of the rural property tax rolls and valuation lists, and the assessment of industrial buildings. Secs. 11 and 12 deal with objections to the rolls and lists and provision is made under Sec. 14 for any person aggrieved by a decision of the official valuer to appeal from such decision to appeal committees appointed by the High Commissioner (Sec. 13).

Appeal Committees will determine all such appeals, and, by Sec. 16 of the Ordinance, will determine also the areas of the categories

Chapter XXIII—Taxation of Land.

of the lands of a village, and the categories as are shown on the Rural Property Tax Roll as finally so determined, and the net annual value of industrial buildings as shown on the valuation list so determined, will provide the data on which the tax will be assessed until such time as it is amended in the manner provided in the Ordinance.

Since, however, the Rural Property Tax Roll will only show the categories of land and the extent of such categories within a division of an area to which the Ordinance has been applied, the procedure for apportioning the tax amongst the owners of the land is provided for in Secs. 18—25.

Provision is made by Secs. 26—29 for maintaining the Rural Property Tax Rolls and Valuation Lists up to date, and for the annual re-apportionment of the tax among owners of land.

The Schedule provides for the division of all the lands of the country in sixteen categories of different descriptions (land with citrus plantations, irrigated land, land with fruit plantations, ground crop land, built-on village areas, etc.). The rate of the tax per dunum is from 825 mils to 8 mils per annum. Certain lands, like lands planted with forest or covered with indigenous forests and uncultivable land, are exempted from the tax.

The tax shall be recovered in accordance with the provisions of the Collection of Taxes Ordinance 1929 (Sec. 32) and shall be a first charge on the property in respect of which it is payable and no transaction relating to such property shall be entered in any Government register until the tax thereon has been paid (Sec. 38).

CHAPTER XXIV—LAND REGISTRATION FEES.

Land Registry fees are collected under the Land Transfer Ordinance 1920 as amended by the Ordinances of 1921—1932. The fees are set out in a Schedule published under Sec. 16 of the Land Transfer Ordinance [1].

The rule is that transactions in respect of which the fees are not covered by the Rules of Fees made under Sec. 16 of the Land Transfer Ordinance and where there is a doubt as to what fees are chargeable are to be referred to the Director of Lands for instruction.

There is a further rule that unless it is otherwise agreed upon between the parties to a transaction, the registration fees in respect of all transactions, except mortgages and discharges of mortgages, are payable by the transferee (or applicant). In respect of mortgages and discharges of mortgages, the fees are paid by the mortgagors.

Scale of Fees in the Land Registry. The scale of fees in Land Registry transactions is 3% on the market value of the property in sales, and in exchanges; 2% on the market value of the property in gifts if the gift is to a descendant or ascendant or wife or husband and 3% if the gift is to any other person; 5% on the rent for one year in a transaction of lease where the lease is for a term of more than 3 years and less than 10 years and 10% on the rent for one year where the lease is for a term of 10 years and over; 1% on the amount of a loan in a transaction of mortgage; $1/2$% on a mortgage in favour of a Credit Bank if the loan is repayable within a period not exceeding one year [2]; the fee payable upon the registration of a mortgage to secure debentures or an obligation of an undefinite amount is calculated on two-thirds of the value of the immovable property given as security [3]; the fee payable on the transfer of a mortgage is $1/2$% of the amount of the secured loan. On the sale of mortgaged

---

[1] See Schedule of Fees in Notice No. 164 under the Land Transfer Ordinance 1920.
[2] Sec. 3 of the Credit Bank (Facilities) Ordinance 1920.
[3] Off. Gaz. No. 239 of 16th July 1929; No. 289 of 16th August 1931; No. 330 of 8th December 1932.

Chapter XXIV—Land Registration Fees.

property at the request of the mortgagee a registration fee of 3% is payable; in addition an execution fee of $2^1/_2\%$ and an auctioneer's fee of 1% is also payable. On the sale and provisional registration of property under Sec. 2 (11) of the Credit Banks Ordinance, 1922, or Sec. 2 of the Mortgage Law Amendment Ordinance 1929, the same fee as set out above is paid, provided that if the former owner redeems the land and the Bank or the Company in whose name such provisional registration is made shall not become the definite owner of the property, the registration fee of 3% shall be refunded [1]).

In successions the fee is $1^1/_2\%$ on the value as registered in the Land Registers or Wergo Registers of the interest transferred by way of succession to descendants or ascendants or wife or husband; 3% on the value of the property as registered in the Land Registers or Wergo Registers transferred by way of succession to brothers, sisters and their descendants; 5% on the value of the property as registered in the Land Registers or Wergo Registers transferred by way of succession to any other heir. The minimum fee is fifty mils in respect of the interest transferred to any one heir [2]). In bequests 10% of the market value of the property is payable if the legatee is not a legal heir. In partitions the fee is $1/_2\%$ on the market value of the property subject of partition. When a certificate of registration based on prescription or other ground is issued for property which does not appear on the Register, a fee of 5% on the market value is payable [3]).

The fee on the registration of Waqf is $2^1/_2\%$ payable on the constitution of land as Waqf if the value of the land is of £P.200, if the value exceeds this amount, the fee is $1/_2\%$ on any amount in excess of £P. 200. One half of the fees levied in respect of the constitution of a Moslem Waqf is paid to the Waqf Administration and one half to the Government Treasury [4]).

The Search fees are 50 mils for every property in respect of which search is made. For the Printed Forms used in a transaction a fee of 50 mils is charged [5]).

For Extracts from the Registers a fee of 40 mils for every one hundred words is chargeable; for the certificate on the Extract 20 mills for every one hundred words is chargeable.

---

[1]) Off. Gaz. No. 235 of 16th May 1929.
[2]) Off. Gaz. No. 210 of 1st May 1928.
[3]) See Appendix V, infra, as to the changes made recently in the Scale of Land Registry Fees.
[4]) Off. Gaz. 15th December 1922.
[5]) Off. Gaz. No. 324 of 3rd November 1932.

The Land Law of Palestine.

A correction fee of 250 mils is payable for every property in respect of which a correction is required.

For the registration of Accretions (Inshaat) [1]), buildings and trees, a fee of 60 mils is payable for property the value of which is less than £P.50; a fee of 110 mils is payable when the value is £P.50 to £P.100; and a fee of 50 mils for each further amount of £P.100; of a value exceeding £P.1000 the fee is £P.1.060 mils.

No fee is payable by the Government or any Department on account of any transaction in the Land Registries [2]).

The Schedule of Fees did not make provision for the fees payable upon the registration of property held as a Charitable Trust, neither did the Charitable Trust Ordinance. A question has arisen as to what fee is payable. In accordance with the general rule set out above the Director of Lands instructed that the transaction must be treated as one analogous to the registration of a Waqf and that fees similar to those prescribed for the registration of a Waqf are chargeable [3]).

Fees on Transfer from an Unofficial Land Book.

The fees [4]) payable on transfer of an entry from an Unofficial Land Book to the Official Register are as follows:

(1) The fee payable on an application for the registration of an interest recorded in an unofficial land book prior to the 1st of October, 1920, is £P.1. No fee is payable on the registration of such an interest in the Official Register;

(2) The fee payable on an application for the registration of an interest recorded in an unofficial land book subsequent to

---

[1]) Ottoman Laws A.H. 1291 and A.H. 1332.

[2]) Off. Gaz. No. 234 of 1st May 1929.

[3]) In Board of Foreign Mission v. the Director of Lands the High Court held that the instruction of the Director of Lands was reasonable. See H.C. No. 46/32, Palestine Post 26th October 1933.

Rules have recently been made by the Chief Justice providing for the fees payable on the registration of a trust in the Land Registry. The fee is $2\frac{1}{2}\%$ on the market value of the property registered as a trust; if the value of the property exceeds two hundred pounds the fee of two and a half percentum is chargeable on the first two hundred pounds, and a fee of one half per centum on any amount in excess of two hundred pounds. On the registration in the Land Registry of any instrument or order of appointment of new trustees, or of a vesting order, in respect of immovable property already registered in the name of trustees, the fee chargeable is two hundred and fifty mils. See Rules made by the C. J. under the Charitable Trusts Ordinances 1924—1925. P. G. No. 487 of 17th January, 1935.

[4]) Collected under the Correction of Land Registers Ordinance, 1926, promulgated in Off. Gaz. No. 160 of 1st of April, 1926, and amended on the 1st of October 1926.

Chapter XXIV—Land Registration Fees.

the 1st of October, 1920, is £P.1. This fee shall be refunded to the applitant if the interest claimed is subsequently registered in the Official Register;

(3) The fees payable on the registration of an interest recorded in an Unofficial Land Book subsequent to the 1st of October, 1920, are similar to the fees prescribed in the Schedule of Fees made under Sec. 16 of the Land Transfer Ordinance, set out above, except with regard to Successions, in which case the fee payable is based on the market value of the land at the date of acquisition and the fee is any case not less than 250 mils.

(4) If an applicant is registered under the Correction of Land Registers Ordinance as the owner of the land on which he has erected improvements after the date of the entry in the unofficial land book on which his application was based and he desires to register such improvements, the fees payable on the registration of the improvements are the Inshaat fees prescribed by the Law of A.H. 1291 as amended by the Law of A.H. 1332.

Fees payable on Land Settlement. In accordance with an Order made by the High Commissioner under the Land Settlement Ordinance, 1928 [1]) the fees payable on registration in the Registers of rights in Land Settlement are as follows:— (1) On registration of a right of ownership of Miri or Mulk land held in divided ownership 10 mils per dunum with a minimum of 50 mils. The same fee is chargeable on the registration of a share in undivided Miri or Mulk land. The fee on a registration of buildings and trees owned separately from the land is 250 mils. (11) On registration of a lease 1 mil per dunum with a minimum fee of 50 mils. (111) On registration of a mortgage half the fee payable on the registration of a right of ownership with a minimum fee of 50 mils. (IV) No registration fee is payable on account of the registration of a partition of Mesha'a land, Cemeteries, land and buildings used for any water supply system owned by a village, buildings and gardens and playing-grounds dedicated for educational purposes, and Metruki land. For the registration of a right of ownership or a lease of land in the name of the Government no registration fees are payable.

Where any right to land registered in an existing registration is recorded without modification, no Land Settlement fee is charged, and where there is modification only the Settlement Officer may waive any fee (Land Settlement Ordinance, Sec. 64 (1) and (2)).

Land Settlement fees payable in Land Settlement may be paid in instalments. The District Commissioner decides at what

---

[1]) Off. Gaz. No. 304 of 1st April 1932.

The Land Law of Palestine.

rate a fee may be paid in instalments and the number and period of instalments.

Fees on actions before a Settlement Officer. The fees payable in Land Settlement on the hearing of actions before a Settlement Officer are now prescribed by an order made under Sec. 62 of the Land Settlement Ordinance 1928, the provisions of which are as follows:—

(1) A Settlement Officer may, at his discretion, in cases of poverty or hardship, remit in part or in whole the payment of any fee prescribed under the Order; (2) a proportional fee of two per centum of the value of the subject matter of the claim shall be levied on the parties to the action in accordance with the decision of a Settlement Officer after hearing the action; (3) If the value of the subject matter is not stated or if the Settlement Officer doubts the exactness of the value stated, the Settlement Officer shall determine the value; (4) The fee shall not exceed twenty pounds nor be less than one hundred mils; (5) If the value of the subject matter of the claim cannot be assessed in terms of money, a fixed fee of one pound and five hundred mils shall be levied; (6) A fixed fee of four hundred mils is levied on each copy of a judgment or decision other than the first copy; (7) A fixed fee of one hundred mils is levied on every page of each copy of any document (other than a judgment or decision). Every one hundred and fifty words or less are deemed to constitute a page [1]).

---

[1]) See Land Settlement Actions (Fees and Payments) Order, 1933, P.G. No. 391 of 28th September, 1933. This order revoked the Order dated the 24th of August, 1928, which provided that the fees charged on the hearing of contested claims in cases before the Settlement Officers were those prescribed by the Rules of Court of 1918 for the hearing of actions as to possession of land. See also Sec. 8 of the Land Settlement (Proceedings) Rules 1928—1934, P.G. No. 423 of 21st February, 1934.

CHAPTER XXV—COURTS DEALING WITH LAND SUITS.

By Sec. 23 of Military Proclamation of 24th June, 1918, it was provided that until further notice the Courts should not give any judgment deciding upon the ownership of land. This proclamation took away all jurisdiction over cases concerning ownership of land from the Sharia Courts and from the Courts of first Instance (District Courts) and this jurisdiction has never been restored. Its effect as to cases pending in the Sharia Courts was to prohibit any further hearing before those Courts[1]).

By Sec. 15 of the Transfer of Land Ordinance, 1920, it was provided that the provisions of this Military Proclamation should remain in force, but that the Courts might, nevertheless, hear actions for Partition in accordance with the Partition Law of A.H. 1332, and also hear actions concerning ownership of land by special fiat of the Attorney General.

In 1921 the Land Courts Ordinance empowered the High Commissioner by Order published in the Gazette to establish a Land Court for such districts as he thought desirable.

Under the Palestine Order-in-Council 1922 the High Commissioner is explicitly authorized to establish Land Courts "for the hearing of such questions concerning the title to immovable property as may be prescribed" (Art. 42). The Land Courts Ordinance 1921, the Transfer of Land Ordinances 1920—1921 like all other Ordinances, etc. issued by the various successive authorities in power in Palestine since the Occupation were declared to be and always to have been valid (Arts. 73, 74).

By Establishment of Courts Order, 1924, made under the Palestine Order-in-Council, 1922 (Art. 42) Land Courts were established, and constituted as follows:—

The Land Courts.

---

[1]) Abd el Rehim v. Mamur Awqaf, Nablus; Off. Gaz. 1st February, 1927. It is further to be noted that even where the land is claimed as Waqf the Sharia Courts are incompetent (Jurisdiction of Civil and Religious Courts Ord. 1925, Sec. 5).

(a) A Land Court for the Jerusalem Division of the District of Jerusalem and Jaffa, and the sub-districts of Hebron and Beersheba, constituted by a British President and one or more judges, sitting at Jerusalem and such other places as the President of the Court may from time to time determine;

(b) A Land Court for the Jaffa Division of the District of Jerusalem and Jaffa and the sub-district of Gaza, constituted by a British President and one or more judges sitting at Jaffa and such other places as the President may from to time determine;

(c) A Land Court for the area served by the District Court of Haifa, constituted by the President of the District Court of Haifa and one or more judges of such District Court sitting for the purpose at such places as the President may from time to time determine;

(d) A Land Court for the area served by the District Court of Nablus, constituted by the President of the District Court of Nablus and one or more judges of such District Court sitting for that purpose at such places as the President may from time to time determine.

This Order which provides also for the establishment of District Courts and Magistrates Courts came into force on 1st September 1924. It makes no reference to the Land Courts Ordinance 1921 nor to the power of the High Commissioner thereunder, but it assumed that the Land Courts established under the Order, are merely in succession to those already existing under the Ordinance of 1921 and have the powers, etc. stated in the Land Courts Ordinance. The Courts Ordinance 1924 constituting the Supreme Court and making various provisions as to judicial organization, etc. refers several times to the Land Court and provides expressly (Sec. 23) that the Ordinance is to come into force on the day on which the High Commissioner should by Order establish the Courts which he is empowered to establish by the Palestine Order-in-Council 1922 and any cases pending in the Land Courts in existence in Palestine at the date of such Order shall be deemed to be transferred as from such date to the appropriate Courts established by such Order in the condition in which they may then respectively be. This appears to make succession clear.

The Establishment of Courts Order 1932. By the Establishment of Courts Order, 1932, which repealed, inter alia, the Establishment of Courts Order, 1924, the following Land Courts were established:

(a) A Land Court for the area served by the District Court of Jerusalem, constituted by the President of the District Court

Chapter XXV—Courts Dealing with Land Suits.[375]

of Jerusalem and one or more judges of such District Court sitting for the purpose at such places as the President may from to time determine;

(b) A Land Court for the area served by the District Court of Jaffa, constituted by the President of the District Court of Jaffa and one or more judges of such District Court sitting for the purpose at such places as the President may from time to time determine;

(c) A Land Court for the area served by the District Court of Haifa, constituted by the President of the District Court of Haifa and one or more judges of such District Court sitting for the purpose at such places as the President may from to time detemine;

(d) A Land Court for the area served by the District Court of Nablus, constituted by the President of the District Court of Nablus and one or more judges of such District Court sitting for the purpose at such places as the President may from time to time determine.

The powers of the Land Court are set out by the Land Courts Ordinance 1921 (Sec. 2) in the following terms:— *The powers of the Land Court.*

The Land Court shall have the following powers:

(a) To call for and record all claims to rights in or over Mulk and Miri and every other class of land.

(b) Where claims to ownership, mortgage, or other registrable rights in or over land are accepted by the Land Court as valid and undisputed, to direct the registration of same in the Land Registry and to demarcate the boundaries of the land over which such rights extend.

(c) Where claims to such rights are accepted by the Court as valid and are undisputed except with regard to the boundaries, to give a decision as to the boundaries and to demarcate them in accordance with the decision.

(d) Where there is a dispute as to the ownership of the land or any rights in or over the land, to hear the case and give a judgment.

(e) To decide upon any dispute arising out of the partition of lands held in undivided ownership.

(f) To enquire into any case where an application is made under the Correction of Land Registers Ordinance, 1920, and to give a judgment whether such correction shall be made.

(g) To hear and decide disputes as to the possession of State lands other than Miri land and to demarcate boundaries in accordance with the decision.

It was, however, provided (Sec. 8) that nothing in the Ordinance was to derogate from:—

(1) the power of Magistrates' Courts to hear actions concerning possession of land or concerning the partition of land in accordance with the Law of 14th Moharrem, A.H. 1332, or

(2) the power of the Legal Secretary (now Attorney General) to allow an action concerning ownership of land to be heard by any District Court.

An appeal lies from the Land Court to the Court of Appeal but only on a question of law [1]).

As to law and procedure the Ordinance provides as follows:—

Sec. 7 (1). The Land Court will apply the Ottoman Law in force at the date of the British Occupation as amended by any Ordinances or Rules of Court issued since the Occupation; provided that the Courts shall have regard to equitable as well as to legal rights to land, and shall not be bound by any rule of the Ottoman Law prohibiting the Courts from hearing actions based on unregistered documents.

(2) The procedure to be followed by the Land Court shall, subject to any Rules of Court, be that laid down in the Code of Civil Procedure as amended. Provided that the Court shall not be bound by the Rules of Evidence contained in that Code or in the Civil Code.

The Section gives wide powers to the Court. Since it is entitled to hear actions based upon unregistered documents, it is necessarily empowered to recognize interests which have not been registered; it is consequently not bound by the explicit provisions of the Ottoman Law already considered requiring the Mulk and Miri owner to obtain a formal title. If in the opinion of the Court an interest should in equity be recognized it will be entitled to recognize it notwithstanding absence of registration. It is, however, to be observed that the Court is not entitled to ignore in this way the provisions of Palestine Ordinances, e.g. Transfer of Land Ordinances. It is only the Ottoman Law which may at its discretion be neglected.

The Land Courts are given power with the consent of the parties to refer to arbitration any dispute arising before it in any matter under the Ordinance. Awards are to be authenticated by

---

[1]) Land Courts Amendment Ordinance 1929 modifying Sec. 3 of the Land Courts Ordinance 1921. For the conditions of Appeal see Land Courts (Appeals) Rules of Court 11th October 1929. (O.G. No. 246 of 1st November 1929).

Chapter XXV—Courts Dealing with Land Suits.[377]

the Court, subject to its powers to remit them to the arbitrators or set them aside on specified grounds, and when authenticated are to have the effect of a judgment of a Court and to be executory (Sec. 5).

Arbitrations directed under this Section are not (semble) submissions under the Arbitration Ordinance, 1926, and the provisions of that Ordinance are consequently not applicable.

Power to order demarcation of land by an owner or occupier is given, and in default of obedience the Court may itself proceed to demarcation (Sec. 9)[1]. The Land Registration Department (i.e. the Land Registry) is directed (Sec. 4) "to carry out the instructions of the Land Court as regards the registration of any rights to ownership, mortgage, or any other registrable rights", and to "issue title deeds in accordance with such instructions".

For the purpose of the Ordinance "land" is "to include houses, buildings and things permanently fixed in the land" (Sec. 10).

It is not clear whether the term can be extended so as to cover easements[2] and the like, but for most if not for all purposes the question is not important since the Land Court can direct the registration of any "registrable" right in or over land and can decide disputes not only as to ownership of land but as to any rights in or over land. Indeed the language of the Ordinance is so broad as to call for some limitative interpretation[3].

Further powers and duties have been conferred upon the Land Court by later legislation. Thus under the Correction of Land Registers Ordinance 1926, Sec. 9, objections to registration under the Ordinance are to be referred to the Land Court. Under Sec. 8 of the Expropriation Ordinance 1926 the amount of compensation payable by promoters under the Ordinance is, in default of agreement,

---

[1] It should be remarked that under Art. 126 Land Code where ancient boundary marks of towns or villages have disappeared new marks are to be fixed by trustworthy persons from the locality with the cooperation of the religious authority. This article does not appear to give judicial power to the religious authority to fix boundaries, and if it is to be interpreted as so doing, such power no longer exists in view of the statutory restriction of the jurisdiction of Religious Courts in Palestine.

[2] As to "land" and "immovable property" see Interpretation Ordinance 1929, Sec. 3 (c) (7). The most comprehensive definition of "land" is that given in the Expropriation of Land Ordinance 1926, Sec. 2, when the term explicitly includes "easements".

[3] An action between co-owners as to removal of pipes installed by the co-owner is not an action as to the ownership of "land" (nor, semble, one as to rights in or over land)—Sheikh Katib v. Darhalli, C.A. 97/32.

The Land Law of Palestine.

to be determined by the Land Court in whose jurisdiction the land is situated. Under Sec. 3 (3) of the Magistrates' Courts Jurisdiction Ordinance 1924—1930 the Land Court has power to hear appeals from judgments of Magistrates' Courts relating to recovery of possession of immovable property and of partitions. The Land Court is also an Appellate Court from judicial proceedings before a Settlement Officer [1]).

Under the Protection of Cultivators (Amendment) Ordinance, 1934 (Sub-sec. (2) of Sec. 19) an appeal from the decision of the Commissions appointed by the High Commissioner under Sec. 19 (1) of the Protection of Cultivators Ordinance, 1933, on a point of law shall lie to the Land Court by leave of the Court on a case stated.

The following Rules of Court relating to the Land Courts have been issued: (a) dealing with procedure in the Land Courts dated 15th May, 1921; (b) directing the registration of copies of the judgments of a Land Court in the Land Registry of the district or sub-district in which the land is situated dated 19th December, 1921; (c) relating to Judgments by Default dated 8th May, 1926 (amended by a Rule dated 16th December, 1928) [2]).

Magistrates' Courts. The jurisdiction of Magistrates' Courts in connection with immovables depends primarily upon the provisions of Arts. 5—7 of the Ottoman Magistrates' Law of 17 Jamad el Awal A.H. 1331. The provisions may be summarized as giving jurisdiction to the Magistrate (a) in claims for recovery of possession of immovables (Art. 5); (b) in eviction of "leased property" (Art. 6); (c) in provisional attachment for debt (Art. 7).

The jurisdiction is now exercised under the Magistrates' Courts Jurisdiction Ordinance 1924—1930 which gives to magistrates in this connection jurisdiction (Sec. 2 (1)—(b)) in actions for the recovery of the possession of immovable property of any value and (Sec. 2 (1) (c)) in actions for the partition of immovable property [3]) and for Muhaya. By Sec. 2 (2) it is provided that no criminal or civil action or counterclaim which involves a decision as to the ownership of immovable property may be heard by a Magistrate.

The provisions as to jurisdiction replace those set out in Sec. 1 of the Magistrates' Courts Jurisdiction Ordinance 1924.

---

[1]) See Chapter XVII on Cadastral Survey and Land Settlement, supra.

[2]) The Court Fees Ordinance 1933 made provision for the fixing of fees, and percentages to be taken in the Civil Courts including Land Courts (See Schedule to Ordinance No. 39 of 1933).

[3]) Compare Law of Partition 14 Moharrem A.H. 1332, Sec. 6.

Chapter XXV—Courts Dealing with Land Suits.[379]

It may be noted that Sec. 10 of the latter Ordinance provides that the provisions of the Ottoman Magistrates' Law and of any amendments thereto concerning the jurisdiction of Magistrates' Courts so far as they are inconsistent with the provisions of the Ordinance are repealed.

Actions for recovery of possession of immovable property may be assumed to include actions for eviction of tenants holding under a lease which has expired or been invalidated though separate provisions were made by the Ottoman Magistrates' law for eviction actions. The provisions of Sec. 20 of the Iradeh as to leasing of A.H. 1299 as amended in A.H. 1332 are still in force in Palestine and recourse may be had to them in eviction proceedings [1]).

But actions for recovery of possession are not limited to proceedings by a lessor against a lessee holding over. They include possessory actions proper i.e. proceedings between two persons each of whom claim ownership to determine which has the better right to immediate possession.

"A decision given in favour of the plaintiff in an action for the recovery of possession does not imply that he is the owner. Consequently if the party who has been ordered to give up possession claims to be owner of the immovable property in dispute the question will be decided in a separate action" [2]).

It is clear from the provisions of Secs. 24, 25 and 26 of the Ottoman Magistrates' law that the holder of a title deed (Kushan) is to be primarily preferred in case of any dispute as to possession [3]). The holder may recover possession against any person interfering with his possession as soon as legal proceedings are taken [4]).

---

[1]) As already pointed out appeals from judgments of Magistrates' Courts relating to recovery of possession of immovable property lie to the Land Court. The Magistrates' Courts Jurisdiction Ordinance 1935 (published as a Bill in P.G. No. 496 of 28th February 1935) provides that where a claim for a sum of money within the Jurisdiction of the Magistrate in respect of rent or profits of immovable property or damage thereto is brought with a claim for recovery of possession of immovable property an appeal in either such claim shall lie to the Land Court.

[2]) Ottoman Magistrates' Law, Sec. 27.

[3]) In Salim Risq Hanna v. Boulos Hanna Risq (L.A. 58/33) the Court of Appeal held that an extract from a Wergo Register was a Sanad of possession within the meaning of Sec. 24 of the Magistrates' Law of A.H. 1331. (Palestine Post 7th November 1934). Cf. L.A. 42/33 reported in Palestine Post 14th January 1935. In this case the Court of Appeal held that a Wergo receipt is evidence not of ownership but of possession only.

[4]) Remark that possession taken "by force" is vitiated and if the holder of a title deed has obtained such possession "he is to be directed to take the proper legal procedure" i.e. (semble) he will be ejected at the instance of the

In case both parties to a possessory action hold deeds the following rules apply:—

If the title deeds emanate from one and the same person or from different persons, preference is given to the older title; but if one of the parties has obtained the property from the other, the deed of the later date is preferred.

The law proceeds to lay down important rules for application in the cases in which the defendant has built or planted or sown crops on the land [1]).

It does not appear that any shorter period of limitation exists for possessory proceedings than for proceedings for the determination of ownership (sometimes termed "petitory" [2]).

Sec. 5 of the Ottoman Magistrates' Law expressly provided that a Magistrate is entitled to hear claims as to a right of user of water which the owner has been prevented from using, without giving a decision on the merits. This express provision suggests, as appears elsewhere in the law, that rights of this description should not be treated as immovable property in Ottoman law for if so treated they would have been already covered by the general provisions in the first paragraph of the Section [3]). The omission of specific provisions to the same effect in the Magistrates' Courts Jurisdiction Ordinance is understood to take the protection of servitudes out of the jurisdiction of the Magistrate and to place it within the exclusive jurisdiction of the Land Courts [4]).

Holy Places. It is provided by Art. 14 of the Mandate that a special commission should be appointed by the Mandatory to study, define and determine the rights and claims in connection with the Holy Places. No such commission has been appointed but by the Palestine

---

person whom he has disseised and be required to start a possessory action against the latter (Sec. 24).

[1]) Secs. 28—33.

[2]) Cardahi in Revue Critique, 1926, at p. 122. In this article to which reference has already been made an interesting attempt is made to compare the possessory proceedings of the Ottoman law with the well-known possessory actions of French law. (Réintégrande, Complainte, Dénonciation de nouvel œuvre). The writer is a member of the Court of Cassation of the Lebanon.

[3]) Compare Cardahi, supra, at p. 217. "The only servitude protected by a possessory action in Ottoman law is the servitude of irrigation (Haq el Shurb) and the servitude of drinking (Haq el Shufa)". The normal remedy for disturbance of servitude in modern Palestine would be an interlocutory injunction.

[4]) See Shems, Manual of Magistrates' Law in Palestine, pp. 10, 12. Though (semble) not immovables, such rights are yet clearly rights in or over land (Land Courts Ordinance 1921, Sec. 2).

Chapter XXV—Courts Dealing with Land Suits.

(Holy Places) Order-in-Council 1924 it was declared that "no cause or matter in connection with the Holy Places or religious buildings or sites in Palestine ....shall be heard or determined by any Court in Palestine" [1]. It appears that no authority for determining such cause or matter exists outside Palestine "pending the constitution of a Commission charged with jurisdiction".

It is submitted that the Order-in-Council should not be interpreted as giving authority to the High Commissioner to decide the "cause or matter". Art. 3 does not state that the "cause or matter" is to be referred to the High Commissioner but that the question whether the cause or matter comes within the terms of Art. 1 is to be so referred and this is the question which the High Commissioner is to decide in accordance with instructions which he receives from the Secretary of State [2].

Judicial proceedings before a Settlement Officer under the Land Settlement Ordinance 1928—1932 and appeals therefrom are dealt with in Chapter XVII on Cadastral Survey and Land Settlement and need not, therefore, be considered here [3]. — Land Settlement Courts.

In 1932 was enacted a novel Ordinance to enable District Commissioners to make Orders as to posseesion of land concerning which a dispute exists which is likely to cause a breach of the peace. This is the Land Disputes (Possession) Ordinance 1932. It was amended by a further Ordinance in 1934. It is not necessary in this place to consider the provisions of these Ordinances in detail. They are designed to provide an administrative remedy for the frequent disputes which arise in Palestine as to rights in land, and have but little relation to the determination of such rights. When any dispute arises concerning any land or water [4] or the boundaries — Land Disputes (Possession) Ordinances 1932, 1934.

---

[1] "Holy Places" are not defined nor are "religious buildings or sites" but questions as to whether any cause or matter is within the scope of the Order-in-Council are to be determined by the High Commissioner (Art. 3).

[2] The contrary view appears to have been taken by the Court of Appeal in Subhi Khadra v. Bishop Hajjar L.A. 2/33 in which it seems to have been suggested that it was for the Court to decide whether the property in issue was a holy place, etc. The report, however, is somewhat obscure.

[3] The question raised in Goldberg v. Rabinovich (L.A. 5/33), referred to on p. 278, supra, as to whether a Settlement Officer can exercise judicial power is now set at rest by the Palestine (Amendment) Order-in-Council 1935. A fresh Art. 38 has been substituted for Art. 38 of the Palestine Order-in-Council 1922 to the effect that in addition to the Courts described in the Order of 1922 any other Courts constituted by or under any Ordinance shall exercise jurisdiction. P.G. No. 496 of 28th February, 1935.

[4] Land or water includes "buildings, crops or other produce of land and the rents or profits of any property" (Sec. 2 (2)).

thereof and the District Commissioner is satisfied that the dispute is likely to lead to a breach of the peace he can require the parties concerned to attend before him and may without any reference to the merits or the claims of any such parties decide if possible whether any or which of the parties is at the date of the order of summons in actual possession of the subject of the dispute [1].

The Ordinance contains detailed provisions enabling the District Commissioner to make orders to secure possession to one party until eviction in due course of law, and to withdraw such order if at any time he is satisfied that there is no longer any likelihood of a breach of the peace [2]. If the District Commissioner decides that non of the parties was in actual possession, or is unable to decide which was so, he is empowered to appoint a manager until a competent Court had determined the rights of the parties [3].

The District Commissioner may depute any public officer, to make a local enquiry if he considers such an enquiry to be necessary and the report of the person so deputed may be read as evidence in the case [4].

Similar procedure to that detailed in Sec. 2 may be applied by the District Commissioner in cases of disputes as to grazing rights, rights of irrigation, etc. In such cases he is empowered to make orders prohibiting interference with or exercise of the alleged right as the case may be until a competent Court has decided whether the right really exists [5].

Orders made for possession or for appointment of a manager "prevent the alienation of the land which is the subject of dispute until a competent Court has determined the rights of the parties thereto". Copies of the order are to be sent to the Registrar of

---

[1] Land Disputes (Possession) Ord. 1932 Sec. 2 (1); (4).

[2] Land Disputes (Possession) Ord. Sec. 2 (6); Land Disputes Possession (Amendment) Ord. 1934, Sec. 2.

[3] Land Disputes (Possession) Ord. 1932 Sec. 3. The District Commissioner is exceeding his power if he makes an order for possession in favour of persons, who were not parties to the proceedings before him or with regard to whom there was not before him any evidence that they had ever been in possession of the disputed land. Haifa Bay Development Co. v. District Commissioner (Northern District) H. C. 92/32. (Palestine Post 26th November 1933; 14th February 1934).

[4] Sec. 5 (1); (2). It is not clear whether the "case" referred to is the case before the District Commissioner or extends to the case before the competent court which decides the issue of rights.

[5] The order is in the nature of an injunction. It is not, however, stated how the order is to be enforced. The Contempt of Court Ordinance 1924 does not apply.

Chapter XXV—Courts Dealing with Land Suits.

Lands who is to "cause a note thereof to be made in the land register". The same procedure is to be followed in the case of withdrawal of the order [1]).

Sec. 2 (10) of the Ordinance of 1932 expressly provides that no appeal shall lie against any order by a District Commissioner made under the Ordinance. In a recent case [2]) it was, however, decided by the High Court that an order made by a District Commissioner in excess of his powers under the Ordinance could be set aside by that Court as being an order not made in the proper exercise of his legitimate judicial discretion. The Amending Ordinance of 1934 makes clear (Sec. 3) that nothing in the Principal Ordinance is to enable a District Commissioner to over ride or vary an order made by a competent Court, a Settlement Officer under the Land Settlement Ordinance 1928—1932 or a Chief Execution Officer.

Under the Protection of Cultivators Ordinance, 1933, as amended in 1934, Boards and Special Commissions have been constituted to hear certain disputes between landlords and tenants. Reference has already been made [3]) to the matters within the competence of these Boards and Commissions. Here it is sufficient to note that though the decisions of the Boards in any matter referred to them under the Ordinance are subject to confirmation by the District Commissioner and when confirmed by him are final, the Order of the District Commissioner must be made in the proper exercise of his legitimate judicial discretion. *Boards and Special Commissions under the Protection of Cultivators Ordinances 1933-4.*

Against a decision of such a Board (and a confirmation by the District Commissioner) no appeal would appear to lie to the Land Court, but following the general principles set out in High Court

---

[1]) Land Disputes (Possession) Ordinance 1932 Sec. 2 (11); Sec. 3 (2). Presumably the "prevention" takes place by reason of the entry in the Register. If the order were by misadventure not notified to the Registrar, an alienation accepted in ignorance of the order would (semble) be valid.

[2]) Haifa Bay Development Co. v. A. D. Commissioner Northern District H. C. 92/32; Palestine Post 26th November 1933. See also judgment in Mohammed Shibl v. A. D. Commissioner Northern District and Haj Khalil Taha H. C. 74/33; Palestine Post 17th February 1934. The High Court held that, though the District Commissioner is not acting as a Magistrate, in so far as his powers under the Land Disputes (Possession) Ordinance relate to matters covered by Sub-section 10 of Sec. 2, the proceedings are to be the same as if they were proceedings before a Magistrate (as regards enforcement of Orders and other like matters). Art. 73 of the Magistrates' Law is applicable and an Order of the District Commissioner executed without due notice having been given to the judgment debtor cannot be considered legally executed. The Order was set aside.

[3]) See Chapter XV— Protection of Agricultural Tenants, supra, p.p. 249 ff.

case No. 92/32 to which reference has been made above, it would appear, by analogy, that if the Board or the District Commissioner have exceeded the powers conferred upon them by the Ordinance, the High Court would appear to have jurisdiction to issue an Order setting aside the decision by the Board and the confirmation by the District Commissioner.

Against a decision of such a Commission, however, an appeal would lie to the Land Court but only on a point of law and by leave of the Court by case stated (Sub-sec. 2 of Sec. 19 as amended by the Protection of Cultivators Amendment Ordinance, 1934). By Sub-sec. 3 of Sec. 19 it is provided that a decision by a Commission is res judicata. A decision by a Board would not appear to be a res judicata.

District Courts.

It is not necessary to do more than to refer briefly to the jurisdiction of the District Courts in matters connected with Successions, Probates, Administration of Estates and Immovables. This jurisdiction is exercised in accordance with the provisions of the Palestine Order-in-Council 1922 (Secs. 38, 40 and 47) and the Establishment of Courts Order 1932. The rule is that the District Court is generally a Court of First Instance in all matters not within the jurisdiction of the other established Courts.

The allotment of Jurisdiction to the Civil Courts under the Succession Ordinance 1923 has already been considered in the Chapter upon Succession and Inheritance [1]). The grant of Probate, Administration of Estates, and the declaration of Successions are matters within the Jurisdiction of the District Court of the District within which the deceased resided or had his place of business at the date of his death; or, if the deceased had no residence or place of business in Palestine, by the District Court of the District within which any property forming part of the deceased's estate is situated; or in default of any such property, by the District Court of Jerusalem [2]).

The competent Court in any proceedings under the Charitable Trust Ordinance 1924—5 is the District Court of the District in

---

[1]) See Chapter VII, p.p. 96—124, supra.

[2]) See Secs. 12, 13 and 23 of the Succession Ordinance 1923; Sec. 25 as enacted by the Succession (Amendment) Ordinance 1932. See also the Succession (Amendment) Rules 1932 (P.G. No. 331 of 15 December 1932).

For the purposes of the Succession Ordinance a District Court may be constituted by the President of the District Court sitting alone or with one or more judges.

Chapter XXV—Courts Dealing with Land Suits.[385]

which any part of the subject-matter of the trust is held or situate [1]).

With regard to Immovables held by Companies, it is to be remarked that The Companies Ordinance 1929 provides that the expression "The Court" used in relation to a Company means the Court having jurisdiction to wind up the Company [2]). And the Court having jurisdiction to wind up Companies is the District Court within which territorial jurisdiction the centre or a branch of the Company's business is situate [3]).

A draft Bill for regulating procedure in execution against both movable and immovable property was published in Official Gazette No. 437 of 3rd May 1934. It is intended to replace the existing Ottoman Law and by Sec. 115 it is declared that the Law of Execution of Judgments dated 28 Nissan A.H. 1330 would cease to have effect in Palestine after its promulgation. The proposals as regards execution against immovable property are to be found in Sec. 28 ff. of the Bill [4]).

Execution of Judgments.

---

[1]) Sec. 42 of the Charitable Trust Ordinance 1924—5.
[2]) Sec. 2 of the Companies Ordinance 1929.
[3]) Sec. 150 of the Companies Ordinance 1929 and Order 4th July 1929 (O.G. 16 July 1929).
[4]) The Bill has not been promulgated up to the time of writing (April 1935) nor is any information forthcoming as to the probable date of promulgation.

APPENDICES.

APPENDIX I—NOTE ON THE PALESTINE (AMENDMENT) ORDER-IN-COUNCIL 1935.

The recent Palestine (Amendment) Order-in-Council, 21st February, 1935 (P.G. No. 496 of 28th February 1935) has the effect of making changes in the jurisdiction of the Religious Courts in matters of personal status consequent upon the new definition of the expression "foreigner" which it has introduced.

By Art. 59 of the Order-in-Council of 1922 the word "foreigner" was for the purpose of the Order limited in its general scope to persons, who were nationals or subjects of a European or American State or of Japan. This provision was intended to restrict the application of the special privileges granted to foreigners by Arts. 60—63 of the Order mainly to those classes of persons, whose affairs would under the old Capitulatory system have fallen within Consular jurisdiction.

By the new amending Order these privileges as to trial have been abolished and the special reason for the limitation in meaning of the term "foreigner" has consequently disappeared.

The new Order gives, therefore, to the term a wider and more natural signification by providing, that for the purpose of Part V of the Order of 1922 the expression "foreigner" means any person, who is not a Palestinian citizen.

Consequent upon this alteration the interpretation of the word "foreigner" in Arts. 53, 54, 58, 64 and 65 of the Order of 1922 is necessarily changed and, as it appears, the exclusive jurisdiction of the Rabbinical and Christian Courts will, henceforth, be limited to persons, who are Palestinian citizens and will no longer extend to Egyptians, Trans-Jordanians, Iraqians and other persons of non-European or American Nationality. In matters of personal status the Civil Courts will apply the law of the nationality to all non-Palestinians when exercising their jurisdiction. Stateless persons must also be treated as "foreigners" notwithstanding the decision in Re Feinstein quoted on p. 99, supra.

Appendix I.

It is not, however, clear, how far this change in the Order-in-Council affects the rules of law and jurisdiction, laid down in the Succession Ordinance 1923. In that Ordinance the meaning of the term "foreigner" stated in Art. 59 of the Order-in-Council 1922 is expressly adopted as governing the use of the term in the Ordinance (Sec. 26 (XIII)). In view of the provisions of Art. 57 of the Order-in-Council of 1922 it must be assumed, the jurisdiction in Succession is still governed by the Ordinance of 1923 notwithstanding the change made by the Order of 1935. If this is so, the Courts of the special Religious Communities still have exclusive jurisdiction to confirm the Will of any member of their Community, not being a foreigner within the meaning of Art. 59 of the Order of 1922, since, though such persons are now foreigners for the purpose of that Order, this fact will not (semble) prevent their being members of the Community. In general also the Civil Courts will still be bound by the older definition when administering the Succession Ordinance.

No doubt it will be found convenient at an early date to revise the provisions of the Succession Ordinance and adapt them to the present policy of the Government.

The (Amendment) Order-in-Council of 1935 dispels also a doubt which has arisen as to the power of the High Commissioner to deal effectively with appropriated Tithes or Taxes. A new article, 16 B, is inserted in the Order of 1922 empowering him to replace Waqf tithes by other taxes and to commute them by annual payments or otherwise to the Waqf or religious or charitable endowment.

APPENDIX II—BILLS RECENTLY PUBLISHED.

Mention may be made of certain Bills recently published in the Palestine Gazette which will no doubt shortly be promulgated as Ordinances.

The proposed Damages Ordinance (Pal. Gaz. 7th March 1935) modifies the provisions of Art. 111 of the Ottoman Code of Civil Procedure by providing that the Courts are not to be bound by provisions in future contracts for sale of or irrevocable powers of attorney given in connection with the sale of immovable property stipulating payment or compensation by way of damages or penalty or otherwise for breach but may enforce such stipulations or award damages as they think fit. This Ordinance will thus introduce into the law of Palestine the equitable doctrine well known to English law, according to which the Courts of Equity gave relief from penalty stipulations in contracts, as to which jurisdiction the English reports provide an abundant jurisprudence (supra, p. 136).

In the Palesine Gazette 28th February 1935 are to be found two other Bills which require mention.

THE MAGISTRATES' COURTS JURISDICTION ORDINANCE 1935 [1]).

This Ordinance is designed to consolidate the Magistrates' Courts Jurisdiction Ordinances by replacing those of 1924, 1930 and 1932 and re-enacting them in an amended form. The amendments do not, however, affect the jurisdiction of the Magistrates' Courts as regards the recovery of possession and partition of immovable property (supra, p. 378).

THE LANDLORDS AND TENANTS (EJECTION AND RENT RESTRICTION) (EXTENSION) ORDINANCE 1935.

This Ordinance extends the Principal Ordinance of 1934 (supra, p. 194) for a further period of one year, i.e. until the thirtieth day of March 1936 and makes various amendments in the Principal Ordinance. (See P.G. No. 501 1st April 1935).

---

[1]) Enacted in P.G. No. 504 of 16th April 1935.

Appendix II.

The Protection of Cultivators Amendment Ordnance 1935.

An Ordinance amending the Protection of Cultivators Ordinance 1933 has been published as a Bill in the Palestine Gazette No. 506 of the 25th April 1935, modifying the definition of "Holding" in the Principal Ordinance (supra, p. 236). The amendment is to the effect that the words "occupied and" in Sec. 2 of the Principal Ordinance have been omitted and "Holding" has been defined to mean a plot of Miri land or any portion of village land held in undivided ownership or tenure "cultivated" by a tenant.

The Bill proposes also to modify the condition under which cultivators of land may claim tenants' statutory rights. Under the present Ordinance a tenant was required to have "occupied and cultivated" a holding for a period of a year before he could claim statutory rights. This is now modified by the amendment of Secs. 3, 4 6, 7 and 10 of the Principal Ordinance (supra, p.p. 237—244) to the effect that the period of cultivation required is:—

"One year or a period necessary to raise two successive crops whichever be the lesser".

Section 19 of the Principal Ordinance as enacted by the Protection of Cultivators (Amendment) Ordinance 1934 (supra, p. 249) has been amended by the insertion of the following Sections:— Sec. 19A, 19B and 19C:—

19A. Where by a decision of a special commission, appointed under section 19 of this ordinance any person is declared to be a statutory tenant of a holding, such statutory tenant shall be entitled to recover possession of the holding and may for this purpose institute proceedings before a magistrate for an order for possession, and a copy of a decision of the special commission purporting to be signed and certified by the chairman thereof shall be admissible as evidence of facts therein in any such proceedings. Provided that no order for possession shall be made by a magistrate pending the hearing of any appeal from the decision of the special commission.

19B. Where any dispute as to whether any person is a statutory tenant of a holding is referred to a special commission appointed under section 19 of this Ordinance and it is proved to the satisfaction of such commission that the person who claims to be a statutory tenant already owns or cultivates an area elsewhere sufficient to enable him to maintain his customary means of livelihood in an occupation with which he is familiar, the commission shall record such fact in their decision, and may dismiss the claim of the person so claiming to be a statutory tenant.

19C. Where any dispute as to whether any person is a statutory tenant of a holding is referred to a special commission appointed under Section 19 of this Ordinance and it is proved to the satisfaction of such commission that the person who claims to be a statutory tenant has cultivated a holding for a period of one year or for a period necessary to raise two successive crops at any time within two years preceding the date of the said dispute the commission shall record such fact in their decision and shall, subject to the provisions of section 19B of this Ordinance, allow the claim of the person so claiming to be a statutory tenant.

391

APPENDIX III—SUMMARY OF CASES CONCERNING LAND LAW IN THE LAW REPORTS OF PALESTINE 1920—1933.

The publication of the Volume of the Law Reports of Palestine 1920—1933 under the editorship of His Honour the Chief Justice took place unfortunately at too late a date to allow of reference in the text to the cases included in the volume. Notes of many of these were happily already in the authors' hands and will be found inserted in the appropriate place in the text. For the convenience of readers we have collected in this Appendix notes of those not previously reported which concern the Land Law and have in reference to each case specified the page of this book on which the subject with which each is concerned will be found treated.

Art. 78 of the Land Code has no application to Mewat. (Kaltoum Ganameh v. Director of Lands. L. R. (Pal.) p. 162). — Mewat Land. (p. 49).

The right to uproot trees planted on ab antiquo Mera must be exercised through the competent authority. (Wadi el Bustani v. Att. Gen. L. R. (Pal.) p. 226). — Land Code, Art. 97. (p. 57).

The Ghor Agreement of 19th November 1921 cannot be treated as a legislative act and the prohibition against disposition does not affect the rights of creditors of the holders. (Att. Gen. v. Chief Execution Officer, Haifa. L. R. (Pal.) p. 774). — Agreement of 19th November 1921. (p. 63).

An action by a Mutwally for a declaration that a lease is void is not one concerning the internal administration of a Waqf. Such an action is within the competence of a Magistrate's Court under Sec. 1 (b) of the Magistrates' Courts Ordinance 1924. (Fuad el Khaldi v. Muhammad Said. L. R. (Pal.) p. 186). — Avoidance of Lease-Waqf. (p. 72).

A claim concerning the ownership of immovable property is within the jurisdiction of the Civil Courts notwithstanding that the claim is to the effect that the land in question is Waqf. (Mamur Awqaf of Nablus v. Saleh el Hamdan and others. L. R. (Pal.) p. 377). — Jurisdiction in Waqf. (p. 73).

The Land Law of Palestine.

Consent to Jurisdiction. (p. 106). Consent cannot be given by a person adjduged insane. (Ibrahim Khoury Farah v. Elias Mitry and others. L. R. (Pal.) p. 331).

For the purpose of giving jurisdiction under Sec. 6 (1) of the Succession Ordinance 1923 there must be either consent in writing or conduct from which consent can be inferred. (Trevich v. Trevich. L. R. (Pal.) p. 109).

Buildings erected on Miri. (p. 128). Art. 906 Mejelle applies to buildings, etc. on Mulk only. It does not apply to Miri. (Yusuf Ibrahim el Asmar v. Hanna Yusef Shami and others. L. R. (Pal.) p. 767).

Sale of land in Execution. Transfer of Land Ordinance 1920-1921. (p. 139). The provisions of Secs. 1 and 2 of the Transfer of Land (Amendment) Ordinance No. 2 of 1921 do not apply to a sale in accordance with the Transfer of Land Ordinance No. 2 of 1921. (Saleh Ibrahim Oufi and others v. Chief Execution Officer, Nablus. L. R. (Pal.) p. 471).

Agreements for Sale not "Dispositions". (p. 140). An agreement for sale of land is not a disposition within the meaning of Sec. 2 Transfer of Land Ordinance 1920. (Yehoshua Hankin v. Ali Qasem. (L. R. (Pal.) p. 574).

Contract of Sale of Land. (p. 140). No action can be brought upon a contract which is null and void under Transfer of Land Ordinance 1920, Sec. 11. (Gabrilovich v. Ali Ibn Hassan. L. R. (Pal.) p. 373).

Pre-emption by Co-owner. (p. 148). If the purchaser against whom pre-emption is claimed is already a co-owner, no ground exists for allowing pre-emption against him by another co-owner. (Ramadan el Haj v. Shakib and another. L. R. (Pal.) p. 46).

Pre-emption. (p. 151). An application for purchase of the land made by the would-be pre-emptor to the purchaser is an effectual bar to pre-emption under Art. 1024 of the Mejelle. (Salimeh bint Ahmed v. Abdallah Yehia. L. R. (Pal.) p. 809).

Servitudes in Miri-Joint interest. (p. 155). A person who has a joint interest in Servitudes over Miri, is entitled to a right of preference (Awlawia) thereover under Land Code Art. 41. (Sheikh As'ad v. Haj Khalil Taha. L. R. (Pal.) p. 159).

Awlawia in Mesha'a. (p. 156). Rights of Awlawia under Arts. 41 and 42 of the Land Code cannot be claimed by persons holding an undivided share in Mesha'a. (Muhammad Hussein v. Jamil Na'aman el Alami. L. R. (Pal.) p. 179).

Preference under Land Code Art. 45. (p. 157). The right of Preference exercisable under this article applies in villages only and not in towns such as Acre. (Abd-el-Rahman Mukhtar and others v. Haj Khalil Taha. L. R. (Pal.) p. 149).

(p. 159). The Court ordered that a right of Awlawia awarded under Land Code Art. 45 should lapse if not exercised within two

Appendix III.

months. (Salem Habib and others v. Palestine Land Development Company. L. R. (Pal.) p. 298).

Under Art. 118 Mejelle a Bei bil Wafa has the effect of a Mortgage. Prescription against under Art. 1660 Mejelle is not possible. (Abdel Salman v. Chief Execution Officer, Jaffa. L. R. (Pal.) p. 490). *Bei bil Wafa-Prescriptive. (p. 163).*

No interest in land is conferred by a Wakalat Dawarya executed since the Transfer of Land Ordinance 1920. (Ismail Muhammad el Nadi v. Rashid Ibrahim and another. L. R. (Pal.) p. 555). *Wakalat Dawaryia. (p. 165).*

The second Mortgagee must be deemed to have note of an agreement by the Mortgagor to pay interest to the first Mortgagee who is, therefore, entitled to priority in respect thereof. Shlomo Steinberg v. Chief Execution Officer, Jerusalem. L. R. (Pal.) p. 538). *Interest due to first Mortgagee. Priority. (p. 171).*

In a mortgage to "order" the creditor whether the original Mortgagee or another can assign his rights under the mortgage. Prov. Law of Mortgage, Art. 7. (George Bishara v. Chief Execution Officer, Haifa. L. R. (Pal.) p. 506). *Assignment of Mortgage. (p. 172).*

A Mortgagor cannot by lease granted after the Mortgage give to the lessee an interest greater than he himself has. Such a lease, therefore, is liable to be determined with the Mortgagor's own interest. (Rothstein and Label v. Chief Execution Officer, Jerusalem. L. R. (Pal.) p. 292). *Lease by Mortgagor. (p. 172).*

However small may be the interest in the mortgaged property of the person seeking to redeem it, yet under Art. 731 Mejelle, he must in order to effect redemption pay the whole debt due. (Tayyan v. Chief Execution Officer, Nablus. L. R. (Pal.) p. 382). *Redemption of part of Mortgaged Property. (p. 173).*

Seeing that there is no Law in this country relating to consolidation of mortgages properties mortgaged by separate deeds must be separately sold. (Petro Abella v. Chief Execution Officer, Haifa. L. R. (Pal.) p. 344). *Sale of Mortgaged Property. (p. 174).*

The President of a District Court cannot order postponment of sale save upon the grounds mentioned in Sec. 2 of Transfer of Land Ordinance No. 2 of 1921. He has no power to make postponment conditional upon payment of debt by instalments. (Vola Shehab v. Chief Execution Officer, Haifa. L. R. (Pal.) p. 764). *Sale of Mortgaged Property. (p. 176).*

On a contract of sale of the property leased being entered into between the Lessor and Lessee the lease becomes null and void in accordance with Art. 442 Mejelle, at least if part of the purchase price has been paid. (Tager v. Cohen. L. R. (Pal.) p. 526). *Merger of Lease. (p. 181).*

A person occupying joint property with the permission of one co-owner is liable for rent under Mejelle, Art. 472, and cannot *Occupation by third person*

The Land Law of Palestine.

of joint Property. (p. 202). claim the benefit of the exception provided by Art. 1075. (Boulos) Hallaq v. Dimiany. L.R. (Pal.) p. 606).

Possession as between heirs. (p. 203). The rule that there is no prescription between co-heirs is exceptional. It does not apply when the parties are not members of the same family and the possession is adverse to the interests of the others. (Musa Shaban v. El Farawi. L.R. (Pal.) p. 630).

A co-heir cannot set up a title as against other co-heirs by proof of possession (Nadim Abdul Rahman v. Abdallah Seilan. L.R. (Pal.) p. 35. Compare L.R. (Pal.) pp. 356; 630).

Mesha'a. Mode of Registration. (p. 207). In view of Land Code, Art. 8, registration cannot be in the names of all the villagers. The proper course is for each plot to be registered in one name with an entry against each plot that it is common land subject to the custom of the village. (Hassan Aly Ayad and other v. Ahmad Muhammad Radwan and others. L.R. (Pal.) p. 82).

Law of Partition. (p. 210). A Magistrate's Court Judgment sent to the Land Registry in compliance with Sec. 6 of the Law of Partition A.H. 1332 is so sent for information only and not for registration. (Mohammad Hussein Ali and others v. Att. Gen. L.R. (Pal.) p. 124).

Right of Privacy. (p. 215). The fact that a new building conforms with the Town Planning Regulations does not bring it outside mischief of Art. 1202 Mejelle, if its windows overlook women's quarters. (Hagenlocher v. Adib el Hannawi. L.R. (Pal.) p. 559).

Excessive Damage. (p. 216). In a claim for abatement of a nuisance the question as to whether or not excessive damage has been caused is a question of fact. (Hassan el Budeiri v. Haj Amin el Husseini. L.R. (Pal.) p. 339).

Rights of Way over Miri. (p. 222). Rights of Way over Miri land can, in the absence of express grant, only be acquired by ab antiquo user. Compare Land Code, Art. 13. (Shukri Aref v. Abraham Shwartz. L.R. (Pal.) p. 242).

Rights of access to Well. (p. 228). The right to take water from a Well in absolute ownership, conferred by Art. 1268 Mejelle is one which cannot be continuously exercised; it is limited to occasional use. (Abd el Latif Hussein v. Haj Abd el Rahman and another. L.R. (Pal.) p. 336).

Land Code, Art. 20. (p. 258). The provisions of Art. 20 of the Land Code are only valid as a defence. Possession for ten years does not entitle the possessor to registration. (Elias Wahby v. Hassan Haj Omar. L.R. (Pal.) p. 87). Cf. L.A. 25/32. L.R. (Pal.) p. 766).

Land Code, Art. 78. (p. 260). The decision of the Council of State, dated 30th December 1322 (Malia) is limited to claims between heirs and persons holding land in partnership. It is, however, not a decision binding upon the Courts. (Mahmud Diab v. Muhammad Aly Selim el Amri and others. L.R. (Pal.) p. 41).

Appendix III.

Now that this decision is officially reported in the volume of the Palestine Law Reports it is presumably idle to contest its accuracy in Law before the Law Courts of Palestine. Its inclusion in the Official Reports must be assumed to show that this interpretation of Art. 78 is definitely adopted in Palestine.

An admission having taken place in an Official Department, viz., the Tabu Department, attention would not be paid by the Court to the statement that it was false. (Khadijeh Abu Khadra v. Amneh Abu Khadra. L. R. (Pal.) p. 1). Cf. Jamila Sarhan v. Ibrahim El Husseini. L. R. (Pal.) p. 432). *Admission in Proceedings before a Land Registry. (p. 308).*

In the absence of overwhelmingly strong oral evidence as to both title and possession, the Court could not accept oral evidence against a kushan. (Yusef Abdul Karim v. Ismail Abdul Rahman. L. R. (Pal.) p. 39). *Evidence against Registered title. (p. 309).*

The Court will not hear oral evidence to disprove an entry in the Land Registers except that such evidence may be heard to prove the customary law of a village (As'ad Dib and others v. Dawud Bdeir. L. R. (Pal.) p. 614). *(p. 310).*

The practice of the Court is to require written evidence to prove that registration as owner was in fact made in respect of a mortgage. (Elias Yaqub v. Khalil Odeh. L. R. (Pal.) p. 44). *Evidence invalidating Registered title. (p. 309).*

A registered title will not be set aside except on production of evidence sufficient to support an adverse title or to corroborate evidence in support thereof. (Afifeh, Rachel and another v. Naim and another. L. R. (Pal.) p. 13). *(p. 309).*

Applications to set aside a registration of ownership in the Land Registry are matters in which the Land Courts have Jurisdiction. (Hegazi v. Chief Execution Officer, Jaffa. L.R. (Pal.) p. 782). *(p. 309).*

Persons who become registered as owners of Mulk by transfer from persons who were themselves registered as Mulk owners are not affected by a prior dedication of the lands as Waqf which there is nothing on the title to suggest and of which they had no notice. (Sheikh Sadik Anabtawi and others v. Faris Shaker and others. L. R. (Pal.) p. 269). *Title by Registration. (p. 309).*

Oral evidence is admissible to prove that the holder of a kushan is registered as the trustee of property which is the common land of a village. (Mahmud Ahmad Salameh and others v. Saleh Ibrahim Ismail. L. R. (Pal.) p. 234). *Mesha'a — Evidence admissible to prove Custom. (p. 310).*

If there is evidence (e.g. a lease) that possession originated in a right less than ownership the possessor must show how he became entitled to possession as owner even though the possession has continued for a term exceeding that for limitation of action. *Possession based on a right less than ownership. (p. 314).*

396   The Land Law of Palestine.

(Khadija bint Ahmed Isleem v. The Armenian Patriarch. L.R. (Pal.) p. 301).

Absence. Where time has begun to run against a party, his departure
(p 351.). from the country does not afford an excuse for not commencing an action so as to prevent time running against him in his absence. (Nir Khanem bint Kubar v. Michael ibn Francis Rahil. L. R. (Pal.) p. 151).

Land Court— A claim for abatement of a nuisance does not involve the
Jurisdiction. ownership of land or any rights in or over land. It is, therefore,
(p. 375). within the jurisdiction of the District Court and not of the Land Court. (Muhammad el Qader v. Schneller. L. R. (Pal.) p. 721).

Land Court— The question of delivery of possession of land is not within
Jurisdiction. the jurisdiction of a Land Court. (Sit Leila bint Mitri v. Sheikh
(p. 376). Mahmud el Aswad and others. L. R. (Pal.) p. 160).

Land Court The Court declined to apply the provisions of Sec. 7 (1) of the
Ordinance Land Court Ordinance 1921 in a case in which the appellant relied
1921. upon an unregistered prewar contract where the consideration for
(p. 376.). the sale had not been paid. (Shukry Kerdahy v. Tempelton. L. R. (Pal.) p. 128).

Magistrates' A claim to a right of Way is not within the Jurisdiction of
Courts— a Magistrate's Court, but is within the Jurisdiction of a Land
Jurisdiction. Court. (Jaber Abu Nassar v. Schneller L. R. (Pal.) p. 89). Cf. L. R.
(p. 378). (Pal.) p. 139).

The Jurisdiction of the Magistrate under Sec. 1 (b) of the Magistrates' Courts Jurisdiction Ordinance 1924 is excluded, if one party claims, that the Land is Waqf, of which he is Mutwally, and the other party claims that it is his Mulk. (Fahmi Quanadilo v. Rida Muhammad and others. L. R. (Pal.) p. 48).

Land Disputes In exercising powers conferred upon him by this Ordinance
(Possession) the District Commissioner is not acting as a Magistrate. An Order
Ordinance improperly made by him under Sec. 2 can be set aside by the
1932. High Court. (Haifa Bay Development Co. v. District Commissioner,
(p. 382). Northern District. L. R. (Pal.) p. 860).

APPENDIX IV—MEWAT AND ITS REVIVER.

The nature of Mewat and the steps which constitute its reviver are stated in the text (pp. 44—51) in accordance with general Moslem authority as followed in the Mejelle. There has been and in some sense it may be said, there still is controversy among Moslem authorities as to the matter. This indeed appears even in the Hedaya [1]). The principle of Reviver of Mewat appears to be derived from a declaration of the Prophet that he who develops and inhabits a piece of land which does not belong to anyone else is entitled to the ownership thereof. In primitive Moslem law, at any rate, dead land which could be so developed was land which had not been developed in the time of Islam even though it might have been developed in the time of Ignorance (Jahalia). Thus there could be reviver of land which had never been developed or which had been developed before Islam but afterwards allowed to go waste. According to that law the permission of the Sultan was not required to the reviver since the right arose directly from the words of the Prophet. This, of course, applied to believers (Moslems) only. In the Hedaya, however, the right of the Zimmee (non-Moslem) to become owner by reviver is recognized though Abu Haneefa was of opinion that the consent of the Imam was necessary.

Land once revived could not be again revived so as to make it the property of the person who developed it. If the owner was not known it fell to the Beit El Mal and the Imam (Sultan) could make orders concerning it in the same way as regards other properties of the Beit El Mal and could concede rights of ownership or occupancy. But it could not by reviver become the property of him who revived it. This opinion is stated also in the Hedaya which, however, appears to treat as Mewat liable to reviver land which has for a long time lain waste or which was formerly the property of a Moslem who is not then known.

---

[1]) Hamilton's Translation, at p. 610.

Much difference existed also as to the nature of the steps which constituted reviver. It seems to have been the opinion of some eminent authorities that actual cultivation was not necessary provided that steps were taken to prepare the land for cultivation and the language of Mejelle Arts. 1275, 1276, which are ambiguous, lend some colour to this view. Thus if irrigation is requisite it was held that the sewer was complete if the drains had been made though no water had actually flowed along them. The Hedaya, however, does not seem to adopt this view [1]).

---

[1]) Ibid, at p. 611.

APPENDIX V—THE TRANSFER OF LAND (FEES) RULES 1935.

Changes have recently been made in the Scale of Land Registry Fees (supra, p. 368). Under the Transfer of Land (Fees) Rules, 1935,[1] the fee for the registration of a lease or sub-lease or transfer of a lease or of a sub-lease is 5% on the rent for one year and not less than 250 mils.

The fees for the registration of a mortgage of specified immovable property to secure a debenture or series of debentures or an issue of debenture stock are those which would be chargeable in respect of a mortgage of such property to secure a loan equal to two thirds of its value as certified by a certificate of two registered land valuers.

The fee for the registration of a Gift or Bequest is 3% on the market value of the properties or rights transferred by way of gift or bequest and not less than 500 mils.

The fee on the registration of a Succession is 1% on the value of the property as recorded in the Land Registers or Wergo Registers whichever is the highest. If the value of the property is not recorded in the Land Registers or Wergo Registers, the fee of 1% is payable on the market value of the whole property or so much of the property as is being registered and the fee is in no case less than 50 mils in respect of the property registered in the name of any one heir. No succession fees are payable:—

(1) if simultaneously with the registration of a succession, a registration of a sale, exchange or partition of the same property is made, or

(2) if the certificate of succession is lodged with the Registrar within twelve months from the date of the death of the registered owner.

---

[1] Rules made under Sec. 16 of the Transfer of Land Ordinance 1920. See P.G. No. 505 of 18th April 1935.

The Land Law of Palestine.

The fee on the registration of a Partition and Sub-Division is:

(a) 100 mils per parcel of land resulting from the partition of a property by the co-owner;

(b) 100 mils for each parcel resulting from a sub-division of a property by the owner.

The rule as regards the fee for the issue of a Certificate of Registration when the property or right does not appear on the Register is as follows:—

(a) If registration is made pursuant to an application lodged within six months from the date of the publication [1]) of these rules no fee is payable.

(b) If registration is made pursuant to an application lodged after six months from the date of the publication of these rules the fee is 2% on the market value of the property or right in respect of which a certificate is applied for.

Correction of the Register is free of charge.

Correction of the terms of a mortgage (except an increase of the amount secured) is free of charge provided that the parties to the mortgage remain the same.

---

[1]) 18th April 1935.

TABLES.

TABLE OF PALESTINE CASES CITED,
Arranged In Alphabetical Order Of Titles.

Title	Page
Abdallah Bey Chedid v. Tannenbaum	109, 118
Abdallah Hussein Haj Ali v. Aaronson	312
Abd el Halik Haj Shaban Tafish v. Ismail Ghalayani	310
Abd el Latif Hussein v. Haj Abd el Rahman and another	394
Abd el Rahman Mustafa and other v. Haj Khalil Taha	392
Abd el Rehim v. Mamur Awqaf of Nablus	373
Abd el Salman v. Chief Execution Officer, Jaffa	393
Abdullah el Hafiz v. Abdel Kasim Salman	265, 309
Abella (Petro) v. Chief Execution Offiter, Haifa	393
Abu Hijla v. Hamed el Yousuf	265
Abu Jafar v. Mustapha	140
Abu Jafar v. Mustapha Bitar	140
Abu Mustafa v. Government of Palestine	260
Afifeh Elias v. Naim Jurius Abiad	267, 310, 311, 395
Agronovich v. Agronovich	173
Ahmed Abu Nyma v. Anglo Palestine Bank	267, 311
Ahmed Mahmud Hejazi v. Chief Execution Officer, Jaffa	309
Ali Pasha Waqf (Mutwally of) v. Government of Palestine	255, 257
As'ad Dib v. Dawud Bdeir	395
Aslin village case	310
Atallah v. Nima and Khalil	164
Attorney General v. Chief Execution Officer, Haifa	391
Attorney General v. Salah	325
Badr v. Hanem	55, 223
Baivqari v. Omar el Mughrabi	313
Bayside Land Corporation v. Segal	323
Beit Lid village case	310
Bishara Assileh v. Fuad Saad	308, 393
Board of Foreign Mission v. Director of Lands	370
Bruchstein v. Barakat	110

The Land Law of Palestine.

Title	Page
Bustany v. Attorney General	391
Chibly Ayoub v. Dib Abou Nawas	236, 250
Cornu v. Ali Ahmed	190, 196
Dajani and others v. Colony of Rishon Le Zion	48, 49
Elias Yakoub v. Khalil Odeh	395
Elias Wahby v. Hassan Haj Omar	394
Eliash v. Director of Lands	90, 94
Estrangin v. Tayan	353
Fahideh bint Nimmer v. Muhammad Abdel Razak and Matalon	314
Fahima Hanem v. Assad Shukairi	353
Fahmi Quanadilo v. Rida Muhammad and others	396
Faram Hadad v. Haj Abdul Wahid Sammer	310
Faris Hamdan v. Osman Bushnaq	279
Feinstein, Re	99, 386
Frank v. Government of Palestine	265
Friedman v. Badie Abdul Karim	312
Fuad el Khaldi v. Muhammad Said and others	391
Gabrilovich v. Alu Abu Duyuk (Ali Ibn Hassan)	392
George Bishara v. Chief Execution Officer, Haifa	393
Goldberg v. Palestine Development Company	106
Goldberg, v. Rabinovitch	278, 381
Government of Palestine v. villagers of Sajad and Qazaza	184
Habib Elias Salem v. Director of Lands and Taha	174
Hagenlocher v. Adib el Hannavi	394
Haifa Bay Development Company v. Distict Commissioner, Northern District	382, 383, 396
Halevi v. Halpern	152
Hallaq v. Dimiany	394
Hankin v. Qasem	344
Harris v. Duchner	140
Hassan Aly Ayad and others (villagers of Aslin) v. Ahmed Radwan	207, 310, 394
Hassan el Budeiri v. Haj Amin el Husseini	394
Hegasi v. Chief Execution Officer, Jaffa	395
Hussein Aba Radwan v. Chief Execution Officer, Jaffa	235
Ibrahim Khouri Farah v. Elias Mitri and others	392
Ismail Muhammad el Nadi v. Rashid Ibrahim and another	393
Jaber Abu Nassar v. Schneller	396
Jamila Sarhan v. Ibrahim el Husseini	395
Kaltoum Ghanameh v. Director of Lands	263, 391

Tables. 403

Title	Page
Kardahi v. Sahyoun	172
Kerdahi v. Tempelton	396
Keren Kayemeth Ltd. v. Beigal	189
Khadija bint Ahmad v. Armenian Patriarch	396
Khadijeh Abu Khadra v. Amneh Abu Khadra	395
Khaledi v. Ottoman Bank	176
Leila bint Mitri v. Sheikh Mahmud el Aswad	396
Litvinsky v. Lippman	136, 144, 311, 312
Mahmud Ahmad Salameh v. Saleh Ibn Ibrahim Ismail	203, 255, 257, 310, 395
Mahmud Diab v. Mohamed Selim	258, 260, 394
Mamur Awqaf v. Syndic of Barsky	189
Mamur Awqaf v. Saleh el Hamdan	391
Mohammad Hussein and others v. Attorney General	394
Mohammad Hussein v. Jamil	392
Mohammed Yahia v. Shaban Aidi	165, 311
Muhammad Qasbash v. Schneller	396
Morcos v. Morcos	111
Muhammad Takrouri v. Abdul Rahim Murib	141, 146
Muhammed Shibl v. Haj Khalil Taha	383
Mukhtar (Abd el Rahman) v. Haj Khalil Taha	392
Musa Shaban v. Abbas el Farawi	203, 255, 394
Musleh v. Yehia	151, 154
Mustafa Sakija v. Jacobson	344
Nader v. Qaraman	312, 313, 349
Nadim Abdel Rahman Serlan v. Abdallah Selim	203, 394
Nir Khanem Kubar v. Michail ibn Francis, Rahil and others	396
Ramadan el Haj v. Shakib and others	392
Rothstein & Label v. Chief Execution Officer, Jerusalem	393
Saadat Hanum (Mutwalli of Ali Pasha Waqf) v. Government of Palestine	255, 262
Sadek Anabtawi and others v. Faris Shaker	395
Saleh Ibrahim Oufi and others v. Chief Execution Officer, Nablus	392
Salem Habib and others v. Palestine Land Development Co.	393
Salim Risk Hanna v. Boulos Hanna Risq	379
Salimeh bint Ahmed v. Abdallah Yehia	154, 392
Sara Litvinsky v. Lippman	311, 312
Shehab v. Chief Execution Officer, Haifa	393
Shehadeh el Aly v. Same	278
Sheikh Asad v. Haj Khalil Taha	392

Sheikh Katib v. Darhalli	377
Sheikh Sadik Anabtawi v. Faris Shaker and others	395
Sheikh Yusuf v. Khalil Ghnubeish	203, 255
Shlomo Friedman v. Badie Bint Abdel Karim	312
Shukairi v. Nour	148, 149
Shukairi v. Moghrabi	148
Shukri Aref v. Abraham Schwartz	394
Shukri Kerdahi v. Tempelton	396
Spectroff v. Agricultural Loan and Land Cooperative Society	158
Sternberg v. Chief Execution Officer, Jerusalem	393
Subhi Khadra v. Bishop Hajjar	381
Tayan v. Chief Execution Officer, Nablus	393
Tager (Shmuel) v. Cohen	393
Trevich v. Trevich	392
Vijansky v. Khojainoff	114, 115
Villagers of Aslin, Re	207
Villagers of Sajad and Qazaza v. Government of Palestine	184
Wadi el Bustani v. Attorney General	391
Yehoshua Hankin v. Ali Qasem	344, 392
Yusuf Abd el Karim v. Ismail Abd el Rahman	395
Yusuf Ibrahim el Asmar v. Hanna Yusef Shami and others	392
Zeide v. Alcaly	140
Zeita village case	310

TABLE OF CYPRUS CASES CITED,
Arranged in Alphabetical Order of Titles.

Title	Page
Aggelidi v. Fudjarbashi	350
Ahmed v. Hassan	258, 263, 264
Ali v. Papa Yanni	216
Anastassi v. Georghi	226
Antoniou v. Joannou	188
Bishop of Kyrenia v. Paraskeva	264
Chacalli v. Kallourena	145
Constanti v. Principal Forest Officer	41, 56
Constantinides v. Theodosi	151, 152
Cristofides v. Tofaridi	131, 151
Delegates of Awqaf v. Kenan	83
Della v. Michael	117
Demetriades v. Liverdou	151
Economou v. Queen's Advocate	19
Emphiedji v. Law	88
Erikzade v. Arghiro	216
Francoudi v. Heirs of Michailides	351
Gavrielides v. Kyriakou	30
Gavrilidi v. Georghi	145
Haji Michael v. Georgeades	225
Haji Michael v. Stilli Nikoli	265
Hanim v. Irikzade	229
Houloussi v. Fiori	226
Houry v. Sabba	153
Houston v. King's Advocate	20, 235
Hypermachos v. Dmitri	103
Jassonides v. Kyprioti	153
Joannes v. Stavrinou	153, 154
Joannou v. Georghou	264
Joannou v. Michael	256

The Land Law of Palestine.

Title	Page
Khanim v. Dianello	70, 80, 83
King's Advocate v. Petridis	31
Koukoulli v. Hamid	190, 193
Kyriakou v. Principal Forest Officer	45, 46, 67, 260, 265
Kyrenia (Bishop of) v. Paraskeva	264
Lambo v. King's Advocate	38
Loizou v. Hanoum	128
Loizou v. Philippou	261
Louka v. Nicola	230
Mehmet v. Kosmo	258, 352, 353
Michael v. Nikoli	265
Monk v. Nicola	255, 352
Mourmori v. Haj Yanni	254
Muzaffer v. Collet	255, 262, 352
Nicolaides v. Jerodiaconos	147, 148, 152, 153
Panayi v. Kathomouta	224, 229, 231
Papa Panayi v. Yaseinidou	225
Pascali v. Toghli	145
Petri v. Petri	145
Pieri v. Philippou	203, 264
Ragheb v. Abbot of Kykko	32, 42
Ragheb v. Gerassimou	19, 225, 227
Romani v. Skoullou	154
Sava v. Paraskewa	265
Sophronios v. Principal Forest Officer	87
Stassi v. Vehim	229, 230, 286, 296
Stavrino v. Queen's Advocate	144, 145
Topal Ahmet v. Agha	145
Tritoftides v. Nikola	193
Tsinki v. King's Advocate	17, 32, 34, 227
Tzapa v. Tsolaki	127, 128, 185, 195
Yemeniji v. Andoniou	22, 253
Yosif v. Nami	153
Zade v. Tsinki	227
Zenobio v. Osman	145, 314

TABLE OF ENGLISH CASES CITED,
Arranged in Alphabetical Order of Titles.

Title	Page
Achillopoulos, Re	115
Agency Company v. Short	256
Angus v. Dalton	215
Bain v. Fothergill	135
Banks v. Goodfellow	112
Colls. v. Home & Colonial Stores	215
Commissioner of Income Tax v. Pemsel	91
Day v. Singleton	135
Elwes v. Maw	232
Gardner v. Mansbridge	126
Mc Cartney v. Londonderry and Lough Swilly Railways	225
Paradine v. Jane	182
Pym v. Blackburn	183
Samuel Johnson & Sons Ltd. v. Brock	256
Secretary of State v. Charlesworth	126
Sutton v. Sadler	112
Tyrrel v. Painton	113
Wigglesworth v. Dallison	232

TABLE OF REFERENCES TO OTTOMAN LEGISLATION.

The Ottoman Land Code A. H. 1274 (1858).

Article	Page	Article	Page
1	1	30	7, 19, 361
2	2, 38, 39, 59	31	29, 30, 35
3	5, 358	32	31, 35, 40
4	8, 9, 76, 77, 359	33	29
5	52	34	34, 361
6	44, 45	35	29, 127, 205, 209
8	64, 394	36	138, 296
9	28, 36, 125, 182	37	296
10	19, 29, 34, 125	38	142
11	28, 125, 126	39	142
12	28	40	138, 296
13	29, 125, 394	41	155, 156, 157, 158, 159, 267, 359, 392
14	32		
15	209, 210, 213	42	155, 156, 157, 159, 392
16	209	43	142, 143
17	209	44	30, 42. 143, 158, 159, 267, 359
18	209, 349		
19	29	45	143, 157, 158, 159, 267, 359, 392
20	251, 255, 257, 258, 259, 261, 263, 265, 348, 352, 394		
		46	155
		47	56, 143
21	128, 348	48	141
22	128	49	22, 30, 42, 133, 158
23	182, 184, 254, 259	50	348, 349
24	7, 19, 361	51	348, 349
25	24, 29, 30, 34, 267	52	348, 349
26	29	53	348, 349
27	138	56	352
28	23, 29, 34	57	352
29	29, 30	58	352

Tables.

Article	Page	Article	Page
59	21, 22, 23, 30, 42, 156, 158, 268, 359	97	45, 54, 57, 59, 207, 391
60	26, 298, 348, 349	98	55
61	22, 348, 349, 352	99	55, 62
62	23, 348	100	54, 55
63	26, 348, 349, 352	101	45, 54
64	25	102	52, 263
65	349	103	44, 45, 46, 48, 50, 263, 268, 358
66	23, 158, 268	104	50
68	20, 298	105	51, 54
69	20	106	29
70	21	107	28, 66
71	21, 26	108	117
72	297	109	116, 117
73	21, 352	110	116, 117
74	267, 352	111	117
75	267, 351, 352	112	344
76	349	113	143
77	23, 24, 26	114	142
78	23, 24, 26, 49, 50, 258, 259, 260, 261, 263, 288, 292, 391, 394	115	179
		116	161
		117	165, 359
81	22, 115, 158	118	166 ff; 167 (note)
82	23, 32	119	143
83	23, 24, 30	120	142
84	20	121	35, 41, 94
85	20	122	86 ff; 354
86	23	123	50, 263
87	23, 24, 27, 268	124	225, 226, 230
89	32, 75	125	222
90	30, 75	126	56, 377
91	45, 57, 58	127	56
92	58	128	28
93	53	130	62, 297
94	53	131	62, 295
95	53	132	41, 294
96	54, 59		

The Land Law of Palestine.

The Tapu Law A.H. 1275 (1858).

Article	Page	Article	Page
1	294	16	24, 25, 295, 359
3	296	20	25, 359
4	296, 359	21	296, 359
5	296	24	143
11	294	25	164, 165
12	25, 47	26	165
13	47	27	165
14	295	30	165
15	296	31—32	349

The Regulations as to Title Deeds A. H. 1276 (1859).

Article	Page	Article	Page
1	261, 263, 266, 295	8	259, 260, 261, 295
3	296	9	295
4	358	10	295
5	47, 358	11	157
6	359	14	296

The Mejelle (The Ottoman Civil Code) A. H. 1285 (1869).

Article	Page	Article	Page
6	52, 207, 218, 220, 222, 262	214	134
7	207	215	134, 202
27	126	216	219
36	207, 222	221	133
37	222	231	141
41	222	232	221
45	222	233	
74	216	235	221
101 ff.	132 ff.	253	131, 134
105	135, 137	262	134
118	166, 393	265—271	134
119	166	282	134
129	37	293	134
142	134	356	134
143	134	369	131, 134
165	41	393—395	134, 142
167	131, 132	396	135
173	131	401 ff.	135
177	137	404 ff.	181
180	132	408	142
185	132	414	127

Tables.

Article	Page	Article	Page
419	213	882	126
421	181	885	126
422	181	886	127, 128
429	182	902	125
441	350	903	127
442	393	906	126, 127, 128, 392
444	181	907	127, 128, 205
458	181, 185	908	127
463	181	926	53
468	181	927	53
472	393	941—942	344
473	181	944 ff.	348
476	181	950—952	155
478	181, 183	955	228
484	181, 182	956	227
494	181	957	344
513	183	958	344
514	183	966	350
516	181	967	350
526	181, 232, 243	968	345
528	181	971	346
529	183	973	345
531	182, 184, 232, 243, 244	974	345, 348
532	182, 184	975	346
586	188	977	345
587	189	978	350
590	186, 187, 241	979	348
596	127	980	348
701 ff.	161, 162	981	345
731	393	982	345
744	171	984	345
750	162, 166	985	345
760, 761	162	986	345
777	202	987	345
830	181	989	346, 350
833—880	103, 105, 136, 137, 142, 151	990	350, 351
839	136	993	350
855	137, 142, 151	998	344
862—867	136	1002	344
872	137	1008	149, 150, 228
877	103, 105, 137, 142	1009	149, 150, 202

The Land Law of Palestine.

Article	Page	Article	Page
1011	149	1163, 1164, 1165	212
1012	148		
1013	150, 157	1166	212, 221
1014	150	1167	221
1016	150	1168	219, 221
1017—1020	147, 148, 155, 160	1169	221
		1170	212
1021 ff.	147, 151, 159	1173	205
1024	392	1174	213
1026	152	1176	213
1029 ff.	152 ff.	1178	182
1034, 1035, 1038, 1039	152, 153, 154, 268	1179	203
		1182	212
1043	151	1186	182
1044	155	1188	203, 212
1045	200, 207	1190, 1191	213
1051	47 (note)	1192 ff.	37, 42, 125, 214, 215
1069 ff.	202	1194 ff.	37, 65, 214
1071, 1072	202	1197	37, 125, 214
1075, 1076, 1077	202, 205, 394	1199	215
		1200 ff.	215, 216, 220
1078	206	1202	394
1083, 1084	202	1204	216
1085, 1086, 1087, 1088	202	1208	216
		1209	216
1107	222	1210	216, 231
1114 ff.	209	1211	231
1127	212	1212	215
1130	210, 211	1213 ff.	53, 215
1131	211	1214	53
1140	211	1215	53
1141	211	1216	52
1143	228	1217	53
1144	228	1218	53
1145	219, 221	1219	228
1146	212	1220	218, 227
1150	211	1223	53
1151	205, 212, 228	1224	207, 216, 218, 220
1153 ff.	212	1226	219
1158	205	1227 ff.	218, 219
1159 ff.	212	1229	220

Tables.

Article	Page	Article	Page
1231	220	1287	226
1232	220, 221	1288	220
1234	50, 223	1289	92
1235	53, 223, 226	1290	219
1236	223	1291	227
1237	53, 223	1293	223
1238	223	1295	223
1239	223, 224, 228, 229, 231	1296	223
1240	125	1297	223
1241	50, 126	1308–1311	205
1242	38, 126		
1243	50	1313	205
1244	38, 126	1316	231
1246	38, 127	1318	221
1248	38, 220, 252	1319	350
1249	38, 223	1321	53
1250	223, 226	1322 ff.	228
1251	223, 224, 225, 226	1327	228
1253	50	1328	228
1256	50	1333	200
1257	38, 126, 127	1431 ff.	196, 197
1258	50	1436	196, 197
1259	50	1441 ff.	196, 197
1262	216	1521 ff.	164
1264	53, 224	1528	164
1265	53, 224, 225	1529	166
1266	53	1591–1594	104, 307
1267	226, 228		
1268	226, 394	1596 ff.	103
1269	226, 228, 229	1644	53
1270	44	1645	59, 222
1271–1274	41, 45, 46	1646	59
		1660–1661	250, 251, 253, 255, 258, 261, 262, 263
1275–1279	45, 48, 397, 398	1662	222, 255, 257, 258, 262
1280	42	1663	255, 292, 352
1281	42, 226	1664	352
1282	42	1665	352
1284	225	1666	256
1285	42	1667	255, 256, 257, 262
1286	42	1668	255

The Land Law of Palestine.

Article	Page	Article	Page
1669	256	1673	254
1670	256, 257	1674	256
1671	256	1675	52, 53, 223, 225, 262, 263
1672	256	1737	308

The Ottoman Law of Disposition A.H. 1331 (1913).

Article	Page	Article	Page
1	263	9	127, 128
3	308	11	127, 128
4	307	12	128, 204
5	32, 33, 35, 39, 182	13	128, 204
6	32, 33, 35	14	128
7	33, 35, 36, 41	15	41, 42, 258, 259, 261
8	33, 35, 36, 41	16	180

The Ottoman Law of Mortgages A.H. 1331 (1913).

Article	Page	Article	Page
1	170	10	174
2	170, 355	11	175
3	170, 172	See also	14, 167, 168, 169, 176, 191, 197, 240
4	170, 172		
5	170, 172	See also Mortgage Law (Amendment) Ordinance 1920 —9	168, 173, 175, 187, 191, 195, 240, 355
6	170, 172		
7	170, 172, 393		
8	173		
9	174		

The Ottoman Law of Leases: Iradeh A.H. (1299). and A.H. 1331 (1914)

Article	Page	Article	Page
1	191	7	193
2	191	8	191
3	191	17	191
4	193	18	191
5	193	See also	14, 182, 184, 185, 186, 190, 192, 195

Tables.

	Page
The Ottoman Forest Law A. H. 1286 (1869) —	
Referred to	13, 38, 51, 58, 66, 85
The Ottoman Laws A.H. 1291 (1875) and A.H. 1332 (1914) of Registration of Inshaat— Referred to	370
The Ottoman Laws of Registration of Mulk Titles A.H. 1291 (1875) and A.H. 1293 (1877) —	
Referred to	13, 42, 43, 131, 132, 144, 163, 263, 266, 296, 297, 306, 307
The Ottoman Laws of Expropriation A.H. 1295 (1879), 1296 (1880), 1332 (1914) —	
Referred to	13, 315, 316
The Ottoman Law of Inheritance A.H. 1284 (1868) —	
Referred to	13, 21, 24, 106
The Ottoman Law of Inheritance A.H. 1331 (1913) —	
Referred to	14, 25, 98, 101, 102, 105, 106, 107, 108, 109, 240
The Ottoman Law of Mussaqafat A.H. 1326 (1908) —	
Referred to	365
The Ottoman Law of Partition A.H. 1332 (1914) —	
Referred to	14, 205, 209, 210, **211**, 213, 228, 280, 376, **378**, 394
The Ottoman Magistrates' Law A.H. 1331 (1913) —	
Referred to	379, 380, 383
The Ottoman Law relating to Foreigners A.H. 1284 (1868) —	
Referred to	306
The Ottoman Code of Civil Procedure — Referred to	133, 136, 187, 189, **198**, 211, 308
The Ottoman Law of Corporations A.H. 1331 (1913) —	
Referred to	14, 60, 160, 307, **354**, 356, 357
The Ottoman Cadastral Law A.H. 1331 (1913) —	
Referred to	269, 299
The Ottoman Law of Societies A.H. 1327 (1909) —	
Referred to	356
The Ottoman Laws regulating the imposition and collection of Tithe —	
Referred to	360, 361
The Ottoman Wergo Law of A.H. 1303 and A.H. 1328 (1910) —	
Referred to	364

TABLE OF REFERENCES TO PALESTINE LEGISLATION.
The Palestine Order-in-Council, 1922.

Article	Page	Article	Page
12	26, 60, 64, 65, 357	53	72, 96, 109, 349, 386
13	60, 64	54	72, 96, 349, 386
24	353	57	98, 387
38	96, 381, 384	58	357, 386
40	384	59	98 (note), 105, 357, 386, 387
42	278, 373	60—63	386
43	309	64	386
46	1, 14, 15, 346	65	107, 386,
47	384	73	364, 373
51—52	12, 72, 86, 96, 109, 114, 304, 346, 348, 349, 350, 351	74	373

Palestine (Amendment)
  Order-in-Council, 1933 . . p. 40
Palestine (Amendment)
  Order in Council, 1935 . . . . . p. 381, 386, 387

The Transfer of Land Ordinance, 1920.

Section	Page	Section	Page
1—2	131, 139, 231	15	373, 376
2	70, 91, 131	16	300
4	70, 131, 139	Transfer of Land Amendment Ordinance, 1921.	233
5	70, 307		
7	131		
8	355	Transfer of Land Amendment Ordinance, No. 2, 1921.	176, 236 300, 392, 393
9	134, 308		
10	167, 168		
11	131, 146, 168		
12	118, 168		

Tables.

THE SUCCESSION ORDINANCE, 1923.

Section	Page	Section	Page
3	106	12	113, 384
4	103	13	113, 114, 195, 384
5	107	15	195
6	115	19	102, 115
7	108, 111, 118, 121, 122, 348	20	195, 347
		22	116, 117, 119
8	121, 122	23	101, 118, 384
9	107	25	384
10	107, 112, 113	26	102
11	107, 112,		

THE LAND SETTLEMENT ORDINANCE, 1928—1933.

Section	Page	Section	Page
2	272, 276, 282, 285, 287	30	270, 271, 272, 275, 282
3	272, 285, 286	31	275
4	272, 285, 286	32	275
5	272, 273, 278	33	280
6	273	34	271
7	273	35	271, 282
8	273	36	283
9	275	37	282
10	276, 289	38	283
11	276	40	281
12	270, 275	42	278, 283, 285, 289
13	213	43	287
14	274	44	287
15	274	45	270
16	271, 274	47	287
17	274	48	282, 287
18	274	49	271, 280
19	274	50	271, 280
21	274	51	271, 280
22	275, 276, 286	52	274, 280
23	273	52 (3)	213, 280
24	274	53	271, 280
25	275	54	280
26	274	55	280
27	272, 275	56	271, 289
28	274	57	278
29	277	58	279

418   The Land Law of Palestine.

Section	Page	Section	Page
59	278, 283, 284, 286, 287	64	271, 279, 371
60	284	66	279
61	271, 275, 276, 284	67	279
62	372	68	269
63	271, 279	69	272

For Reference to:
The Acquisition of Land for the Army and Air Force Ordinance 1925.
The Antiquities Ordinance 1929.
The Arbitration Ordinance 1926.
The Charitable Trusts Ordinance 1924-5.
The Commutation of Tithes Ordinance 1927-8.
The Companies Ordinance 1921.
The Companies Ordinance 1929.
The Concealment of Crops Ordinance 1923.
The Cooperative Societies Ordinance 1933.
The Correction of Land Registers Ordinance 1920-22.
The Correction of Land Registers Ordinance 1926.
The Cotton Exemption from Tithe Ordinance 1925-7.
The Courts Ordinance 1924.
The Credit Banks Ordinance 1922.
The Exemption from Tithe Ordinance 1929.
The Expropriation of Land Ordinance 1926-32.
The Palestine (Holy Places) Order-in-Council 1924.
The Interpretation Ordinance 1929.
The Jurisdiction of Civil and Religious Courts Ordinance 1925.
The Land Courts Ordinance 1921-1929.
The Land Disputes (Possession) Ordinance 1932.
The Forest Ordinance 1926.
The Landlords and Tenants Ordinance 1933-5.
The Land Law (Amendment) Ordinance 1933.
The Magistrates' Courts Jurisdiction Ordinance 1924, 1930, 1935.
The Mahlul Land Ordinance 1920.
The Mewat Land Ordinance 1921.
The Mining Ordinance 1925-33.
The Mortgage Law (Amendment) Ordinance 1920, 1929.
The Municipal Corporation Ordinance 1934.
The Mussaqafat Tax Validation Ordinance 1932.
The Palestine Jewish Colonisation Association Ordinance 1924.
The Partnership Ordinance 1930.
The Protection of Cultivators Ordinance 1929-1933-4.

Tables.

The Public Lands Ordinance 1926.
The Registration of Land Ordinance 1929.
The Religious Communities Organization Ordinance 1926-1934.
The Rural Property Tax Ordinance 1935.
The Sand Drift Ordinance 1922.
The Seed Loans Ordinance 1929.
The Survey Ordinance 1929.
The Tax on Immovable Property of Corporate Bodies (Abolition) Ordinance 1933
The Tobacco Ordinance 1925.
The Town Planning Ordinance 1921-9.
The Treaty of Peace (Turkey) Ordinance 1926.
The Urban Property Tax Ordinance 1928-1932.
The Weights and Measures Ordinance 1928-33.
The Width and Alignment of Roads Ordinances 1926-7.

SEE INDEX.

TABLE OF ABBREVIATIONS.

A.H.	Anno Hegira (Moslem Era).
Cf.	Compare.
C.A.	Civil Appeals.
C.L.R.	Cyprus Law Reports.
D.C.	District Court cases.
H.C.	High Court cases.
Ibid.	Ibidem. In the same place.
Infra.	Below.
L.A.	Land Appeals.
L.C.	Land Court.
L.R. (Pal.).	The Law Reports of Palestine 1920-1933
L.T. L.T.R.	Law Times Reports.
Loc. Cit.	Loco Citato. In the place quoted.
Op. Cit.	Opus Citatum. The work already quoted.
O.G. Off. Gaz. P.G. Pal. Gaz.	The Official Gazette (or the Palestine Gazette) published by authority of the Palestine Government.
P.C.	Privy Council cases.
P.N.	Public Notice.
Supra	Above.
Semble.	It seems so.

421

CORRIGENDA.

Page 10	line 6 (from bottom)	for	Wakf	read	Waqf
" 22	" 3	"	and	"	land
" 42	footnote	"	Subject	"	subject
" 71	" "	"	Lale	"	Laloe
" 111	" "	"	there ore	"	therefore
" 140	" "	"	Alealy	"	Alcaly
" 143	" "	"	suprd	"	supra
" 222	line 14 (from bottom)	"	cutttng	"	cutting
" 237	" 11	"	contracto	"	contract to
" 256	footnote	"	Michai	"	Michael
" 260	" "	"	1332	"	1322
" 300	" "	"	Registraion	"	Registration
" 304	line 4 (from bottom)	"	rsgistered	"	registered
" 310	" "	"	Farah Wahis Sammer	"	Faram Wahid Sammar

INDEX.

	Page
Abou Hanifa, Referred to	153
Abou Sounoud, Quoted	4
Absence	
Meaning of	351
Absent co-owners	206, 396
Effect of—upon prescription	255, 257, 352, 353, 396
Different kinds of	351, 352
In relation to rights to Tapu	351
No legal excuse in Pre-emption	151, 396
And see generally Chapter XXI	
Absentee heirs, right of Tapu	267
Acquisition of Mulk	38
Acquisition of Land for Army and Air Force Ordinance	
Powers of expropriation in	89
Pre-emption under	159, 160
Powers of leasing under	195
Arbitration Board under, for assessment of compensation	323
Acquisitive prescription	289
Admission in Land Registry proceedings irrebutable	308, 394
Adverse possession in Land Settlement areas	288, 291, 292
Agreement to sell is no "disposition"	140, 392
Agri deserti	3
Agricultural Bank	
Properties purchased by Ottoman	178 ff.
Agricultural Land	
Restriction on leasing of	300
Agricultural Loans	179
Agricultural Tenants	
Protection of	232 ff.
Resumption of Holding of	247
See also Cultivation	
Antiquities, Antiquities Ordinance 1929	38, 195, 316, 317

Index.

	Page
Appendices	386, 391 ff.
Appropriation of land	
Unlawful	125 ff.
In good faith	127 ff.
Aqueduct	
On Mewat land	42
Right of	218, 219, 228 ff.
And see Watercourse	
Arable Fields	5
Arbitration Ordinance 1926, Referred to	377
Archaeological Sites	
When expropriated fall within public lands	67
Army, Acquisition of Land for	89, 159, 160, 195, 316, 317, 323, 331
Attachment	
of land for Government Debts	178
See also Execution Law.	
Auction, Sale by	
of Mahlul	26 ff.
of Mahluls of Takhsissat	80, 81
of Mahluls of Ijaratein	81
of Mortgaged property	175, 176
Baltalik	
Meaning of	19, 51
Rights of villagers in	58
Bedl Misl	
Meaning of	7, 8, 17, 23, 358
Payable for revived Mewat	46, 358
Dedication by way of Waqf	77
Payment of in case of exercise of right of preference	157, 158
Right of State in case of prescription	260, 261
And see Tapu Value	
Bei bil Istighlal, Explained	164 ff.
Bei bil Wafa	
Meaning of	165 ff.
Bei bil Wafa not prescriptive	393
Beisan	
Agreement with villagers of	62 ff., 391
Betterment Tax	329
Bills recently published	388

The Land Law of Palestine.

	Page
Block (Registration)	269
Block plans	269
Boards under the Protection of Cultivators Ordinance 1933—34	249, 383
Boundaries	
Delimitation of in case of Metruki pastures	56
Disputes as to	56 (note), 381
Demarcation of by Land Courts	377
Breach of contract of sale	135 ff.
Building, Buildings	21—24, 29
Accessory to land	133
Separate ownership of buildings and land	30, 40, 41, 157, 158, 392
Right to Tapu of heir of Mulk on Miri land	21
Right of preference of owners of Mulk	
Right to tapu where Mulk buildings disappear	23, 32
Law as to ownership of buildings on Miri	21, 28, 30, 31, 39, 392
must not be erected on Metruki	54
may be dedicated as Waqf	84
on Ijaratein Waqf	82 ff.
on Muqata'a Waqf	116
registration of, Inshaat	304
Succession to Mulk buildings on Miri	115
Right of preference by owners of	148 ff., 155, 158, 159
erected on land without consent of owners	125 ff.
on land forming part of mortgaged property	172
Partition of	212
Prescription as regards	267
Burial	
forbidden in Miri land	29, 34
effect of in creating Waqf	69 ff.
Byzantine Law	2
Cadastral Law (Ottoman)	269, 299
Cadastral Survey	269, 298, 378
Calendar	15, 22
Canon Law	12
Cemetery	34
Certificate of Registration, See Kushan	
Charitable Institutions	356
Charitable Trust	
Fees on registration of	370

Index.

	Page
Joint tenancy under	199
Law relating to	15, 88 ff.
Powers of trustees of	89 ff., 195
Nature of	90, 91
Declaration of	90, 91
Charitable Trusts Ordinance 1924—1925	89, 92, 93, 94, 195, 199, 355, 356, 357, 370, 384, 385
Christian Courts, Christian Law	
Application of Canon Law of in Palestine	12, 15
Jurisdiction of Courts in Waqf	72 ff., 85 ff.
in succession	99 ff, 386
in case of Wills	98 ff, 386
Certification of heirship by	96 ff.
Jurisdiction in administration of estates of absentees	346, 347, 349
Limitation of jurisdiction of	386
Citizen of Palestine defined	386
See Foreigner	
Civil Court	
Jurisdiction in Waqf	72 ff., 85 ff.
Jurisdiction in Succession	98 ff., 100, 101 ff, 384 ff., 387
Law applied in matters of Succession	100, ff., 386
Wills provable in	113 ff.
Jurisdiction as regards estates of minors	346, 347, 349
Commissions and Boards under Protection of Agricultural Tenants Ordinance	249 ff, 378, 383, 388
Communities	
list of having jurisdiction in matters of personal status	99
as corporations	354, 356
Commuted Tithe	361 ff.
Commutation of Tithes Ordinance 1927	361 ff.
Company	
Debentures of	177
as trustee of charitable trust	93 ff.
Mortgage by	171, 177
Restrictions upon ownership of land by	355, 356, 385

The Land Law of Palestine.

	Page
Expropriation of land from	330
Companies Ordinance 1921 (and 1929), Referred to	93, 177, 355, 356, 385
Compensation for Disturbance of Agricultural Tenants	241 ff.
„ „ Improvements made by „ „	243 ff.
„ „ Preparation to „ „	245 ff.
Concealment of Crops Ordinance 1923, Referred to	362
Condition	
Transfer of Miri on	138
Gift under	142
Consent to jurisdiction of Non-Moslem	
Religious Courts	120, 392
Consul	
Order of November 1922 as to powers of	120
Contentious proceedings	121
Contract stamps	191
Co-operative Society	
Mortgages and Debentures of	171
Co-operative Societies Ordinance, Referred to	356
Co-owners, Co-ownership	
Right of tapu of	21
Right of pre-emption of	148
Right of preference by	156
Lease by	182
Classes of	199
Powers of	202 ff.
Absence of	206
in Mesha'a	206 ff.
Repairs by	205, 350
Partition of benefit by	213 ff.
Prescription between	203 ff., 255.
Watercourses, etc.	214 ff., 228 ff.
And See generally Chapter XIII	
Copyhold	28
Corporation	
unknown to Moslem Law	354
unknown to older Ottoman Law	206, 354
Ottoman Law as to	14, 60, 160, 307, 354
Tax on land owned by	357, 364
as trustee of charitable trusts	355
Foreign corporations	355, 356

Index.

	Page
Preference to villagers in land sold by	160
See Municipal Corporations Ordinance	190-192, 193, 335
And see generally Chapter XXII.	
Correction of Land Registers Ordinances	
Referred to	273, 304 ff., 356, 370, 377
Summarised	305 ff
Applications by charitable and religious institutions under	356, 357
Objections to registration under, referred to the Land Court	306, 375, 377
Cotton Exemption from Tithe Ordinances 1925-7	363
Court	
See Civil Court, Sharia Court, Land Court, Magistrates, Rabbinical, Christian	
Courts Ordinance 1924, Referred to	374
Credit Banks Ordinances, 1920-22	170, 176, 177, 187, 195, 355, 368, 369
Provisions as to mortgages by	176 ff.
Leasehold interests may be mortgaged under	169
Powers of leasing by mortgagee under	176, 177, 195
Receiver under	177
Relief to borrowers under	177
Creditors	
Rights of secured	161 ff.
" " unsecured	179 ff.
And see generally Chapter XI	
Cultivation	
Object of Tapu grant to secure	19
Effect of want of in Miri	20, 21, 25
of Mewat	41, 46 ff.
not allowed if pasture assigned as Metruki	54
Unauthorised cultivation of land	125 ff.
Contracts of (muzaraa)	195 ff.
in case of absent co-owners	195 ff.
non-cultivation by minor, etc.	349
Land under	3, 4
Cultivators,	15, 195, 222, 232 ff.
Protection of	248
Custom modifying law	1, 222
Custom of grazing	248
Customary tenure	310, 394, 395

The Land Law of Palestine.

	Page
Cyprus	
Ottoman Land Law in	1, 20
And for references to cases see Table of Cases	
Daftar Daimi	
Meaning of	298
Daftar Kassam, Entry in	117
Daftar Khani	
Establishment of	18, 294
Mulk titles transferred to	16, 296
represented by Land Registry in Palestine	18, 24, 296
See Land Registry, Registration.	
Daftar Mahlulat	298
Daftar Shamsieh	297
Damage, Excessive	
Sale of mahlul revocable for	26, 28, 29, 268
Revocation of partition for	212
Provisions of Mejelle in case of	41, 132, 216, 394
to neighbouring properties	214 ff., 216
Provisions of Land Code	143, 394
Damages	
upon breach of contract for sale of land	135, 136, 145, 388
in case of unathorised cultivation	127 ff.
liability to pay for owerflow of sewers	215
Ordinance 1935 (Bill)	388
Dastour	16
Dead land	
See Mewat	
Debentures	
Provisions of law as to	177, 399
Deceit	
Actions for between transferor and transferee of Miri and Mevqufe land	143
Dedication	
Method of dedication as Waqf	69 ff.
And see Waqf	
Deed	
See Kushan	
Delivery on sale, gift, etc.	134 ff.
Demarcation of Land by a Land Court	377
Director of Lands, Referred to	273, 355, 360
duty of in connection	

Index.

	Page
with Agricultural Tenants	246 ff.
with Possesory Titles	291 ff.
Disposition of Land	
Definition of, in land Settlement Ordinance	287
Prohibition of transactions in land after British Occupation	299
Formalities of disposition of land	300 ff.
Dedication of Waqf is	70, 91, 132
Definition of Transfer of Land Ordinance, 1920	131, 189, 190, 221
Effect of unregistered disposition	144, 145, 146
of leasehold interest	188, 189
of Mahlul	24, 25, 26
See Tables for references to Articles of Ottoman Law of Disposition	
Under Transfer of Land Ordinances	14, 28, 138, 145, 146
See generally Chapters VII, XVIII, IX	
Disposition Law of 1331	
Referred to	14, 204
For references to Articles See Tables	
District Court	
Jurisdiction of	374, 384, 385, 396
Disturbance, compensation for to tenants	241 ff.
Dowry	
registration of dowry rights	303
Dunum	
Meaning of	295 (note)
Sale by	143
Duress	
Effect of upon dispositions of Miri or Mevqute	143
Will made under	104
Effect of upon running of prescription	255, 257
Easement	
Defined	217 ff.
in English Law	217 ff.
Action regarding	377
And see Servitudes	
Egyptian Courts	
Judgments of referred to	72, 121, 122, 123, 124, 137
Egyptians	386

The Land Law of Palestine.

	Page
Emancipation	
Who may effect	345
Emirieh land	
Meaning of	3, 5
Emphyteusis	10
English Courts,	
judgments of, See Tables	
English Law of sale	129 ff.
English Law	
Referred to	28, 37, 53, 129, 135, 136, 137, 163, 182, 183, 388
Eviction of Tenants	241 ff.
Evidence of entries in Tapu Books	308, 395
Evidence of witnesses not heard against a Kushan	309, 395
Exchange of Land, See also Sale	129 ff., 135
Execution Law of 1332, Procedure under	176 ff., 180, 187, 235, 385,
Expropriation Ordinances (1924) 1926-1932	53, 89, 159, 195, 316,
Referred to	317, 319, 322-331, 377
Expropriation	
Assessment of Compensation in	323
Acquisition by Agreement in	322
Notice to Treat under	322, 323
" " " on whom served	323
" " " withdraval of	326
Entry into possession under	323
Damage from	325
Appeals in matters of compensation	325
Payment of Compensation into Court	325
Land vested in Promoters	326
Betterment Tax	329, 330
Expropriation from persons under disability	330
Promoter defined	319
Undertaking defined	319
English Law of	319
Gratuitous expropriation for roads	327
Land expropriated for road	52, 327
Expropriation of Waqf	79, 82
Pre-emption under Expropriation Ordinance	159, 326, 327
Compulsory leases under	195, 318
Compensation payable upon to be determined	
by Land Court	318, 323, 377

Index.

	Page
Ottoman Law of	13, 315, 316, 317
Fees (Land Registry)	368, 369, 399
" Succession	369
" Partition	369
Feragh	
transfer of tessaruf of Miri land by way of	137, 296
Feragh bil Wafa explained	164 ff.
Fiefs (Military)	4, 5
Floating charge	177
Flooding, non-cultivation by reason of	20
Foreign corporations	355
Foreigner	
Right to hold immovables in Ottoman Empire	13, 306
in Palestine	306, 386
Right of dowry of	304
Jurisdiction in succession over	98 ff., 386
Meaning of term, under Order-in-Council	98, 386
Law governing succession to	98, 105
Abolition of incapacity to inherit land	116
Abolition of privileges to trial	386
Stateless person is	386
Foreshores as Metruki	53
Forest	
Reserves	66
Waqf forests	66, 85
See Forest Ordinance, Woodland	
Forests Ordinance, 1926	
Provisions as to forest reserves	58, 66 ff.
Care of forests	66
See also Baltalik, Woodland	
Fraud	143
Ghaib	
distinction between Ghaib el Munqata and Ghaib	351
And see Absence	
Ghair Mazbuta, Awqaf	72
Ghair Sahiha, Awqaf	75, 76
Ghor (Beisan) Agreement	62 ff., 391
Gift	
law as to	129, 136, 139, 142
no pre-emption in	151

The Land Law of Palestine.

	Page
by minors	349
Grants	3, 4, 19, 26
Grazing, custom of	248, 382
Guardians	
of minors	345
of persons of unsound mind	348 ff., 350
Powers of, in connection with land	349
Rights to tapu can be exercised by	349
Expropriation of land from	330
Guedik, Meaning of	75
Hajr, Meaning of	344
Hamuleh, Meaning of	208, 209
Hanafite rite	11, 45
Haq el Awlawia	
See Preference	
Harim	
of well	42, 226, 227
of springs and trees	42
overlooking	215 ff., 394
Hatt Hamayoun	97, 120, 121
Hedaya	
Quoted	11, 19, 44, 45, 46, 133, 134, 147, 150, 153, 154, 155, 183, 184, 196, 211, 213, 219, 221, 226, 228, 351, 397, 398
Heirs	
Possession by, not adverse possession	203 ff., 394
Provisions of Land Law Amendment Ordinance 1933 as to possession by	204 ff. 347
Highway	
classified as Metruki	53
Obstruction of	53
Prescription does not run against public rights in	263
See Leases, Leasing, Hire	
Hikr, Meaning of	10, 74 (note)
Historical sites	
Expropriation of	316
Hodgets of Religious Courts	308, 312
Holding	
Definition of under Protection of Agricultural Tenants Ordinance 1933—4—5	236, 388

Index.

	Page
Holy Places	
Claims to	380
The Palestine Order-in-Council 1924 relating to	381
House	
Sale of, what included in	141
Right to support of	231
See also Building, Buildings.	
House and Land Tax—See Wergo.	
Hypothec	168 ff.
Idda	
Succession of divorced wife during	209
Ifraz Urfi	209
Ihya, Meaning of	47 (note)
And see Reviver	
Ijara (Muajele)	80
Ijara Wahida	
Meaning of	9, 10
Law relating to	80, 193
Succession to interests under	101
Lease of	193
Ijara Zemin	
Referred to	17
substitute for tithe	361
Ijaratein	
Nature of	9, 10, 74, 80, 81 ff.
Mahluls of	81 ff.
Raqabe of	82, 83 ff.
Condition for creation of	83 ff.
Prescription in case of	262
Inheritance of interests in	13, 100, 101
no right of pre-emption over	160
can be sold for payment of debts	179, 180
Sale and purchase of by guardians	350
Lease of	193
Mortgage of	164, 165, 166, 176
See also Mussaqafat; Mustaghilat; Leases.	
Immemorial User	220, 224, 225 ff., 394
Immovable property	11, 37
held by Companies	385
Sale of	129 ff.

The Land Law of Palestine.

	Page
Improvements	
Compensation for, to Agricultural Tenant	243 ff.
Incapacity	
Right of preference notwithstanding	157
Will made by person under	104
Abolition of incapacity to inherit	116
Prescription does not run during period of	255
See also Minor, Unsound Mind, Prodigal.	
Inheritance	
Law of, applicable in Civil and Religious Courts	100 ff.
Jurisdiction in matters of	96 ff., 384
And see Succession, Will.	
Inheritance to Ijaratein	
Law as to, applied in Palestine	101
Inheritance to Miri	
Law of, applied in Palestine	100 ff.
Inheritance to Miri (Law of 1331)	
Referred to	14, 24, 25, 100, 116, 122
Inheritance to Mulk	
Law of, applied in Palestine	103 ff., 116
Inheritance to Muqata'a	
Law as to, applied in Palestine	101, 116
Insane	
Person incapable to give consent	392
And see generally Chapter XXI	
Inshaat	
Registration of	301, 304
Fees on registration of	370
Interpretation Ordinance 1929	
Referred to	22, 37, 60, 135, 139, 353, 357, 377
Intiqal, Meaning of	100, 117
Iqtaa, Meaning of	3, 5
Iraq	
Ottoman Land Law in	1
The term Miri in	6
Iraqians in Palestine (foreigners)	386
Irrigation	68, 228, 382
Irsad, Meaning of	76
Istibdal of Waqf	74

Index.

	Page
Jewish Religious Law	12
Jiftlik	
Pasture grounds attached by usage to	55
Jiftlik lands included in State Domain	61 ff.
of minors	349
Joint ownership	200 ff, 202
" " of roads, watercourses and walls	227
Joint tenancy by trustees	199 ff.
Judgments, Execution of	385
Judgments of Courts	385
Juridical personality—See Corporations.	
Jurisdiction of Civil and Religious Courts Ordinance	
Referred to	72, 73, 373
Jurisdiction in matters of Succession	96 ff., 109 ff., 120, 384 ff, 386,, 392
Jurisdiction in Winding up of Companies	385
Khali Land included in Mewat	44
Khalit, Meaning of	150, 156
See also Servitude	
Kharaj Moukassamah and Mouwassaf	2, 360
Kharaji Land, Meaning of	2, 3, 39, 360
Kishlak	
Meaning of	56
Registration of	56, 57
Payments in respect of	361
Kushan	
equivalent to Title deed	18, 295, 379
Issue of	18, 19, 295
Character of	18
Form of (Turkish)	295, 307
Execution of	295, 296
Application for, in respect of unregistered land	304
Validity of	307 ff., 379
Lake	
Bed of, classified as Metruki	53
Land left by recession of great lakes are Mubah	50, 223
Land	
defined in Transfer of Land Ordinance	70, 91, 131
defined in Land Courts Ordinance	377
defined in Land Settlement Ordinance	285

The Land Law of Palestine.

	Page
Land Books (Unofficial)	305
Land Code, Ottoman	
Character of	1, 2
For references to Articles, See Tables	
Land Commission, Appointment of	300
Land Court	
Land Court Ordinance 1921-1929, Referred to	301, 309, 310, 323, 376
Jurisdiction of	375, 376, 380, 395, 396
Appeals from	376, 380
Law applied by	373, 374, 375, 376, 380
Reference to arbitration by	377
Appeals in Land Settlement	277, 378
Rules of Court of	378
Establishment and constitution of	373, 374, 375, 376, 380, 384
And see generally Chapter XXV	
Land Disputes Possession Ordinance 1933-1934	222, 381, 382, 383, 396
Land Law (Amendment) Ordinance 1933	15, 22, 26, 27, 28, 40,
Referred to	41, 50, 59, 61, 117, 141, 169, 170, 187, 237, 253, 254, 267, 347, 353, 360
Landlords and Tenants Ordinance 1933, 1935	
Referred to	194, 388
Land Registry	
in Palestine	6, 18, 299 ff.
Scope of registration in	6, 298
Closing of, after British Occupation	299
Re-opening of	299
Organisation of	300 ff.
Regulations by Director of	300 ff.
Fees (Scale of)	368, 369, 399
Refund of Fees of	369
See Daftar Khani, Registration.	
Lands Department	300
Land Settlement Ordinance 1928-1933, Referred to	269 ff., 271 ff.
Land Settlement	15
Cadastral Survey	269, 378
Registration Block	269 ff.
" Parcel	272 ff.
Settlement of Rights	270 ff.
Definition of land in	272
Settlement Areas	272

Index.

	Page
Definition of village	272
Preliminary Notice of	272 ff.
Settlement Notice	273 ff.
Schedule of Claims	273, 274
Memorandum of Claim	273
Village Settlement Committee	274
Government rights in Land Settlement	274
Claim in, publicly investigated	275
Courts of	381
Schedule of Rights	275, 283, 286, 289
Administrative Powers of Settlement Officer in	275
Judicial powers of Settlement Officer in	275, 276
Law to be applied in	276
Commissioner of Lands (as Controller of Land Settlement)	276
Appeals from decisions in	277
Appeals decided in Chambers	278, 279
Partition in	213, 279
Partition Schedules in	279, 280
Fees in	279
Offences in	279
Penalties in	279
Minimum (or Minima) of areas of Parcels in	280
Parcellation of Village Mesha'a in	281
Registration of land in	281
Character of Registered Title in	283
Correction of clerical errors in	284
Prescriptive Title in	284, 288 ff.
Possessory Title in	284, 288 ff.
No compensation for errors in	285
Conflicting rights in	285
Land defined in	286
Rules regarding proceedings in	372
Fees payable in	371, 372
Servitudes in	286
Adverse possession as prima facie right in	288
Leases for more than 3 years	286

The Land Law of Palestine.

	Page
Land Tax See—Wergo	
Land Transfer Ordinance, Referred to	15, 131, 233 ff., 271 ff., 286, 309
Lausanne, Treaty of, Referred to	60, 67, 257
Law Reports of Palestine, Referred to	391 ff.
Leasehold	
Mortgage of	169, 177, 196
See leases, Leasing	
Leases, Leasing	
of Waqf land	391
Miri land may be leased	36, 182 ff.
Leases of public lands	60, 62, 68
Powers of trustees of charitable trust	195
Leases exceeding three years included under "disposition"	189
Law of in Mejelle	181
Interest created by lease	184
Transfer of	185, 186
Registration of leases	187, 188, 189
Powers of by mortgagee, etc.	189, 191, 192, 195, 393
Lessee cannot prescribe against lessor	258 ff.
of jiftliks of minors	349
Sale of property leased	187, 188
Power of lessor to re-enter	189
Lease for more than 3 years in Land Settlement	286
Lease of Mortgaged property	393
Merger of	393
And see Ijara Wahida, Ijaratein.	
See generally Chapter XII	
Legal ownership	5
Licence distinguished from Servitude	219 ff.
Light, Right to	
Law in Mejelle as to	215 ff.
Limitation of Actions	250 ff., 312
distinguished from Prescription	251 ff.
And see generally Chapter XVI	
Lunacy	344
Magistrates	
Magistrates' Courts Jurisdiction Ordinances 1924-1930 and 1935, Referred to	378, 379, 380, 388

Index.

	Page
jurisdiction of Magistrates' Courts in land questions	267, 374, 378, 379, 380, 396
Majority, age of	346, 347
Mahalla	
See Village	
Mahlul land	
Meaning of	25
Disposal of	26, 359, 360
Notification of land becoming	21, 25
cannot be changed into Mewat	49
classified as Public Land	67 ff.
Sale of Mahluls of Takhsisat	80
Sale of Mahluls of Ijaratein	81
Prescription of State's right to	259, 261, 267
Mewat land cannot be Mahlul	49
No possessory Title to Mahlul land	292
Mahlul Land Ordinance 1920	
Referred to	15, 19, 20, 25, 26, 88, 261
Anoted	25
Effect of, upon prescriptive right	261
Malia	
Meaning of	6
Calendar	16
Mandate of Palestine, Referred to	380
Market places classified as Metruki	53
Mazbuta	
Awqaf Mazbuta, Disposition of	74, 138
Meadow land	
Tapu grant of	28, 29
becoming Mahlul	20
Meadows	5, 28
Mefqud	
See Absence	
Mejelle	
Compilation of	1, 11
English translations of	47, 48
Law of sale in	132
And for reference to Articles	
See Tables	
Mera	
See Pasture	

The Land Law of Palestine.

	Page
Mesha'a Land	
Mode of registration of	394, 395
Partition of	208 ff.
Transfer of share in	206, 302
Nature of	206 ff.
Report of Commission upon	206, 207, 208 ff.
Awlawia in	392
Metruki land	
Meaning of	7, 8, 52
Classes of	52, 59, 67
New Metruki	59
Prescription in relation to	263
Claim to in Land Settlement	274
Pasture and Woodland as	45
And see generally Chapter IV	
Mevqufe Land, Meaning of	8, 9
And see Waqf	
Mewat land	
Meaning of	7, 44 ff.
Grant by Bedl Misl of	358
Transmutation into Mulk	41
may be granted as Metruki	59, 67
Reviver of	44 ff, 391, 397
falls within public lands	67
Prescription in case of	263 ff.
No possessory Title to Mewat land	292
And see generally Chapter III	
Mewat Land Ordinance 1921, Quoted	15, 46, 47, 263, 292 (note)
Mines, Minerals	
Ownership of minerals in Miri land	28
Licences to extract stone, etc.	
in communal Metruki	57
vested in High Commissioner	64 ff.
Powers of High Commissioner over	64 ff.
under Mulk land	64 ff.
Leasing of	195
And see Mining Ordinance	
Mining Ordinance 1925—33, Referred to	28, 38, 57, 60, 65, 66, 195, 316
Sec. 30 ff. ” ”	195
Sec. 35 ” ”	65

Index.

	Page
Minor, Minority	
Provisions of Mejelle as to	344, 345
Right of pre-emption affected	153, 156, 158
Leases of property of	195, 350
Effect of minority upon running of prescription	255, 257
Law in Mejelle as to guardians of	345
Minority under Commercial Code	347
Provisions of Land Code as to	348, 349, 350
Powers of President District Court as to estate of	347 ff.
And see generally Chapter XXI	
Miri Land	
Origin of	4, 6, 7, 17, 18
Definition of	5
Proprietary interest of State in	6, 17
Dedication by way of Waqf	75 ff.
Registration of interests in	8, 9, 28, 29, 32
Inheritance of (Law as to)	14, 24, 100 ff., 116, 122
User of	28
Rights of holder of	28 ff.
Transformation into Mulk of	40
Charitable trusts of	94 ff.
Rules as to disposition by sale or exchange of	35, 137 ff
Gift of	136, 142
Succession to	96 ff., 100
Right of preference over	155 ff.
Unauthorised cultivation, etc. of	125 ff.
Mortgages of, before British Occupation	161 ff.
Present law of mortgages of	170 ff.
can be sold for payment of debts	166 ff.
Partition of benefit not applicable to	210, 213 ff.
Servitudes over	216 ff., 392
Prescription in case of	255, 353
cannot be left by Will	36
cannot be made Waqf	36
subject to Tithe	36, 360, 361
Cemetery on	34
Mahlul of	61
See generally Chapter I	

442   The Land Law of Palestine.

	Page
Monasteries, land attached ab antiquo to	86 ff.
Mortal Sickness	
Transfer of Miri and Mevqufe made in	134, 142
Acknowledgment in, may operate as Will	104
Mortgage	
Formalities upon registration of	303
Forms of, before British Occupation	161 ff.
Prohibition of, after British Occupation	167 ff.
Mortgages during prohibitory period	167
Present law of	167 ff., 393
to Credit Bank	176 ff.
by Company	177 ff.
Notice of leases to mortgagees	171 ff., 189–191, 192
of minors' property	349
priority interest in	393
Assignment of	393
Redemption of	393
Registration fees	399
Mortgage Law of 1331	
Mortgages under	14, 167, 170—175
amended	175, 176
Provisions set forth as amended	
by Mortgage Law (Amendment) Ordinances	
1920 and 1929	168, 176, ff , 355, 369
Moslem and non-Moslem	
Inheritance between	96 ff., 116
Rules as to certification of succession to	
respectively	118 ff.
Moslem Calendar	15
Moslem Council	
powers of, over Waqf	74
Moslem Courts	
See Sharia Courts	
Moslem Religious Law	8, 11
Muajelle	6, 80, 358, 359
Mubah	
Meaning of	50
Public rights over	50
what are	50 ff., 67, 126, 223 ff., 226
Mudawara Lands, Meaning of	61 ff.

Index.

	Page
Muddet Safar	
Meaning of	352
Effect in suspending prescription	257
Muhassils, Replacement of feudetaries by	5
Muhayeh	
Explained	210, 213
Jurisdiction of Magistrates as to	378, 380
Partition of	210, 213, 229, 378, 378
Mukhtar	
Duty as to notification of Mahlul	21
Certificate by on disposition of land	300, 301
Map of property to be registered signed by	302
Mulhaqa	
Awqaf, disposition of	74
Mulk	
Meaning of	2, 4
Waqfs of	8, 75
Registration of titles of, transferred to Darfar Khani	13, 296
Mulk trees and buildings on Miri	21-24, 29-31
Rights to tapu by heir to	21
Rights to tapu on disappearance of	23
Right of owner to	37, 43, 307
Ways of acquiring of	38
Classes of	38 ff.,
Right of State to take on failure of heirs to	42
Interests in must be registered	43, 296
Charitable trusts of	89 ff.,
is in principle titheable	360, 361
Dispositions by sale and exchange of	42, 129, 131-135
Gifts of	136 ff.,
Succession to	103 ff.,
Wills of	103 ff,.
Right of pre-emption in	147 ff.,
Unauthorised cultivation of	125 ff
Mortgages of before British Occupation	161 ff.,
Present law of mortgages of	170 ff.,
can be sold for payment of debts	166 ff.,
Servitudes over	216 ff.,
Mulk streams and watercourses	227, 228
Partition of	209 ff.,

The Land Law of Palestine.

	Page
Partition of benefit in	210, 213
Prescription in case of	253 ff., 353
Transmutation of Miri into	40
See Trees, Buildings.	
See generally Chapter II	

Mulk Mahlul
Disposition of	42
Prescription against claim for	258, 260, 261

Multazims, Replacement of Feudatories by	5, 294, 295
Municipal Corporations Ordinance, Referred to	190—192, 193, 335, 356

Muqata'a Bedl Ushur
Meaning of	24

Muqata'a Waqf
Nature of	10, 42, 83
Law relating to	83 ff.,
Registration of	85, 296
Inheritance to interests in	85, 100, 101, 116
Interests in available for payment of creditors	180
Prescription in case of	253
Qadima	85

Musakat, Contracts of	195 ff.,
Musaveghat Conditions, Meaning of	349

Mussaqafat (Waqf)
Mussaqafat Tax Validation Ordinance 1932	
Referred to	365
Meaning of	9, 13, 79, 82
Registration of	85
Application of Law of Disposition to	138
Application of Law of Mortgages to	164
can be sold for payment of debts	165 ff., 179
Unlawful occupation of	128
Partition of	211
Tax on	365
And see Ijaratein, Muqata'a.	

Mustaghilat Waqf
Meaning of	9, 13, 79 ff.
Registration of	85
Application of Law of Disposition to	138
Application of Law of Mortgage to	164
can be sold for payment of debts	166 ff., 179
Unlawful occupation of	128

Index.

	Page
And see Ijaratein, Muqata'a Waqf.	
Mustaheki Tapu, Meaning of	19
Mustesna	
Awqaf Mustesna	74
Non-Moslem Waqf as	85 ff., 354
Disposition of	138
Mutessarif	7
Mutwally	71 ff., 82
Power of leasing of Waqf property by	195
Muzaraa, Contracts of	195 ff.
Nam Mustaar, See Nominee	
Neighbourhood, Natural rights by reason of	214 ff., 218
Noksan Arz, Meaning of	127, 128
See also Damages	
Nominee	
Registration in name of	206, 306 ff., 356, 357
Now prohibited	206 ff., 307, 357
Non-contentious proceedings	120 ff.
Options	134, 152—154
Ordinances of Palestine Government	15
Otlak, Meaning of	51
Ottoman Calendar	15, 16
Ottoman Land Law	
Origin of	2, 5, 13, 14
Application in Palestine of	
Land Code	1, 15, 16
Laws subsequent to Code	14, 15
Ottoman Law of Execution	385
Ottoman Penal Code, Art. 264, Referred to	34, 52, 53
Ownership as distinguished from possession	5, 6, 7, 288 ff.
Palestine Jewish Colonisation Association Ordinance	
1924, Referred to	356
Palestine Order-in-Council, Referred to	1, 12, 15, 64 ff., 97 ff., 278, 386
Palestinians	386
Parcel as Registration unit	272
Parcellation of Land	273
Partition	
of waqf	85, 211
Report of Mesha'a Commission on partition	
of Mesha'a	208 ff.

The Land Law of Palestine.

	Page
Provisions of Mejelle as to	202 ff.
Revocation of	212 ff.
of benefit	209, 213
of private roads	228
What passes on	212
of land of minors and lunatics	349, 350
Jurisdiction in	210, 376, 378, 394
Reinforced by prescriptive rights	209
Fees on	369, 400
Partition Law of A. H. 1332	
not applicable in Land Settlement Areas	213
Referred to	14, 204 ff., 209, 210, 280, 376, 378, 394
Partition in Land Settlement	213, 279, 280
Partnership Ordinance 1930, Referred to	200, 201 ff.
Partnerships	196 ff., 200 ff.
Party Walls, Law in Mejelle as to	231
Pasture, Pasture Grounds	5, 7, 19, 20, 28
Tapu grant of	19, 223
becoming Mahlul	20
Breaking up of	28, 391
Assigned for inhabitants of village	54
Customary right of	222, 223
Delimitation of	53, 55
Action concerning communal pastures	59, 222, 223
Path, Demarcation of	286
Patriarchial Courts, See Christian Courts	
Peace, See Treaty of Peace (Turkey) Ordinance 1926	
Pernalik, See Woodland.	
Personal Status	
Matters of within meaning of	
Palestine Order-in-Council	96 ff., 123, 386
Plans (Survey)	
See Block plans. Survey of Palestine.	
Plantation, See Trees	
Pledge, Law of	161
Pollution of Water, excessive damage caused by	214, 218
Possession adverse between co-heirs	394
Possession distinguished from Ownership	57, 288 ff., 290
Possession valid as defence only	394
Possession, Recovery of	378, 379

Index.

	Page
Possessory Title	290, 291
Power of Attorney, Irrevocable	162 ff.
Preliminary Notice of Settlement	272 ff.
Pre-emption	
Prescription as regards	268
Definition of	147
Grounds for exercise of right of	147, 148
Order of exercise of right of	150, 151
Applicable only to Mulk	147, 149
Conditions for exercise of right of	151, 268
in streems	231
in case of sale by promoters of expropriated land	327
by co-owner	392
And see generally Chapter X	
Preference, Right of	
in Waqf property	160
Right of, Referred to	143, 147, 155
Grounds for exercise of	155 ff.
distinguished from right of pre-emption	156, 157
prescription of rights of	267, 268
under Land Law Amendment Ordinance 1933	159
under special Ordinances	159, 160
in Mesha'a land	392
not applicable to villages	392
Preparation	
Compensation to Agricultural Tenants for	245 ff.
Prescription	
as regard Waqf	262 ff.
of actions to enforce servitudes	252
Nature of	250 ff.
Moslem law as to	251 ff.
Periods of fixed by Mejelle	253 ff.
Doctrine of discussed in Mejelle	253 ff.
Commencement of period of	255 ff., 262 ff., 353
Suspension of	255 ff., 349
Provision as to, in Land Law (Amendment) Ordinance 1933	254, 353
Interruption of	255, 256, 353
in relation to Miri land	255, 257, 258 ff., 353
in partition	209 ff.

The Land Law of Palestine.

	Page
as bar to action in Land Settlement	299
between co-heirs	254, 353, 394
Title by, in Land Settlement	265, 289, 290
See Immemorial user	
Prisoner of War, effect of non cultivation in case of	20
Probate of Wills	113, 384 ff.
Prodigals	344 ff., 350
Profits à prendre, nature of	217 ff., 222
Progress Notices of Land Settlement	273
Promoter	
See Expropriation.	
Promulgation of Ottoman Laws	14
Protection of Cultivators	15, 194, 222, 232 ff.
Protection of Cultivators Ordinances 1933-4 Referred to	235 ff., 300, 378, 383, 384, 388
Puberty	344, 345
Public Lands	
High Commissioner's power over	26, 27, 59, 60
Definition of	59, 60
Classes of	61 ff., 67
Leasing of	68, 195
Public Lands Ordinance, Referred to	68, 195
And see generally Chapter V	
Qesmat	
See Partition.	
Quarter, Building of new	33
Rabbinical Courts, Rabbinical Law	
Application of Rabbinical Law in Palestine	12
Jurisdiction of Rabbinical Courts in Waqf	72, 85
” ” ” in Succession	106 ff., 118, 386
” ” ” in case of Wills	111, 386
Certification of heirship	96 ff , 386
Jurisdiction in administration of estate of absentee	351
Limitation of jurisdiction of	386
Railway premises	67
Raqabe	
Meaning of	3, 4, 7, 17, 222 (note)
Grant of by Sovereign	49
Prescription of right of action for	41, 258

Index.

	Page
of communal Metruki	52, 57
of revived Mewat	46
of Miri Waqf	75
Prescription against claim for	258
of Ijaratein Waqf	81
Receiver under Credit Banks Ordinance	177
Refund of Land Registry fees	369
Register of Title Deeds	18
Registration Fees	300, 399
Registration of Land	
Principles of, under Ottoman Law	18, 263, 294
Extension to Mulk Titles	43, 296
of yaylak and kishlak	56
of land held on charitable trust	94, 355. 356, 357
of servitudes	221, 263, 296
in Palestine at present	299, 300 ff.
in case of Succession	303
Correction of Land Registers	304 ff., 356, 357
Registration in name of nominee	306, 355, 356, 357
Rights of a registered owner	309
Effect of want of	265, 266, 307, 311 ff.
Mortgages in name of company	175
Registration of leases	189 ff.
Prescription and Registration	263 ff.
Power of Land Court to direct	375, 378
Fees on	368
Registration of Land in Land Settlement	281 ff., 289
Registration of Waqf transactions	297
Registration of Land Ordinance 1929, Referred to	265, 284, 288, 289
Registered Title, validity of	263, 264, 265, 266, 268, 307, 310, 311, 395
Regulations as to Title Deeds 1276, Referred to	13, 18, 259, 260
For reference to Articles, See Tables.	
Religious Communities Organization Ordinance 1926-1934, Referred to	356
Religious Courts	98 ff., 106 ff., 119, 276, 277, 386
Consent of jurisdiction of	120 ff., 392
Religious Law, Moslem	8, 11, 12
" " Christian	12
Renounciation of interests under Succession	101

	Page
Restriction of Rent	194, 245 ff.
Restrictions in Land Registration	299
Reviver of Mewat land	44, 48 ff., 397
Rice Fields, user of Miri land as such	28
Right to Tapu	19, 21
Riparian owners	223, 224
Rivers, Private	224, 228
Rivers, Public	229, 231
Classified as Metruki	53
are Mubah	223, 224
Prescription does not run against public rights in	224, 263
Roads	
Width and Alignment of Roads Ordinance 1926-7	53, 54, 328
Expropriation of land required for public roads	53, 327
Private roads	218, 219, 227
Prescription of rights to private roads	263 ff.
Roads and Works Ordinance 1927	53
See also Way	
Royalty on Mines	65, 66 (note)
Rudjhan, See Preference	
Rural Property Tax Ordinance 1935, Referred to	366 ff.
Sacred (Moslem) Law	
Rules as to Iqtaa	3
relating to Waqf Sahiha	8, 75, 257
Schools of	11
Application in Palestine of	11, 12
relating to Wills	103 ff.
Sale	
Law relating to	129
Effect of on lease	187, 189, 349
What passes on	141
of property of minors	347, 349, 350 ff.
of things not in existence	132, 133
Contract of	145
See also Auction, Disposition, Options.	
Sand Drift Ordinance 1922	
Land reclaimed under may be applied as Metruki	59

Index.

	Page
Scale of Land Registry Fees	369
Schedules of Rights	270 ff., 289
Sea	
Bed of, classified as Metruki	53
Land reclaimed from	41
Seas are Mubah	223 ff.
Seed Loans Ordinance 1929, Referred to	179
Servitude	
in Miri	392
Registration of	221, 263, 286
Right of pre-emption by owner of	149 ff.
Nature of	216 ff.
Prescription in case of	222, 252, 263
Creation of	218 ff.
Sale of	221
Actions regarding	377
See Easements, and see generally Chapter XIV	
Settlement of Rights	270 ff., 273 ff., 290
Sewers, Partition of jointly owned	228
Overflow of	214 ff.
Sharia Courts	
No jurisdiction in matters of ownership	373
Jurisdiction in waqf	72
Jurisdiction in case of succession and wills	96 ff., 118
Jurisdiction in case of minors and absentees	344 ff, 351 ff.
Shia, Meaning of	11
" Succession to	103 ff.
Shirket el Akd, Nature of	200 ff.
Shirket el Ibaha, Nature of	200 ff.
Shirket el Mulk, Nature of	200 ff.
Shufa. See Pre-emption	
Sipahis	
Meaning of	4, 5
Replacement by Multazims, etc.	5, 294, 295
Hearth tax imposed by	363
Title deeds issued by	295
Sites within towns and villages	2
Slavery, Referred to	344
Societies, Ottoman Law of, Referred to	356
Specific Performance could not be enforced	136 ff.
Springs in Mewat land	42

The Land Law of Palestine.

	Page
Squatters	3
State Domain. See public lands	
Stateless persons	99, 386
State Land	3
See Miri land and Public land	
Statutory Tenant, Definition of	236, 388, 389
Stillicide, Law in Mejelle as to	220
Succession	15, 19
Failure of	21
Formalities on registration of	203
Rights under	96 ff.
Certification and Registration of rights under	117 ff.
Fees on	369, 399
See also Inheritance, Will.	
See generally Chapter VII	
Succession Ordinance 1923, Referred to	93 ff., 102 ff., 195, 384, 387
Suni, Meaning of	11
Support, Right to	214 ff., 231
Supreme Moslem Council	74, 331
Survey Ordinance 1929, Referred to	269
Survey (Public) of Palestine	269 ff.
Syed Amir Aly, Law of Waqf and Wills	69, 103 ff.
Syria, Ottoman Land Law in	1
Takhsisat Waqf, Origin of	9
" " Character of	9, 75
Distinction between true and untrue Takhsis	75 ff.
Tithes from	363
Tapu, Tapu fee, Tapu grant	6, 7, 358
Meaning of	7, 8, 9, 358
Resemblance to lease	17
Scope of	19, 259
Revocation of payment of	25, 26
Tapu Law 1275, Referred to	13, 47, 294
For reference to Articles, See Tables.	
Tapu Misl	7, 27, 358, 359
Tapu, Right to	
Mahlul subject to	14
of former holder in case of non cultivation	20
of designated persons in case of failure of successors	21
Condition of exercise of	21

Index.

	Page
Persons entitled to in case of failure of successors	21 ff.
Non heritable character of	23
in case of disapearance of mulk trees and buildings	23 ff.
Period for exercise and formalities upon exercise of	22, 27, 268
cannot arise over mulk	42
Minority and Insanity in relation to	349 ff.
Absence in relation to	351 ff.

Tapu Value
Meaning of	27, 358, 359
Assessement of	359, 360
Excessive damage caused by unfair	28, 268
And see generally Chapter XXIII	

Tax on Immovable Property of Corporate Bodies (Abolition) Ordinance 1933, Referred to	364
Taxation of Land	358 ff.
Tax Collectors and Tax Farmers	5
Tax (Waqf), Replacement of	387
Tenancy in Common, Nature of	199
Tenants Agricultural, Protection of	232 ff.
See generally Chapter XV	
Tessaruf, Meaning of	7, 17, 33
Dedication by way of waqf	76 ff.

Threshing floor
Miri land may be set apart as	34
but not without special kushan	34
set apart ab antiquo for inhabitants of a place	54
Excessive damage to	215

Timar, Meaning of	4
Abolition of	5, 6

Tithe
Exemption from Tithe Ordinance 1929	363
Tithe paying land	2, 39, 42, 360
Dedication by way of Waqf	76 ff.
Incidence of and Amount of	361, 362 ff.
Commuted	361 ff.
from Waqfs, replacement of	387

The Land Law of Palestine.

	Page
Title Deeds	6, 18, 131, 261, 266, 267, 271, 283, 308 ff.
Tobacco Ordinance 1925, Referred to	363
Town Planning	
Area and Scheme of	334
Establishment of new villages under	34 ff.
before and after the Occupation	332, 333
Central and Local Commissions of	333 ff.
Outline and detailed Schemes of	337 ff.
Approval of Schemes	339
Expropriation of Land for Scheme	340
Land may be given in exchange	340
Financial Provisions	341
Betterment Tax	341
Compensation for Injury	342
Penalties	334
Owners may be compelled to accept land instead of money	340
Town Planning Ordinance, 1921—1929, Referred to	34, 35, 38, 316, 327, 328, 329, 333—343
Transfer, See Disposition	
Transfer of Land Ordinances, 1920-1, Referred to	15, 139 ff., 176, 233
For references to Articles, See Tables.	
Transjordanians	386
Treaty of Peace (Turkey) Ordinance 1926	60, 257
Trees	21-24, 29, 34
Circuit of	42
Separate ownership of trees and land	29
Right to Tapu of heir of Mulk trees on Miri land	21
Right to Tapu where Mulk trees disappear	21, 30
Trees growing naturally on Miri	29
Law as to ownership of trees planted on Miri	29, 30, 267
Trees planted on Mewat	41 ff.
must not be planted on pasture assigned as Metruki	54
may be dedicated as Waqf	75
on Muqata'alu Waqf	83 ff.
Registration of Inshaat	304
pass upon sale of land	141
Succession to Mulk trees on Miri land	115

Index.

	Page
Right of preference by owner of	148 ff., 155, 158 159, 267
planted on land without consent of owner	125 ff.
on land form part of mortgaged property	172
overhanging	215 ff.
Partition of	212
Prescription with regard to	267
See also Forests, Woodland.	
Tribute paying land	2, 39, 42, 360
Trust	15, 69, 354
Fees on registration of	370
Trustees for Debenture holders	178
Trustees for Charitable Trusts	195
Unlawful appropriation	128
Unofficial Land Books	305 ff., 370
Unregistered Transfers	144—146, 298, 310
Unsound Mind, Person of	
Leases of property of	350
Effect of insanity upon running of period of prescription	257 ff.
Law in Mejelle as to	348
Guardian of	348, 349
Provisions of Land Code as to	349, 350
Partition of land of	349, 350
cannot buy or sell land	349, 350
Certification of	348
Urban Property Tax Ordinance 1928-1932, Referred to	302, 365
User (Immemorial)	220, 224
User of Miri land	28
" of Water	225 ff. 380
Ushurie Land, Meaning of	2
Validity of Registered Title	307 ff.
Valuation of land	301
Village	
Right to Tapu by inhabitants of village	21
New village on Miri	35 ff.
Provisions of Town Planning Ordinance as to construction of	35
Provisions of Public Notice of 1924 as to construction of	35
Metruki assigned for inhabitants of	54

Rights of action of inhabitants of	59
Rights of inhabitants to take forest produce	50, 51
Rights of preference by inhabitants of	157, 267, 268
Water rights of	160
Prescription does not run against communal village rights	263

Vines, See Trees
Wakalat Dawaria, Explained — 165, 393
Wakalat ma Haq el Ghair, Explained — 164 ff., 227, 231, 311
Walls — 214 ff.
Waqf

Meaning of	8, 9, 69, 75, 354
Constitution of	35, 41, 70, 71 ff.
Administration of	70, 73
Classes of	73
Inalienability of	71
Jurisdiction in matters of	72, 391
Lease of	195, 391
Claims in Land Settlement on behalf of	274
Powers of Supreme Moslem Council as to	74
Sahiha and Ghair Sahiha	75 ff.
Transformation into charitable trusts of	92 ff.
Ijaratein Waqf	9, 10, 74, 80 ff.
Muqata'a Waqf	83, 296
Waqf forests	66, 85
Non-Moslem Waqf	85, 354
Dispositions of Waqf land	132
Prescription in case of	253 ff., 259 ff.
Takhsisat	75 ff., 363
Expropriation from	72, 89, 330
Tithes from	363, 387
Fees on registration of	369

Waqfieh — 69 ff.
Waqf-Mahlul — 81

And see generally Chapter VI

Water, Watercourses

Law of Mejelle as to jointly owned watercourses	214 ff., 227 ff.
Rights of, in Mejelle	218 ff., 223 ff.
Rights of, in Land Code	230 ff.
Effect of sale or partition of land on	212, 221
Sale of	221 ff.

Index.

	Page
Public streams	223 ff.
Private streams	227 ff.
Subterranean waters	226
Prescription of rights to	257
Possession cannot be taken of flowing water	37 (note)
Claims as to right of user of	380
Disputes as to right to, under Land Disputes (Possession) Ordinances 1932, 1934	381
And see Aqueduct, Rivers, Public land.	
Way, Right of	396
How acquired	214, 215 ff.
Effect of sale or partition on	212, 221
Law in Mejelle as to	214 ff. 218, 227
Law in Land Code as to	29, 125, 227, 394
Prescription of rights of	262, 263, 344
Weights & Measures Ordinance 1928-33, Referred to	295
Wells	
Circuit of	42, 394
on Mewat land	32, 41
on Miri land	32
Waqf may be created of	73
Public wells	223 ff., 226
Right to dig	223 ff., 226, 227
Wergo Registration as evidence of possession	379
Nature and incidence of	363, 365 ff.
Production of Wergo certificate on disposition of land	302
Exemption from payment of	365
Width and Alignment of Road Ordinances, Referred to	328
Will	
Miri land cannot be left by	33, 102 ff.
Ijaratein interests cannot be left by	102 ff.
Moslem law as to	103 ff.
Law as to of non-Moslem in Palestine	107, 387
in Civil form	111
Probate of	113
Winding up of Companies, Jurisdiction in matters of	385
Woodland	
Tapu grant of	7, 19, 28

458. The Land Law of Palestine.

	Page
becoming Mahlul	20
Breaking up of	28, 58
Breaking up of by co-owner	204 ff.
Wrongful appropriation of land	125 ff , 128
Yaylak	
Meaning of	56, 57
Registration of	57
Payment in respect of	361
Year	
Meaning of	253
Youklama	
Meaning of	295 ff., 312
Ziamet	
Meaning of	4
Abolition of	5, 6, 363
Zukur	
System of, applied in Partition	208 ff.